FROMMER'S

ISRAEL
ON $30 AND $35
A DAY

by Tom Brosnahan

Assisted by Nancy J. Keller

1988–89 Edition

Published by Prentice Hall Press
A Division of Simon & Schuster, Inc.
Gulf + Western Building
One Gulf + Western Plaza
New York, New York 10023

ISBN 0–13–506361–2

Manufactured in the United States of America

CONTENTS

MAPS

This book is dedicated to the hope for greater understanding and tolerance among all the peoples of the Middle East.

IMPORTANT NOTES

THE $30 AND $35 DAILY BUDGET, which provides the title for this book, is intended to cover the basics: room and board. By adopting our philosophy and following our recommendations, you'll be able to live in Israel for that modest amount. Other costs of an Israeli vacation—transportation, entertainment, souvenirs—will be added to the basic budget, but these costs are different for each person. If you're content to take buses, visit museums, and just roam the winding streets of Old Jerusalem, your extra costs will be minimal. Those who fly to Eilat, rent scuba gear, or take in a nightclub will end up paying more. It's up to you.

Establishments recommended in this book are generally moderate in price, not rock-bottom. Thus the book can be used with safety by people of all ages and both sexes.

A NOTE ON CURRENCY: In the recent past, Israel has suffered from the highest inflation rate in the world. But in August 1985 the Israeli government introduced a "new" shekel which was stabilized by links to the hard currencies of Israel's major trading partners. This system of stabilization worked quite well, and the value of the **New Israeli Shekel (NIS)** remained at 67¢ U.S. until January 1987. At that time, the shekel was devalued slightly to its current value of NIS1.62 to $1 U.S., making each shekel worth about 62¢ U.S.

The exchange rate may change by the time you arrive in Israel, but any bank or newspaper will tell you the current rate. In any case, it looks as though the days of shekel hyperinflation are over.

Some prices in Israel's tourism-related businesses have always been quoted only in dollars. For instance, all but the very cheapest hotel-room rates, rental-car charges, and airline tickets are always and *only* quoted in dollars, and I have followed that practice in this book. As for other costs normally quoted in shekels, such as bus and taxi fares, restaurant meals, and admission fees, I have given the shekel prices, and also the U.S. dollar equivalents calculated at the rate of NIS1.50 to $1.

Remember that Israel has a Value Added Tax (VAT) of 15%, added to most purchases made in shekels. You can avoid it in many cases—hotel rooms and dining room bills, rental cars, airplane tickets, purchases which you will take home with you—by paying with hard currency (dollars, marks, francs, etc.) in the form of notes, traveler's checks, or credit cards denominated in hard currency.

A NOTE ON SAFETY: Many readers ask me, "Is it safe to travel to Israel? What about all that fighting?" The Middle East has a well-deserved reputation for violent conflict, but you will see virtually none of this during a visit to Israel. The invasion of Lebanon, for instance, made big headlines and frightened many prospective visitors. But it took place in Lebanon, *not Israel*! Unless there's full-scale war in Israel proper, which is unlikely considering the country's strong defenses, you have little to fear. Don't postpone a visit just because of headlines.

A NOTE ON HOTEL PRICES: Everywhere in Israel, most hotel room prices are quoted in U.S. dollars. Also everywhere, a 15% service charge is added to your room bill, whether you pay in shekels or dollars. I've *included* this inevitable 15% markup in the room prices I quote, so you needn't add anything to these prices. By the way, it is the custom in virtually all hotels except the very cheapest ones to include a huge—often buffet-style—Israeli breakfast in the price of the room. Unless I specifically mention otherwise, you can assume that you will receive breakfast with your room at no extra charge.

ACKNOWLEDGMENTS: A travel guidebook is a complex work, with hundreds of facts and recommendations on every page, any of which can go out of date in a second. I'd like to thank several people for helping me to make this guide as complete as possible, and to keep it right up to date. Greatest thanks go to my tireless assistant, Nancy J. Keller; thanks also to Aviva Lavi of El Al Israel Airlines Ltd. in New York, to Raphael Bar-Yaakov of the Public Relations Department of the Ministry of Tourism in Jerusalem, to Ruth Weinstein of the Haifa Tourism Development Association, and to Tzippi Moss and Allan Rabinowitz of Jerusalem. Finally, I must thank all those readers of this book who took the time and trouble to write me cards and letters, recommending new establishments, adding facts on historical points, and generally sharing their travel experiences with me. *Toda raba!*

ISRAEL ON $30 AND $35 A DAY

1. The Land and the People
2. A Short History
3. $30 and $35 a Day: Hotels and Restaurants
4. We Love to Get Mail!
5. The $25-A-Day Travel Club

NO PLACE ON EARTH is filled with fascination and significance to equal that of Israel. Millions upon millions of Jews, Christians, and Muslims look to this as the Holy Land where Solomon reigned in all his glory, Jesus died on the cross, and Mohammed visited during a miraculous journey.

Religion is the basis of Israel's political importance as well. Were it not for the sacred character of the land, few people would choose this narrow strip of land between sea and desert as the choicest place to live. But Jews have been living here, in larger or smaller numbers, since Old Testament times. Christianity began here two millennia ago. And in the very early days of Islam, before Mecca became a sacred city, Muslims prayed in the direction of Jerusalem.

All three religions have battled to capture and hold this holy territory: Israelites fought Canaanites, Jews fought Romans, Muslim armies invaded and Crusader armies drove them back. In the present century Muslim Turks were driven out by the Christian British, and the British in turn were driven out by terrorist groups of Zionists and Palestinian Arabs. These pitched battles over the land sacred to God and man alike are among the great ironies of history.

Israel looms large in the great political happenings of our times. It's the place where an ancient people's dream of a homeland finally came true after thousands of years and unnumbered tribulations. But great movements of peoples are never smooth, and the making of Israel left others—Palestinian Arabs, both Christian and Muslim—feeling displaced the way Native Americans must have felt when faced with the invasion of America by Europeans.

1. The Land and the People

For all its triumphs and troubles, Israel is a surprisingly small place. Not counting the West Bank territories of Judea and Samaria, or the empty Negev, the country is about the same size as Massachusetts, or Wales and Monmouthshire. Starting from Jerusalem, you can drive down to Jericho, along the Dead Sea to Masada, inland to Beersheba at the edge of the Negev, north to Tel Aviv,

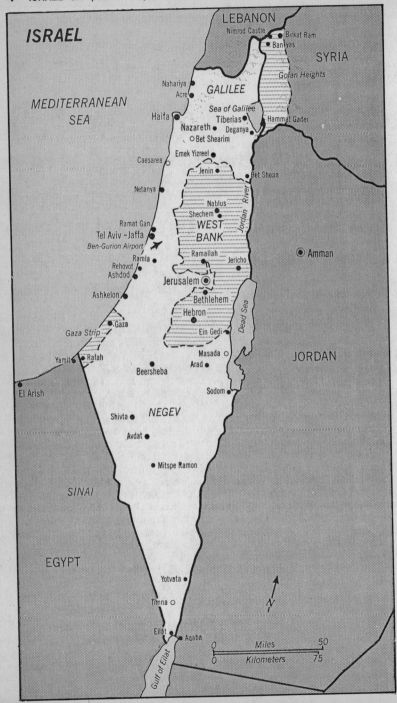

then all the way up to the Lebanese border, the Golan Heights, and around the Sea of Galilee, returning to Jerusalem, and the distance would be only about 600 miles. Driving at the speed of the fabled Israeli *sherut* drivers, you could do it in a day. Don't, though. As for population, the entire country counts less than four million—the population of a largish city in Europe or America. But Israel is special: it's not at all surprising that in the minds of many first-time visitors, it looms larger than life.

In ancient times this land was looked upon as a corridor between the richer, lusher lands of Egypt and Mesopotamia. When drought threatened, people were forced to go north or south to reach the fertile lands fed by mighty rivers. But in 20th-century Israel, modern farming and irrigation have made marginal land wonderfully fruitful, and the warm Mediterranean sun makes for a long growing season. The diligence and hard work of Israeli farmers is legendary: they love the land as much as life itself.

Modern agriculture and dedication can make the desert bloom, but that's not to say Israel is all desert—far from it. In biblical times the land yielded abundance which acted as a powerful lure to the Israelites wandering in the deserts of Sinai. You can check that best-of-all guidebooks to Israel, the Bible, for confirmation: Moses sent spies into Canaan to report on the land, and they returned with figs, pomegranates, and a single bunch of grapes so huge that two men were needed to carry it back to the Israelite camp (Numbers 13:23). The **Israel Ministry of Tourism** has adopted this as their symbol: two men, each bearing an end of a pole, with an immense bunch of grapes suspended from its middle.

Today the wines of Mount Carmel are famous, as are Jaffa oranges and Israeli avocados. Besides fruits and vegetables, Israel is rich in livestock. Sheep, goats, and cattle did well in Abraham's time, and they thrive even better today. Scenes of "shepherds keeping watch over their flocks" are a common sight.

Agriculture is important, industry even more so. Israelis learned at an early stage the importance of manufacturing their own tools, arms and weapons, airplanes and machines. Many raw materials must be imported, but many more are found here in abundance. The Dead Sea, heavily saturated with minerals, has only begun to be exploited. The one great lack is oil. With Iranian supplies cut off and Israeli-held Egyptian fields turned back to their former owners, Israel is faced with enormous oil bills.

Most tiny countries have a uniform topography. They're either sandy or rocky, mountainous or flat, high or low, lush or arid. The people who live in such small countries may vary greatly, but usually they possess certain "national" characteristics. Their foods and fashions, customs and cussing, wares and wants possess a thread of similarity.

About the only thing Israel has in common with such countries is size: it is tiny. And about the only thing *all* Israelis have in common is that they're Israelis.

THE LAND: Traveling north to south, east to west, you can't help marveling at the changes in the land: stretches of sandy shores . . . lush and rich valleys and mountainsides . . . rambling foothills and flat plains . . . skybound snow-capped peaks . . . body-parching hot wilderness climbing from the mineral-saturated waters of the Dead Sea, lowest and possibly stillest spot on earth . . . lifeline oases in desert regions that vary from shifting sands to hard, cracked mud to the awesome and frighteningly beautiful multicolored crags and crevices of the Negev. So you can't really say Israel is uniform! But wherever you go, one thing is for certain: there you'll find traces and remnants of uncountable centuries of civilization.

THE PEOPLE: Israel's peoples match their land in variety. They vary greatly in looks, customs, speech, personalities. Their particular needs are as different as the countries from which they came, whether they arrived to stay in Israel last week, last year, five or six generations ago—or if they happen to be of the few who are descended from "original" stock.

True, with difference comes divergence. Quite astounding progress has been made to bring them together; but Israel is still a country of assorted peoples—and this, to us, is a positive feature of the country. Hebrew—the language excavated, reconstructed, and reclaimed after thousands of years of disuse—has probably done more to unite the people than anything else. And the fact that 85% of Israelis are Jewish is also a strong bonding element—whether the individual translates his or her Judaism into strict and orthodox adherency or into a sort of nationalism separate from any religious ideology. The parliamentary democracy of Israel gives all citizens a voice in government (which gets a bit confusing at times), and race, creed, or color set no limitations on citizenship—another point of growing unity, as is compulsory military service for both sexes. Then, too, every effort seems to be made to provide the best possible education, housing, medical, sanitation, technical, and spiritual services and rights for everyone. Of course, any "melting pot" has its tensions, and Israel has its share.

AESTHETICS, RELIGION, AND NATIONALISM—ISRAEL'S BOON AND BANE: Israel is special, if not sacred, to more faiths than any other land in the world. Today for at least 15 different Jewish sects, several Christian sects, Muslims, Druze, Baha'is, Samaritans, Circassians, Karaites, Bedouin, and on and on and on, Israel is holy, and although many of the groups claim the land as "their own," the differing faiths are practiced side by side. This calls for daily tolerance, not just of those who adhere to creeds different from yours, but of those who supposedly practice what *you* preach! For instance, there are Jews who visit Israel and return home shaking their heads in woe because it isn't "Jewish" in the way they personally practice or understand Judaism. A Yemenite will tell these visiting Jews that items such as gefilte fish are "gentile" foods—most confusing! Christians traveling in Israel are often perplexed by certain Israeli Christian groups, those who charge entrance fees at holy shrines, those who subdivide famous churches (with actual lines of demarcation on walls and floors) among different sects of Christianity. Protestants are often amazed to find most holy places tended by Catholics; Catholics are surprised to find their Israeli counterparts functioning as they did hundreds (or thousands) of years ago, instead of following modern practices that have spread to most parts of the Catholic world.

And then there's nationalism, which translates here to Zionism. Yes, Israel is the Jewish homeland, fired with a national spirit akin to religious fervor, yet equally secular and political. Many people visit the country today to express or increase their Zionist feelings. Though Israel was founded by dint of Zionism, the form it takes these days disappoints those Zionists who have been removed from the tide of daily life in Israel. Zionism has changed through the years among Israelis themselves, perhaps not so much among those who are Zionists only in spirit. That is not to say that Israelis do not welcome visiting Jews to their country (as a matter of fact, they consider such a visit "a natural action for any Jew"); it is to say, rather, that they welcome everyone to their land, happily, but without great fuss. Israel has come of age.

NO PLACE NAME IS EVER SPELLED THE SAME WAY TWICE: One of the

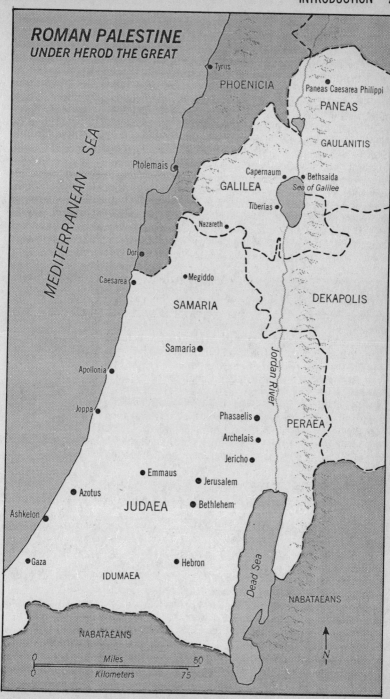

ROMAN PALESTINE
UNDER HEROD THE GREAT

MEDITERRANEAN SEA

PHOENICIA

Tyrus

Paneas Caesarea Philippi

PANEAS

GAULANITIS

Ptolemais

Capernaum

Bethsaida

GALILEA

Sea of Galilee

Tiberias

Nazareth

Dor

Megiddo

Caesarea

SAMARIA

DEKAPOLIS

Samaria

Jordan River

Apollonia

Joppa

Phasaelis

PERAEA

Archelais

Jericho

Emmaus

Jerusalem

Azotus

JUDAEA

Bethlehem

Ashkelon

Gaza

Hebron

IDUMAEA

Dead Sea

NABATAEANS

NABATAEANS

N

Miles   50

Kilometers   75

first things you'll notice in Israel is the place names: no name seems to be spelled the same way twice. Is it Jaffa, Joppa, or Yafo? Safed, Safad, Zfat, or Zefat? Lake Tiberias, the Sea of Galilee, or Kinneret Lake?

The confusion stems partly from Israel's long history and influence on many cultures, partly from the myriad of peoples and languages here, and partly from Hebrew. The lingua franca of modern Israel is undoubtedly Hebrew, the resurrected language of biblical times. Written in its own alphabet, Hebrew must be transliterated into the Latin alphabet for non-Hebrew-speakers. Vowels are not normally written in Hebrew (they do the same strange thing in Arabic), and so in transliteration you get such unpronounceable words as Sde (for Sede) and Sderot (Sederot). Further confusions are added by sounds like the guttural "kh" sound, a rasping in the back of the throat usually rendered as "ch," but pronounced very differently from the "ch" in "church." You might come across "Hen" and "Chen," which are the same Hebrew word, but have nothing to do with chickens or Chinese restaurants. The word is pronounced more like "khen."

How does one cope? The only way is to pronounce the word you want and compare it to the one you've found. If it sounds the same, it probably is: Mikveh Israel, Miqwe Yisra'el, Elot-Elat-Eilat, Tiberias-Teverya. . . .

2. A Short History

It's simply amazing: you can open the Bible to the tenth chapter of the book of Genesis, and from that point on the Bible becomes a guidebook to Israel.

This is not legend or theory. You can actually follow in the footsteps of Abraham, Isaac, and Jacob, stop where they stopped, see what they saw, and thrill to the feelings they must have experienced in the Promised Land.

Recorded Jewish history goes back to the hypothetical creation of the world some 5,740-odd years ago. Incredibly, most of this history is accurate, as confirmed by recent archeological discoveries. But a history so deep and full of universal significance is almost impossible to grasp in its entirety, so I've simplified things by giving a rundown of its major periods. The outline that follows will at least enable you to match up the dates of any archeological site, ancient tomb, or world-class event that seizes your interest while you are in Israel.

A HISTORICAL OUTLINE: Modern scientific methods have revealed men living in the Holy Land from the Old Stone Age, some 600,000 years ago, so we'll start our incredible survey there.

Old Stone Age (600,000 to 12,000 B.C.): Cave men, hand axes, hunting, fire.

Middle Stone Age (12,000 to 7500 B.C.): *Homo sapiens*—man—begins to gather and cultivate grain; more sophisticated tools.

Late Stone Age (7500 to 4000 B.C.): First villages are founded, including Jericho; animal husbandry, irrigation, and pottery begin.

Chalcolithic (Copper) Age (4000 to 3200 B.C.): Copper used in tools; towns grow; designs show on pottery; a culture develops at Beersheba.

Early Bronze (Canaanite) Age (3200 to 2200 B.C.): Towns are fortified, temples and palaces built.

Middle Bronze (Canaanite) Age (2200 to 1550 B.C.): The Age of the Patriarchs; Abraham's travels; trade develops; the Hyksos invade Canaan and Egypt.

Late Bronze (Canaanite) Age (1550 to 1200 B.C.): Israel captive in Egypt;

the alphabet develops; the Exodus from Egypt; Ten Commandments delivered on Mount Sinai; Israel conquers the Promised Land.

Early Iron Age (1200 to 1020 B.C.): Period of the Judges; Philistine invasion from the sea.

Middle Iron Age (1020 to 842 B.C.): The united monarchy under King Saul and King David (1000 B.C.); Jerusalem becomes the capital of the kingdom; in 961 King Solomon builds the First Temple; golden age of Israelite culture and power.

Late Iron Age (842 to 587 B.C.): Period of the later kings and prophets; in 587, destruction of the First Temple.

Babylonian and Persian Periods (587 to 332 B.C.): Israel captive in Babylon, followed by Persian domination; the Second Temple is built; times of Ezra and Nehemiah.

Hellenistic and Maccabean Periods (332 to 37 B.C.): Domination by Alexander the Great, by the Ptolomies and Seleucids; the Maccabean struggle; Hasmonean dynasty.

Roman Period (37 B.C. to A.D. 324): Herodian dynasty; birth of Jesus, his ministry and crucifixtion; wars against Rome; destruction of the Second Temple and of all Jerusalem (A.D. 70); fall of Masada (73); Talmud and Mishnah compiled; Bar Kokhba's revolt against Rome (132–135).

Byzantine Period (324 to 640): Jewish revolt, Byzantine domination; Jerusalem Talmud completed; Persian invasion and sack of Jerusalem (614); Arabs conquer the entire Middle East.

Arab Period (640 to 1096): Jerusalem surrenders (637); Arab Empire capital first at Damascus, later Baghdad; joint Christian-Muslim protectorate of Holy Places; many Christian pilgrimages.

The Crusades (1096 to 1291): First Crusade (1096–1099), sack of Jerusalem, Crusader kingdom under Godfrey of Bouillon; Second Crusade (1147–1149); Saladin captures Jerusalem (1187), but does not sack it; Third Crusade (1189–1192); Fourth Crusade (1202–1204).

Ottoman Turkish Period (1291 to 1917): Mongols, Mamelukes, and Seljuks replace Arabs and Byzantines as overlords of the Holy Land; Ottomans conquer Palestine; Suleiman the Magnificent rebuilds Jerusalem (mid-1500s); Jews expelled from Spain and Italy welcomed into the Ottoman Empire; Napoleon's campaign in Egypt and Palestine (1799); Zionism begins with Herzl (1860–1904), publication in 1896 of *The Jewish State;* First Zionist Congress (1897).

British Mandate (1917 to 1948): League of Nations grants Great Britain the "mandate" to govern Palestine (1920); Sir Herbert Samuel, first high commissioner; Jordan becomes a separate kingdom (1923); Arab attacks on Jews (1929); Jewish immigration restricted; Pan-Arab Congress (1937) in Syria; Arab and Jewish terrorism; King David Hotel blown up (1946); British Mandate ends on May 14, 1948, and the State of Israel proclaimed on same day.

RECENT HISTORY: In the beginning of Israel's history there was a grim determination—born partially out of the horrors of World War II—to hang on, to protect every sand dune, to force life out of the desert. Then conditions grew more stable. Israelis became a little more like other people. Television, the good life, and a certain cockiness were infused into the overall picture. This was particularly apparent during the heady days after the Six-Day War in 1967. Suddenly Israel was no longer a struggling state hanging on tenaciously to its hard-won independence. Land areas had more than trebled. Infusions of new immigrants swelled the country's Jewish population. The economy was burgeoning and tourism was increasing at a rate greater than ever before.

Israel, with its artifacts, excavations, and kibbutzim, always had a lot to offer. After the 1967 war, it had more. Most important of all, there was united Jerusalem, the Western (Wailing) Wall, the Levantine veneer of the Old City. For the Christian, Israel became a synonym for the entire Holy Land. Both sides of Jerusalem were joined together. Barbed-wire fences and the Mandelbaum Gate border post became things of the past. Bethlehem, once virtually inaccessible from Israel, was only minutes away from Jerusalem. Jericho, believed to be the oldest city in the world, and Hebron, where the ancient Hebrew patriarchs were buried, were open to visits. In the north, the Golan Heights provided a double meaning: tranquility in Galilee and a new area for tourist inspection.

In the opposite direction, there was a new accessibility to the great historic wilderness called Sinai. Eilat, once considered by Israelis as the end of the world, awoke one morning with a deep and dependable tourist hinterland. The craggy isolation of the Santa Katarina Monastery, at the base of Mount Sinai where Moses was believed to have received the Ten Commandments, provided an unforgettable experience. Command cars, Jeeps, buses, and airplanes began penetrating the desert that had once sustained the ancient Israelites during their 40-year odyssey.

In those days the mood was optimistic. No one any longer questioned the premise that Israel was on the map for good. World economies were booming, and there was a tremendous quantity of expendable wealth. The major items were hotel accommodations and airline space, and an empty hotel room in July was as rare as summer rain in the desert.

But the country experienced a sharp change in fortune in October 1973. The completely unexpected Yom Kippur War had a sobering effect on the entire nation. The price was steep. Over 2,500 young men were killed, losses proportionately higher than the casualties the United States sustained during the entire Vietnam War. While the war ended with Israel closer to Cairo and Damascus than ever before, the initial setbacks and the high cost in lives shook the nation's confidence, plunged the people into despair, and tarnished the image of national heroes. In a backlash voters turned against the Labor party, which had led the state since its foundation, and elected a new government dominated by the right-of-center Likud.

A few weeks after he assumed office in 1977, Prime Minister Menachem Begin asked President Ceausescu of Rumania to arrange a meeting with President Sadat anywhere in the world. This set in motion a series of events highlighted by President Sadat's dramatic visit to Jerusalem, the conclusion of a framework for the Middle East peace agreement in Camp David, and the treaty with Egypt in March 1979 terminating 30 years of war between the two countries. Accordingly, Israel withdrew from the Sinai, and Mount Sinai with the Santa Katarina Monastery reverted to Egypt. With the state of peace it remains open to tourists from Israel.

Even with the Egyptian-Israeli peace agreement, all has not been smooth sailing, however. The 1982 invasion of southern Lebanon put further strains on Israel's relations with its neighbors, and provoked a great deal of debate in every sector of Israeli society. But the withdrawal from Lebanon, the coming to power of a coalition "National Unity" government, and a vigorous effort to solve the country's serious economic problems may be the prelude to better times.

3. $30 and $35 a Day: Hotels and Restaurants

Israel is not an inexpensive country. A brittle economy and inflationary trends have pushed consumer prices skyward. An Israeli-made raincoat or bathing suit often costs 20% to 30% more in Tel Aviv than in New York. A meal in one of the country's better restaurants can easily cost $25. The price of a room in a luxury hotel would not only devour our $30 to $35 allotment, but eliminate meals the next day.

And yet, paradoxically, the very seriousness of the situation and the high competition for tourist dollars have produced a reaction that is working for the overseas traveler. It's becoming clear that the Israeli shekel, despite devaluations, is still overpriced as far as tourists are concerned. Many hotels are holding last year's prices firm rather than increasing them, and the trend seems to be catching on. Except at peak vacation, holiday, and pilgrimage periods, when maximum prices are charged and occupancy rates approach 100%, hotels are willing to haggle a bit over room prices. You should know this, and keep it in mind when you're looking over hotels. The slightest hesitation over price on your part may well bring swift and gratifying reductions.

Also, there has been a proliferation of clean, unpretentious restaurants serving acceptable meals at affordable prices (about $8). The seaside resorts of Netanya and Nahariya are squarely devoted to the postulate of popular tourism. Kibbutz guesthouses, providing clean, comfortable lodging and wholesome, tasty food, are attracting ever-larger numbers of people. Some of the kibbutzim (collective farm settlements) even have arrangements where you can offset the cost of room and board with good, honest toil.

So while the postulate of $30 and $35 a day is not easy, it certainly is not impossible. It requires a certain ingenuity, a willingness to experiment, and a spirit of adventure, but the practicalities are all there.

The aim of this book is to show you how to function in Israel at the lowest of costs: first, because I think more and more people should be encouraged to travel in Israel, and second, because I believe low-cost Israel is the most interesting Israel. For Israel is an informal and vigorous country that bears little resemblance to the staid luxury-class hotels in which the higher-living tourists will be staying. .

THE $30- AND $35-A-DAY STANDARD—WHAT IT MEANS: The $30- and $35-a-day budget (for room and meals) in Israel is based on necessary expenses per person per day—and there's nothing impossible or gimmicky about that goal. You can stay in comfortably unostentatious hotels, hostels, or hospices, and you'll find that there are many such places in each and every area this book covers. That leaves adequate money for lunch, dinner, and occasional splurges.

In general, plan to budget $15 to $25 per person per day for lodging (including that huge Israeli buffet breakfast), and $10 to $20 for lunch and dinner. If you're willing to stay at youth hostels, to have falafel for lunch and a modest meal for dinner, you can actually visit Israel for as little as $15 or $20 per day. And if you prefer to travel almost-first-class, staying in very comfortable though not quite luxurious hotels, and dining in some of the fancier restaurants, you can do so for the moderate splurge of only $45 to $55 per person per day.

You'll find, by the way, that the hot summer weather will decrease your appetite for the meat-and-potatoes type of meal, and that you'll be eating more and more dairy, vegetable, and salad meals—which are healthy, plentiful, and relatively inexpensive.

People traveling alone will, of course, have to pay more per person for a room than two people traveling together. But couples will find many good-quality hotel rooms with private facilities available all seasons of the year within their budget.

You will notice that I have also mentioned some restaurants and hotels slightly out of budget range. These are to be considered "splurges"—and particularly worthwhile ones. They all represent considerable value for the money, worth the extra expenditure should you be able to save elsewhere.

A WORD ABOUT PRICES: Rates quoted for most hotel rooms in this book are in dollars only. The Israel Ministry of Tourism, the Israel Hotel Association, and hotels themselves always quote their room rates in U.S. currency rather than in shekels. Only a few small hotels and pensions will quote you room or bed rates in shekels.

All Israeli and most West Bank hotels add a 15% service charge onto your hotel bill—it's inevitable, and has nothing to do with "extra" services. To make your life simpler, the inevitable 15% has *already been included* in the room prices I quote, so you need do no quick arithmetic to determine what you'll actually pay. These prices are *per room,* single or double, and not per person. The hotel may quote prices differently: "Double room for $15 per person plus 15% service." Well, I've just done all the work for you by multiplying $15 by 2 and the total ($30) by .15 (15%) and adding in this service charge to get the actual room price of $34.50.

If you pay in hard currency (dollars, marks, francs, etc.) in the form of notes, traveler's checks, or credit card, you won't be subject to Israel's 15% VAT (Value Added Tax), a tax that is normally added onto the price of any shekel purchase. Thus it's a good idea to put hotel restaurant meals and drinks and such on the hotel bill rather than paying for them on the spot with cash shekels. Every time you pay in shekels, you're paying that tax, whether it's shown as a separate charge or hidden in the total price.

Reductions for Children

Children up to the age of 6 years are allowed a 50% reduction on the extra-person rate if they stay in the same room with their parents. From 6 to 12 years old, children receive a 30% reduction.

Breakfast Is Included

It's important to realize that virtually every hotel in Israel and the West Bank provides a large breakfast to each guest for no additional charge. Often the breakfast is a kosher buffet, long tables packed with salads, eggs cooked various ways, breads and rolls, fruits and vegetables, cheeses, dips, cereals, juices, even pickled fish. Unless I mention otherwise, you can assume that breakfast comes with your room, for no extra charge.

Renting an Israeli Apartment

You may like to know about a service called **Homtel,** Suite 612, 1170 Broadway, New York, NY 10001 (tel. 212/686-9343). Homtel is an agency through which you can arrange to rent an apartment or private home in Israel. If your visit is going to be lengthy, this may save you money on lodgings. Homtel has an office in Israel as well, at 33 Dizengoff St., Tel Aviv (tel. 03-289-141).

On- and Off-Season

Israel's hotels fill up during certain seasons and holidays, and you should be prepared with advance reservations, secured by a deposit. Generally speaking, hotels are busiest during July and August, and on the major Jewish and Christian holidays such as Passover, Easter, Rosh Hashannah and Yom Kippur, Hanukkah and Christmas. For detailed information, and a full list of precise holiday dates, see Chapter IX, "Details, Details!" under "Holidays."

Off-season is generally November through February (except for Hanukkah–Christmas–New Year's). In Eilat, though, that's the busiest season of the year due to the almost perfect, sunny weather here when it's chilly up north. In summer Eilat is like an oven and prices are lower. Precise on-season and off-season information is given in each chapter. Note it. There's money to be saved on hotel rates off-season.

I can't stress enough that you should start the reservations process very early. It can take three weeks for a letter to cross the seas and continents to Israel (by air!), and another three for the reply. Assume two weeks' "turnaround time" (for the hotel to go through its paperwork), and you've logged two months—and the answer you get might be "full up"! Also, if you wish a confirmation, enclose International Reply Coupons (on sale at any post office) to pay the return postage. Hotels, which can run up huge postage bills, look very favorably upon requests that include IRCs.

You might also like to know that a direct-dial telephone call to Israel from the United States, early in the morning (before 8 a.m. EST), lasting three minutes, will cost something like $5. Ask the operator, or check your phone book, for rates before you call. Even if you can't dial direct, you may be eligible for the low direct-dial rate. Remember also that when it's 7 a.m. EST in New York, it's 2 p.m. in Israel. Also, that many Israelis will not answer the telephone during the Sabbath (Friday evening to Saturday evening).

4. We Love to Get Mail!

I cannot stress too much that you, the reader, are the reason this book exists. I've done my best to help you discover the real Israel, at a very down-to-earth price. If you've found this book useful, write and tell me so. If you've had problems at one of the recommended establishments, or just some general travel difficulty, write and let me know so I can work out the bugs and help other travelers to avoid bad times.

Israel on $30 and $35 a Day has become a clearinghouse for low-cost hotel and restaurant finds, and budget travel tips, contributed by its savvy, aware readers. If you've come across any particularly appealing hotel, restaurant, bargain, or interesting travel information, please don't keep it to yourself. Send your letters and suggestions to Tom Brosnahan, Prentice Hall Press, One Gulf + Western Plaza, New York, NY 10023.

Incidentally, I *personally* read each and every letter, postcard, telegram, epistle, and note-in-a-bottle that comes in from readers of *Israel on $30 and $35 a Day*. In most cases, I fire off a reply in a short time. So do it—write me a note!

5. The $25-A-Day Travel Club—How to Save Money on All Your Travels

In this book we'll be looking at how to get your money's worth in Israel, but there is a "device" for saving money and determining value on *all* your trips. It's the popular, international $25-A-Day Travel Club, now in its 25th successful year of operation. The Club was formed at the urging of numerous readers of the $$$-A-Day and Dollarwise Guides, who felt that such an organization could provide continuing travel information and a sense of community to value-minded travelers in all parts of the world. And so it does!

In keeping with the budget concept, the annual membership fee is low and is immediately exceeded by the value of your benefits. Upon receipt of $18 (U.S. residents), or $20 U.S. by check drawn on a U.S. bank or via international postal money order in U.S. funds (Canadian, Mexican, and other foreign residents) to cover one year's membership, we will send all new members the following items.

(1) Any *two* of the following books

Please designate in your letter which two you wish to receive:

Frommer's $-A-Day Guides
Europe on $25 a Day
Australia on $25 a Day
Eastern Europe on $25 a Day
England on $35 a Day
Greece including Istanbul and Turkey's Aegean Coast on $25 a Day
Hawaii on $50 a Day
India on $15 & $25 a Day
Ireland on $30 a Day
Israel on $30 & $35 a Day
Mexico on $20 a Day (plus Belize and Guatemala)
New York on $45 a Day
New Zealand on $25 a Day
Scandinavia on $50 a Day
Scotland and Wales on $35 a Day
South America on $30 a Day
Spain and Morocco (plus the Canary Is.) on $40 a Day
Turkey on $25 a Day
Washington, D.C., on $40 a Day

Frommer's Dollarwise Guides
Dollarwise Guide to Austria and Hungary
Dollarwise Guide to Belgium, Holland, & Luxembourg
Dollarwise Guide to Bermuda and The Bahamas
Dollarwise Guide to Canada
Dollarwise Guide to the Caribbean
Dollarwise Guide to Egypt
Dollarwise Guide to England and Scotland
Dollarwise Guide to France
Dollarwise Guide to Germany
Dollarwise Guide to Italy
Dollarwise Guide to Japan and Hong Kong
Dollarwise Guide to Portugal, Madeira, and the Azores
Dollarwise Guide to the South Pacific
Dollarwise Guide to Switzerland and Liechtenstein
Dollarwise Guide to Alaska
Dollarwise Guide to California and Las Vegas
Dollarwise Guide to Florida
Dollarwise Guide to the Mid-Atlantic States
Dollarwise Guide to New England
Dollarwise Guide to New York State
Dollarwise Guide to the Northwest
Dollarwise Guide to Skiing USA—East
Dollarwise Guide to Skiing USA—West
Dollarwise Guide to the Southeast and New Orleans
Dollarwise Guide to the Southwest
Dollarwise Guide to Texas

(Dollarwise Guides discuss accommodations and facilities in all price ranges, with emphasis on the medium-priced.)

Frommer's Touring Guides
Egypt
Florence
London
Paris
Venice
(These new, color illustrated guides include walking tours, cultural and historic sites, and other vital travel information.)

A Shopper's Guide to Best Buys in England, Scotland, and Wales
(Describes in detail hundreds of places to shop—department stores, factory outlets, street markets, and craft centers—for great quality British bargains.)

A Shopper's Guide to the Caribbean
(Two experienced Caribbean hands guide you through this shopper's paradise, offering witty insights and helpful tips on the wares and emporia of more than 25 islands.)

Bed & Breakfast—North America
(This guide contains a directory of over 150 organizations that offer bed & breakfast referrals and reservations throughout North America. The scenic attractions and schools and universities near the homes of each are also listed.)

Dollarwise Guide to Cruises
(This complete guide covers all the basics of cruising—ports of call, costs, fly-cruise package bargains, cabin selection booking, embarkation and debarkation and describes in detail over 60 or so ships cruising the waters of Alaska, the Caribbean, Mexico, Hawaii, Panama, Canada, and the United States.)

Dollarwise Guide to Skiing Europe
(Describes top ski resorts in Austria, France, Italy, and Switzerland. Illustrated with maps of each resort area plus full-color trail maps.)

Fast 'n' Easy Phrase Book
(French, German, Spanish, and Italian—all in one convenient, easy-to-use phrase guide.)

Honeymoon Guide
(A special guide for that most romantic trip of your life, with full details on planning and choosing the destination that will be just right in the U.S. [California, New England, Hawaii, Florida, New York, South Carolina, etc.], Canada, Mexico, and the Caribbean.)

How to Beat the High Cost of Travel
(This practical guide details how to save money on absolutely all travel items—accommodations, transportation, dining, sightseeing, shopping, taxes, and more. Includes special budget information for seniors, students, singles, and families.)

Marilyn Wood's Wonderful Weekends
(This very selective guide covers the best mini-vacation destinations within a 175-mile radius of New York City. It describes special country inns and other

accommodations, restaurants, picnic spots, sights, and activities—all the information needed for a two- or three-day stay.)

Motorist's Phrase Book
(A practical phrase book in French, German, and Spanish designed specifically for the English-speaking motorist touring abroad.)

Swap and Go—Home Exchanging Made Easy
(Two veteran home exchangers explain in detail all the money-saving benefits of a home exchange, and then describe precisely how to do it. Also includes information on home rentals and many tips on low-cost travel.)

The Candy Apple: New York for Kids
(A spirited guide to the wonders of the Big Apple by a savvy New York grandmother with a kid's-eye view to fun. Indispensable for visitors and residents alike.)

Travel Diary and Record Book
(A 96-page diary for personal travel notes plus a section for such vital data as passport and traveler's check numbers, itinerary, postcard list, special people and places to visit, and a reference section with temperature and conversion charts, and world maps with distance zones.)

Where to Stay USA
(By the Council on International Educational Exchange, this extraordinary guide is the first to list accommodations in all 50 states that cost anywhere from $3 to $30 per night.)

(2) A one-year subscription to *The Wonderful World of Budget Travel*

This quarterly eight-page tabloid newspaper keeps you up to date on fast-breaking developments in low-cost travel in all parts of the world bringing you the latest money-saving information—the kind of information you'd have to pay $25 a year to obtain elsewhere. This consumer-conscious publication also features columns of special interest to readers: **Hospitality Exchange** (members all over the world who are willing to provide hospitality to other members as they pass through their home cities); **Share-a-Trip** (offers requests from members for travel companions who can share costs and help avoid the burdensome single supplement); and **Readers Ask . . . Readers Reply** (travel questions from members to which other members reply with authentic firsthand information).

(3) A copy of *Arthur Frommer's Guide to New York*

This is a pocket-size guide to hotels, restaurants, nightspots, and sightseeing attractions in all price ranges throughout the New York area.

(4) Your personal membership card

Membership entitles you to purchase through the Club all Arthur Frommer publications for a third to a half off their regular retail prices during the term of your membership.

So why not join this hardy band of international budgeteers and participate in its exchange of travel information and hospitality? Simply send your name and address, together with your annual membership fee of $18 (U.S. residents) or $20 U.S. (Canadian, Mexican, and other foreign residents), by check drawn on a U.S. bank or via international postal money order in U.S. funds to: $25-A-Day Travel Club, Inc., Frommer Books, Gulf + Western Building, One Gulf +

Western Plaza, New York, NY 10023. And please remember to specify which *two* of the books in section (1) above you wish to receive in your initial package of members' benefits. Or, if you prefer, use the last page of this book, simply checking off the two books you select and enclosing $18 or $20 in U.S. currency.

Once you are a member, there is no obligation to buy additional books. No books will be mailed to you without your specific order.

Chapter I

GETTING THERE

1. Before You Leave Home
2. Going by Air
3. By Ship from Greece and Cyprus
4. Travel to Egypt or Jordan
5. Arrival, and Travel Within Israel

THE STATE OF ISRAEL is located on the far-eastern end of the Mediterranean, no less than 6,000 nautical miles from New York. By all rights it should cost a small packet to travel to Israel; and the widespread belief that a trip to Israel definitely is expensive has stopped many tourists—particularly the budget tourist—from ever dreaming of attempting the trip.

The fact is that under certain circumstances it costs less to fly to Israel than to fly to Rome or Athens! And with that provocative statement, I begin our study of the cheapest ways to get to the place under discussion.

1. Before You Leave Home

Every experienced budget traveler knows that an enjoyable, low-cost trip begins quite some time before boarding an aircraft. Study airline fare tables looking for special low-cost flights. Look at Israel's holiday calendar to see whether you'll be there on any busy holidays, in which case you should have hotel reservations. Expect to pay a premium—up to 15% or 20%—on holidays. Or decide to visit Israel when hotel prices are down and airlines are offering promotional fares.

Make sure your passport is up-to-date. Study the books and maps you've gathered so that you'll know what's what and what's where even before you land at Israel's Ben-Gurion International Airport. Throughout this book are names and addresses of organizations that can help you have an enjoyable stay, but often you must contact them in advance. Want to use the Youth Hostels, or stay at a congenial, low-priced Christian hospice, or take a cycling tour, or plant a tree? You may have to make advance preparations. Be advised.

To help you with all these details, I'll provide some tips on packing and reading up before you go.

EVERYTHING YOU ALWAYS WANTED TO KNOW ABOUT ISRAEL: More questions, about electrical current, Customs, Tourist Information Offices, how to use the telephone, or what the weather's like? Don't neglect the marvelously detailed Chapter IX, "Details, Details!" and the fact-packed Appendix at the back of this book.

TRAVELING WITH CHILDREN: Israel is a young country with a young population. After a week in the country, you get used to the surprising number of babies, prams, and playgrounds. If you plan to travel with a small child, you'll have lots of local company.

The better hotels, and even most of the smaller ones, will know whom to call for babysitting services, so the front desk is your first resort. Request a sitter as early as possible—even at breakfast time—on the day you'll need one. If you plan to stay in the hotel for the evening, but not in your room, ask if the hotel can utilize your room telephone as an intercom. That way the switchboard operator or front-desk clerk can notify you if the baby begins to cry.

Car seats are available from rental firms, but again, you must reserve one as early as possible. It may have to be brought from some other rental station.

Disposable diapers, called *tafnukim*, are sold at some drugstores in Israel. Expect them to be relatively expensive. But when you're traveling, perhaps you'll figure that the convenience is worth it.

Not all restaurants will have highchairs, but many will (remember all those baby sabras!) and others are usually happy to work out ad hoc accommodations for members of the next generation.

TRAVEL FOR THE HANDICAPPED: A handy and detailed guide entitled *Access in Israel*, "A Guide for the Disabled and those with problems getting around," is published by Pauline Hephaistos Survey Projects, 39 Bradley Gardens, West Ealing, London W.13, England. The charitable organization that publishes the guide does not charge a set price, and in fact will send you a copy for free. But it actually costs them about £2 to publish each copy, and they ask that you make a contribution in a similar amount, if you can, to cover publishing, research, and (in addition) postage and handling.

The 122-page guide includes useful maps of easily traversed routes, including Jerusalem's Old City; a handy guide to hotels, Kibbutz Inns, youth hostels, and their conditions of access. It even covers access and transportation situations at the major airports from which you might commence or terminate your flight, such as New York's JFK, Chicago's O'Hare, London's Heathrow, and Lod's Ben-Gurion.

PACKING: Everything you'll need in Israel you can buy right there, but if you prefer to come prepared, here's a list of items you'll find useful or necessary: a stopper for sink or tub, as many hotels don't have them; a plastic bottle of soap liquid for your wash-and-wears; tissues to carry at all times, as many public rest rooms lack paper (or at least the kind you're used to). Add sunscreening lotion, sunglasses, and a shade hat, and consider all three utterly vital necessities from May to October. Insect repellent is another item I wouldn't travel without, especially if I'm headed for the Dead Sea or desert regions. If you're planning on long walks or hiking, a canteen will come in handy. Cosmetics and personal toiletries come next, and a plastic bottle of astringent can be mighty welcome when you're touring around. Some travelers include a supply of tablets for relief of miscellaneous aches and upsets. Then they stuff in some extra rolls of film, safety pins, and a small sewing kit. Again, you can buy all such things in Israel, but the prices are quite high on some of these items, whether locally made or imported.

As for clothing, there are no hard-and-fast rules on what is or isn't proper gear. You'll see almost everything, from ancient dress to modern fads and fashions, so let comfort guide your personal selection of styles. However, do try to select fabrics that you can personally wash and dry, because that's the best way to keep clean in this land where laundry services usually take about a week and cost like crazy. Dry cleaning is expensive too (especially in hotels), and can take up to four days, unless you up the ante for "express" service of one or two days. So it's really best to take easy-wash and quick-dry fabrics, plus a few plastic clothespins with hangers attached. You'll find clothing for all climates in such fabrics.

Speaking of fads and fashions: Jeans, shorts, and the like are acceptable, but not everywhere—bring along a long-sleeve shirt or modestly long skirt to wear when visiting synagogues and other religious places. Without such coverings, you'll not be allowed to enter and/or will seem offensive.

It's also a good idea for women traveling alone to avoid short-shorts, very short skirts, or tank tops. The male inhabitants of the Holy Land can be very Mediterranean at times.

Whatever else you pack will depend on the season, but try to travel light, with just one suitcase per person. Keep in mind too: even those on a tight budget do shop along the way.

Summer

The hot weather of summer usually lasts from mid-May to the beginning of October. The evenings are cool or reasonably cool. Jerusalem, Safed, and the inland regions are dry. It is moist along the coast. Eilat and the deserts are very dry. You will be happy to wear a sweater or jacket in Jerusalem after the sun goes down. The days are hot all over.

Nevertheless, there are a few precautions you should take, and the most important of these is to remember that the sun is unusually strong—so wear a hat!

Second, take clothes that are "cool" and will allow your body to breathe. This is very important, because you will perspire a lot. And because of the lack of humidity, you will hardly be aware of it—*if* your clothes allow the moisture to evaporate. Arnel and nylon fabrics may be nonwrinkle, but they are also nonbreathing. Cotton with a combination of Dacron and Rayon is much to be preferred.

When I refer to "cool" clothing, I don't mean that you should take many sundresses; in fact, dresses that expose much of your body to the sun cancel out the protection of wearing a hat. Rather, loose short sleeves that will cover your shoulders fit the requirement. Even the olive-skinned person who tans easily can burn in this sun, so use common sense to protect yourself. I found that salt tablets often help to beat the heat.

While choosing which clothes to pack, keep in mind that both men and women should wear tops with sleeves, and skirts or trousers when visiting holy sites of any faith. Visitors with sleeveless tops or shorts will not be allowed in, or may offend religious sensibilities.

Winter

From November through early March is "winter" in Israel. Not winter as you know it, with heavy coats, mufflers, snow-wear, and cozy fires, but rainy-season winter—more like a chilly April. It's a good idea, in that time of year, to bring several sweaters of different weights, so that you can peel them off or pile them on, depending on the day and the location. Jerusalem tends to be chilly in winter (down to freezing), while Haifa and Tel Aviv often have spells of warm spring-like weather in December and January.

Of course, your staple apparel for winter is a good waterproof raincoat, a rain hat, an umbrella, and a pair of sturdy, comfortable boots. For women, a pair of warm slacks and socks can also give you a much-needed extra layer of warmth in an unheated Jerusalem hotel. And finally, a wool or knit ladies' suit, or corduroy skirt and jacket, can be used for all occasions—touring, evening out, traveling—depending on whether you wear a sweater or an evening blouse with the outfit.

In Her Suitcase, Take:

    one pair walking shoes
    one pair sandals
    one pair rubber sandals
    4 sleeveless drip-dry blouses
    2 cotton skirts
    3 daytime dresses (drip-dry)
    one bathing suit
    one bathing cap
    2 pair slacks
    one wool sweater (also doubles for evening wear)
    one pair medium-heel shoes
    one dark-colored cotton dress for evening
    one cotton sun hat (for beach and city)
    underwear
    sunglasses
    washcloth and soap
    pharmaceuticals, including salt tablets, aspirin, suntan cream, zinc ointment (for sun blisters), toothpaste, talcum powder, toilet paper, and personal items
    5 folding plastic hangers, 4 plastic combination clothespin hangers, one stretching clothesline

In His Suitcase, Take:

    one pair sneakers (or sandals)
    one pair rubber sandals
    one pair walking shoes
    one bathing suit
    5 drip-dry shirts
    3 pair slacks
    one pair shorts
    one tie (you may never need it, but just in case)
    one sports jacket
    underwear
    sunglasses
    washcloth and soap
    sun hat
    personal items, such as brush, shoe polish, shaving equipment, and toilet paper

BOOKS ABOUT ISRAEL: For tourists who take their traveling seriously and want to bone up on Israel, there are several good books that can greatly add to the enjoyment and appreciation of your stay.

The single most helpful book I've come across is *The Penguin Shorter Atlas of the Bible,* by Luc. H. Grollenberg. Much more than a mere atlas (though it does have useful maps), it is a detailed but fascinating history of the land from earliest times through the times of Jesus to the destruction of Jerusalem by the Romans.

One need hardly mention such bestsellers as *Masada, Exodus,* and *The Source.* Werner Keller's *The Bible as History,* now available in paperback, reads like a suspense novel, although it's actually an archeological survey of the biblical remnants uncovered in Israel and the surrounding countries. A fascinating, well-written book, *A History of the Holyland,* edited by Michael Avi-Yonah, is another good selection. You'll also see Josephus' *The Jewish Wars* on every English-speaking Israeli's bookshelf. Ruler of the Galilee during Roman times—and a sometime traitor—he was also a historian who provided historical commentaries and anecdotes about almost every area you'll see in Israel. In fact, his section on the Masada battle is the most often quoted of all historical texts, in terms of factual accuracy. More recently, Yigal Yadin wrote two very readable accounts about Bar Kokhba and Masada, detailing history, archeology, and excavated finds; each is handsomely illustrated. His latest book now deals with the ancient site of Hatzor.

Also check out:

Footloose in Jerusalem, by Sarah Fox Kaminker, a series of guided walking tours in Jerusalem; *The Arab-Israel Conflict: Its History in Maps,* by Martin Gilbert, tracing the history of the conflict from the turn of the century to the present day; *A Life,* the autobiography of Jerusalem's famous mayor, Teddy Kollek, written with his son, Amos; *The Israel I Love,* by Noel Calef; *The Natural History of the Land of the Bible,* by Azaria Alon; *The Autobiography of Abba Eban; The Rabin Memoirs,* by Itzhak Rabin; *The Revolt,* by Menachem Begin; *My Life,* by Golda Meir; *Story of My Life,* by Moshe Dayan; Samuel Katz's *Battleground—Fact and Fantasy in Palestine;* and *Raquela: A Woman of Israel,* by Ruth Gruber.

2. Going by Air

FARES: Air fares are in a constant state of flux, buffeted by deregulation and by ever-changing oil prices. The following fares, therefore, from El Al are guidelines and correct *only* at press time.

The year is divided into periods (low season, high season, shoulder, etc.), and each type of ticket has different fare periods. Thus, if you buy a 6- to 90-day excursion ticket, you can fly at the low winter rate up to April 3; but if you buy a 6- to 60-day APEX super-saver fare (for several hundred dollars less), you can fly at the winter rate only until March 23. You'll have to check with your travel agent for exact dates. Do it early. You can save yourself up to $200 by flying on the last day of the winter fare period rather than 24 hours later when the new fare period begins. (Obviously, the flights on the last day of a fare period fill up quickly!)

Sunshine 6- to 60-Day Super-APEX Fare

Priced at $899 to $919, depending on when you fly, this is the cheapest round-trip fare regularly offered by El Al from New York to Tel Aviv. You must stay at least 6 days and not more than 60; your ticket must be bought at least 14 days in advance (if not, there's a $100 surcharge). No stopovers are permitted. If you cancel, you must pay a $100 penalty; if you change your return date, $100; if you fly within a week of the beginning of Christmas or Passover, there's a $100 surcharge.

Normal 6- to 180-Day Excursion Fare

Costing about $944 to $1,164, this one has fewer restrictions.

Special Economy-Class Fare

These are special promotional fares, offered only from time to time, and in very limited quantities. If you can get one, you've got a real bargain, as they range from $639 in winter to $749 in summer, round trip. There's no minimum stay, the ticket is good for a year, there's no advance-purchase requirement, and you're allowed one stopover in Europe—all for less than half the normal Economy fare!

Youth Fare

This one is for anyone who, ". . . at time of commencement of travel, has reached his/her 12th but not his/her 24th birthday," according to El Al's official tariff. It costs slightly more than the excursion fare, but it's good for a year and you can change your plans as you like.

Normal Fares

Normal fares are the ones where you buy your ticket whenever you like, change your plans as you like, cancel if you want to (for a full refund). Another advantage of a normal, full-fare ticket is that if your flight is delayed or postponed, the airline picks up the tab for meals and lodging—something they aren't required to do for the cheaper fares. El Al has First Class, Business Class, and Economy. One-way fares are exactly half of these round-trip fares. In Economy you pay $2,690. In Business you pay $2,958. In First Class, the fare is $4,422 round trip. Children pay 50% of these fares; infants, 10%.

Charter Flights

You may think that the advent of airline deregulation has put an end to cheap charter flights. Not so! Chartering a whole plane and filling it with budget-minded travelers is still one of the best ways to save money on a flight.

The advantage, then, is price. The disadvantages are these: the flight may be cancelled due to insufficient demand; it may be delayed on departure, sometimes for quite a number of hours; you are committed to fly on specific flights, and it may be impossible to switch to other flights (though you can often sell your tickets on the open market). If you lose your ticket, or if you get to the airport late and miss the flight, you lose your money. Period.

Since all charter airlines must meet government regulations just like the scheduled airlines, your flight should be just as safe as on a regular, scheduled airline. (In fact you may end up flying on one of the big scheduled airlines; the word "charter" can also denote a block of seats on a scheduled flight.) And though a charter airline does occasionally go bankrupt, you can protect yourself by making sure that your payment is made not directly to the charter operator or airline, but to its escrow fund; this way, in the unlikely event that your flights don't operate as planned, you can get your money back directly from the escrow bank.

If you're certain of your plans, and keep an open mind and a tolerant attitude, a charter flight can save you hundreds of dollars.

The list of companies operating charter flights to Israel changes from season to season, but you can get up-to-date information, and you can buy your ticket, from any travel agent. Here are some examples of charter flights from New York to Tel Aviv, current only as of this writing:

Tower Air, Hangar 8, Second Floor, JFK International Airport, Jamaica, NY 11430 (tel. 718/917-8500, or toll free 800/221-2500), weekly flights for as little as $769 off-season.

Sunbeam Travel, Suite 904, 274 Madison Ave., New York, NY 10016 (tel. 212/725-8835, or toll free 800/247-6659), operates weekly charters for $549 to $599 in high season. You can reserve a seat for the outbound flight, but leave your return date open, as long as you return within 120 days (four months). The freedom of an open-return ticket is nice, but keep in mind that there are only a few flights a week, and certain returning flights may fill up early.

TFI Tours International, 34 W. 32nd St., New York, NY 10001 (tel. 212/736-1140, or toll free 800/223-6363, or 800/235-9834) runs a weekly charter flight that costs $399 one way, $699 round trip, year round.

Package Tours

You can get even lower prices for air travel if you book an inclusive tour. You'll find that the tour price is far, far below the normal sum for the air fare, hotels, tours, and meals involved. If a tour fits your plans, don't hesitate because you always went freelance before. The more loosely organized tours are as good as traveling by yourself. The only difference is that you combine your purchasing power with that of others to take advantage of bulk rates, a sort of "travelers' mutual fund."

El Al Israel Airlines, Ltd., has its own program of **"Milk & Honey Vacations,"** which include all the highlights of the country at prices that are simply incredible. For example, the **"Sunsational Israel"** tour, available from mid-November through mid-March (except for mid-December through early January), gives you round-trip air transportation from New York to Tel Aviv, five nights' hotel room in Jerusalem or Tel Aviv, a Hertz rental car for five days (you pay gas, mileage, and insurance), and numerous discount coupons good at shops, restaurants, and attractions in Israel. You get all this for only $779 per person.

Purchased separately, these travel services would cost a minimum of $1,000, if you figure that the bargain Sunshine Super-APEX Fare alone is $779, the car is priced at $18 per day ($90 total), the hotel would be at least $20 per person per day ($100 total), and the coupons represent further savings.

This astoundingly low tour price assumes that two people will travel together, each paying the tour price and sharing a hotel room. You must pay somewhat more if you fly from Chicago, Los Angeles, or Miami, if you want a hotel fancier than three stars, and if you want a hotel room just for one person alone (the "single supplement"). Also, keep in mind that you will have some other expenses, particularly for the car, such as mileage at 24¢ per kilometer, insurance at $10 per day, and gas at $2.15 per gallon; also, you'll be paying for meals, and some tips at the hotel. But any way you look at them, these tours represent marvelous value-for-money.

There are plenty of other El Al Milk & Honey Vacations. These are set up slightly differently from the "Sunsational Israel" program, as you pay for air fare and land arrangements separately. But the savings are equally impressive, and hotels are of a higher grade, being either four-star or deluxe. The 12-day/10-night **"Israel Discovery Tour"** gives you three nights in Tel Aviv, two in Galilee, and five nights in Jerusalem for $429 to $619 plus air fare, depending on when you fly and what grade of hotel you choose. The **"Israel Plus Tour"** is similar, but with six nights in Tel Aviv (15 days and 13 nights total), for $529 to $789 plus air fare. If you'd like some guided travel and some time on your own, look into the **"Israel at Leisure Tour,"** a 22-day/20-night program which gives you six nights in Tel Aviv, two in Galilee, and 12 in Jerusalem; your schedule is free for that entire second week, and you use Jerusalem as your base for further explorations of Israel in depth, on your own. The price for all this is $679 to $1,060, plus air fare.

The Milk & Honey Vacations program also includes an offer for a junket to Eilat priced at $180, including round-trip flight from Tel Aviv, three nights at the luxurious Sonesta Hotel, and breakfast every day. There's a Cairo tour too, with round-trip flight from Tel Aviv, three nights at the Ramses Hilton, and airport transfers, for just $249. Any travel agent can give you all the details, and make your reservations for you, at no extra charge. Look into these tours if they are at all in accord with your travel plans. Why pay more, and get less, by doing it on your own?

WHO FLIES TO ISRAEL: Fourteen international airlines fly from New York to Tel Aviv. The first airline one thinks of is **El Al,** Israel's national carrier and the pioneer in nonstop service (10½ hours) between New York and Tel Aviv.

The other major carrier on the New York–Tel Aviv route is **TWA,** with 19 flights per week during the summer, including nonstop New York–Tel Aviv service three days a week, and 16 flights per week that make one stop (Paris, Rome, or Athens). They offer a plethora of fares, including excursions, APEXs, and full tours including hotels and land transportation. Some travelers report that security checks take less time on TWA than on El Al.

El Al's Check-In Service

Passengers on El Al flights who are leaving from Jerusalem, Tel Aviv, or Haifa can avail themselves of El Al's in-city check-in service. The Jerusalem office, 12 Hillel St. (tel. 02-246-725), opens especially for this purpose every evening (except Friday and eves of holidays) from 6:45 to 11 p.m. In Tel Aviv, El Al's in-town terminal (tel. 03-625-252), next to the Central Railway Station in northern Tel Aviv, is open from 4 p.m. to midnight every day except Friday (on Saturday it opens after the end of the Sabbath). In Haifa, early check-in is presently at the El Al office, 80 Ha-Atzma'ut Rd. (tel. 04-641-166), corner of Khayat, in the port area only a block from the Paris Square Carmelit station, open each evening except Friday from 6:30 to 10 p.m. It's scheduled to move, however, so check for a new address.

Some details you should know about early check-in: you can check in only the night before your flight is scheduled to depart; early check-in is not applicable to all flights (you cannot check in early for night flights, for instance); you must have your ticket, passport, and money for the airport departure tax (about $10 in shekels) when you check in, just as though you were at the airport. Your bags will be inspected right there in the El Al office, and then sent directly to the aircraft. The next day, you need arrive at the airport only in time for passport control, security check, and boarding, for which you must figure one hour and 15 minutes. Without early check-in, you're required to be at the airport 2¼ hours before flight time. This is no idle deadline, by the way. You could miss your flight if you ignore this time limit.

ISRAELI DEPARTURE TAX: There's an Israeli government departure tax of about $10, levied in new shekels, when you check in for your flight. You can pay in dollars, but the rough-and-ready exchange rate at the check-in counter will cost you money. A better plan is to save slightly more than $10 in shekels for check-in time, then after checking in, spend whatever is left on a snack, a drink, or a newspaper.

3. By Ship from Greece and Cyprus

Several car-ferries make the journey to Haifa from Venice, Piraeus (Athens), Heraklion (Crete), Rhodes, and Limassol (Cyprus). Ships include the Stability Line's *Vergina* and the Sol Maritime Services' *Sol Phryne,* which are either Greek- or Cypriot-flag vessels.

The usual route is Piraeus, Rhodes, Limassol, Haifa, with each port being reached on a different day. Standard itinerary calls for departure from Piraeus (Athens) on Thursday, arriving in Haifa on Sunday. The route and departure days are the same for the ships when they leave Haifa; that is, departures are on Sunday. These schedules can change according to the seasons, so use them as a general indication only; get the latest details in Piraeus or Haifa (see below).

While several of these ships have good accommodations and service, others are not so hot. Conditions can change from season to season, so check out the ship in advance, if you can, just the same as you'd look at any hotel room before registering. It's also a good idea to pack some food along, even if you intend to buy your meals on board. Sometimes the dining rooms run out of food before everyone has dined. Don't depend on buying food in the ports of call either, as arrival and departure might be in the middle of the night.

Sample fares, between Piraeus and Haifa, port taxes included, are given in the table below. Students and youth are entitled to a 20% discount, and anyone who buys a round-trip ticket is entitled to a 20% discount. Sorry, only one discount per person.

Fares Between Piraeus and Haifa
(Per person, port taxes included)

Accommodation	January–May	June–September
Deck chair (no meals)	$67	$72
Reclining seat (no meals)	$77	$82
4- to 6-berth cabin, washbasin, and three meals	$137	$152
2- to 4-berth cabin, washbasin, and three meals	$162–$192	$172–$212
2- to 4-berth cabin, shower, toilet, and three meals	$212–$232	$232–$262
Private car (according to length)	$96–$160	$106–$160
Motorcycle	$60	$60

By the way, if you plan to take your car, you can get a 20% reduction for a round-trip ticket, or 10% if you're a member of an auto club.

Tickets

For tickets in Athens, go to the **Sol Maritime office** at 4 Filellinon St. (tel. 323-3176), which is near Syntagma (Constitution) Square; in Rhodes, the office is at 11 Amerikis St., and in Limassol at 1 Irini St. The agent in Haifa is Jacob Caspi Ltd., 1 Natan Kaiserman St. (tel. 04-674-444), in the port area. Kaiserman is a tiny street which begins at 76 Ha-Atzma'ut St.

The **Stability Line's office** is in Piraeus at 11 Sahtouri St. (tel. 414-3312); the agent in Haifa is Multitours Passenger Lines, 55 Ha-Namaz St. (tel. 04-674-485 or 663-570), in Haifa's port area.

4. Travel to Egypt or Jordan

Signature of the Israeli-Egyptian peace treaty was a dream-come-true for Israeli and foreign tourists alike. Now you can visit both of these ancient-modern lands in one trip. It's easy, and it's inexpensive. As for Jordan, that's trickier.

Basically, there are four routes that will interest you: between Cairo and Tel Aviv by air, between the same points by land (bus or car), between Sinai and/or Cairo and Eilat, and between Jerusalem and Amman. Travel into Sinai is discussed in detail in Chapter VIII, "The Dead Sea and the Negev." The other routes are discussed immediately hereafter, but before I get on to that discussion I should note that it is more difficult to get from Cairo to Israel than vice-versa. No real problem, just that the Egyptians have not yet begun actively to encourage travel to Israel. Information may be a bit scarce and hard to come by, but rest assured that it can be done, and a little perseverance will bear fruit.

FROM ISRAEL TO EGYPT: If you would like to include Egypt in your itinerary, you should get a visa before leaving the States. An Egyptian tourist visa can be obtained by visiting or writing to the Egyptian mission nearest you: Egyptian Embassy, 2310 Decatur, Pl. NW, Washington, DC 20008 (tel. 202/234-3903); Egyptian Consulate, 1110 Second Ave., New York, NY (tel. 212/759-7120); or Egyptian Consulate, 3001 Pacific Ave., San Francisco, CA 94115 (tel. 415/346-9700). You can get a visa in Tel Aviv, but it will be an awful lot faster at home. By the way, visas, stamps, and airport and exit taxes for travel to Egypt may end up costing as much as $25.

In addition, if you enter Egypt as an independent tourist (not part of a tour or group), you will be required to convert about $150 into Egyptian pounds at the commercial exchange rate. The rate may be, say, 83 Egyptian piastres to the dollar, rather than the 135 piastres (1.35 Egyptian pounds) you'd get for the same dollar at the Tourist Exchange Rate from a bank in Cairo. This amounts to a travel tax of about $50. The conversion requirement seems to be a leftover from the days of Soviet influence. It is supposed to assure that you change money legally to cover your expenses (that's why tours and groups are exempted —their expenses are assumed to be covered by payment through legal channels). The black-market rate for Egyptian pounds is probably well above the official rate (as of this writing) of 135 piastres to the dollar.

By Land

You cannot drive an Israeli rental car into Egypt, and that includes Sinai.

If you make the trip in your own vehicle you must obtain a permit to take a vehicle into Egypt from the Consular Section, Ministry for Foreign Affairs, Hakirya, Romema, Jerusalem (tel. 02-235-111).

For most of us, then, going into Egypt by land means going by bus or shared taxi (*sherut*).

By Bus: You can easily get from Tel Aviv to Cairo and back by signing up for one of the daily (except Saturday) bus tours offered by every travel agency. Buses leave from Jerusalem, pick up more passengers in Tel Aviv (if not already full), and then head off for Cairo. The trip takes 10 to 12 hours. Sign up just for the one-way bus ($17 to $25), the round-trip bus ($30 to $40), or a tour which gives you hotel, or hotel and sightseeing, or the works: a full-blown guided tour of all the Nile's treasures. Students get good discounts. For more information on this Cairo Express, contact **Galilee Tours,** 3 Ben-Sira St., Jerusalem 95181 (tel. 02-246-858), 142 Ha-Yarkon St. (tel. 03-221-372) or 42 Ben-Yehuda St. (tel. 03-203-311) in Tel Aviv, or any Israeli travel agent.

Food and Drink Along the Way: Whether you go by bus or sherut, you should pack some food and beverages. Refreshments and sustenance bought at points along the route will be expensive, low quality, and perhaps even dangerous to your health.

By Sherut: The trip by sherut from Jerusalem or Tel Aviv to Cairo works out to cost slightly less than the bus. You progress in stages, starting from the sherut stands at Damascus Gate or Herod's Gate (Jerusalem) or the Central Bus Station (Tel Aviv). For less than $10, a big eight-seat Mercedes driven by an Israeli or Palestinian Arab will whisk you to the border. It's a good idea to reserve your seat in the car a day or so in advance.

From the border, a shuttlebus takes you to the Egyptian side. After formalities there, you board another shared taxi (called *servis,* "sehr-*vees,*" in Arabic) to the Suez Canal. You take a free ride on the ferryboat across the canal, and hop into yet another servis at Qantara for the final leg to Cairo. Charges for transport on the Egyptian portion of the journey work out to about $10 as well. The servis should drop you in Cairo's Ramses Square, near the railway station. For the return journey, you start from Ramses Square in a servis headed for Qantara.

By Air

El Al has four flights a week between Cairo and Tel Aviv, and similar service is operated by **Air Sinai.** Cost is $122 one way, $244 round trip, and the flight takes about 45 minutes.

For the El Al flight, contact any travel agent; in Cairo, contact El Al's agent, Salah Nabhan & Co., 5 El-Makrizi St., Zamalek (tel. 699-912 or 699-795).

Air Sinai can be contacted in Tel Aviv at 114 Ha-Yarkon St. (tel. 03-246-038 or 246-442). The Air Sinai office in Cairo is in the Nile Hilton, Tahrir Square (tel. 740-777 or 750-666).

You should look into tour packages if you plan to go by air. The basic air fare is not cheap, and if you have to spend in these lofty ranges, you might as well get a cut on the hotel and land arrangements. A tour will give you this cut in price.

Keep in mind also that you must pay an Israeli airport departure tax of $10 on all flights to Egypt from Ben-Gurion ($5 from Eilat).

FROM ISRAEL TO JORDAN: You can, in fact, cross between Israel and Jordan on the Allenby Bridge near Jericho, but it takes a good deal of advance planning before you leave home, and a capacity to endure some hassles. First, a summary of the political situation.

As far as Jordan is concerned, the Israeli-Jordanian border is in Jerusalem, not at the King Hussein Bridge (as the Allenby Bridge is known in Jordan). And as Jordan and Israel are technically still at war, you may not travel to either country if your passport bears any evidence of your having visited the other one.

To visit Jordan, you must also have a valid visa. You cannot obtain a Jordanian visa in Israel, since Jordan has no diplomatic representation there; and you can't get one at the Allenby/King Hussein Bridge "border" point since there is technically no border there. Though you can get a Jordanian visa in, say, Cairo or Nicosia (Cyprus), it is a much better idea to get one before you leave home. Contact the Jordanian Embassy, 3504 International Dr. NW, Washington, DC 20008 (tel. 202/966-2664), and they'll send you a visa application. You then must send your passport off to be stamped. Allow at least two weeks for this process.

When you enter Israel, you must convince the Immigration Officer not to stamp your passport directly. An obliging officer will stamp only the immigration form that you carry in your passport while in Israel.

Your trip to Jordan will no doubt start from Jerusalem or Jericho. It's a good idea to ask around in East Jerusalem or in Jericho about current conditions for the border crossing. West Bank residents, as quasi-Jordanian citizens, are allowed to travel from the West Bank to the East Bank; Israeli citizens are not.

As you start your journey, be aware that only vehicles (minibuses, taxis) specially licensed by the Israeli military authorities will be allowed to pass the first checkpoint on the approach to the Jordan River crossing point. If you hire a taxi without a special permit, the driver will have to drop you well short of the border, and you'll have to arrange for another cab to complete this journey ($20 for a five-minute ride!). Some taxi drivers don't know about this special permit business.

From East Jerusalem, reserve a seat ($12) in the minibus operated by **ABDO Taxi and Travel Service,** 42 Saladin St. (tel. 02-272-973 or 281-865), which will take you all the way to the final checkpoint; or you can hire a taxi at the Damascus Gate ($25 to $30), or in front of Jericho's Municipality building ($10 to $15), but be sure the driver has that all-important permit.

The border is not open at all on Saturday and closes at 1 p.m. on the other six days, so you must start early. You end up at the Israeli border station. It's air-conditioned, has rest rooms, a small snackbar, and a combination post office / currency-exchange office. It's a good idea to buy some Jordanian dinars here, as I didn't see any currency-exchange place on the Jordanian side. The currency-exchange office is also where you buy your exit permit, $13 a person. You also pay a couple of dollars for stamps for your luggage. After going through the border formalities, you then wait anywhere from a few minutes to an hour or more for a Jordanian bus to carry you across the bridge, at another $5 per person. If you look quickly, you can spot the Jordan River, just a stream really. Note also the bunkers bristling with machine guns on both sides. This is not a friendly border. The bus will drop you at the Jordanian border station, where the usual passport inspection takes place. After that, you're on your own. Taxis are available to take you into Amman for about $20.

You should note that you may find it difficult to recross from the East Bank to the West Bank. You'll need a special permit from the Jordanian Interior Ministry. It's best to plan your itinerary so that you leave Jordan for Egypt, Turkey, or Cyprus. If you've entered Jordan other than via the West Bank, you should find it easier to get a West Bank travel permit, which means that you can fly into Amman, visit Jordan, get a West Bank permit, and continue to Jerusalem. Stephen Zatland, a reader from Harrow, Middlesex, England, went from Turkey via Syria to Jordan in August 1986. He writes to say that "the Amman-to-Jerusalem journey went much quicker than expected. I left my Amman hotel at 7 a.m. by JETT bus, and was sitting in my Jerusalem hotel by 10:30 a.m." Note that Mr. Zatland had no Israeli stamp in his passport.

5. Arrival, and Travel Within Israel

Actually, there are various ways of arriving in Israel these days: by ship to Haifa, across the Allenby Bridge from Jordan, through the Sinai from Egypt. But these streams of tourists represent the merest trickle when compared with the flood of people touching down at Ben-Gurion International Airport.

BEN-GURION INTERNATIONAL AIRPORT: Israel is a small country, and Ben-Gurion International Airport, at Lod on the outskirts of Tel Aviv, serves the whole country. Other, smaller airports exist in Jerusalem, Tel Aviv, Haifa, Rosh Pinna, and Eilat. But most points in Israel are so easily accessible by bus and sherut (more on this in a minute) that few people spend the relatively large amount of money to fly.

After landing and passing through Immigration and Security, you'll be in the Arrivals Hall waiting for your baggage. There are lots of people on hand to help you here, including a fully staffed office of the Ministry of Tourism, a hotel reservations desk, rental-car desks, and a desk for the Voluntary Tourist Service representative (see Chapter IX under "Information" for details). Whether your need is for a map, a hotel room, or the number of the bus to Haifa, they'll be able to provide it.

From the Arrivals Hall you pass through Customs, in the British "Red" or "Green" passage system. Then you're outside, *in Israel.*

TRANSPORTATION FROM THE AIRPORT:
After walking down the long path lined with eager relatives and friends awaiting arriving passengers, you turn left to find a warren of bus lanes and stops, and rental-car and tour offices.

Buses

To Jerusalem, Egged operates buses more or less every half hour at a price of NIS3.50 ($2.35). The trip takes about 45 minutes. Schedules are posted by the bus ticket window which is in the low building amid the bus stops. Going by bus, you can be at your hotel in Jerusalem within two hours after your plane has landed.

To get to Tel Aviv, take the United Tours (tel. 03-298-181) Airport Shuttle Service bus 222 for NIS2.20 ($1.45) which departs at least once an hour, usually more frequently, between 4 a.m. and midnight (on Saturday, noon to midnight). It leaves the airport, stops at the El Al Air Terminal at the Central Railway Station, then stops near the Bnei Dan Youth Hostel, and then travels all along the waterfront boulevard named Ha-Yarkon Street, stopping at each cluster of hotels. The trip from the airport to your hotel should take a half hour or less.

There are also buses to Haifa and several other points directly from the airport. Check the schedules next to the bus ticket window.

Sheruts

The Israeli sherut (*"service"* in Hebrew) is a jitney cab which goes from city to city or point to point within a city. These days they're mostly long, limousine-like Mercedes-Benz cars. Sherut drivers will accost you as soon as you exit from the air terminal, asking if you want to go to Jerusalem or wherever. They won't depart until their eight-passenger car is full (or almost so). Sherut fares are about 25% higher than the bus; service is often faster and more comfortable. Sherut service from the airport to Jerusalem is highly regulated, with a fixed fare (about $4) for the trip from Ben-Gurion to almost any point in Jerusalem (except outlying places like Ein Kerem, Hadassah Medical Center, etc.). The price posted on the sign by the parked sheruts will probably be out of date—shekel prices rise frequently. Notice what the other passengers are paying, and then pay exactly the same, not a penny more, for the trip right to your hotel door.

All set to go? Here's some detailed information on inland transport to peruse while you cruise to your hotel.

BUSES WITHIN ISRAEL:
Most city and intercity bus routes are operated by two cooperative shareholder companies, Dan and Egged. Their equipment varies widely. Depending on the whim of fortune, you'll take your intercity bus ride in either spanking-new buses with red upholstery and efficient air conditioning or in a run-down, torn-upholstered, dirty-windowed, breathlessly hot bus. There's no way to control it.

Buses run from about 5:30 a.m. till late evening, though some routes operate until midnight. If possible, you should avoid bus travel at rush hours (7 to 8 a.m. and 4 to 6 p.m.). On Friday and the eves of Jewish holidays buses run only until an hour or two before sunset. East Jerusalem and the West Bank have partial bus service on Friday evening and Saturday, and Haifa has partial service on Saturday, but otherwise there is no bus service throughout the country from Friday afternoon till Saturday evening.

Both Dan and Egged have discount fare plans for both city and intercity buses. For instance, when you get to Jerusalem, Tel Aviv, or Haifa, the first time you climb on a city bus, don't just buy a single-fare ticket. Instead, ask for one of the multifare cards that are right at the driver's fingertips next to the single-fare tickets. If you are a senior citizen or a student, show your identification. The driver will sell you a multifare card at a regular, senior, or student discount. The color of the card is different for each category. The next time you get on a bus, the driver will punch your card. At less than 35¢, city bus tickets are not expensive. But why pay even that when you can pay much less?

As for intercity travel, Egged offers 14-, 21-, and 30-day passes good for unlimited travel throughout the country. Ask at any Egged Tours office for details.

Egged's central office is at 15 Frishman St., Tel Aviv (tel. 03-242-271), not far from the Israel Government Tourism Office. Egged is open Sunday through Thursday from 7 a.m. to 8 p.m., on Friday from 7 a.m. to 2 p.m.; closed Saturday. Students can apply for discounts here. For further information, in Jerusalem call 02-523-456 or 528-231; in Tel Aviv, call 03-432-777.

Egged has restaurants in 19 central bus stations, where prices are considerably cheaper than restaurants with the same level of food and service elsewhere. They are kosher.

The Dan bus company's main office is in the Hadar Dafna building, 39 Shaul Ha-Melekh, Tel Aviv (tel. 03-253-411). Ask there, or at any bus station, about discounts on Dan lines.

TRAINS IN ISRAEL: Trains are even cheaper than buses, but they link only six cities—Jerusalem, Beersheba, Dimona, Tel Aviv, Haifa, and Nahariya (with local stops made along the way). Although the vintage of some of the trains is rather ancient, they are usually roomy, and the railroad tracks run through some of central Israel's most beautiful areas. Just as you should experience the bus ride to Eilat, so too you really should make the trip from Tel Aviv to Jerusalem by train. The route is through the beautiful Judean Hills, a winding, mountain-clinging ride through a parched and rugged landscape.

By the way, when you're traveling by bus or sherut, you'll notice unused railroad tracks running seemingly to nowhere, in various parts of the country. These abandoned tracks are a throwback to the British Mandate times, when these railway lines connected Israel with Jordan, Egypt, and Lebanon.

Note: The International Student Identity Card holder obtains a 25% train discount.

Excepting the Sabbath and religious holidays, trains run daily. Operations close earlier on Friday and prior to holidays.

There are two train stations in Tel Aviv: the **Central** (sometimes called "North"; tel. 03-254-271) and the **Tel Aviv South** station (tel. 03-822-676).

SHERUTS: These are jitney-type taxis, which charge slightly more than a bus. They supplement city and intercity bus routes and often go where the bus doesn't go. On Saturday in many parts of the country they are the only transportation available.

Figure about 25% more than the bus fare if you want to know how much the sherut will cost. All sherut fares are about 25% higher at night, by the way.

Special rates for children are available. There is no charge for a child under 5 traveling with an adult. Two children under 5 pay one adult fare. For each additional child under 5, the full fare is required.

Sheruts usually make regular stops, but by and large they'll let you off at any bus stop in or out of the city along their routes, and you can reserve your seat in advance on a long trip. (Israel also has regular taxis, so when you hail what looks like a cab, make sure you ask if it's a sherut before you get in—it is an expensive difference.)

FLIGHTS WITHIN ISRAEL: If you can afford it, and if traveling overland on hot days just isn't your cup of tea, then by all means use **Arkia,** Israel's inland air service. There are no flights on Saturday, but otherwise daily flights connect Tel Aviv with Eilat and Rosh Pinna (Safed/Tiberias), Jerusalem with Eilat and Rosh Pinna, and Haifa with Eilat. Other flights are scheduled according to demand, as the seasons change. A round-trip flight from Tel Aviv to Eilat, for example, costs $124.

Arkia also sponsors very popular air tours, including journeys from Tel Aviv and Jerusalem to Eilat and even to Santa Katarina, in Egypt's Sinai. Or you can design your own tour, gather a group of people, and charter an Arkia aircraft, from nine-seaters to Boeing 737s.

Arkia Offices

You can book tickets and check flight schedules at the following Arkia offices:

Tel Aviv: 11 Frishman St. (tel. 03-233-285), and Sde Dov Airport (tel. 03-426-262).

Jerusalem: Klal Center, 97 Jaffa Rd. (tel. 02-225-888).

Haifa: 84 Ha-Atzma'ut St. (tel. 04-643-371).

Eilat: Downtown Airport (tel. 059-73141), or New Tourist Center (tel. 059-76102).

Information on Arkia flights is also available at the Israel Government Tourist Office in New York, Empire State Building, 350 Fifth Ave., 19th Floor, New York, NY 10118 (tel. 212/695-2998).

Shahaf Charter Ltd.

Another Israeli carrier with inland routes is Shahaf Charter Ltd., which operates five round-trip flights weekly between Tel Aviv and Eilat for as little as $99 per person, round trip. They also run charter flights from Tel Aviv and Haifa to Cyprus (Paphos) twice weekly. The word "charter" means that the air fare and frequency of flights vary with the number of people who sign up to go. You can reach Shahaf at 228 Ben-Yehuda St., Tel Aviv (tel. 03-452-735 or 442-297); or 210 Jaffa Rd., Jerusalem (tel. 02-383-554 or 380-151); or in the Richeter Center, Hatmarim Boulevard, Eilat (tel. 059-74508).

RENTING CARS: This is a desirable way to travel in Israel, if you can afford it. Rent-a-car agencies, both the international ones such as **Avis, Hertz, Budget,** and **National (Europcar),** as well as local agencies, rent small cars at about $16 to $24 a day, plus a 24¢- to 28¢-per-kilometer charge, rates depending on the season, the company, and the size of the car. These rates are for such cars as Fiats and Autobianchis.

Driving is one of the best ways to see Israel. And should you feel that car renting is too great a luxury for your budget, remember that with your new-found mobility you can stay at any of the camping-bungalow sites, and thus recoup in low hotel accommodations your car-rental splurge. Also, if you have three or four people in the car, you're almost operating your own mass transit!

Even so, car rental can turn out to be extraordinarily expensive if you don't realize what's involved. Let's run down the costs, item by item.

The very cheapest cars are often not available, even though their rental prices are widely publicized by agencies. So let's assume you end up renting the "B" group of economy cars, such as Ford Fiesta, Peugeot 104, Daihatsu Charade, or Talbot Samba. Your best deal will be on a weekly, unlimited-kilometrage basis. As the deductible on the agency-provided collision insurance is a staggering $750 to $1,000, you'll want to protect yourself against that much liability for damage to the car. So you must initial the little block that shows you want the collision damage waiver insurance, which will cost $6 to $10 per day. Thus a balance sheet of what you'll actually end up paying for a week's vehicular liberation may look like this:

Basic weekly charge, unlimited kilometers	$275
Collision damage waiver, 7 days @ $6 per day	42
Gasoline, 100 liters @ 60¢ per liter	60
Total	$377

This works out to a frightening $53.85 per day, for about the cheapest car truly available, at the best rates offered by the big companies.

These figures are an average of going rates. You'll save significant sums by shopping around. Be sure to ask in advance what the collision damage waiver will cost, because—as you can see from the figures above—it ends up being a significant sum. If one firm offers a weekly rate of $250, but with an enormous collision damage waiver fee, you may be better off going with another company which charges $260, but only $20 for a week's collision damage waiver.

By the way, you should not be misled by firms offering extremely low daily rental rates such as $6 or $8. The daily rental rate is only a small portion of the total rental bill. If the daily rental rate is $8, but the collision damage waiver is also $8 and the kilometer charge is 30¢, a day's rental for a 175-kilometer (78-mile) trip from, say, Tel Aviv to Jerusalem and back will still end up costing a whopping $68.50! You could do the trip by taxi for about the same price.

You can save some money by renting from a small, local company. The rental can turn out quite well, but you must be extra-cautious: Does the advertised price include any insurance at all? You'll assume that it does, but sometimes it doesn't. My word of advice: Assume that a small, local company wants to do a respectable business and make its customers happy, but proceed slowly, deliberately, and check everything that should be checked. At the first sign of off-color dealing, leave and go try another firm.

Incidental Facts

Age minimums for rentals vary from company to company, but usually you must be 21 to rent. You may pay more for insurance if you're under a certain age in the early 20s. There are no toll roads or bridges within Israel, so this is not a cost. Parking is usually on the street, and often free. Gasoline comes as 91 octane at about 50¢ per liter, and 96 octane at about 60¢ per liter. Rental cars are often "required" to have the higher octane gas. These gas prices work out to about $1.90 to $2.27 per U.S. gallon. When you return the car, the rental company will estimate—to their advantage—the amount of gas needed to fill the tank. As rentals do not include gas, this estimate will appear on your bill. Therefore it's a good idea to make sure the fuel gauge on your rental car reads "full" when you return the car, to avoid such estimates. Either way you'll pay, but this way you pay less.

Car-rental offices are everywhere in Israel. If you don't happen to pass the one you want, your hotel or any travel agent will be glad to arrange the rental. It's a good idea to reserve a car as far in advance as possible. Except in holiday periods, a day in advance should be enough. The point is that you should not expect to walk into a rental office and drive away a half hour later in the car of your choice. The earlier you reserve, the more certain you can be of getting the car you want, when you want it.

Caution

In renting cars, tourists are cautioned to deal only with reputable companies, not to sign a contract without reading it thoroughly in a language completely understood, and to make sure of proper and full insurance coverage.

DRIVING IN ISRAEL: Although Israel honors an American driver's license, they prefer you to have an International Driver's License, which should be obtained in advance in your hometown. The local automobile club, called **MEMSI**, has its main office in Tel Aviv at 19 Petah Tikva Rd. (P.O. Box 36144, Tel Aviv 61360; tel. 03-622-961). Office hours are 9 a.m. to 3:30 p.m., to noon on Friday; closed Saturday. It offers AAA members: (1) information on touring, hotels, car hire, etc.; (2) emergency assistance on the roads, patrolled by radio-controlled yellow vans with MEMSI's name and emblem; (3) legal and technical advice; (4) guarantor of letters of credit issued by A.I.T. and F.I.A. clubs; (5) acceptance of members of affiliated clubs without paying a registration fee.

Provided a tourist's foreign car registration is valid and he is in possession of a valid driving license, he may bring his car into Israel for a period of up to one year. No Customs document or deposit of Customs duty is required.

But before you decide to bring in a car or even drive in Israel, you should understand that this is a tough country for autos. Auxiliary roads are rarely wide and straight, and once you're off the main highways, you're faced with winding, narrow mountain roads—particularly in the Golan Heights and the Negev.

Besides the roads themselves, there are many other problems confronting a driver in Israel. The main problem is the Israeli driver himself; brashness on the road is his national sport. The Israeli's driving habits, especially those of taxi drivers, directly reflect two main components of his personality: aggressiveness and impatience. You will see cars taking daredevil chances and overtaking regularly on blind curves and without any sensible regard for oncoming traffic, narrowly squeezing back into their lane only by a hair's breadth. Such foolishness (or should I say fearlessness and recklessness?) has caused tragedy and death on Israel's roads to an extent way out of proportion to the number of cars in the country.

Other hazards? First, rains bring up loose gravel and dirt, and make for unstable, slippery conditions. Flash floods occur in the desert during the rainy season, often gutting low sections of the highway.

The number of cars in Israel has doubled during the past few years, so Israel now has real, honest-to-goodness traffic jams. The increase in cars has also exacerbated the parking problem in the big cities, and you may hunt in vain for a legal space. The Israelis have taken to that horrible European habit of parking on the sidewalks. By the way, in Jerusalem, when you park on the street during daylight hours, you must display a parking card in the passenger window. This is a strip of paper with punched tabs for the hours of the day. You tear a tab to designate the month, day, and hour when you parked. Cards can be purchased at newsstands or from lottery-ticket vendors. The cards are supposed to take the place of parking meters. It's nice not to see parking meters in the Holy City, but an awful lot of the parking cards end up littering the street.

Gas stations are plentiful enough on main roads, except that on Saturday some of them are closed. And on Saturday and Jewish holidays it's virtually impossible to have a flat tire repaired in the Jewish sections of Israel.

ISRAEL MILEAGE CHART

With Distances in Both Miles and Kilometers

	Ashkelon		Beersheba		Eilat		Haifa		Jerusalem		Netanya		Tel Aviv		Tiberias	
	km	mi	km	mi	km	mi	km	mi	km	mi	km	mi	km	mi	km	mi
Akko (Acre)	174	109	231	143	474	294	23	14	181	112	86	53	118	73	56	37
Ashkelon			63	39	306	190	151	94	75	47	88	55	56	35	191	127
Beersheba	63	39			243	151	208	129	83	52	145	90	113	70	248	165
Bethlehem	145	90	76	47	319	198	168	104	10	6	105	65	73	45	208	139
Eilat	306	190	243	151			451	280	326	202	388	241	356	221	491	327
Haifa	151	94	208	129	451	280			158	98	63	39	95	59	70	47
Hebron	117	73	48	30	291	181	168	104	37	23	132	82	100	62	201	134
Jericho	115	71	119	74	364	226	146	91	35	22	122	76	98	61	181	121
Jerusalem	75	47	83	52	326	202	158	98			95	59	63	39	198	132
Lod (Airport)	54	34	98	61	341	212	112	70	51	32	49	30	18	11	152	101
Nahariya	184	114	241	150	484	301	33	20	191	119	96	60	128	79	66	44
Nazareth	161	100	218	135	461	286	38	24	135	84	73	45	105	65	32	21
Netanya	88	55	145	90	388	241	63	39	95	59			32	20	103	69
Tel Aviv	56	35	113	70	356	221	95	59	63	39	32	20			135	90
Tiberias	191	119	248	154	491	305	70	43	198	123	103	64	135	84		
Zefat (Safed)	227	141	284	176	527	327	74	46	234	145	139	86	171	106	36	24

Chapter II

JERUSALEM, THE HOLY CITY

1. On the Way
2. Orientation
3. Where to Stay
4. Where to Dine
5. The Sights of Jerusalem
6. Jerusalem's Nightlife

DESPITE EVERYTHING it's endured, Jerusalem is a serene and peaceful city as old as time itself, with streets that seem to breathe an almost hypnotic lassitude. It ranks among the two or three cities of the world with the longest record of continual habitation. Needless to say, its citizens have seen everything, and there's a solidity about them and their city that has withstood the test of time and will obviously continue to endure.

Few cities have such a special mood to them as does Jerusalem. For one thing, it is the most exotic of Israel's three principal cities, partly because it is the holiest of the three as well as its capital. To many of the religious immigrants from Middle Eastern and North African countries (who now comprise over 50% of Israel's population), going to Israel means going to Jerusalem.

On Jerusalem's streets you'll recognize the long-bearded Hasidic element, in broad fur hats and black garments. Perhaps less recognizable, but equally well represented, are Europeans, Asians, Americans—quite literally peoples from the world over. Along the eastern streets, outside shops and business areas, Arab men sit in the sunlight—heads usually covered with flowing scarves called *kefiyas*—drinking coffee. Arab women—often draped head to toe and wearing hand-embroidered dresses—scurry around, laden with bundles. Within the walls of the Old City, most people live as they have for some 2,000 years, in somnolence and a mixture of fragrances. If you've ever thought New York was a melting pot, wait until you see Jerusalem.

The city's oldtime residents take an uncommon pride in living in Jerusalem —for a number of reasons. Some fought for the city during the war; some venerate the city for its religious meaning; some just regard it as the perfect place to live in Israel, with its cool, crisp evenings and sweet, clear days. Israelis who have lived in Jerusalem and moved to another part of the country somehow always return to Jerusalem to retrace the charming dignity of its streets, the aged grace of its neighborhoods, the memories of a youth spent among its golden-stoned byways.

1. On the Way

Back in biblical times, it used to take many days for a pilgrim to travel from the Mediterranean coast to Jerusalem. Today the ride requires less than an hour, or if you have a particularly aggressive sherut driver, around 35 minutes. Whatever the speed you travel, the last part of your gradually ascending ride will undoubtedly be one of the most dramatic and memorable phases of any journey you've ever made.

There are many ways to enter Jerusalem, or to "go up" to the city, as the Hebrew word, implying a physical and spiritual ascension, expresses. From the north, you can either take the Jordan Valley way passing through Tiberias, Bet Shean, and Jericho, and enter Jerusalem from the east, or an alternative, a beautiful way between mountains passing Jenin, Nablus, and Ramallah. The third and longest way is via Afula, Hadera, and the coastal plain to Tel Aviv, and reaching the city from the west. The southern entry is Beersheba through Hebron and Bethlehem.

The newer road from Tel Aviv—finished in 1979—is a 57-km (34-mile), four-lane highway. It passes by beautiful countryside and the Ben-Gurion Airport, en route to the Latrun area which bisects a wide natural pass between the Judean hills and the coastal region—an area that's known bloodshed since biblical days, when Joshua prayed for the sun to stand still over Gibeon and the moon to remain over this **Ajalon Valley** (Joshua 10:12). Locals know the Scriptures well, and mark with interest every square foot of ground that has biblical significance, but they are quicker to note that it was in this valley that over 1,000 Israelis died during the 1948 War of Independence, trying to take **Fortress Latrun** in what can only be described as human-wave assaults. Because of its crucial position on the approach to Jerusalem, Latrun became a battlefront once again in the 1967 war. The blood-saturated plain was cleared and planted with life-supporting crops, which, other than the pock-marked and deserted former police station (Fortress Latrun) and the romantic and peaceful **Latrun Monastery,** are all that you'll see today. (Although locals and tourists look searchingly at the still-haunting fortress, they seldom stop there. But often they enter the road to the Trappist monastery, where the monks have two distinctions: they've vowed not to speak, and they make—and sell—cheese and excellent wine. The vineyards surrounding the monastery are theirs, as is much of the land on both sides of the road.)

Directly past the monastery, the road forks to the left to Ramallah, then straight ahead to Jerusalem. From here on, you'll be climbing even higher, through steep but lovely terraced hills.

The last leg of the trip is a steep ascent up a corridor strewn right and left with wrecked military vehicles. The smashed, overturned trucks and tanks, lying in the sun beside the road, are mute reminders of the men and equipment sacrificed in the 1948 war to keep this pass open. Were it not for that sacrifice—similar to the one at Latrun—the population of Jerusalem, cut off and under continuous bombardment, might have starved to death.

2. Orientation

To get around Jerusalem easily, you've got to understand how the city grew.

A century ago, when Victorian pilgrims and early Zionist settlers arrived at the fabled city of Jerusalem, they found a living, breathing medieval town still enclosed in its towering walls. It was a romantic vision—until they set foot inside

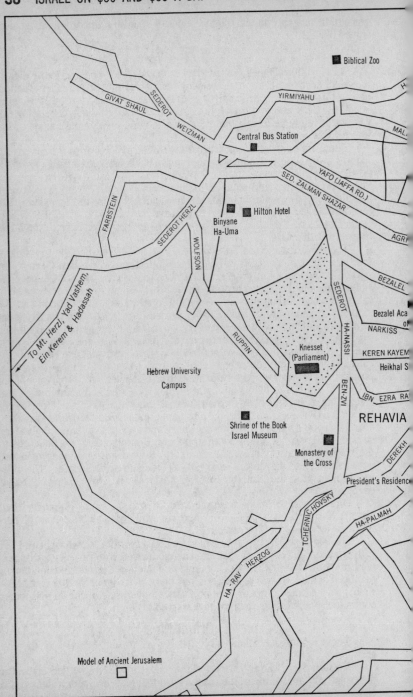

Biblical Zoo

GIVAT SHAUL

SEDEROT WEIZMAN

YIRMIYAHU

H

MAL

Central Bus Station

YAFO (JAFFA RD.)

SED. ZALMAN SHAZAR

FARBSTEIN

SEDEROT HERZL

Hilton Hotel

Binyane
Ha-Uma

AGRI

WOLFSON

BEZALEL

Bezalel Aca
of

To Mt. Herzl, Yad Vashem,
Ein Kerem & Hadassah

SEDEROT HA-NASSI

NARKISS

RUPPIN

KEREN KAYEM

Knesset
(Parliament)

Heikhal S

IBN   EZRA RA

Hebrew University
Campus

BEN-ZVI

REHAVIA

Shrine of the Book
Israel Museum

DEREKH

Monastery of
the Cross

President's Residence

TCHERNICHOVSKY

HA-PALMAH

HA-RAV HERZOG

Model of Ancient Jerusalem

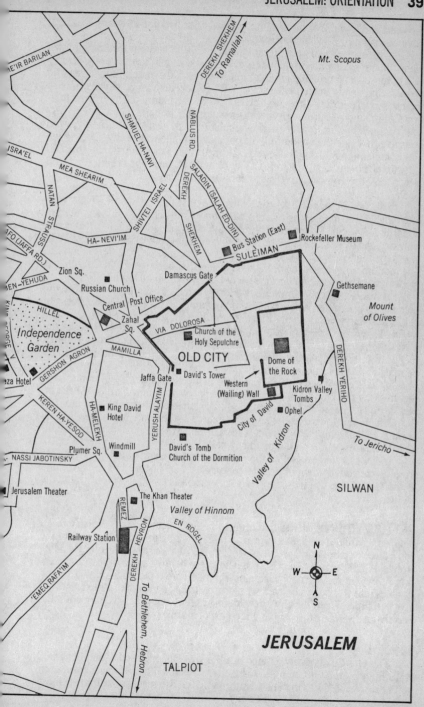

JERUSALEM

the walls and found that the quaint medieval town had not-so-quaint medieval sewerage running down its streets.

A few of the town's straighter streets had been laid out by Roman town planners, but most of the tortuous maze had just grown by itself over the centuries. As more and more pilgrims and Zionists arrived, the antique public facilities proved completely inadequate. "Colonies" of new arrivals began to establish themselves in enclaves—the American Colony, the German Colony, the Russian Compound—scattered over the surrounding hilltops of Judea. As the decades of the 20th century passed, the population of Jerusalem-outside-the-walls grew to equal, and then to exceed, the population of the walled city. By 1948 the new colonies had been knitted together in an arc that almost surrounded the Old City on the north, west, and south. (The Mount of Olives, to the east, remained largely unsettled.) Now, in effect, there were two Jerusalems: the Old and the New.

In the fateful year of 1948, the United Nations voted to establish two states: one Israeli, the other Palestinian. Jerusalem was to remain a united, international city. But the U.N. had no way to enforce its will, and the new jurisdictions were decided by war instead. The State of Israel was established in this 1948 War of Independence, but Jerusalem was split down the middle from north to south. The modern western section remained in Israeli hands, but the Old City and the modern section north of it became part of the Kingdom of Jordan.

From 1948 to 1967 there were two Jerusalems, and pilgrims on a visit to the holy places of Old Jerusalem came via Amman. The people of East Jerusalem held Jordanian passports, but they did not think of themselves as Jordanians, really. They were Palestinians, caught between the new State of Israel to the west and the young Kingdom of Jordan to the east. The two halves of Jerusalem met only at heavily guarded checkpoints, where travelers with the proper credentials could pass from one armed camp to the other.

In the Six Day War of 1967, East Jerusalem came under Israeli control and the city was reunited once again. With the accomplishment of **Yerushalayim Hashleyma** ("United Jerusalem"), the city began to resume its normal life. But the distinctions of two decades largely remain: East Jerusalem and the Old City are still predominantly Palestinian (Christian and Muslim Arabs) in population, and West Jerusalem is predominantly Israeli.

Today's United Jerusalem, half a million people and growing, is a far cry from the medieval town of a mere century ago. Its history has given it three distinct areas, and so I'll use those areas as the basis for guiding you around the Golden City.

GETTING YOUR BEARINGS: The fact that Jerusalem is three cities in one is a help rather than a hindrance. It won't take you long to get a clear idea of the city's three ethnopolitical areas, and thus to feel at home as you stroll its winding streets. A free, detailed map is a great help (see below under "Tourist Information"), but be forewarned: Jerusalem sprawls across the Judean hilltops and tumbles into the valleys between. Maps may trace the winding streets, but will give you little idea of the city's bewildering up-hill-and-down-dale topography. Start by memorizing this simple three-part division:

The Old City

The Old City is easily defined: it's the area still enclosed within the grand walls built by the Ottoman Turkish sultan, Suleiman the Magnificent. Seven gates provide access to the Old City through its massive walls, and two of these gates you must get to know right away.

Jaffa Gate (*Sha'ar Yafo* in Hebrew, *Bab el-Khalil* in Arabic), at the end of Jaffa Road (Derekh Yafo), is the main access from West Jerusalem.

Damascus Gate (*Sha'ar Shekhem* in Hebrew, *Bab esh-Sham* or *Bab el-Amud* in Arabic) is the main access to the Old City from East Jerusalem.

When you get lost in the labyrinthine alleys of the Old City, as inevitably happens, you can find your way out again by simply intoning the magic name of either gate, in the appropriate language, to any Old City denizen. He'll point you on a course out of the maze with a sympathetic word or two.

West Jerusalem

To the west and south of the Old City is the modern Israeli city, a huge area of residential, commercial, and industrial development punctuated by high-rise hotels and office towers. Extending far to the south and west, and encroaching on the east, the "New City" (as it's sometimes called) holds the Knesset, one of Hebrew University's two large campuses, the Israel Museum, and—far out on a distant hilltop—the Hadassah Medical Center. Broad avenues twist and turn along the tops of the Judean hills to connect West Jerusalem's outlying quarters with the century-old downtown area.

Downtown West Jerusalem is centered on **Zion Square** (Kikar Ziyon), where **Jaffa Road** intersects with **Ben-Yehuda Street.** A few short blocks west of Zion Square is **King George V Avenue** (Rehov Ha-Melekh George), which joins Ben-Yehuda and Jaffa Road to form a triangle. Many of the hotels, restaurants, and businesses you'll want to know about are in or near this triangle.

East Jerusalem

Not quite so modern and sprawling as the western part, East Jerusalem is nevertheless a bustling 20th-century cityscape lying north of the Old City. Its compact business, commercial, and hotel district starts right along the Old City's north wall on **Sultan Suleiman Street,** near the Damascus Gate. **Nablus Road** (*Derekh Shekhem* in Hebrew) and **Saladin Street** (*Salah ed-Din* in Arabic) are East Jerusalem's main streets. With Sultan Suleiman Street they form a triangle useful in orientation.

During the years when East Jerusalem was part of Jordan, it suffered somewhat because its people were not true Jordanians, and because Jordan's capital was Amman. Most money for development went to Amman rather than Jerusalem. But East Jerusalem is undergoing its own construction boom these days as the Israeli government encourages citywide growth. Even so, there are still lots of green swaths and open land between downtown East Jerusalem and Mount Scopus, topped by Hebrew University's hilltop campus.

Due east of the Old City, the **Kidron Valley** lies between ancient Jerusalem and the Mount of Olives (*Et-Tur* in Arabic). On the slopes of the Mount, facing the Old City, is the Garden of Gethsemane. Farther down the valley is the Palestinian town of Silwan. All of this area was under Jordanian control from 1948 to 1967.

East Jerusalem has two bus stations: one for national routes (mostly to the West Bank towns), and another for city-bus routes. For national routes, go to the station on Sultan Suleiman between Nablus Road and Saladin Streets. For city buses, go up Nablus Road from Damascus Gate a long block, and you'll see the bus lanes on your left.

By the way, city plans call for construction of a brand-new bus station for East Jerusalem, to be located right at the intersection of Ha-Nevi'im and Sultan Suleiman, facing Damascus Gate. The old bus station, right beside what many Christians believe to be the hill of Golgotha, would then be turned into a park.

USEFUL FACTS: Here's a quick and handy list of facts to smooth your way through Jerusalem.

Babysitters: Israel, the country that invented the kibbutz and its "Children's House," has ample provisions for babysitters. Often a sitter will speak some English. The easiest way to find a sitter is to ask at the front desk of your hotel.

Banks and Moneychangers: In general, banking hours are 8:30 a.m. to noon or 12:30 p.m.; on Sunday, Tuesday, and Thursday there are also hours from 4 to 5 p.m. Some banks stay open longer hours during the high summer season. Take your passport whenever you change money at a bank. Many of the city's banks have branches in West Jerusalem on Ben-Yehuda Street, Jaffa Road, and King George V Avenue. As for moneychangers, they have offices in and around Damascus Gate in the Old City, and are open for business most of the day, every day. Their activities are perfectly legal, and not black market.

Bookstores and Newsstands: Jerusalem has lots of them, with the greatest concentration within two blocks of Zion Square. The **Heatid Bookstore,** 38 Jaffa Rd. (tel. 02-244-753), sells new books, including lots of Penguins. **Book Shuk Distributors,** 5 Ha-Havazelet St. (tel. 02-224-894), just off Zion Square near the Alba Pharmacy, has both new and used books. **The Book Shop,** 6 Yosef Du Nawas St., off 36-38 Jaffa Rd. (no phone), sells new and used books; if you buy a new book and have them stamp it here, you can later sell it back at a good price. The **Librairie Française Alcheh,** 30 Jaffa Rd. (tel. 02-234-681), sells French books; it's between Zion Square and the central post office. For scholarly books, history, serious Judaica, and weightier reading, the place to go is **Ludwig Mayer Ltd.,** 4 Shlomzion Ha-Malka St. (tel. 02-222-628); the store was founded in 1908. Perhaps the most available bookseller throughout Israel is the **Steimatzky** chain, with five branches in Jerusalem, including those at 39 Jaffa Rd. (tel. 02-223-654), 9 King George V Ave. (tel. 02-240-494), in the Hilton Hotel, in the King David Hotel, and on the Cardo in the Jewish Quarter of the Old City (tel. 02-271-101). Steimatzky shops always have good selections of current magazines and newspapers.

Consulates: Many countries do not accept Jerusalem as Israel's legal capital, and so embassies remain in Tel Aviv while Jerusalem is served by consulates. The **U.S. Consulate** has two locations. Apply first to the Consular Section, in East Jerusalem near the YMCA Aelia Capitolina Hotel at the intersection of Nablus Road (Derekh Shechem) and Pikud Ha-Merkaz Street (tel. 02-234-271). The West Jerusalem consulate building is at 18 Agron St., just down the hill from the Jerusalem Plaza Hotel (same phone). The **British Consulate** is in East Jerusalem's Sheikh Jarrah quarter on the Mount of Olives Road (Derekh Har Ha-Zetim; tel. 02-282-481). There is no Canadian consulate in Jerusalem; contact the embassy in Tel Aviv at 220 Ha-Yarkon St. (tel. 03-228-122).

Crime in Jerusalem: Jerusalem is perhaps the safest city in Israel, but be cautious in the crowded streets and bazaars of the Old City, where a thief can snatch your watch, wallet, necklace, or earrings in a second, and disappear without a trace. Otherwise, observe the normal precautions, and you'll be very safe. To call the police, dial 100.

Laundry: Take it to **Gallery Wash,** in the Jewish Quarter of the Old City on the Street of the Jews (Rehov Ha-Yehudim), south of the Street of Chairs. It's open from 8 a.m. to 5 p.m. Sunday through Thursday, to noon on Friday. The price to wash, dry, and fold a small load of wash is NIS8 ($5.35).

Libraries: The U.S.I.S. sponsors the **American Library,** on Keren Ha-Yesod Street between the Jerusalem Plaza and Moriah hotels. The **British Council Library** is next to the YMCA Aelia Capitolina Hotel in East Jerusalem.

Medical Services: You can get a list of English-speaking doctors and dentists from the consulate, and often from your hotel's front desk as well. In **emergencies,** dial 101 for Magen David Adom (Red Shield of David), Israel's emergency first-aid service. For medical emergencies requiring hospitalization, dial 102. Magen David Adom has a clinic in Romema, near the Central Bus Station, and also a mobile intensive-care unit (tel. 02-523-133) on call 24 hours a day. For the Rape Crisis Center, dial 02-245-554. The *Jerusalem Post* lists under "General Assistance" the names and addresses of duty **pharmacies** that stay open nights and on the Sabbath.

   Post Office: Jerusalem's **Central Post Office** is at 23 Jaffa Rd., near the intersection with Shlomzion Ha-Malka Street. General hours for all services are 7 a.m. to 7 p.m. Sunday through Thursday, though limited services (telephone and telegraph) are open nights and on the Sabbath. **Branch post offices** in West Jerusalem are on Keren Kayemet Street, corner of King George V Avenue; and on the little passage between Shammai and Hillel Streets, opposite the Orion Cinema. East Jerusalem's main post office is opposite Herod's Gate, at the intersection of Saladin, Ibn Sina, and Sultan Suleiman Streets. The Old City post office is next to Christ Church Hospice and opposite the entrance to the Tower of David (Jerusalem City Museum), inside Jaffa Gate.

   Rest Rooms: Jerusalem is well provided with them. Virtually every café and restaurant has facilities for its customers, and there are municipal facilities as well. Near Zion Square, walk up Ha-Rav Kook Street. At the Western Wall in the Old City, go to the north side of the square; another facility is near St. Anne's Church and St. Stephen's Gate. Look for signs that read "WC," "OO," or that have standard symbols such as profiles of a man and woman.

ENTERING JERUSALEM:

Coming from Tel Aviv, Haifa, or Ben-Gurion International Airport, you'll climb into the Judean hills and enter the city along the four-lane highway which narrows to become Weizmann Boulevard (*Sederot Weizmann*). The boulevard soon changes names and is called Jaffa Road (*Derekh Yafo*), an appropriate name as this street was once the main path out of the city and down to the ancient port at Jaffa (*Yafo* in Hebrew). The city's Central Bus Station, for most Egged intercity buses, is right on Jaffa Road not far past the intersection with Herzl/Yirmiyahu Boulevard, virtually across the street from Jerusalem's large convention center named Binyane Ha-Uma.

   From the Central Bus Station, Jerusalem city buses fan out to all parts of United Jerusalem: Check below ("Where to Stay,") and find a hotel that meets your needs. Then come back here to find out how to reach your hotel by bus or sherut.

GETTING TO YOUR HOTEL BY CITY BUS . . . :

When you arrive at Jerusalem's **Central Bus Station,** you're faced with the problem of getting to your chosen hotel. If it's a Friday evening you must take a cab or sherut if one is available, because all city and intercity buses stop running an hour before sundown and don't start up again until Saturday evening. At other times of the week you can still take a cab, which is recommended if you're completely exhausted after a long flight; or you can catch the appropriate city bus for the mile-or-so ride to Zion Square, or beyond.

   Should you be busing up to Jerusalem from the south or east (Bethlehem, Hebron, or Jericho), your bus may arrive at the East Jerusalem bus station on Sultan Suleiman Street near the Damascus Gate.

   Just before you exit from the Central Bus Station, look above the exit doors and you'll see a large sign which tells you which city bus to catch for a certain destination, and also where to catch it. The system works like this: the board shows a bus number, and then (in English) the high points of its route. Bus 9, it says, goes to Hebrew University's Givat Ram campus, the Israel Museum, and the Knesset. Right beside this information is a symbol that indicates where you can catch the bus. There are four boarding areas, each bearing a letter and a symbol. To get to Area A, symbolized by a square, you simply head out the bus station door and you're there. To get to Area B (a triangle), Area C (a circle), and Area D (an octagon), you go out the bus station doors and down the stairs into an underpass beneath Jaffa Road. Go up the stairs at the opposite end of the underpass for Area B; for C and D, keep walking straight along the path and follow the signs.

Here are some of the **most important destinations,** and the buses that take you there:

Abu Tor (and Railroad Station)—7,8,21,30
American Colony (East Jerusalem)—23,27
Bet Ha-Kerem—6,16,17
Damascus Gate (Old City)—27
East Jerusalem—23,27,99
Ein Kerem—17
German Colony (South Jerusalem)—4,14,18,24
Ge'ula Quarter—3,9,39
Israel Museum—9,17,24
Jaffa Gate (Old City)—3,13,19,20,30,80,99
Jewish Quarter (Old City)—1,38
King George V Avenue—7,8,9,10,14,31
Mount Scopus—9,23,26,28
Mount Zion—38
Railroad Station—5,7,8,21,30
Yad Vashem—13,17,18,20,23,24,27,39,40,99
Zion Square—4,18,22

When you come out to Jaffa Road from the Central Bus Station, look left up Jaffa Road and you'll be looking east toward the center of the city.

Bus Tickets and Fares

A normal, simple, full-fare city bus ticket costs 50 agorot (a half shekel, 33¢). But if you ask the driver for a *kartisiya* (that's "kahr-tee-*see*-yah"), he'll sell you a pass good for 25 trips, for which you pay NIS10 ($6.10), normally the fare for 20 trips, so you get 5 trips free. The pass is punched each time you board a bus.

Students pay reduced fares of 30 agorot (20¢), and can buy special discount kartisiya, as well.

. . . AND BY SHERUT: You've arrived in Israel by plane, and you've packed yourself into a stretched Mercedes with various other travelers on their way to Jerusalem. Good! You're in a sherut, or shared taxi. The fare is a fixed rate, and the driver must—without charging an extra *agora*—take you to the hotel of your choice anywhere in United Jerusalem. He may try to charge you for the hotel drop. Don't pay anything more than the flat-rate airport-to-anywhere-in-Jerusalem charge.

For the return trip, by the way, your hotel will be glad to call in advance and make an appointment for a sherut to pick you up. If you'd rather do it in person, you should know that the two locations with lots of sherut offices are: outside Damascus Gate in East Jerusalem; and at the intersection of Ben-Yehuda Street and King George V Avenue, right near the City Tower, in West Jerusalem. The office of Nesher sheruts, known for their airport service, is here.

TOURIST INFORMATION: There's an information desk (tel. 03-971-485 or 971-487) in the Arrivals Hall of Ben-Gurion International Airport. It's staffed by helpful and knowledgeable **Ministry of Tourism** people. After you're done with passport control and while you're waiting for your luggage, go to the desk and ask for city maps, brochures, and the answers to any questions you might have. A hotel reservations desk nearby will help you find a room for the night if you wish.

When you get to downtown West Jerusalem, direct your feet and your questions to the **Tourist Information Office** (tel. 02-241-281 or 241-282) at 24 King George V Ave., which is just a few blocks off Jaffa Road near the intersection of King George V Avenue and Hillel Street. (*Note:* That's Hillel Street, not to be confused with the nearby Ben-Hillel Street.) The office is open Sunday through Thursday from 8 a.m. to 5 p.m., on Friday and holiday eves to 3 p.m.; closed on Saturday.

The city maintains its own useful information bureau separate from the government one. It's the **Jerusalem Municipal Tourist Information Office,** 17 Jaffa Rd. (tel. 02-228-884), going toward the Old City, open from 9 a.m. to 12:30 p.m., on Friday till noon; closed Saturday.

In the Old City there's another government **Tourist Information Office** just inside Jaffa Gate, a few steps down on the left (tel. 02-282-295 or 282-296), and this one has the advantage of being open on Saturday from 10 a.m. to 2 p.m.; other days it's open from 8 a.m. to 5 p.m. (to 4:30 p.m. on Friday).

Want to find out what's cooking in terms of nightlife? After 6 p.m. call this special number, 02-241-197, and you'll get a Tourist Office recording that tells you what's happening tonight.

3. Where to Stay

Moderately priced hotels are scattered throughout Jerusalem: in the Old City, in bustling West Jerusalem, in Arab East Jerusalem, up the slopes of the Mount of Olives, and in several neighborhoods farther from the center of town. Each of the three main hotel areas below also has at least a few inexpensive hostels or hospices which are just perfect for the traveler in search of plain but clean accommodations at bargain prices. As for the four- and five-star luxury high-rise hotels, they're all in West Jerusalem except for the Intercontinental, perched atop the Mount of Olives.

How does one choose where to stay? If you want medieval ambience, if you expect to spend most of your time in the Old City, then find a room there. If you want a lot of time in the Knesset, Israel Museum, Jerusalem Theater, or if you want a lot of nighttime ambience and activity, or if you need many kosher restaurants close at hand, stay in West Jerusalem. As for East Jerusalem, its hotels are in general much closer to the Old City than West Jerusalem's, and are comparable in price. East Jerusalem boasts the best Arab restaurants, which serve up what many consider the tastiest food in the entire city; but none of them is kosher. The streets of East Jerusalem abound with colorful scenes of daily life during the sunlit hours, but are fairly quiet at night, with not much to do. Whatever basis you choose for your decision, don't choose that of race: Palestinian vs. Israeli. All visitors, of whatever race or religion, are equally welcome, equally well treated, and equally safe no matter where they stay in Jerusalem.

RESERVATIONS, FACILITIES, ETC.: Jerusalem's hotels are busiest in the spring at Passover and Easter, during the high-tourist-season months of July and August, and in September or October during the Jewish High Holidays (Rosh Hashannah, Yom Kippur, Succoth, Simchat Torah), and of course at Christmas. Check your calendar and get reservations if you plan to be here during any of the busy times. If you arrive without reservations, ask at the airport for help in finding a room (see above under "Orientation, Tourist Information"), or if all else fails, arrive in Jerusalem early in the day so you can nail down a room that's being vacated before someone else does.

In high summer, it's good to consider a room with air conditioning if the weather's hot, and especially if you're in a modern building. The older stone buildings often have thick walls which keep the room cool without air conditioning. Jerusalem is about the coolest spot in Israel during the hot months.

Jerusalem is also about the chilliest spot in Israel during the cold months, from December through February. Most moderately priced hotels will offer you an electric heater for your room at no extra charge. Be sure they do. Second-best is an air-conditioning unit with a heater control—these tend to be noisy. Central heating is fine, but only if it's turned on! Many times you'll find the level of heat depends on the number of guests registered at the hotel. Where you are the only guest, or almost so, you had better make sure to have an electric heater. The central heating will probably not be fired up.

Also, in the winter you can expect the Israeli breakfast that comes with your room to be less inspired and varied than during the boom months of summer. It should always be plentiful, though, and you should ask for more of this or that, have them make you an omelet or fried eggs, as you wish. Traditionally, the guest gets as much as he wants, even though the seasonal selection of foods is more limited.

OLD CITY ACCOMMODATIONS: You won't come across any high-rise (or even low-rise) luxury palaces in the Old City, just a few budget to moderate-priced one-, two-, and three-star hotels. Besides these, several Christian-run hospices (open to all regardless of religion or nationality) provide plain but very clean and respectable lodgings and meals for surprisingly good prices.

Jaffa Gate is the place to start your search for a good Old City hotel, hospice, or hostel. Most are only a few minutes' walk from the gate or from Omar Ibn El-Khattab Square, which is the open space just inside the gate.

Hotels

Twenty paces inside Jaffa Gate, turn left on Latin Patriarchate Street and a short distance up on the right you'll find the **Gloria Hotel** (P.O. Box 14070; tel. 02-282-431 or 282-432). The entrance is up a flight of steps; from there you take an elevator up one more level to the hotel desk, where an English-speaking clerk awaits you. Rooms here, renovated in 1987, have either twin or double beds, bathrooms with showers, central heating, and telephones. All are centrally heated, and the rooms are relatively large—and quiet—considering the cramped quarters of the Old City. The dining room in which you take your breakfast and in which you can opt to have lunch or dinner, overlooks the Tower of David and West Jerusalem. For its good location, modernish facilities, and three stars, the Gloria is moderately priced: one person pays $23 to $32.25, two pay $46 to $55.25, breakfast and service included. Students get a 10% reduction in low season.

Just a short distance farther up Latin Patriarchate Street, which becomes Jawalden Street, on the left-hand side at no. 4 is the **Knights Palace Hotel** (P.O. Box 14020; tel. 02-282-537), built in 1874 and called "palace" quite aptly. The huge old stone building, with steep stairs, very old heavily carved furniture, Gothic-type arches, and high ceilings, was originally part of the Latin Patriarchate; it later became a religious seminary, and eventually (1954) a pilgrimage hotel for Knights of the Holy Sepulchre. Now the hotel welcomes any and all visitors to Jerusalem. When you first enter, through wrought-iron outer gates and heavy front doors, you encounter a large beautiful statue of the Madonna and Child. The hotel is both palatial and spartan, as might befit the noble knights. But rooms are comfy, and the tiny add-on bathrooms are functional, if not commodious. Location is excellent, and quiet; prices are $15 to $26 single, $32 to $36 double, for the 40 rooms, continental breakfast included.

Christian Hospices

Pilgrims and tourists began to arrive in Jerusalem in great numbers during the late 1800s. To accommodate them, various sects and national groups constructed buildings and compounds complete with dining facilities, rooms, and even chapels. Pilgrims could stay here, among their coreligionists, safely and inexpensively.

Today Jerusalem's Christian hospices serve a similar purpose, although there are no rules excluding visitors of other religious beliefs or nationalities. Accommodations are by definition simple, inexpensive, and safe; meals are the same. A hospice is not a hotel, however, and you should note these differences: there is usually a curfew, after which gates and front doors are locked (although sometimes you can enter after curfew by making arrangements in advance with the night porter); meals are table d'hôte—a set menu with no choices—and you may be required to take breakfast and supper; and you won't find any cafés, bars, discos, or similar entertainment spots in a hospice.

One of the best and most convenient hospices is **Christ Church** Hospice (P.O. Box 14037, Jerusalem 91140; tel. 02-282-082), the Anglican hospice right next door to the Tower of David. Go through Jaffa Gate, turn right as the street does, and the entrance gate to the courtyard is on your left, right next to the little post office and across the street from the ornate entrance to the Tower of David. Through the big iron gates you'll find a flagstone courtyard with trees and benches, an Anglican church, a small office, and a wide variety of accommodations. Rooms with one bed, twin beds, or three or four beds are all priced at $25 per person. This includes bed, breakfast, and service. Add $5 for lunch, and $7 for dinner. The gates to Christ Church Hospice close at 11 p.m., and stay locked until 6 a.m., except by special arrangement. As with most good hospices, this one is heavily booked during the summer months and at Christian holidays—best to reserve in advance for those times.

Staying at the 100-room **Casa Nova,** 10 Via Casa Nova (P.O. Box 1321, Jerusalem 91013; tel. 02-282-791), takes you back to the time of Crusaders and Saracens—but with modern conveniences. The stone hospice boasts an impressive lobby and dining room with vaulted ceilings and massive marble pillars. Rooms have shower, toilet, and central heating, and come with three meals a day for $42 to $44 double; pay a few dollars less if you don't want lunch. Doors are closed from 11 p.m. to 5 a.m. To find the Franciscan-run Casa Nova, walk through Jaffa Gate, past Latin Patriarchate Street on your left, and then take the next street on your left, which is Greek Catholic Patriarchate Street. This takes a sharp turn to the right after a while, but you keep going straight, up a narrow alley. Casa Nova is the long building right there on the left-hand side of the alley. Go up a ways and look *back* to the left to see the heavy door. There's no sign, but you'll note "Casa Nova" in wrought iron over the door.

The **Evangelical Lutheran Hostel,** St. Mark's Road (P.O. Box 14051, Jerusalem 91140; tel. 02-282-120), is also a short distance from the Jaffa Gate. Go through the gate and keep going straight; the street turns into steps as it enters the market. Go down the steps (this is David Street) to the first "street" or passage on the right-hand side, called St. Mark's Road. Follow this, and the signs, to the hospice. Do it in daylight, as the signs are hard to see at night. Inside the enclosure are a garden and fountain with patio tables, a squeaky-clean German guesthouse with private double rooms ($25 per person, shower fee and breakfast included), and cheerful youth-hostel dormitories where a bed costs a mere $5 per person per night (no breakfast). You must be between the ages of 16 and 32 to stay in a dorm. Note that curfew is at 11 p.m. A fully equipped kitchen is available for your use. At Easter, Christmas, and during the summer, reserve in advance and get a confirmation.

A less comfy but still very suitable hospice is the one at the **Ecce Homo Convent,** 41 Via Dolorosa (P.O. Box 19056, Jerusalem 91190; tel. 02-282-445), operated by the Roman Catholic Sisters of Sion. Here, singles pay $22 for bed and breakfast in a room with private bath; doubles pay $37.50. There are two dormitories which are divided into cubicles, each with a bed, sink, closet, and mirror, for which one pays $11 for bed and breakfast. Simpler dorm facilities, for women only, cost a mere $4. The door closes at 11 p.m. and reopens at 5:45 a.m. The convent is a bit difficult to find if you're not familiar with the Old City. The easiest route is through the Damascus Gate in East Jerusalem, down the steps inside the gate, then straight into the market along El-Wad Road. El-Wad meets the Via Dolorosa at the Austrian Hospice; turn left here and walk up the slope on the Via Dolorosa. Look for the "bridge" above the roadway, called Ecce Homo Arch. The convent is here, on the left-hand side.

A Youth Hostel

The **Old City Youth Hostel** (*Moreshet Yahadut* in Hebrew—P.O. Box 7880; tel. 02-288-611) will rent you a bed at rock-bottom rates if one is available. The hostel tends to be very crowded in summer, but if you're low on bucks and really want to stay in the Old City, check it out. Have your IYH hosteler's membership card to get the lowest rates: $4.50 to $5.75 for bed and breakfast, $2.50 to $3.15 for lunch or dinner. The hostel is locked tight from 9 a.m. to 5 p.m. You can check in between 5 and 9 p.m.; curfew is at 11 p.m. To find the hostel, go through the Jaffa Gate and bear right, up the hill, on Armenian Orthodox Patriarchate Road. Pass Christ Church Hostel on your left and the police station on your right, and turn left at the next street, St. James or Or Chayim Street. Follow St. James to Ararat Street and turn left; then follow the signs along the labyrinthine way. Keep walking past Syrian Convent Road on your right, then turn left (there's a sign). The hostel is very near the end of a dead-end street. By the way, the hostel's official address of 72 Ararat St. is of almost no use in finding the place.

WEST JERUSALEM ACCOMMODATIONS: Where you stay in West Jerusalem depends on your needs and your budget. A moderately priced hotel room? An incredibly inexpensive youth hostel bed? A spartan-but-clean pension? What about a rented room or apartment in a private home? All of these options are yours for the asking. Let me make a suggestion. Take a hotel room for the first few days of your stay, just to get the lay of the land. While staying in the hotel, explore the possibilities for lower-priced accommodations if you intend to stay for any period of time—a week or more. Several agencies rent rooms in private homes, and small apartments. (You'll find all the information on these farther along in this section under the heading "Rooms and Apartments for Rent.") Also, a few of the hotels listed below can provide housekeeping accommodations, usually rooms with small kitchenettes, allowing you to save money by fixing your own meals.

Virtually all of the hotels and pensions in West Jerusalem that serve meals are careful to abide by *kashrut,* the dietary laws.

The axis of downtown West Jerusalem, the "New City," is Ben-Yehuda

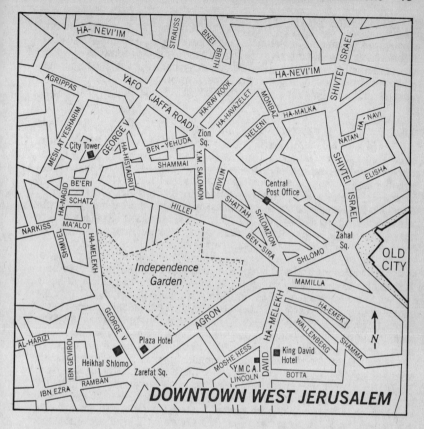

DOWNTOWN WEST JERUSALEM

Street, which climbs a gentle slope starting from Jaffa Road at Zion Square, and reaches King George V Avenue only a few blocks away. You can always identify the intersection of Ben-Yehuda and King George from virtually anywhere in the city: just look for the vertical black-and-white stripes and bevelled top of the City Tower–Eilon Tower Hotel skyscraper which looms above the intersection. The tower, one of Jerusalem's most prominent landmarks, is an office building; the Eilon Tower Hotel occupies the upper floors.

Hotels Near Zion Square

The 22-room **Ron Hotel,** at 42A Jaffa Rd. (Jerusalem 94222; tel. 02-223-471), virtually in the square, is a real study in graceful decline of old-fashioned elegance. Through its gracious portal is a tiny registration booth; up a flight of steps are the modernized rooms, all (except one) with showers in the private bathrooms. Nice little extra touches make the Ron a pleasurable place to stay: individual reading lamps, colorful and bright decor, thick comforters for chilly winter evenings. In the halls and public areas you'll note lots of mirrors, marble floors, and vaulted ceilings. Readers of this book are exempt from the 15% service charge. Prices for all this, without service charge, are $28 single, $40 double.

At the eastern edge of Zion Square, toward the Old City, a small street named Ha-Havazelet runs north off Jaffa Road. Half a block up Ha-Havazelet on the left-hand side is the **Kaplan Hotel** at 1 Ha-Havazelet (tel. 02-224-591). The Kaplan is a bleak-but-clean hotel in the style of a simple European pension, actually two apartments converted to take in guests. Mrs. Wasserman, the kind proprietor, or her assistant, Nathan Teig, will show you the rooms, all of which have cold running water (shared bathrooms in the hall). Some of the rooms are quite large, others small. You won't get breakfast with your room here—or any other meals, for that matter—but the price is low: $14 to $17 single, $20 double, all in.

Hotels Near the City Tower

On Ben-Yehuda Street go right to the top of the street where Ben-Yehuda meets King George V Avenue. The City Tower looms above, the blocky Hamashbir Lazarchan department store squats at the base of the tower, and a mysterious ruin emblazoned with gold letters that spell "TALITHAKUMI" (see Mark 5:41) occupies part of the department store's front lot. King George V Avenue is lined with little shops, boutiques, restaurants, and eateries; traffic alternately whizzes by and waits at red lights. The sidewalks of King George are heavily peopled day and night. Besides being a major thoroughfare, King George is a favorite place for strolling, window-shopping, and munching.

On King George between Ben-Yehuda and Jaffa Road are three places to stay, neatly covering the price range from moderate to budget to rock-bottom. Turn right onto King George from Ben-Yehuda, and at no. 15 on the right-hand side you'll see the cheapest of the lot. **King George Hostels, Ltd.** (tel. 02-223-498) operates a youth-and-tourist hostel where guests stay in four-bedded bunk rooms for the rock-bottom price of $6 per person; private rooms go for $15; breakfast costs another dollar or so. A hostel card is not essential here, and there's no age limit, although guests tend to be the young and adventurous.

A bit farther along King George V Avenue, this time on the left-hand side, a well-disguised doorway at no. 10 leads to the **Hotel Klein** (tel. 02-228-988). Mrs. Klein offers homey, pension-style rooms for $14 to $18 in the winter and $16 to $19 in summer; no breakfast, although guests have use of the kitchen. A simply furnished apartment with private bath and kitchen goes for $26. Be aware that Mrs. Klein's place is up four flights of steps, 72 in all, and watch the street noise when you choose a room.

The two-star **Hotel Palatin**, 4 Agrippas St. (Jerusalem 94301; tel. 02-231-141), is actually a few steps off King George V Avenue, an advantage which results in quieter rooms. Look for the traffic lights on the left—that's Agrippas Street. A few steps up Agrippas you'll spot the hotel sign on the right; the entrance is just around the corner on Aven Israel Street. The Palatin is considerably more expensive than the modest hostelries just mentioned, and so it should be. Its 29 small, telephone-equipped rooms have been thoroughly modernized recently, done in bright and cheery colors; all have private bath with shower, and wall-to-wall carpeting. The pleasant dining room serves kosher cuisine, including an Israeli breakfast which comes with the room. Singles cost $28.75 to $32.25; doubles are $41.50 to $43.75. The lobby is one flight up, as are some of the rooms. Climb the stairs for the rest of the rooms.

There's a nice, friendly family-run pension just up the hill from the City Tower skyscraper. From the intersection of Ben-Yehuda Street and King George V Avenue, walk uphill with the City Tower on your right and bear left on Shmuel Ha-Nagid Street. Go one very short block and turn right on Bezalel Street. At no. 4, right across the street from the original Bezalel art school, is the **Noga Hotel** (P.O. Box 7723; tel. 02-224-590). The Noga is at the top of three flights of stairs. The very plain rooms are supplemented by a kitchen open to guests. The owners, Mr. and Mrs. Kristal, don't live at the pension, so guests don't feel they're imposing when they use the kitchen. The charge is $12 single, $16 to $18 double, without breakfast. If you get no answer at the pension phone number, try the Kristals' home (tel. 02-661-888).

Another inexpensive hostelry is the **Hotel Eretz Israel** (tel. 02-245-071). Finding it is tricky, though. Here's how: At the top of Ben-Yehuda Street, turn left onto King George V Avenue and walk south toward the imposing neo-Temple bulk of Heikhal Shlomo, the Great Synagogue and seat of the Chief Rabbinate. Cross Ha-Rav Avida Itabbi Akiva Street, and the towering Jerusalem Plaza Hotel will be looming ahead on the left. Before you come to the Jerusalem Plaza, look to your left into what seems to be a vacant lot at 51 King George. A sign announces the Hotel Eretz Israel. Walk down, under the sign, behind the trees. The stone building harbors a simple, tidy pension on its upper floor where rooms with running water cost $14 single, $26 double, without breakfast. You'll like the proprietors here.

Only a few blocks north of Zion Square is the simple, inexpensive **Hotel Zefania**, 4 Zefania St. (tel. 02-286-384 or 272-709), right at the corner with Strauss/Yehezkel Street. Bonuses here are use of kitchen facilities and a TV lounge. As the hotel is in the orthodox Ge'ula quarter, women must dress modestly, especially in summer. In exchange, they get a neighborhood that's quiet and safe. Rates are $10 single, $12 double, $18 to $20 for three or four, in rooms with private bath. Buses 1 and 27 run between the hotel and the Old City; nos. 4 and 9 go to downtown West Jerusalem.

A Youth Hostel and a Hospice: Not all that far from the City Tower are two more rock-bottom choices. The **Bet Bernstein** (tel. 02-228-286) is a youth hostel affiliated with the Israel Youth Hostel Association. It's at 1 Keren Ha-Yesod St. (that's the continuation of King George), corner of Agron Street, beside and behind the Center for Orthodox Judaism. The 75 beds go at the standard youth hostel rate of $5.50 to $6.50 for bed and breakfast, and in addition you get an air-conditioned dining room, lounge, reading room, etc. The daily curfew is at 11 p.m. Because of its prime location right near the Jerusalem Plaza Hotel, Bet Bernstein is usually filled early on summer days. Write in advance if you can.

For spotless accommodations and ultimate respectability, you can't beat the **Rosary Convent Hostel,** 14 Agron St. (P.O. Box 54; tel. 02-228-529), not far from the Or-Gil and Jerusalem Tower hotels. Each person pays $15 for bed and breakfast in a room with toilet and shower; for bed only, the rate is a low $13 per person. Lunch or dinner costs $7. It's not a big place, though, with only 49 beds.

The YMCA

When is a YMCA a three-star hotel? When it's in Jerusalem. This dramatic building, its tall tower rising to challenge the bulk of the King David Hotel directly across the street, is more than a community center for the city's Christian Arabs and foreign pilgrims. It holds 68 guest rooms, most of them with shower, two with bathtubs, a few without private bath. All rooms are quite basic and simple, but clean and proper, and the price is excellent for this status location: $27.50 to $34.50 single, $41.50 to $46 double, service charge and continental breakfast included. The YMCA is at 26 King David St. (tel. 02-282-593).

For Families

The modern, luxurious 301-room **Hotel Moriah Jerusalem,** 39 Keren Ha-Yesod St. (tel. 02-232-232), is one of Jerusalem's best places to stay. Rating four stars, it charges $85 to $103.50 double as normal rates. But a special family plan allows two parents and two children to stay in a large room for only $78.25, bounteous buffet breakfast and service charge included. That's an amazing

$19.55 per person, well within our budget. This rate is for off-season, but even in high summer and in holiday periods, the somewhat-higher family rate constitutes one of the city's indisputable lodging bargains. The Moriah Jerusalem, reachable by bus 4 or 7 along King George V Avenue, is located on Keren Ha-Yesod, which is the continuation of King George V Avenue, near the intersection with King David Street. It's just around the corner from the YMCA and the King David Hotel.

The Big Splurge

I don't really expect readers of this book to be staying at the elegant **King David Hotel**, King David Street (Jerusalem 94101; tel. 02-221-111), but I'm sure most readers will be curious as to what that privilege costs. Rates depend on the type of room and its view, and range from $100 to $157.50 single, $113.75 to $171.25 double in summer. During peak travel periods (holiday periods), all rates increase by $23 per room; in winter, rates are about 15% lower. The luxurious five-star King David is Jerusalem's status address, and has been so since the hotel was built during the British Mandate. With seven restaurants and bars, a swimming pool, and numerous shops, plus a superb location with panoramic views of the Old City, it's the city's compleat lodging. You might want to take a stroll through the lofty public rooms, admire the view from the patio, and have something refreshing just to catch a little of the ambience.

Farther Out

Other sections of West Jerusalem hold interesting places to stay, although you'll have to depend on buses for transportation to downtown and to the Old City.

West, in Bet Ha-Kerem: West of downtown, and south of the Central Bus Station, is Jerusalem's residential Bet Ha-Kerem quarter. Bus service to the center of town is frequent (except, of course, on the Sabbath), and out here you're close to Mount Herzl, Yad Vashem, and Hebrew University's West Jerusalem campus.

The best bus service between downtown and Bet Ha-Kerem is provided by the no. 20 bus along Jaffa Road and Herzl Boulevard.

Not quite in Bet Ha-Kerem, but on the way to it, is **Apartotel, Ltd.,** in the Nordau Towers at 214 Jaffa Rd. (P.O. Box 13100, Jerusalem 91130; tel. 02-381-221), corner of Sarei Israel Street, a block from Binyane Ha-Uma and two blocks from the Central Bus Station. Half-hotel and half-apartment-building, Apartotel offers small, medium, and large flats by the week and month. Maids come in to spruce things up three times weekly, and to change linens twice a week. Each flat has a fully equipped kitchenette, and you pay nothing extra for utilities (except outgoing phone calls). Washers and dryers, babysitting service, and even grocery delivery service are yours for various reasonable fees. Apartments have two to six beds (plus child's cot), and cost anywhere from $280 to $322 double per week; monthly rates save you a bit of money over weekly rates. (At Jerusalem three-star hotels, two people would pay between $300 and $400 for a week's room with breakfast, so you can see how much you save.) It's best to reserve your apartment, and put down a deposit, in advance.

In Bet Ha-Kerem proper is another apartment-hotel, the **Neveh Shoshana,** at 5 Bet Ha-Kerem St. (Jerusalem 96343; tel. 02-521-740 or 524-294). Get off the bus at Haft Square and walk along Bet Ha-Kerem Street to the hotel, which will be on your left. For a cheerful, modern room with bath and kitchenette one person will pay $25, two will pay $35, and you can pay $3.50 extra for breakfast, or fix your own.

Two blocks down Bet Ha-Kerem Street around the curve from the Neveh Shoshana is the **Pension Har Aviv**, at 16a Bet Ha-Kerem St. (tel. 02-521-515). (You can also enter from Denmark Square: get off the bus there, and walk down Bet Ha-Kerem Street. Look for the little sign on the left after about a block.) The Har Aviv is set back from the street in a verdant if small yard, and the 15 rooms all have terraces so you can enjoy the peace, quiet, and clean air. Rooms with private showers and toilets cost $28.75 single, $41.50 double, breakfast and service included. Full kosher lunches and dinners are available at moderate charges. The family-operated Har Aviv is classified as a two-star hotel.

Far West, Toward Ein Kerem: Scattered around the hilltops southwest of downtown are several youth hostels and hospices, good places to stay if you're adventurous and also impecunious.

The **Louise Waterman Wise Youth Hostel** (P.O. Box 16350, Jerusalem 96465; tel. 02-423-366 or 420-990) is part of the hostel federation. With 310 beds (124 in the new guesthouse), it's Jerusalem's biggest IYHF hostel. Rates are the standard $5.30 to $8 for bed and breakfast, the higher rate being for hostelers over age 18. A kitchen is here for your use, or you can buy inexpensive hostel meals; the hostel is centrally heated. To get to the hostel, you've got to get to the Bayit Vegan quarter: catch a bus (no. 13, 17, 18, 20, 24, 26, 39, or 40) going west in Zion Square, along Jaffa Road, or at the Central Bus Station. Get off at the Mount Herzl stop and ask for Pisgah Street (Rehov Ha-Pisgah). The hostel is a few steps down the street, on the right at no. 8.

In the village of Ein Kerem itself is the hospice at the **Sisters of Sion Convent** (P.O. Box 3705, Bet Ha-Kerem, Jerusalem 91037; tel. 02-415-738). It will appeal to those looking for a quiet religious retreat and a full-pension plan (room and three meals). Before venturing all the way out to Ein Kerem, however, call them to see what's available.

Some 12 km (7½ miles) west of jerusalem, just north of the highway to the airport and Tel Aviv, lies the Arab village of Abu Ghosh. Very near it is the three-star **Kiryat Anavim Kibbutz Hotel** (Kiryat Anavim 90833; tel. 02-348-999 or 348-850), with all the services of a fine, comfortable hotel, yet with the tang of kibbutz life all around. Of the 93 guest rooms, 52 have private baths, and heating and cooling systems; the rest have private showers, and central heat. Several of the rooms can comfortably lodge a family of three or four. A big bonus, besides the spacious grounds and uncluttered openness, is a large swimming pool. Of course, the hotel has its own restaurant, snackbar, and cocktail bar. Rates include breakfast, and range from $33.25 to $43.75 single, $39 to $57.50 double, depending on the time of year and the comforts of the room. Buses run to Kiryat Anavim and Abu Ghosh from the Central Bus Station.

South of the Old City: A few more lodging possibilities exist to the south of the Old City, not far from Jerusalem's quaint railroad station. Two hospices and several hotels are worth looking at here, in the Abu Tor and Talpiot quarters.

Only a few steps from the railroad station and the Khan Theater is **St. Andrews Hospice** (Church of Scotland—P.O. Box 14216; tel. 02-717-701). It's situated on a small hill, surrounded by a garden and boasts panoramic views of Mount Zion and the Old City. The hospice's lounge contains a fine portrait of General Allenby, who captured the city from the Ottomans in World War I; the general also laid the cornerstone of St. Andrew's Church in 1927. Most of the hospice's guest rooms have private bath, and all have central heating. The directors and staff offer a warm Scottish welcome to visitors, and charge $23 per person for bed and breakfast, about $8 for dinner. Prices change somewhat according to the season. Catch bus 4 or 7 along King George V Avenue or Keren Ha-Yesod Street, and get off at the Khan Theater stop. You'll see the hospice atop the hill, the banner of St. Andrew waving proudly from its tower.

St. Charles Hospice (P.O. Box 8020; tel. 02-637-737) is not far from St. Andrews Hospice. Located in the German Colony section of the city on Jan Smuts Street, the hospice is appropriately Teutonic in theme and administration, but travelers of any nationality or religion can stay here—if they can find a place. The 10 single and 15 double rooms are plain but immaculate, and usually full. Six have private bathroom, and are priced at $26 per person, breakfast and dinner included. Write in advance for reservations.

As for hotels, you'll want to know about the **Apt Hotel,** 9 Bet Ha-Arava St., in the Talpiot section of Jerusalem (tel. 02-719-131), a small apartment hotel in a quiet neighborhood not far off the route of bus 7. For $45 double, you get a small living room, a similar bedroom, and a private bath with both tub and shower. Use of a fully equipped communal kitchen is open to all, as is use of a comfy little lounge. An extra person in a room costs another $5. To find the Apt, catch bus 7 heading south along King George V Avenue or Keren Ha-Yesod Street and ask the driver to let you off in Talpiot at Bet Ha-Arava Street. The hotel is then a short five-minute walk along that street, on the left.

Another choice south of Talpiot is the big, ultramodern **Zohar Hotel,** 47 Leib Yaffe St., Arnona (P.O. Box 8261, Jerusalem 91082; tel. 02-717-557). This dramatic smoked-glass block rates three stars, and has 120 air-conditioned rooms, each with private bath and shower, telephone, radio, and wall-to-wall carpeting, plus a pleasant air-conditioned indoor "patio" at the center of the hotel. Views from the guest rooms are over the Judean hills. Rates are $36.75 to $39 single, $46 to $50.50 double, for bed and breakfast. Dinner costs about $10. You definitely get value for money, but give up none of the comforts, by staying outside the center of town. Take bus 7 south and ask to get off at the hotel. By the way, a group of town houses next door to the hotel bears the same street number, 47. Look for the distinctive smoked-glass exterior of the hotel.

Rooms and Apartments for Rent in West Jerusalem

Another choice you have in Jerusalem, as well as in most larger towns and cities, is to rent a room in a private home or boarding house. Should this appeal to you (it's a good way to get to know the "real" Israel), check the classified section of the daily *Jerusalem Post,* where you'll surely find several ads for rooms in or near Jerusalem. Then, too, keep your eyes open for small signs tacked to store and shop windows—often seen, they're usually in rather bad English or French or German, and announce rooms to let by the week, or more, or less.

A service with some important extras is offered by Mr. and Mrs. Eliezer Schecter of **A Home Away From Home,** 27 Ussishkin St. (P.O. Box 7769, Jerusalem 92463; tel. 02-636-071). The Schecters will find you a very comfortable furnished apartment for $400 to $900 per month, and pick you up and take you to the bus station to catch a tour. The cost for these services and others is $13 to $15 per person per day.

EAST JERUSALEM ACCOMMODATIONS:

You'll find numerous hotels in East Jerusalem, in the downtown area and on the Mount of Olives. All pilgrims to the Holy Land stayed in this part of town during the 20 years of Jordanian control. Hoteliers here have long experience in hospitality to foreign visitors.

Almost all two- and three-star East Jerusalem hotels contain a telephone, toilet, hot-water shower/bath, and central heating in each room. And the warmth of hospitality is very much in the Arabic tradition.

East Jerusalem's hotels are located in downtown East Jerusalem, on or near Saladin Street; and on the way to, and on top of, the Mount of Olives.

The following recommended hotels are discussed more in order of location than by price, since in East Jerusalem you often find "budget" hotels side by side with moderately priced or "big-splurge" hotels. All prices include your room, 15% service charge, and breakfast, unless otherwise noted, and are current during the summer months (rooms are cheaper in winter). Also, the majority of East Jerusalem hotels raise their prices by 20% to 25% during the Christmas and Easter holidays.

Downtown Hotels and Hospices

The first thing you ought to get straight is that **Saladin Street**—the main thoroughfare, the Fifth Avenue of this part of town—is spelled Saladin, Salah ed-Din, Salah Eddine, Salach A'Din, and Salah E-Din. It's all the same street.

Take a look at the map: Saladin Street begins opposite Herod's Gate and runs north for about half a mile. It roughly parallels Nablus Road, which begins at Herod's Gate and meets Saladin at the crest of a hill near the American Colony Hotel. The center of the downtown area is roughly a triangle formed by Saladin, **Port Said,** and **Rasheed Streets.** Port Said Street is frequently called **Az-Zahra Street** and Rasheed is sometimes called **Rachidya Street.**

As you come down the street from Zahal Square and West Jerusalem, over the crest of a hill at the Notre Dame Hospice, you will continue parallel to the old fortress wall. The street you are on is Ha-Zanhanim, which becomes **Sultan Suleiman.**

Just past Damascus Gate look across Sultan Suleiman Street and you'll see the big black letters of the **Pilgrims Palace Hotel** (P.O. Box 19066; tel. 02-284-831) staring you in the face. (It's on the western side of the East Jerusalem bus station—which means rooms on that side tend to be noisier.) The big limestone two-story, 95-room hotel has three stars and a convenient location. One flight up is the lobby, which has quite an array of stuffed chairs and sofas as well as a broad expanse of windows offering exciting day or night views of the Old City walls (across the street) and the busy folks bustling around them. It's not an opulent place, but it does have a corner bar (souvenir shop too). As for the rooms: spic and span, centrally heated and air-conditioned, with phones, toilets, and shower/baths . . . the works! Singles start at $28.75 to $35.75, doubles at $43.75 to $50.50. Students get a 15% discount.

Along Saladin Street: Saladin Street begins at the modern post office, and there, on the opposite side of the street, you'll see the 31-room, two-star **Rivoli Hotel** (P.O. Box 19599; tel. 02-284-871). Rooms here are cheerful enough, with cream-colored walls and a bright wool blanket on each bed, and each has phone, central heating, wall-to-wall carpeting, shower/bath, and toilet. Ten rooms have air conditioning as well. The Rivoli boasts an opulent lounge, two TV rooms, and air-conditioned public areas. The service is usually all you'd want it to be, in the rooms or in the restaurant. The price? $20 single, $30 double, breakfast included.

The one-star **Savoy Hotel,** right around the corner at 5 Ibn Sina St. (P.O. Box 19766; tel. 02-283-366), is elevator-equipped and heated. All 17 rooms have private bath or shower and toilet, but are basically of the no-frills variety. Rates are $12 to $15 single, $20 to $24 double. Students get a 15% discount, even during high season.

Farther up Saladin, at no. 6 (next to the Universal Library Book Store, biggest, best-stocked bookstore in this part of Jerusalem), is the five-story, two-star, elevator-equipped **Metropole** (tel. 02-282-507). All 30 rooms here have phones, central heating, and fully equipped bathrooms. The cost is $20.75 single, $36.75 double; rates are slightly lower off-season. From the pleasant roof garden (where lunch and dinner are served in the summertime) you can view Mount Scopus, the Mount of Olives, and the Rockefeller Museum. The Metropole is, by the way, the traditional stopping place for Arab pilgrims, Muslim and Christian.

Right next door to the Metropole is the **New Metropole Hotel,** 8 Saladin St. (P.O. Box 19614; tel. 02-283-846). The New Metropole boasts air-conditioned rooms, an elevator, and a three-star rating, not to mention its good downtown East Jerusalem location. Room prices are $25.25 single, $39 double.

At 18 Saladin St., opposite the Capitol Hotel, is the 30-room, two-star **Lawrence Hotel** (P.O. Box 19129; tel. 02-282-585). Central heating, and showers or baths in each room here, which you've come to expect in this part of Jerusalem, but what you don't expect is the elevator. In the spacious (but a bit musty) lobby, sedately furnished with glass-topped tables, is a well-equipped (tiny) gift shop. There's carpeting in the rooms, but few frills outside of that—just the necessities. Rates are $20.75 single, $36.75 double. Discounts are offered to students.

The **Capitol Hotel** (tel. 02-282-561), across Saladin Street from the Lawrence, offers luxury at moderate prices. Its 54 four-star rooms all have private bathrooms with tubs, plus telephones and radios (TVs on request); an elevator, central heating, and air conditioning, a bar, and a private parking lot add to the four-star classification, and yet prices are surprisingly low by Jerusalem standards: $25.25 to $30 single, $36.75 to $43.75 double, and that includes breakfast and service charge. Prices are somewhat lower when business is slack.

Turkish Mansion Hotels: The Ottoman Empire ruled Palestine for centuries, finally relinquishing it to General Allenby's armies in World War I. Magnificent vestiges of Ottoman rule remain, however. Besides Sultan Suleiman's great walls around the Old City, the Turks left many mansions and palaces. Several of these have been converted to hotels, and you can get a whiff of Ottoman glory by staying in one. Both of the following hotels are near the upper reaches of Saladin Street.

Behind the Christmas Hotel, technically at 10 Abu Obideah El-Jarrah St. (you'll have to circle the block), is the 22-room **New Orient House** (P.O. Box 19312; tel. 02-282-437), opposite an orphanage school. The New Orient really looks like what it once was: the residence of an important family during Turkish rule. Its dining room is straight out of that era—light-blue walls, vaulted archways, massive hanging fans. Note the unique bar made from pounded copper. The house was—and still is—owned by the Husseini family, who played host to Kaiser Wilhelm of Germany, King Abdullah of Jordan, and Emperor Haile Selassie of Ethiopia within its walls. Rooms are adequate, if not as exciting as the public rooms, and they're outfitted with bathrooms, phones, and central heating. Singles are $19.50; doubles run $32.25. Slight reductions off-season.

Romantically Middle Eastern in feeling, with beautiful gardens and an unforgettable atmosphere, the **American Colony Hotel** (P.O. Box 19215, Jerusalem 97200; tel. 02-282-421), once the home of Khaldi, a Turkish pasha, is practically in a class by itself. The four-star, 102-room hotel is within the walled courtyard just past the top of the hill where Saladin Street and Nablus Road meet. Some rooms here are outfitted with mother-of-pearl cocktail tables, copper trays, feenjons, and ornate gold and blue ceilings. You'll find an intriguing duality in these rooms: antique Arab and Turkish furnishings and modern tile bathrooms. In the cloister-like lobby above the garden, archeological finds are displayed in glass cases. There's a swimming pool. The garden, ablaze with crimson and orange flowers, sends up a 20-foot palm tree. Potted plants and mosaic tables lend atmosphere to the sitting rooms and lounges. Only 13 of the rooms here are in the museum-like old building; the rest are in slightly less august buildings across the courtyard. Rates are $62 to $103.50 single, $85 to $126.50 double, breakfast and service included. Even if you decide you can't afford the American Colony's four-star luxury, come for the famous Saturday-afternoon buffet, and take a turn through the public rooms upstairs in the main building.

Along Nablus Road: Starting from Damascus Gate, Nablus Road (or Derekh Schekhem) heads north roughly parallel to Saladin Street—parallel, that is, until they curve to meet.

Several blocks up Nablus Road, past the street named Pikud Ha-Merkaz, you'll come to the **YMCA East**, at no. 29, also known as the **Aelia Capitolina Hotel** (P.O. Box 19023; tel. 02-282-375). Just past the American Consulate's Consular Section, the YMCA is a 57-room, three-star hotel in everything but name. The Israel Hotel Association rates it as such. Actually, it seems even grander. The imperial-looking lobby—with its brass lamps, great pillars, archways, and low couches—resembles a sheik's sitting room. Rooms in the four-floor hotel are clean and airy, each with phone, bathroom, and central heating. There's a swimming pool in the basement and squash and tennis courts outside. Beyond the lobby's grillwork, brass tables, and mosaic fountain is a coffee bar and a new grill room. In the garden in front of the hotel stands a directional marker, noting that New York is 5,785 miles away; Baghdad, 543 miles; London, 2,290 miles; and Cairo, 256 miles away. Singles are $26.50 to $32.75; doubles are $48.25. The Aelia Capitolina takes men, women, and couples, just like any hotel. An added bonus: Buses to downtown come right by its front door, and the British Council library is right next door.

Walk just a bit farther up Nablus Road from the Aelia Capitolina and you'll be approaching the English Gothic spires of St. George's Cathedral on the right. At the point where Nablus Road and Saladin Street meet, in the imposing cathedral compound, is **St. George's Hostel** (P.O. Box 19018; tel. 02-283-302). The 45-bed Anglican/Episcopal hostel is housed in a cloister around its own veddy English garden. Accommodations are comfortable and congenial, and cost $18.75 per person, breakfast and service included. Although St. George's is at a noisy corner, that's all to the good. It's supremely quiet within the thick stone walls, but buses to all parts of town are right outside your door.

On and Off Harun er-Rasheed Street: Another main street in downtown East Jerusalem is Harun er-Rasheed (or Rashid) Street, which starts from Herod's Gate behind the post office; as you start up Harun er-Rasheed Street, the Rockefeller Museum is up on its hill to your right. This part of town has an interesting collection of places to stay, in all price ranges.

Starting up Harun er-Rasheed Street, the modest two-star, 15-room **Pilgrims Inn** (tel. 02-284-883) will be on your right about half a block down. Run by the same people who own the fancier Pilgrims Palace by the bus station, the Pilgrims Inn has refurnished rooms equipped with showers and telephones, and central heating. There's a small dining room and coffeeshop. The location is a handy one, and prices are negotiable if business is not heavy: $20.25 to $22.50 single, $30 to $32.25 double, breakfast and service included of course.

Slightly farther up Harun er-Rasheed Street, on the right at no. 6, is the large and modern **Holyland East Hotel** (P.O. Box 19700; tel. 02-284-841), a 99-room hostelry with modern bathrooms (with tubs), air conditioning and central heat, telephones and radios in all rooms. As you enter the lobby, you may have the feeling you're in a well-run and orderly hotel in America or Europe—the careful arrangement of plumpish sort-of-modern chairs and tables is Western indeed. Be sure to avail yourself of the pleasures of the roof garden, with a wonderful view of everything. Chances are that your room here will have a balcony and a view of the Mount of Olives. For these three-star comforts one person pays $30 to $32.25, and two pay $41.50 to $46, less when the various Muslim, Jewish, or Christian holidays, or the prime summer months, don't fill the hotel.

Backtrack a few steps now, to El-Azfahani Street, which begins at a point between the aforementioned two hotels. Go down El-Azfahani and then turn right on El-Masudi to get to the **Victoria Hotel,** 8 Masudi St. (P.O. Box 19066; tel. 02-286-220). The 54-room Victoria is the last in the Pilgrims Palace chain, a large and comfy place on a very quiet street only minutes from the Old City. All the rooms have telephones, and tubs in the bathrooms, plus central heating and (in some) air conditioning. You can rent a TV for use in your room on request. Expect lower rates off-season (although not in the dead of winter, when the Victoria tends to close, sending its potential customers to the larger Pilgrims Palace), but in spring, summer, and fall, you'll pay about $22.50 single, $32.25 double, with breakfast as usual.

Back on Harun er-Rasheed Street, climb up the slope and turn left on Az-Zahra (or Zahara) Street to find the **Azzahra Hotel** at 13 Az-Zahra St. (P.O. Box 19026; tel. 02-282-447). A small, congenial family-run place on a quiet cul-de-sac, the Azzahra can boast a dozen rooms with bathtubs and another dozen with showers; all have telephones and pastel-colored walls. A wonderful garden patio is yours to enjoy in good weather (which is almost all the time). For these comforts, plus breakfast and the 15% service fee, the total price is $18.50 single, $32.25 double. The Azzahra rates two stars.

At the top of Harun er-Rasheed Street, where it intersects with Az-Zahra Street, is a sort of plaza where several streets come together. Turn right (east) and you'll be on Nur ed-Din Street, which curves behind the Rockefeller Museum. Nur ed-Din is more or less the continuation of Az-Zahra Street.

A few steps along Nur ed-Din Street, on the left-hand side, is where you'll find Doris and Farid Salman's 25-room **Jordan House,** 12 Nur ed-Din St. (tel. 02-283-430), one of Jerusalem's most distinctive, intriguing hotels. Constructed from rough-cut local stone, it sits amid a grouping of pine trees, a panorama of the Mount of Olives behind it. The owners are dealers in antiquities and this accounts for the splendid Middle Eastern furnishings within. The Arabic decor begins in the lobby and hallway and continues into the rooms. Look again at those cushions, copper tables, old brass lamps, and assorted objets d'art: they're the real thing, heavy and ornate, not the kind you find in some tourist shops hereabouts. In the older rooms are magnificent oil lamps (now electrified, of course), highlighting the venerable old look. The bathrooms are new, though. Rooms at Jordan House go for $30 single, $46 double.

On Wadi el-Joz Street: A bit farther from the center of things, Wadi el-Joz Street winds through the valley and city district of the same name, to the north of the Rockefeller Museum, and also through the neighboring district of Sheikh Jarrah.

There's a **YWCA** on Wadi el-Joz in Sheikh Jarrah (tel. 02-282-593). A big, solidly built, Jerusalem-stone three-star hotel, it is supported by round pillars. Shiny marble floors create a feeling of opulence. Bedrooms at the elevator-equipped Y have private baths, central heating, and throw rugs on the floors. There is a large dining room and a snackbar on the premises. Single occupancy is $27.50 to $32.25; double occupancy, $46.

Vienna East Hotel, 47 Wadi el-Joz St., Sheikh Jarrah (tel. 02-284-826), is elevator-equipped and heated. Some of the 39 bedrooms, which are painted in pastel colors and carpeted, have terraces; all have baths or showers. Rates are $20.75 to $27.50 single, $23 to $32.25 double. Students get a 10% discount. Off-season rates are a bit lower.

Starvation Budget

Jerusalem Student House, also known as the **Jerusalem Hotel** (P.O. Box 20606; tel. 02-283-282), is at 4 Antara Ben-Shaddad St., just off Nablus Road to the left behind the city bus depot (which is only a block or so up Nablus Road from Damascus Gate). Its 15 rooms all have private baths with showers and although the rates aren't strictly starvation budget, they're very low for what you get, and liable to be lower if business is slack. Singles go for $17.25 to $23, doubles for $32.20, with automatic reductions in effect off-season. You'll meet other young people here.

The **Ramsis Youth Hostel Student House,** 20 Ha-Nevi'im St. (tel. 02-284-818), off Sultan Suleiman Street and just a few steps from Damascus Gate, has recently been renovated. It has clean dormitory beds for $3 to $5, private double rooms for $11, and all the other necessary services: kitchenette, television set, dining room where breakfast is served, and free storage of luggage. The hostel has an 11 p.m. curfew.

Mount of Olives Hotels

Up here the view is grand and biblical—churches and mosques everywhere, among hillsides of golden stone cypress trees. One drawback worth noting, however, is that bus service to and from this area is not as regular or fast as one would like. Buses 42 and 75 run up from the East Jerusalem bus station on Sultan Suleiman Street near the Damascus Gate, at well-spaced intervals, and only bus 75 operates on Saturday. But despair not: you can call a sherut from any hotel up here, and for a loadful (seven people) the cost will be quite reasonable.

On a quiet hillside off Mount of Olives Road are several good hotels. The first is the two-star **Astoria Hotel** (tel. 02-284-965), which has a nice outdoor terrace. The 23 rooms here are decorated in the Western idiom, and each is fully equipped: bathroom (tub or shower), phone, and central heating. Singles are $19.50, and doubles are $32.

Up the hill on the same side is the three-star, 45-room **Commodore Hotel** (P.O. Box 19715; tel. 02-284-845). This is a tidy, well-groomed place, with a big, handsome lobby (look for the painting of Petra on the wall), an elevator, and rooms with all the conveniences. Singles are $25.25; doubles are $32.25.

At the top of the hill on the Mount of Olives Road, you turn right and pass through the Arab village of Et-Tur and continue past two hospitals. The steeple of the Russian church will be on your left and at a bend in the road to the left you'll see the **Mount of Olives Hotel** (tel. 02-284-877). The distinguishing features of this two-star, 63-room hotel are its tent-like, red-cloth bar and its proximity to the Church of the Ascension, just next door. Rooms are simply furnished, all with bathtubs or showers, and central heating; some have phones. Singles are $18.50, and doubles are $34.50, including continental breakfast.

4. Where to Dine

Jerusalem has such a selection of restaurants, dairy bars, lunch counters, snack shops, delicatessens, and cafés that it's bewildering at first. I'll help you sort it all out by recommending several of the best places of each kind, grouped first according to location, and then according to the type of food and services provided.

Here's what to expect: in the Old City and East Jerusalem you'll find mostly Middle Eastern cuisine. Falafel stands abound, as do those serving shwarma (slices of mutton stacked on a vertical spit, grilled, and carved for sandwiches). The sit-down restaurants are usually quite plain in decor, but very fancy as far as the food goes: full meals start with an assortment of mazza (hors d'oeuvres and salads) such as hummus, olives, eggplant purée, pickled vegetables, and on and on. Main courses can be steak, chicken, fish, or chops. Shellfish and pork are prohibited to good Muslims as they are to Jews, but in restaurants catering to Christian Arabs you will find these dishes. Virtually no kosher restaurants exist in the Old City (except in the Jewish Quarter) or in East Jerusalem.

In West Jerusalem the dining scene is quite different. Pizza parlors, hamburger stands, Viennese-style cafés (often called "conditory," an Anglicization of the German *konditorei*) good for breakfast, a snack, or afternoon tea. Full restaurants in West Jerusalem serve American, Indian, Spanish, Italian, Central European, and Middle Eastern cuisine, and most of them are kosher. Don't assume that the Jewish cuisine you know from home will be served in every West Jerusalem restaurant. Bagels, for instance, are usually eaten here as a street snack picked up from a vendor, and not ordered with cream cheese and lachs (lox) in a restaurant. A bagel in an Israeli restaurant would be like a hot pretzel in a New York restaurant!

Those unfamiliar with kosher food may find a few surprises as well. The kosher prohibition against serving meat and milk products at the same meal is the most noticeable law of *kashrut*. What it means is that you can order a hamburger, but not a cheeseburger. At breakfast you'll be served eggs and various cheeses, yogurt, etc., but no small breakfast steak will be on the menu, and your spaghetti won't come all bolognese, with a sauce of both meat and cheese. Since you'll probably order meat at dinnertime, the borscht you order as a first course won't come with sour cream—you see how it works.

A NOTE ON SABBATH DINING: You need to know a few things about the Sabbath dining problem. Actually, it's not Sabbath dining that's the problem, but the lack of it. On Friday and eves of holidays, Jerusalem's shops, offices, and restaurants close around 2 p.m. Most of the restaurants don't reopen until Saturday evening. The problem for hungry tourists is a very real one.

Saturday's breakfast is usually provided by your hotel, and by Saturday's dinnertime, restaurants will be open again. That leaves Friday's dinner and Saturday's lunch. Of these, Friday is definitely the bigger problem. Friday evening at home with the family, relaxing and enjoying the beginning of the Sabbath after a hard week's work, is a revered tradition among Israelis, whether they're strictly religious or liberal and secular. Having to work Friday evening would be like an American's having to work Sunday morning: Who wants to? But what do the hungry tourists do?

Here are some answers. If you're looking for a kosher meal, you're pretty much out of luck, so you should eat a hearty lunch on Friday, and buy snacks or picnic supplies for Friday evening. You won't need much since you will awake to the huge Israeli breakfast on Saturday. If you aren't concerned about *kashrut*, you can head for East Jerusalem's many Arabic restaurants, which do a booming business on Friday evenings. As for Saturday lunch, the same solutions apply. One or two cafés may be open in West Jerusalem at this time, but you should not depend on this. Rather, plan ahead.

THE NOBLE FALAFEL: The noble falafel is virtually a Middle Eastern way of life. Found in most Arab countries as well as in Israel, falafel is everyone's favorite snack or inexpensive light lunch. Classically, it consists of chickpea (garbanzo) meal mixed with herbs and spices, formed into balls and deep-fried. The balls are stuffed into the pouch of a loaf of flat bread, leaving room for shredded cabbage, pickles, hot peppers, olives, and half a dozen other garnishes. Finally, a few spoonfuls of creamy tchina (sesame purée dressing) are ladled on top, and the struggle to get one's mouth around this tempting but unwieldy assemblage begins.

There are variations: the Egyptians, for instance, like their falafel made from *fool* beans rather than chickpeas. And in the interests of economy some Jerusalem falafel purveyors mix in an unconscionable quantity of breadcrumbs from leftover pita with the chickpea meal.

How to tell a good falafel? Split a ball and see how much bread it has in it. If it's all chickpea meal, see how many you get for your money. Stuff-it-yourself falafel places are ideal—you never cheat yourself. What should you pay? Well, the price is rarely posted, and can vary from customer to customer. Currently it can be anywhere from 80 agorot (55¢) to NIS1.50 ($1); NIS1 (65¢) is about right. Ask first, or watch to see what a local person pays. West Jerusalem's falafel center is the intersection of King George V Avenue and Agrippas Street, near Jaffa Road.

EATING PLACES IN THE OLD CITY: Luckily for tourists, the Old City is well provided with snack stands and budget-priced restaurants serving Arab cuisine. As you'll be out to see the sights, a quick snack or a simple, inexpensive meal will probably fill the bill. Arab cuisine being what it is, the snack or meal is bound to be tantalizing and delicious.

First I'll describe eateries convenient to the principal city gates, and then we'll rove the bazaars in search of exotic, inexpensive fare.

Near Jaffa Gate

Just inside the gate on the left are several snack stands at which you can order a falafel sandwich or one made with shwarma (grilled mutton) for about NIS1.50 ($1). The pouch of flat bread filled with fried chickpea balls or spicy mutton and salads may be all you can eat. If not, try a sit-down meal at one of these restaurants.

Abu Seif & Sons, 17 Omar Ibn El-Khattab Square (tel. 02-286-812), is my first choice in this category. Modest-looking from the outside, it has two floors and is open from 8 a.m. to 9 p.m. every day except Sunday. On Saturday the management prepares many different dishes and the food is all fresh. Appetizers such as hummus, tomato salad with tchina, eggplant salad, or soup, cost a uniform NIS2.25 ($1.50). In the more exotic department, you can purchase potatoes, grape leaves or marrow stuffed with meat, spinach with beef or lamb, or roast meat with rice, and the three-course meal will cost you NIS12 ($8), tip included.

Near Damascus Gate

One of the city's most important places, Damascus Gate is curiously devoid of restaurants. Perhaps this is because downtown East Jerusalem, with its marvelous Arab eateries, is right close by. In any case, you won't starve here for my favorite falafel stand in all Jerusalem is inside the gate at the bottom of the flight of stairs. Usually a man selling fruit of the season will be standing right next to it, so you can make a filling, delicious, and very inexpensive lunch right on the spot. For dessert, wander along Suq Khan ez-Zeit Street, to the right as you face the falafel stand, and let your eyes roam over the mouthwatering sweets and pastries in the Arab sweet shops on the right-hand side of the street. Stop in at **Abu Sair Sweets,** also called **Nablus Sweets** (tel. 02-284-043), for some baklava, or try burma (pronounced "*boor*-mah"), a cylinder of toasted shredded wheat stuffed with pistachio nuts and flavored with honey. The price you pay to sit and have a portion of such as Eastern delight depends on the one you select. Burma, with those expensive pistachios, will cost more than a plain crumpet-like kata-yeef. It's best to ask what the price will be before you sit down.

Farther along Suq Khan ez-Zeit Street is a natural-juice bar serving freshly made carrot juice, and juices of fruits in season. Prices are posted on the wall.

Near Herod's Gate

The northernmost of Old Jerusalem's city gates, Herod's Gate is just opposite the beginning of Saladin Street. Inside the gate and down a short way on the right is one of Jerusalem's best and most famous starvation-budget eateries.

Uncle Moustache's Restaurant and Tea Room (tel. 02-273-631) may well be the ultimate budget eating spot in the Old City. Uncle Moustache's is the simplest of storefront cafés, located about 20 yards inside Herod's Gate, on the right-hand side. It's indistinguishable from all the other tiny storefront cafés that line these broad courtyard steps except for Uncle Moustache—a gentle, big-bellied man with a black handlebar moustache—and the lowest of low-priced menus. A cheese omelet with rice or chips and salad is NIS3.50 ($2.35), hummus and tchina with salad in a pita even less, and a main course of chicken, kebab, shishlik, liver, or fish, all served with rice or chips, and salad is NIS4.50 ($3). Open daily from 7 a.m. to 10 p.m., till midnight in summer.

In the Jewish Quarter

The revivified Jewish Quarter of the Old City also has restaurants worthy of special mention. For instance, try the **Mitspe Ha-Kotel Panorama Restaurant and Café** (tel. 02-280-618), a kosher cafeteria in Batei Mahse Square, at the heart of the Jewish Quarter. Located up a flight of stairs at one side of the square, the restaurant has the advantages of self-service and low prices. Figure to spend less than NIS12 ($8) for a main course, dessert, and beverage—no tip, of course. The restaurant is open for lunch and dinner daily, closing for the Sabbath.

EATING PLACES IN WEST JERUSALEM: It would be no exaggeration to say that downtown West Jerusalem has an eatery on almost every corner. One can hardly walk 20 paces without passing a place that sells pizza, falafel, hamburgers, spaghetti, steaks, or Sachertorte mit schlag. There's no trouble locating a place to have a bite.

But some bites are tastier than others in this culinary maelstrom, and the suggestions below will help you chart your course. Here are some general guidelines: Jaffa Road between the main post office and King George V Avenue has something for everyone, from pubs through snack stands and cafés to full restaurants, plus several places to buy delicatessen-style picnic supplies. Rivlin Street, off Zion Square, is West Jerusalem's trendy restaurant street, lined with interesting places serving everything from steaks through natural foods. Luntz Street has a huge deli and several good general-purpose restaurants. Ben-Yehuda Street has mostly Central European–style cafés, and King George V Avenue has some restaurants, but is lined mostly with quick snack and lunch counters.

Here are West Jerusalem's restaurants, then. Most are kosher, but check to make sure before you buy: look on the sign out front, or on the posted menu.

Near Zion Square

Just about the nicest place for a light lunch, tea, or supper (except on Friday) is the **Ticho House** coffeeshop, on Abraham Ticho Street off Ha-Rav Kook Street (tel. 02-245-068). Walk out of Zion Square on Ha-Rav Kook, and Ticho Street is on the left before you reach Ha-Nevi'im. You enter the house through its shady grounds and terrace café. Ticho House was built, complete with Persian garden, in the 1880s as the villa of one Rasheed Agha. Later it became the home of Dr. Abraham Ticho and his wife, the artist Anna Ticho. It is now part of the Israel Museum. There's a permanent exhibition of Mrs. Ticho's drawings, and another holding Dr. Ticho's collection of Hanukkah lamps. In the café, either indoors or outdoors, you can order crêpes (savory or sweet), soups, salads, sandwiches (hot cheese and herbs is a favorite), or the daily special platter. Most items cost between NIS2 ($1.35) and NIS5 ($3.35). Drinks include real espresso coffee, wine, and beer. Service is friendly, and the kitchen is kosher. The coffeeshop is open Sunday through Thursday from 10 a.m. to 11:45 p.m., on Friday from 10 a.m. to 3 p.m., and on Saturday from the end of the Sabbath till 11:45 p.m. The museum is open Sunday through Thursday from 10 a.m. to 5 p.m., (till 10 p.m. on Tuesday), till 2 p.m. on Friday.

Leah and Ernest Brumer's **Europa Restaurant,** 48 Jaffa Rd. (tel. 02-228-953), is a Hungarian eatery situated on the upper floor of a building overlooking Zion Square. It's fancier at dinner than at lunch when paper placemats and napkins are replaced by white, orange, or purple cloths. A stuffed quarter chicken comes with a choice of rice, carrots, baked potato, spinach, or dumplings. Sweet-and-sour pot roast, a specialty, is another good choice. Leave room for a dessert of palacsinta (dessert crêpes). Open Sunday to Thursday from noon to 10 p.m., on Friday till 3 p.m. For a full meal of soup or appetizer, main course, and the luxurious dessert, expect to pay NIS25 ($16.75) to NIS30 ($20); lower that by 28% if you forgo the dessert. The Europa is kosher.

A window display of pastries and cakes will lure you into the **Café Navah,** 44 Jaffa Rd. (tel. 02-222-861), Zion Square's upscale café, where Jerusalem's best go to see and be seen. Glimmering mirrors, white and gold trim, and marble floors surround you as you settle into a comfortable booth or take a tiny table. The Navah menu offers light meals as well as the pastries which have already tempted you. Settle down with soup and a sandwich, or a luncheon plate of cold cuts and salads, and your bill will come to less than NIS10 ($6.65), all in. Alcoholic drinks are served as well as coffee, and Navah is open daily, all day, except on the Sabbath.

Pie House, 5 Hyrkanos St., next door to the Jerusalem Hotel (go up Ha-Havatzelet out of Zion Square and turn right; tel. 02-242-478), is a wood shack that will surprise you with its size and rustic quaintness once you get inside. The place is a favorite hangout for journalists. A few outdoor tables are set up in good weather, and this is a good, quiet place for your afternoon coffee and cake. Salads, stews, and full-course meals fill the menu, but steak and fish are also available. The star attraction is the three-course daily special dinner, a huge repast including soup or salad, main-course platter, and dessert, for less than NIS10 ($6.75).

A few steps farther on you'll see **Home Plus,** 9 Heleni Ha-Malka St. (tel. 02-222-612), about a block northeast of Zion Square. This attractive, unusually upbeat (for Jerusalem), mod establishment calls itself a "café/restaurant," and has a well-stocked bar, an excellent sound system playing the latest cool hits, and two floors of light, open café sitting areas. The menu lists a variety of light meals, including soups, spaghettis, and sandwiches, and you can easily throw something together for NIS15 ($10). Hours are easy: Home Plus is open 24 hours a day, except on the Sabbath.

The hamburger has come to Israel with a vengeance. The most visible of several small burger chains is **MacDavid,** 40 Jaffa Rd., at Eliashar Street (tel. 02-222-989), just a few steps out of Zion Square toward the Old City. A burger, french fries, and soft drink costs NIS5.20 ($3.50). This Holy City branch of the MacDavid chain is kosher; in sinful Tel Aviv, however, you can order a cheeseburger!

You'll find the entrance to the **Ma'adan Restaurant,** 35 Jaffa Rd. (tel. 02-225-631), to be an unprepossessing aluminum doorway. Down the stairs in the white arched and stuccoed interior are simple tables covered in red cloths. Light pours through a colored-glass window, dispelling the cave-like feeling as you order from a menu in English which lists stuffed vegetables (including stuffed vine leaves) and such oldtime Israeli favorites as shishlik and goulash. Portions are of good size and tasty, if simple, and prices are moderate: I had shishlik (beef shish kebab) with rice and a soft drink for NIS10 ($6.65), tip included. The daily special plate costs a bit less. Come for lunch or dinner, except on the Sabbath.

For Picnic Supplies: One of the best places for picnic fare is the **Picnic Grill,** 57 Jaffa Rd. (tel. 02-224-195), between King George V and Even Israel Streets, where you can also eat at the counter. But it's cheaper to take the food with you: NIS8 ($5.35) for a whole grilled chicken, half price for half a chicken. A nine-ounce portion of salad (there are 13 kinds) costs NIS2 ($1.35); rice-filled vegetables, about the same. Open from 8 a.m. to 8 p.m., closed Friday from 3 p.m. until Sunday morning.

Also very good for picnic fixings is the **grocery store** at 44 Jaffa Rd., across the street and down a bit from the Picnic Grill. Take advantage of these places. You can eat much better, for lower cost, than if you took similar meals in a sit-down restaurant.

Along Rivlin Street

Walk out of Zion Square on Jaffa Road, toward the Old City. The first street on your right is Rivlin Street.

Down at the end of Rivlin Street at no. 7 is a tidy café and dairy restaurant. Called **Café O'clock** (tel. 02-247-501), it's hardly the place for clock-watchers in the usual sense, though there is a big old clock over the doorway. Run by immigrants from Holland (who also speak half a dozen languages, including English), this is the place for a light lunch or supper, or a pleasant afternoon tea. Salads, omelets, sandwiches, and particularly the luscious desserts are on the bill of fare. A mountainous plate of salad, for instance, with a glass of wine and some fresh bread, will set you back NIS9 ($6), all in. The café is open for lunch and dinner—and later—every day, except for the standard Sabbath closing.

On Salomon Street

Starting right in Zion Square, and running parallel to Rivlin Street, is narrow Salomon Street. It harbors several good wining-and-dining establishments.

Off the Square, 6 Salomon St. (tel. 02-242-549), is appropriately named as it's only a short block off Zion Square and down a passage on the right. This is a *glatt kosher* dairy restaurant that's extremely popular. The secrets of its success are several: congenial, rustic dining rooms with a patio for summer; good food; and a tempting variety of dishes. Choose from soups (onion, mushroom, yogurt), salads (Greek, niçoise, country), pot pies, crêpes, fish, and wonderful desserts including pies made from blueberries, pecans, apples, and mixed fruit. Beer and wine are served. You can dine well on a pot pie or soup and salad here for NIS10 ($6.65), or you can have soup, fish, dessert, and wine, and spend two or three times that much. Whichever way, you will get your money's worth. Off the Square is open from noon to midnight daily; closed from 3 p.m. Friday until the end of the Sabbath on Saturday.

Just a few steps farther along the street is the **Tavlin Restaurant,** 16 Salomon St. (tel. 02-243-847), a cozy little place with a kosher dairy menu which includes corn soup, artichoke-heart salad, and spaghetti served several ways. Tavlin's crêpes come with fillings of mushrooms, bleu cheese, spinach, onion, or Bulgarian cheese; the broccoli-and-almond pot pie is delicious. You get good country bread and butter with whatever you order. Expect to pay NIS10 ($6.65) to NIS15 ($10) for a good meal here; you'll rarely spend more. Service at Tavlin is Sunday through Thursday from 11:30 a.m. till midnight, on Friday till 3:30 p.m., and on Saturday from an hour after the end of the Sabbath till midnight. Wine and beer are served, and some evenings there's live jazz piano music.

On and Off Ben-Yehuda Street

West Jerusalem's main thoroughfare, and the side streets running from it, can provide many solutions to the problem of sustenance. Starting from Zion Square and climbing up the slope, here is a tour of Ben-Yehuda dining places.

Go in either of the two entrances to the **Derby Grill Restaurant,** at 2 Ben-Yehuda St. or 1 Luntz St. (tel. 02-244-454), and you'll find a small, cozy, bright, and upbeat place with a grill counter and small tables in two long, narrow rooms. Woodwork and ceramic tiles add spice to the decor. From the menu (in English, of course), I chose hummus, which was superb, and shishlik, which turned out to be three enormous skewers of large, charcoaled chunks of beef. A plate of pickled peppers and olives, and a basket of flat bread, came with the meal at no extra charge. With an enormous glass of beer, and the tip, I paid NIS20 ($13.35), but the dinner would easily have fed two people. The Derby is open daily for lunch and dinner, except on the Sabbath.

At 5 Ben-Yehuda, just out of the square, is **Moshiko Falafel & Shwarma** (tel. 02-222-605), where the Middle Eastern delicacy of spit-roasted lamb comes to you in a sandwich made with flat pita bread for NIS2.50 ($1.65). A similarly substantial pita sandwich of falafel costs NIS1.50 ($1). The kitchen is kosher.

A few steps out of Zion Square along Ben-Yehuda brings you to Luntz Street, on the right. Luntz Street, now a pedestrian way, is famous for **Heppner's American-Style Deli,** 4 Luntz St., on the left (tel. 02-221-703). Bare and boldly colored, with lots of sidewalk tables, Heppner's is not exactly one's vision of a cozy New York corner deli, but it really delivers when it comes to food and prices. Long lists of dishes and prices are posted here and there: a falafel plate consisting of falafel, hummus, tchina, pickles, pita bread, and salad costs only NIS4.70 ($3.15), and other such filling platters based on chicken, pot roast, tongue, or a hamburger are about the same. Three-course meals, unbelievably, are just slightly more expensive. Heppner's is kosher, and is open almost all the time, except on the Sabbath.

Next door to Heppner's is the **Rimon Café** (tel. 02-222-772), a posh café with handsome hardwood tables surrounded by brass-trimmed chairs inside, chrome-trimmed outside. The specialty here is freshly baked cookies, cakes, and other desserts—just look at them all in the display cases. You can also get good light meals consisting of soup and, say, a tuna or cheese platter. Expect to pay NIS4 ($2.65) to NIS5 ($3.35) for pastry and coffee, only slightly more for a light meal.

The **Liber Vegetarian Restaurant,** 10 Ben-Yehuda (tel. 02-222-007), is a modest little place with very good, interesting food, plus one of the most impressive line-ups of desserts I've seen in a long time. The menu is eclectic: fish (cooked, gefilte, or pickled) for NIS8 ($5.35), spaghetti, vegetarian main courses at NIS6 ($4), and toasted cheese all share the same menu, along with the aforementioned desserts. The kitchen is kosher. Wine and beer are served. Get one of the few sidewalk tables if you can.

The **Shemesh Restaurant,** behind the Shemesh grill counter at 21 Ben-Yehuda (tel. 02-222-418), is a marvelous, almost luxurious, place for relaxing meals and interesting people. House specialties are baked lamb and steak à la Shemesh, at NIS25 ($16.65), other choices for only half as much. Every first course is NIS4 ($2.65), as is the meat, bean, or chicken soup. There's a good selection of wines. Fresh fruits make a great dessert. Open noon to midnight, it has soft lights and a restful atmosphere. Closed Friday night and Saturday until evening.

Too much? Then the **Shemesh grill counter,** facing on Ben-Yehuda, has food from the same kitchen for less. As for the grills, they're right before your eyes. If you order chicken livers or shish kebab, the meat will be tossed on the grill, done to your order, and served with french fries and salad. With a bottle of Maccabee beer and the tip, you pay NIS5 ($3.35).

The tiny **Taami Restaurant,** 3 Shammai St. (tel. 02-225-911), near the corner with Ha-Histadrut Street, is always jammed at lunchtime by workers with more appetite than money. The food is great, the price delightful: stuffed cabbage, stuffed vine leaves, or stuffed squash for NIS2.30 ($1.55); more substantial kebabs, shishliks, and "chicken steaks" cost only NIS7.50 ($5). Taami serves seven days a week, at lunch and dinner.

Ben-Yehuda Street Cafés: In summer, most put tables out on the pedestrian mall. But all year round the cafés are the right place for a delicious breakfast of pastries, eggs, cheeses, and coffee or tea. Most serve light lunches too, and although prices are higher than in the no-frills eateries along King George V Avenue, standards of service and atmosphere are higher as well.

Among the most prominent and attractive places is the **Café Atara,** 7 Ben-Yehuda (tel. 02-225-008). Besides coffee for NIS1 (65¢) to NIS2 ($1.35) and beer, you can enjoy sandwiches, Swedish hors d'oeuvres plates, lasagne, and even fried onion rings at the outdoor tables, all for around NIS3 ($2) to NIS6 ($4). Atara is kosher.

The **Café Alno,** halfway up Ben-Yehuda Street on the left-hand side, is typical of the city's cafés. Various set breakfasts fill the menu early in the morning until 11 a.m.; in the afternoon, soup with good dark bread, coffee, and cake take over. Coffee, from plain American to fancy Viennese, costs NIS1 (65¢) to NIS2.25 ($1.50), and pastries about the same. The mood inside is neighborly, newspaperly, and very *gemütlich*.

The **Café Max,** 23 Ben-Yehuda St. at the intersection with King George (tel. 02-233-722), shines even in the shadow of the tall City Tower across the way. Coffee and cake are always offered and always good, but you can also get omelets, blintzes, or a varied Swedish plate of hors d'oeuvres, or any of a multitude of sandwiches, all priced from NIS3 ($2) to NIS6.50 ($4.35). The bonus, again, is the congenial café atmosphere, a step up from the normal lunch counter. Café Max is open from 7 a.m. to midnight, except for the normal Friday-evening to Saturday-evening Sabbath closing.

On and Off King George V Avenue

On the half mile of King George V Avenue, starting at Jaffa Road and going to Agron Street, is a greater concentration of eateries than at any other place in all Jerusalem. Starting at the busy intersection of Jaffa Road and King George, here's the rundown:

For pizza, there are lots of choices. **Pizzeria Rimini,** 15 King George V Ave. (tel. 02-226-505), for instance, is actually an informal sit-down restaurant where you can order any of 17 different pizzas, or other Italian specialties, among them antipasto and fettuccine. It's not cheap though, and a fancy pizza plus a bottle of beer can run you NIS10 ($6.65). From what I've tasted, you're better off sticking to the lower-priced pizzas anyway. Although they're not really authentic, they're good and filling.

A good pizza stop is **Richie's New York Pizza,** 7 King George V Ave. (tel. 02-244-130), across from the Agrippas Street intersection and just a few doors down from Ben-Hillel Street. Besides the pizza for NIS1.50 ($1) NIS1.80 ($1.20) per slice, Richie's has a marvelous bulletin board. Many of the notices are in English, or English and Hebrew, and they tell of rooms and apartments to rent, babysitters wanted or available, and used stuff for sale. Kosher; closed for the Sabbath.

Another King George eatery, with good food, low prices, and large portions, is the **Marvad Haksamim** (Magic Carpet) at no. 12 (tel. 02-231-460). You could fill yourself here on soup and stuffed eggplant for little over NIS6 ($4), or a filling, spicy goulash for only a little more. Get fancier if you like, and have steak, chicken, or liver—they're all offered. I had a big, delicious portion of turkey shishlik, chunks of turkey skewered and charcoal grilled, with rice and vegetable, and a soda, for NIS10 ($6.65). There's a menu in English; the Carpet flies daily for lunch and dinner, except on the Sabbath.

Near the YMCA and King David Hotel

You really should take a stroll over to the YMCA, actually a three-star hotel, and the massive King David Hotel, browse in the antique shops on King David Street (Rehov Ha-Melekh David) near the intersection with Agron Street, and enjoy this part of town. When you do, you can have a bite in the low-priced self-service fountain shop at the **YMCA** (closed Sunday). Milkshakes, ice-cream sodas, hamburgers, and similar red-white-and-blue fare are the specialties, and low prices are the rule. If you choose to eat in the dining room, prices go up, but are still in the moderate range. The "Y" is a good choice for Sabbath dining, also.

Want to sniff around the **King David Hotel** and look as though you belong? Head for the **coffeeshop,** which serves light meals (soups and appetizers, potato latkes, sandwiches, yogurt, omelets, blintzes, etc.). Now, you'll pay more (about NIS15, $10) for your light lunch here than you would on King George V Avenue, but after all, this is the King David. The person sitting next to you might well be a famous diplomat, Knesset member, world business magnate (yes, really!). Part of what you're paying for is the atmosphere and the thrill.

Farther southeast along King David Street, at the corner with Mapai, is the **Garden Restaurant,** a shady refuge from the busy street. Behind the fence and the vines, up a few steps, is a patio dappled with sunlight and shade, an informal neighborhood atmosphere, and simple, standard fare such as wienerschnitzel, roast chicken, soups, and salads. Many people come here to linger over a meal or a cool drink. Expect to pay between NIS12 ($8) and NIS16 ($10.65) for the experience.

Near Zahal Square and New Gate

Just across Ha-Zanhanim Street from New Gate in the Old City walls rises the massive, tawny bulk of the **Notre Dame of Jerusalem Center** (tel. 02-289-

723), crowning the hill and visible from all of East Jerusalem. The center, operated by the Pontifical Institute, shelters a guesthouse, arts-and-crafts shop, social and cultural offices, and a dining room and coffeeshop named the Twin Towers (one look at the building and you'll know why). The nonkosher English-language menu is a mix of Middle Eastern and North American favorites, with a daily special platter at both lunch and dinner priced at only NIS7.50 ($5). It's open and serving every day of the week.

Specialty Restaurants

When you want something special, you're willing to go get it, regardless of location. Here are some of West Jerusalem's special places, none of them very far from Zion Square.

Italian Restaurants: How would you like to dine at a little Italian country villa built of stone, with a nice patio, rustic wood tables, and excellent cuisine? Without much work, you can imagine just that when you dine at **Mamma Mia, 18 Rabbi Akiva** (tel. 02-248-080), a kosher Italian dairy restaurant. The old Jerusalem stone house is set amid trees, and entered by a verdant walk. The Italian owners make their own white and green fettuccine, ravioli, cannelloni, gnocchi, and other favorites, including pizza. Though authentic, this is not a fancy place, so a full meal from minestrone to cannoli need cost only NIS15 ($10) to NIS20 ($13.35). Mamma Mia is a bit difficult to find, so read carefully: go to the Jerusalem Tower Hotel on Hillel Street. On the opposite side of the street, notice Rabbi Akiva (or Aqiba) Street. Follow this; there's a dead-end alley to the right, and then Rabbi Akiva itself turns right. The restaurant is on the right, set back from the street. Coming from this direction, the sign is in Hebrew; the English is on the opposite side.

For Chinese Food: In recent years there has been a flowering of little Chinese restaurants in Jerusalem (of all places), and one of them is not far from Zion Square. Across from the Central Post Office is **Chinese Express,** 28 Jaffa Rd. (tel. 02-228-739), which touts its wares with doggerel: "Need a nosh? Want to fress? Hurry to Chinese Express!" Start with hot-and-sour soup or eggrolls; then go for chicken prepared with garlic or almonds or as chow mein; have beef with green peppers or spicy vegetables. The food, while not super-authentic, is tasty and filling, and served up at once, or to go. Soups and starters are priced at NIS2 ($1.35), most main courses with meat cost NIS8 ($5.35), and there's a daily special lunch of soup, rice, and main course for only NIS9 ($6). Beer and soft drinks are served, and hours are the familiar lunch and dinner ones, except on the Sabbath.

Vegetarian Restaurants: Besides the aforementioned Liber Vegetarian Restaurant on Ben-Yehuda Street, West Jerusalem has two fine vegetarian places where the food is tasty, healthful, and inexpensive.

Julie and Rudy Touitour of San José, California, tipped me off to **Mifgash Bavly,** 54 Ha-Nevi'im St. (tel. 02-222-195), just two short blocks from Zion Square up Ha-Rav Kook Street. Here, a big old house sits back from the busy street, its lower floor serving as a winter dining area, its front yard set with tables in spring, summer and fall. The assortment of foods, from soup through gefilte fish to eggplant moussaka, and especially the healthful and delicious salads, is vast, and most plates cost NIS2 ($1.35) or less! The exception is a fish filet platter for less than NIS5 ($3.35). The Bavly is good for Sabbath dining too, as it's open for lunch and dinner every day except Sunday.

Convenient to the Central Post Office is **Ha-Meshek Vegetarian Restau-**

rant, 14 Shlomzion Ha-Malka St. (tel. 02-226-278), a small kosher dairy place with lots of platters featuring salads, cheeses, and vegetables. For heartier fare, order a soya "hamburger" or "hot dog." Few plates are priced above NIS8 ($5.35), and most are half that. The restaurant itself is cheery and bright, with light wood walls hung with paintings and prints. Hours are 11 a.m. to 10 p.m. Sunday through Thursday, on Friday till 3 p.m.; closed Saturday. I'm indebted to Ian Baker of London, England, for recommending that I sit down and tuck in at Ha-Meshek.

Yemenite Cuisine: Jewish immigrants from Yemen have contributed a great deal to Israeli culture. You may already have noticed their exceptionally ornate costumes and fine antique jewelry. Here's your chance to sample their cooking.

Ruchama, 3 Yaavetz St. (or Ya'abetz; tel. 02-246-565), is on a tiny side street which begins between 47 and 49 Jaffa Rd. A few doors in from Jaffa Road, enter the gate on the left and pass into an airy summer-dining patio and several cozy all-weather dining rooms. Decor is simple, consisting of Yemenite handcraft tools and costumes, which are elaborately worked and colored. Yemenite food is similarly inspired: sometimes made from the cheapest ingredients such as oxtail, trotters, or tripe, the results are rich, savory, spicy, and delicious. The soups, of calves' foot, oxtail, or beef, are hearty and filling at NIS4.50 ($3). Try the specialty, melawach, a flaky pastry filled with chopped meat, chicken, or mushrooms, and served with chopped tomatoes and spices, for NIS10 ($6.65) to NIS12 ($8); a dessert version comes filled with honey. Ruchama is kosher, and is open daily from 10 a.m. till midnight, except on the Sabbath. Thanks to my friend Shel Horowitz of Northampton, Massachusetts, for mentioning his good meals at Ruchama.

For Tea and Pie: Though you can consume these treats at numerous places around Zion Square, one place specializes in them, and draws a young, congenial crowd. It's called **Don't Pass Me By Tea and Pie,** 4 Nahalat Shiva St. (no phone; turn down the alley at 33 Jaffa Rd.). The two small, homey rooms in the stone building are open daily except on the Sabbath from 2 p.m. to midnight, and are usually humming with quiet conversation, candlelit at night. Have coffee or tea, fruit juice (banana, pineapple, or orange), hot or cold cider, or even a cocktail, and a slice of pie, and you will pay about NIS7 ($4.65) to NIS9 ($6). Note that there is no other food—only pies and cakes—so come for afternoon tea or dessert, not for a light lunch.

EATING PLACES IN EAST JERUSALEM:
The Arab section of town is not wall-to-wall with eating places, as West Jerusalem sometimes seems to be. But East Jerusalem's small downtown area has a good variety of eateries ready to satisfy pennywise or extravagant, tame or adventurous appetites. The downtown area is so small, I'll group East Jerusalem's eateries according to type rather than location.

What are you out for? Your first venture into the *1001 Nights* world of authentic Middle Eastern cuisine? Then the thing to do is choose from among the restaurants listed below. Just a snack? See the section on cafés. What about a special occasion, last-night-in-Jerusalem sort of blowout, with a zillion-course dinner, intense Arabic decor, authentic music, dancing girls, the works? Look to the section on nightclub restaurants to satisfy your desire.

This is the area in Israel to get acquainted with authentic Arabic cuisine. Ask for *mazza* before your meal, and you will be served a large variety of small, spicy salads to scoop up with pita, plus assorted hot and cold appetizers. In most Arab restaurants, mazza can often make up a meal in itself and is especially good with cold beer after the movies at night. After your meal, try Turkish coffee with *hehl*, pronounced "hell." It is cardamom that adds the pungent aroma to the thick, sweet coffee and is claimed by Arabs to have a wonderfully calming effect on an overfull stomach. Arab cookery concentrates heavily on lamb, served several ways, and rice, often topped with nuts. The English-speaking waiters in most Arab restaurants will be glad to recommend their restaurant's specialties and are unendingly patient about describing each dish in detail.

Restaurants

For your first Arabic meal in Jerusalem—whether it's your first-ever taste of Arabic food or your hundredth—I heartily recommend the **National Palace Restaurant** (tel. 02-282-139), in the National Palace Hotel at the corner of Az-Zahra and Al-Masudi Streets. As you enter the swinging doors, you'll notice a very unobtrusive, almost plain decor consisting of a few plants and '50s architecture. At first the restaurant doesn't seem to befit the hotel's four-star status, but wait until you taste the food!

The menu lists all sorts of things, but you should know that in Arabic restaurants the clients depend a great deal on the waiter: ask what's good and fresh, what he recommends, how it's prepared. A long discussion with the waiter is the proper Arabic prelude to a well-orchestrated meal. You simply must start with a selection of mazza: brain salad, hummus, olives, pickles, eggplant purée, etc. You can simply ask the waiter to bring an assortment. If he brings too many or includes something you don't want, don't hesitate to let him know and he'll gladly remove it from your table and from your bill. Each plate of mazza costs about NIS2.50 ($1.65) here.

Then proceed to the main course. Perhaps shish kebab, grilled liver, grilled spring chicken, or grilled mutton marinated in yogurt and served over rice. The main course can run NIS8 ($5.35) to NIS12 ($8). For dessert, have burma (toasted shredded wheat, stuffed with pistachios and soaked in honey), or baklava, or a crème caramel (flan). Wine is about NIS9 ($6) the bottle, but to do it in truly Arab style, order a small bottle of arak (an anise-flavored brandy similar to pastis, ouzo, or anisette; Golden Arak is the best). Mix it with water to taste (about half and half), over ice, and sip it slowly during the meal. It's powerful, wonderful stuff!

What will all this cost? For two people, with wine or arak, service, and tip, about NIS36 ($24) to NIS45 ($30). You can do it for less; it's hard to spend much more.

The National Palace Restaurant is open from 7 a.m. to 10 p.m. seven days a week. The Roof Garden is open in good weather. You should know that on the eve of the Moslem Sabbath—Thursday evening—and all day Friday, you may not be able to order alcoholic beverages. The same goes for Muslim feasts and holidays.

The **Philadelphia Restaurant,** 9 Az-Zahra St. (tel. 02-289-770), is comfy, cozy, even a little fancy, and always crowded with happy diners. The restaurant's formula for success is sure-fire: excellent Arabic food at very moderate prices. Menus are printed in Arabic, English, and Hebrew. Start with a rich, savory lentil soup, go on to stuffed peppers or lamb chops, finish up with baklava, and your bill will come to NIS15 ($10) or less, drinks and tip included. To find the restaurant, enter the passageway at 9 Az-Zahra, turn left, and go down the stairs. It's open daily from noon to midnight. By the way, the restaurant takes its name not from Pennsylvania's City of Brotherly Love, but from Amman's name in ancient times.

At the end of the passageway at 9 Az-Zahra St. is the **Dallas Restaurant** (tel. 02-284-439), fancier and a bit more expensive. The restaurant's name, in this case, does indeed come from its American counterpart, and the television series that made it famous.

For seafood, East Jerusalem's **Dolphin Restaurant,** at the corner of Harun er-Rasheed and Az-Zahra Streets (tel. 02-282-788), has a simple decor, but a tempting menu which includes shrimp, St. Peter's fish from the Sea of Galilee, and various Mediterranean fishes. The decor is pleasant, though not fancy, and prices are good, ranging from NIS16 ($10.65) to NIS18 ($12) for main-course platters of fish or shrimp. Shellfish tend to be among the more expensive items, of course. The Dolphin is open every day for lunch and dinner.

Al-Umayyah Restaurant, on Sultan Suleiman Street between the Damascus and Herod's Gates (tel. 02-282-789), is always booming on Friday evenings. Many nonkosher diners from West Jerusalem make the pilgrimage to East Jerusalem on that evening and fill the Umayyah's tables. But this very serviceable restaurant also offers good food and decent prices every other day of the week. The menu—in French, German, English, Arabic, and Hebrew—lists many lamb and chicken dishes, and even pigeon stuffed with rice, all priced between NIS8 ($5.35) and NIS11 ($7.35). The daily special platter, a huge offering of various treats, costs only NIS13 ($8.65), plus drinks. Hours are 8:30 a.m. to 10 p.m. daily.

A Café

La Gondola Tea Room, 8 Az-Zahra St. (tel. 02-283-504), serves tea and light fare on a beautifully carved wood balcony. Ice cream, tea or coffee, sandwiches, etc., are in the NIS1.50 ($1) to NIS5 ($3.35) range. Open daily from 9 a.m. to 8 p.m.

Nightclub Restaurants

Let's be truthful, now. Some restaurants in East Jerusalem are unabashedly touristic, catering to those who entertain a romantic stereotype of things Arabian: tents and dancing girls, savory concoctions served in a lavish, exotic, slightly naughty setting. Why not? The Palestinian businessman of East Jerusalem rides in a Peugeot, a Ford Cortina, or a Mercedes, and not on a camel. Three-piece suits have taken the place of the flowing jellaba here. But if they can throw colonial banquets in Montréal and medieval feasts in London, surely East Jerusalem should not be denied its bit of fun. And it *is* fun, partly because of the Cecil B. deMille setting, but mostly because the food is good, and not the least because, if you order the table d'hôte meal, the total price is known in advance.

On Harun er-Rasheed Street is **Hassan Afendi al-Arabi** (tel. 02-283-599), where there's a uniformed doorman, and patrons are ushered upstairs to an ornate dining room. Besides the traditional lamb and mutton and vegetable dishes, which are delicious, they offer grilled pigeon (an Arab delicacy). Come with a group and you can order (in advance) an Arabic banquet at about NIS35 ($23.50) per head consisting of ten salads (mazza), a mixed grill of shish kebab, kufta, etc., then baklava and Turkish coffee. A less sumptuous banquet is priced at NIS26 ($17.25), which can be served to a group or to single patrons. You can even pay with MasterCard. Try that in any other Bedouin tent.

5. The Sights of Jerusalem

Any understanding of the sights of Jerusalem, apart from their sheer physical beauty, must first be based on an appreciation of the city's history, an evolution that shaped the destiny of the Western world. What follows are the bare essentials of the city's remarkable history.

A QUICK HISTORY: In Genesis 14, it is recorded that Abraham visited Melchizedek, "king of Salem"; this is the first known reference to Jerusalem. Not until 800 years later did the Jews settle in the city. Then, in 1000 B.C., King David captured Jerusalem, at the time a Jebusite city. David brought the Ark to Jerusalem from his former capital, Hebron. On Mount Ophel, a hillock to the south of Temple Mount, David built his city and declared that henceforth Jerusalem would be the capital. Under the reign of his son, Solomon, Jerusalem grew in importance. Solomon built the great Temple (960 B.C.), and constructed a magnificent palace. Jerusalem, and Israel, prospered under Solomon's rule. After his death, the kingdom split in two, Israel to the north and Judea to the south, with Jerusalem becoming Judea's capital. After seeing a succession of kings, prophets, and invaders, Jerusalem fell to the armies of Nebuchadnezzar, who in 586 B.C. destroyed the Temple, sacked the city, and carried off many thousands of Jerusalem's inhabitants into exile in Babylonia. But Babylonia soon fell to the Persians, and Cyrus, in 540 B.C., allowed the Jews to return to their homeland and rebuild the Temple. This was carried out under the prophets Zechariah, Ezra, and Nehemiah.

Jerusalem fell under the domain of Alexander the Great in 331 B.C. The Hellenistic rule passed to the Selucids, and it was against their domination that (under the Hasmonean priests and kings) the Maccabees staged their famous revolt—between 167 and 141 B.C.

The next 80 years of the Jewish Hasmonean era were the penultimate years (until 1967) that the Jews were to rule over Jerusalem.

Pompey claimed Jerusalem for Rome in 63 B.C., and in 37 B.C. Herod (whose father converted to Judaism) was appointed king of Judea. He was a frantic builder, and remnants of his constructions are seen throughout Israel today. Herod rebuilt Jerusalem, and in particular designed a palatial Temple area more magnificent than Solomon's. (Thus far, scholars and archeologists believe that the present Western Wall is a remnant of Herod's Temple, not Solomon's—but excavations down to the wall's foundations are shedding further light.) Herod died in 4 B.C. The city that he built, with its fortress and towers and aqueducts, was the Jerusalem that Christ knew.

Under Pontius Pilate, the Roman procurator, Christ lived, preached, was imprisoned, and crucified. According to certain Christian traditions, the Church of the Holy Sepulchre marks the site of the crucifixion, and the Via Dolorosa is the way he trod, carrying the cross, from prison to Golgotha.

An unsuccessful rebellion against Roman rule brought Vespasian's armies to deal with the Jews. In A.D. 70 he starved out the population of Jerusalem and destroyed the city and its Temple. Bar Kokhba's revolt returned Jerusalem to the Jews for three short years, but in A.D. 132 Emperor Hadrian leveled the city, rebuilt it with the name "Aelia Capitolina," erected statues of Roman gods, and decreed that henceforth Jews were forbidden entry to the city.

Emperor Constantine, a convert to Christianity, turned Jerusalem into a Christian city and opened the gates to Jewish and Christian pilgrims so they could visit the holy places. Constantine built the first Church of the Holy Sepulchre, and Justinian, 200 years later, rebuilt and enlarged it. Caliph Omar, in 639, began the Muslim occupation—and shortly thereafter (687–691), Caliph Abd el-Malik built the Dome of the Rock. After the first Crusader invasion in 1099, Jerusalem changed hands several times—between Crusader and Muslim (most notably Saladin). Five centuries later the Ottoman Turks, also Muslims, conquered Jerusalem. From 1517, the Turkish rule lasted exactly 400 years—until General Allenby marched through Jerusalem's Jaffa Gate at the head of a British regiment in 1917.

The British Mandate—a mixed blessing for both Arabs and Jews—lasted until May 15, 1948. The day the British left, Jerusalem, and all of Israel, again became a battlefield. Once again this city was besieged, almost entirely surrounded by Jordanian forces, and pinched off from the rest of Israel. Cut off from supplies of food and water, the Israeli section held out—although the "Jewish Quarter" within the Old City walls was abandoned and destroyed. At the second truce, the Israelis held the western half of Jerusalem and the Jordanians the eastern half. A no-man's-land was marked out along a line that divided Jerusalem.

On June 5, 1967, within minutes of the outbreak of the Egyptian-Israeli war, Jordanian shells began pounding West Jerusalem. The next day the Israelis returned the fire, went on the attack, and in 36 hours the entire city, East and West, was in Israeli hands.

GENERAL INFORMATION: Don't try to see Jerusalem's sights in a day, or two days for that matter. In fact, anyone trying to "do" Jerusalem in less than three days is guilty of criminal haste.

For the purposes of organization, since there is so much to see, the sightseeing section here is divided into four parts: inside the Old City walls; downtown East Jerusalem; Mount Scopus, Mount of Olives, Valley of Kidron; and West Jerusalem, the "New City."

But before you set out to any of these areas, remember that tourists can get a **"combined ticket"** to six Jerusalem sights which represents a 50% reduction on admission prices to such places as the Rockefeller Museum, Solomon's Quarries, the Citadel (David's Tower), and so forth. The discount book must be used during two weeks. Ask about it at I.G.T.O. or the **Jerusalem Tourist Information Office,** the latter at 34 Jaffa Rd. (tel. 02-228-844). The **I.G.T.O. office** in the Jaffa Gate and the Municipality Information Office are excellent sources of local information (tel. 02-282-295). Open Sunday through Thursday from 8 a.m. to 6 p.m., on Friday from 8 a.m. to 3 p.m., and on Saturday from 10 a.m. to 2 p.m. The Municipality Office is open the same hours, except for Friday when it closes at 1:30 p.m. until Sunday morning.

The **Christian Information Center** (P.O. Box 14308; tel. 02-287-647), inside Jaffa Gate on Omar Ibn El-Khattab Square near the Anglican Hospice and opposite the entrance to the Tower of David, has a list of all the daily and special services celebrated by the dozen or so Christian sects in the city. Visit them to find out which church to attend when, and for other useful information and guidance on Christian sites and ceremonies. The center is open Monday through Friday from 8:30 a.m. to 12:30 p.m. and 3 to 6 p.m. (till 5:30 p.m. in winter), on Saturday for the morning hours only; closed Sunday and holidays.

SPECIAL TOURS AND WALKS: Before you set out to explore this most fascinating of cities, there are several touring possibilities you should know about: a special tour bus, guided walking tours, and a guide-yourself walk along the top of the massive Old City walls.

Bus No. 99

First of all, the no. 99 bus, the **Jerusalem Circular Line.** Egged (tel. 02-531-286) operates a bus that leaves the Tanus (or Tannous) building, its Jaffa Gate terminus, every hour on the hour from 9 a.m. to 5 p.m. Sunday through Thursday, 9 a.m. to 2 p.m. on Friday (none on Saturday). This bus stops at 34 of the most visited sites throughout the city, from the Mount of Olives to Yad Vashem. You can buy a single tour ticket for NIS1.50 ($1)—a great way to get a quick rundown of what the city has to offer, and where it is—a full-day ticket, or a two-day ticket. With these, you can get off and back on the bus as many times as you like during the validity of your ticket. Buy tickets, and pick up a map of the route, at the Egged Tours office in Zion Square, 44a Jaffa Rd. (tel. 02-224-198), at the Central Bus Station (tel. 02-534-596), or right at the Jaffa Gate terminal building (tel. 02-247-783).

Ramparts Walk

You can walk virtually all the way around the Old City on the walls built by the Great Ottoman Turkish sultan in the 1500s. Enter at Damascus Gate, the Lions' Gate, Zion Gate, or Jaffa Gate, buy your ticket—NIS1.50 ($1) for adults; 75 agorot (50¢) for children—and you can exit and reenter the Ramparts Walk for 48 hours (72 hours if you buy on Friday). The entire circuit of the walls is about 2 ½ miles, or less than an hour's walk. The best place to enter is Damascus Gate. The reason? They've excavated the Roman-era gate which stands to the left and below the gate built by Suleiman the Magnificent. Within this Roman gate, which would have been extant in Jesus' time, there's a small museum worth a quick visit. Count your change after you buy your ticket here.

By the way, it's not a good idea for single women to walk alone on the ramparts, whether during the day or at night.

Guided Tours

On any guided tour that includes holy places, of whatever religion, you must dress modestly. This means no shorts (men or women), no sleeveless shirts or blouses, and women should have a head covering. In general, avoid very informal attire (T-shirts, etc.).

The **Sheraton Jerusalem Plaza Hotel,** 47 King George V Ave., at Agron Street (tel. 02-228-133), sponsors free tours of various areas. Drop by the hotel to pick up a schedule, or check "Events in the Jerusalem Region," issued by the Israel Government Tourist Office. Meet in the lobby of the hotel at 8:50 a.m. for any tour.

The **Society for the Protection of Nature in Israel,** 4 Hashfela St. (tel. 02-222-357), also sponsors various tours. Check with them for details.

Various commercial concerns will take you on guided tours of the city which emphasize its history and archeology. For instance, **Archeological Seminars Ltd.,** 34 Habad St. in the Jewish Quarter (no phone), will guide you through the Jewish Quarter, Temple Mount, the Temple Mount Excavations, the City of David (Ophel), or the Christian and Muslim Quarters of the Old City for NIS6.75 ($4.50) per tour or three tours for NIS16.50 ($11). Tours run Sunday through Friday. For information, ask at the Cardo Information Center in the Jewish Quarter of the Old City.

Walking Tours Ltd. will show you the historical and archeological highlights of the Old City or the Mount of Olives for NIS10.50 ($7) per tour (less for students). Tours depart from the Tower of David. For information, inquire at the Tourism Office just inside Jaffa Gate, to the left.

READER'S WALKING TOUR SELECTION: "Walking tours of the Jewish Quarter, the Old City, Shiloah water tunnel, and surrounding archeological sites are sponsored by the **Young Israel** movement. The office is located in the post office on Tiferet Israel Street, just off the main plaza in the Jewish Quarter of the Old City (tel. 02-287-065 or 285-737)" (Ellen Kaufman, Forest Hills, N.Y.).

SIGHTS OF THE OLD CITY: An uneven rectangle of 40-foot-high wall encloses the **Ir Ha-Kodesh,** the holy city, the Old City. The wall is at least 400 years old (some portions, in fact, date back more than 2,000 years), built by Suleiman

the Magnificent and repaired several times since. In their present form the grandiose towers, battlements, and sentry walks are quite handsome, with the new parks and gardens beneath them in full bloom. At night the walls are impressively illuminated by golden lights.

Main gates into the wall are the **Jaffa Gate,** entered from Mamilla-Agron Street or Jaffa Road, and the **Damascus Gate,** entered from Ha-Nevi'im or Nablus Road. Israelis call Damascus Gate **Sha'ar Shchem.** In all, there are eight gates in the Old City fortress-wall.

The Old City itself is divided into five sections—the **Christian Quarter,** the **Armenian Quarter,** the **Muslim Quarter,** the **Jewish Quarter,** and **Temple Mount** (Mount Moriah), the latter housing the Western (Wailing) Wall, the Dome of the Rock, and El Aksa Mosque.

The Local Populace

It is really impossible to generalize about the people of Old Jerusalem. They run the gamut from Christian to traditionalist Muslim to the bearded rabbi to a mob of kibbutz youngsters sharing the tourist sights with you. The two dominating themes of the area, however, are religion and tourism. Both these factors are evidenced everywhere.

You move from the sanctity of a church to the tumult of the bazaar. You're alone in the huge plaza of the Western Wall one moment and then you're suddenly accosted by a swirling, noisy band of Arab youngsters. You stare at a shop window and, before 60 seconds pass, you're not only drinking hot coffee with the owner, but perilously close to purchasing brassware that you'd never dreamed of acquiring. It's reverence and fun all mixed together, and neither of these components will ever be forgotten. And despite the fact that the city is united and part and parcel of Israel proper, the dominating motif of this part of the capital is Arab. The food is Arabic. The language is Arabic. The customs are Eastern. Bartering for goods is a way of life. Unlike the rest of Israel, children will ask for handouts. You'll also be approached by a plethora of would-be guides, offering cut-rate expertise. As a general rule of thumb, if you're going to be guided—and it's not a bad idea—make certain that your mentor is officially licensed by the Ministry of Tourism.

A Note About Islam

You will discover, inside the Old City, that Muslims venerate many of the shrines sacred as well to Jews or Christians. To the Muslim, the patriarchs were holy men and Jesus was a prophet, though not the final one. Islam, in fact, is closer to Judaism than to Christianity, closer to the nomadic-type culture of the patriarchs than to the Trinity of Christianity. The Muslim is dedicatedly monotheistic: there is but one God, Allah, and the only way is to submit to his will. A Muslim's principal beliefs center on monotheism, praying five times a day, fasting in daylight hours during the month of Ramadan, making a pilgrimage to Mecca, and giving alms. Thursday sunset to sunset on Friday is the Muslim Sabbath. Like Jews, Muslims are enjoined from eating pork. Gambling and drinking alcohol are also prohibited to Muslims, and they may not make paintings or sculptures of human beings or animals. The men may marry up to four wives—but only the very rich can afford this.

Through Jaffa Gate

The citadel tower at the entrance is called the **Tower of David.** It marks the place where stood three towers built by Herod near his palace. Today it is the

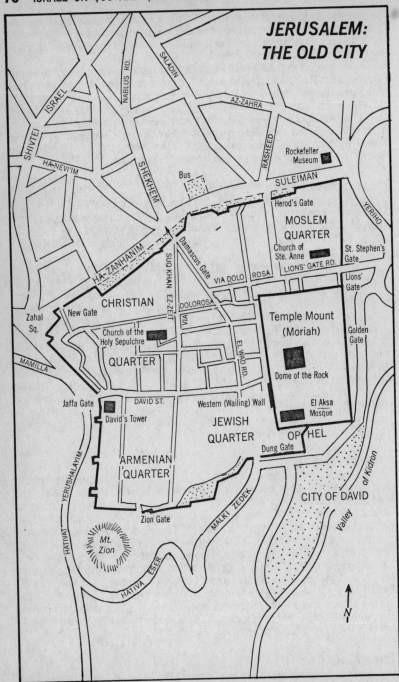

JERUSALEM:
THE OLD CITY

Jerusalem City Museum (tel. 02-285-770), showing ancient maps of Jerusalem. It also houses an exhibit of 66 dolls in ethnological dress of the diverse population of this region. It's open Sunday to Thursday and on Saturday from 8:30 a.m. to 4 p.m., on Friday and holiday eves until 2 p.m., for NIS2.50 ($1.65) per person. The Tower of David is also the setting for a **Sound and Light show** (held nightly from sometime in March to mid-November, except on Friday and holiday eves), the theme of which is the Old City's biblical history. Performances in English are at 8:45 p.m. Dress warmly, as evenings are chilly here even in summer.

Jaffa Gate is said to have been widened to its present size for the visit of Kaiser Wilhelm and his entourage in 1898. Here Allenby entered Jerusalem in 1917. The Balfour Declaration Ceremony, soon thereafter, was held here as well.

As you come inside the courtyard, you'll see a road heading off to the right, past the moat. This route leads into the **Armenian Quarter,** a quiet residential area of small churches that parallels the wall; the road leads to the Western Wall and the Dome of the Rock.

In the Armenian Quarter are many green courtyards and ancient buildings, including the splendid **St. James Cathedral,** the **Church of the Holy Archangels** (said to be from the Early Medieval period), the **Gulbenkian Public Library,** the **Library of Manuscripts,** and the **Helen and Edward Mardigian Museum of Armenian Art and History** (tel. 02-282-331); the last is open daily except Tuesday from 10 a.m. to 5 p.m. for NIS1 (67¢)

If you head straight into the bazaar (the *suq*) from the Jaffa Gate, you'll enter **David Street,** bustling with shops vending bushels of mother-of-pearl and olive-wood rosary beads, other religious crafts and souvenirs, maps, and household items. If your first destination is the Church of the Holy Sepulchre, then take the first left off David Street to **Christian Quarter Road.** This latter takes you right to Christianity's most hallowed shrine.

But if the Western Wall and Temple Mount is your first goal, then continue straight along David Street. It changes its name halfway to **Chain Street** (Silsileh, Shalshelet). Follow the signs to "The Wall." On your first trip you may think you forgot to take a turn somewhere and that you're lost in a maze of narrow bazaar streets and noisy, crowded shops. The air grows heavy with spices and fragrances, the throughway fills with milling people and donkeys, and the archways blot out the sky from view. As the smell of spices becomes stronger, the little street shrinks further, and soon it is a teeming mob scene of shoulder-to-shoulder traffic.

Finally, however, you arrive at the **Gate of the Chain,** an entrance to the Noble Enclosure (Haram es-Sharif), otherwise known as **Temple Mount.** The Western Wall, at this point, is off to your right.

The Jewish Quarter

Let's take a detour through the Jewish Quarter on our way to the Wall and Temple Mount. By doing so, you'll save an uphill walk, for the Wall lies well below most of the quarter.

King David (1000 B.C.) built his city on the Ophel, south of Temple Mount. Over the centuries the city spread northward, up the slope. In the time of King Hezekiah, around 700 B.C., the area now known as the Jewish Quarter was a wealthy suburb crowded with rich houses and defended by a mighty Broad Wall. But the wall and its many towers were not strong enough to keep out Nebuchadnezzar of Babylon, who conquered Jerusalem and laid waste the Jewish Quarter in 586 B.C.

The area was again leveled in A.D. 70 by Roman armies intent on ending

Jewish inhabitation of the city forever. The burnt remains of a house destroyed in that conflagration have been uncovered.

Once the Jewish inhabitants were driven out, the Romans, and later their Byzantine successors, rebuilt the city. You can visit several impressive vestiges of Byzantine times, including the vast, ruined church called the Nea, and the southern end of the city's major north-south thoroughfare, the Cardo Maximus.

When Jerusalem fell to the Crusaders (1099), they promptly pillaged it, but later rebuilt many parts in the architecture of the day.

The Jewish Quarter's most recent destruction came during the 1948 war, when it was virtually flattened by Jordanian artillery. But since 1967 the quarter has been rebuilt and revitalized, and now boasts a high concentration of synagogues and yeshivas, as well as many comfortable homes—continuing a tradition of Jewish residence that began almost 3,000 years ago.

Because of its periodic destruction, most historical remains in the Jewish Quarter are fragmentary. Don't expect the glories of Solomon's city, or even Justinian's, to leap at your consciousness. Rather, look at these fragmentary remains as stone souvenirs of a momentous, not to mention tumultuous, past.

The sights of the Jewish Quarter are well marked, and many little signs guide you here and there. Explanatory plaques with diagrams are mounted at significant points. The whole area is like one immense outdoor museum, and you should have no trouble finding your way around. Here are the highlights:

The Cardo Maximus: This recently excavated 6th-century street was Roman and Byzantine Jerusalem's main drag, bordered by stately columns and lined with posh shops. What you see now, some eight feet beneath the level of the bordering Street of the Jews (Rehov Ha-Yehudim), dates from the mid-500s. The original street is said to have been laid out by Hadrian (117–138) when he rebuilt the city as Aelia Capitolina.

The southern portion of the Cardo is open to the sky; the rest is beneath some modern buildings. As you walk northward along the reconstructed Cardo, past the shops, you can see some Crusader-era arches above, and, to either side, excavations that reveal fragments of the city's defensive walls dating from the First Temple period, about 700 B.C.

Old Yishuv Court Museum: Of the houses here that have been rebuilt, one of them, at 6 Old Yishuv Court, is now a museum—appropriately named the Old Yishuv Court Museum (tel. 02-284-636). It belongs to the Weingarten family, whose great-great-grandfather lived in it in the 18th century. Within, the displays reflect Ashkenazi and Sephardic lifestyles from the middle of the 19th century to the end of Turkish rule in 1917. The living quarters, kitchens, and several very important synagogues have been restored. The museum is open Sunday through Thursday from 9 a.m. to 4 p.m. for a NIS3 ($2) admission fee.

The Burnt House: When Jerusalem was destroyed in A.D. 70 on orders of Vespasian, this house, belonging to a temple priest, was burnt along with the rest, though its occupants held out for a month after the Lower City fell. It's now a museum, with a fine slide show, open Sunday through Thursday from 9 a.m. to 5 p.m., on Friday to noon, for an admission of NIS2 ($1.35).

The Nea: Once the city's second-grandest church, the Nea (or "New" in Greek) was later lost in the rubble of history. The building's foundations were rediscovered during recent excavations. You can view the very unimpressive remnants of this church, built by Justinian in 543, from 9 a.m. to 5 p.m., for free.

Other Places: Many other Jewish Quarter buildings are today recalled by only a single arch, doorway, or minaret. You can inspect a few arches from the Crusader Church of St. Mary of the Teutonic Knights (1128). Then there's the minaret from the little Mosque of Omar, and behind it a single broad, graceful arch, rebuilt from the ruins of Ha-Hurva, the Ashkenazi synagogue of Rabbi

Yudah He-Hasid. The rabbi came to Jerusalem with his disciples in 1700; the first Hurva was built in 1740, a later one in 1864.

Between the minaret and the Hurva arch is the **Ramban Synagogue,** of Rabbi Moshe ben Nahman.

You'll also want to take a look at the complex of four small **Sephardic synagogues** named for Rabbi Yohanan Ben-Zakkai, whose school occupied this site during the Second Temple period. The four in the complex are the one named for the rabbi himself, another for Eliyahu Ha-Nevi, the Central Synagogue, and the Istanbuli Synagogue. During Muslim rule, no church or synagogue was allowed to exceed the height of the nearest mosque, so to gain headroom, the foundations of these synagogues were laid well below ground level.

The **Tiferet Israel** (or Yisrael) **Synagogue** (Ashkenazi) was founded by Nisan Bek and inaugurated in 1865. Dedicated to the Hasidic Rabbi Israel Friedmann of Ruzhin (the synagogue's name means "Glory of Israel"), it was destroyed in the War of Independence and recently restored.

Now that you've got a feeling for Jewish life in Jerusalem, it's time to visit Judaism's greatest shrine, just down the hill from the Jewish Quarter.

The Western Wall

This is the **Ha-Kotel Ha-Ma'aravi.** It was formerly called "Wailing" because the Jews have traditionally come here to bewail the loss of their Temple. It is the holiest of Jewish sites, a remnant of the wall that once supported the Temple Mount. During the night and early in the morning, the large blocks of the wall are covered with dew, which tradition claims are the tears shed by the wall that weeps with its mourners. For over 2,000 years, at this place and wherever they have lived in the diaspora, Jews have bemoaned the loss of the Temple: "For the temple that is desolate, we sit in solitude and mourn." They prayed for forgiveness for their transgressions, and they prayed that God might one day give Jerusalem back to the chosen people. On June 14, 1967—Shavuoth—the way to the Wall was opened for the first time. A quarter-million Israelis walked from Mount Zion through the Dung Gate to renew their contact with this symbol of Israel and its long past.

For centuries the Wall had stood 60 feet high and 91 feet long, towering over a narrow alley 12 feet wide which could accommodate a few hundred worshippers standing. To make room for the stream of pilgrims after the Old City was restored to Jewish hands in the Six-Day War, the Israelis bulldozed the Moors Quarter facing the Wall to create a plaza that could accommodate tens of thousands. They also made the Wall about 6½ feet higher by digging down and exposing two more tiers of ashlars from the Second Temple which had been underground for centuries. Apart from the traditional area that is still reserved for prayer and worship, archeologists have exposed an area down at the southern end and uncovered remains from various periods.

At the prayer section of the Western Wall, grass grows out of the upper cracks. The lower cracks of the chalky, streaked, yellow-white blocks have been stuffed with bits of paper containing prayers. Black-robed Orthodox Jews are always seen standing at the wall, praying and chanting and swaying. If you care to go down to the Wall but are hatless, you can acquire a head covering, at no cost, at the little stand at the top of the path. Women may borrow shawls and short skirt coverings.

The separate section at the extreme right of the Western Wall is reserved for women, who are not allowed at the other section, in keeping with Orthodox Jewish tradition. Services are held here daily; no photography or smoking is permitted on the Sabbath.

The exposed portion of the Western Wall dates from the Second Temple, perhaps just before the time of Jesus. The wall built at that time to retain the western part of Temple Mount was actually much wider and deeper than the portion you can see readily today. For an idea of how big the original construction was, enter the doorway located between the men's rest rooms and the public telephones, on the plaza's northern side. Entry is allowed here, for free, to men and women on Sunday, Tuesday, and Wednesday from 8:30 a.m. to 3 p.m., on Monday and Thursday from 12:30 to 3 p.m., and on Friday from 8:30 a.m. to noon; closed Saturday.

You enter from the bright, hot plaza to a cool, dark labyrinth of vaults and chambers, pitfalls (now rendered safe by lamps, grates, and barriers) and passages. After a while you make your way to a viewing area behind a prayer room filled with the devout at their devotions. The prayer room is off-limits to women, except in the viewing area.

From the platform of the viewing area, the Wall is clearly visible. Shafts have been sunk along the surface of the Wall to show its true depth. The arches in this man-made cavern date from various periods, from the Herodian (100 B.C. to A.D. 100) to the Crusader (1000 to 1200) periods.

Temple Mount—Dome of the Rock

Take the staircase to the right of the Western Wall to Temple Mount, **Mount Moriah.** This is the **Haram esh-Sharif,** the Noble Enclosure of the Muslims. When David first came to Jerusalem, he purchased the flat rock on Moriah from Orhan the Jebusite, who had used it as a threshing floor. II Chronicles 3 relates that "Solomon began to build the house of the Lord at Jerusalem on Mount Moriah." The Second Temple (Solomon's was destroyed by Nebuchadnezzar in 586 B.C.) was first built between 525 and 520 B.C., and later enlarged and beautified by Herod shortly before the time of Christ. The Temple Mount you see here is a stone-paved platform, about 30 acres in area. There is a small admission to the two mosques at the Mount. Visiting hours are 8:30 to 11 a.m., 12:15 to 3 p.m., and 4 to 5 p.m. Neither mosque may be visited on Friday or Muslim holidays.

The **El Aksa Mosque** is the first shrine you come to. Leave your shoes outside, and enter a broad open hall hung with chandeliers. (You won't miss your shoes—the floors are covered with Oriental rugs.) The mosque's lofty ceilings are embellished in Byzantine design. Stonework keeps the mosque's interior cool and comfortable in summertime. Up front, past rows of great marble pillars, is a wood-partitioned platform that had been reserved for King Hussein when he came here to pray. A separate women's prayer chamber, in blue decor, is at the right.

Leave El Aksa, reclaim your shoes, and turn right. Walk across the open expanse of stone-covered pavement. If a guide has not yet proffered his services, he's sure to do so at this point. Many guides with the official badges of the Ministry of Tourism work on Temple Mount. Most of them know their stuff, and can get you into places you wouldn't get in by yourself. But settle on a price in advance, and make it clear what you want to see for that price.

Over at the far end of the pavement is a corner in the city walls. Some say this is the **"pinnacle of the Temple"** where Satan took Jesus to tempt him (Matthew 4:5). You can get a marvelous view of the Mount of Olives and the Kidron Valley from here.

A stairway leading down into the walls from this point takes you into **Solomon's Stables** (here's where a guide is essential—to unlock the door). Beneath the pavement is a vast chamber said to be the stable for Solomon's thousands of horses. Actually, the "Solomon" referred to is probably the Ottoman Sultan Suleiman (or, Solomon) the Magnificent, who rebuilt the walls. Today the stables hold thousands of pigeons, which have left their mark indelibly on the walls and floors. Take the trouble to see Solomon's Stables only if you're enthralled by vast underground pigeonholes.

Heading straight across the broad open temple deck, you'll pass **El-Kas,** the fountain where Muslims perform their ritual ablutions before entering their holy places. It is equipped with a circular row of pink marble seats, each with a faucet.

The golden-domed **Dome of the Rock ("Mosque of Omar")** is reached by heading straight across the platform under the Roman archway. The mosque's interior is every bit as fantastically ornate as the outside, a geometric display of blue, green, yellow, and white tiles. Anyone intrigued by Arabic art and architecture will go into ecstasies here. Inside, plush red and green carpets line the floor. There is not a piece of wall or ceiling space without some design on it. The marble is not white as it is at the Aksa; here it is striped gray and streaked purple. Stained-glass windows cap the ceiling at the top of the dome.

Everything in this beautiful Muslim sanctuary (built in A.D. 691) centers on the rock that occupies the middle of the shrine. Traditionally, this is the spot where Abraham, in 1800 B.C., prepared the sacrifice of his son, Isaac, at the Lord's command. On this rock, the Jewish religion was founded. Genesis 22 relates how Abraham followed God's instructions to go to Moriah and sacrifice Isaac, his only son. Isaac, puzzled, said to his father: "Behold the fire and the wood: but where is the lamb for a burnt offering?" Abraham built the altar and bound his son, but an angel intervened and told him to lower his knife. God told Abraham that because he did not withhold his only son, he would be blessed: "Thy seed will multiply as the stars of Heaven and the sand which is upon the seashore . . . because thou hast obeyed my voice." Later, around this rock, the Temple of Solomon was built.

To Muslims, the rock is equally holy ("the third most important shrine in Islam, after Mecca and Medina"), not only because of Abraham's near-sacrifice, but because from this rock Mohammed ascended to heaven. (Mohammed said that one prayer at this rock is worth a thousand anywhere else.) Footprints of Mohammed are pointed out on the rock—which is about 30 feet by 30 feet, rising six feet above the floor.

Next to the rock, a few strands of Mohammed's hair are kept in a lattice-work wooden cabinet. A stairway leads under the rock to a cave-like chamber where glass partitions have been built so that pilgrims will stop eroding the sacred rock: for centuries it has been chipped away by the faithful who wanted to bring home a memento.

From the flat courtyard surrounding the two mosques you have a wonderful view. There's usually a gusty wind blowing across the flat expanse. To the south, the Valley of Jehosophat (Valley of Kidron) and the hilltop, tree-bordered U.N. Government House (Mount of Contempt). To the east, the lower slopes of the Mount of Olives, the Russian Magdalene Church, the Tomb of the Virgin, and on top of the Mount of Olives, the Intercontinental Hotel (also called "Seven Arches") and the high-steepled Russian Monastery.

Head north down the steps, past the Antonia, the remnants of Herod's fortress-castle, and through Bab en-Nazir to reach the Via Dolorosa. From here it is just a short walk, crossing El-Wad Road, to the Holy Sepulchre.

Ophel Archeological Park

South of the Western Wall, near the Dung Gate, is the entrance to the Ophel Archeological Park, just the place for a quick trip back to the time of the Book of Kings and the prophecies of Isaiah and Micah. As you stroll among the ruins of the Jerusalem of almost 3,000 years ago, use your imagination to reconstruct the great prophet advising King Hezekiah to form an alliance with the Assyrians, rather than with the Egyptians, for the defense of Israel. Perhaps Isaiah lived in a house built on foundations recently unburied and restored. The park is open for wandering Sunday through Thursday from 9 a.m. to 5 p.m., on Friday to 3 p.m.; closed Saturday. Admission costs NIS1.50 ($1), half price for children.

Dung Gate

The gate in the city wall nearby is Dung Gate. Many stories surround the origin of this name. One story is that the name resulted from the debris from each consecutive destruction of Jerusalem that was pushed out into the valley below. Another is that the area above the wall extending to the gate region was, in fact, the Jerusalem garbage dump. Rubbish was heaped on the wall and in the gate area because, according to one story, the rulers of Jerusalem were cruel; yet another version has it that the rubbish dump kept the wall hidden so that, for the time being, no further harm would come to it. Take your pick.

Beyond Dung Gate is the Valley of Kidron and Mount Ophel, where David built his city.

Via Dolorosa

This is the **Way of the Cross,** the route followed by Christ from the Praetorium, the Roman Judgment Hall, to Calvary, scene of the crucifixion. Over the centuries, millions of pilgrims have come here to walk the way that Christ took to his death. Each Friday at 3 p.m. priests lead a ceremony for pilgrims along Via Dolorosa (starting in the Monastery of the Flagellation at the tower of Antonia), and prayers are said at each of the 14 Stations of the Cross.

You can enter the **Sanctuaries of the Flagellation and the Condemnation,** where Jesus was whipped and judged, daily from 8 a.m. to noon; afternoon hours are 2 to 6 p.m. from April through September, 1 to 5 p.m. from October through March. In the sanctuaries are some of the original paving stones of the Lithostrotos, the pavement from Jesus' time.

The Sanctuary of the Condemnation marks the first Station of the Cross. As you leave the sanctuary to follow the Via Dolorosa, keep in mind that many of the Stations are not well marked. If you miss one, ask and someone will point it out to you. It may only be an unobtrusive sign, or a number engraved in the stone lintel over a door. Some Stations are behind closed doors; knock and a monk or nun will probably be there to open up for you. There's a rest room opposite Station 3.

Station 1: Jesus is condemned to death. *Station 2:* Jesus receives the cross (at the foot of the Antonia). *Station 3:* Jesus falls for the first time (Polish biblical-archeological museum). *Station 4:* Jesus meets his mother. *Station 5:* Simon the Cyrene helps Jesus carry the cross. *Station 6:* Veronica wipes Jesus' face. *Station 7:* Jesus falls the second time (at bazaar crossroads). *Station 8:* Jesus consoles the women of Jerusalem. *Station 9:* Jesus falls the third time (Coptic Monastery).

The five remaining Stations of the Cross are inside the Church of the Holy Sepulchre. *Station 10:* Jesus is stripped of his garments. *Station 11:* Jesus is nailed to the cross. *Station 12:* Jesus; dies on the cross. *Station 13:* Jesus is taken down from the cross and given over to Mary. *Station 14:* Jesus is laid in the chamber of the Sepulchre and from here is resurrected.

Church of the Holy Sepulchre at Golgotha

Two Oxford University astrophysicists have determined that Jesus was crucified on Friday, April 3, in the year A.D. 33. They reached this conclusion after examining biblical and Babylonian records, and employing the most up-to-date astronomical data and methods. So that's when it happened, and this is where it happened.

A feeling of clutter and compartmentalization reigns within, for the church itself is cared for by five different sects—Roman Catholic, Armenian Orthodox, Greek Orthodox, Abyssinian Coptic, and Syrian Orthodox. Each denomination has its own traditions, and its own ownership of space—right down to lines drawn down the middle of floors and pillars. The decor, partitioned and changed every few feet, is a mixture of Byzantine and Frankish styles. To say there is no overall church plan is an understatement.

Monks and nuns show you the various Stations inside the church—the marble slab as you enter, the Stone of Unction where Jesus was anointed, the site of Calvary on the second floor, the marble tomb in the sepulchre. Candles light the way to reveal a piece of the true cross (in Armenian territory).

The church evolved thusly: After Constantine had converted to Christianity, his mother, Queen Helena, came on pilgrimage to the Holy Land. She searched out the area of the crucifixion and found part of the wood thought to be from the true cross. Over this spot Constantine built the first church, and two centuries later Justinian enlarged it. Fire, earthquake, and the Persians destroyed the church, but the Crusaders rebuilt it in the 12th century.

If you're in Jerusalem during Easter week, you can attend many of the fascinating services, based on ancient Eastern church traditions, that are held at the Church of the Holy Sepulchre—most notably the Service of the Holy Fire, and the dramatic pageant called the Washing of the Feet.

St. Anne's Church

Just inside St. Stephen's Gate, on the right, is the Church of St. Anne, a particularly beautiful 12th-century Crusader church erected in honor of Mary's birthplace. It is built next to the **Pool of Bethesda,** the site where Jesus is believed to have healed the cripple. The seminary gardens here are attractive and conducive to meditation. As the church is just a few blocks east of the Sanctuaries of the Flagellation and the Condemnation, at the beginning of the Via Dolorosa, you might want to visit the Church of St. Anne before following the Stations of the Cross. St. Anne's is open from 8 a.m. to noon and 2 to 5 p.m. (till 6 p.m. in summer), for free; closed Sunday.

Just a few steps into the city from St. Anne's, a small streetside rest spot has been built where some foundation stones of the Second Temple were uncovered. The trees planted here are sycamores, to bring to mind the New Testament passage about Jesus' entry into Jerusalem prior to that fateful Passover holiday: "There was a man named Zaccheus . . . and he sought to see Jesus . . . and could not . . . because he was little of stature. And he ran before, and climbed up into a sycamore tree to see him: for he was to pass that way" (Luke 19:2–4).

Through Damascus Gate

Everyone says this is the handsomest and showiest of the gates. Maybe so, but it won't by any means dazzle you. The walls here are just a bit more ornate than those at the other gates. Inside, all is as Middle Eastern as can be. Cafés line a wide entrance street; Arabs sit inside and out smoking water pipes and watching you as you watch them. The game they're playing is *shaish-baish*, a sort of backgammon; others play dominos. Music emanates from these coffee-houses, and occasionally a donkey joins in, protesting at the crowds that block his way. Whether you take **El-Wad Road** to the left, or **Suq Khan ez-Zeit** to the right, the way becomes very narrow and all is mobbed, surging confusion. You'll see stalls of spices, silversmiths, craft shops, pastries, blanket shops, mosaic-tile barber chairs, shoe stores, fruit and vegetable stands.

Turn down the **Street of the Spices.** You wouldn't believe there were so many spices and nuts. Decked out in open sacks, you'll see (and smell) curry, cocoa, sesame, pepper, and all kinds of beans. For a bazaar street you won't soon forget, turn down **Suq El-Lahhamin** (Butcher Street); it's to the left of the Holy Sepulchre, at the junction with Dabbaga Road. The narrow bazaar manages to get even more narrow, the light grows more scarce, and the slabs of fresh meat hanging out in front give you pause. There are no tourist shops in here, just repair shops and heaven knows what else. The smells become thicker and sweeter, punctuated by an occasional pungent odor. The chief attraction about this particular suq is its anything-can-happen air.

You can't really get lost here. If you just continue on, you're bound to get where you want to go after another five minutes. The area, incidentally, is well patrolled by policemen, some of whom are actually ex-Jordanian policemen.

Notice that the shops nearer the gates are uncovered to the sky. Notice also the meticulous attention to arrangement in certain shops—thousands of pieces of fruit piled in perfectly symmetrical stacks, kitchen gadgets and household appliances in conspicuously well-arranged patterns of yellow baskets, purple hangers, and green sponges.

Mount Zion

This is an important location, the site of an impressive cluster of buildings, and can be easily spotted from almost any point in Jerusalem. The building with a tower is the Dormition Abbey, and on the same site is King David's Tomb and the Room of the Last Supper (Coenaculum) above it.

Entrance to the grounds is a short walk after passing through Zion Gate. Proceed down a narrow alley bounded by high stone walls, and turn left to reach **King David's Tomb.** It's open daily, including the Sabbath, from 8 a.m. to 6 p.m. (till 2 p.m. on Friday). Cover your head when you enter the room.

Whether or not this is actually the tomb of the great king who lived 3,000 years ago is unproven, but the notion has been passed down from generation to generation for centuries.

Near King David's Tomb is a doorway and flight of stairs leading to the **Coenaculum, or Upper Room,** legendary sight of the Last Supper, at which Jesus sat with his disciples to celebrate the Passover Seder and "took bread, and blessed, and brake it, and gave to them, and said, Take, eat: this is my body." The ceremony inspired the Mass, or service of communion, celebrated countless times throughout the world since then, commemorating that fateful seder. Again, the room's authenticity is debatable. Athough tradition furnishes the only evidence that this was the room, yet tradition is tenacious, and may well be correct.

In the cellar of a building near King David's Tomb is the **Chamber of the Holocaust** (tel. 02-716-841), an eerie room lit by candles and dedicated to the memory of the six million Jews slain by the Nazis. The chamber is open for visits Sunday through Thursday from 8 a.m. to 5 p.m., on Friday to 1 p.m.; closed Saturday.

Close by, the graceful **Dormition Abbey** (tel. 02-719-927) stands, according to tradition, on the spot where Mary fell into eternal sleep. It was erected in 1906 on a plot of land presented to the German kaiser by the Turkish sultan. Inside the church are an elaborate golden mosaic, a crypt containing particularly interesting religious artwork, and a statue of Mary, around which are chapels donated by various countries: the Austrian Chapel is a memorial to its slain prime minister and the Hungarian chapel depicts famous saints and Hungarian kings. From the tower of the church there's a good panoramic view of the surrounding region. No visitors allowed between 1 and 3 p.m.

Vis-à-vis Mount Aion road is a **peace memorial,** a slender pillar with a tangle of metal at the bottom. The inscribed legend is Isaiah's swords-intoploughshares admonition, and the memorial itself is a gift from Abie Nathan, Israel's celebrated flying and sailing "peacenik." Nearby is a road winding to the right, clear up to the top. Jerusalemites call it the "Pope's Road," since it was built especially for the pope's visit several years back. During its construction part of a ceramic aqueduct was uncovered. Believed to have been built during the Second Temple era, it runs though hills and valleys for 45 km (27 miles) to Solomon's Pool. Parts can be seen today in the area of Hativat Yerushalayim Street south of Mount Zion.

SIGHTS IN EAST JERUSALEM: The modern part of East Jerusalem is not a very large area, and you can probably cover its major sights in half a day.

The Rockefeller Museum

Start at the Rockefeller Museum (tel. 02-282-251) on Sultan Suleiman Street near Herod's Gate. Visiting hours are 10 a.m. to 5 p.m. Sunday through Thursday, to 2 p.m. on Friday, Saturday, and eves of holidays. Admission costs NIS4.50 ($3) for adults, NIS3 ($2) for children.

Architecturally, this is a handsome place, with a castle-like tower and cloister gardens in the middle. The top of the Moorish castle-turret was badly shot up during the Six-Day War, and in fact the entire museum was once pockmarked from shells and machine-gun fire. But the damage to the displays was scant; and there was no damage at all to the Dead Sea Scrolls, which were wrapped up and tucked away in the basement.

The northern and southern galleries contain one of the most extensive archeological collections in this part of the world. Much of the treasure here was excavated in the areas of Acre and the Galilee by American and English archeologists in the 1930s. Pottery, tools, and household effects are arranged by periods—Iron Age, Persian, Hellenistic, Roman, Byzantine. In the south gallery's Paleolithic section are displayed the bones of Mount Carmel Man, "an extinct race combining the characteristics of Neanderthal and Modern Man which lived in Israel about 100,000 years ago."

Zedekiah's Cave

Head back down along the walls until you are just across from the East Jerusalem bus station (between Herod's and Damascus Gates). Here you'll see an entrance leading down under the walls into Zedekiah's Cave, or Solomon's Quarries, which tradition calls the source of the stones for Solomon's Temple. To Masons the spot is considered the origin of their group, the builders of Solomon's Temple. Jewish and Muslim legends claim that tunnels in those caves extended to the Sinai Desert and Jericho. The quarries are called Zedekiah's Cave, since in 587 B.C. King Zedekiah was supposed to have fled from the Babylonians through these tunnels, to be captured subsequently near Jericho. You can enter the caves from 9 a.m. to 4:30 p.m , seven days a week, for NIS1 (65¢), half price for children. An illuminated path leads you far back into the caves and under the Old City.

The Garden Tomb

Head up Nablus Road (Derekh Shechem) now, opposite Damascus Gate. Look for a side street named Conrad Schick Street on the right, and follow it to the Garden Tomb (tel. 02-283-402), a typical rock-hewn tomb of the 1st century

A.D. The lovely grounds, and the tomb itself, are open to visitors from 8 a.m. to 12:15 p.m. and 2:30 to 5:15 p.m., for free (donations accepted) every day except Sunday. There is a Protestant service in English at 9 a.m. on Sunday; it's open to all, but otherwise the Garden Tomb is closed on that day.

In 1867 Dr. Conrad Schick discovered this tomb, which fits closely the description of the biblical one in which Jesus was interred. In 1883 General Gordon, hero of China and Khartoum, visited the tomb on his way to Egypt, and had a vision that this was indeed the tomb of Jesus, and the general's enthusiasm lent popularity to the belief. The tomb was finally excavated in 1891, and whether it is "the place" or not, it is certainly very similar: near the site of the crucifixion, hewn from the rock, a new tomb, not an old one reused, made for a rich man and situated in a garden. The gardens are beautiful, lush, peaceful, and fragrant, and the sepulchre itself vividly recalls the tumultuous times of Jesus and Pontius Pilate. Today the site is well cared for by the Garden Tomb (Jerusalem) Association of London, England.

The Tourjeman Post

Continuing up Nablus Road, you'll pass the East Jerusalem American Consulate building. Nablus Road goes to the right of the consulate. Take a detour, though, to the left, for a look at a grisly landmark.

The **Tourjeman Post Museum** (tel. 02-281-278), near the confluence of Shivtei Israel–St. George Street and Nablus Road, is easily identifiable: just look for the old Turkish house turned into a fortress. This was an Israeli command post during the 1948 War of Independence, and as long as Jerusalem was divided (until 1967). The Mandelbaum Gate, the only passage between Israel and Jordan during that period, was just up the street. Today the Tourjeman Post is a museum dedicated to the history of Jerusalem divided (1948–1967). It's open Sunday through Thursday only, from 9 a.m. to 4 p.m. Admission is NIS1.50 ($1) for adults, NIS1 (65¢) for children.

St. George's Cathedral

From the Tourjeman Post, go north to the intersection and turn right. Before you will be the Gothic towers of St. George's Cathedral, Holy Land headquarters for the Anglican church. Feel free to pass through the courtyard for a look at the handsome church. The complex also contains a religious college, a school, a hostel for travelers, a nice little garden, and residences.

Tombs of the Kings

As you come out the gate from St. George's, turn right (north) and circle around the complex to get on Saladin Street. You'll notice, as you circle, the gate to the American Colony Hotel just to the north of St. George's.

Behind St. George's, on the left-hand side as you head down Saladin Street, is a gate marked "Tombeau des Rois." This is the Tomb of the Kings, administered by the French Republic, open from 8 a.m. to 12:30 p.m. and 2 to 5 p.m. Monday through Saturday; closed Sunday. Admission costs NIS1.50 ($1).

Some 15 or 20 feet down a stone stairway, you'll see a hollowed-out courtyard, in which are several small cave openings. Inside one of them, four sarcophagi, covered with carvings of fruit and vines, rest in a crypt-like chamber. It's been over 100 years since scholars discovered that, in fact no kings are buried here (rather, the family of Queen Helena of Adiabene, who converted to Judaism in Jerusalem around A.D. 50)—but what's in a name?

Coming down Saladin Street, in the direction of the Old City walls, you'll pass the **Ministry of Justice**, on the right. Farther down, across the street, is the **Albright Institute of Archeological Research**. Just after it, on the left, you'll find Az-Zahra Street, a modern thoroughfare of bookshops, restaurants, and hotels, leading to the Rockefeller Museum.

SIGHTS AT MOUNT SCOPUS, MOUNT OF OLIVES, VALLEY OF KID-RON: You reach Mount of Olives Road either by driving north up Saladin
Street or by taking a left turn at the wall, just past the Rockefeller Museum. If you want to go by bus, go to the East Jerusalem bus station and take no. 75, the one that goes to the village of Et-Tur. Another bus, no. 42 from the municipal bus depot on Nablus Road, goes through Et-Tur all the way to the Intercontinental Hotel. For Hebrew University, take no. 4a, 9, or 28.

Mount Scopus

From Sheikh Jarrah (on Nablus Road), the road heads up past the Mount Scopus Hotel and proceeds, gradually curving, past Shepherds's Hotel. Now you're on Mount Scopus Road, and at a bend in the road, to your left, you'll see the **Jerusalem War Cemetery**, resting place for British World War I dead. To the left—past tombstones identifying soldiers of the Royal Welsh Fusiliers, Black Watch, and Devonshire Regiment—are several gravestones of Jewish Legion soldiers who died along with the British in World War I. You are now on Mount Scopus—**Har Hatsofim,** which means "Mount Observation."

About 100 yards farther along the ridge is the checkpost through which passed the fortnightly convoy of Jewish police that tended to the Mount Scopus university complex for 19 years. The Mount Scopus **Hadassah Hospital** is on your left. Lining both sides of the roads are university buildings, the result of a fast and furious building program that was launched to place these units back in operation as part of the Hebrew University complex. Today you'll see dorms housing 3,000 students, and the construction continues. From the Truman Research Institute (a pink stone building) there's a fine panoramic view: the Seat of the Rabbinate, Mount Zion, the Dome of the Rock. Tours are given daily, except Saturday, at 11 a.m. from the Sherman Building.

A view of a different nature can be had from the outdoor **amphitheater** across the road: here, on April 1, 1925, the Hebrew University was opened in a ceremony attended by such notables as Lord Arthur Balfour, Sir Herbert Samuel (then high commissioner for Palestine), Chaim Weizmann, Haim Nahman Bialik (the foremost Hebrew poet of the day), and Rabbi Kook, then chief rabbi of Palestine. The Mount Scopus university buildings were in Israeli hands during the first ceasefire of the 1948 war, and although the enclave was surrounded by Arab-held territory, it received a "demilitarized" status. Police and civilian caretakers, in two-week shifts, looked after the buildings over the succeeding 19 years—while another hospital and university compound was built in Givat Ram, West Jerusalem. The view to the east is magnificent—the parched, tawny Judean Hills falling in endless small waves down to the Dead Sea.

During the Six-Day War, the university compound held out against great odds. It was defended by the 120 "policemen" who were there on duty. Over the years they had smuggled up an impressive cache of small arms and light artillery—piece by piece—and when the occasion arose, as many Israelis suspected it one day would, the weapons were ready for use.

The Best View in Jerusalem

The road skirting the ridge proceeds past the high-towered **Augusta Victoria Hospital,** an Arab Legion bastion during the Six-Day War (its tower is peppered with bullet holes) and the Arab village of Et-Tur, the Mount of Olives, the Jewish Cemetery, and the Intercontinental Hotel. From the Hebrew University on Mount Scopus, and the Intercontinental Hotel, you have absolutely the most exciting views that Jerusalem has to offer. Come here early in the morning and see all of Jerusalem below in a soft, pinkish hue of limestone white. Return in the late afternoon and you will see why the city is called Jerusalem the Golden.

Mount of Olives

Here you'll find half a dozen churches—and the oldest **Jewish Cemetery** in the world. It was this cemetery that religious Jews had in mind when they came to die in the Holy Land, and many legends have emerged to surround it throughout its long, long history (start down the path on the right and you'll come to the **Tomb of the Prophets,** believed to be the burial place of Haggai, Malachi, and Zechariah). Many Jews have believed, perhaps still do, that from here the route to heaven is the shortest, since God's presence is always hovering over Jerusalem; others have held that here, on the Mount of Olives, the resurrection of the dead will occur—so you can imagine the anguish many Jews felt when the Intercontinental Hotel was built over the easternmost perimeters of the old cemetery, and when the Jordanians used some of the tombstones in the construction of army barracks.

Farther back up the road, on the southern fringe of Et-Tur, stands the **Mosque (and Chapel) of the Ascension** (ring the bell), marking the spot where Jesus ascended to heaven. Interestingly enough, this Christian shrine is under Muslim control. Muslims revere Jesus as a prophet and believe in the doctrine of the ascension. Jesus, they believe, will raise Mohammed on Resurrection Day.

Just a few steps away is the **Church of the Pater Noster,** built on the traditional spot where Christ instructed his disciples on the Lord's Prayer. Tiles along the walls of the church are inscribed with the Lord's Prayer—in 44 languages. The **Carmelite Convent** and **Basilica of the Sacred Heart** are on the adjoining hill.

From up here you can see a cluster of churches on the lower slopes of the Mount of Olives. All can be reached either from here or from the road paralleling the fortress wall, diagonally opposite St. Stephen's Gate (Lion's Gate).

If you head down the path to the right of the Tomb of the Prophets, you'll come to the only church in this area built along contemporary architectural lines. It is **Dominus Flevit,** a Franciscan church marking the spot where Jesus wept over Jerusalem. The Russian Orthodox **Church of Mary Magdalene,** topped off strikingly with onion-shaped spires, is next (open Tuesday and Saturday from 9 a.m. to noon and 2 to 4 p.m.); it was built in 1888 by Czar Alexander III. The Roman Catholic **Garden of Gethsemane** (open 8:30 a.m. to noon and 3 p.m. to sunset, April to October; 8:30 a.m. to noon and from 2 p.m. to sunset in winter) adjoins the **Basilica of the Agony (Church of All Nations),** containing a piece of the rock at which Jesus is said to have prayed the night before he entered Jerusalem for the Passover supper. The mosaic façade of the church is impressive: it shows God looking down from heaven over Jesus and the peoples of the world (16 nations' worth of "peoples" contributed to the building of this church in 1924). Next door, past beautifully tended gardens of ancient olive trees and bougainvillea, is the **Tomb of the Virgin,** a deep underground chamber housing the tombs of Mary and Joseph.

Valley of Kidron

This is the depression between the foot of the Mount of Olives and the Old City walls. It runs south, between Mount Ophel (where David built his city) and the Mount of Contempt. Just under the wall here, roughly in front of the El Aksa Mosque, are two tombs: **Absalom's Pillar** and the **Tomb of Zechariah.** At one time religious Jews would throw stones at Absalom's Pillar (*Yad Avshalom*), in condemnation of Absalom, who rebelled against his father, King David. A hand (the *yad*) is used to top the conical monument.

The Valley of Kidron is also known as the **Valley of Jehoshaphat.** The book of Joel 3:2, 12, records that here the judgments will be rendered on Resurrection Day: "Let the heathen be awakened, and come up to the Valley of Jehoshaphat, for there will I sit to judge all the heathen round about." Muslims hold to a similar belief. They believe Mohammed will sit astride a pillar under the wall of the Dome of the Rock. A wire will be stretched from the pillar to the Mount of Olives, opposite, where Christ will be seated. All mankind will walk across the wire on its way to eternity. The righteous and faithful will reach the other side safely; the rest will drop down in the Valley of Jehoshaphat and perish.

About 200 yards down the valley is the **Fountain of the Virgin,** at the Arab village of **Silwan.** This spring is the **Gihon,** whose waters anointed Solomon king and served as the only water source for ancient Jerusalem. During the Assyrian and Babylonian attacks (8th century B.C.), King Hezekiah constructed an aqueduct through which the waters could flow into the city. **Hezekiah's Aqueduct** is still there (underneath the church commemorating the spot where Mary once drew water to wash the clothes of Jesus), and its interesting expanse, ending up at the **Pool of Siloam,** can be negotiated—but not too easily. It's about 1,600 feet long, and the depth of the water is 10 to 16 inches. The walk takes about 40 minutes; best to have a flashlight with you. You can walk through from Sunday to Thursday between 8:30 a.m and 3 p.m., on Friday and holiday eves till 1 p.m. Entrance is free, but give the caretaker a tip.

The City of David

Above the Gihon spring, but below the Dung Gate, lie the ruins of King David's city, built around 1000 B.C. You can enter daily from 9 a.m. to 5 p.m., for free, and follow the paths along the steep hillside past the excavated piles of stone, some identified by plaques in English. Even the imagination fails here, as it is difficult to reconstruct in the mind's eye how this very primitive town must have appeared.

THE SIGHTS OF WEST JERUSALEM: From three high vantage points in the city, you'll be able to obtain a picture of Jerusalem's general layout that will be most helpful in your touring. It would be wise to include these three sights among your first stops.

The first view is from **King George V Avenue,** between the Jewish Agency building (which consists of a large courtyard housing a trio of connected administrative buildings) and the Heikhal Shlomo, the domed, imposing Seat of the Rabbinate. From here, you can look directly out over Independence Park (Gan Ha-Atzma'ut) clear across the Old City wall, beyond which lie the Mount of Olives and the Ascension Site (on the left). In the distance, the cream and orange stone of Jerusalem's houses blends into the earth itself. On the right side, bordering the park, is the West Jerusalem building of the American Consulate, with its tall flagpole; at the extreme right of this panorama stands the oddly Victorian King David Hotel, a big rectangular building; at its right, slightly in the foreground, is an impressive building, the Jerusalem YMCA. Its tall tower, flanked by domes, suggest some mammoth minaret and mosque, giving it an exotically Eastern flavor. Away off to the right, on a clear day, the landscape blurs into a maze of mountains, the biblical range of Moab and Gilead.

For an even broader panoramic view, take the elevator up to the top of the YMCA's 152-foot **Jesus' Tower.** Hours are 9 a.m. to 3 p.m and tours run Monday through Saturday; the fee is minimal. Once at the top, the entire city spreads around you, and you are able to really see Jerusalem. Now on to the sights of West Jerusalem, one by one:

The YMCA

One of the most outstanding landmarks of the city was built in 1928 from funds donated by a Montclair, New Jersey, millionaire, James Jarvie. The YMCA (tel. 02-227-111) has a swimming pool, tennis couts, lecture hall, and gymnasium. The Y also holds organ concerts Saturday mornings at 11:30—on the largest pipe organ in the Middle East.

Herod's Family Tomb

This burial cave, discovered in the late 19th century, is off King David Street, just a few steps down from the King David Hotel. Used as an air-raid shelter during the 1948 war, it is believed to be the tomb of some member of Herod's family rather than his actual burial site (that's called the Herodion and is in the mountains south of Bethlehem). Open from 10 a.m to 1 p.m. Monday through Thursday for a small entrance fee.

King David Hotel

This is the famous hotel blown up in July 1946 by Israeli underground fighters—an act that hastened the departure of the British from Israel. The entire right wing of the building was subsequently rebuilt, and if you look closely, you can see the difference in the stone. (The bomb was hidden in a milk container in the basement, in what is now the grill room.) The outdoor patio here is a lovely place for a drink, but the lobby of the hotel should be experienced just for its own sake. It is something out of a bygone era, and if you let your imagination go, you can visualize British ladies in long skirts, their gentlemen in white double-breasted panama suits, with Arab sheiks in flowing gowns seated nearby. Kissinger has been a frequent guest at the King David, and it was the official World War II residence of Haile Selassie of Ethiopia. Incidentally, when the hotel was built, in 1934, the designers thought to give each public room an "ancient" influence.

Windmill and Yemin Moshe

There's no confusing Jerusalem with Holland, but all the same, the windmill across from Mount Zion has piqued many a tourist's curiosity. As it happened, Sir Moses Montefiore, the British philanthropist, visited Palestine a century and a half ago and was appalled by the ghetto conditions of the Jews in the Old City. He decided to build them a new residential section just outside the walls, and soon New Orleans philanthropist Judah Touro joined in the project, becoming the first American Jew to contribute to Israel. The new quarter was called Yemin Moshe, and the Philanthropists even provided a windmill for the grinding of flour. Standing on the upper part of Yemin Moshe, facing the Old City ramparts, the windmill was an important observation point during the 1948 War of Independence. In fact the entire Yemin Moshe quarter was under persistent siege during the war, taking the full brunt of the attack, hopelessly surrounded a dozen times but still managing to hold out. The windmill, now a museum dedicated to Montefiore, may be visited, for free, Sunday through Thursday from 9 a.m. to 4 p.m., till 1 p.m. on Friday; closed Saturday. Tourists and residents alike swarm the area at all times, peering into the artists' galleries that have been fashioned out of the original homes. After the 1967 war, the Jerusalem Municipality offered help and grants to artists to reconstruct the houses and stables and convert the area into a small artists' colony. As the area became more and more desirable, and thus expensive, many artists could no afford to live there, and wealthy foreigners began buying up the property. Famous local poets, novelists, and about a dozen artists live here now. If you're around in August, don't miss the special art fair centering around the square next to the windmill.

An exact replica of the Liberty Bell in Philadelphia stands in the center of Jerusalem's **Liberty Bell Garden,** surrounding the Windmill. The seven-acre garden has a picnic area, and future plans include a large children's playground and an entertainment area.

Near the Montefiore Windmill is a row of old stone buildings called **Mishkanoth Sha'ananim,** built by Sir Moses Montefiore in 1859. It was the first venture of settlers outside the city walls. Today the building is used as a residence for visiting artists and official guests of the government.

Jewish Agency Compound

The three connected buildings, around a big courtyard on King George V Avenue, were the seat of the "secondary" government under the British Mandate. The Jewish Agency headquarters is here, as is the Jewish National Fund and Keren Ha-Yesod (UJA buildings). These two giant institutions still play a major role in immigrant absorption and the reclamation of land. There are various displays—the Golden Book, recording donors' names, and the Zionist Archives. Free films about Israel are shown occasionally at noon.

Heikhal Shlomo

At 58 King George V Ave., facing the large main park, Gan Ha-Atzma'ut, is the imposing **Great Synagogue** and **Seat of the Rabbinate** building, styled along the lines of King Solomon's Temple. Square at the bottom and domed on top, the lofty building offers quite a view from its uppermost balcony. It houses the country's highest religious offices. Free tours from 9 a.m to 1 p.m. Sunday through Thursday, till noon on Friday. Weekly programs here—religious and folk songs, lectures and readings—mark *Melave Malka,* the end of the sabbath and the beginning of the new week. For times of these traditional festivities, check at Heikhal Shlomo, your hotel, or the Tourist Information Office. Don't miss the **Sir Isaac and Lady Edith Wolfson Museum** (tel. 02-635-212), with an outstanding collection of religious and traditional objects, maps, coins, and the entire interior of an old Italian synagogue.

Rehavia

A turn to the west from King George V Avenue, either at the Jewish Agency compound or at the Kings Hotel, will bring you into Jerusalem's handsomest residential section: Rehavia, with its middle- and upper-class, tree-lined, quiet streets. Main streets are Ramban, Ussishkin, Abarbanel, Ben-Maimon, Gaza, Alfasi.

Some sights along the way include the **Prime Minister's Residence,** at the corner of Balfour and Smolenskin; the **Alfasi grotto** (also called the Tomb of Jason), on Alfasi Street, a frescoed and inscribed tomb discovered by builders while they were digging foundations (open from 10 a.m. to 4 p.m.); and the **Monastery of the Cross,** built by Gregorian monks in the 11th century, and now maintained by the Greek Orthodox church. According to tradition, the beautiful monastery is located on the spot where stood the tree from which the Cross was made. Its interior is splendidly medieval. If you don't want to walk down the rocky hillside from Rehavia to the monastery, take bus 9 or 16. South of Rehavia, in Kiryat Shmuel, is **Bet Ha-Nassie,** the president's residence.

Bezalel Academy of Arts and Design

Located behind the City Tower, off King George V Avenue at 10 Shmuel Ha-Nagid St,, the school was founded in 1906; many of Israel's artists have attended classes here at one time or another. The name Bezalel is that of the Old Testament's famous artist, Bezalel Ben-Ouri, "full of divine inspriation in the art of combining cloths, working gold, silver, copper, precious stones and woods" (Exodus 31:2–11); Bezalel built the Holy Tabernacle for the tribes of Israel while they were wandering in the desert on their way to the Promised Land. (The museum that used to be here is now part of the Israel Museum.) The academy's five departments are: fine arts, environmental and industrial design, graphic design, ceramics, and gold- and silversmithing.

Jerusalem Artists' House

Next door to Bezalel, at 12 Shmuel Ha-Nagid st. (tel. 02-223-653), a flurry of cultural activities centers around exhibitions of the Jerusalem Artists' Association. Evenings of chamber music, concerts readings, jazz, and art lectures are scheduled each year (for specifics, check with the Tourist Office or at the office here); there's a restaurant and a club where tourists are welcome—open Sunday to Thursday from 10 a.m. to midnight, closed Friday and open Saturday nights. On the main floor, paintings and sculpture of all 430 member artists are exhibited and sold (if you buy, they'll ship your purchases). Upstairs and throughout the building are general exhibitions in August and the spring; special exhibitions, featuring about three artisis at a time, change every three weeks during the rest of the year. When you visit here, don't miss a close look at the beautifully carved outside doors, the crenellated roof and dome, and the garden sculpture. Open from 10 a.m. to 1 p.m. and 4 to 7 p.m. Sunday through Friday and 10 a.m to 1 p.m on Saturday; free entrance.

Prophets Street

Called **Rehov Ha-Nevi'im,** this is the "Christian Street" of West Jerusalem, housing a variety of missionary societies and foreign churches. From Zion Square, in the heart of downtown Jerusalem, go right up any of the two or three narrow streets branching off north, up the hill.

On Prophets Street you'll find the **Swedish Theological Seminary,** the **Christian Missionary Alliance,** the **American Bible Institute,** and branching off at Abyssinian Street, the splendid **Abyssinian** (Ethiopian) **Church,** with a Lion of Judah carved on the gate above the courtyard. The reason for the Lion of Judah (emblem of the late Emperor Haile Selassie of Ethiopia): the Ethiopians believe that the Queen of Sheba was an Ethiopian empress and that on her first visit to Jerusalem she received the Lion of Judah emblem from King Solomon. Haile Selassie himself traced his royal lineage to the meeting of King Solomon and the Queen of Sheba.

Mahane Yehuda

Just off Jaffa Road, half a mile west of Zion Square, is an old market quarter where the streets are named for fruits and the atmosphere is at its liveliest on

Wednesday and Thursday, when the streets are jam-packed. Here, in a square off Mahane Yehuda and Jaffa Road, stands a war memorial commemorating the success of the Israelis' homemade secret weapon used in the defense of Jerusalem. It threw a small shell, did a bit of damage, but made such an earsplitting roar that, as legend has it, it scared the devil out of the enemy.

Binyane Ha-Uma

This imposing auditorium on the northwestern part of Jaffa Road, just opposite the Central Bus Station, often has interesting exhibitions. King-size conventions take place on the premises, and it is the concert hall for the Israel Philharmonic Orchestra. The Tourist Office has a schedule of current doings.

Mea Shearim

A visit to this religious quarter north of Zion Square is bound to be informative, and at the same time either fascinating or chilling, depending on your attitude. The stronghold of an extreme sect of Jewish orthodoxy since 1887, Mea Shearim derives its name from the account of Isaac, son of Abraham: "Then Isaac sowed in that land, and received in the same year a hundredfold [*Mea Shearim*] and the Lord blessed him" (Genesis 26:12).

Center of the mystical Hasidic religious sect, Mea Shearim, with its winding alleys, could have been taken from a classical picture of the Eastern European ghetto. The customs, clothing, and language fill out the picture. Here you can see scribes painstakingly copying the Scriptures by hand. Long-bearded men in black gowns trudge the streets. On their heads they wear beaver-fur hats or sometimes more broad-brimmed black hats. Young boys with pale white faces wear bobbing side-curls (*payot*), short black pants, and high black socks. The married women, according to strict Orthodox tradition, wear wigs and scarves over their shaved heads. Dozens of tiny shops sell religious ornaments and artifacts, and almost every other door is either a Talmudic school or a synagogue. Many residents speak only Yiddish in conversation, regarding Hebrew as too sacred a language for everyday use. These fiercely religious Russian and Polish Jews are fighting what they consider the blasphemous modern life of Israel. Some of them don't even recognize the laws of the Israeli government. One group, called the Guardians of the City (Neturei Karta), claim that no State of Israel can exist before the coming of the Messiah. The sect has frequently clashed with police in demonstrations protesting autopsies, driving on Saturday, and mixed swimming pools.

Long-sleeve dresses, lengthy skirts, and head coverings are *musts* for women visiting the synagogues; in fact, they are recommended for all women touring this area. And since photographs represent "graven images" to some residents here, and are considered just plain taboo by others, you're strongly advised to resist all temptation to snap pictures in this area.

In fringe areas around this Ashkenazi—or Eastern European—section are other religious neighborhoods, composed of Yemenite, Bukharian, and Persian Jews.

Russian Compound

Along Jaffa Road from Zion Square, look up to your left (north) before coming to the main post office to see the **Russian Orthodox church,** an edifice that looks as if it was lifted from the heart of Leningrad. The green-domed cathedral and surrounding land long remained the property of the Russian church (the Israeli government rented some of it for administrative offices). In 1965 Israel finally purchased the compound from Russia. Once this structure was the world's largest "hotel"; it could accommodate 10,000 Russian pilgrims at one time (that was in the 1920s, when the Russians were the most numerous pilgrims to Israel). A permanent exhibit stands in the **Hall of Heroism** (tel. 02-233-209), which once served as the Mandate's Jerusalem Central Prison (see the cells and execution chambers). It focuses on Jewish underground activities of the pre-1948 period. Visiting hours are Sunday through Thursday from 9 a.m. to 4 p.m., on Friday till 1 p.m.; closed Saturday. There's an admission fee of NIS2 ($1.35). Coming by bus, take no. 18, 20, or 56.

Inside the compound, by the way stands **Herod's Pillar** (circled by an iron fence), thought to have been intended, once upon a time, for Herod's Temple.

Sanhedrian Tombs

Go up Shmuel Ha-Navi, off Shivtei Israel Street, to northeast Jerusalem's beautiful public gardens of **Sanhedria** (or take bus 2 from Jaffa Gate). Called either the Tombs of Sanhedria or the Tombs of the Judges, this is where the judges of ancient Israel's "Supreme Court" (during the first and second centuries) lie buried. The three-story burial catacomb is carved out of rock, with many an intricate feature—some niches have rolling stone closures. The gardens are open every day from 9 a.m. to 4 or 5 p.m.; the tombs are closed Saturday.

The Biblical Zoo

Located in a natural animal haven, a glen shaded by tall fir and cypress trees in the section named Romema, the **Jerusalem Biblical Zoo** (tel. 02-814-822) is undoubtedly one of the most unusual animal collections in the world. Here, Prof. Aaron Shulov of the Hebrew University's Biology Department has gathered together almost all of the plants, 100 animals, and 30 birds mentioned in the Bible. Many of the animals in the zoo are still indigenous to Israel; even today you can find jackals, wild boar, wildcats, porcupines, wolves, gazelles, camels, eagles, and vultures throughout the country. In front of the gazelle cage is a plaque reading: "I adjure you, O daughters of Jerusalem, by the gazelles and the hinds of the field" (Song of Solomon 2:7). In front of the lion's cage, the sign reads: "As a roaring lion and a greedy bear, so is a wicked ruler over an indigent people" (Proverbs 28:15).

Not all the animals and rare birds in the zoo still exist in their natural state in Israel, though. Certainly the lion doesn't. Nor does the crocodile: "The great crocodile that lieth in the midst of his streams" (Ezekiel 29:3).

Hours are 8 a.m. till dark; there's a free tour on Sunday at 2 p.m. (Though the zoo is open Saturday, no tickets are sold—so buy them beforehand at one of the ticket agencies or at the zoo.) Take bus 28 going north from the Central Bus Station.

Major Christian Landmarks

Although many of the more important Christian monuments are located in the eastern section of Jerusalem, the western side has a number of historic churches and monasteries that you can visit.

Terra Sancta: Once the temporary quarters of the Hebrew University, the splendid-looking Franciscan church in the garden is on the corner of King George V Avenue and Gaza Road (Derekh Aza).

Notre Dame de France: From the roof here is a splendid view of the Old City of Jerusalem. Situated on Shivtei Israel Street at Zahal Square just opposite New Gate in the Old City walls, this monastery was built by the Assumptionist Fathers in 1887 to serve as a pilgrim's hostel. The church, on the old border, was the scene of heavy fighting during the 1948 war. It is a hospital, restaurant, and hostel too.

Pontifical Jesuit Monastery: Around the corner from the King David

Hotel, it has a large biblical library and archeological collection. Open from 9 a.m. to noon daily except Sunday.

St. Vincent de Paul: Belonging to the order of the Sisters of Charity, this convent is at the end of Agron Street, near the American Consulate.

San Rosaire: Also on Agron Street, right next to the American Consulate, the convent belongs to the Order of the Sisters of the Holy Rosary.

St. Peter of Ratisbone Monastery: Next to the Yeshurun Synagogue, on Shmuel Ha-Nagid Street, this is one of the city's newer sanctuaries, founded in 1874. It belongs to the Fathers of Zion order and has a boy's orphanage.

Church and Monastery of St. John: This 5th-century Franciscan sanctuary is located in Ein Kerem, built on the site said to be the birthplace of St. John the Baptist. Take bus 17.

Church of the Visitation: A Franciscan church, dedicated to the visit of Mary, mother of Jesus, and to Elizabeth, mother of St. John the Baptist, it's also located in Ein Kerem. Bus 17.

Monastery of St. John of the Desert: The grotto where St. John is believed to have spent his early years is the site of the Franciscan monastery, on a hillside some two miles outside of Ein Kerem. Bus 17 and then a long walk.

Benedictine Monastery: Built over the site of a 12th-century Crusader's church in Abu Ghosh, five miles outside Jerusalem on the main road to Tel Aviv. Bus to Abu Ghosh.

Church of Notre Dame of the Ark: Served by the Sisters of Saint Joseph, this is near a famous statue of the Virgin holding the infant Jesus in her arms which dominates the surrounding countryside. Bus to Abu Ghosh.

St. Andrew's Church of Scotland: Built by the people of Scotland, this Presbyterian church is situated on a hilltop near Abu Tor and the railroad station.

Monastery of the Cross: In a valley below the residential section of Rehavia, the monastery stands on the site where the tree was cut for the Cross. It has a beautiful garden and a medieval church with restored mosaics.

Greek Orthodox Monastery: Built over the foundations of a medieval church at Abu Tor, it is called the Church of Evil Counsel, and contains interesting catacombs and crypts.

Monastery of Saint Simeon: Part of the Greek patriarch's summer residence, the monastery and church are on Katamon Ridge.

Russian Orthodox Cathedral: Just off Jaffa Road, the green-domed edifice was originally constructed after the Crimean War for pilgrims of the Russian Orthodox faith. (See "Russian Compound," above.)

Russian Church of St. John: Identified by its bright-green steeple, this sanctuary is located in Ein Kerem. Bus 17.

Abyssinian Church: Off Ha-Nevi'im Street in Mea Shearim, the elegant building with the Lion of Judah framing the entranceway is the spiritual home of the Coptic Ethiopian clergy.

Hebrew University

Take bus 24 or 28 to the **Givat Ram** campus, which from the distance looks like an architect's model—with clean, functional lines for its modern buildings and landscaped grounds. Located in the midst of rolling hills, the Hebrew University (tel. 02-882-819) is one of Israel's most dramatic accomplishments, with 14,000 students on this and the Mount Scopus campus.

Mosaics adorn the entranceways to the various buildings on the campus. See especially the **Belgium House Faculty Club, La Maison de France, the Physics Building,** and the huge **National and University Library** (changing exhibits of Jewish bibliographical lore and data) at the far end of the promenade. And don't miss the mushroom-shaped synagogue behind the library. The 21st-century-looking gymnasium and the swimming pool are interesting structures on campus.

Free tours start daily except Saturday and Jewish holidays at 9 and 11 a.m. from the Administration Building. You can stop for lunch in the cafeteria of the Administration Building, or in the Jewish National and University Library. Tours of the Mount Scopus campus leave at 11 a.m. from the Sherman Building.

The older and original site of the Hebrew University and Hadassah Hospital on Mount Scopus is described earlier in this chapter.

Model of Ancient Jerusalem

Next, take the road opposite Mount Herzl (or bus 21 or 99 from downtown) and follow the sign pointing to the Holyland Hotel. A short walk from the hotel's entrance brings you to a garden in which stands a painstakingly complete, perfectly scaled-down model of Jerusalem (tel. 02-630-201) as it was in the time of the Second Temple. This is Herod's Jerusalem, a grand, opulent place of palaces, mammoth walls, and elegant towers. This impressive project is the result of years of collaboration by a team of architects, historians, archeologists, and builders, led by Prof. M. Avi-Yonah. Open daily from 8 a.m. to 5 p.m. in winter, to 6 p.m. in summer (on Friday to 4 or 5 p.m.). Admission is minimal.

Government Quarter—Kiryat Ben-Gurion

Opposite the university, on Kaplan Street, is an assortment of buildings comprising most of the government quarter. Most impressive of the government buildings is the **Parliament (Knesset);** tel. 02-554-111). A $7-million structure of peach-colored stone, this elegant landmark on Jerusalem's "Acropolis" has a 24-foot-high Chagall mosaic in the reception hall, and contains a synagogue, separate kitchens for meat and milk dishes (you can stop for a moderately priced meal in the cafeteria), and exhibition rooms. The entranceway, a grillwork of hammered metal, is the work of the Israeli sculptor Polombo, who did the dramatic doors at Yad Vashem.

The Knesset is Israel's third Parliament building—and the first permanent one. Previous Parliaments were convened in a converted cinema in Tel Aviv and a converted bank (Bet Froumine) in downtown Jerusalem at the junction of King George V Avenue and Ben-Yehuda Street, which now houses the Government Tourist offices. The Menorah that stood in the park next to that last Knesset is now positioned across from the entrance to the new one. Open for guided tours of the building on Sunday and Thursday from 8:30 a.m. to 2:30 p.m.; reached by bus 9, 24, 28, or 99. You must have your passport with you. You can attend a session of Knesset on Monday, Tuesday, or Wednesday from 4 to 9 p.m. The Knesset recesses during Jewish holidays and the summer.

Israel Museum

Opened in May 1965 to great fanfare, the Israel Museum complex (tel. 02-698-211 or 698-213) lies on Ruppin Street, just south of the Knesset (buses 9, 17, 24, and 99). Israelis say it's the largest museum between Rome and Tokyo.

The complex is an outstanding example of modern Israeli architecture.

There are five main components: the **Bezalel Art Museum,** the **Samuel Bronfman Biblical and Archeological Museum,** the **Billy Rose Art Garden,** the **Shrine of the Book,** and the **Ruth Youth Wing.**

Collections of Jewish ceremonial artifacts, gleaned from Israel's many historic sites and going back thousands of years, form the bulk of the collection at the first two. On view here are decorative pages from centuries-old Torahs—from Iran, Italy, and Singapore. In one room there are dozens of Hannukah lamps, silver Torah ornaments, serving trays, shofars, and an exhibit of costumes worn by Jewish women in Yemen on festival occasions. There are two reconstructed synagogues, one 17th-century Italian, the other 18th-century German. The art museum shows the work of Israeli contemporaries and also contains period rooms. The Bronfman-Bezalel complex, in the main building and adjoining wings, houses a gift shop well stocked with books, prints, and posters. Outside, to the right of the stairs, is the museum cafeteria (moderate prices).

Three important new pavilions have been added in recent years. One contains an impressive collection of pre-Columbian Central American art from 2000 B.C. to A.D. 1550; another is a separate building housing ancient glass; and the third is the Walter and Charlotte Floersheimer Pavilion for Impressionist and Post-Impressionist Art with works by Corot, Monet, Renoir, Degas, Gauguin, Matisse, etc.

Another recent addition is an **archeological garden** between the Shrine of the Book and the Youth Wing complex. It contains classical Greco-Roman sculptures, sarcophagi, and mosaics, most of which were discovered and excavated in Israel.

Free guided tours of the museum are conducted in English on Sunday, Wednesday, and Thursday at 11 a.m., and on Tuesday at 4:30 p.m.

The Billy Rose Art Garden, on a 20-acre plot, has been impressively landscaped by the renowned Japanese-American artist, Isamu Noguchi. In the garden cf semicircular earth-and-stone embankments is a 100-piece sculpture collection, much of it donated by Mr. Rose. The outdoor sculpture garden, on successive pebbled slopes, houses both classical and modern European, American, and Israeli works—Rodin, Zorach, Henry Moore, Picasso, Maillol, and Channa Orloff.

Head toward the edge of the hill at the end of the sculpture park for a magnificent 180° panoramic view: from right to left, the Parliament and government buildings, the university, and the hills directly ahead; and to the left, the levels of cypress, golden and pink stone, rich brown slopes. All the hues of Jerusalem's stone are seen from here, a spectrum of browns, cream shades, and whites.

Then there's the Shrine of the Book, with its distinctive onion-shaped top, contoured to resemble—in 275,000 glazed white bricks—the jar covers in which the Dead Sea Scrolls were discovered. In addition to housing the prized Dead Sea Scrolls and the Bar Kokhba letters, the underground shrine is the exhibition site for many additional finds from Masada.

Specifically, the Shrine of the Book exhibits the scrolls and documents discovered at three sites at the Dead Sea: Qumran Cave (2nd century B.C. to A.D. 71), the Nahal Hever Cave (post-135 A.D.), and Masada (2nd century B.C. to A.D. 73). The Shrine is constructed inside like a series of underground caves; the entrance corridor displays letters in Aramaic telling of real estate leases 2,000 years back. There's also a marriage contract, dated April 5, 128 A.D. In the circular underground chamber are the shreds of parchments from Leviticus, Psalms, and Isaiah. The best-known exhibit here is the Dead Sea Scroll, "The War of the Sons of Light Against the Sons of Darkness." Down the steps are rare finds from the Bar Kokhba period, including a perfect large glass plate, nearly intact baskets, tools, utensils, vessels.

Museum hours are Sunday, Monday, Wednesday, and Thursday from 10 a.m. to 5 p.m. The main building is open on Tuesday from 4 to 10 p.m. (nighttime, when the buildings are illuminated, is an excellent time to visit). There are tours daily at 11 a.m. The Billy Rose Garden and the Shrine of the Book are also open on Tuesday from 10 a.m. to 10 p.m. On Friday, Saturday, eve of holidays, and holidays, the museum is open from 10 a.m. to 2 p.m. (If you go on a Saturday or holiday, you have to buy your tickets ahead of time from the museum, a local ticket agent, or your hotel.) Entry costs about NIS3 ($2), or NIS5 ($3.35) if you want to see the Shrine of the Book as well.

And More Museums

L. A. Mayer Memorial Museum of Islamic Art, 2 Hapalmach St. (tel. 02-661-291), is another Jerusalem museum worth visiting. The name explains the types of exhibitions. Admission costs NIS3 ($2), less for students and children. Open Sunday through Thursday from 10 a.m. to 1 p.m. and 3:30 to 6 p.m., plus Saturday and holiday eves from 10 a.m. to 1 p.m.

In the courtyard of the Society for the Protection of Nature in Israel (SPNI), at 13 Heleni Ha-Malka St. (tel. 02-249-568), is an **Agricultural Museum.** Displays demonstrate agricultural methods from ancient times. The building, the Sergei Hostel, itself is interesting, having been constructed to house Russian Orthodox pilgrims in the days of the czars.

The **Museum of Natural History,** 6 Mohilever St. (tel. 02-631-116), displays local flora and fauna; closed in August.

The **Musical Instrument Museum,** at the Rubin Academy of Music on Smolenskin Street, holds a collection of ancient and modern instruments from all over the world.

The **Taxation Museum,** 32 Agron St. (tel. 02-228-978), is the second museum of its kind in the world devoted entirely to aspects of taxation and collection in ancient Israel, during the diaspora and in Israel today.

Ammunition Hill Memorial and Museum (tel. 02-828-442), at the top of Givat Ha-Tachmoshet (Ammunition Hill), between Sheikh Jarrah and Ramot Eshkol, is dedicated to the reunification of Jerusalem and the Six-Day War. Its setting is the scene of the fiercest fighting in the city. You can walk through bunkers and trenches, and five exhibition halls display weapons used in the war, maps, battle plans, and suchlike. Take bus 4, 9, 25, 28, 39 or 99. Open Sunday through Friday from 9 a.m. to 4 p.m.; closed Saturday.

The **Pontifical Biblical Institute,** 3 Paul Botta St. (tel. 02-222-843), near the King David Hotel, houses a rich archeological collection, including an Egyptian mummy; by appointment only.

Mount Herzl

Take bus 17, 17a, 18, 20, 21, 23, 24, 26, 27, 39, 40, or 99 to Herzl Boulevard, and soon you'll come to Mount Herzl, the resting place of Theodore Herzl, prophet and visionary, who predicted and worked for the founding of Israel 40 years prior to World War I. Mount Herzl is located at the end of the Bet Ha-Kerem section. Down the road from the Herzl cemetery, inside an entrance made of slabs of orange Jerusalem stone, is a military cemetery where thousands of Israeli men and women who died in battle are interred. Particularly stirring is the memorial to the sailors who died at sea. Tablets on the floor at a pool of water quote Psalm 69: "I will bring my people from the depth of the sea."

In the **Mount Herzl Cemetery,** a large black monolith marks Herzl's interment. Herzl's wife and his parents are buried there too.

Facing Yad Vashem is the final resting place of Vladimir Jabotinsky and his wife. After years of controversy, the body of Jabotinsky, revisionist philosopher, was moved here from abroad.

The **Herzl Museum** (tel. 02-531-108) is on the grounds, and entrance is free (same for the park). April through October, the park is open from 8 a.m. to 6:45 p.m. daily; museum hours are 9 a.m. to 6:45 p.m. daily, on Friday to 1 p.m.;

closed Saturday. The park and museum close at 5 p.m. during the winter. The museum has a replica of Herzl's Vienna study with his own library and furniture.

Yad Vashem Memorial

Down the road from Mount Herzl is a ridge called **Har Ha-Zikaron** (Mount of Remembrance), dedicated to the six million Jews murdered by the Nazis. The **Avenue of the Righteous Among the Nations,** lined with trees in tribute to non-Jews who helped save Jewish lives during the Nazi era, leads into the memorial.

In all the world there is no more terrifying a memorial than the massive structure atop this hill. Here the Israelis have constructed a rectangular building whose lower walls are formed out of mammoth, uncut boulders. The heavy entrance gate by David Polombo is an abstract tapestry of jagged, twisted steel, an anguished, agonizing pattern of shapes. Inside is a huge stone room, like a crypt, where flames in the middle shed an eerie light over the plaques on the floor: Bergen-Belsen, Auschwitz, Dachau. . . . In here, there is no poetry or weeping or sermonizing. The almost hallucinatory mood captured in the design and architecture of the memorial is unbelievably moving.

The building to the left has a permanent exhibition of photographs and effects relating to the slaughter of World War II, a period forever inscribed in history as the Holocaust. Other exhibits include an **art museum,** containing works made under the harshest conditions imaginable, and the **Hall of Names** which contains over three million pages of testimony, the names, photographs, and personal details of those who perished in the Holocaust.

On the crest of the western slope of the Mount of Remembrance stands a 20-foot-high monument dedicated to the 1½ million Jewish soldiers among the allied forces, partisans, and ghetto fighters.

Below the monument one can see the excavations for the **Valley of the Destroyed Communities,** commemorating the 5,000 European Jewish communities that disappeared during World War II.

Across the hill is an **archive building,** probably the most complete library and permanent testimony to that awful time. Yad Vashem (tel. 02-531-202) is open from 9 a.m. to 5 p.m., on Friday till 1:45 p.m.; closed Saturday. Any of the buses to aforementioned Mount Herzl will bring you here.

Ein Kerem

From Herzl Boulevard, the route to the Hadassah Medical Center, you'll have a beautiful view of this enchanting village, nestled on a hillside of tall cypress and olive groves and scattered through with monasteries and Christian holy places. Ein Kerem is the birthplace of John the Baptist, as well as the place where Mary visited Zachariah and Elizabeth before Jesus was born. A Stone Age spring in the village is called **Mary's Well,** or the Virgin's Fountain, and most churches have displays of archeological finds. The **Church of St. John** and the **Church of the Visitation** are especially worth seeing.

There are several good restaurants here, and an interesting art gallery named Bet Ma'yan (operated by an art colony) in an old Arab house right next to Mary's Well. Bus 17 goes directly to Ein Kerem.

Absalom's (Stalactite) Cave

A favorite excursion for tour bus groups is to Absalom's Cave (tel. 02-911-117), 20 km (12 miles) west of Jerusalem along the road out of Ein Kerem. In a region of limestone, it's not surprising that there should be caves filled with awesome geological formations. Being so close to Jerusalem, neither is it surprising that the cave should also be filled with tourists. Yet the scenery along the road from Ein Kerem to the moshav of Nes Harim, a mile from the cave, is by itself worth the pleasant excursion.

Egged will take you on a tour to the cave and nearby sights for $15, or you can take a bus from the Central Bus Station to Nes Harim for a fraction of that.

Hadassah Medical Center

The largest medical center in the Middle East, the $30-million Hadassah Hebrew University Medical Center stands on a hilltop several miles from downtown Jerusalem. Take bus 19 or 27 from Jaffa Gate, Jaffa Road, Agron Street, King George V Avenue, or Bezalel Street.

This project contains a medical school, nursing school, hospital, dental and pharmacy schools, and various laboratory buildings. Hadassah, the Women's Zionist Organization of America, was the sponsor here, and in the hospital's synagogue is displayed the organization's most important acquisition: Chagall's 12 exquisite small stained-glass windows depicting the 12 tribes of Israel. Medical Center tours, including a look at the Chagall windows, leave at 8:30, 9:30, 10:30, 11:30 a.m. and 12:30 p.m.; Friday tours are at 9:30, 10:30, and 11:30 a.m. No tours on Saturday or holidays. Half-day tours of all projects cost NIS15 ($10) per person and are by reservation: telephone 02-416-333 at least a day in advance.

Just want to grab a quick look at the Chagall windows? Well, plan to arrive at the synagogue between 2 and 3:45 p.m. Sunday through Thursday, when it's open to the public without need of a tour. Admission costs NIS1.50 ($1), less for students.

To better accommodate the 140,000 annual visitors to the hospital, the **Tannenbaum Tourist Center** was opened in 1984. It has a cafeteria and provides all necessary information on hospital facilities, tours, etc.

Kennedy Memorial

About seven miles from downtown Jerusalem, in the same general direction of Hadassah Medical Center, **Yad Kennedy** is reached by following the winding mountain roads out past the Aminadav Moshav. Opened in May 1966, the 60-foot-high poured-concrete memorial is designed in the shape of a cut tree trunk, symbolizing the president whose life was cut short in its prime. Inside it is virtually barren—an eternal flame in the center of the floor, a shaft of light from an opening in the roof illuminating a bust of the late president. Said to be visible on a clear day from Tel Aviv, 40 miles away, the mountaintop memorial is encircled by 51 columns, each bearing the emblem of a state of the Union, plus the District of Columbia. The city bus 20 stops quite a distance away. Be prepared to take a cab and have the driver wait.

To the west is the village of **Batir,** site of a stronghold that witnessed the last Jewish revolt against the Romans, in A.D. 135, by Bar Kokhba. The view from the parking lot is breathtaking—a never-ending succession of mountains and valleys. In one valley you can see the railroad tracks running from Jerusalem to Tel Aviv.

The monument and adjoining picnic grounds are part of the **John F. Kennedy Peace Forest.**

THOSE WHO "TOURED" BEFORE YOU: In Jerusalem, as throughout most of Israel, if you give your imagination some rein, you can feel that peculiar identification with history, the kinship with thousands of travelers from myriad cultures who have passed this way over the past 4,000 years.

In biblical times the Hebrew farmers trudged up this road on the agricultural holidays to bring their offerings to the Holy City. The Pharaoh's legions and Roman Centurions came this way, as did Crusader forces and armies of pilgrims —Christian, Jewish, and Muslim.

Traveling to Jerusalem has always been colorful. In the 12th century a tourist to Jerusalem had to hire mercenaries to protect him on the trip, since the area was rife with bands of robbers who made their living by preying on the pilgrims. The pilgrim caravans were supervised by guides equipped with maces and spears and shields. Then came the Arab occupants who charged enormous road taxes to the weary pilgrims for the right to use the pass. In the 19th century Austrian Emperor Franz Josef made the trip, and he was the first man ever to use a carriage to do so. And then, during the Ottoman period in 1908, an American tourist came, bringing a motor car with him, and after the sensation he created, mechanized transport became the rule of thumb. The pilgrimage to Jerusalem forever lost some of its uniqueness, but now many more people can make the trip.

Great ones for keeping alive the biblical traditions of years gone by, the Israelis have instituted an "**Aliya le'Regel**" (walking pilgrimage) to Jerusalem, which takes place each year around Passover/Easter and Succoth time. Thousands participate, and during this three-day excursion period you can see them walking along this road just as their ancestors did—youngsters from the kibbutzim, columns of paratroopers, female soldiers, athletic middle-aged residents who've made the hike for years, and footsore tourists who like the drama of the thing and become swept up in the fervor attached to this march. If you are in Israel in the spring around Passover time or in the autumn during Succoth, do catch this event. (Overseas visitors need pay no registration fee and are guests of the March Command for all meals, camp accommodations, and evening programs during the march. To register, contact the Government Tourist Office.) And if walking up and down hills isn't your idea of fun, then be sure to catch the procession as it comes into Jerusalem. Pick out a spot near Jaffa Gate and watch them strut by.

AND NOW, A SWIM: You have a choice of many pools if you want to take a dip in Jerusalem on a summer's day. One of the cheapest (but most crowded) is the **Jerusalem public pool,** 43 Emek Refaim St. (tel. 02-632-042). On Saturday and holidays, when Israeli's pack the pools, the price goes up. Open from 8 a.m. to 5 p.m.

The **Bet Tailor,** on Zangwil Street in Kiryat Yovel (tel. 02-414-362), is open from 8 a.m. to 4:30 p.m. Take bus 18.

During the week you can use the pool at the **YMCA Aelia Capitolina Hotel** on Nablus Road (tel. 02-282-375), payment allowing for a 45-minute swim.

Outside Jerusalem, in the Judean hills, **Kibbutz Shoresh** (tel. 02-533-477) has built a pool high on a hilltop; it's endowed with such country-club amenities as lounge chairs, a lifeguard, and a snackbar. From April 29 to October 10 the pool, called Shoresh, is open from 8 a.m. to 5 p.m. It's rarely crowded and the scenery is marvelous. Buses 65 and 401 leave from the Central Bus Station.

A handsomely situated pool is at **Kibbutz Ma'ale Ha-Hamisha** (tel. 02-539-872), out in the Judean Hills. It's in the middle of a pine forest and you can picnic in the shade of the tall trees. Admission on Saturday and holidays is for members only. Buses 63 and 403 from the central station.

Last, don't forget the pool at **Kibbutz Ramat Rachel** (tel. 02-715-711). The admission allows you to use both the pool and the tennis courts.

The **Turkish Bath** (Ha-Hamam Ha-Turki), 36 Yehezkel (tel. 02-287-542; buses 4, 9, 25, and 35), was built by the Bukharian Jews over 90 years ago as one of their first endeavors upon arriving in Jerusalem. It was designed according to the ideas of typical Roman Empire bathhouses. You have a choice of hot, tepid, or cold pools, a steam room, or the dry-heat sauna. One of the rooms has three slabs of marble, each a different temperature, and they are believed to be beneficial for many sorts of aches and pains. After you've tried them all, head for a "resting room," where you may relax upon colored cushions and sip coffee and imagine yourself in a harem of long ago. Entrance is a few dollars; a visit to the hairdresser or a massage are additional options; you can also get soap, or rent a robe, towels, or hair dryer. There's a snackbar on the premises. Hours for the baths are, not surprisingly, according to gender: for men, the baths are open Sunday, Tuesday, and Thursday from 11 a.m. to 11 p.m. and on Friday from 10 a.m. to 3 p.m. For women, the hours are Monday and Wednesday from 11 a.m. to 11 p.m.

6. Jerusalem's Nightlife

At night it's almost possible to forget that Jerusalem is the Holy City—almost. Although there are plenty of cinemas, cozy bars, theaters, nightclubs, and even a few discos, Jerusalemites are somehow always conscious that this is sacred ground. The variety of nighttime activity, the volume level, the naughtiness—in none of these can Jerusalem even come close to her seacoast sister Tel Aviv. Perhaps that's as it should be.

Never fear. You'll find a lot to do at night here, and it needn't be expensive at all.

INFORMATION: By all means, be sure to buy the *Jerusalem Post* on Friday morning, for the thick Friday edition of the paper carries within it the magazine section. The magazine contains an exhaustive list of things going on in the week to come: television and radio schedules, movie programs, concerts, theater offerings, special events. If it's not Friday yet and you're in need of info, the daily edition of the *Post* still has a lot to offer.

Another excellent source of information is the flyer "Events in the Jerusalem Region," prepared by the Tourist Office and handed out for free at the office at 24 King George V Ave. (corner of Hillel), in hotel lobbies, airline offices, travel agencies, etc. There's a new edition of "Events" each week.

Finally, should you be at a loss for something to do right now, this evening, dial 02-241-197 after 6 p.m. and a recorded message will outline some of tonight's best opportunities—in English.

THEATER: The boldly modern **Jerusalem Theater**, 20 David Marcus St. (tel. 02-667-167), corner of Chopin (in the Rehavia district near the President's House), opened its doors in 1975. Original Israeli plays and Hebrew translations of foreign classics and modern works are performed in the theater's main hall; visiting troupes also use the main hall for performances in foreign languages. The theater's Auditorium is the home of the Jerusalem Symphony Orchestra and the Israel Chamber Ensemble. (The Israel Philharmonic Orchestra performs in Binyane Ha-Uma, the convention center near the Central Bus Station.)

Jerusalem's other prominent theater is the antithesis of the first. The **Khan** (tel. 02-718-281) is an ancient Ottoman Turkish caravanserai, a sort of Middle Eastern motel where caravans could house their men, animals, and goods safe from marauders. Refurbished and opened in 1968, the Khan complex has a theater, a café-restaurant, a bar (tel. 02-718-283) for drinks, dancing, and music, and the Khan Club. At the club, one pays a high admission charge to see the nightly show (at 10 p.m.) of Israeli folksingers, lively traditional dances, and yourselves (there's always a hearty sing-along). Have reservations.

By the way, performances at the theater are usually in Hebrew, but there are often chamber music concerts and other cultural events.

The atmosphere at the Khan truly harks back to Turkish times: rough-walled, candlelit in many places. After its days hosting camel caravans, the Khan became a beer garden for the German Knights Templar in the 19th century. During the British Mandate it was used as an ammunition depot, and after the British withdrawal as a carpenter's shop.

The Khan is almost across from Jerusalem's railway station in David Remez Square. You can walk there from King David Street. Start from the YMCA and King David Hotel, and simply head southeast, straight through Plumer Square and toward the Scottish castle (St. Andrew's Church and Hospice) on the hill ahead. The Khan is at the foot of the hill. By bus, catch a no. 4, 7, 8, 10, or 14 anywhere along King George V Avenue going south (away from Jaffa Road).

For English-language theater, check what's on at the **Jerusalem Hilton** (tel. 02-536-151), which often hosts small theatrical presentations open to the public. The Hilton is next to Binyane Ha-Uma.

CONCERTS:
The Jerusalem Theater, as mentioned above, plays host to the **Jerusalem Symphony Orchestra,** and the Khan to chamber music concerts. When the **Israel Philharmonic** comes to town it performs in the convention center, Binyane Ha-Uma, near the Central Bus Station and the Jerusalem Hilton.

Lots of other locations are used for concerts: the **YMCA,** on King David Street (tel. 02-227-111); **Pargod,** at 94 Bezalel St. (tel. 02-231-765); **Tzavta,** at 38 King George V Ave. (tel. 02-227-621); **Wise Auditorium** at Hebrew University; the Hilton's **Little Theatre;** and the **Anglican School** at 82 Ha-Nevi'im (Prophets) St. Check the *Jerusalem Post* for details of what's going on.

CINEMA:
Israelis are inveterate movie-goers. The hottest flicks in Europe and the States usually show up here very soon after release, almost always in the original language, with Hebrew subtitles. This goes for cinemas in West Jerusalem only; in the eastern part of the city, the films come mostly from Arab countries. They're in the original language too—Arabic, without subtitles.

West Jerusalem's cinemas are scattered throughout the city. Although the *Post* carries notices of current film offerings, the notices never carry addresses or telephone numbers of the movie houses. Here's a list of the most prominent cinemas, with addresses, locations, and phone numbers:

Cinema 1 (tel. 02-415-067), in Kiryat Ha-Yovel, out past Mount Herzl on the way to Hadassah Medical Center. Catch bus 18 on King David Street, in Zahal Square, or along Jaffa Road. The no. 18 runs in a circular route, so it doesn't matter which direction you take.

Cinematheque (see below).

Eden, 5 Agrippas St. (tel. 02-223-829), half a block off King George V Avenue on the left.

Edison, 14 Yeshayahu St. (tel. 02-224-036); from the intersection of King George V Avenue and Jaffa Road, walk up Strauss Street (the northern continuation of King George), turn left on Ha-Nevi'im, then right on Yeshayahu.

Habira, 19 Shamai St. (tel. 02-232-366); Shamai is one block southeast of Ben-Yehuda Street, and roughly parallel to it.

Kfir, 97 Jaffa Rd. (tel. 02-242-523), in the Klal Building (called Merkez Klal). You won't see a street number; ask any passerby.

Orna, 19 Hillel St. (tel. 02-224-733), near the Jerusalem Tower Hotel.

Or-Gil, 18 Hillel St. (tel. 02-234-176), near the Jerusalem Tower Hotel.

Orion, along an alley between Hillel and Shammai Streets (tel. 02-222-914), which is a block southeast of Ben-Yehuda, and roughly parallel to it.

Ron, 1 Rabbi Akiva St., off Hillel (tel. 02-234-704).

Semadar, 4 Lloyd George St. (tel. 02-633-742), in the German Colony just south of the railway station three blocks. Take bus 18 heading east along Jaffa Road or King David Street and get off just after the station (ask the driver). Chances are that other passengers will be going to the same movie.

Besides these movie houses, there are other places that screen films: the Jerusalem Hilton, the King David, the Jerusalem Theatre, the Israel Museum, Tzavta (38 King George V Ave.), etc.—see the notices in the *Post.*

You should know about the **Cinemathèque** (tel. 02-724-131), or Israel Film Archive, Jerusalem. Located in its own building near the railway station, the Cinemathèque is the scene of nightly (and Tuesday and Friday afternoon) screenings of the classics, the experimental, and the arcane. Films are in the original language most times, with Hebrew and (usually) English subtitles.

Members of the Cinemathèque get first grab at seats, but half an hour before screening time the remainder are put on sale to one and all for about NIS3 ($2) each. Pick up the *Jerusalem Post* for a notice of what's on, then follow these directions: Get to the traffic intersection between the railway station and Plumer Square. St. Andrew's Scottish Hospice and Church is right on the hill above you. Now, walk down the slope to the northeast, toward the Old City, and soon you'll come to the Cinemathèque, built into the hillside above the Hebron Road.

CLUBS: Nightclubbing in Jerusalem is not necessarily subdued, although even the lively places offer only good clean fun. All the large hotels have their nightclubs, or you can try a night out at the **Jerusalem of Gold Nightclub** (tel. 02-718-880), in the basement of the Abu Tor Observatory at 5 Ein Rogel St. Folk dancing show begins at 8:30 p.m., the main feature at 9:30. It's not cheap, but the admission price—about NIS20 ($13.35)—includes all the wine or soft drinks you can consume.

DRINKS AND CONVERSATION: The cafés on **Ben-Yehuda Street** are a fine place to see and be seen, meet and be met. Some move tables and chairs out onto the pedestrian portion of the street in fine weather, and nothing could be better.

Another good place to look for action is along **Rivlin Street,** described above under restaurants (West Jerusalem). Parallel to Rivlin is **Salomon Street,** which runs between Zion Square and Hillel Street. Here you'll find a few pubs, including **Champs,** where the volume-level of the music tends to be stratospheric.

Drinks, dinner, conversation, and gallery-going are all combined at the **Jerusalem Artists' House Restaurant and Club,** 12 Shmuel Ha-Nagid St. (tel. 02-232-920), up the hill from the City Tower. An extremely attractive club always filled with witty and interesting types, Jerusalem Artists' House sponsors a host of activities. Drop in for a beer or a drink. It's especially active on Saturday nights, and especially welcoming to foreign tourists (everyone there is very cosmopolitan).

The **American Colony Hotel,** on Nablus Road in East Jerusalem (tel. 02-282-421), has a cozy cellar bar and a continuing series of "Jazz in the Cellar" performances. Check the *Post* for details.

OTHER THINGS TO DO: In summer the Old City becomes quieter in the evening; in wintertime it's virtually deserted after 7 p.m. Taking a stroll along the quiet alleyways, listening to your footsteps echo from the golden stone, pondering the tumult, triumphs, and tribulations that have taken place *right here*—this can turn out to be a highlight of your trip.

An alternative is to take bus 75 from East Jerusalem Bus Station on Suleiman Street and go to the top of the Mount of Olives to watch dusk creep over the city, the lights coming on, and the call to prayer rising from a minaret in nearby Silwan.

During the warmer months, a **Sound and Light show** is featured in the Citadel of David at Jaffa Gate. Check on times and tickets in advance, and then come dressed *much* more warmly than you think necessary. Think: stone fortress, night breezes, sitting rather than walking. You may ignore this warning if you like, and join in the nightly chorus of whispered exclamations, "I never thought it would be this cool at night!"

Chapter III

THE WEST BANK

1. Bethany, Jericho, the Dead Sea, and Qumran
2. Bethlehem
3. Hebron
4. Ramallah, Shechem, Nablus, and Samaria

JERUSALEM IS THE BEST jumping-off point for visits to the majority of West Bank sites described here. Most of them are within an hour's drive of the city. Consequently, you will find few hotels described in this chapter—mainly places to visit, among them the sites that are holiest and most meaningful to Judaism and Christianity. I would recommend that you take a Bible with you on these outings, for in few other places on your trip to Israel will the mountains and cities described in both the Old and New Testaments come alive with such drama. Jesus was born in Bethlehem, Abraham entered the land of Canaan in Samaria, the patriarchs are buried at Hebron, and Mount Gerizim at Shechem looks much the same today as when Joshua described it.

THE WEST BANK TODAY: Many changes have taken place since the Israelis first occupied the West Bank, now designated by Israelis as Judea and Samaria (biblical names). For the first six months after the Six-Day War, all visitors to this area needed military permits, soldiers were everywhere to be seen, hotels were not functioning, and a nighttime curfew was in effect. Now life has become normal again. Hotels are operating in Bethlehem and in the crossroads town of Ramallah; more restaurants have opened in the area. There are Ministry of Tourism offices in Bethlehem and Ramallah. Green-and-white signposts in English guide you to all the major points of interest.

It is still wise, however, to stick to the main roads—the routes are marked clearly—and not wander off by yourself through the hills around Hebron and Nablus. Around Jericho, which is close to the border, be sure to observe carefully the round red sign crossed by a horizontal white bar. That means "No Entry" and broaches no arguments. Don't pass that sign or you may find yourself an unwelcome guest in a military zone.

If there are any changes affecting travel in these parts, you can get details from the tourist offices in Israel. If you have questions or concerns while in the area, stop in any local police station. Another word of caution: Leave politics alone. The future is unclear and the less political the verbiage, the better.

SIGHTS TO EXPECT: The character of this area is different from that of all other parts of the country—make no mistake about it. The landscape is more biblical, the atmosphere more bucolic. Everywhere you drive you will see Arab women walking by the roadside balancing great loads on their heads. Donkeys, urged on by old men or little boys, groan under their burden of olive-wood twigs. In sharp contrast, the most common car you'll see driven by Arabs in the West Bank is a Mercedes-Benz sedan. The reason: The car is assembled locally. From Bethlehem to Hebron and from Ramallah to Nablus, you'll see men in headdress riding in these Mercedes cruisers. Many more women wear the veil in these parts, a custom the Christian Arab women in Nazareth and the Galilee seem to have discarded.

1. Bethany, Jericho, the Dead Sea, and Qumran

GETTING THERE: Various means will get you to the cities and towns in the Jordan Valley.

To Bethany there's even a city **bus**, no. 43, which departs from the municipal bus depot on Nablus Road (Sha'ar Shechem), not to be confused with the East Jerusalem bus station on Sultan Suleiman Street, nearby. Bethany is just on the other side of the Mount of Olives.

No doubt you're going farther than Bethany, however, and for this you must catch a bus from the Central Bus Station on Jaffa Road (tel. 02-521-121). (For more information, see Chapter II on Jerusalem, "Orientation.") Those who plan to head south to the Dead Sea and Qumran will have to catch another bus from Jericho. All this takes time, and it's doubtful you could bus-hop quickly enough to see everything and still make it back to Jerusalem at a decent hour. There are faster ways than bus-hopping, however: read on.

Sheruts run to Jericho from the Damascus Gate taxi stand, and they're considerably faster than the bus—too fast, in some cases. The price is a bit higher, but the time saving is well worth it. It's a good idea to drop by the taxi stand the day before and talk with the drivers about rates and schedules so as to avoid waiting and haggling.

TOURS: **Egged Tours,** 44a Jaffa Rd. in Zion Square (tel. 02-231-604 or 224-198), or at the Central Bus Station, will be glad to sign you up for a half-day tour of Jericho, the Dead Sea, and Qumran. The tour runs every day but Saturday, and costs about $17 per person. Virtually any travel agency in East or West Jerusalem can set you up with a tour to these places at a similar price; the Arab companies even run on Saturday.

BETHANY: On the western slope of the Mount of Olives lies the village of Bethany (*El-Azariya* in Arabic). Its fame comes from the fact that Jesus lodged here with Simon the Leper before that fateful Passover which saw his crucifixion. He also performed one of his most notable miracles here, according to the Gospel of St. John: raising Lazarus, brother of his followers Mary and Martha, from the dead.

Four churches and one mosque have stood on the same site, commemorating the raising of Lazarus. The first was built in the 300s, the second in later Byzantine times, the third by the Crusaders (100s), and the last by the Franciscans in the early 1950s. Traces of the earlier churches, including some nice mosaics, are present in the modern church. The tower is left from a fortified Benedictine monastery built in the 1100s by Queen Melisende, wife of Fulk of Anjou, Crusader king of Jerusalem from 1131 to 1143.

A stairway leads down into the tomb of Lazarus, open from 8 a.m. to 6 p.m. every day, with a lunch break from noon to 2 p.m. Tip the caretaker.

ON THE ROAD TO JERICHO: The trip from Jerusalem to Jericho and the Dead Sea is only a 45-minute ride. You'll soon notice the difference in elevation between Jerusalem's 2,700 feet *above* sea level and Jericho's 1,300 feet *below* sea level.

Take a good look at the hills around Bethany—the arrangement of houses on orange and limestone slopes, the pine groves, the sheep grazing on the hillocks. It's as serene, pastoral, and biblical a landscape as you'll see anywhere in the Holy Land.

A turn in the road here reveals an excellent view of Jerusalem—you'll recognize the Mount of Olives, the Russian church, Mount Scopus, the Augusta Victoria Tower. Then, abruptly, as the turn in the road ends, you're in the wilderness of Judea. The sky here is pale blue; the land sandy and chalky, with patches of sunburnt green scrub and scattered trees. Many Bedouin live here, and though you'll seldom see their tents, you often see the Bedouin with their sheep, goats, and donkeys. The sight of a black-clad Bedouin woman surrounded by a flock of black goats, in sharp contrast with the stark whiteness of the landscape, is startling and timelessly beautiful. Startling, too, are the strange rock patterns wrought by centuries of erosion. One of the loveliest sights to look for: the eternal shepherd leading his flock.

Inn of the Good Samaritan

As the road continues, you'll find yourself surrounded by mountains, but not really the same as the saw-toothed mountains of the Negev. Note the artistry with which road workers have carved passes in the mountains. The walls have been specially contoured to expose the interesting color gradations to best advantage: you see pastel-toned streaks of rose, pink, orange, and soft greens in the rock walls bordering the highway. About halfway along this route a very distinctive pointed mountain appears. As you get closer you'll notice something different about its crest: on it stand the ruins of an old Crusader fortress. Here you'll see signs pointing to side roads on the right and left. To the right, within sight of the main road, is what is known as the Inn of the Good Samaritan, supposedly the site where Jesus' parable of the Good Samaritan took place. What is definitely known is that this site has always been an important roadmark. A Roman road once passed here, as did others even before that, including an ancient caravan route. The present inn is of Turkish construction, some 400 years old, with a large entranceway and huge rooms leading off on either side of it. Each room has arched windows and wall niches (supposedly for fires). The entranceway opens into a huge central courtyard. In the middle of the courtyard is a large circular stone cooking area, and a well so deep the bottom of it can't be seen. There are also stone troughs. Much of what is found in the courtyard is said to date from Roman times, when the site was a military stronghold.

Wadi Kelt

Back on the main road, follow the sign pointing left to the St. George Monastery (Khoziba), where monks live near a spring named Wadi Kelt, whose waters have quenched the thirst of centuries; it once ran through the aqueducts of Herod's time and today continues to irrigate part of Jericho. On the banks of Wadi Kelt are the remains of winter palaces of the Hasmonean and Herodian periods. Much of interest has been uncovered here during archeological digs.

Nebi Musa

Now the main road curves down more steeply, and you soon come upon a Jordanian encampment that was used during the Six-Day War. Within the encampment are several ancient buildings on a site called Nebi Musa—according to Muslim belief, the "Tomb of Moses" (the Bible cites Mount Nebo as Moses's burial place). A right turn off the road here (there are signs pointing to it) will take you to this abandoned city-like cluster of buildings—abandoned, that is, by all but the dead, for all devout Muslims wish to be buried here. The cemetery is a fascinating holy site.

As the drive takes up again, you'll descend into the Jordan Valley, from which you'll make a left off the main highway to go to Jericho. As you travel toward Jericho, you'll notice hundreds of mud huts, once occupied by refugees. Today they are empty, but when occupied after the war, these Jericho camps formed the largest refugee village in Jordan. These desolate camps are quite a contrast to Jericho, which is a blooming, sweet-smelling oasis, so fertile and lush that it seems a miracle in this dry, sun-baked countryside. Underground streams feed the soil here, and the combination of heat, low altitude, and fresh water makes the many tropical plants and fruit grow all year. This year-round paradise is a spot sun-worshippers and vacationers have been coming to for some 4,000 winters.

JERICHO: Jericho is one of the world's oldest cities—some claim it's the oldest. Archeologists have discovered habitations, in several strata, of civilizations that date back 9,000 to 12,000 years. This is the Jericho Joshua conquered, and parts of the walls that came tumbling down are still here. Jericho was the first city captured by the Israelites after their 40 years in the wilderness. The tribes approached it from the other side of the Jordan River, sent in spies, and to the blasts of trumpets blown by priests, the city was attacked and captured. To the east of Jericho is the place where the Israelites crossed the Jordan into the Promised Land.

Orientation

Jericho is not a large town, but it is spread out. Public transportation is minimal, so you'll find yourself walking a mile or two during your visit, or taking a taxi (if you find one).

Coming into town from Jerusalem, you'll first skirt the downtown area, with the **Baladíyah** (see below) and the market, passing along Jaffa Street just to the east of these landmarks. If your bus or sherut continues to head north, stay in it! That way you can cut the walking in half. Heading north, you'll get on **Ein es-Sultan Street.** You'll finally come to a fork in the road. Just along the right-hand road is **Tel es-Sultan,** also called **Tel Jericho,** which is the ruined city of Old Jericho. The left fork goes behind the **Mount of Temptation Restaurant,** and after a kilometer uphill, a sign points left to the **Mount of Temptation** and **Qarantal,** the Greek Orthodox Monastery of the 40 Days.

Caliph Hisham's Palace is about 4 km (2½ miles) along the right fork, past Old Jericho. It would take you about two hours to walk there, visit the site, and walk back to Old Jericho.

Old Jericho

The man-made hillock of **Tel es-Sultan,** or Old Jericho, is not very interesting—at first glance. For century upon century men and women lived here, building defensive walls and houses, discarding refuse, until this "dustbin of history" reached its present impressive height.

Jericho was an old town when Joshua conquered it. Some say the site had been inhabited for 6,000 years before the Israelite victory. Archeologists and geologists, true to their scientific calling, report that Joshua's powerful trumpets may have been materially aided by an earthquake. (When you tour the ruins, don't expect impressive palaces and temples. Remember, we're talking about a Late Bronze Age civilization here!) The National Parks Authority has spruced up the site, added modern facilities, and now charges admission. Old Jericho is open from 7 a.m. to 6 p.m. in summer, slightly shorter hours in winter.

Across the road from Old Jericho is the cool, shady oasis of **Ein es-Sultan,** the Sultan's Spring, also called Elisha's Fountain. The fountain, of course, has its story and its biblical connection. In II Kings 2:19–22 is the story of how the Prophet Elisha cast salts into Jericho's water source and miraculously purified it: the bitter water turned to sweet.

Mount of Temptation

The left fork near Old Jericho leads uphill, the sad panorama of a ruined refugee camp spread out below. At the crest of the hill, a road heads up to the left. As you come to the top of this slope, the golden cliffs of the Mount of Temptation rise before you cross the valley. Hanging precariously to the steep cliff-face is the Greek Orthodox Monastery of the 40 Days (Qarantal; in Arabic, Deir el-Quruntul), built in late Ottoman times (1890s) and open to visitors daily from 8 a.m. to noon and 3 to 4 p.m. According to the Gospels, Jesus went into the wilderness and fasted for 40 days following his baptism by John the Baptist in the waters of Jordan. During this time he was tempted by Satan, who showed him "all the kingdoms of the world" from an "exceeding high mountain." According to legend, that sometimes questionable source, this was the high mountain. It is unquestionably a marvelous view from the top, but you've got to walk to get there, and, as the summit is supposedly off-limits, you may only get as far as the monastery—worthwhile in itself. A cave within the monastery complex is said to have been Jesus' wilderness home during the ordeal. The monastery is open to visitors every day except Sunday.

Caliph Hisham's Palace

Proof that Jericho was a popular wintering place for royalty is right before your eyes at the ruins of Caliph Hisham's magnificent palace, not far from Old Jericho. Take the right fork at the northern end of Ein es-Sultan Street, and pass between Old Jericho and Elisha's Fountain, and after 2½ km (1½ miles) you'll come to a sign pointing toward Hisham's Palace. Turn right, as the sign indicates, and follow the little road 1½ km (a mile) to the ruins.

The palace is a fantastic blend of Romanesque and Arabic architecture and mosaics. Be sure to see the several good groups of mosaic work: in the bath-house and the guest hall particularly (climb the stairs behind the guest hall, which take you inside for a better view). When you get back to Jerusalem, visit the Rockefeller Museum, where you can see the best of the carved stone and stucco work from this palace, plus a model of the entire site.

Archeologists place Hisham's Palace in the Omayyad Dynasty of the 7th and 8th centuries, and inscriptions show it was built in A.D. 724 as a winter resort. Unfortunately, it was destroyed soon after by an earthquake (Hisham never even set foot in it!), but today is worth seeing for the many well-preserved bathhouse structures, heating systems, pools, and sauna-like chambers. The pillars and stone carvings are elegant, and one magnificent mosaic depicts two gazelles feeding under a pomegranate tree, while a lion feeds on a third gazelle. Admission to the site, which is now under the jurisdiction of the National Parks Authority, is slightly over a dollar for adults, less than half that much for children and students. Outside the palace, you can buy cool drinks; inside, near the museum area, is an electric water cooler.

Hours are the same as at other National Parks sites: 8 a.m. to 5 p.m. (to 4 p.m. on Friday) in summer; closing is an hour earlier in winter.

Lunch in Jericho

Jericho has several cafés, with sign names in Arabic and Hebrew, where you can get refreshments or full meals at lunchtime. The cost is low, and the meals are strictly local. I found that the most enjoyable way to lunch downtown is to take a walk around the **Municipality** (ask for the **"Baladíyah"**—it looks like Jericho's version of Courthouse Square, U.S.A.), stopping in at the shops lining its sides. There are loads of fresh vegetables and fruits for sale here, as are inedible but fun-to-look-at items such as cooking utensils, shoes, sacks of dried tobacco, and soaps. At an indoor/outdoor bakery you can get two enormous round rolls—like big bagels with sesame seeds—which you can take to a nearby merchant, who will sell you a Coke and let you sit on his low stools while you munch and sip. The entire transaction will cost you about a dollar.

Perhaps the most convenient spot for lunch is the **Mount of Temptation Restaurant** (tel. 02-922-659), right next to Old Jericho at the fork in the road—you can't miss it. The prices are not bad, even for a place right in the midst of the tourist crush: NIS6 ($4) will buy you filling portions of salads and hors d'oeuvres; for NIS9 ($6) you can fill up on meat dishes, with free seconds. A large platter mixing generous portions of all these things costs only NIS11 ($7.35). There are other restaurants right next door, but can you resist a restaurant named "temptation"?

Halfway between the center of town and Old Jericho are numerous garden restaurants lining both sides of the road. Their fortunes, and the quality of food and service, rise and fall with the passing tourist tides. Lunch here can be very pleasant, well away from the crush next to the Old Jericho site. Pick the restaurant that looks most active, and this should assure fresh supplies and a good variety of dishes.

TO THE DEAD SEA AND QUMRAN: Buses 421, 444, 486, and 966 will take you to Qumran from Egged's Central Bus Station in Jerusalem. Otherwise, head back through Jericho to the main road and continue the southeasterly descent, following the signs to Qumran and Ein Gedi. En route, in the distance, is a row of dark trees along the Jordan River. The building in front of them is the Abyssinian-style **Monastery of John the Baptist,** built on the spot where John the Baptist is said to have baptized Jesus. You're now in the Jordan Valley, and here the land is flat, with sprinklings of shrubbery and interesting erosion formations.

After turning onto the road running along the Dead Sea in the direction of Qumran, you'll see buildings scattered between the road and sea; these were once Jordanian military encampments.

As you drive by you'll of course notice how extremely still the Dead Sea is. It's like this most of the year, but when there's a storm, especially one with a south wind, the sea becomes wild and very dangerous. The mountains along this stretch are sand-colored with black-hued, fierce-looking peaks. When the mountains turn to a reddish hue, you're near the **Qumran Caves.** A side road leads up to the **Qumran Village,** where the Dead Sea Scrolls were found in a cave in 1947 by a Bedouin shepherd boy.

Qumran

Archeological finds have indicated that this area was first settled in the 8th century B.C. and that those who wrote the scrolls lived here around the end of the 2nd century B.C. It appears the place was deserted during Herod's reign (37–4 B.C.), but resettled soon afterward by members of the same sect, usually called the Essenes. The Romans conquered the area during the A.D. 66–70 wars, and it's been largely deserted since then. Today, though, many people visit the area for various reasons. Kibbutzniks love to bring their children here to show them "the world's oldest kibbutz" (so-called because here the Essenes evidently lived a collective community life). It's said that the historian Josephus Flauvius lived in the area for three years. It's also been speculated that the idea of monastic celibacy originated here with a certain group of Essenes who believed in devoting their entire lives to divine study and work.

The excavated Essene settlement is a rather small-scale outdoor museum of trenches, pottery sheds, step-down baths, cisterns, bakery sites, and cemetery plots. You can see all the excavations from the top of the village tower. Near the ruins are the caves where the first scrolls were found. High above, in the mountains, are more caves.

Since 1967 the Qumran site has been all fixed up by the National Parks Authority and now has a modern air-conditioned snackbar.

Einot Zuqim
Three kilometers south lies Einot Zuqim, or Ein Feshcha. If you go on a Saturday you'll have to fight half of Jerusalem for elbow room. But on a weekday this popular **swimming** place receives much less traffic. There are three pools for children only. By noon, the pools can be murky, and you may find an occasional fish or two joining you. So if the pools find little favor in your eyes, walk on to the sandy, clean beach nearby, where you can dip in the Dead Sea. Admission fee to the area includes the cost of a shower after your swim and a storage bag for your clothes. On the beach you'll also find shady shelters and a bungalow clinic. It may surprise you to learn that enough people get ill enough here to justify this clinic, which is staffed by two nurses. The problems almost always come from overexposure to the sun. So be smart and protect yourself— drink as much as you can, keep your head covered, and don't stay in the sun too long! Also, try to avoid all pools, and the area in general, between noon and 3 p.m. The heat is murderous during those hours all year long, although it's far worse in summer.

If you swim in the Dead Sea, please be kind to yourself—wear shoes to protect your feet from the sharp stones that cover the beach and shore; don't let the water get in your eyes or touch your sunburn because the salt will really smart. If you have any scrapes, insect bites, or recently shaved areas, expect them to tingle in the salty water, but remember that it's healing rather than harmful. When you get out, hot showers are available to wash off the thin residue of minerals and oils from your body. Local folk, by the way, don't bathe till bedtime in order to get all possible benefits from the water's richness. Also, make certain to rinse your bathing suit in fresh water.

The Nature Reserves Authority has outfitted the springs with dressing rooms, rest rooms, and a buffet eatery that also sells postcards and souvenirs. Einot Zuqim is open from 8 a.m. to 3 p.m. in the winter, to 4 p.m. in the summer.

From here, it's only 51 km (31 miles) to Masada, with Ein Gedi 30 km (18 miles) en route, along the sea-skirting road. From there, you could travel on to Sodom and the fast highway to Eilat, or to Arad and Beersheba and then on to the central, but slower, highway to Eilat. See Chapter VIII, "The Dead Sea and the Negev," for details.

2. Bethlehem

ON THE ROAD TO BETHLEHEM: To reach Bethlehem, which is only seven miles south of Jerusalem, you can take the Arab bus 22 (East Jerusalem bus station; 50 agorot, 35¢) or Egged bus 34 or 44 (Nablus Road bus depot); or take a 20-minute drive in a sherut (leaving from Damascus Gate); or drive out in

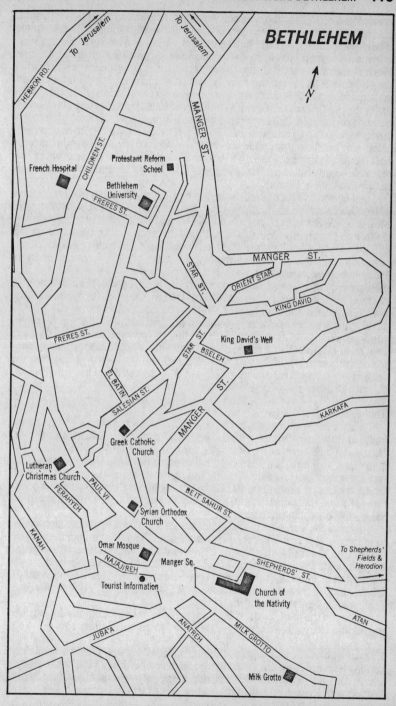

your rented car. Then, too, you can walk it, as pilgrims do yearly at Christmas. If you have the time, the latter course is very interesting though the heavy traffic is bothersome. It should take between 2 and 2½ hours. Head out past the Jerusalem railway station at Abu Tor, and simply keep going straight on Derekh Hevron, the main road near the Talpiot section, past Jerusalem's new industrial area on your right. From there on the landscape changes. Small boys ride past you on donkeys, and farmers work in the fields on either side of the road. Eventually the road passes the Greek Monastery of Elias, then past an old two-story building on the right that once was a hospital. From here, take a look left to the tallest mountain, the one with a flat top—that's the Herodion. The road takes a sharp turn here; olive trees line the right now, and the low hills beyond the trees host the Arab village of Bet Jallah (biblical Gelo), birthplace of the prophet Nathan. Now you're at the northern edge of Bethlehem (the biblical name of this road is Bethlehem Efrata).

An alternative road, for drivers, totaling 20 km (11 miles) from Jerusalem to Bethlehem, is even more fascinating than the walk. This road starts from the Mount of Olives, cuts through Sur Baheer, and winds its way in hilly curves down into the Hebron Valley. As the road descends, notice the caves on the hillside around you. They are inhabited—and have been for centuries. Some cave entrances are covered by flapping blankets, some by arrangements of bramble bushes, others by a door. Apart from farmers, Christian hermits and monks have lived in these caves down through the centuries. The road leads up to the U.N. headquarters, atop the Hill of the Evil Counsel, then joins another road at Mar Elias and continues on to Rachel's Tomb.

By the way, near Rachel's Tomb on the Jerusalem–Bethlehem highway, you'll see a sign bearing the legend "Herodion, 15 km" and pointing to the east. *Don't take this road!* It's a perilous one-laner which qualifies as the longest continuous refuse dump in the Holy Land. At its end you'll find yourself on the eastern outskirts of Bethlehem, where you'd be anyway if you had simply come through Bethlehem.

Rachel's Tomb

This unprepossessing little shrine, just past a bus stop, is a low rectangular building with clean Turkish lines and dome, built in 1860 by Moses Montefiore. Rachel, wife of Jacob and mother of Joseph, is revered by Muslims, Jews, and Christians. (Men need a head covering to enter the shrine, by the way.) The outer room is empty; the inner room, the cupola, contains the tomb of Rachel, where dozens of women are usually seen praying and weeping. You can visit Sunday through Thursday from 8 a.m. to 5 p.m. (till 6 p.m. in summer), on Friday to 1 p.m.; closed Saturday.

Across the street from the tomb are several shops for souvenirs, crafts, arts, rugs, and religious items. Just past the tomb, you'll see an open courtyard circled by a low wall with a few olive trees and a few small houses rising behind another wall. Take a long look at the latter, almost unnoticeable in this ramshackle area. The stones there are part of a water pipe made 2,000 years ago. Inside, the wall is hollow, and once conducted water from King Solomon's Pools (not far from here) to Jerusalem.

Back on the road, take the left-hand fork just ahead and continue past olive groves and vineyards—another 1½ miles and you are in Bethlehem.

IN BETHLEHEM: Bethlehem is the birthplace of Jesus. Pilgrims have been coming here to see the traditional cave and manger of Jesus' birth for 16 centuries. In the Old Testament, Bethlehem is mentioned several times, first in connection with Rachel, who died there after giving birth to Benjamin, her second and Jacob's 12th son. Bethlehem was also the place where Ruth, the Moabite girl, married Boaz in one of history's most famous love stories. Joseph visited Bethlehem. David, a descendent of Ruth and Boaz, was born in Bethlehem and tended his sheep in the hills of Judea. From Bethlehem he went out to fight Goliath; later he was summoned from Bethlehem by Samuel to become king of Judah.

To Israelis, Bethlehem is Bet Lechem, "house of bread"; to Arabs, Bet Lahm, "house of meat."

Your bus, sherut, or taxi will take you to the throbbing heart of downtown Bethlehem—**Manger Square.** No doubt it goes back to Jesus' time as the center of town where the principal inns were located. Even today it boasts many hotels and restaurants, banks, shops, and offices. Manger Square is not particularly attractive, filled as it is with parked cars, buses, tours, and tour groups. Make your way to the great heap of stone east of the square, for that is the Church of the Nativity.

Bethlehem at Christmas

There are special telephone booths for tourists to phone Christmas greetings home with the bells of Bethlehem pealing in the background. . . . Restaurants and coffeehouses stay open all night during Christmas season, and some banks operate until midnight. . . . Rates in Bethlehem, Nazareth, and even some Jerusalem hotels, go up during the holiday period. Be sure of your accommodations before you arrive. . . . Weather gets very cold, especially at night—it might even snow. . . . *Most important:* Admission to Bethlehem on Christmas Eve is usually restricted to tourists holding special tickets; these can be obtained free from the I.G.T.O. offices in Jerusalem, Tel Aviv, and Haifa, or on December 24, from the Ben-Gurion Airport.

By the way, there are actually three Christmases celebrated in Bethlehem: Catholics and Protestants hold their services on December 24 and 25, the Orthodox churches on January 6, and the Armenians on January 17 and 18.

Church of the Nativity

This is the principal shrine of Bethlehem, a fortress-like structure facing the paved expanse of Manger Square. On Manger Square, by the way, you'll find official guides, working in rotation, who will offer their services for a fee of about $3. Hire one if you wish to see the shrine in every detail.

You enter the famed church—the oldest in the country—through a doorway so low that you have to bend over to go through it. Legend has it that the doorway was made that small to prevent the unbelievers from riding into the church on horseback. It does make you pause for a moment to bow and show reverence . . . perhaps another motive.

The basilica of the church is divided into five naves by four rows of pinkish Corinthian pillars. As the Church stands on its disciples, so the building is supported by its pillars, and every pillar bears the picture of an apostle. Several dozen gilded lamp fixtures hang from the rafter-like oaken ceiling. The floor is stone and wood, with occasional trap-door openings that reveal the original mosaic floor beneath. Up front, beyond a magnificent silver-and-gold chandelier, is the Altar of the Nativity, equally ornate with gold and silver decoration. The Greek Orthodox occupy the area to the right of the altar, the Armenian denomination the area to the left. Armenian, Greek, and Franciscan priests are responsible for the care and preservation of the church.

On either side of the altar, narrow stone staircases lead underneath to the manger, scene of Christ's birth. Simply lit by hanging lights, the grotto is in the wall of the cave, marked by a silver star.

Don't be afraid to poke around a bit. For instance, if you find your way to the grand, shiny Franciscan church on the northern edge of the Church of the Nativity, you'll see a small stairway on the right at the back of the nave. Descend. Here is a maze of rock-hewn rooms and chambers, part of which is a portion of the original stable where Jesus was born. Later used as catacombs for martyred innocents, the stable rooms here look much more "authentic" than the marble-clad portion under Greek Orthodox control.

Also down beneath the church is a cave-like chamber where St. Jerome translated the Bible from Hebrew into Latin.

Back upstairs, leave the church via the courtyards of cloisters and convents. Notice the difference in dress of the various priests who administer the church—the Greeks in long black robes, bearded, and with their long hair tied into a bun; the Armenians in purple- and cream-colored long robes; and the Franciscans in simple brown.

The construction of the church (A.D. 326) goes back to the time of the mother of Constantine the Great, Queen Helena, who made a pilgrimage to the Holy Land in the early part of the 4th century. She searched out the grotto of Christ's birth, and then Constantine built a church over the spot. The Emperor Justinian, 200 years later, found the original church destroyed (probably by an earthquake), and built a new church on the old site. The present church is a restoration of both early churches—carried out by the Crusaders, which explains its fortress-like appearance.

Other Bethlehem Sights

There's the **Milk Grotto,** run by the Franciscans (open from 8 to 11:45 a.m. and 2 to 5 p.m. daily). This is the place where Mary, in nursing the infant Jesus, is said to have dropped some milk which, according to certain traditions, promptly turned the rocks of the cavern chalky white. Visits made here by nursing mothers are supposed to help their lactation. Packets of the powdered stone are sold as souvenirs.

By heading back toward Jerusalem for a few blocks, and turning a sharp right at the appropriate sign, you can make your way to the **Shepherds' Fields** along either Shepherds' Street or Bet Sahur Road. Taxi or private car is the easiest way to go, but you can also take a no. 66 Egged bus, or no. 52 Arab bus. Driving to where the shepherds, "keeping watch over their flocks by night," saw the miraculous star, you'll pass by Arab villages in which both church steeples and minarets share the skyline—as in Bethlehem itself. Actually, there are two Shepherds' Fields, the ones maintained by the Roman Catholic church and the others by the Greek Orthodox church. Both are east of Bet Sahur, where the road forks. Take the right fork for the Greek fields, the left for the Roman. You can walk from Manger Square to either set of fields, visit for half an hour, and walk back, and the entire expedition on foot will last about two hours. An alternative plan is to walk to the Greek fields, visit, and then wait for the Egged no. 66 or Arab no. 52 bus, and take it to the Herodion.

Want to see more of this interesting half-Christian, half-Muslim, and virtually all-Arab town? Walk out of Manger Square to the right of the mosque which is at the opposite end of the square from the Church of the Nativity. This is Paul VI Street, Bethlehem's main drag—although it is certainly more a pedestrian street than a throughway. Paul VI Street, named after the pontiff who visited here, winds past cobblers' shops, a smithy, coffeehouses, hole-in-the-wall stores both ancient and modern, people buying supplies, children playing. Up the hill, you'll come to the striking **Evangelical Lutheran Christmas Church,** with a very handsome minaret-like steeple. Past the church, on Abdul Nasser Street, are a few of Bethlehem's better hotel bargains.

Where to Stay

Should you decide to stay the night in Bethlehem, you've got a good, if small, collection of hotels from which to choose. The newest and best are only a short walk from Manger Square along Paul VI Street.

At the corner of Paul VI Street and Freres Street is the new **Grand Hotel Bethlehem** (P.O. Box 18; tel. 02-741-440), a shiny, modern place complete with a snappy lobby, restaurant, and cocktail lounge. The bright and colorful guest rooms have large windows, twin beds with scarlet spreads, private baths, wall-to-wall carpeting, and central air conditioning. Rates for a double room are $40 to $50, breakfast included. This is Bethlehem's most comfortable place to stay.

The **Bethlehem Star Hotel** (P.O. Box 282; tel. 02-743-249), on Al-Baten Street, at the corner with Freres Street, has just about everything: it's modern, with friendly staff, on a quiet street, not far from the center of town, and some of the 54 rooms even have views of the cityscape. Some rooms have showers; others have tiny tubs too. There are even some triples, perfect for the couple with a child. There's an elevator so you needn't climb steps. Prices in season are $23 single, $36 double, breakfast and service included. To find the hotel, walk out of Manger Square on Paul VI Street and keep glancing up the side streets on your right. Pretty soon you'll see the hotel and its sign, about a block away up the hill.

About the best place to stay in Manger Square is the **Al Andalus Guest House** (P.O. Box 410; tel. 02-741-348), on the south side of the square in the arcade. All you'll see is a doorway and a sign, but upstairs are shining-clean rooms with gleaming tile showers and colorful curtains and spreads. Cheerful and welcoming, the rooms look either onto Manger Square or to the hills of Judea. The centrally heated rooms rent for $22 single, $33 double, breakfast and taxes included, as always.

Set in a garden to one side of Manger Square is the 25-room **Palace Hotel** (tel. 02-742-798), which provides good accommodations for the price. Right next to the church, and surrounded by the sounds of tolling bells, the Palace was built by the Greek Orthodox Committee. It has a large dining room, a colorful sitting room with a view of the city from its bar, and many attractive rooms, all with private bathrooms and many with balconies looking out toward the Judean Hills. The doubles are equipped with wide twin beds; there are only two single rooms. All are accented with bright Oriental throw rugs and have central heating. Yet the price is a low $16 single, $27.50 double, without breakfast.

You can get good accommodations at the **Handal Hotel** on Abdul Nasser Street, off Paul VI Street, a 10- or 15-minute walk from Manger Square (P.O. Box 12; tel. 02-742-494). Here there are 40 double rooms, all with private bath or shower, wall heater, electric cooler, telephone, and balconies. The rooms are spacious and well maintained. There's a dining room. From March 1 to October 31 bed with breakfast costs $20.75 single, $34.50 double. Add a surcharge of 25% during Christmas and Easter weeks. Rates are a bit lower off-season. Continental breakfast is included.

Where to Dine

There are several restaurants close to Manger Square that are clean and cheap. The closest is right on the square, in the **New Tourists Shopping Center**, opened in 1971. The center's a neat two-story building packed with shops, a band, and the **Granada Grill Bar** (tel. 02-742-810), which is where we're heading. The Granada is a small, modern place, where music is always playing. There's counter service downstairs—and speaking of the counter, take a look at the wooden sign above it: "Patience, Passion, Penitence, Prudence, Penalty." Upstairs you'll find tables and chairs, and a service charge. Hot meals, snacks, and drinks are served on both levels. Nearly all the appetizers, including hummus, tchina, eggplant, or Oriental salad cost NIS2.50 ($1.65); mixed grill, lamb chops, or shishlik run about NIS9 ($6); for the exotic-minded, grilled pigeon or a plate of kibbeh (lamb or beef meatballs served with a condiment of cedar-tree seeds) provides a culinary adventure.

The **Al Andalus Restaurant** (tel. 02-743-519) caters to tourist groups with a NIS12 ($8) set meal consisting of soup or grapefruit (depending on the season), salad, and a main course of roast beef, chicken, kebab, or veal cutlet with vegetable and potatoes, and fruit. You can also order à la carte here: kufta (ground beef in spices) baked in tomato or tchina sauce with potatoes or rice for NIS6 ($4) to NIS9 ($6); hamburgers, salads, and omelets for about the same. Open daily from 8 a.m. to midnight.

If you want something more substantial try the **St. George Restaurant** in the Municipality Building, next door to the Government Tourist Office (tel. 02-743-780). Out front are umbrella tables for al fresco dining; within, the cream-colored walls are adorned with murals of Bethlehem, and tables are covered with red cloths and graced with flowers; background music further enhances the ambience. Try the roast pigeon stuffed with rice, meat, and almonds for NIS15 ($10), or a platter of six different kinds of vegetables for less than NIS6 ($4). Open daily from 8 a.m. to about 11 p.m. or midnight.

TO HEBRON VIA THE HERODION: Either of two roads will take you to our next stop, Hebron. Those driving will want to make a loop of it, going down one way and coming up the other. If you don't have your own car, however, you can take (infrequently) a no. 66 Egged bus or a no. 52 Arab bus, or hire a taxi to run you out to the Herodion and then back to Bethlehem to catch your bus or sherut to Hebron. Try to find a few other people in Manger Square or the Church of the Nativity to share the cost of the taxi—about NIS18 ($12) for the entire car, round trip.

By the way, if you're driving from Jerusalem to the Herodion, go via Bethlehem—don't take the road marked "Herodion, 15 km" near Rachel's Tomb, north of Bethlehem.

To get to the Herodion from Bethlehem, head out of town on the road to Bet Sahur and the Shepherds' Fields. After a while, signs will point to a right fork for the Herodion, 9 km (5½ miles) from Bethlehem. From the bus stop, it's a one-kilometer (half-mile) walk to the top of the hill.

Herod the Great had ambitious plans for this dry mountaintop in the barren hills of Judea. He reshaped the entire mountaintop into a perfect cone, and then built a lavish palace on top, complete with a mikve (ritual baths), storerooms, and 200 marble steps leading down the mountainside. Herod even piped in water, at enormous expense.

The Herodion, finished in the 1st century B.C., was only one of Herod's grand palace-fortresses; another was atop Masada.

The Herodion is cared for by the National Parks Authority, open from 8 a.m. to 5 p.m. (closes at 4 p.m. on Friday) every day of the week. Admission is NIS2 ($1.35) for adults, a fourth of that for kids.

From the Herodion, you can continue along the country road, which will eventually bring you to the main highway at the town of Halhoul. Turn left to get to Hebron, which is roughly 26 km (15½ miles) from the Herodion.

3. Hebron

Of the biblical sites in the Holy Land, none is more affecting than the Tomb of the Patriarchs in the Cave of Machpelah, where Abraham and Sarah, Isaac and Rebecca, and Jacob and Leah are buried. You can read all about it in the Bible's first book, Genesis, starting with Chapter 23. This is history that is significant for adherents of all three great religions, a direct link between us and the Middle Bronze Age.

Yet, sadly, Hebron is not a peaceful place. Conflict between Hebron's Arab citizens and the Israeli settlers at nearby Kiryat Arba is constant and violent, with frequent serious injury, and even death. You'll want to check with the Government Tourist Office on the current situation before you go. Depending on conditions, here's how you should visit Hebron:

If conditions are very tense, *don't!* If there's been a minor flare-up of tensions, go on an organized tour. The bus tours do not run if the situation is known to be dangerous. If things seem peaceful, you can go by public bus or sherut, but do your best to look like a foreigner, not an Israeli. About the worst way to visit Hebron is by rented car. With Israeli license plates, it will be assumed that the driver is an Israeli too; rental-car insurance often does not cover glass breakage.

ON THE WAY: The distance is only 33 km (20 miles), the road wide and in good repair, and you should figure on a 30-minute drive over the twisting southward route. Beautiful villas line part of the road on the outskirts of Bethlehem; the road then dips close to the picturesque village of **Bet Jalla,** to the right in the nearby hills. Farther along come rich fields, more villas and new homes. Soon you pass a big archway (on the right) spanning a road leading to the nearby villages of **Husan** and **Nahhalim.** The archway honors St. George, depicted on horseback in the arch's center. This is the road David took from Bethlehem to carry his brother's food to the battle area in the Valley of Elah, where he subsequently met up with Goliath.

Solomon's Pools

Soon you'll see signs, and a left turn to Solomon's Pools. If you haven't eaten, this is a good place for lunch—either a picnic or a sit-down meal at **King Solomon's Gardens,** a small café opposite the first of the three large rectangular pools. Tall pine trees and flowery shrubs make this a shady, restful spot.

There's been some quibbling about the exact origin of the pools. Most hold that they're really the work of Herod, who brought the water here by aqueduct from springs near Hebron. Others argue that these pools were indeed built by Solomon as part of his grand scheme for supplying Jerusalem with water. Some say part of the water is from three nearby wells that belonged to Solomon's good—and wealthy—friend, Itam. And many claim the pools' origin can be found in the Book of Ecclesiastes: "I made me pools of water, to water therewith the wood that bringeth forth trees." An adjoining spring, **Ein Salah,** is considered the one referred to by Solomon in the Song of Songs: "A garden enclosed my sister, my spouse, a spring shut up, a fountain sealed."

Whatever the case, it's clear that these pools were an important source of water for the Herodion, and more important, for Jerusalem, from at least the time of Herod the Great (37–4 B.C.) to the time of modern Israel. The Romans kept the pools and aqueducts in good repair, the Ottoman Turks built a fort (now in ruins) to defend them, and the British kept the system in good working order until the end of the Mandate.

Meanwhile, back on the road: houses become fewer, and terraced slopes reach almost to the highway. The vines and trees are heavy with grapes, apples, peaches, figs, and plums. This is a fertile area—the best land in this whole rich region.

Where the road takes a sharp left, look on the facing mountainside for three ancient wells. Two of them are marked by window-like holes in the rock walls; the third is marked by a tall structure with built-in arches. These are **Itam's Wells,** which fed Solomon's Pools and which are still in use today. As the highway levels out now, you pass more fields—often divided by low rock walls —and occasional side roads leading to nearby villages.

Kefar Etzion

Halfway between Bethlehem and Hebron a green road sign points to a right fork leading to Kefar Ezyon or Etzion. At Etzion, a settlement has been reactivated (after being completely destroyed in the 1948 war), and you'll find the new **Etzion Youth Hostel** (groups only) with its adjoining popular-priced restaurant.

The Etzion region is a graphic example of recent Middle East history. It was originally settled by fervent religious Zionist farmers. Not only were the complex and its inhabitants wiped out in the convolutions resulting from the declaration of a Jewish State, but every trace of the settlements was eliminated. By 1949 it was as if there had never been a Jewish presence in Hebron.

After the Six-Day War, tremendous local pressures were exerted on the Israeli government for the settlement of the captured West Bank. At least one out of every two Israelis (including not only the right-wing Likud, but the powerful religious parties represented in the government) believes that the area is historically a part of the rest of the country and that there has been a significant Jewish imprint in the region for well over 3,000 years. Because of international pressures, the Israeli government was cautious about approving the establishment of new Jewish settlements. The West Bank was not like the Golan Heights (virtually deserted after the war) nor the coastal strip of Sinai (with only a small, indigenous Bedouin population). The West Bank was highly populated, well settled, and highly developed. In the case of Hebron, however, the pressures were irresistible. A new Etzion Bloc was established and the volunteers were the very sons and daughters of the original settlers.

Halhoul

Nearing the large village of Halhoul, where the road from the Herodion comes in, construction and donkey traffic increase noticeably. Farmers operate roadside stands and rich fields often are stripped with plastic to protect them from birds and insects. Entering the village, note the ancient well and stone cave-like structure looming on the left. A road here leads off to the **Tombs of Nathan and Gad.** In the center of "town"—a few buildings lining the main road —there's the bustle of local people shopping for daily needs, or smoking and sipping coffee in the café. Although there's nothing to warrant stopping here, it's a colorful area, with many people and lovely houses farther on dotting the roadsides and surrounding hills.

Abraham's Oak

Once past town, a left turn will take you to **Ramat Al Khaled,** where you'll find Abraham's Oak, supposedly on the site where Abraham pitched his tent and met the three angels who announced that Sarah would bear Isaac. Here's where he built an altar, and where David was anointed king. The oak, although very old, is hardly 3,000 years old—perhaps 500 or 600 years. Another biblical legend surrounds the dust of the Hebron fields, out of which God, some speculate, created Adam. Adam and Eve are also considered by some to be buried in Hebron in the Cave of Machpelah.

A little farther north is the **Valley of Eshkol,** from whence Moses' spies returned carrying clusters of grapes, symbol of the fertility of the Promised Land. (This picture—two men in robes carrying bunches of grapes on a long stick— has been adopted as the official tourist emblem of Israel.)

Another left, farther along the highway, leads to **Kiryat Arba,** a new Israeli town near Hebron. Ahead the highway splits: Beersheba is to the right, and Hebron, our destination, is immediately beyond the left fork.

IN HEBRON: Artifacts provide a useful message about the past, but human beings are a preview of the future. So even if Hebron had nothing more to offer than its contemporary history, we would find the city fascinating. Israel calls the region the West Bank, Jordan sees the city as an integral part of the Hashemite Kingdom, the Hebronites regard themselves as Palestinians.

Certainly, the people of Hebron have had their ups and downs with the Jews, and vice versa. In 1929 and 1948 there was bloodshed sufficient to decimate the local Jewish population, and relations between Jews and Arabs here have been difficult ever since.

Taking the main road through Hebron, you'll first pass lovely villas and a few shops and grocery stores. At one point, islands of trees, flowers, and greenery divide the highway lanes, after which the archeological **Museum of Hebron** will be on your left (nearby are several places for cool drinks). On the right is the **Israel Government House.**

When you see a glass factory, a pottery factory, and a woodwork factory side by side in a huge three-story building on your left, you'll be in the shopping district (photo shops, tailors, tiny clothing stores, shoe stores, grocery stores, etc.). In this area you'll see a roadside pillar pointing to Abraham's Tomb; when the road forks, bear left toward the tombs. Shortly there's another sign, a red one, pointing out the **Jewish Cemetery.** Dating back 3,700 years, this cemetery was almost entirely destroyed during the 1929 slaughter, but people still come here to pray and stand in awe. Hereabouts the road narrows until it is just barely two lanes and leads by shops of shoemakers, carpenters, leather workers, and saddle makers (who outfit camels and donkeys). Coming into the vegetable area, the road widens and the **Muslim Cemetery** is to the right.

And now there's an open expanse and a sign guiding you left to Abraham's Tomb.

Tomb of the Patriarchs

Enclosing the **Cave of Machpelah,** the tomb is what gives Hebron its designation as one of Israel's four "Holy Cities"—the others being Jerusalem, Tiberias, and Safed.

To religious Jews who now can worship at the sacred Tomb of the Patriarchs, the holy experience is second only to worshipping at the Western (Wailing) Wall in Jerusalem. Genesis tells how Abraham bought his family burial cave from Ephron for 400 silver shekels. Tradition has it that Hebron is thus one of three places in Israel that Jews can claim by virtue of having purchased the property; the same claim is made for the Jerusalem Temple and the Tomb of Joseph.

The tombs of Abraham, Isaac, and Jacob (and their wives) are housed in a fortress built by Herod. The walls range from 40 to 60 feet high. You may visit the tombs between 7:30 and 11:30 a.m. and 1:30 till 4 or 5 p.m. From 11:30 a.m. to 1:30 p.m. devout Muslims worship inside, and no other visitors are allowed. No non-Muslim visitors are permitted on Friday, which is the Muslim Sabbath, or on Muslim holidays.

Inside the walls, the Muslims built a mosque around the tombs. The square main basilica is richly decorated with inlaid wood and ornate mosaic work reminiscent of the Dome of the Rock. Inscriptions from the Koran run along the walls. In the main section you will see the tombs of Isaac and Rebecca, red and white stone "huts" with green roofs. Looking inside, you'll see the richly embroidered drapes covering the cenotaphs. ("Cenotaph," according to Webster, means "an empty tomb in honor of a person buried elsewhere." The real tombs are supposed to be underground, beneath the cenotaphs.) In an adjoining courtyard are the gold-embroidered tapestries covering the cenotaphs of Abraham and Sarah—behind a silver grating. Just opposite is the tomb of Jacob and Leah, with a 700-year-old stained-glass window. A shrine to Joseph is right next door, but the authentic tomb of Joseph is generally thought to be at Nablus.

4. Ramallah, Shechem, Nablus, and Samaria

This route takes you north into biblical Samaria, the land of Canaan that Abraham first saw over 4,000 years ago, the scene of great events involving Jacob, Joseph, Joshua, and the rulers of the northern kingdom.

You should remember that there have been periods of unrest in these West Bank towns. The mayor of Ramallah was seriously wounded and crippled for life by a bomb planted in his car a few years ago. Charges were brought against an extreme right-wing Israeli group. Military rule here is sometimes strict. Check with the Government Tourist Office on current conditions, join an organized tour if things seem iffy, and avoid driving a rental car with Israeli license plates. Identify yourself as a foreigner, and remember that this is not Israel, or Samaria, or the West Bank, or the Administered Territories, or even Jordan to the local people, but rather Palestine.

ON THE ROAD: From Jerusalem you climb above Mount Scopus, following the signs to Ramallah. The road passes **Shu'afat,** biblical Gibeah, Saul's capital when he became the first king of Israel. This is a prosperous region. About seven miles out of Jerusalem you'll find yourself in the "better" suburban quarter of what was Jordanian Jerusalem: new development areas of high-rise apartments give way to posh private villas. The mountains reveal themselves off to the left, as does a particularly distinguishable building with a high tower. This is the **Tomb of the Prophet Samuel,** and it rises above the scattered buildings of more new suburban projects. (A left turn a bit farther on leads you through the valley to the tomb site.)

One of the most prominent buildings you'll pass on the main road, on the right, is the **Semaris Hotel.** Used now as a lecture hall, it once was considered the best hotel by tourists in Jordan. After passing it, note the Ramallah Arak factory to the left—it's small, but produces a well-known quality brew, arak (the licorice-scented liquor; an absinthe derivative, it's powerful but slow-acting stuff —so if you're not used to it, drink carefully). Ramallah is around the next bend of the road. And the closer you get, the more television aerials you see on the horizon.

RAMALLAH: Arabic for "the Heights of the Lord," Ramallah is a cool, high town, once the most popular summer resort in Jordan ("Switzerland of Jordan"). You will see elegant villas on hillsides green with pine groves. At 2,900 feet, Ramallah sits some 300 feet higher than Jerusalem. A Christian and Muslim town, Ramallah is quite well off, with many good restaurants, hotels, and shops.

Should you stop for a while in Ramallah, make sure to see the town's large, beautiful park, which contains a well-equipped children's playground. You might also want to see **King Hussein's former palace,** a pleasant but unostentatious building.

El Bira, the town east of Ramallah, is considered to have been the first caravan stop on the ancient Jerusalem–Galilee route. Neither Ramallah nor El Bira has any biblical sights to see these days, though.

Once past Ramallah, a road on your left will take you on a shortcut to Jericho (34 km, 20½ miles), via the Arab village of **Taiybah.** You'll see a large compound on your right as you continue; it was once a Jordanian hospital, and in the hills farther on is what was once a Jordanian training camp. The buildings are still in use . . . by the Israelis. At this point you'll begin to notice an occasional shepherd with his flock—it might take you back to biblical days, when this was the area of the Tribe of Benjamin.

Bethel

Two miles farther on is the Arab village of **Betin**—biblical Bethel, "House of God." This is one of the key places mentioned in Genesis 12. "I will make thee a great nation and I will bless thee, and make thy name great." Abraham passed into Canaan in Shechem, "And he removed from thence unto a mountain on the east of Bethel, and pitched his tent . . . and there he builded an altar unto the Lord" (Gen. 12:1–8). It was also to Bethel that Abraham and Lot returned from Egypt, "with their flocks and herds and tents." Later, as described in Genesis 28, the Lord appeared to Jacob in a dream: ". . . and behold a ladder set up on the earth, and the top of it reached to heaven: and behold the angels of God ascending and descending it. And, behold, the Lord stood above it, and said, I am the Lord God of Abraham thy father, and the God of Isaac: the land whereon thou liest, to thee will I give it, and unto thy seed." Jacob was in awe; and because his home was visited by God, he named it "House of God," Bethel, and set up a stone pillar at the spot marking the ladder. The hill today is called **Jacob's Ladder,** but unless you have a guide to point it out, you'll never find it.

After a bit of countryside, a few large buildings are seen on either side of the road, and a smaller paved road leads left and down into a small valley. The buildings are schools, new since the Six-Day War, built for the children of the village below. Part of this lovely village is also a refugee camp, but it's hard to tell which part, as the entire village looks so well kept and pretty, with most houses painted blue and lavender. Here you'll see a mosque with a difference—it's the only mosque tower with glass windows. When the muezzin calls villagers to prayer in this extremely windy village, he simply opens one or more of the windows and closes them immediately afterward to guard against the chill wind. The people here work mostly at agricultural tasks, and they tend trees bearing almonds, figs, apples, peaches, and olives—you'll note large groves lining the road and nearby hills.

The next village you'll see is **Bir Zeit,** which means "the Oil Well," and a bit farther along is the village of **Ein Sinya,** with its cluster of old and new buildings on the left, some dating back to Turkish times. Farther along, high in the hills, is the town of **Sinjil,** the Arab name for the settlement of the French monk St. Giles, who lost his life here.

Shiloh

Now the road twists and turns through low hills covered by groves of olive trees. Soon you'll see a five-foot stone pillar pointing to the ruins of ancient Shiloh on the left: Shiloh is where the Tabernacle and the Ark of the Covenant were once housed. It is also the place where the men of Benjamin's tribe, short of women, carried away the daughters of Shiloh who were innocently dancing in their vineyards.

Valley of Dotan

As you pass Shiloh, note the natural Canaanite agricultural terraces still being worked in the hills. The steep winding road here was constructed originally by the British. It snakes down toward the village of **Lubban,** and the rich fields in the Valley of Dotan. Pull over before you descend and take in the magnificent view of the valley and Lubban. You have to look carefully at first to find the village, as it blends in so perfectly with the slopes. This area, in biblical times, was famous for myrrh and other incense. This industry still exists and tobacco is also grown here. Between Shiloh and here is the area where Saul met the Philistines, and Eli prophesied doom for Shiloh, then capital of the land. The territory from Shiloh northward belonged to the tribe of Manasseh. Entering the valley, you'll see houses begun in Turkish times and repaired and refurbished throughout the years. Many were, and still are, called *khans* and once served as wayside inns for travelers, housing both animals and men within their walls.

As you continue on, keep an eye out for the small villages that dot the surrounding hills. And along the roadside, depending on the season, you'll see boys and men selling fruits, fresh or dried figs, and such. The earth of the valley is plowed to show its rich redness, in sharp contrast to the chalky sand color of the hills. A bit of history: The Valley of Dotan was where Joseph was sold into slavery. One of the Via Maris roads ran through here, and the area was part of a caravan route traveled over by many, including the Maccabees.

SHECHEM: Just before you reach Nablus, the largest town of the West Bank, you'll want to stop on its southern outskirts for Jacob's Well, Joseph's Tomb, and biblical Shechem. At Shechem, Abraham first entered the land of Canaan. The town was built much earlier by Shechem, Hamor's father. Jacob lived here, built an altar, and dug a well. Joshua also built an altar at Shechem and summoned the tribes together, "half of them against Mount Gerizim and half of them over against Mount Ebal" (which are on either side of Shechem). Joshua united the tribes in a covenant ceremony which is considered the beginning of the Israeli nation (Josh. 8:30–35). Joseph, who was sold into slavery in the Valley of Dotan, was buried here. Archeological remains of ancient Shechem show that it was a large city; some of the finds are displayed in the Rockefeller Museum in East Jerusalem. Archeologists have long puzzled over why Shechem, if it was such an important place, was situated in such a vulnerable position—in a pass between two mountains, Ebal and Gerizim.

The Samaritans

Mount Gerizim became very holy to the Samaritans, who today believe it to be the authentic Mount Sinai as well as the site of **Abraham's Altar,** where he prepared to sacrifice his son, Isaac. The present-day Samaritans will show it to you, between the rocks at the summit of Gerizim. (Others believe the near-sacrifice took place on Mount Moriah in Jerusalem.) The Samaritans, who celebrate many of the traditional Jewish holidays, will be glad to point out altars built by Adam and Noah on Gerizim. (Moses and Joshua also attached great significance to Mount Gerizim. See Deut. 6, Josh. 8.) About 275 Samaritans live here these days, calling themselves the children of the Tribes of Manasseh, Aaron, and Efraim. Other remnants of that proud tribe are to be found south of Tel Aviv in Holon.

Originally descended from the tribes of Israel, the Samaritans are those who remained behind when the Babylonians carried off the population of Israel in the 6th century B.C. When Cyrus released the Jews and they returned to Israel after a 60-year absence, the Samaritans wanted to help them reconstruct the Temple. The Jews refused their help, declaring that the Samaritans were no longer Jews, that they had intermarried with the Assyrians and Babylonians and had adopted pagan customs. The factions split and remained split down through the centuries, the Samaritans claiming that they and only they have continuously inhabited Israel and kept the traditions pure. They also claim themselves to be the keepers of a Pentateuch (the first five books of Moses) which they say came to them from Aaron, Moses's brother. If this is the case, it's the oldest biblical scroll in existence; you can see it in the Samaritan synagogue in Shechem.

On Passover, the Samaritans of Shechem are joined by those from Holon; together they sacrifice a lamb on the site of Abraham's Altar, observing, they say, the tradition begun by their forebears 25 centuries ago.

Jacob's Well

In Shechem too is the **Convent of Jacob's Well.** You'll recognize it by its two large metal doors. Ring the electric buzzer to notify the convent's sole monk that you'd like to enter the locked gate. As the doors open, you see a beautiful cluster of well-tended small gardens. To the right is a tiny station for prayer, housing a picture of Jesus and the Woman of the Well, another name for this convent. Directly ahead are two blue pillars, mounted with ancient Roman capital stones that support a new ceramic arch leading to the shrine and the huge unfinished church. In 1912 the Russian Orthodox church began building this enormous basilica, but work stopped with the onset of the First World War. Later, this and all other Russian Orthodox holy places were turned over to the Greek Orthodox church, which still maintains them.

The outside walls were part of a Byzantine church that once stood on this site. Inside the basilica area, with its three separate nave sections, the larger and central section is sheltered with tent-like fabrics and contains a cross atop a broken Roman pillar. Here is held the Feast of the Samaritan Woman. Two painted cement buildings, looking much like guard stations, cover and secure two 18-step passages leading down to the chapel and well. Although the small, beautiful chapel looks older, it was built in 1910, on the site of the earlier chapel, which was built in the times of Queen Helena, mother of Constantine. Rich and intimate, the chapel is hung with shining incense burners and paved with painted tiles; its walls are covered with old paintings and icons, most depicting Jesus and the Woman at the Well. In the center is Jacob's Well, with wrought-iron fixtures and a metal pail—a bit incongruous amid so much elegance.

The well itself is 115 feet deep (89 feet before you reach water level). The topmost structure is Greek; beneath it, lining the interior of the well for about 13 feet, is stonework dating back to Byzantine, Roman, and Mameluke times. The balance is believed to be original well stone from Jacob's day. The water, besides being cold and sweet, is supposed to have special properties; indeed, oldtimers here will tell you of the days, 70 or 80 years ago, when Russian Orthodox pilgrims came by the thousands to this shrine. In those days several monks were needed to aid the pilgrims and maintain the shrine; today's lone vigil is kept by a solitary monk. You may buy religious souvenirs here and you can come away with small brown bottles of the well water for whatever donation you care to leave.

Joseph's Tomb

From here it's 100 yards north to the traditional site of Joseph's Tomb, in a little white, domed house, similar in appearance to Rachel's Tomb. Since this was the land parceled out by the Lord to the Patriarchs, the Israelites brought Joseph's bones back from Egypt and placed them in Shechem, "in a parcel of ground which Jacob bought of the sons of Hamor, the father of Shechem, for a hundred pieces of silver: and it became the inheritance of the children of Joseph" (Josh. 25:32). This is one of the three places—along with the Jerusalem Temple and the Patriarch's Tomb in Hebron—that religious Jews claim is historically theirs by right of documented purchase.

NABLUS: The largest West Bank town, with houses piled up like white chalky soap bubbles on the hillsides, Nablus is somewhat modern and business-like compared to, say, Hebron, which has nearly the same population but which looks hundreds of years older . . . and drearier. Nablus is in fact a business center, home of the local soap-making industry and equally known for the sweet, sticky baklava pastries made here. The name Nablus is the Arabic contraction of the Greco-Roman city built here, Neapolis. It was founded by Titus who named it Flavia Neapolis in honor of his father, Flavius Vespasian.

We'll quickly pass through the town, noting what's around: the large complex to the right is an old Arab-British prison, still being used, and farther on are beautiful villas and a lovely small mosque with a huge blue-green dome and stained-glass windows. Past here, to the left, the Casbah area starts—this is the older quarter and strictly off-limits to tourists. Within it is the dome of another mosque, and above it, on the hillside, is the Samarian quarter, opposite a Muslim cemetery. The streets are filled with black-veiled Muslim women and headscarfed men, and the outskirts are scattered with more beautiful villas that almost touch the next small village. The road winds on through small villages between low hills and mountains and eventually forks: right to Samaria; left is a shortcut to Netanya.

SAMARIA: The road to Samaria curves downward, and by paying attention, you'll note the many caves in the area and small houses built into the hillsides. Women sit in front of their houses near the road working with stitchery or wool and you may see a group of them working together to sift or grind grain beside the road. On the hill to the right is Samaria (**Sebastia** today), and as you climb the Israeli road, watch for niches in the mountainside. These were discovered when the road was being built—they're burial caves, many of which were found filled with ancient sarcophagi dating back to around 800 B.C. Today this is a tiny Samarian village, its winding narrow streets topping ruins from the days of Ahab, the Romans, Byzantines, and Crusaders. The small, poor houses often are made or propped up with bits of stone and pillars from past eras. The main square, if I may call it that, has an outdoor café where you can get cold drinks.

The entire region of Samaria was occupied by the tribes of Ephraim and Manasseh, the children of Joseph, in biblical times. Samaria was once the capital of the Kingdom of Israel. Inside the village a mosque has been built within an old Crusader cathedral. Beneath it, reputedly, is the tomb of Elisha, the prophet, and also the head of John the Baptist, brought here by Herod Antipas at the request of Salome. The hills bear witness to the Roman city that once stood here: ruins of a hippodrome, columns, towers, a theater, palace walls.

At an earlier time, however (around 876 B.C.), Omri founded the capital of the Kingdom of Israel here. His son, Ahab, married Jezebel, daughter of a Phoenician king. She brought Baal and other idolatrous pagan gods to the people of Israel. The prophets fought her, particularly Elijah, who challenged the priests of Baal in the famous cliffside battle on Mount Carmel. Samaria remained the capital under Jeru and Jeroboam, but the Old Testament recounts bad times of transgression, corruption, vice, and drunkenness. In 725 B.C. the Assyrians plundered Samaria, ending the Kingdom of Israel, and carried off 25,000 of its inhabitants.

To Jenin, Nazareth, and the Jordan Valley

The road moves on past **Dotan**, traditionally the city where Joseph was sold into slavery by his brothers, to Jenin. Take a left at the square in the middle of this little town and follow the road north. From here you can head north to Afula and thence to Nazareth and Haifa, or east to the Jordan Valley and the Sea of Galilee.

TEL AVIV–JAFFA

COMPARED WITH JERUSALEM, Israel's largest metropolis is a gawky, incoherent mass of undistinguished architecture and frantic commotion. Highlighted against Haifa, Tel Aviv is unkempt, noisy, and hopelessly uncoordinated. The city doesn't have the saving grace of Beersheba—the wide expanse of lapping wilderness and desert. Nor does it compare favorably with the Red Sea coral empire of Eilat. It isn't cleanly fashioned like Arad, and its questionable beauty is a light-year removed from the pious serenity of Safed.

And yet Tel Aviv is where the action is. It is the brash, polyglot microcosm of all of Israel.

Before 1909 the area on which modern Tel Aviv stands was a dismal landscape of sand dunes. Jackals howled in the evening at sites where you now hear the roar of diesel engines. Snakes and lizards slithered around Dizengoff Square, where locals now sip their drinks at crowded outdoor cafés. Bedouin camped in black tents on the sand flats above the sea, in the exact spot where the Dan, Hilton, Plaza, Ramada, and many more plush hotels are fast converting Tel Aviv's seafront into a Middle Eastern Miami Beach.

As Israel's most cosmopolitan city (the population of Greater Tel Aviv is over a million), Tel Aviv is unique, a perfect product of the 20th century—bold, crowded, and impolite, lacking the mannered graces of an earlier time, and indifferent to the aesthetics of architecture. It has pizza parlors, nightclubs, and acres and acres of apartment buildings. To an idealistic kibbutznik, the mere mention of its name conjures up an image of Gomorrah in its worst depravity.

But for all that, Tel Aviv is the cultural, business, and entertainment center of Israel. The newspapers are published here (excepting the *Jerusalem Post*), the books are published here, the concerts are given here, and the theaters thrive here. Say what you want, this is the commercial and fun capital of Israel—a city born of necessity, growing up too fast to worry about its style or appearance.

A BIT OF HISTORY: Back in 1906 the Jews of Jaffa (the old port of Tel Aviv) decided that they were tired of their cramped and noisy quarters in that Arab city. With a boost from the Jewish National Fund, a group of them decided to build their own city on Jaffa's northern outskirts. In 1909 they bought 32 acres, and under the leadership of Meir Dizengoff, 60 families (about 250 people)

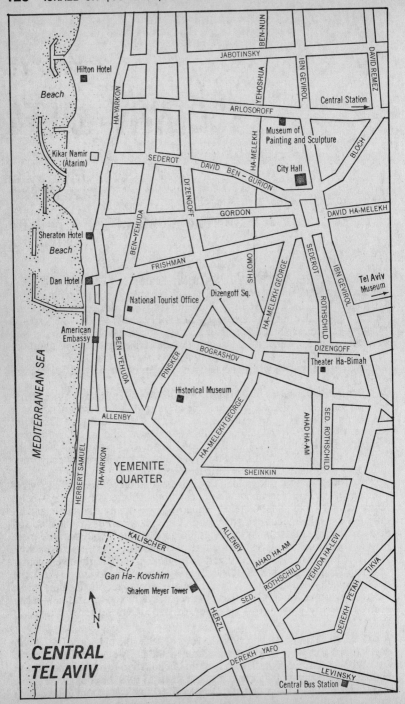

CENTRAL
TEL AVIV

staked out their claims. A famous photograph of these people, who had sufficient sense of history to pose for the occasion, recalls the moment. You'll probably see this picture at one time or another at some exhibition in Israel: the 60 posed families, stuffed into their fluffy Victorian clothes. Dizengoff, in his invocation address, prophesied a town of 25,000; his hopes have been exceeded 40 times over.

Most of the pioneers' wealth went into the building of a fine school, the famous Herzlia Gymnasium (Palestine's first high school), which was modeled after an ancient drawing of Solomon's Temple but emerged resembling a Turkish fortress. Later, they turned their tents into cottages and named their first thoroughfare Herzl Street. They argued with the encamped Arabs over their rights to the land, persevered, and by the time World War I began, the city's population had grown to 3,000.

During the war the Turks dispossessed the residents of Tel Aviv, but they all came back when General Allenby's British army dispossessed the Turks. Subsequently the Balfour Declaration launched a wave of immigration, and by 1921 Tel Aviv had blossomed into a separate town from Jaffa, elected Dizengoff mayor, and became home to 15,000 residents.

The city's motto, "I shall build thee and thou shalt be built," inspired many of the immigrants who came into Israel from Jaffa port to stay right in Tel Aviv and do their building—instead of pioneering in the malarial swamps of the agricultural settlements. Sporadic fighting with Arab neighbors in Jaffa accompanied Tel Aviv's early history.

By the outbreak of World War II, Tel Aviv was a small metropolis of 100,000 people, and in that capacity, the city played host to 2 million Allied soldiers who passed through Tel Aviv during the war. Although most of Israel escaped the ravages of that war, Tel Aviv was bombed by Italian and Vichy French planes.

After the war, Tel Aviv became a center of Israeli dissatisfaction with the British Mandate policy that prevented Jewish refugees from entering Israel. Once, in 1946, 20,000 British soldiers placed the entire city under rigid curfew while a search was conducted for underground members. After interrogating almost the entire population of 110,000 residents, the British made two arrests. In 1948, just as the British were pulling out of Israel, the Israelis launched an attack against Jaffa, headquarters for Arab guerrillas and snipers: Jaffa's Arab population, dispersed to Arab-controlled areas, thereupon fell from 50,000 to 5,000.

Once the British were gone, Tel Aviv really began to mushroom. The city's suburbs spread out in three directions. Between the establishment of Israel in 1948 and the present time, the population of the greater Tel Aviv region has grown many times larger.

1. Orientation

Tel Aviv and Jaffa (Yafo in Hebrew) together form a large urban area. With the many suburbs—Ramat Gan, Bnei Brak, Petah Tikva, Bat Yam, etc.—the urban area becomes a sprawl daunting to any newly arrived traveler. But don't give up. The Tel Aviv–Jaffa you'll get to know is actually only the downtown seafront section, extending east only to the thoroughfare of Ibn Gevirol Street. Granted, this is still a six-kilometer (four-mile) strip at least one kilometer wide, but of this only certain sections are of interest to us as the commercial, cultural, and entertainment centers. The rest of the turf is residential, and only interesting if you have relatives or friends who live there.

Coming from Ben-Gurion International Airport, at the confluence of several major arteries—Petah Tikva Road, Haifa Road, and Arlosoroff Street—is the **Central Railway Station** (sometimes called North Railway Station because it is in the northern reaches of the city). The **Central Bus Station** is in southern Tel Aviv, surrounded by Levinsky, Levanda, Shalma, and Har-Ziyon Streets. The **South Railway Station** is just south of Kibbutz Galuyot Boulevard, the main road to Jerusalem.

GETTING AROUND: From the Central Railway Station, take city bus 20 or 64 to Dizengoff Square, Ben-Yehuda Street, and Allenby Road, also to Namir Square and the waterfront Ha-Yarkon Street. Bus 27 runs between the Central Railway terminal and the Central Bus Station.

From the Central Bus Station into town, take no. 4 to Allenby Road, Ben-Yehuda Street, Namir Square, and Ha-Yarkon Street; take the no. 5 to Dizengoff Square, Ha-Yarkon Street, and the youth hostel.

LANDMARKS: Perhaps the easiest landmark to recognize in Tel Aviv is the white 34-story shaft of the **Shalom Mayer Tower (Migdal Shalom)**, in southern Tel Aviv, at the southern end of Allenby Road. Less conspicuous, but more important for our purposes, is the area where Allenby Road meets Ben-Yehuda Street. This is **Moghrabi Square** (also called **Bet Be-November Square**). Between Moghrabi Square and the waterfront is a short section of Allenby Road, which ends in Allenby Square at the water's edge. Here you'll find an unlikely congeries of things: Tel Aviv's old, ruined Opera House (in which the very first Knesset sessions were held in 1948); several good budget hotels; and Tel Aviv's small and surprisingly unsinister red-light district.

Dizengoff Square, which is actually more of a circle, has an elevated pedestrian plaza with a big fountain perched above busy Dizengoff Street near the intersection of Pinsker and Zamenhoff Streets. If any one place can be described as the very heart of Tel Aviv, throbbing and pulsating, this is it.

West of Dizengoff Square on the waterfront is Tel Aviv's oldest luxury hostelry, the **Dan Hotel**, at Ha-Yarkon and Frishman Streets. Here also you'll spot the big United States Embassy building (the U.S. still does not accept Jerusalem as Israel's capital—no doubt because of Jordanian claims—and maintains its embassy here in Tel Aviv).

North of the Dan Hotel, the huge hotels march along the beach: the Sheraton, the Ramada Continental, the Diplomat, the Plaza, the Hilton. Right next to the Plaza Hotel, where Ben-Gurion Boulevard joins Ha-Yarkon Street, is **Namir**, or **Atarim**, **Square** (Kikar Namir), a modern multilevel plaza with restaurants and outdoor cafés, shops, and services. Namir Square is a popular place for an evening stroll or an early-morning cup of coffee in the open air.

All the way at the northern end of Tel Aviv, just south of the Yarkon River, is a quaint section of small streets filled with restaurants, clubs, and cinemas popular with a youngish university crowd, a fine place for a prowl after dark. Crossroads for this area is the intersection of Dizengoff and Yirmiyahu Streets.

Inland, at the center of town, **Malchei Israel Square,** where Ibn Gevirol Street, Ben-Gurion Boulevard, and Frishman Street meet, is dominated by Tel Aviv's city hall and a great plaza. Another important inland location is **Tzimoret Square,** with the Ha-Bimah National Theatre and Mann Auditorium (home of the Israel Philharmonic). Tzimoret Square is bounded by Dizengoff, Tarsad Ahad Ha-Am, Rothschild, and Marmorek Streets.

Finally there's **Jaffa (Yafo),** actually a fairly large sister city, although we're interested mostly in the picturesque hilltop section known as Old Jaffa.

INFORMATION: The **Israel Government Tourist Office,** at 7 Mendele St., near the corner with Ben-Yehuda just south of Frishman Street (tel. 03-223-266 or 223-267), is open from 8:30 a.m. to 5 p.m. Sunday through Thursday; on Friday and holiday eves the hours are 8:30 a.m. to 2 p.m.

By the way, the corner of Mendele and Ben-Yehuda Streets is Tel Aviv's "Tourism Corner." Besides the Israel Government Tourist Office, you'll find several travel agencies offering cut-rate flights, plus offices of Egged Tours and United Tours, and car-rental agencies. Bring your travel questions here.

Voluntary Travel Service

In the lobbies of many three-, four-, and five-star hotels you may spot a small desk with a sign saying **V.T.S.** on it. The cryptic initials stand for Voluntary Travel Service, and the cheery person behind the desk has donated his or her time to helping tourists with questions. Don't hesitate to quiz these thoughtful native Tel Avivans on any point in question, from museum locations to theater ticket purchases.

USEFUL FACTS: Israel's largest city is fairly easy to handle. Here are some useful facts to make it even easier.

Banks: In general, banking hours are 8:30 a.m. to noon or 12:30 p.m.; on Sunday, Tuesday, and Thursday there are also hours from 4 to 5 p.m. Some banks stay open longer hours during the high summer season. Take your passport whenever you change money at a bank. Alas, Tel Aviv does not have Jerusalem's good collection of moneychangers. The banks are all over, however, particularly on Ben-Yehuda and Dizengoff Streets.

Bookstores and Newsstands: There are eight **Steimatzky** branches in Tel Aviv, including those at 107 Allenby Rd. (tel. 03-299-277), 109 Dizengoff St. (tel. 03-221-513), 4 Tarsat Ave., near Ha-Bimah Theater (tel. 03-280-806), and in the Diaspora Museum (tel. 03-429-264). There's also **Quality Books,** 45 Ben-Yehuda St. (tel. 03-234-885), between Mendele and Bograshov.

Consulates: Many countries do not accept Jerusalem as Israel's legal capital, and so embassies remain in Tel Aviv. The **U.S. Embassy** is at 71 Ha-Yarkon St. (tel. 03-654-338), not far from the Dan Hotel. The **British Embassy** is at 192 Ha-Yarkon St., corner of Arlosoroff (tel. 03-249-171), north of Namir (Atarim) Square up near the Hilton. The **Canadian Embassy** is at 220 Ha-Yarkon St. (tel. 03-228-122), north of the Hilton.

Crime in Tel Aviv: Israel's largest city has less crime than most cities its size, but there is still enough that you must observe the normal precautions. Don't walk in deserted areas, especially the beaches, after dark. To call the police, dial 100.

Laundry: Take it to 63 Ben-Yehuda St., near Bograshov, which advertises "six hours cleaning and laundry." Hours are 7 a.m. to 1:30 p.m. and 3:30 to 6 p.m.

Medical Services: You can get a list of English-speaking doctors and dentists from the embassy, and often from your hotel's front desk as well. The **Dental Association** has a clinic at 49 Bar Kokhba St. (tel. 03-284-649), open on Friday from 6 p.m. to midnight and on Saturday from 10 a.m. to 2 p.m. and 8 to 10 p.m., treating dental problems at times when dentists would not be receiving patients. In **medical emergencies,** dial 101 for Magen David Adom (Red Shield of David), Israel's emergency first-aid service. For medical emergencies requiring hospitalization, dial 102. Magen David Adom has a mobile intensive-care unit (tel. 03-240-111) on call 24 hours a day. For the Rape Crisis Center, dial 03-234-819. The *Jerusalem Post* lists under "General Assistance" the names and addresses of duty **pharmacies** that stay open nights and on the Sabbath.

Post Office: Tel Aviv's **Central Post Office** is at 132 Allenby Rd. General hours for all services are 7 a.m. to 7 p.m. Sunday through Thursday, though limited services (telephone and telegraph) are open nights and on the Sabbath. **Branch post offices** are on Ha-Yarkon at Trumpeldor, at 3 Mendele St. next to the Hotel Adiv between Ha-Yarkon and Ben-Yehuda, and just off Dizengoff Square on Zamanhof Street.

2. Where to Stay

Tel Aviv's construction boom in recent years has resulted in the rise of many new three-, four-, and five-star hotels, but this is hardly good news for the budget traveler. Off-season (roughly from November through March), Tel Aviv's three-star hotels offer very good bargains. Many cut their rates during this whole period; others keep the cuts to the months of January and February. In a three-star hotel, you're pretty much assured of getting good value for money: elevators, rooms with shower or tub, balconies, telephones, perhaps a radio. But prices in summer can be at the high end of our budget.

Luckily for us, Tel Aviv still has a decent number of older hotels and pensions, well maintained in most cases, although far from luxurious. Besides price, there are other considerations when selecting a room here.

If one word could describe Tel Aviv's hotel situation, that word would be "noisy." Some 90% of these establishments are built directly on the main streets —**Ben-Yehuda, Allenby,** and **Ha-Yarkon.** And for sheer diesel roar and motor-scooter cough, Tel Aviv is unsurpassed in all the world. I once stayed in a conveniently located hotel on a busy corner, facing on the street, and soon discovered that not only was an afternoon nap impossible, but the sound and fury outside the window didn't abate till well after midnight.

Therefore, more than any other commodity—the bathroom, the shower, the plaster job on the ceiling—make sure you value the location of your Tel Aviv room. Don't take a room facing on the main street, unless of course it has air conditioning and soundproof windows. Get off the heavily trafficked streets or take a room in the back. Sightseeing is a tiring business and you need your rest. (Strangely enough, Tel Aviv hoteliers don't seem to realize that rooms in back, away from the noise, are highly desirable; they charge precisely the same for front and back rooms.)

Here, then, are Tel Aviv's budget hotels. Unless otherwise noted, the prices given below include a filling Israeli breakfast and also the 15% service charge levied by virtually all Israeli hotels.

NEAR ALLENBY SQUARE AND MOGHRABI SQUARE: The heart of down-

town Tel Aviv, where Allenby Road meets the sea, is one of the city's older sections. Hastily built to house the city's burgeoning population half a century ago, the modest stucco buildings are now chipped and cracked, much the worse for wear. Urban redevelopment is restoring or replacing whole neighborhoods hereabouts, but for the time being these aging buildings offer good lodging buys. You may spot a streetwalker or two, but you may do that in the lobby of any posh hotel also, and the presence (now dwindling) of "ladies of the night" doesn't seem to add danger to the area. The location, right smack in the center of town, couldn't be better.

The one-star **Nes Ziona** is at 10 Nes Ziona St., off Ben-Yehuda and one block from Allenby (tel. 03-656-587). This gray-façaded hotel of three stories is on a quiet street two blocks from the sea. Of its 21 rooms, 15 have showers and 6 have sinks only. It is very simple and clean; the highlight is the lounge-lobby

wherein paintings of local artists are displayed. Per-person rate, without breakfast, is $13 for one, $18 for two, a night. Three in a room will be cheaper. No
meals.

The **Moss Hotel,** 6 Nes Ziona St., just northwest of Moghrabi Square (Tel
Aviv 63904; tel. 03-651-655), has three stars, as you can readily guess when you
see its tall, modern façade. With 70 rooms, all equipped with tubs in the bathrooms, central heat and air conditioning, radios, and telephones—you'd think
the place is a cut above the rest. Bar, coffeeshop, dining room, private parking,
and a good location are welcome extras. For the price, it's a good deal: $28.75
single, $38 double, $51.75 triple, breakfast and service all in—you can even pay
by credit card.

Down Allenby Road

Walk out of Moghrabi Square inland along Allenby Road, and at 56 Allenby you'll come to the Atara Café. Turn right and walk down the pedestrian
street that's there, between nos. 54 and 56. At the far end of it, cross the street
and there on the right will be the lace-curtained doorway of the **Hagfalil Hotel,**
23 Bet Yosef St., corner of Hillel Ha-Zaken (tel. 03-655-036). The nine rooms
are extremely well kept, and although none has a bath, there are two bathrooms
nearby. For a nice kosher Israeli breakfast you'll have to pay a bit more, as the
rooms are very low-priced: $8.75 to $12.25 single, $17.50 to $20 double. This
small place is often full, so it's best if you write to Shmuel Rosen, the friendly
owner, in advance.

A Hostel

Not far into the Yemenite Quarter is a private youth hostel called **The
Home,** 20 Al-Sheikh St. (tel. 03-656-736), a veritable clearinghouse for information on all aspects of low-budget travel, as well as an extremely cheap place to
bed down. Take bus 4 from the Central Bus Station, get off at the fifth stop, cross
the street, and find the alley at 56 Allenby Rd. Walk down the alley, take a right,
then a left, and you'll see The Home on the left. For NIS6 ($4) you get a dormi-
tory bed, for NIS15 ($10) a private room with two beds, plus hot showers and
use of a kitchen. Floor space for a sleeping bag is a mere NIS4 ($2.65). The
music is good, the drinks cheap, the company congenial, the accommodations
rock-bottom.

NEAR THE U.S. EMBASSY AND DAN HOTEL: Let's take Bograshov Street
on the south, Frishman Street on the north, and Ben-Yehuda as our thoroughfare, and we've got another neighborhood with good budget hotel finds. First,
let's see what's on Ben-Yehuda itself.

Along Ben-Yehuda

On Ben-Yehuda between Bograshov and Shalom Aleichem Streets, at no.
35, above and behind the KLM office, is the **Ora Hotel** (Tel Aviv 63807; tel.
03-650-941). An elevator services its five floors, and there's a carpeted bar. The
hotel's entrance is to the left side of the KLM office. Sleek and modern, the
three-star Ora holds 54 rooms with the usual three-star comforts: elevator, radios and phones in the rooms, tubs in the bathrooms, air conditioning and central
heating throughout. The three single rooms go for $23; if you're alone in a dou-
ble, you pay $26.50 to $28.75; two in a double costs $36.75 to $41.50. Breakfast,
as usual, is included.

At **The Hostel,** 60 Ben-Yehuda St. (Tel Aviv 63431; tel. 03-287-088 or 281-500), you must walk up 80 steps to the fourth floor. What you'll find are dorm rooms, doubles, and triples going for $4 (students) or $4.50 (nonstudents) per person; $11.75 for a double; and $15.25 for a triple. Hot showers in each room, fresh linens daily, use of a kitchen are some of the services. You must stay outside the hostel between 10 a.m. and 2 p.m. each day. No meals are served, and the Hostel is not affiliated with the IYHA. Look for it down at the end of a passageway near the corner of Mendele.

Along Ha-Yarkon

At the **Imperial Hotel,** 66 Ha-Yarkon St., corner of Trumpeldor (Tel Aviv 63902; tel. 03-657-002), you'll be staying in a new and modern building. The 49 rooms have wall-to-wall carpeting, private baths, air conditioning, and telephones, all at moderate prices: $20 to $26 single, $36.75 double, $44.75 triple, breakfast included. The Imperial is a two-star hotel with three-star accommodations.

The extremely basic and equally cheap **Excelsior,** 88 Ha-Yarkon St. (tel. 03-655-486), is at the corner of Bograshov. Here front rooms face the sea and back rooms have balconies. All 24 rooms have showers and toilets, some have baths and air conditioning (heaters are available). Room-only rates are $16 to $18 single, $20 to $25 double.

Just to the south is the **Maxim Hotel,** 86 Ha-Yarkon St. (Tel Aviv 63903; tel. 03-653-721), near the corner with Bograshov. New and modern, the Maxim offers you the important conveniences—like air conditioning—in its 60 rooms, and then tempts you with sea views from its front-facing rooms. All but eight of the rooms have tubs; the eight have showers. The slightly higher figures are for the sea-view rooms, of course: $21.75 to $25.25 single, or $36.75 to $40.25 double.

A cozy three-star hotel decorated with lots of colors is the 68-room **Adiv,** 5 Mendele St. (tel. 03-229-141 or 229-144). It has a popular self-service restaurant. Rooms have baths, radios, carpeting, heating, and air conditioning. Rates are $34 single, $45.50 for a double room. The Adiv is a good, clean, centrally located choice right next to the Israel Government Tourist Office.

All of the aforementioned hotels are on the land (east) side of Ha-Yarkon. There is a hotel on the sea (west) side, however. Although it's stretching our budget a bit, some readers will no doubt want to consider the luxurious four-star **Concorde Hotel,** 1 Trumpeldor St. at Ha-Yarkon (Tel Aviv 63451; tel. 03-659-241). This 92-room hostelry is part of the Basel Group. All rooms have radio, telephone, and air conditioning, and many have views of the sea, which is just across the esplanade. The hotel has its own garage. Despite its posh appointments, four-star rating, and excellent location, the Concorde has quite reasonable prices for what you get: $48 single, $60 double, breakfast and service included. Children get reductions of 50% (till age 6) or 30% (till 12). Winter rates are a few dollars lower.

Near Kikar Namir

Namir Square, also called Atarim, is surrounded by hotels, including the Plaza, the Diplomat, and the Carleton. All of these seafront hotels are well beyond our budget. But if you cross the street to the land side of Ha-Yarkon, prices go down dramatically, and quality remains excellent.

The three-star **Hotel Florida,** 164 Ha-Yarkon, a half block south of Ben-Gurion Street (tel. 03-242-184), has 52 modern rooms with tub baths, wall-to-wall carpeting, radios and phones, central heat, and air conditioning. Some

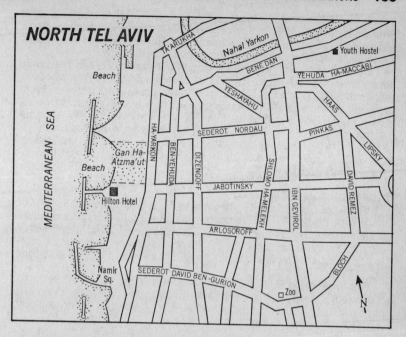

rooms even have views of busy Namir Square and of the Mediterranean, and yet the price is a moderate $27.50 to $30 single, $39 to $41.50 double.

Near Dizengoff Square

The **Dizengoff Square Hotel,** 2 Zamenhoff St., corner Dizengoff Square (tel. 03-296-181), is the only hotel at Dizengoff Square, just about the busiest part of town. Here you'll be a stone's throw from fancy shops, banks, a post office, a supermarket, cafés, restaurants, everything. It is an excellent location in terms of transportation, for there is a virtual army of buses on Dizengoff to take you practically anywhere in town. The modern, 54-room hotel itself, with balconies in front overlooking the action on Dizengoff Square, has three stars. Double-occupancy rate is $40.25; singles pay $28.75, with a few small singles priced at $23.

Up North, Near the Hilton

On Ha-Yarkon Street, out near the Tel Aviv Hilton, is the three-star **Shalom Hotel,** at no. 216 (tel. 03-243-277). It is a modern, five-story structure housing 48 rooms, 36 doubles with bath and 12 singles with shower. All the front rooms have balconies providing fine views of the Mediterranean and Independence Park. Done up in understated contemporary hotel fashion, the rooms come complete with air conditioning, central heating, and telephones, and cost $34.50 in a single room, $46 in a double during the summer, a few dollars less off-season. Students receive a 10% discount. Breakfast, included in the room rate, is served. In front of the hotel is the popular Stagecoach Restaurant (see below for a description).

Twenty-four air-conditioned, radio- and telephone-equipped rooms in a modern hotel with all services—that's the **Hotel Armon Ha-Yarkon,** 268 Ha-

Yarkon St. (Tel Aviv 63504; tel. 03-455-271 or 455-272), just across the street from the big Hotel Tal. It's a small, friendly place only a block from the beach and two blocks from the nightlife action of Little Tel Aviv. Rooms are priced at $30 single, $39 double, all in. Lots of good restaurants nearby.

Due east of the Hilton, at 201 Dizengoff St., corner of Vilna, is **The Greenhouse** (Tel Aviv 63462; tel. 03-235-994), a hostel charging $6 a day for a bed in a four- or five-bed dorm room. Sheets and blankets, hot showers, use of the kitchen, a sitting room with TV and soft drinks, and friendly staff are all included in the low price. If you come into the Central Railway Station or the El Al Terminal, just shoot down Arlosoroff to Dizengoff. From that intersection, it's only a block north to the hostel. You can also take bus 5 from the Central Bus Station, or no. 222 right from the airport. By the way, the Greenhouse also rents efficiency apartments—see below.

Private Rooms and Apartments

The **Israel Government Tourist Office** at 7 Mendele St., near the corner of Ben-Yehuda (tel. 03-223-266/7), compiles and prints a list of agencies and individuals who rent rooms and apartments. Though they will not make a contact or reservation for you, and they cannot guarantee the quality of service or accommodations, the tourist office staff will be glad to give you a copy of the list for free.

The **Greenhouse Hostel**, 201 Dizengoff St. at Vilna (tel. 03-235-994), described above, also rents one-room flats with bedroom, shower and toilet, and balcony. Up to four people can share a flat, which makes this a very good deal for families. Rent is by the week, priced at $150.

The Youth Hostel

Tel Aviv's **B'nei Dan Youth Hostel** (tel. 03-455-042) is at 32 B'nei Dan St. (the street just south of the Yarkon River), about midway between Ibn Gevirol and Weizmann Boulevards. Bus 5 will take you there, starting at the Central Bus Station, through Dizengoff Square, up Dizengoff Street to Yehuda Ha-Maccabi, whence you walk. Other buses on different routes are 24, 25, 27, and 66. The 250-bed hostel has a kitchen, store, and air conditioning, and charges $5 for bed and breakfast to those with a Hostel Association card, $6 to those without; those 18 years or under get a slight discount.

3. Where to Eat

In Israel's most cosmopolitan city, you can find a wide variety of cuisines. Of course, typical Israeli cuisine is the most widespread and popular, and prices for native food are certainly going to be lower than for the imitated foreign dishes.

To keep your food costs low in Tel Aviv, here are a few tips to follow: Breakfast is usually provided by your hotel, so you have only lunch and dinner to consider. You might make one a big three- or four-course meal at the many restaurants that advertise reasonably priced fixed menus. Several such restaurants are recommended below, but you can find many more—often with sandwich boards outside advertising their prices—along Allenby, Ben-Yehuda, and Dizengoff Streets, and at the Central Bus Station. You might make the other meal a lighter one, consisting of a pita stuffed with steak or shwarma and salad, plus a fruit drink, at the open stands that line either side of Dizengoff and that can be found readily enough on Allenby Street. Even cheaper is a falafel-stuffed pita, with salad.

As elsewhere in Israel, the least expensive restaurants in Tel Aviv are the small, family-owned vegetarian spots and those serving Middle Eastern fare.

For the latter, the tastiest food in the entire city is served up in the Yemenite quarter of town, in the maze of streets that surround the Carmel Market, off Allenby Street.

And now for specific suggestions.

ALONG BEN-YEHUDA STREET: Starting from Ben-Yehuda Street near Frishman Street, we'll look at a few choice places on this major thoroughfare. The first is an old favorite, open all week for lunch (only), including on the Sabbath.

One of the best lunchtime bargains in all Tel Aviv is found at the **Restaurant Vienna,** 48a Ben-Yehuda (no phone), tucked back in a passageway close to the corner of Bograshov. This tiny gold-walled restaurant, with tables covered in checkered cloths, is open daily from 11 a.m. to 3:30 p.m. Select one of three set-price lunches for NIS8.50 ($5.65), NIS9.70 ($6.45), or NIS12 ($8). À la carte, you might order goulash or wienerschnitzel for about NIS7 ($4.65). Don't be surprised if you have to wait in line for a table or be asked to share your table with others—the Vienna has been in business for a long time and is deservedly popular. The Vienna is not kosher; happily for tourists, it's open for lunch on the Sabbath (Saturday).

The **Osteria Ristorante da Lelio e Fiorella,** 44 Ben-Yehuda, at Bograshov (no phone), advertises that it serves *"vera cucina italiana"* (authentic Italian cuisine) prepared by *"padroni italiani"* (Italian owners). This tidy little nonkosher corner place has an attractive sense of Italy in its small tables spread with red-and-white-checked cloths, tawny curtains, and bar. A few tables are set outside on Bograshov Street in good weather. The trattoria menu has most of the old-favorite Italian dishes, and the plate of the day allows you to enjoy one selected by the chef for less than NIS10 ($6.65), plus tip and beverage. Come for lunch or dinner from 10 a.m. to midnight any day of the week.

Burger Ranch, 21a Ben-Yehuda (tel. 03-657-365), is open Sunday to Thursday from 10 a.m. to 10:30 p.m., on Saturday from 5 p.m. to midnight, and closes on Friday at 3 p.m. The menu reflects the decor: the selection of burgers is branded on wood with a real branding iron. It's an easygoing place, with Americanesque fare. A hamburger on a bun is NIS2.50 ($1.65) to NIS6 ($4) topped with cheese, pineapple, or onion. A quartered chicken with chips is about NIS6.30 ($4.25). There is a counter inside and tables and chairs outside. Eat in or take out.

At the kosher **Grill Center** ("Pinat Ha-Grill"), 2 Ben-Yehuda (tel. 03-296-894), next to the Moghrabi Cinema, right off Allenby Street, is a large self-service restaurant. The restaurant recently renovated and modernized, offers chicken with chips and pita, schnitzel in pita, a hamburger, and kishke, just to name a few items. Soup, salad, a main course, and beverage will set you back about NIS9 ($6). Open Sunday to Thursday from 10 a.m. to 10 p.m., closing Friday at 3 p.m.

In the same vicinity, **Nes Ziona,** 8a Nes Ziona St. off Ben-Yehuda near Moghrabi Square (tel. 03-652-855), is well known for its authentic and delicious Hungarian fare. It's a homey place with walls covered in imitation wood and wallpaper, and curtained windows. For NIS15 ($10) to NIS20 ($13.35), you can order a full meal beginning with an appetizer of chopped liver, soup, or gefilte fish, proceeding to a main course of goulash, chicken, schnitzel, or roast beef—all served with two side dishes, and winding up with a dessert of apple compote, blintzes, or strudel. Open Sunday through Thursday from noon to 10 p.m., till 3 p.m. on Friday, closed Saturday.

ALONG ALLENBY ROAD: Starting on the stretch of Allenby Road that runs between Allenby (or Knesset) Square and Moghrabi Square, we'll now examine

the culinary possibilities as you stroll south from the axis of Moghrabi Square for a block or two. This area has several very good but inexpensive restaurants which cater to the budget-conscious travelers who stay in the area's inexpensive hotels.

At 13 Allenby is the **Long Seng Chinese Restaurant** (tel. 03-655-685), only a half block from the Hotel Riviera. Small and plain but very tidy, the Long Seng usually offers a set-price meal such as hot-and-sour soup, sweet-and-sour pork, or beef with bean sprouts, dessert, and tea for NIS12 ($8). This is about the cheapest price for a full meal. A more elaborate eight-course dinner for two is priced at NIS37.50 ($25) total. You can order à la carte, but it will cost more. Hours are noon to 3 p.m. and 6 to 11 p.m. Saturday through Thursday, on Friday from 6 to 11:30 p.m.

"Weight Watchers" will appreciate knowing that the **Atara Café and Self-Service Restaurant** at 54 Allenby (look for the sign that says "Cafeteria-Dairy Meals-Fish"; tel. 03-656-653) is where their Israeli counterparts meet and try not to overeat. They serve hot and cold vegetable dishes from 6 a.m. to 11 p.m. daily, on Saturday evening to midnight, on Friday until 5 p.m. There are two prices for everything, depending on whether you help yourself at the counter and sit in the front section, or sit in the rear section and are served at your table. A low-calorie meal of grilled fish and salad with two vegetables can be had for NIS6 ($4), self-service. A standard breakfast of two rolls, cottage cheese, butter, jam, coffee or tea—table service only—is priced at NIS3.75 ($2.50).

THE YEMENITE QUARTER AND CARMEL MARKET: Walk along Allenby
Road from Moghrabi Square. At the Atara Café (54 Allenby) mentioned above, turn right and walk along the pedestrian alley to the closely packed grid of little streets at its far end. This is the **Yemenite Quarter**, a section of squat houses and shops, exotic by day, dimly lit and shadowy at night. Don't let the neighborhood's appearance rattle you. The people here are honest and respectable, if a bit boisterous, and it's a perfectly safe area to traverse. This is one of the first parts of Tel Aviv, built in 1909 when the Jews decided to leave Arab Jaffa and start an all-Jewish city.

The tangled streets of the Yemenite Quarter harbor several restaurants serving the tastiest Middle Eastern food in all Tel Aviv and some of the best in the country.

If you enter the Yemenite Quarter as described above, turn right at the end of the pedestrian alley, then left onto Najara Street. Down at the far end of Najara Street is the **Maganda Restaurant**, 26 Rabbi Meir St. (tel. 03-659-990). The Maganda has recently been completely rebuilt, and is now airy, modern, and very attractive. The cuisine is Yemenite, strictly kosher, and includes grilled meats such as lamb shishlik and kebab at NIS7.50 ($5) to NIS15 ($10). The menu is in English as well as Hebrew. Hours are noon to midnight Sunday through Thursday; closed Friday, and Saturday till after sunset. Expect to spend about NIS15 ($10) to NIS24 ($16) for a full meal here.

The **Zion**, at 28 Peduyim (or Yihye) St. (tel. 03-657-323), a half block from the Maganda, serves authentic kosher Yemenite dishes, and kicks in a bit of atmosphere too. You walk down several stairs into the center room of the restaurant, which is plain and overlighted. Off the main room are several small anterooms, with flagstone floors, stained-glass doors, and romantic dim lights. Slip into one of the anterooms ("Zion Exclusive") for dinner, but keep in mind that prices are higher in this section, and that the hours differ. The cheaper section is open from noon to 11 p.m., on Friday until 3 p.m.; the "Zion Exclusive," closed all day Friday and on Saturday until sundown, is open from noon to 3:30 p.m. and 6:30 p.m. to midnight. As for the food at the Zion, it is uniformly excellent. Try one of the spicy soups, a salad appetizer, and you'll pay NIS15 ($10) to NIS24 ($16) for the full meal with a kebab main course, with delicious vegetables or chips on the side. Such a feast will be accompanied by pita, olives, and peppers for just slightly more. Try experimenting with choices on the menu and ask the English-speaking waiter to be your guide.

Peduyim Street is a pedestrian way, and is packed with other little restaurants. This gives you a choice, and also adds to the atmosphere. You really feel something delightfully different here.

To get to **Shaul's Inn** (tel. 03-653-303), turn west down Ge'ulah Street off Allenby. A very short half block down Ge'ulah, take a diagonal left turn—this is Ha-Ari Street, the first street on the left. Walk along Ha-Ari, and turn right onto Rabbi Meir Street, then quickly left onto Kehilat Aden Street. Shaul's Inn is a block down, on the left.

Shaul's Inn is probably the most expensive kosher restaurant in the Yemenite Quarter, but it is one of the best. Address is Kehilat Aden Street, corner Elyashiv. Nicely atmospheric, with heavy wooden chairs, flagstone floors, and a large photomural of a Yemenite wedding on one wall, this restaurant can get packed out to the street on Saturday nights. Stick to the main room on the ground floor; downstairs, where there is an intimate restaurant and bar, the prices go up by over 100%. English is spoken here, and the waiters will help you choose from the Middle Eastern specialties. The "Specialty of the Inn" is the lamb's breast stuffed with rice and pine nuts—deliciously tasty. Have a Turkish or Greek salad (scoop it up with pita), or a gorgeous stuffed eggplant, cabbage, or pepper. At Shaul's, you can eat very reasonably by choosing from such dishes as shishlik or kebab, and a full meal need cost no more than about NIS18 ($12) to NIS27 ($18). Hours: noon till midnight, on Friday till 3 p.m., on Saturday after sundown.

Gamliel Restaurant, 38 Ha-Kovshim St. at Ezra Hassofer, one block east of the sea (tel. 03-658-779), is the domain of owner Gamliel, whose specialties are different kinds of meat- and rice-filled vegetables at NIS4.50 ($3) a serving. This is an especially attractive place, with an interior terrace, lots of greenery, an aquarium, and splashing fountains. If you feel brave, try some of the regional specialties—pigeon spleens or beef lungs. But less adventurous diners needn't worry. They can order lamb shishlik or kebab. Save room for dessert of Bavarian cream. Open Sunday to Thursday from noon to 12:30 a.m.; closed all day Friday until Saturday evening. Kosher.

Owner Oda Nagi takes great pride in his **Restaurant Nagi,** at 22 Gedera St. (no phone), behind the Allenby Cinema. If you don't want the pickles and pitas placed on your table automatically, have them taken away or you'll be charged for them. Try the goulash soup for NIS2.50 ($1.65). A main course of kebab, shwarma, steak, or liver (not to mention spleen, kidneys, lungs, or lamb testicles) is NIS5.25 ($3.50) to NIS10 ($6.65). Open in winter from 8 a.m. to 7:30 p.m. Sunday to Thursday, closed Friday from 3 p.m. until Sunday morning. Open till 10 p.m. in summer.

IN AND AROUND DIZENGOFF SQUARE:

On Dizengoff Street, steak-and-pita, shwarma, and hamburger stands abound, especially around Dizengoff Square, where the street takes on the aspect of both Times Square and the Via Veneto. These are quick-service places, with a grill in the middle and possibly a rôtisserie for the shwarma. Frankly, I find the shwarma far tastier than the steaks, which are frozen and then quickly defrosted over the flaming grill, and all the spicy salad stuffed around the steak can't change the often low quality of the meat.

By the way, Dizengoff Square is the place to come for a bite on Saturday, when most of the other places are closed. Numerous restaurants and snack-shops open in mid-morning and serve edibles all day.

Some Money-Saving Tips

Do some comparison-shopping when you buy falafel. Sometimes the price for falafel is posted (in English), sometimes it's not. Watch and see what a local pays, and insist on paying only that much (yes, tourists sometimes get over-charged). Make sure your falafel is good, with real chickpea meal, not just bread dough. A good falafel should cost about NIS1.20 (80¢) to NIS1.80 ($1.20).

In the dozens of cafés around Dizengoff Square, a cup of coffee costs about NIS1.35 (90¢) to NIS2.50 ($1.65), perhaps a bit more for special brews such as cappuccino. Before you sit down to order, take note: Are people drinking coffee here, or are they sticking to tea, soft drinks, and beer? The quality of coffee varies greatly from place to place.

For a glass of beer in a café, you can pay anywhere from NIS1.50 ($1) to NIS5 ($3.35), depending on size, brand, and the establishment. Draft beer in large glasses gives you the best value for the money if your intention is to sit, sip, and watch the parade of pedestrians.

Dizengoff Restaurants

Although Dizengoff Street near Dizengoff Square harbors few elegant, at-mospheric dining places, you can still find establishments that provide a modi-cum of decor, good food, moderate prices, and menus offering more than just snack fare. Here are my favorites, starting with several restaurants right around the "circular square."

A few steps north of the circle you can easily spot the popular **Derby Bar,** 96 Dizengoff (no phone), busy all day and evening. It combines the atmos-pheres of a sidewalk café and a modern cafeteria with low prices and a vast menu to draw the crowds. A Greek salad and a kebab, with dessert and bever-age, need cost no more than NIS15 ($10); a hamburger served in flat bread, with a soft drink, costs less than half that amount.

Food like mother used to make can be found at the **Restaurant Naknikiya Ha-Kikar,** at 4 Dizengoff Square (tel. 03-280-939). In this small and simple place you can enjoy gefilte fish (slightly sweet), chopped liver, or kreplach in chicken soup or sauce for NIS2.50 ($1.65), and those stick-to-the-ribs food like tcholent and kishke for twice as much. Chicken or goulash with vegetables is NIS9 ($6). Open Sunday to Thursday from 8 a.m. to 10 p.m.; closed Friday afternoon until Saturday evening.

Students get a 10% reduction at **Pundak 91,** 91 Dizengoff St. (tel. 03-225-941), a Middle Eastern/European eatery with mirrored walls inside and green chairs at yellow tables on the sidewalk out front. You can choose from about 17 kinds of salad—NIS3 ($2) for a small plate, double that for a large. Kebab in a pita, or shwarma is NIS4.50 ($3). Open daily from 8 a.m. to 1 a.m.

The Artists' Place: Less than two blocks north of the square, on the left-hand side, stands the **Kassit Restaurant,** 119 Dizengoff (tel. 03-223-855), a hangout of artists and writers for many years. Though many of these worthies no doubt come for the company, others arrive for the daily special menu priced at only NIS7 ($4.65). For that low price you get soup or salad, schnitzel or meatballs or calves' liver, and coffee or tea. Indoor and outdoor tables accommodate thrifty diners, the walls are an eclectic gallery of sketches and paintings, and a canopy of trees shades the sidewalk from the brilliant sun. Kassit is open daily, all day.

For Seafood: Tel Aviv has several restaurants specializing in seafood, all of them something of a splurge for readers of this book. Among these pricey but worthy places is the **Stern Dolphin Restaurant,** 189 Dizengoff St. (tel. 03-232-425), just south of Arlosoroff. Soft light illuminates a decor that is pleasant, though neither simple nor elegant. The menu shines with all of those treats so difficult to find in Israel, including shrimp, calamari, trout (served with olives and nuts, or with apples and mushrooms), and lots of other fish. You can finish up with Bavarian cream or baklava, have a half bottle of wine, and spend NIS40 ($26.75) per person. If you choose something other than shrimp, and have only a glass of wine, you need spend only NIS26 ($17.25) or so. The Stern Dolphin is open from noon to midnight, seven days a week.

For Italian Meals: The area around Dizengoff Square holds a few nice Italian eateries, and Dizengoff Street running northeast out of the square holds some more. In general, street numbers 90 and higher indicate addresses on Dizengoff Street northeast of the square. These restaurants are all within a block or two of the square itself.

Pizzeria Capri, 107 Dizengoff St. (tel. 03-220-602), is convincingly Italian —wrought ironwork, cozy little trattoria-style tables set with candles and flowers—until you note the South American travel posters which add splashes of color to the walls. The owner is from South America in fact, although his menu is mostly Italian: lasagne, pasta, ravioli, cannelloni, calamari, antipasto, and of course pizza in 14 varieties. As an Israeli touch, liver and schnitzel are served up too, but none of the food is kosher. If you start with soup or a salad, go on to a filling pizza or pasta dish, and finish up with ice cream, fruit salad, or chocolate mousse, your bill should come to NIS12 ($8) to NIS18 ($12), service charge (10%) included. Add a dollar or two more if you want fish, shrimp, calamari, or schnitzel, and a glass of wine or bottle of beer. The Capri is a dependable all-the-time eatery, open from 9 a.m. to 1 a.m., seven days a week.

A cafeteria called the **Numero Uno,** 89 Dizengoff St. (tel. 03-225-978), offers an array of Italian foods. Spaghetti (of course), cannelloni with mushrooms, lots of things in tomato sauce with cheese on top. And there's pizza or a cheese omelet, and nothing on the menu costs more than NIS9 ($6). A dessert specialty is a crêpe made with apples, pineapple, cheese, or strawberries (in season), whipped cream, nuts, and chocolate syrup. Open from 8 a.m. to 1 a.m.; closed from Friday at 4 p.m. to Saturday at 7 p.m.

Thirteen varieties of pizza are offered at **Pizzeria Rimini & Coffee Shop,** 93 Dizengoff St. (tel. 03-221-681), ranging in price from NIS6 ($4) to NIS9 ($6). Pasta, meat dishes, wine, and liquor are also available. Pizzeria Rimini is at five other centrally located addresses: 4 Malchei Israel Square (tel. 03-263-987), 24 Ibn Gevirol (tel. 03-266-177), 3 Ahuzat Bait St. (tel. 03-253-287), Namir Square (tel. 03-288-800), and 262 Ben-Yehuda St. (tel. 03-457-050). All are open daily from 11 a.m. to 1 a.m.

For Hamburgers and Subs: On Dizengoff Street, just at the northeast side of Dizengoff Square, you may have noticed in the jumble of little shops and eateries some signs advertising "South American Sandwiches" or "Sandwiches Argentinos." To a New Yorker it's a hero or a grinder, to a Bostonian it's a sub, to a Philadelphian it's a hoagie—an immense sandwich stuffed with all sorts of meat or cheese, salads, and vegetables. These places often allow you to stuff your own roll, and the charge per sandwich is only NIS1.50 to NIS3.75 ($1 to $2.50). You can pick up a large salad for about the same, and then consume your hefty purchases indoors, outdoors at sidewalk tables, or up by the fountain in Dizengoff Square.

Just a bit farther northeast out of the square on Dizengoff Street, turn left onto Frishman Street and just on the right at no. 39 you can't fail to spot **MacDavid** (tel. 03-220-826). The Israeli version of you-know-what is an amusing replica, even down to a sign that keeps tabs on "Hamburgers Sold to This Day" (over a million at last count). Order a Big MacDavid with cheese (yes! this one's not kosher), a bag of french fries, and a cold Maccabee beer, and you'll pay NIS7 ($4.65), just a plain burger and a soft drink will cost only half that price. Get one of the sidewalk tables if you can. MacDavid is open from 9:30 a.m. to 1 a.m.; on Friday they close from 3 to 7 p.m., and then reopen until 2 a.m.; Saturday hours are 10:30 a.m. to 1 a.m.

An alternative cure to a fit of burgermania is the Dizengoff Square branch of **Burger Ranch,** 109 Dizengoff, just north out of the square on Dizengoff Street, west side. With a glass-enclosed sidewalk seating area and competitive prices, it's one of the most popular places here.

A Classic Café: The **Rowal,** 111 Dizengoff (tel. 03-225-838), has much to offer. Walk past the cold case filled with tempting cakes, down the passage and up the stairs. You'll enter an airy, attractive room with a streetside balcony, bamboo furniture, tidy napery, and attentive staff. The selection of pastries and cakes is positively Viennese in its extravagance, and one enormous portion with a "Cappuccino" (really a kaffee mit schlag) will set you back about NIS5 ($3.35) to NIS8 ($5.35). For lunch or supper, try soup and salad, or a burger, for about NIS7.50 ($5). The Rowal is plush, attractive, genteel and quiet, yet not really expensive, and it's open on Saturday.

For People-Watching: You hardly need tips on people-watching as Dizengoff is sprinkled with good sidewalk cafés along most of its length. But if you're at a loss on where to start, head for the **Acapulco Inn,** 105 Dizengoff (tel. 03-237-552), at the corner of Dizengoff and Frishman. It's got all the winning elements of a great people-watching place. As in most cafés, light meals such as hummus or Greek salad are served for NIS2 ($1.35), as well as coffee, pastries, beer, and wine.

You'll enjoy both the people and the food at **Cherry,** 166 Dizengoff, corner of Ben-Gurion (tel. 03-240-300), as both are eclectic. The people tend to be young and upscale, but really come from all parts of Tel Aviv life. The food and drink fill a long list which includes sandwiches, ice-cream sundaes, a dozen salads, milkshakes, frozen yogurt, quiches, fish, and every conceivable sort of drink from cognac through Southern Comfort to mango juice or Sanka. Prices depend very much on what, and how much, you eat and drink, but a sandwich and a beer will set you back about NIS10 ($6.65), tip included. Coffee and cake will cost only about half that much. Cherry is always crowded, from its opening at 9 a.m. to its closing after midnight, seven days a week.

Make Your Own Meals

Tired of eating in restaurants and snackshops? Want to relax in your hotel room, nibble on cheeses, pickles, olives, cold meats, fresh bread, and sip some nice wine? You can get all the ingredients you need—including the wine—at the **Supersol,** a supermarket on the American plan located at 79 Ben-Yehuda St., between Mapu and Smolenskin, on the left as you head north. It's a fascinating cross-cultural experience, shopping the way the Israelis shop. Labels on many products are in English as well as Hebrew; pointing to what you want at the huge deli counter in the back seems to work just fine. There's another such supermarket next to the cinema in Dizengoff Square. Bon appétit!

IN AND AROUND NAMIR SQUARE: The Namir Square (Kikar Namir) complex is a must for daytime or evening strolling—it's Tel Aviv's answer to Ghirardelli Square, complete with cafés, ice-cream parlors, restaurants, and shops. There are plenty of small food stands where you can buy food to go; in this category you might try a strawberry whip for NIS2.50 ($1.65) from **Fruit House.**

The most popular eating place here by far, and for years, is the local branch of **Pizzeria Rimini** (tel. 03-288-800), which is no simple pizza joint but a full Italian restaurant serving such things as bistecca alla gorgonzola (steak in bleu cheese sauce) and fettuccine al chef. The pizzas are good, varied, and priced from NIS6 ($4) to NIS10 ($6.65). There are both indoor and shaded outdoor dining areas. Expect to pay from NIS10 ($6.65) to NIS24 ($16) for a full dinner here. Hours are daily from 11 a.m. to 1 a.m.

Also on the plaza at Namir Square is the **Rondo Restaurant** (tel. 03-287-704), with attractive wicker patio furniture, some view of the sea, and lots of possibilities for people-watching. The specialty here is grilled meats, from burgers through lamb chops to steaks, all accompanied by a vast serve-yourself salad bar. The bill for a meal will run from NIS15 ($10) to NIS40 ($26.75). The Rondo is open daily for lunch and dinner.

In your Kikar Namir explorations, don't neglect the nether regions: beneath the plaza level are warrens of little cafés, bars, and nightspots, most of which serve light meals accompanied by music, usually rock.

A few blocks north along Ha-Yarkon Street, opposite the Hilton, is the Hotel Shalom at 216 Ha-Yarkon, and in front of the hotel is the popular **Stagecoach Restaurant** (tel. 03-241-703). It's heavy on the western movie-set saloon decor, which ends up being delightfully amusing. There's live music each evening. The menu lists huge hamburgers, bowls of chili, and salads, which will cost you about NIS12 ($8) to NIS20 ($13.35) when you add in a beverage (draft beer is a specialty) and the tip. Not kosher; open for lunch and dinner every day.

NEAR HA-BIMAH AND MANN AUDITORIUM: Tel Aviv's center of culture is the area a block west of the intersection of Dizengoff Street and Ibn Gevirol Street. Along with the Ha-Bimah National Theater, Mann Auditorium, Z.O.A. House, and Helena Rubinstein Pavilion, the area includes places to get a bite before the performance. I'll describe what's available by starting at that important intersection, Dizengoff and Ibn Gevirol, and will then head north along Ibn Gevirol.

Right at the intersection, at 22 Ibn Gevirol, corner of Kaplan (Kaplan is the continuation of Dizengoff), is a branch of the **MacDavid** hamburger chain (no phone). The burgers, if not absolutely authentic, are none the worse for that: they're tasty, and priced right. Figure NIS3.75 ($2.50) for a simple burger and soft drink. If you're hungry, go on to more elaborate burgers, french fries, desserts, or even a roast beef sandwich. MacDavid is open from 9:30 a.m. to 1 a.m.; closed on Friday from 3 to 7 p.m., then open until 1 a.m. On Saturday, hours are 10:30 a.m. to 1 a.m.

Down the block from MacDavid are many other little eateries. At the far (north) end of the block, at no. 24, is an outlet of **Pizzeria Rimini** (tel. 03-266-177), where you can order a small pizza for as little as NIS6 ($4) and consume it at a sidewalk café table to boot.

Another great light-meal idea is to try a **boureka.** These delicious pastries are filled with such things as cheese and spinach, and served hot or cold. There's a boureka place at the northwest corner of the Dizengoff and Ibn Gevirol intersection, right across Ibn Gevirol from MacDavid.

Go a bit farther north on Ibn Gevirol, in the next block, and you'll come to several cafés, including the **Café Ministore** (tel. 03-265-373) at no. 30. Outdoor tables shaded by awnings make up the café-dining area. Help yourself (self-service) to blintzes, pizza, coffees, cool drinks, and desserts. The **Whitman's Milk Bar** (no phone) next door takes the overflow when the Ministore fills up.

UP NORTH BY THE YARKON RIVER: In daylight, the neighborhood just south of the Yarkon River is nondescript, if pleasant. But each evening it becomes a different place, with lights blazing from restaurants, lines forming at the doors, and windows filled by scenes of happy diners.

The neighborhood, sometimes called Little Tel Aviv, is centered on Yirmiyahu Street, a short street near the point where Ben-Yehuda and Dizengoff Streets meet, a block from the bend in the Yarkon. Take a bus or a cab north on Ha-Yarkon, Ben-Yehuda, or Dizengoff Streets all the way to Yirmiyahu.

Wandering the maze of streets surrounding Yirmiyahu will disclose all sorts of restaurants: steakhouses, seafood grills, vegetarian eateries, and blintz parlors of every description. American, Israeli, Chinese, European, and Middle Eastern cuisine are all represented here.

About the best-known restaurant in these parts is **Little Old Tel Aviv,** also known as **Mandy's Candy Store,** 300 Ha-Yarkon St. at Ha-Sira Street (tel. 03-450-109). At Mandy's you can order practically anything: crêpes, hamburgers, calamari (squid), steaks and kebabs, ice cream, pies and cakes, boiled beef and tcholent, pasta, soups and salads. The drink list is equally bewildering, proffering everything from sangría to Irish coffee. Staff are friendly and efficient, and you can pick your decor as there are a myriad of rooms, nooks, porches, and booths. Most of Mandy's is done in mod-Victorian, with exposed brick, old furniture and mirrors, period pictures, and leafy plants. Sound like fun? It is, though prices are not low. The best deal is to choose one of the daily specials from the blackboard, which might be soup and a salade niçoise (lettuce, tomato, cucumber, sliced boiled potato, black olives, and anchovy filets) for NIS10 ($6.65), service included. Drop in just for dessert, or afternoon tea, and a slice of chocolate cream cake with a cup of coffee will set you back about NIS8 ($5.35), all in. Hearty three-course meals cost about NIS20 ($13.35). Mandy's is open from noon to half past midnight Sunday to Friday, till 1:30 a.m. on Saturday.

The quaint café-restaurant at 265 Dizengoff St., corner of Yirmiyahu, is actually a Russian place called **Pirozki** (tel. 03-457-599). The restaurant's name appears frequently on its menu, as pirozkis (soft dough envelopes stuffed with various things) are the specialty. I had the meat-and-mushroom pirozki, the most expensive one, which came with a side of coleslaw. It was simply enormous. With a glass of beer, and a dessert of dried fruit with honey and whipped cream, tax, and tip, the bill came to NIS24 ($16). The crowd here is a mixture of young and old, seated in the cozy, tiny inner room, or upstairs, or in the glassed-in sidewalk area. Not kosher; open daily for lunch and dinner, until after midnight.

Ethnic Restaurants

In recent years, northern Tel Aviv has seen a veritable explosion of restaurants specializing in ethnic cuisine. Now you can take your pick among several Chinese, Thai, Moroccan, Italian, Hungarian, and Russian places. Here are some of the best:

For Italian fare, you'll love the quaint façade and cozy interior of **Me and Me, The Pizzaria,** 293 Dizengoff St., at Ta'Arukha (tel. 03-443-427). This is the Italian cuisine branch of a downtown steakhouse of the same name. Here the fare includes a dozen kinds of pizza, plus various pasta dishes including spaghetti, fettuccine, and lasagne, most priced around NIS9 ($6). Calamari (squid), antipasti, and shrimp cocktail are also on the menu, along with veal scaloppine. The fanciest main courses can run twice the aforementioned price. Me and Me is not kosher, and is open seven days a week from noon until after midnight.

Luckily for discriminating diners, Israel has recently seen a dramatic increase in the number of Thai-Chinese restaurants. The food can be wonderful (especially the Thai dishes), the prices moderate. Tel Aviv's hottest place in this regard is the **Red Chinese Restaurant,** 326 Dizengoff, at Ben-Yehuda (tel. 03-448-405). Last time I was there, I sat with dozens of happy Tel Avivans helping themselves to wonton and hot-and-sour soups, and chicken, pork, beef, and seafood dishes for about NIS15 ($10) to NIS23 ($15.35) per person. Wine and beer are served. Hours, every day, are 1 to 3:30 p.m. and 7 p.m. to midnight.

For sheer glitz and variety, the prize goes to **Suki Yaki,** 302 Dizengoff St., at Yirmiyahu (tel. 03-448-273 or 443-687), three floors of dining rooms in which you can sit down to Chinese, Thai, and Japanese dishes. Make your way through the gleaming black and glinting chrome, find a table, and study a menu that includes pork, beef, chicken, and squid for NIS10 ($6.65) to NIS14 ($9.35) per plate. On Sunday and Monday there's a 20% discount for diners paying in cash. Come to dine anytime from 12:30 p.m. to 12:30 a.m.

For Pastry and Coffee

North Tel Aviv's most pleasant European-style café is the **Conditory London,** 15 Yirmiyahu, between Dizengoff and Ben-Yehuda (tel. 03-546-1218). Pleasant, shiny, and modern, the glass-fronted refrigerator cases hold a heaven of savarins, eclairs, tarts, and other delightful diet-busters. Coffee comes in various ways, and there are many other drinks served as well. Expect to pay about NIS6 ($4) for coffee and pastry here. It's open daily from breakfast until after dinner.

Good, Cheap Hummus

Tramping around northern Tel Aviv one hot afternoon, I sought refuge and sustenance at a tiny eatery called **Asli,** 338 Dizengoff, at Ta'Arukha (tel. 03-441-965). The motherly lady behind the counter suggested (in French) that I try the hummus, which I did. It was fantastic, and with two rounds of flat bread and a soft drink, it made a simple, delicious lunch for a grand total of NIS3.65 ($2.45). Asli has no sign or menu in English, just a few glassed-in sidewalk tables and a counter with the kitchen behind it. The lady speaks French and Hebrew, but no English. The word for hummus, luckily, is universal. It's open from breakfast through early evening; closed Saturday.

Blintzes, Blintzes

Although you can find any manner of cuisine hereabouts, the specialty is definitely blintzes (or crêpes, if you prefer), thin pancakes filled and rolled up. The filling might be spiced spinach, mushroom goulash, eggplant, vegetables, white cheese, sour cream, kashkeval, chocolate whipped cream, nuts, apples, or fruit cocktail—just about anything interesting and delicious. The thing to do is ask for an order of savory blintzes—two to an order, about NIS8 ($5.35)—as a main course, and another order of two sweet ones for dessert for a bit less.

Among the coziest and friendliest of the blintzerias is the one named **Shoshana & Uri Hungarian Blintzes,** 35 Yirmiyahu (tel. 03-450-674), half a block east of Dizengoff Street. Dinner is the only meal served (from 6 p.m. to 1 a.m., except Friday), and the blintzes are kosher. I had a bowl of vegetable soup, two sweet blintzes made with apples, raisins, and cinnamon, and a soft drink for NIS12 ($8), all in. Other desserts, plus wines and liqueurs, are also served.

For Natural Foods

The **Banana Natural Foods Restaurant,** 334 Dizengoff, north of the intersection with Yirmiyahu Street (tel. 03-457-491), offers vegetarian fare in a fittingly natural setting. The window is filled with plants, chairs and tables are unfinished wood, and the ceiling has wooden beams. Only fresh, natural foods are served. Juices and soups are NIS3 ($2); a salad of beets, cabbage, carrots, pecans, and mint leaves, or steamed veggies and brown rice, and homemade healthy cakes will cost NIS10 ($6.65). Natural juices (with vodka, if you like!), beer, and wine are served. Open Sunday to Thursday from noon to midnight, on Saturday from 1 p.m. to midnight; closed all day Friday.

JAFFA RESTAURANTS: People come down to Jaffa for sightseeing during the day, and for expensive dinners and some nightclub action after dark. For the purposes of this book, we can do without the expensive dinners, and the nightclubs, discos, and bars are covered later on in the section on that subject. Here's what you need right now: tips on where to have lunch or a pick-me-up without busting your budget.

Right in the square by the St. Peter Convent and Roman excavations are a number of restaurants, most of them fairly expensive. The **Restaurant Yamit,** 16 Kikar Kedumim (tel. 03-825-353), with its open-air terrace filled with tables and chairs, its view of the sea and of the square, is about the most popular spot for a cool drink or a cup of coffee. The Yamit has a full menu, including some set-price meals costing NIS18 ($12) to NIS24 ($16), or you can order just a salad or a sandwich for about NIS6 ($4).

Old Jaffa, appropriately, has a good Arabic restaurant, just down the hill on the south side of Kikar Kedumim. It's **Al-Sheich Deeb,** 15 Kikar Kedumim (tel. 03-824-688), the Jaffa branch of a restaurant which grew famous at a location on the highway to Herzliya. The indoor room here is stuccoed and atmospheric of Old Jaffa, and the several small sunny patios out front have umbrella-shaded tables. As you study the menu, you will see that overeating here is a distinct possibility, as the food is tempting and the prices reasonable. There are spicy soups, creamy hummus, tangy salads based on cauliflower or cabbage or chopped eggplant, and lots of grilled meats and fish. Seafood is priced according to size and season, but you can have a meal of salad and grilled lamb for as little as NIS15 ($10), or only slightly more if you go all out. Al-Sheich Deeb serves lunch and dinner every day.

For your heavy tuck-in, however, you must forsake the top of the hill altogether. Walk in front of St. Peter's and along **Mifraz Shlomo Street** down the hill, enjoying the sweeping view of Tel Aviv. At the bottom of the hill, before you reach the main intersection with the clock tower, is a warren of little eateries on the right. Most have both indoor and outdoor eating areas, and all are very plain and simple. If you don't get a menu, ask prices before you order. Your Hebrew may be rusty or nonexistent, but your eyes and nose will tell you all you need to know. The charcoal grills smoke all day, cooking up fresh fish, shish kebab, and other treats; salad, dessert, and side dishes are there for you to point to. Have some fish or kebab, a salad, dessert, and a soft drink, and the bill will come to less than NIS16 ($10.65); it'll be delicious, and you'll be full. This is where the Jaffans eat, not up at the top of the hill.

Not far from this group of restaurants is another that you might want to consider. Mifraz Shlomo Street meets the main drag at the bottom of the hill near the clock tower. Turn left and you're on **Yefet Street.**

The **Tripoli**, on Yefet just opposite the Clock Tower (no phone), is a family-run restaurant that specializes in couscous for NIS9 ($6); other choices are charami (a fish in piquant sauce), mafrum (potatoes stuffed with meat in a sauce), and green peas with meat and a stuffed vegetable. Chips and salad are served with all the above. Drinks here are classed as "strong," "cold," and "hot." The Tripoli is open from 8 a.m. to 1 a.m., closing Friday at 4 p.m. until Saturday at 7 p.m.

CAFÉ LIFE: Tel Aviv's sidewalk coffeeshops enjoy a far-flung reputation. Nothing delights an Israeli more than to sit out at night surrounded by friends and watch the evening walkers stream by. Two areas are traditionally popular for this pastime: Dizengoff Street and the Herbert Samuel Esplanade—**Ha-Boardwalk**—which runs along the sandy beach (women take note: it's best to walk or sit in pairs in this second area, particularly at night). Before you pick out a seat for yourself at one of these cafés, however, make sure you understand that you will have to pay up to three times as much here for coffee as you would anywhere else. But no one will force you to order more than a single cup. If you're café-ing by day, and it's hot, cool off with a coffee ice-cream soda, one of the most popular Israeli drinks, or apple cider, very refreshing and tasty. And if you want to conserve your pennies, order tea, Tempo (like Seven-Up), Crystal (plain soda water), or Orangeade, all of which are fairly cheap.

Outdoor café life on Dizengoff Street starts near Dizengoff Square, and works northward. The "scene" is pretty packed most nights, but its real crescendo is reached on Saturday nights after the movies let out. Before you settle on one café, it's fun to take a stroll from one end of the area to the other, checking out the different types of places and crowds, and keeping in mind that you can sit and eat a meal as well as simply have coffee or dessert.

4. The Sights of Tel Aviv–Jaffa

There's much to see and do during the daytime, and all of it is either free or very inexpensive. After a look at city tours, I've set forth the places you'll want to visit, grouped according to the general areas in which they're found: (1) near or along Allenby Street; (2) along Rothschild Boulevard; (3) along or near Dizengoff Street; (4) near Ha-Yarkon Street and the Yarkon River, and (5) elsewhere.

TOURS: The **Association for Tourism of Tel Aviv–Jaffa** (tel. 03-438-214 or 232-581) leads a free walking tour of Old Jaffa on Wednesday mornings. See the section on Old Jaffa for details.

Another good source of guided tours is the **Society for the Protection of Nature in Israel,** 4 Ha-Shefela St. (tel. 03-382-501). These tours are for individuals or families, for a fee.

ALLENBY STREET: This long street, which begins at the seaside, was named after the British general who took Palestine from the Turks in 1917. It is a street of furniture stores, bakeries, bookstores, kiosks, and screeching buses. Allenby Street is what non–Tel Avivans mean when they speak about "one of those typical Tel Aviv streets—if you know what I mean."

Between Montefiore and Ahad Ha-Am Streets, on Allenby, at no. 110, is the domed **Great Synagogue** (1926), quite handsome since extensive exterior renovations were completed in the 1970s. It is the largest synagogue in Tel Aviv.

Go around the corner to Ahad Ha-Am Street; one block down is the 34-story **Shalom Mayer Tower** (Migdal Shalom). It is an outstanding commercial shopping center, housing a large department store, shops, and offices. The view from the **Observatory** can be magnificent, by the naked eye or by the telescopes set out for that purpose. Take the glass elevator to the top. There is a café up top too—but all this is hardly half of what goes on at Shalom Tower. There is **Mayerland,** an amusement park with many kinds of rides, arts-and-crafts booths, and the typical goodies that go with such installations, such as cotton candy, ice cream, and popcorn. The **Wax Museum** depicts events in Israeli history, personalities, and in some cases sensational news items. The amusement park, observatory, and wax museum are open Sunday to Thursday from 9 a.m. to 7 p.m., on Friday and holiday eves till 2 p.m.

The department store, called **Shalom Stores** (tel. 03-652-131), can sell you everything from shoelaces to furniture; you can have your hair done, be photographed, eat in one of the many restaurants, even mail a letter in the post office. Open daily from 9 a.m. to 5 p.m., till 1 p.m. on Friday. Take bus 1, 4, 12, 25, or 30.

Back now to Allenby. At no. 115 is **Hamashbir Latzarchan,** another department store, this one is part of a chain throughout the country. Open from 8:30 a.m. to 7 p.m. daily, but only till 2 to 3 p.m. on Friday. It, too, offers a huge assortment of merchandise, from the basement with kitchenware, a milk bar, and a supermarket, on up through its escalated levels.

Carmel Market and the Yemenite Quarter

Going uptown, where Allenby Road approaches Magen David Square, a six-sided intersection, you'll find a colorful market area, the **Carmel Market** (Shuk Ha-Carmel), an open-air affair of vegetables, fragrant fruit, and shining kitchenware. There are vendors selling everything from food to clothing on open tables along the main street. Many have their own songs, which tell you all about the price and quality of what is being sold. Sometimes one vendor sings against another in a competitive duet. The market runs into side streets, large and small, one side favoring dry goods, and the other dried beans, fruit, nuts, and spices in all colors and fragrances, sold from sacks. Opposite the market, at the King George Street intersection, is where freelance housepainters gather, simply hanging around and waiting for a floor to scrub or a wall to paint.

Kerem Ha-Teimanim (the **Yemenite Quarter**) is near the Carmel Market and if you are eager for a meal, you are near the source of some of the best Middle Eastern dishes you can find anywhere (see "Where to Eat"). It is a network of narrow lanes and alleys and despite its exotic quality, it's a perfectly safe place to be. If you get a bit lost, just ask—people will be helpful.

At Allenby Street near the sea you can pick up Ha-Yarkon Street, the hotel, café, and embassy row; and Herbert Samuel Esplanade for Tel Aviv strolling.

ROTHSCHILD BOULEVARD: The center of Tel Aviv's cultural life is at the northern end of tree-lined Rothschild Boulevard. Clustered here together are the Ha-Bimah Theater; a youth museum, the big Mann Auditorium, home of the Israel Philharmonic (IPO), and lovely Gan Yaakov Park. Farther south along Rothschild, in the center of the island at Nahlat Benyamin Street, is the impressive **Founder's Monument,** depicting the three phases of Tel Aviv's history. The bottom of the bas-relief tier shows the workers of 1909 digging and planting, while snakes and animals form a lower border. The middle level shows the Herzlia Gymnasium (which was demolished in 1959 and rebuilt in the northern part of the city); the uppermost section is modern Tel Aviv, with the Ha-Bimah Theater, Bialik's home, and many modern houses.

Ha-Bimah National Theater (tel. 03-283-742) is the nation's first and best-known repertory theater. Founded in Moscow in 1918 by the renowned Stanislavsky, it moved to Palestine in 1928. The great Russian artist inspired the group and it went on to achieve a fantastic reputation, both in Palestine and at other great theaters throughout the world. They presented the first Hebrew translations of plays by Shakespeare, Molière, Shaw, and O'Neill. All performances are in Hebrew.

Around the corner at 6 Tarsat Blvd. is the **Helena Rubinstein Pavilion** (tel. 03-287-196), which exhibits the works of artists Israeli and foreign. Open Sunday through Thursday from 10 a.m. to 1 p.m. and 5 to 7 p.m., on Saturday from 10 a.m. to 2 p.m.; closed Friday. Bus 5, 18, 25, or 63.

The **Mann Auditorium** (tel. 03-295-092), which can seat 3,000 concertgoers, is the permanent home of the Israel Philharmonic Orchestra. Bronislaw Huberman founded the orchestra in 1936 by bringing together many renowned European musicians who had become refugees in Israel. Since then, some of the world's leading conductors and soloists have appeared with the Israel Philharmonic: Arturo Toscanini, Serge Koussevitzky, Leonard Bernstein, Arthur Rubinstein, Isaac Stern, Jascha Heifetz, Yehudi Menuhin, and Zubin Mehta (music director since 1969). Yet even now that the magnificent concert hall has been built, the orchestra continues to give performances in other towns, carrying on a tradition that began during the War of Independence, when they played just behind the lines for the troops near Jerusalem and Beersheba. The orchestra is on vacation during August and September.

At **Independence Hall,** 16 Rothschild Blvd. (tel. 03-653-942), you can see the "cradle" of Israel's birth. Hours are 9 a.m. to 1 p.m. Sunday through Friday. Meir Dizengoff, the first mayor of Tel Aviv, lived here, and it was in this same historic house that the independence of Israel was declared in 1948.

Bet Eliyahu–Bet Hagana, the **Hagana Museum** is a fascinating place, well worth a visit. It's at 23 Rothschild Blvd. (tel. 03-623-624), home of Eliyahu Golomb, a former Hagana general. The museum records the history of the Israeli military from the time of the farmfield watchmen at the beginning of the century down through the War of Independence. Here are interesting photos, documents, uniforms, scale models, and weapons. On the third floor you see the various ways the Israelis hid arms inside farm machinery to escape British detection, and how they stealthily manufactured hand grenades and Sten guns in clandestine kibbutz workshops. There's one homemade grenade with the letters USA stamped on it—so that, had a Hagana soldier been caught with the bomb, the British wouldn't have suspected that it had been made locally. But the joke here was that "USA" were the first letters of three Yiddish words meaning "Our piece of work." Other items relate to the Arab riots of 1937, the World War II Jewish Brigade that fought with the British throughout the Mediterranean and Middle East, and the bizarre authorization papers printed during the *Exodus* affair.

Almost all of the explanatory captions in this four-story museum are in Hebrew—but never fear, the museum has stationed a group of English-speaking interpreters and guides.

Entrance hours are 9 a.m. to 3 p.m., till 12:30 p.m. on Friday; closed Saturday. Take bus 1 or 4.

DIZENGOFF SQUARE: Dizengoff Square comes to life at night. Lights flash from overhead advertisements, a cinema marquee calls to you in no uncertain terms, motorcycles roar by, and lovers stroll arm-in-arm.

Just down the street from the circle is Dizengoff Street's famous stretch of sidewalk cafés, peopled with Tel Aviv's brand of bohemia and café society.

At the center of the plaza suspended above the roadway is a huge **sculpture-fountain** by Yaacov Agam named *Water and Fire.* Five large concentric metal rings are painted so that when the rings turn, the painted surfaces produce differing effects of light and color. At the same time, jets of water shoot upward from the rings, and at the top of the sculpture, in the midst of the shooting water, rises a jet of flame! Music accompanies the whole marvelous display in a show that lasts for 20 minutes. Agam's computerized sculpture begins to play at 11 a.m., noon, and 1, 4, 5, 6, 7, 8, 9, and 10 p.m. If you come a few minutes early, you may be able to get a seat on one of the benches surrounding the sculpture.

HA-YARKON STREET AND THE YARKON RIVER: Ha-Yarkon Street, which parallels the seafront, is the thoroughfare of most of Tel Aviv's hotels. Like two other main streets—Dizengoff and Ben-Yehuda—it terminates at the Yarkon River.

Traditionally, the Yarkon was the scene of picnicking and rowboat excursions along its serpentine, tree-canopied waters. But the Yarkon River Diversion Plan, which pipes off water to the Negev, substantially depleted this river—which never was much more than a large stream in the first place.

Although not the same as punting on the Thames, boat rides on the Yarkon River are definitely a nice diversion. Bus 24 or 26 to the end of Ibn Gevirol will bring you to the Yarkon River; bus 1, 4, or 5 takes you to within easy walking distance. Boats can be rented from 9 a.m. until midnight (except when it rains). One firm is called **Tikvah-Dagon** (tel. 03-412-921). Ice cream and soft drinks are on sale here too. There is a second operator, **Irgun Ha-Yarkon,** whose pier is near where Yirmiyahu Street meets the river (tel. 03-448-422). They offer the same equipment plus a motorboat ride.

There have been free outdoor concerts in the Yarkon Park for the past number of summers. Check the newspapers or the Government Tourist Office for dates.

Beyond Power Station Reading IV is **Sde Dov** airport. East of the airport, on the Abba Hillel Street, is the country's "Yankee Stadium," a sports arena that seats 30,000 soccer-mad spectators.

Ha-Aretz Museums

Plan to visit Tel Aviv University, the Ha-Aretz Museum complex, and Beth Hatefutsoth on the same trip north of the Yarkon River, as all of these sights are right together in Ramat Aviv. A smart way to do it is to catch a bus that goes all the way to the top of the hills to Beth Hatefutsoth, then bus or walk down through the university campus to Ha-Aretz. For the trip back into Tel Aviv, several buses pass Ha-Aretz, and many more pass along Derekh Haifa (Haifa Road), a ten-minute walk downhill from Ha-Aretz.

The **Ha-Aretz Museum Complex** (tel. 03-415-244) lies within a large enclosure which also encompasses Tel Qasile, an ancient mound in which 12 strata of past civilizations have been discovered. Selected artifacts from Tel Qasile are displayed in the appropriate museums.

Besides Tel Qasile, Ha-Aretz has eight attractions. The **Kadman Numismatic Pavilion** has exhibits chronicling the history of coinage and monetary systems. The **Glass Pavilion** has a fine, rare collection of glass vessels spanning 3,000 years of civilization, from 1500 B.C. to A.D. 1500. The **Ceramics Pavilion** shows how pottery was made, decorated, and used during the ages, and even has a reconstructed dwelling from biblical times complete with pots. In the **Ethnography and Folklore Pavilion,** a wealth of Jewish ethnic art and handcrafts is on display. Household and religious items, jewelry, and costumes are set in scenes from daily life to make their place in the Jewish home readily recognizable. The **Nechushtan Pavilion** is devoted to mining and metallurgy as it was practiced in the Timna Valley near Eilat, in Arava, and in Sinai in biblical times. The **"Man and His Work" Center** holds displays showing how men and women have earned their daily bread in Israel since ancient times, and some of the tools that helped them earn it. For astronomy shows, there's the **Lasky Planetarium.** An especially pleasant addition to the complex is a park called **Landscapes of the Holy Land,** a large expanse in which scenes once familiar in Israel will be revived and reconstructed for modern visitors.

Admission to the entire museum complex costs NIS4 ($2.65) for adults, NIS3 ($2) for students and seniors. The museums are open daily from 9 a.m. to 1 p.m. (on Saturday from 10 a.m. to 1 p.m.); there are evening hours on Tuesday from 4 to 7 p.m.

Take bus 24, 25, 27, or 45.

Tel Aviv University

If you continue on these same buses, you will come to Tel Aviv University (tel. 03-420-111). It has a handsome, multifaceted campus and an extensive library. Thirty-five buildings house the widest spectrum of studies of any university in Israel and its enrollment of 18,000 students is the largest as well. The faculties encompass fine arts, the humanities, history, Jewish studies, law, medicine, the sciences, engineering, business administration, and there are special colleges and research institutes. Courses for English-speaking students are given here.

Bet Hatefutsoth

Among the most fascinating museums in all of Israel is Bet Hatefutsoth, the **Nahum Goldmann Museum of the Jewish Diaspora** (tel. 03-425-161). The museum is in Ramat Aviv on the campus of Tel Aviv University, off Klausner Street, inside the Matatia Gate (University Gate 2). The best way to get there is by taking one of the buses which goes directly to this gate: no. 25, 45, 49, 74, 86, or 274. Taking any other bus involves a long, hot, uphill walk across the campus.

The museum was the brainchild of Dr. Nahum Goldmann, founder and first president of the World Jewish Congress. In the huge, beautiful, strikingly modern museum building are countless artful exhibits which chronicle the 2,500-year history of the Jewish Diaspora. The collection is not so much a treasury of relics as a history lesson: here is what happened to the Jewish people, and what they accomplished, between the time when they were driven from Israel and when they returned. Photographs, documents, replicas of artifacts, maps, and scale models vividly bring to life the communities, synagogues, households, and workshops of Jews living in dozens of countries. Among the highlights of the exhibits are these: a model of a 13th-century Jewish community peopled by over 100 tiny figurines of men, women, and children clad in period dress and engaged in their various occupations; films showing the traditional Jewish life in Eastern Europe, Greece, and Morocco; scale models of famous synagogues, including one in China in 1653. For a small fee you can get a computer print-out on any of 3,000 Jewish communities—perhaps the home of your ancestors. You can pick up a headset and listen to a dialogue (in English) between a 13th-century monk, Pablo Christiani, and a Jewish scholar, Nachmanides, about whether or not Jesus was the Messiah. There's a dairy cafeteria on the premises. The museum is open Sunday through Thursday from 10 a.m. to 5 p.m. (on Wednesday to 7 p.m.). Admission costs NIS4 ($2.65) for adults, NIS3 ($2) for students and seniors.

ELSEWHERE: The **Tel Aviv Museum,** 27 Shaul Ha-Melekh Blvd. (tel. 03-257-

361), houses temporary as well as permanent exhibitions—paintings, drawings, prints, sculpture, photography, etc., of both Israeli and foreign artists from the 16th century to the present. Films, concerts, and lectures are also offered to the public. It's open Sunday to Thursday from 10 a.m. to 2 p.m. and 5 to 9 p.m., on Saturday from 11 a.m. to 2 p.m. and 7 to 10 p.m.; closed Friday.

Bet Bialik Museum, 22 Bialik St. (tel. 03-651-530), was the home of the great Hebrew writer Haim Nachman Bialik, and it remains for all to see just as it was when he died. His 94 books, with translations in 28 languages, are there, as are articles, correspondence, paintings, photographs, and an archive of hundreds of his manuscripts. Moshe Ungerfeld, who manages the museum, was a great friend of Bialik's, if you know Hebrew or Yiddish he will tell you many interesting stories about him. It is a favorite visiting place of school classes. Open Sunday through Thursday from 9 a.m. to 7 p.m., till 1 p.m. on Friday; closed Saturday.

Just up the street is the **Museum of the History of Tel Aviv,** at 27 Bialik (tel. 03-653-052). Photographs, models, a film (in English), and documents tell the story of the city's founding and early history. The museum is housed in Tel Aviv's former City Hall, and is open on Sunday, Monday, Wednesday, Thursday, and Friday from 9 a.m. to 1 p.m., on Tuesday from 4 to 7 p.m.; closed Saturday. Admission costs NIS2 ($1.35) for adults, NIS1.50 ($1) for students.

Another museum is the **Israel Theater Museum,** 3 Melchet St. (tel. 03-292-686), housing historic memorabilia and documents of the Jewish and Israeli theater. Open Sunday to Thursday from 8 a.m. to 1 p.m. Buses 4 and 5.

The **Ben-Gurion House** is open to the public. It stands at 17 Ben-Gurion Blvd. (tel. 03-221-010), not far off Dizengoff. The personal items belonged to Paula and David Ben-Gurion and are shown as they were when they lived here. The library comprises some 20,000 books and was bequeathed by Ben-Gurion himself. The great man's scholarship and breadth of acquaintance with knowledge are very impressive. Most of the signs in the museum are only in Hebrew, but this will not detract much from your visit, as furnishings are mostly familiar, except perhaps the bedroom, with blocked-in window, used as a bomb shelter. You can visit the Ben-Gurion House free of charge Sunday through Thursday from 8 a.m. to 2 p.m., on Friday to 1 p.m., on Saturday from 11 a.m. to 2 p.m.; it's also open on Monday and Thursday evenings from 5 to 7 p.m.

The **Jabotinsky Institute,** 38 King George St., Metzudat Zeev (tel. 03-287-320), is a historical research institute devoted to the study of the activist trend in the Jewish Resistance Movement. Here, archives are preserved connected with the activities of Nili, the Jewish Legion in World War I, the Revisionist Movement, Betar, Irgun Zevai Leumi, Fighters for the Freedom of Israel (Lehi), etc. Jabotinsky was a poet, writer, journalist, soldier, and founder, during World War I, of the Jewish Legion, which helped Allenby's forces liberate Eretz Israel from Turkish rule. He called into being many of the abovementioned groups and movements as well. Attached to the institute is a museum devoted to his life and activities—a collection that sheds a very interesting light on Israel's dramatic history. Open most days from 8 a.m. to 3 p.m., on Tuesday till 8 p.m., and on Friday to 1 p.m. Take bus 13, 24, 25, 26, or 61.

Israeli painter Reuven Rubin captured on canvas the spirit and the sights of Mandate Palestine, nascent Israel. Though the holy cities of Jerusalem and Safed were among his favorite subjects for painting, he also did scenes of Tel Aviv, his home city, in its very early years. For a look at his home and his paintings, make your way to the **Rubin House,** 14 Bialik St. (tel. 03-658-961), not far from Bet Bialik (see above); it's open on Sunday, Monday, Wednesday, and Thursday from 10 a.m. to 2 p.m., on Tuesday from 10 a.m. to 1 p.m. and 4 to 8 p.m., and on Saturday from 11 a.m. to 2 p.m.; closed Friday.

Safari Park (tel. 03-776-181 or 744-981) is out of town at Ramat Gan, but it's really just a short bus ride (no. 30, 35, or 45) from anywhere in Tel Aviv. The park is a wide-open plain (250 acres) where African animals roam free. For obvious reasons, visitors must remain in closed vehicles while traversing the five-mile trail. Private motorists can drive around as much as they want for their admission fee of NIS5 ($3.35) per adult, NIS4 ($2.65) per child. You will have the opportunity to see the mighty lion, massive elephant and rhino, towering giraffe, swift gazelle, gnu, eland, impala, and zebra, and the feathered ostrich, flamingo, and stork. These and many more will make your visit memorable. Open daily from 9 a.m. until 3 or 4 p.m., until 6 p.m. in summer, until 2 p.m. on Friday.

The **Tel Aviv Sailing Club,** in Marina Atarim (P.O. Box 16285; tel. 03-202-596), can be found in front of Namir (Atarim) Square between the Carlton and Hilton hotels. You can rent a sailboat here by the hour, with or without skipper. The marina is open from 9 a.m. to 5 p.m. daily. An alternative is merely looking —and it's a pretty sight too, seeing those bright white and striped sails out on the waves.

JAFFA:
Jaffa, now an integrated component in the sprawling Tel Aviv–Jaffa complex, has a long and colorful history, dating back to biblical times. It was the principal port area of Palestine prior to the British decision to create a new harbor in Haifa. The old Middle Eastern town of bazaars, peeling buildings, and narrow cul-de-sacs is rich in history and legend. The old Arab site was noisy, dirty, sleepy, and indigenous to a different age. Many of the earliest Zionist settlers opted for Jaffa before Tel Aviv began to emerge out of the northern sand dunes. Crusaders, pilgrims, and occasional merchants considered the city the "port of Jerusalem," although alighting meant trudging several yards through the water or riding the back of an Arab porter, and cargo was physically manhandled from rowboats by chains of men.

Jaffa and Tel Aviv were like two trees planted too closely together. In the beginning, Tel Aviv fell under the austere shadow of the Arab enclave. Afterward, the trend was reversed. The old section of the city has become the starlit patio of Tel Aviv, providing an exceptional view, fine restaurants, the best artists' section in the country, refurbished streets and shops. The beachfront is being claimed for luxurious new hotels, the largest edifice being the Laromme.

To get to Jaffa from Tel Aviv, take bus 10, 25, 26, or 28. If you're walking, simply head south from the Shalom Tower building on Herzl Street, which eventually runs into Jaffa.

A Bit of History
Why the name? One legend has it that Jaffa was built just after the flood by Noah's son, Japhet—and hence the city's name. Another explanation is that the word "Yafah," which means "beautiful," is the town's namesake. At any rate, this is the port, the Bible tells us, where Hiram landed the Lebanon cedars for King Solomon's Temple; and from here Jonah embarked for his fabulous adventure with the whale. The Greeks were here too, and they fostered the legend that a poor maiden named Andromeda, chained to a rock and on the verge of being sacrificed to a sea monster, was rescued by Perseus on his winged white horse. Today tourists are shown this rock. (Things haven't changed much: one historian notes that as far back as 58 B.C., and continuing into the Middle Ages, tourists were being shown the alleged broken chains that bound Andromeda and the skeleton of the fabulous marine monster that nearly did her in.)

The Crusaders came this way of course. Richard the Lion-Hearted built a

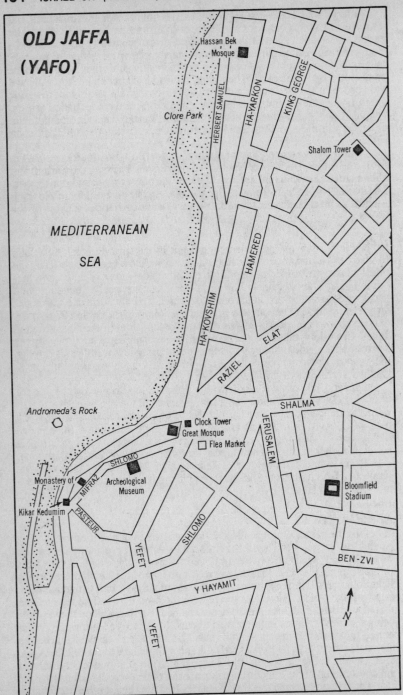

OLD JAFFA
(YAFO)

Hassan Bek
Mosque

Clore Park

MEDITERRANEAN

SEA

Andromeda's Rock

Clock Tower
Great Mosque
Flea Market

SHLOMO

Monastery of
MIFRAZ
Archeological
Museum

Kikar Kedumim
PASTEUR

YEFET

SHLOMO

Y HAYAMIT

YEFET

HERBERT SAMUEL

HA-YARKON

KING GEORGE

Shalom Tower

HAMERED

HA-KOVSHIM

RAZIEL

ELAT

SHALMA

JERUSALEM

Bloomfield
Stadium

BEN-ZVI

N

citadel here, which was promptly snatched away by Saladin's brother, who slaughtered 20,000 Christians in the process. A few hundred years or so later Napoleon passed through, a few Jewish settlers came in the 1890s, and Allenby routed the Turks from the port in 1917.

Countless ships have sunk in Jaffa port, although none so tragically as the fleet back in the 2nd century B.C., when, persecuted by Jaffa's Greek rulers, the Hebrew citizens were lured aboard ships, taken out to the high seas, and cast overboard. This was a major factor in the subsequent revolt of the Maccabees.

Of capsized ships, one Jewish legend notes that all the sunken treasure in the world flows toward Jaffa, and that in King Solomon's day the sea offered him this rich bounty, thereby accounting for the king's wealth. According to the legend, the treasure has once again been accumulating since Solomon's time—to be distributed by the Messiah on the Day of the Coming "to each man according to his merits."

Today Jaffa still shows traces of its romantic and mysterious past. The city is built into a kind of amphitheater on the side of a hill, thereby doubling the protection afforded by the bay, enclosed as it is by a natural promontory. The imaginative development project on the top of the hill is rapidly altering Jaffa's overall face.

Orientation

The streets from Tel Aviv run into Jaffa's Jerusalem Avenue and Tarshish Street where a great stone tower and the Turkish mosque called Mahmudiye (1812) remind you of the city's former occupants.

Although the 1948 war reduced Jaffa's Arab population to 5,000, the city, as you'll plainly see, has retained an Eastern character, and indeed most of the 100,000 Jewish population here is from the North African and Middle Eastern countries. In Jaffa's shops, you'll hear mainly Arabic and French, with some Rumanian, Hungarian, and Yiddish thrown in for good measure. On the streets, Jaffa's children yell in Hebrew. Jaffa's Eastern flavor is captured most definitely in the **Flea Market** (as you enter Jaffa, turn left onto Olei Zion Street just past the Clock Tower). Combing through these stalls and shops (open every day but Saturday) will produce everything from antique Bulgarian costumes to contemporary junk.

To the right past the Clock Tower, on Mifratz Shlomo Street and up the hill, is the section called Old Jaffa.

Walking Tours

Jaffa's Ottoman Clock Tower, at the intersection of Jerusalem and Mifratz Shlomo Streets, is the first landmark you'll see. From here, the **Association for Tourism of Tel Aviv-Yafo** sponsors a free walking tour of Old Jaffa each Wednesday morning, starting at 9:30 a.m.

Old Jaffa

The reclamation of Old Jaffa—only a short time ago a slum-like area of war ruins and crumbling Turkish palaces—has proven one of the most imaginative of such projects in all Israel. Atop the hill and running down in a maze of descending streets to the sea are artists' studios and galleries, outdoor cafés, fairly expensive restaurants and gift shops, all artfully arranged among the reconstructed ruins. Climb to the top of the hill and wander through the lanes (named for signs of the zodiac). At the summit is Kikar Kedumim, the central plaza, and at one side of it, the Franciscan **Monastery of St. Peter,** which was built above a medieval citadel. You can visit the church for prayers on Sunday. Opposite the church is an excavation area, surrounded by a fence, where you can inspect remnants of a 3rd-century B.C. catacomb. Facing the catacomb is a hilltop garden, Gan Ha-Pisgah, atop which, surrounded by trees, is a white monument depicting scenes from the Bible: the conquest of Jericho, the near-sacrifice of Isaac, and Jacob's dream.

Past the church gardens, on the sea side of the hill, is a small and charming café. Wander through the elaborately decorated and lit dome-roofed room and out onto the deck, from which the all-encompassing view of Tel Aviv and the Mediterranean coastline is superb. Incidentally, Andromeda's Rock is the most prominent of those blackened stones jutting up from the floor of the bay. The view is the most brilliant in the morning sunlight. At night it takes on more of a fairytale aura, with the Tel Aviv lights glittering on the curved coastline, especially when viewed from the gardens behind and below.

Jaffa's Port

Frank Carpenter, that venerable travel writer of the '20s, solemnly declared that the harbor of Jaffa is one of the worst in the world. In his 1926 *Holy Land* book, he recounted how the small boat that took him from his liner to the port bobbed up and down so much that his luggage was soaked. Worse yet, he reported, was the treatment accorded to passengers of steerage and third class who came into this port. They "were hung over the sides of the deck of the steamer by the arms, and dropped into the boats, twelve or more feet below. Some of the women screamed as they fell, making the rocks re-echo with their cries, as though the beautiful Andromeda were still chained there."

Oldtimers in Israel recall similar experiences during the days when they landed at Jaffa port. Several people who immigrated in the '20s have told me it was the custom to be transported ashore on the shoulders of Arab porters who waded through the water.

Today, replaced by the modern harbor at Haifa and the newest port, at Ashdod, Jaffa port basks only in former glories.

Simon's House

Christian tradition places the house of Simon the Tanner next to the lighthouse of the port, at the site of a small mosque. Acts 10 recalls St. Peter's visit to Simon's house in "Joppa."

To reach Simon the Tanner's House (tel. 03-836-792), walk through the main square away from the St. Peter Convent, heading south. At the southern limits of the square, where it meets the road, look right and you'll see steps descending into the shady valleys of Old Jaffa. This is Shimon Ha-Burski Street, and at no. 8 is Simon's house, open from 8 a.m. to 11:45 a.m. and 2 to 4 p.m. (till 6:30 p.m. in summer) every day.

Museum of Antiquities

The **Museum of Antiquities of Tel Aviv–Jaffa,** also called the **Jaffa Museum,** is at 10 Mifratz Shlomo St. (tel. 03-825-375), facing Tel Aviv's seaside promenade. From the top of the hill in Old Jaffa, walk from Kikar Kedumim past the Monastery of St. Peter and down the hill on Mifratz Shlomo Street toward the Clock Tower. The museum will be on your right before you reach the bottom of the hill.

The museum building was a Turkish administrative and detention center during the previous century. Care has been taken to preserve its vaulted ceilings and archways. Displays in the five halls are of objects and finds that have been concealed beneath Jaffa for hundreds to thousands of years and were excavated from 30 sites within the city. They cover a time span from the fifth millennium

B.C. ending with the Arab period. The museum is open Sunday through Friday from 9 a.m. to 1 p.m. (on Tuesday only from 4 to 7 p.m.), and on Saturday from 10 a.m. to 1 p.m. Admission costs NIS2 ($1.35) for an adult, NIS1.50 ($1) for a student.

The Flea Market

Tradition has it that you can get the best buy here early Sunday morning. If you are the first customer on the first day of the week, the seller hopes a quick sale will bring him luck through the week. The market is a tight group of alleys east of the Clock Tower. You can weave your way in and out sorting through a mixed array of treasures and junk. The kinds of merchandise change from time to time, but copper, brass, and jewelry are always to be found. Bargaining is the order of the day and expected. In the end it really comes to how much the item is worth to you, but feel free to indulge in lengthy haggling. Even if there is a little language problem, you can get a lot understood with your hands. It's great fun even if you don't buy anything.

SWIMMING IN TEL AVIV: Tel Aviv's seashore is within walking distance of Dizengoff Square. A promenade runs the entire length of the beach. The cleanest beach in the city is at Clore Park. Most beaches have free showers and facilities for changing clothes.

A word of caution: Swimming at Israeli beaches can be dangerous. Every summer the local papers report an all-too-high number of drownings. The problem is an unpredictable undertow that can be hazardous even for a strong swimmer. It's safe, however, to swim at beaches where guards are stationed. Elsewhere it's risky, and you shouldn't do it; but if you have to be defiant—don't go swimming alone. In any case, it's best to pay attention to the safety symbols, in the form of small flags, along Israeli beaches. The color of the flag tells the story: *black* means *absolutely no swimming* in the area; *red* warns you to be especially *cautious; white* indicates that *the water's fine,* so jump right in.

There's a **swimming pool** open year round at Gordon Street (tel. 03-233-241), on the beach facing Namir Square. The pool is open from 4 a.m. to 5 p.m., till 6 or 7 p.m. in summer.

In a slightly more remote location, the **Bat Yam Beach,** three miles south of Jaffa, is wide and sandy, and gets crowded only on hot Saturdays in summer. From Moghrabi Square, you can get a sherut going there. Also bus 10, which begins its run at the City Hall.

For complete information on seaside resorts, see Chapter V, "The Golden Coast."

Facing Kikar Namir and the Hilton is the **Hof Hadarim** (Orange Beach), more generally known as the Hilton Beach. Entrance and use of changing rooms are free; you can rent lockers and deck chairs. A snackbar and restaurant are also on the premises.

THE SUBURBS: Within half an hour of Tel Aviv are some eight or so suburban residential communities, many of which were born when Tel Aviv ran out of elbow room. Before I go into the somewhat brief particulars, please note that for detailed data on accommodations in Herzlia, Bat Yam, and other nearby coastal areas, see Chapter V, "The Golden Coast."

Bat Yam

Meaning "Daughter of the Sea," Bat Yam is 3½ miles south of Tel Aviv, right on the beach. It is a summer resort community, with fine wide beaches. Population: 130,000.

Holon

Half a mile southeast of Bat Yam, Holon was founded in 1933 by settlers who eventually transformed the shifting sand dunes into an aggressively industrial city. (Present population: 120,000, most of whom work in textiles, metalworking, leather goods, and nylon products.) Yet despite all this industrialism, Holon is a garden community of parks and tree-lined streets. In the town is a handsome old-age home—a collection of modest bungalows, pretty gardens, a library, and community dining hall. There's also a Samaritan Colony here.

Ramat Gan

"Garden Heights" is what this one means, and it's located, gardens and all, two miles east of Tel Aviv. Also an industrial community, Ramat Gan is the upper-middle-class suburbia of Tel Aviv, with many private houses, flourishing gardens, and a population of 150,000. In the large garden opposite the police station stands a striking monument to the heroism of an Irgun fighter, Dov Gruner, who was captured when his group raided a British police station, and was later hanged, in 1947, in Acre prison. The statue, a small struggling lion wrestling with a big powerful lion, symbolizes the clash between the young Lion of Judah and the great Lion of England. Inscribed are the words: "A few against many."

In Ramat Gan, the "village" of **Kfar Ha-Maccabia**—which looks like a group of college dormitories—was built by sports enthusiasts to accommodate the international athletes who participate in the Maccabee Games. But since the games are held once every four years, and in order not to let the investment go to waste, the rooms are rented out between games, the swimming pool remains in use, and the dining room offers first-class service and kosher meals.

Also in Ramat Gan is **Bar Ilan University** which emphasizes Judaic studies in conjunction with major academic subjects. The campus accommodates 1,100 students, of whom 750 are from abroad. The faculties include humanities, Judaic studies, languages and literature, social sciences, natural sciences, and mathematics, and there are professional schools of education, social work, and law. Tours are conducted on weekday mornings, and they visit the computer center, the central library, and the scientific laboratories, among other things. For further information, call 03-357-461 or 718-506. Guests may dine in the cafeteria. Take bus 43, 45, 64, 68, 70, 164, or 400 from Tel Aviv.

B'nei Brak

This one's an Orthodox Jewish community founded in 1924, located one mile east of Ramat Gan. The town houses a cluster of yeshivas and other religious institutions.

Petah Tikva

Meaning "Gate of Hope," Petah Tikva was begun as a moshav in 1878, built with the help of Baron Benjamin Edmond de Rothschild. A stone archway commemorates Rothschild's influence on this town of 115,000. The Petah Tikva synagogue was the first to be built in a Jewish village in modern times. Seven miles east of Tel Aviv and highly industrial, Petah Tikva is nevertheless surrounded by about 1,500 acres of orange groves.

Savyon

Organized by a South African group, Savyon is a posh community, eight miles southeast of Tel Aviv. Many expensive villa-type houses are found here—also a tennis club, swimming pool, and gardens of iris, tulip, and gladioli.

Zahala

Zahala is a pleasant garden suburb which started out as a community for the families of career army personnel.

Herzlia

Ten miles north of Tel Aviv, Herzlia was founded in 1924 as an agricultural community. Later it made the switch to industry, and now it earns much of its income from a spate of luxury hotels on the seafront (see Chapter V).

5. Nightlife

Not having to worry about Jerusalem's weighty sanctity, Tel Aviv throbs with activity after sundown. It doesn't matter what the season or the weather is, strollers are out on the boulevards, people-watchers crowd the cafés, clubs and discos throb and crash, restaurants are packed.

Tel Aviv's single most popular nighttime activity is strolling, sipping, and munching along the seaside promenade or in the vicinity of Dizengoff Square. This diversion costs very little, is always amusing and often exciting (especially if you're on the prowl for someone of the opposite sex). For something more organized, try a cinema, concert, ballet, opera, or theater performance.

INFORMATION: First thing to do when you plan your nighttime activities is to have a copy of the *Jerusalem Post,* preferably the Friday-morning edition, which contains the weekend magazine with all its listings of things to do and see. Next thing to do is pick up a copy of "Events in the Tel Aviv Region" from the Tourist Office at 7 Mendele St., or from a hotel lobby. Armed with these sources of information, you're ready to explore Tel Aviv by night.

HIGH CULTURE: Jerusalem has many cultural offerings, but Tel Aviv is the true cultural center of Israel. Mann Auditorium is the home of the **Israel Philharmonic,** but there are many other musical groups besides: the **Israel Chamber Orchestra,** which often performs in the Tel Aviv Museum, is just one. Concert and recital halls are scattered throughout the city. The *Post* has all the details.

The **Israel Ballet** is also centered in Tel Aviv, often performing at Bet Hayal, the Soldiers' House, 60 Weizmann Blvd. at the corner of Pinkus Street.

Theater presents a problem. Performances abound, with the **Ha-Bimah National Theater** as the flagship of the art, but most are in Hebrew, which might damp your enjoyment somewhat unless you're fluent. Look for the notices in the *Post* that indicate English-language performances.

DISCOS AND CLUBS: Along with the sidewalk cafés, Tel Aviv is rife with discos. Their prices vary. Some are on rather tacky-looking streets, but that's no indication they'll be cheap; the atmosphere can be very different inside. Check the prices carefully before you start downing the drinks.

As for full-fledged nightclubs, they tend to be in the larger hotels, or in Old Jaffa (see below). Many charge for cover and drinks at "international" (high) rates; again, check prices carefully.

In Tel Aviv proper, a number of clubs and organizations are dependable for good evening entertainment. For current offerings, check the *Post* or "Events in the Tel Aviv Region."

Bet Lessin, 34 Weizmann (tel. 03-256-222), has dancing and jazz most nights.

Up the street at 30 Weizmann is **Hamlin House** (tel. 03-266-188), with folk dancing classes and performances several times a week.

The club called **Tzavta**, 30 Ibn Gevirol St. (tel. 03-250-156), specializes in Israeli music, both folk and popular.

ZOA House, 1 Daniel Frisch St. at the corner of Ibn Gevirol (tel. 03-259-341), has a variety of activities, including English theater and play readings, Israeli folksinging with guest performers, lectures, concerts, art exhibitions, and celebrations in honor of Israeli and American holidays.

For Students Especially

Up at **Tel Aviv University**, the students' club is called **Focus**. The disco here is open all year, on Friday and Saturday evenings from 10 p.m., with an entrance fee. Monday and Wednesday nights there's folk dancing at 7 p.m.; Tuesday at 7 p.m. it's '60s rock-and-roll. Other activities at the university include film evenings and concerts; you can also use the swimming pool and play tennis here. Reductions are granted on all events to holders of the International Student Identity Card. Buses 13, 24, 25, 27, 45, 74, and 79 go to the university; for further information on events here call the Student Organization at 03-423-004 or 413-619 between 8 a.m. and 4 p.m.

At the Hotels

A singer and a pianist appear nightly at the **Dan's Bar**. . . . At the **Hilton**, you'll find the **Coral Piano Bar**. . . . The **Plaza** has the **Marina Bar**. . . . At the **Ramada Continental** there's a pianist nightly at the **Europa Bar**. . . . The **Basel** has a very pleasant bar. . . . And best of all, the **Beach Bar** at the **Grand Beach**, where there's dancing nightly at the pool and dining at the rooftop **Barbecue Bar**.

Around Town

Owned by a former American, **Bernie's Bottle Club (BBC)**, 231 Ben-Yehuda St. at Dizengoff Street, also up north by the Yarkon River (tel. 03-451-629), is a favorite with foreign embassy staffs, U.N. personnel, and American and Canadian tourists. The flags of these favored groups are suspended from the ceiling. You can order reasonably priced light food—bacon and eggs, sandwiches, burgers, etc.—and the bar is well stocked. Beer begins at NIS3 ($2), mixed drinks at NIS4 ($2.65). Open daily from 8 a.m. to 1 a.m.

Right near City Hall, at 17 Kikar Malchei Israel, corner of Ben-Gurion, is the **Prince of Wales Pub** (tel. 03-222-658), where after a few drinks you'll almost think you're in London. Sandwiches from NIS4 ($2.65) to NIS6 ($4), drinks the same. Open daily from 11 a.m. to 2 a.m.

Budget Nights in Tel Aviv

One of the least expensive forms of nighttime entertainment in Tel Aviv is to stroll around and people-watch. You might even take a romantic stroll to a lovely little park which juts out on a promontory 100 feet above the rolling surf. It's called **Gan Ha-Atzma'ut**, and it's located north of the Hilton Hotel, on upper Ha-Yarkon Street.

Then there are the **movies**. Tel Aviv has at least two dozen cinema houses, and they don't dub the English or American films. You can enjoy first-run shows for NIS4 ($2.65) to NIS6 ($4). Also enjoyable is the rare experience of seeing what, to the Israeli, is a foreign film, and watching others crane their necks to read the Hebrew subtitles, while you sit back and enjoy the English soundtrack.

JAFFA NIGHTLIFE: Between them, Tel Aviv and Jaffa are the nightlife centers of Israel. Their clubs have been the breeding ground for almost every Israeli singer who has gone on to international popularity. But the real center of things

—Israel's Montmartre—is located in Old Jaffa, on the side of the hill that slopes down toward Tel Aviv, where creative minds have taken wrecked Turkish baths and once-grand palaces and wrought several different and very esoteric clubs. They are, however, almost all wildly expensive and should be prudently saved for that one "big splurge" evening out of your Israeli vacation.

A very exotic club is **Yoel Sharr's Omar Khayam,** 5 Netiv Ha-Mazaloth (tel. 03-825-865), a huge room in an old Arab mansion, with lofty vaulted ceilings and stone walls. Omar Khayam abounds with atmosphere—fish netting strung about, soft candles on every table. Top Israeli singers and pianists appear nightly. Open from 9:30 p.m. until 1:30 a.m. The show starts at 10:45 p.m., but come earlier to get good seats. The show is in Hebrew and English. Admission, including one drink, costs NIS18 ($12).

Glowing among the trees up the hillside behind the Jaffa Museum is the **Caravan Night Club,** 10 Mifratz Shlomo (tel. 03-828-255), whose high-arched windows offer a magnificent view of the Tel Aviv–Jaffa area. (Framed by two mosques and the tall Jaffa minaret in the foreground, and bounded by the Mediterranean breakers on the west, the Tel Aviv coastline gracefully curls northward in a busy, crowded, serpentine panorama.) The club opens at 8 p.m. There is dancing until 10:30 p.m., when there is a show of international artists (including striptease). Dancing is resumed after the show. Cover charge is NIS8 ($5.35) to NIS10 ($6.65), depending on the day of the week. Alcoholic drinks begin at NIS5 ($3.35). Closing time is about 2 a.m.; closed entirely on Sunday.

One of the most popular clubs in Jaffa, **Michel's Aladin,** at 5 Mifratz Shlomo (tel. 03-826-766), just down from the St. Peter Convent, is housed in an 800-year-old building that was once a Turkish bath. The cavernous nightclub is down a flight of stairs, and it's usually packed. The rollicking show features a four-piece combo, singer, and belly dancer. Entrance is free on weeknights, NIS5 ($3.35) on Friday, NIS8 ($5.35) on Saturday, which includes a drink. The club is open daily, except Sunday.

Another club to consider is **The Cave,** right in the main plaza at 14 Kikar Kedumim (tel. 03-829-018): singers, dancers, and a folklore troupe.

Chapter V

THE GOLDEN COAST

1. Ashkelon
2. Ashdod and Environs
3. Bat Yam
4. Herzlia
5. Netanya
6. Caesarea and Vicinity
7. Acre (Akko)
8. From Nahariya to the Border

THROUGHOUT ITS LONG, long history, the land now called Israel has played host to pilgrims seeking solace, penance, union, communion with the deity or deities they most fervently believed in. Today these pilgrims still come, but there's a new kind among them, with a different but equally fervent kind of an old worship: sun worship. What they seek is a rich golden tan, and for this they flock to their own particular mecca—the long, unbroken strip of Israel's eastern Mediterranean shoreline, where they bask in the sunshine and sea.

These pilgrims are of every class and nationality. Some move bag and baggage into first-class resorts; others drop their backpacks on the sands and dig in for a fortnight. In between, there are pleasant accommodations for everyone.

Like the rest of the country, the shore strip combines the old and the new in uniquely Israeli juxtaposition. There's neon and chrome side by side with biblical and even prebiblical ruins. And there's much to do: beaches of sand, pebbles, or rocks with fascinations on, in, or under the waters. Sports enthusiasts can swim, fish, dive, boat, ski, or surf. Good sightseeing here, and good relaxation.

1. Ashkelon

Although the beach winds much farther south, the southernmost tourist accommodations are found in a thriving community that's grown up over the ruins of civilizations buried in its sands for 25 centuries. One of the five Philistine city-states (the others were Gath, Gaza, Ekron, and Ashdod, all within today's Israel), Ashkelon was an important caravan stop. Here's where Delilah snipped Samson's hair and strength, where Herod was born, where Romans and Crusaders rallied. Today the territory called the Sands of Ashkelon includes **Migdal** and **Givat Zion,** the oldest of the contemporary areas; **Afridar,** built in 1952 by a South African development company; **Samson District;** and **Barnea.**

The city can be reached by Egged bus no. 300, 301, or 311 from Tel Aviv in one hour and 15 minutes.

Ashkelon is not a large town, but it's very spread out. Your bus will come into town from the highway on Ha-Nitzahon Road. You'll pass by Migdal, the Old City, on your right and end up at the Central Bus Station on Ha-Nitzahon in the newer part of town. With a hotel reservation in hand, you can start out by city bus or taxi to your chosen hotel. Without a reservation, you'd better make some calls from the bus station to find a room. Ashkelon has only a few hotels, but to check them out on foot, carrying luggage, would be impossible.

For our purposes, the part of town one must get to know is Afridar. In **Afridar Center,** with its conspicuous Clock Tower, is the **Tourist Office** (tel. 051-32412), banks, shops, restaurants, cafés, a cinema, and the small Ashkelon museum. Early on during your stay in Ashkelon, check out Afridar Center. The town's only budget hotel is within ten minutes' walking distance of the center—if you're not lugging a suitcase.

Some Israelis think that Ashkelon has the perfect climate, blessed by cool breezes from the sea, but modified by the dryness of desert winds. It definitely does have good weather, and on a summer night you'll appreciate those breezes.

ACCOMMODATIONS: You should know, first, that Ashkelon's hotel prices operate under a special framework. This fast-growing beach town charges its highest rates from mid-July till the end of August, and during Passover and the September holidays. This all has to do with Ashkelon's weather, a commodity that local residents discuss with fanatic possessiveness, not unlike the Miami Beach taxi drivers who always talk as if they own the weather. You will probably be offered rain insurance: for every day it rains, beginning on the second day of your stay, you get to stay a day free—breakfast included!

Samson's Gardens (Ganei Shimshon), 38 Sonnebend (or Ha-Tamar) St. (P.O. Box 5049, Afridar, Ashkelon; tel. 051-34666), has 22 rooms, all with bath or shower, radio, and air conditioning. And as the name suggests, it's situated in a garden; all rooms have terraces overlooking it. Guests can use the pool at the nearby King Shaul Hotel at reduced rates. Kosher meals are available. Single occupancy is $17.25 to $19.50; double occupancy, $35.75 to $40.25.

An inexpensive alternative to hotels is to stay in a private home. Generally, this costs $10 a night. To find out about home accommodations, contact the **Government and Municipal Tourist Office,** Afridar Center (tel. 051-32412).

Camping

Ashkelon has a beautiful and extensive camping ground—a 15-acre swath of lawns dotted with trees and marble pillars, located inside the seaside **National Antiquities Park.** Caravans and bungalows are available for hire year round for $10 to $12 per person. There are three to four beds in each bungalow; the large caravans (trailers) can accommodate six; the smaller ones, four. Three shower and toilet areas contain ample facilities. For food, there are a grocery store and a restaurant, or you may purchase bottled cooking gas for your own equipment.

For further information, you may write to the campsite at P.O. Box 5052 (tel. 051-36777). Or contact the Israel Camping Union, P.O. Box 53, Nahariya (tel. 04-923-366). Members of the Israel or International Camping Union will receive a 5% to 10% discount on certain items.

BUDGET MEALS: The **Ma'adan Café,** in Afridar Center, opposite the Municipal Tourist Office (tel. 051-31925), has both indoor and outdoor seating. You might order a dairy plate here with cheese, hard-boiled egg, and salad, a platter of four appetizers, a fish meal or cold cuts and salad for about NIS9 ($6). Open from 9 a.m. to 8 p.m., till 11 p.m. in summer.

Down in Migdal, the old section of town, are various lunch-counter eateries, and there's one at the Central Bus Station as well. With such limited dining possibilities, it's not difficult to see why many visitors arrange for half or full board at their hotels. You can too.

WHAT TO DO IN ASHKELON: Ashkelon offers a wide variety of activities. The main source of information on all the goings-on is the **Government and Municipal Tourist Information Office,** Afridar Center (tel. 051-32412). It's open from 9 a.m. to 1 p.m., on Friday to 11:30 a.m. You can obtain up-to-date information on everything from picnicking in the national park to seasonal events, such as the Arts and Crafts Fair in July or August.

A Little Archeology

Exactly what happened at Ashkelon over the last 4,000 years is a chapter of history still waiting to be written. What Ashkelon really needs is a rich archeological expedition, for only occasional pokes and gropes have thus far been made into the sand-covered cities of antiquity that lie within its boundaries. At one point along the shore, you'll see where some scientists have made a tentative longitudinal slice into the cliff, revealing a network of pillars and caves several strata deep that seem like a mysterious royal basement from Ashkelon's past.

It's a virtual certainty that further excavations will reveal important historical treasures, because the Bible mentions Ashkelon frequently. When King Saul was killed by the Philistines, David lamented: "Tell it not in Gath, publish it not in the streets of Ashkelon, lest the daughters of the Philistines rejoice."

Some scholars of Greek legend claim that Ashkelon—and not Crete—may have been the original home of Aphrodite, goddess of love. Here, too, Herod built great works of marble and granite, and the Arab settlers who came later called Ashkelon "the bride of the east."

When the Crusaders and Muslims fought over the city, Ashkelon, like so many other Israeli locations, fell into utter ruin. Later builders took the ruins of Roman staircases, Hellenistic pillars, and Crusader stonemasonry, and used all these materials for building houses around Jaffa and Acre.

National Antiquities Park

As you'd expect, the main sights are archeological in nature. For example, take a walk along the sea in a southerly direction, and you'll see bits and pieces of pillar and column poking through the sand, just waiting for that excavating team we've been hoping for. Toward the end of the public beach section, you'll then come to a staircase leading into a park. Proceed through the park, and you'll soon come upon the sunken arena (the "Sculpture Corner") that houses Ashkelon's handful of finds: a headless Winged Victory supported on the shoulders of a childlike Atlas, Isis and child, and grouped pieces of colonnade from Herod's collection of carved capitals, "Stoa of a Hundred Columns."

There's also a refreshment stand here—in case you're weary from the walk through the park.

The Painted Roman Tomb

Practically hidden in the sand dunes, this interesting sight is just north of the Shulamit Gardens Hotel, on the beach. This Roman burial cave is the work of an artist who had a happy and secure vision of the afterlife. Romance and eternal springtime abide in the paintings here—reclining nymphs and their pitchers of water, marsh birds nesting in a stream thick with fish. On the ceiling are nude children playing, greyhounds and gazelles, birds and clusters of grapes. The gods Apollo and Demeter look down from between some vines, assuring the entombed man, whoever he was, that things in the afterlife are really pretty good. Open daily from 9 a.m. to 3 p.m., for free.

Public Beaches

Ashkelon has several public beaches. Swim only if there is a lifeguard present, since the water tends to have tricky currents. All beaches are free and seldom crowded.

2. Ashdod and Environs

Another of those five Philistine city-states, Ashdod today is newer than Ashkelon, and also of a different nature. It is said that this will be Israel's largest commercial and trading sea gateway, and in fact the town's prize possession is its modern, fully equipped harbor, where the Israeli navy's Nautical School is located. From the Observation Post here, you can see big ships cruising and loading and also get a view of this rapidly developing town with its nearby industrial area.

Ashdod is growing wildly: everywhere you go the ground is being readied for more factories or plants, new high-rise apartments or schools, more shops or hotels. One of Israel's "planned" cities, it's all built on sand dunes which accounts for its lack of grass lawns and such except in specially nurtured areas. If you want a garden here the first thing you have to come up with is soil, but somehow that doesn't seem to discourage the 70,000 folk who live here (about 60% Sephardic Jews, plus many from India) and carefully tend their greenery.

Ashdod has three shopping centers, and the largest is nearest the hotels and beach areas. From its large courtyard you can see an attractive modern building with a tile wall mural facing the main street; it's the local absorption center where many new immigrants live for several months and study Hebrew. In the shopping center you'll find cinemas, department stores, shops, and banks, plus a pharmacy, deli shop, newsstand, and bookstore.

WHERE TO EAT: Ashdod has a number of inexpensive eating places both in the center of the small city and in the port area. They feature the typical Middle Eastern and European fare. As for recommendations, it's catch-as-catch-can; you'll find that variety, quality, and price are all on a par at whatever place you find. The town also has its share of falafel stands, and for pizza during the hours of 9 a.m. and midnight (on Friday till 3 p.m., on Saturday from 6 p.m.), there's **Pizza Don Pedro** in Mercaz Mischari Alef (Commercial Center A), with pies hot from the oven beginning at NIS4 ($2.65).

IN THE ENVIRONS: There are two ways of heading north from Ashdod. The easier and faster way is along the coastal road, which intentionally misses several of the population centers in the region. The inner road, however, connecting with Gedera—once the northern tip of the Negev until Israeli farmers pushed the desert back beyond Beersheba—is well worth the extra effort and time.

Rehovot and the Weizmann Institute

Without returning to the coastal highway, you can reach Rehovot from Gedera; there's also a road directly off the coastal highway. Either way, it's a short drive to Israel's foremost scientific establishment—the **Weizmann Institute of**

Science (tel. 08-482-111). You enter through a gateway on Rehovot's main street, and as soon as you're inside the grounds you'll feel as if you've stepped into another world. This is a beautiful compound of futuristic buildings, lawns of the deepest golf-course green, lily ponds, and colorful gardens—all, apparently, for the spiritual satisfaction of the hundreds of scientists at work here.

Dedicated in 1949 in honor of Israel's first president (himself an important chemist), the institute grew out of the Daniel Sieff Research Institute, established in 1934. Conducting both fundamental and applied research, the Weizmann Institute also has a graduate school where about 500 students work for their doctorates. The majestic buildings, in a pastoral, tranquil setting, have been a drawing card for scientists from all over the world.

On the grounds are the Wix Library, where there is an exhibition on Dr. Weizmann's life; the Wix Auditorium, where audio-visual shows on the institute's activities are shown at 11 a.m. and 3:15 p.m. daily (except Friday when they are shown at 11 a.m. only); and the residence of the late Dr. and Mrs. Weizmann, built in the 1930s. The residence is open daily except Saturday and Jewish holidays from 9 a.m. to 3:30 p.m.; admission is NIS1 (65¢). Near the residence is a simple tomb marking the Weizmanns' resting place and a Memorial Plaza dominated by a Holocaust Memorial depicting the Torah being snatched from flames. A restaurant on the premises serves light dairy meals.

Rishon-le-Zion

Should it be an unusually hot and thirsty day, you'll be well advised to stop off in nearby Rishon-le-Zion, home of Israel's wine industry. Here you can catch a free tour of the wine cellars, refreshingly concluded with samples of the local stock (no tours, however, late Friday afternoon or Saturday).

Free wine shouldn't be your only object here, though, because this is an important historic site—one of the first Jewish settlements in Israel. Started in 1882 by a group of idealistic Russian Jews escaping czarist persecution, Rishon-le-Zion nearly didn't make it. Things went from bad to worse for the settlers, who suffered not only from inexperience with agricultural techniques, but from Arab marauders, malaria, squalid living conditions, and a rapidly degenerating morale. Finally, they sent an emissary to see Baron Rothschild in Paris. The financier and philanthropist aided the cause by dispatching agricultural experts to help the settlers find water and transplant young French vines. (This was the benefactor's first enterprise in Israel.) The vines from Beaujolais, Bordeaux, and Burgundy took hold, and in 1887 the Israeli wine industry was born, under the name **Carmel Oriental.** Today these wines are generously exported and can be found throughout the world. (Zichron-Yaakov, south of Haifa, is also a leading wine center.)

History was again made in Rishon-le-Zion, which means "First in Zion," when Naftali Imber wrote "Hatikva," Israel's national anthem, in this very village.

3. Bat Yam

Although there are numerous public beaches between Ashdod and Tel Aviv, Bat Yam ("Daughter of the Sea") is one of the most pleasant. On the southern fringes of Tel Aviv–Jaffa, and boasting an ever-growing population of 130,000 inhabitants, Bat Yam is a popular resort area.

GETTING TO BAT YAM: It couldn't be easier. Wherever you are in Tel Aviv–Jaffa, look for one of the following city buses headed south: nos. 10, 18, 25, and 26. Bat Yam borders on Tel Aviv–Jaffa, so the journey may take as little as 5 minutes or as long as 20, depending on your starting point.

Once you arrive in Bat Yam, look for Rothschild Bouelvard. Your bus (no. 10, at least) will probably head down Rothschild to the waterfront. The waterfront street is Ben-Gurion Boulevard (also sometimes called Ha-Nesi'im). Virtually all of the tourist hotels are arrayed along Ben-Gurion to get the benefit of the sea view, so you should start your hotel explorations at the intersection of Rothschild and Ben-Gurion, near the northern end of Bat Yam's beach. The Tourist Office is right here.

TOURIST INFORMATION: The Municipal Tourist Information Bureau (tel. 03-589-766) is a few doors north of the Rothschild–Ben-Gurion intersection, in the same building as the Via Maris Hotel and the Kontiki Restaurant, fronting on Ben-Gurion Boulevard. The office is well organized due to tourism's importance in Bat Yam's economy. Hours are 8 a.m. to 2 p.m. Sunday through Thursday (with evening hours on Tuesday and Wednesday from 4 to 6:30 p.m.), to 1 p.m. on Friday; closed Saturday.

HOTELS AND RESTAURANTS: As all of touristic Bat Yam is arrayed along Ben-Gurion Boulevard facing the sea, we'll simply start at the northern end, at the intersection of Rothschild and Ben-Gurion Boulevards, and walk along to the last hotel at the southern end. If a hotel and a restaurant are near to one another on Ben-Gurion, they'll be near to one another in this description as well. The distance from the northern end of Ben-Gurion to the last hotel is over a mile, so you may not want to walk it all if you're carrying bags.

Several possibilities for accommodation and dining are right here, in the large building at the northern corner of the Rothschild–Ben-Gurion intersection. Besides the Tourist Office, the building shelters the **Via Maris Hotel,** 43 Ben-Gurion (or Ha-Nesi'im) Blvd. (tel. 03-860-171). With 27 air-conditioned rooms, the Via Maris might be looked upon as your typical Bat Yam seafront hotel. Most (22) of the rooms have showers, a few (5) have tubs; all have telephones and central heating, though you're liable to want the air conditioning more than the central heat. Prices are about standard for a Bat Yam hotel: $25.25 single, $36.75 double, breakfast included. The outstanding feature of the Via Maris is its convenience to restaurants, the Tourist Office, and buses to Tel Aviv–Jaffa.

Right across the street from the Via Maris, and a few steps from the tourist office, is **Chez Raymond,** 47 Ben-Gurion (tel. 03-872-348). A nice, open sidewalk café with booth-like wooden tables and benches, Raymond's specializes in such light beach fare as blintzes, pizzas, and salads for about NIS5 ($3.35) to NIS7 ($4.65), but beware! To make the café-sitters pay their way, Raymond's charges upward of NIS4 ($2.65) for a beer, half that much for a mere soft drink. Raymond's is open every day.

A few doors down on Ben-Gurion is the **Bat Yam Hotel,** 53 Ben-Gurion (tel. 03-871-646), with 20 tastefully furnished rooms, two-thirds of them equipped with showers, the rest with tubs. As with all Bat Yam hotels, rooms on the front have that marvelous sea view. Air-conditioned and centrally heated throughout, the Bat Yam also boasts a television lounge, a cocktail bar, a kosher dining room, and a sidewalk café. Rates include breakfast, of course: $26.50 single, $38 double in season, about 10% less off-season (mid-November to the end of February, excluding the busy Christmas–Hanukkah–New Year's season). Students get a 10% reduction if they're not too busy.

One of Bat Yam's few three-star hotels is the **Armon Yam,** 95 Ben-Gurion (P.O. Box 3240, Bat Yam 59131; tel. 03-582-424), a large and modern hostelry of 66 rooms, all with tubs in the bathrooms and balconies on the front. The standard luxuries are here: elevator, air conditioning, radios and telephones in the rooms. Prices are a bit higher than the rest of Bat Yam's hotels, which are two-star. At the Armon Yam you pay $26.50 single, $38 double, all in.

Finally, security buffs will like the highly recommended **Sarita Hotel,** 127 Ben-Gurion Blvd. (Bat Yam 59560; tel. 03-589-183)—there's actually a safe for storing valuables in every room. Each of the ten rooms also has a tub in its private bathroom, plus the requisite air conditioning, radio, and telephone. The Sarita, some distance from the center of Ben-Gurion's hotel-and-restaurant concentration, has its own little dining room, so you needn't starve way down south here. Prices, perhaps because of the Sarita's slightly out-of-the-way location, are cheap: $25.25 single, $34.50 double, breakfast and service included.

4. Herzlia

Herzlia, ten miles north of Tel Aviv, is one of Israel's most famous beach resorts. It was founded in 1924 as an agricultural center, but the years have changed its face and purpose. Perhaps, for accuracy's sake, I ought to admit that the real twist in the village's fortunes came about as the result of the unexpected growth of Tel Aviv. As the large Israeli metropolis grew northward, the beaches of Herzlia suddenly became much more accessible and a good deal more desirable. Today when you're talking about Herzlia, you're talking about luxury. The entire waterfront area is studded with fine hotels, none of which falls within the budget of this book. Fine restaurants abound in Herzlia, as do some of the country's most expensive villas. A disproportionate number of foreign diplomats reside in Herzlia; their neighbors are airline captains and other high-earners.

An Egged bus ride from Tel Aviv to Herzlia takes about 45 minutes; a special bus service run by United Tours connects the Herzlia hotels with downtown and north Tel Aviv. From Herzlia you take another bus, no. 29 or no. 90, to the beach. (If you tell the bus driver that you want to go to the beach, he'll let you out at the connecting bus stop near the highway, saving you a trip into town.)

The Herzlia beach is lovely, but expensive by Israeli standards. Best beaches are the **Zebulun,** near the Daniel Hotel; the **Sharon,** next to the Sharon Hotel; and the **Accadia,** between the Accadia and Daniel hotels. One additional word about the beach: A dangerous undertow exists and bathing is strictly prohibited when a lifeguard is not on duty.

HOTELS: Herzlia's sprawling layout is pretty confusing for the first-time visitor. Luckily, a few landmarks are known to everybody, and if you go with these, getting around should be easy.

The luxury Sharon Hotel, right on the beach, is a major landmark. Inland just a block is Shalit Square (Kikar Shalit), which you can use as your base of operations. Several inexpensive hotels and restaurants are right in Shalit Square, or nearby. By the way, this whole beachfront section of town is known as Herzlia Petuah, to differentiate it from the inland city, on a hill to the east.

Once you find Shalit Square, ask anyone for Ha-Ma'apilim Street. A few steps down Ha-Ma'apilim at no. 29, on the right, is the two-star **Hotel Cymberg** (Herzlia Beach 46752; tel. 052-572-179), a pretty villa-type hotel around an extremely tidy garden and lawn. Rooms are entered from a shady veranda. Each has its own little air conditioning unit, shower, light-colored walls, and eye-catching textiles. In the dining room, Swiss rough wooden chairs maintain the rustic cabin effect. Art and craft objects hung or placed around the public rooms add a great deal of charm, and all in all, the Cymberg is an oasis of peacefulness with its well-cared-for, quiet atmosphere, still maintained by the Cymberg family who built it 40 years ago when Herzlia Beach was considered to be out in the middle of nowhere. The Cymberg has only 11 rooms (seven with showers, four with tubs); the cost here, breakfast and service included, is $25 to $28 single, $35 to $42 double. All rooms have refrigerators; those on the higher end of the price range also have their own private veranda.

Three blocks east of the square, the **Tadmor Hotel,** 38 Basel St. (Herzlia 46660; tel. 052-578-321), is a sort of Israeli institution. Hotel staffs from all over the country train here, and chefs are assiduously cultivated and launched from the Tadmor. There is a radio in each of the 63 air-conditioned rooms; large gardens and a fine park with a children's playground are additional highlights. You pay a premium for the Tadmor's three-star rating: $29 to $34 single, $39 to $49 double. The hotel is open all year, and rates are several dollars lower off-season. If you're driving up to Herzlia from Tel Aviv, look for Basel Street to the left off the main road.

RESTAURANTS: Best place to look is in **Shalit Square,** for this pleasant little plaza is surrounded by snackshops, ice-cream parlors, and small restaurants catering to locals and the beach crowd alike.

Should you find yourself famished while at the beach, look for the **Zevulun Restaurant,** between the Daniel and Sharon hotels, right on the beach. A modest café-restaurant with tables both inside and out on the terrace, and a small playground out back, the Zevulun's specialty is fish—not surprisingly. Let your eyes roam the interior and you'll discover plastic mock-ups of the most popular platters served in the restaurant (a trick used extensively in Japanese eateries). A meal of seafood or lamb chops with fries runs NIS15 ($10) to NIS20 ($13.35); a hamburger or kebab with fries, NIS9 ($6).

5. Netanya

Located about 21 miles from Tel Aviv and a third of the way up to Haifa, Netanya is regarded as the capital of the Sharon Plain, the rich and fertile citrus-grove area stretching from the outskirts of Tel Aviv to Caesarea. Perched on verdant cliffs overlooking the Mediterranean, it is also the center of Israel's diamond industry. Founded in 1929 as a citrus center, the seaside town has for many years been a popular flocking place among Israelis. Lately, however, tourists have been joining them, for they've discovered Netanya to be quiet and convenient, charming and hospitable, geared to service and in easy reach of several areas, including Tel Aviv and Caesarea. It's a sizable town, with all sorts of cafés, hotels, and shops—but the real appeal remains the sunny beach and quiet.

A handsome park parallels the beach—and the coast itself has achieved great popularity with Scandinavian visitors who take dips in December and January. Most everybody else waits until April or May, when the weather at the attractive beach in this pleasant garden town is near perfect.

The city of 125,000 is easily accessible from everywhere in Israel. Several express buses ply the route between Netanya and Jerusalem. Connections are available from Haifa, and there is regular bus and train service from Tel Aviv. Sherut service is most frequent, followed by bus and then train; also, the train station is some distance from the center of the city. Netanya buses (nos. 601 and 605) leave Tel Aviv at an average of about every 15 minutes during most of the day. Buses from Tel Aviv to Netanya operate until 11:30 p.m. The last bus to Tel Aviv departs at 11 p.m.

Shoppers and bank customers, take note! Netanya is one of those towns that closes down between 1 and 4 o'clock each afternoon, so plan to do your business before, or after, the afternoon siesta.

ORIENTATION: Netanya is a big town, but it's not really difficult to find your way around.

The main coastal highway is known as the **Haifa Road.** Coming north on Haifa Road from Tel Aviv, you will pass the Railway Station on the right just before the big intersection with **Herzl Street,** Netanya's main east-west boulevard. Those coming by train can catch a bus at the station which goes to the Central Bus Station, downtown.

Turn left (west) onto Herzl Street, and about six blocks down the street is the Central Bus Station, right where Herzl meets Weizmann–Benyamin Boulevards. Another six blocks along Herzl and you're in the great expanse of **Ha-Atzma'ut Square,** right by the sea, in the very heart of Netanya. Most of the hotels and restaurants recommended below are within a few blocks of the square.

The square, being the town's primary promenade, has been enlarged in recent years, and now extends up Herzl Street all the way to Dizengoff Street. On weekends (Friday night through Saturday night), it's blocked off for a pedestrian mall a block farther still, up to the corner of Herzl and Stamper Streets.

Around this square you'll find everything you need, including eateries of many kinds, pubs, discos, cinema, hotels, the tourist information office, banks, post office, and more. In addition to the lovely beach, one of Netanya's favorite sports, both day and night, is to sit at one of the many cafés with tables and chairs placed out on the square, watching the variety of people strolling by.

USEFUL FACTS: The **Tourist Information Office** is in a little modern kiosk (tel. 053-27286) at the southeastern corner of the square, over by the trees and the beachfront gardens. Hours are 8:30 a.m. to 2 p.m. Sunday through Friday; closed Saturday and holidays. From May through the end of August, the office is also open from 4 to 7 p.m.; afternoon hours, September until October 15, are 3 to 6 p.m. This tourist office is an especially helpful one, and you can come here with any questions you may have, about Netanya or even other places in Israel. While you're here, be sure to pick up a copy of "Kan Netanya," the monthly booklet listing special events, entertainment, and services in Netanya.

If you're traveling by bus, you might also want to stop into the tourist office for a bus schedule giving the complete rundown on all buses coming into and out of Netanya. There's a timetable all drawn up, and you might find it clearer than the information you'll get at the bus station.

Want something to read? Check out **Pompan's Bookstore,** 9 Herzl St. (tel. 053-22476). You'll find a wide selection of books, magazines, and newspapers in English and other languages, plus crossword-puzzle books and useful maps. It's open Sunday to Thursday from 7 a.m. to 1 p.m. and again from 4 to 7:30 p.m., on Friday until 2 p.m.; closed Saturday.

HOTELS: You needn't go far out of Ha-Atzma'ut Square to find a hotel, either cheap or expensive. The clean, pleasant, well-maintained hotel room is almost a Netanya specialty because of the large German-Jewish population.

Netanya is a beach town, oriented toward warm-weather vacationers. Being a seasonal place, prices are seasonal too. Generally speaking, high season is from mid-July through the end of August, plus Jewish holidays, and low season is November through February; between these times the prices will be somewhere between the high- and low-season rates.

Be sure to check for heating and/or air conditioning, if you think you'll need them, depending on the weather and the season. In winter, days can be balmy but nights can get chilly.

By the way, all of Netanya's hotel kitchens are kosher.

In Ha-Atzma'ut Square

Right on the square, on the north side through a tiny doorway, is the modern and tidy **Hof Hotel,** 9 Ha-Atzma'ut Square (P.O. Box 1009, Netanya 42271; tel. 053-22825 or 31304). Each of the 30 rooms has its own air-conditioning unit, telephone, clock radio, and wall-to-wall carpet; 12 rooms also have balconies with tables and chairs overlooking the square. Central heat, elevator, piano bar, tubs as well as showers in the private bathrooms—for these conveniences, the prices are moderate: a single in-season is $33; a double, $44; and off-season rates drop to $21 single, $25 double.

On the south side of the square, just a few steps around the corner of Ussishkin Street, is the four-star **Hotel Goldar,** 1 Ussishkin St. (P.O. Box 1150, Netanya 42272; tel. 053-38188). With four-star luxuries like color TV, radio, tub and shower, air conditioning, and balconies in all of its 150 rooms, the Goldar's prices are about the same as at the three-star hotels facing the seashore: $33 single, $50 double in high season; $23 single, $32 double in winter. There's also a swimming pool here, parking, and a rooftop cafeteria with a lovely sea view, and tables both inside and out.

Right across from the Goldar is the **Atzma'ut Hotel,** 2 Ussishkin St. (Netanya 42272; tel. 053-22562). This two-star hotel occupies the fourth and fifth floors of a building with an elevator. All 20 rooms have showers, some have toilets while others are close to toilets down the hall, and most have little balconies overlooking the square. Prices are $23 single, $35 double in high season; $14 single, $28 double in low season. You may be able to bargain it down even lower in winter, when the hotel is competing for customers.

On King David Street

King David Street (Rehov Ha-Melekh David) is the main street going north out of Ha-Atzma'ut Square. Along this wide and pleasant street are a good number of budget hotel choices.

On the left as you stroll up King David Street is the **Hotel Ginot Yam,** 9 King David St. (Netanya 42264; tel. 053-41007). A three-story building near the corner with Bialik, the Ginot Yam is literally a stone's throw from the sea. It was completely renovated in 1984, and now rates three stars. By the time you read this book, the new top floor should be finished, giving the hotel a total of 55 rooms, all with heat, air conditioning, phone, clock-radio, wall-to-wall carpeting, shower (some with bathtub), and a TV on every floor. You couldn't find a cleaner, better-kept place. Prices are $34 single, $42 double in season, dropping to $23 single, $28 double in winter.

On your right heading up King David Street, the first thing you'll see as you leave the square is the three-star **King David Palace,** 4 King David St. (P.O. Box 1060, Netanya 42264; tel. 053-42151 or 42152). All 60 rooms have telephone, TV, radio, heat, and air conditioning, and all except those on the first floor also have balconies. If you get the sea side, you'll be facing right onto the park and the sea beyond it. Prices are $32 single, $40 double in high season; $25 single, $32 double in winter.

Next up the street on your right is the **Maxim Hotel,** 8 King David St. (Netanya 42264; tel. 053-39341). It's listed as a three-star hotel, but it has all the facilities of a four-star establishment, including a swimming pool, dancing room, bar, and so on. Since it's been put together with the former Hotel Gan Ha-Melekh next door, the hotel now has 140 rooms, including 60 suites that come for the same price as the other rooms. All come with all comforts, and the sea-view rooms have balconies with sliding glass doors. Prices here are $35 single, $52 double in high season; $21 single, $26 double in winter.

The modern, 64-room **Topaz Hotel** is a long two blocks from Ha-Atzma'ut Square on the left at 25 King David St. (P.O. Box 1137, Netanya 42264; tel. 053-36052 or 91229). Fully air-conditioned and carpeted, the Topaz is a fine, bright, clean, cheerful, full-service hotel rated at three stars. There are some large rooms here, with four or five beds, all rooms have tubs in the bathrooms, and fully half the rooms come with kitchenette. Prices for a room with kitchenette (but no breakfast) are the same as for rooms with no kitchenette but including breakfast: $35 single, $45 double in high season; $24 single, $32 double in low season. You must present your copy of this book to obtain these special prices; otherwise, it will be 15% higher.

South of Ha-Atzma'ut Square

On the south side of Ha-Atzma'ut Square, several main streets and side streets will lead you to a dozen other budget hotel choices. All of these establishments are only a short walk from the beach and from the busy square.

Let's start along Gad Machnes Street, the one closest to the seashore. Head for the Tourist Information Office kiosk at the southeast corner of Ha-Atzma'ut Square—that's where Gad Machnes Street begins.

Along Gad Machnes Street: Just a short distance from the kiosk is the **Hotel Margoa**—actually two Hotel Margoas, the Margoa "A" on your left and the Margoa "B" on your right, by the sea. For either hotel, the reception, as well as the dining, are done at the **Margoa "A,"** 9 Gad Machnes St. (Netanya 42279; tel. 053-34434). Each hotel has 35 rooms, with heat and air conditioning, plus wall-to-wall carpeting. All the rooms in Margoa "B" have balconies, facing either toward the sea or toward town and the square; some of the rooms in Margoa "A" have a balcony too. You'll pay $30 single, $42 double here in high season; $21 single, $26 double in winter.

Next door to the Grand Yahalom is the three-star **Yahalom Hotel,** 11 Gad Machnes St. (Netanya 42279; tel. 053-35345). Fairly large, with 48 rooms, the Yahalom has an arrangement whereby you can stay at the Yahalom and take your meals and your pleasures at the Grand Yahalom if you like. Swimming pool, sidewalk café, bar, kosher dining room, air conditioning, and radio and telephone in the rooms—all this, plus balconies (although without a sea view, really). Prices are definitely three-star, at $34.50 single, $50.50 double in high season; $21 single, $28 double off-season. If you're coming in winter, the three-star Yahalom may be closed if there are not enough guests to warrant keeping it open, in which case you'll be housed at the Grand Yahalom—which is not bad, either, since its off-season rates are not that much higher: $29 single, $35 double.

The **Metropol Hotel,** 17 Gad Machnes St. (Netanya 42279; tel. 053-38038), is a wonderful bargain for a two-star establishment, and here's why. Although they were once separate facilities, the two-star Metropol and the four-star Grand Metropol have now been joined together, so that the only difference is in the rooms themselves, which, since the joining of the two buildings, are reached through the same lobby. The two-star guests share all the privileges of their four-star counterparts, including swimming pool, sidewalk café, bar, dining room (the food is the same), wide-screen TV in the lobby bringing in channels from all over the world, and air conditioning and heat in the rooms. Prices are $26 single, $40 double in high season; $17 single, $28 double in low season. But here's a special tip for winter travelers: the two-star hotel sometimes closes during the slow season, and if it does, the guests that have booked for the two-star hotel are lodged in the Grand Metropol for the same two-star price.

Next up the street is the newly renovated **Hotel Sironit,** 19 Gad Machnes St. (P.O. Box 1047, Netanya 42279; tel. 053-40688). All 62 rooms have wall-to-wall carpet, air conditioning and heat, telephone, radio, and bathtub or shower; 20 come with sea view. Prices here are $36 single, $48 double in high season; $23 single, $28 double off-season.

Next along Gad Machnes, on the opposite (west) side of the street, is the innovative **Residence Hotel,** 18 Gad Machnes (tel. 053-33777). Billing itself as "Netanya's most luxurious three-star hotel," the Residence is building its clientele by offering cut-rate prices. As of this writing, any of the 96 rooms with balcony, private bath, radio, telephone, air conditioning, and view of the sea, costs $43 single, $65 double in high season; $22 single, $30 double in low season. Try to get a room on the sea side here—the view is spectacular from your private balcony (balconies are on the sea side only), and being eight stories tall, if you get an upper room you'll really have a bird's-eye view.

Going up the hill a bit, on the beach side, you'll see the new **Princess Hotel,** 28 Gad Machnes St. (Netanya 42279; tel. 053-36061), near the corner of Ussishkin Street. This is a large, fancy place, with 147 rooms full of every convenience. Again, try for the rooms with a sea view. You'll pay $36 single, $49 double in season; $23 single, $28 double in the off-season.

Finally, as you're nearing the corner of Ussishkin Street, you'll come to the **Palace Hotel,** 33 Gad Machnes St. (Netanya 42279; tel. 053-37631), a large and fairly impressive establishment boasting 71 guest rooms and all the usual three-star services. The hotel is blissfully air-conditioned throughout, although guests can step outside to the terrace for a sun-roast every now and then if they like. Some of the rooms have the sea view, but most do not; however, the lovely terrace overlooks the sea, and there is a nice dining room, ballroom, bridge and table tennis, and TV in the lobby. Prices are $35 single, $46 double in high season; $21 single, $25 double off-season.

Just around behind the Palace, at 29 Rishon-le-Zion St. (Netanya 42279; tel. 053-23655), is the quaint, cozy **Hotel Daphna.** Rating only one star, the Daphna is a converted home with a surprising 17 rooms, all with showers and toilets, but little in the way of frills or fripperies. Prices reflect this austerity, however, and are gratifyingly low, remaining the same all year at $19 single, $23 double with breakfast, or $16 single, $19 double with no meal.

Ussishkin–Karlebach–Gad Machnes Intersection: Three streets come together forming an intersection behind the Palace Hotel. Gathered on or near this little crossroads are these choices:

Those looking for a boldly modern hotel with a decent location and reasonable prices might try the **Galei Ha-Sharon Hotel,** 42 Ussishkin St. (Netanya 42273; tel. 053-25125 or 41946), corner of Gad Machnes. Although it's a small, three-story, 25-room hotel, the Galei Ha-Sharon somehow achieves a surprising feeling of spaciousness. The rooms, while not luxurious, are fine—all with shower in the bathroom, shuttered balcony, and wall-to-wall carpet. There's also a cozy bar, and color TV in the lobby. Prices are $23 single, $34 double in high season; $16 single, $20 double in low season.

Kitty-corner from the Galei Ha-Sharon, at 4 Karlebach St. where Karlebach meets Ussishkin, is the two-star **Mizpe-Yam Hotel** (tel. 053-23730). Twenty-eight rooms here, in an older but well-kept building with five floors and an elevator to serve them. The decor here is very pleasant, with a covered patio full of plants, giving it a tropical feel, and beautiful wicker furnishings in the patio as well as in the lobby, which has a piano and bar, a stone patio out front, a handsome dining room with flowers on the tables, and best of all, a penthouse sun roof with lawn furniture and flower boxes all around. Rates are $25 single, $35 double in high season; $18 single, $28 double off-season. During the low season you can probably get a lower price, so be sure to ask; and in summer, you can get the best deal in Netanya by staying in the rooftop dormitory room with prices the same as at youth hostels, that is, around $5.

Right behind the Mitzpe-Yam at 3 Jabotinsky Blvd., is the **Landa family guest house** (Netanya 42277; tel. 053-22634). The sign out on the sidewalk reads "Motel—Rooms for Rent." Some of the rooms come with separate kitchens, others with private shower and toilet; there are also five four-room/two-bath furnished apartments complete with kitchen. No meals are served here, but you can buy food at the little store across the street. There's a common room upstairs for color TV in the evening. Prices are $10 for one person, $6 to $8 per person when there are more than one, except for July and August when rates go up by about $3.

Along Ussishkin Street: Between the aforementioned intersection and Ha-Atzma'ut Square is another hotel choice, the two-star **Hotel Ruben,** 25 Ussishkin St. (tel. 053-23107), with 27 air-conditioned rooms with bath or shower, wall-to-wall carpeting, swimming pool, and nice gardens surrounding. The Ruben charges these rates: $28 single, $37 double in season; $19 single, $21 double off-season.

On Dizengoff Street

Dizengoff Street is about three short blocks from the seashore, and parallel to it. Three blocks is hardly a long distance to walk, but you'll still pay lower prices here than if you are staying in proximity to the sparkling Mediterranean. To explore the whole length of Dizengoff Street, walk to the end of the pedestrian mall that forms Ha-Atzma'ut Square. The mall ends at Dizengoff, where you'll turn right (to the south). None of the hotels mentioned below is more than four blocks from the square.

The first hotel you'll come to is the **Hotel Grinstein,** 47 Dizengoff St. (tel. 053-22026), one block south of the square. All 40 rooms have balcony and private bathtub. This is not a fancy place, but on this quiet, tree-lined street, it's fine for a stay at $30 single, $35 double (prices remain the same all year).

Half a block south past the Grinstein, on the other side of the street, is the quiet **Hotel Gal Yam,** 46 Dizengoff St. (P.O. Box 1029, Netanya 42439; tel. 053-22603). Renowned as "the first hotel in Netanya," the Gal Yam has almost an acre of lawns and gardens, 22 rooms with bath or shower, balconies, and a pleasant, peaceful atmosphere. Each balcony has special shutters which you can open or close according to the weather, using it for a sitting room if you wish. There's a homey lobby, with both a piano and TV. You may eat in the dining room, or if you prefer, in the lovely gardens to the front or rear of the hotel. Prices are in the two-star range of $18 single, $32 double in season; $14 single, $25 double off-season.

If you continue to walk down Dizengoff Street, you'll come to Jerusalem (Yerushalayim) Street. Cross it, and you're on Chen (or Hen) Street, Dizengoff's "extension." Two blocks down Chen Street on the left is the **Scandinavian Service Center Orit,** 21 Chen St. (tel. 053-66818), entered by the main door around the corner to the right. There are only seven rooms here, and in high season it's usually full with Swedish guests, who enjoy the bright, clean rooms and friendly Swedish management. Rooms here are simple, but do have private shower and toilet, and prices stay the same all year: $14 single, $23 double.

Private Rooms and Apartments

One of the best ways to save money on accommodations, particularly if you plan to stay in Netanya for some time, is to rent a private room or apartment. Consult the **Municipal Tourist Information Office,** Ha-Atzma'ut Square (tel. 053-27286), for listings of rental agents. The office is open Sunday through Friday from 8:30 a.m. to 2 p.m., plus 4 to 7 p.m. May through the end of August, 3 to 6 p.m. from September until October 15; closed Saturday and holidays. The actual rental arrangements will generally be handled by local agents. And you'll have to pay an agent's fee, which is a flat 10% of the total rental (no extra charge if meal arrangements are made, fortunately).

Room rentals are available for at least three to four days, apartments for a week or more. Most of them are within walking distance of the sea.

Rooms in private homes come with sheets and blankets, and guests may use the refrigerator and stove. The cost without meals is about $7 to $12 per person.

In an apartment, you are provided with basic furniture requirements. The place is cleaned up before you arrive, but the onus of upkeep is on you for the length of your stay. What is known as a two-room flat (living room, one bedroom, kitchen, bath, balconies) costs about $450 per couple per month. A three-room flat (two bedrooms plus) costs $535 to $700 per month. A four-room flat (three bedrooms plus) costs $795 for the same period. Considering that the larger apartments can accommodate six to eight people, the daily average cost per bed is really quite low.

And bear in mind that these are *summer* rates. Prices in the off-season drop to a half or even a third of this. The apartment that cost you $600 from June through October might easily cost $200 to $250 in the off-season, with a single room going for maybe $100 to $150. Be sure to bargain for the best off-season rates.

If you plan on taking a room or an apartment during the high season (July to September), you should make arrangements in April or May.

Send a deposit (the usual deposit is about a third of the monthly rental)—which you'll probably lose if you cancel close to arrival time. You definitely won't get back the agent's fee. In return you'll receive a contract and exact information about what you'll be renting.

The agency recommended by the Tourist Information Office as of this writing is **S.O.S.,** located right behind the tourist information kiosk at 2 Gad Machnes St. (tel. 053-40487), in the same building as the Diamimon diamond center. They handle all the arrangements for renting either rooms or entire apartments, for whatever length of time you choose, and will assist you with every aspect of the rental.

Other agencies handling apartment rentals include **Nobil-Greenberg,** 2 Ussishkin St. (tel. 053-28735); **David Gafen,** 7 Herzl St. (tel. 053-39372); **Anglo-Saxon Real Estate Agency,** 7 Kikar Ha-Atzma'ut (tel. 053-28290); and **Signal,** Kikar Zion (tel. 053-23198).

The Youth Hostel

Netanya doesn't have an IYHA Youth Hostel right in town, but there's the **Emek Hefer Youth Hostel** (tel. 053-96032) in nearby Kefar Vitkin, 6 km (3½ miles) to the north, a small village easily accessible by bus. Kefar Vitkin does have its own lovely beach, but since the village is set back from the sea, it's a bit of a long walk (or a short bus ride, with buses going frequently). Prices at this hostel are the same low rates as for all the official IYHA hostels: $5.50 for IYHA members, $6.50 for nonmembers, breakfast included. The hostel has 150 beds, including family rooms, and a kitchen for guests' use.

RESTAURANTS: Naturally, the first place one thinks of eating in Netanya is at one of the lovely little sidewalk café-restaurants that line Ha-Atzma'ut Square. Here you can find just about anything your heart desires, and if it's not here, it's only a short walk along Herzl Street.

To make sure you're not disappointed, no matter where you eat, pick a place that's doing a thriving business. Remember the restaurant-goers' golden rule: "Never sit down in an empty eatery!" Sure, late at night all the places might be empty. But if it's lunchtime and the cafés all around are full, don't go into that invitingly quiet, empty one. Another warning: Try to pick a restaurant where the service charge is already included in the quoted prices—look at the menu, or the posted price list, and it will (or will not) say "Service Included." And watch out for drink prices. Two beers at some of these places can end up costing more than the fish you ordered as a main course.

Now for some place-by-place recommendations, starting down by the sea.

Right on the northwest corner of the square is the **Restaurant-Pizzeria La Terrasa** (no phone), on the corner of Ha-Atzma'ut and King David Streets, an open-air restaurant announcing itself as a "Grill-Fish-Italian-French Kitchen." It features several combination fixed-menu meals, ranging in price from NIS10 ($6.65) to NIS20 ($13.35), with the most expensive combo including salad niçoise, couscous, fried fish or pepper steak or Cordon Bleu or calamari, potatoes, wine, and dessert. Open from 11 a.m. to 11 p.m. daily.

The **Renaissance Restaurant,** 6 Ha-Atzma'ut Square (tel. 053-28653), offers Israeli fare with a slight international accent. The decor is attractive and modernistic, with tables both inside and out under the flowered awning. An order of kebab or hamburger topped with egg, schnitzel or an omelet, served with salad and chips, is about NIS9 ($6), and an American waffle—a waffle topped with three scoops of ice cream, fruit cocktail, chocolate and strawberry syrup, and loads of whipped cream—goes for NIS10 ($6.65).

On the other side of the square, the **Oriental Restaurant** at 4 Ha-Atzma'ut Square features a self-service buffet Arabian dinner for NIS10 ($6.65) to NIS15 ($10). Open from 10 a.m. to midnight daily.

At **Restaurant Tahiti,** on the north side of the square, the emphasis is French and Italian rather than Polynesian. You can get spaghetti, lasagne, or ravioli for NIS6 ($4) to NIS8 ($5.35), or a nice seafood dinner including fish, shrimp, or calamari prepared in any of several ways (fried, butter garlic, au gratin, or provençal), plus french fries and salad, for NIS14 ($9.35) to NIS18 ($12). A vegetable, onion, and mushroom goulash comes for NIS5 ($3.35). Open daily from 11 a.m. to 1 a.m.

Restaurant Miami, 2 Herzl St. (tel. 053-32600), is generally acknowledged to have the best shwarma in town, priced at NIS10 ($6.65). Other Middle Eastern delights are similarly enticing, with selections like lamb steak, veal schnitzel, the special house shishlik, or a hamburger coming for the same price. Open from 9 a.m. to midnight Sunday through Thursday, on Friday until 4:30 p.m., on Saturday from 6 p.m. to midnight. If you have a large group, you might want to call for a reservation at this popular kosher restaurant.

Another place for a superb meal is the **"Ha-Nassi" President Restaurant and Café Bar,** 5 Herzl St. (tel. 053-22952). This is an ultra-kosher restaurant specializing in traditional Jewish dishes. You can order a multitude of meats from the grill or the oven; a full meal will cost about NIS9 ($6) to NIS15 ($10). The house specialty is the Saturday meal, a traditional Sabbath feast, served from 11 a.m. to 2 p.m. for NIS15 ($10), which must be paid in advance. Open Sunday through Thursday from morning until midnight or 2 a.m., closing an hour before the Sabbath on Friday, and on Saturday from 11 a.m. to 2 p.m. only.

At 1 Herzl St. is the **Conditory Espresso Ugati** (tel. 053-22604), a Central European pastry shop just perfect for devotees of those sinfully delicious, heavily creamy confections favored in Berlin and Vienna. Don't make a meal of it here, but do drop in for afternoon tea or after-dinner coffee—and a pastry from the refrigerator case out front. You can get espresso here, of course, but if you'd like a shot of brandy with your blintzes, they have that too. Open from 8 a.m. to midnight every day but Friday, when it closes at 3 p.m.; open on Saturday from 6 p.m. on.

Right around the corner, at no. 1 Ha-Rav Kook St., is the **Pundak Ha-Yam Grill Bar** (tel. 053-24880). A plain, no-nonsense grill with meats sizzling on the grill, hard-working waiters, and a minimum of decor, it is nonetheless a top favorite with locals. Reasons? The grilled meats are prepared fresh, to your order, before your eyes; service is quick, portions are huge, and prices are moderate. Order shishlik, steak, heart, or liver, and you'll get a salad, french fries, a plate of spaghetti, and several rounds of flat bread too—all for NIS10 ($6.65), and only half that if you order hamburger or sausages as your main course. There's another Pundak Ha-Yam in the restaurant complex right down on the beach, serving the same food for the same prices. Open from noon to midnight daily, except for Friday when it closes at 3:30 p.m.

A Liquid Pick-Me-Up

Don't overlook the **juice bar** at the corner of Herzl and Dizengoff, on the left-hand (north) side. Freshly squeezed orange, carrot, and grapefruit juice are served here in season, at moderate prices considering the nutritive value of these wholesome refreshers. Open from 8 a.m. to 1 a.m. daily in summer, until 7:30 or 8 p.m. in winter according to the weather; closed for the Sabbath, reopening Saturday evening.

For Ice Cream

Although ice cream is available at many places around the square, everybody's favorite seems to be **Ice Cream Vitman,** on the northeast corner of Herzl and Dizengoff Streets. With its many umbrella-shaded tables squeezed onto the corner, it's a popular place both day and night, serving a big ice-cream sundae for NIS3 ($2), three scoops in a large waffle cone for NIS2 ($1.35), or NIS2.50 ($1.65) if you get nuts, fruit, and whipped cream too. Open from 8 a.m. to midnight every day.

For Pizza

Pizza Don Pedro, 7 Herzl St., has 'em lining up for slices of the hot, savory stuff for only NIS1.50 ($1) to NIS1.70 ($1.15) per giant-sized, delicious slice, depending on toppings. Grab yours anytime from 10 a.m. to 2 p.m. and again from 4 until 10 or 11 p.m.; closed Friday at 2 p.m., opening again on Saturday at 4 p.m. You can sit under the awning at one of the sidewalk tables and enjoy a beer with your pizza for only NIS1.30 (85¢) more, watching the people stroll by.

Another popular pizza spot is **Pizza Rimini,** 3 Herzl St., where you can get a slab-to-go for NIS1.50 ($1) to NIS1.80 ($1.20), or sit down at the nice sidewalk tables to enjoy spaghetti, fettuccine, or ravioli on the full Italian menu for NIS5.50 ($3.65) to NIS9 ($6). Open from 10 a.m. to 3 p.m. every day.

Closer to the beach, just around the corner from the square at 2 Ussishkin St. is **Los Argentinos** (tel. 053-64246), a tiny place that prides itself on being the only kosher pizzeria in Netanya. You can sit here for a break from the hubbub of the square if you can find a table, or you can take away a slice of pizza or an empanada (a Spanish-origin snack something like a piroshki, that is, fried bread filled with egg, tomato, and spices) for NIS1.60 ($1.05). Open from 10:30 a.m.

until 1 or 2 a.m.; closing for the Sabbath on Friday afternoon, reopening Saturday evening.

At the Central Bus Station

The **Egged Bus Station Restaurant** here as elsewhere offers some of the least expensive food in town. It's a self-service place, and you can get a three-course meal for about NIS5 ($3.35). Open from 5:30 a.m. to 3:15 p.m. and 4 to 9 p.m.; closed for the Sabbath.

WHAT TO DO: The main attraction at Netanya is, of course, the lovely **beach.** In addition to lots of sand, swimming, and sun, you can enjoy the attractions in the beach complex, with restaurants and snackshops, beach chairs, and shade under large public umbrellas, a basketball court, and a gymnastics field. You can rent a sailboard, and get lessons on how to use it. You'll see people fishing up on the rocky breakwater. The water is great for swimming—you can go out pretty far before it starts to get deep. There's a lifeguard on duty, and do swim in the approved area; it's posted not to swim beyond a certain point.

Of course it's beautiful to see the sun set into the Mediterranean, and in the high tourist season, student patrols keep watch to make sure everything is okay. Still, be cautious at night here. The lifeguards leave the beach when it *starts* to get dark. Be sure you stay where you see other people, and if you're a woman alone, be extra-cautious. During the winter the student patrols are not around, and it's not a good idea to hang around the beach, or the parks on the cliffs, at night.

Netanya Activities

During the 90% of the year when the sun is in full bloom, you bake under the Mediterranean sun, swim in protected areas, fish, boat, stroll, and while away the hours in a sidewalk café. In other words, you relax and enjoy yourself.

July and August are the most active months here. Each week, in the amphitheater of **Gan Ha-Melekh park,** running along the beachside cliffs just north of the square, there are community sings and screenings of full-length feature films, for free, plus evening entertainment in Ha-Atzma'ut Square by top Israeli singers and folklore groups. Also in the square are weekly programs for children, starting at 6:30 p.m., with magicians, clowns, and so on. In addition to the weekly events, you'll find classical and light music and songs in the Gan Ha-Melekh park amphitheater Sunday through Thursday from 5:45 p.m. until sunset.

In July, there is a one-week **art exhibit** on Ha-Atzma'ut Square (Sunday through Thursday from 5:30 to 11 p.m.; closed Friday; on Saturday from 8:30 p.m. to midnight). . . . For the more cerebral, a **chess tournament** is held in the city yearly during May and June. The location varies. The event is a big draw, and every two years there's a match for international contestants. The games start at 3:30 p.m. and last until 10 p.m. For further information, contact the Tourist Information Office or the Israel Chess Federation, 6 Frisch St., Tel Aviv (tel. 03-258-102).

If you'd like to **meet an Israeli citizen,** apply three days in advance at the tourist office and you'll soon find yourself invited to a home for a friendly chat and a cup of coffee.

Sports and Games

Sport activities abound in Netanya.

Horseback riding is available at two locations. The Ranch (tel. 053-93655), near Havezelet Ha-Sharon Village, has horseback riding daily from 8 a.m. till sunset; take bus 17 or 29 from the Central Bus Station. There's also the Cactus Ranch, on Itamar Ben-Avi Street (Tobruck), also open daily from 8 a.m. until sunset.

There's **lawn bowling** at the Wingate Institute (tel. 053-96652), except during the month of May.

Surfing and sailboarding can be arranged at the Kontiki Club down on the Netanya beach—lessons too—open daily from 8:30 a.m. until sunset.

Mini-golf—18 holes—is on Nice Boulevard, after the Dan Hotel, open daily from noon until 11 p.m. April through September (check for hours during other months).

Squash and tennis are featured at the Elizur Sports Center (tel. 053-38920) at the end of Radak Street (take bus 8 from the Central Bus Station), open daily from 6 or 8 a.m. until 5 to 10 p.m. (call to check which hours are on what days).

Other **tennis courts** include the Maccabi Courts on Ha-Hashmonaim Street (tel. 053-24054), open daily from 8 a.m. to 10 p.m., on Friday to 6 p.m.; the Green Beach Sports Center (tel. 053-51466) in Netanya South (bus from Central Bus Station); and the Residence Hotel, 18 Gad Machnes St. near Ha-Atzma'ut Square (tel. 053-33777), by appointment only.

If you're not up for a dip in the sea, you'll find **swimming pools** at the Green Beach Sports Center (open April till October from 9 a.m. to 6 p.m.) and at the Elizur Sports Center (open May to September, Sunday to Thursday from 6 a.m. to 6 p.m.); see above for details on these sports clubs. Many Netanya hotels have swimming pools as well.

Community folk dancing is held every Saturday, beginning at 8 p.m. April through the end of October, in Ha-Atzma'ut Square; it's free.

If you happen to be in Netanya during **Succoth** (the Feast of Tabernacles), come to Ha-Atzma'ut Square for four free evenings of **folklore** featuring the various ethnic groups living in Israel, with dance, song, and typical traditional snacks.

Duplicate bridge is played every Monday and Thursday at 8:15 p.m. at the Women's League House, 5 MacDonald St.

Bingo evenings are Sundays at 8 p.m. at the Americans and Canadians Association, 28 Shmuel Ha-Naziv St. (tel. 053-30950).

Chess Club meetings are every Monday from 7 to 10 p.m., at the Library, 30 Shmuel Ha-Naziv St.

Open House for Tourists is held every Monday, Tuesday, and Wednesday from 9:30 to 11:30 a.m., at the British Settlers Association, 7 Ha-Matmid St., and also on Wednesday at 4 p.m. at the WIZO House, 13 MacDonald St. (tel. 053-23192).

Many **international social clubs** hold regular meetings in Netanya, including Rotary, Lions, Hadassah, Freemasons, International Toastmistress, Pioneer Women, B'nai B'rith, the American and Canadian Association, the British Settlers Association, and WIZO. Ask at the Tourist Information Office, or see the brochure "Kan Netanya," for times and places.

A Visit to a Diamond Factory

Israel is the number-one spot in the world for cutting and polishing diamonds, and Netanya is Israel's number-one diamond center, with two large factories. If you're in the market to buy, you can probably save about 20% by buying here. Prices range from $35 to $150 for simple necklaces or rings, up to infinity for highest-quality investment diamonds and jewelry ensembles.

Even if you're not interested in buying, a visit to the **Netanya Diamond Center,** 31 Benjamin Blvd. (tel. 053-37463 or 22233), two blocks south of the Central Bus Station, is still a fascinating experience.

When you arrive at the door, you'll be asked which language you prefer, and a guide will meet you to show you around in your chosen tongue. First you'll see a model of a South African mine, complete with model railroad. Then your guide leads you past rows of cutters and polishers, explaining what happens to the diamonds in every phase of their transformation from raw stone to finished jewelry. There's a gem museum on the premises, and be sure to ask to see the 12-minute film telling the story of the diamonds as they proceed from the South African mines to you. Finally, you emerge into a showroom of jewelry so lovely you've probably never imagined anything like it, with diamonds of all shapes and sizes in every possible combination, and other precious stones as well. There's no pressure to buy, so after looking around, you can just say a polite "thank you" to your guide and be on your way. If, however, you have questions or need further help, you'll be given expert, courteous service.

Netanya Diamond Center has another location too, at 90 Herzl St. near the entrance to Netanya (tel. 053-34624 or 34730), with a larger showroom but no gem museum, geared more toward larger volumes of visitors. Both locations are open the same hours: 8 a.m. to 7 p.m. daily, on Friday until 3 p.m.; closed Saturday.

Netanya's other diamond factory outlet is **Diamimon,** located right near the beach in Ha-Atzma'ut Square, at 2 Gad Machnes St. (tel. 053-41725 or 91182). Here, too, is a lovely showroom, and craftsmen busy at work cutting and polishing away, but it's all on a much smaller scale. Nonetheless, it's worthwhile to stop by here since you'll undoubtedly be in the area anyway, and if you're thinking of making a purchase, you might want to compare prices. Open in summer from 8 a.m. to 10 p.m. Sunday through Friday, on Saturday from 6 to 10 p.m. Winter hours are until 7:30 p.m. every day but Friday, when it closes at 2 p.m.

When you visit Diamimon, go up one more flight of stairs and visit the cafeteria above, featuring displays of exotic clothing worn by the Jews of Yemen, and art of Jews in many countries. The cafeteria has a beautiful sea view too.

You can also compare prices at **Dorit Jewellers,** 8 Herzl St. (tel. 053-33440), on the corner of Dizengoff Street, which prides itself on "honesty and special value."

Nightlife

There's no problem finding plenty of things to do around Netanya after a day at the beach. Everything in Ha-Atzma'ut Square is open until around midnight or later, and the square is alive with strollers, sippers, and diners on a warm evening. Be sure to check with the Tourist Information Office for special events and activities of all kinds, in addition to those listed above; there's quite a lot going on, especially during the summer months.

Discos and Nightclubs: If it's a nightclub or disco you're looking for, you've got a number of choices.

For the 18-year-old set, there's **La Terrasa** piano bar just behind the La Terrasa restaurant on the corner of Ha-Atzma'ut Square and King David Street, down by the sea. Although the sign says it's a piano bar, I found rock 'n roll videos playing instead of a pianist. Open from 4 p.m. to 4 a.m. every day.

Another place young folks will enjoy is the discothèque **Plaisance,** also on the north side of the square, entered through a tiny doorway beside the Renaissance Restaurant. The NIS10 ($6.65) admission fee also buys your first drink. This is an over-18 membership disco club, but tourists are welcome. Open daily from 9:30 p.m. to 4 a.m.

Near here, around through the little passageway just a bit farther inland, beside the Whitman Restaurant, is **The Place.** Actually, once you go down the long flight of stairs and get inside, it's two places—one a discothèque nightclub, and over to your right, a piano bar. The disco is ultramodern, with multilevel seating, sunken dance floor, fountains, and an aquarium, and features all the latest disco hits. In the piano bar, you'll find music in mixed styles depending on the clientele; for example, you might find a singer of Israeli folk tunes. The price of admission entitles you to use the facilities of both clubs, and includes the first drink. On Friday and Saturday nights, admission is NIS13 ($8.65) per person; during the week, it's NIS10 ($6.65)—and only the males pay; females are admitted free. Open from 9:30 p.m. to 4 a.m. every night, for ages 18 and over.

Pubs: Prefer something a little more mellow? A couple of nice pubs are located just a little farther back from the sea.

Walking inland down the square from the sea, look to your right when you get to Dizengoff Street and you'll see, on the right-hand side of the street, a neon sign sporting a mug of draft beer and a carved wooden sign announcing the **Uris Pub,** at 26 Dizengoff St. Walk down the flowered walkway to the wooden door and you'll find a friendly pub atmosphere, with stools at the bar, wooden tables indoors, or patio tables out back in the garden to choose from. Depending on when you come, you may find nice American music on the jukebox or amateur live music—you can even bring your guitar and play, if you like. A new artist is on exhibit every month to decorate the walls. You'll find an assortment of wines, beers, and cocktails, plus a menu of sandwiches and omelets for about NIS6 ($4). Open from 8 p.m. until 1 or 2 or sometimes even 5 a.m., depending on the crowd.

Another popular pub is **The Magnet,** at 14 Herzl St., with four different sections: a wooden bar when you first enter the door, an upstairs pub with wooden tables, an open patio in the rear, and a piano bar with cozy stuffed chairs, featuring music ranging from jazz and blues to classical. International customers are invited to plunk a tune on the piano or a note on the guitar when there's no performance scheduled. In addition to the bar selections, there's a menu of hamburgers, kebab, schnitzel, pizza, and other assorted goodies for about NIS8 ($5.35) to NIS10 ($6.65). Open nightly from 4 p.m. to 5 a.m.

Across from here is **Pub Beer,** 15 Herzl St., an open-air place which features sidewalk tables and music on the jukebox. Open from 9 a.m. to 1 a.m.

EN ROUTE TO CAESAREA:
On the coastal highway just north of Netanya, in Kefar Vitkin, there's a large gas station, **Paznon,** with a great snack restaurant that's open from 7 a.m. to 1 a.m. daily, and a gift shop flanking it. While you have the car tanked up, you can fill up on the specialty of this American-owned place: pancakes. Two of them with maple syrup will cost you NIS2.5 ($1.65). More exotic varieties—with salami, apple sauce, coconuts, cherries, lemons, raisins, cheese, or an egg—cost more. Many other choices are available, ranging from hummus or tchina in a pita to grilled chicken with chips—and even a version of Mexican chili.

Two new holiday villages have sprung up on the shores of the Mediterranean at **Mikhmoret** ("Fishing Net"), a village between Netanya and Caesarea. There's easy access by bus, and you have a full range of activities to choose from, including many sports, horseback riding, aerobics, entertainment, special activities, a private beach, and even a child-care program with special fun activities planned for the kids. This little bit of lavish holiday heaven is called **Nueba on the Mediterranean** (tel. 053-96397). Call to check on open dates and prices; as of this writing, Nueba is open from April to October only, with full board (including three meals and all activities) priced at $33 per person per day in the busiest times (July and August), $25 the rest of the time, and 20% less for children.

Mikhmoret's other holiday village, Sun Club (tel. 053-96065 or 96070), may also be open only seasonally; call to check for details.

6. Caesarea and Vicinity

This is one of my favorite places in Israel. Among Caesarea's beautiful excavations you get an inspired feeling for the tide of history that has washed Israel's shores.

Located about a third of the way from Tel Aviv to Haifa, behind an immigrants' village and a cluster of banana groves, Caesarea has been the scene of considerable activity and development—archeological digs, a luxury hotel, a golf course and country club.

Caesarea is the spectacular city of Herod the Great. Herod set out to construct a port to equal Athens, and judging from scientific reconstructions, he probably succeeded. The magnificent harbor town was dedicated to Augustus Caesar, emperor of Rome from 27 B.C. to A.D. 14. It later became the largest city in Judea, the chief port, the governor's residence, and the home of Pontius Pilate. Despite its splendor, it was also a cruel Roman city, and within its gates hundreds of Jews and Christians were thrown to the lions following the revolt of A.D. 66.

Ancient Caesarea was a diplomat's city, a merchant's city, and a sportsman's city—a cosmopolitan delight for the sophisticates of the time. Its grandeur lasted for about 300 years, but ultimately the Arabs took the town from the Byzantines in the year 640.

Some 400 years later (1107), the Frank Crusaders reconquered Caesarea, and among the treasures they recovered was what was reputed to be the famous Holy Grail, the green crystal vessel from the Last Supper, which figured in so many of the Arthurian romances. It was taken to Italy, where it is preserved in the Cathedral of San Lorenzo, in Genoa, becoming known as the "Sacro Catino." Saint Louis (Louis IX) later built a fortress here, in 1271, and most of the Crusader remains we see here today date from his time.

GETTING THERE: To get to Caesarea by bus, you must first take a bus to Hadera and transfer from there. Buses run to Hadera from Tel Aviv, Netanya, or Haifa, roughly every 30 to 45 minutes. From Hadera, bus 76 leaves hourly for Casearea, departing Sunday through Thursday at 9, 10, and 11 a.m., and 12:30, 3, 4, 5, and 6 p.m. On Friday the last bus leaves Hadera at 12:40 p.m. No buses run on Saturday. The return bus leaves Caesarea about 20 minutes after each inbound arrival.

A TURBULENT HISTORY: But before getting into archeological detail, let's take a quick look at the momentous events that took place in this now-placid spot. Caesarea was a port. That fact was significant from start to finish. The first port city here was constructed by colonists from Sidon in the 300s B.C., and named after Sharshan, king of Sidon. The name was later Hellenized to Straton, and the town called Straton's Tower.

Around 90 B.C. the town was conquered and rebuilt by Alexander Jannaeus (died 76 B.C.), Hasmonean king of Judea. But Rome annexed all of Judea in 63 B.C., and the town of Straton's Tower along with it.

It was Herod the Great (37–4 B.C.) who enlarged and beautified the town considerably, added a spectacular harbor, called Sebastos, and named the city in honor of his Roman suzerain and benefactor, Caesar Augustus. By the year of Herod's death, Caesarea was among the grandest port cities of the eastern Mediterranean.

The first century of the Christian era saw bad times for both the Christian and Jewish populations of Caesarea. Besides persecution by their Roman overlords, the two communities fought between themselves.

Caesarea is mentioned in the New Testament as the place where the Holy Ghost was first given to the Gentiles (Acts 10 and 11), a significant and controversial event in the development of Christianity. Caesarea figures prominently in the story of the apostle Paul, who was here warned not to go to Jerusalem; he went anyway, returning in chains to stand trial for heresy. After his imprisonment and subsequent trial in Caesarea, it was from this port that he was sent to Rome, in the year A.D. 62, to stand trial again there, at the capital of the Roman Empire. (See Acts 21:8–14; Acts 23:23–25; and Acts 25 and 26.)

Caesarea, as the headquarters of Roman rule in Israel, had been a tinderbox for a long time, as the Jews increased in resentment of the Roman militaristic domination of their land. Tensions came to a head in the '60s; pogroms against the Jewish population began, and culminated in a brutal massacre of 2,000 Jews in the Caesarea amphitheater. Many more were sent to Rome and sold into slavery. With these atrocities, all Judea rose in revolt. The rebellion saw the Roman destruction of Jerusalem in A.D. 70, and the valiant but hopeless defense of Masada in 73.

A later rebellion, that of Bar Kokhba in 131, saw upward of 500,000 Jews die throughout the country. The greatest sages of the time, including Rabbi Akiva, were brought to the amphitheater of Caesarea, tortured in public, and burned alive.

Under the Byzantines, things got better. Caesarea was home to a succession of important church scholars, including Eusebius (264–340), who codified the rules of the young church. During the 400s, it became the seat of a metropolitan bishop responsible for all the Christian communities of the eastern Mediterranean. A small but significant Jewish community thrived throughout this period.

The Talmud mentions a number of judges or rabbis who lived in Caesarea, particularly R. Abba, R. Adda, R. Hanina, R. Assi, R. Hosheya, R. Hezekiah, and R. Ahava b. Zeira (Eruvin 76b; Jerusalem Talmud, Shab. passim), and also refers to the synagogue of Caesarea, situated near the harbor (Jerusalem Talmud, Berakhot 3:1, 6a, et al.).

The Arab invasions put an end to this time of growth, in 640. Under the caliphs, Caesarea did not play a big part in world affairs. Muslim rule continued until 1101, when Baldwin I and his Crusader army landed in Caesarea and slaughtered the entire Arab population.

During the conquest, Baldwin's troops discovered what they thought to be the Holy Grail, the famous vessel from which Jesus had drunk at the Last Supper. The Crusaders began construction of a church at the spot where St. Paul was said to have received his condemnation, but building was interrupted when Saladin arrived in 1187. Caesarea changed hands several times during the following century, even though St. Louis had built up its walls in 1252 to an impressive strength. When Muslim armies again took the town (in 1265 and 1291), they did their best to pull down the defenses, remembering that this had been Baldwin's beachhead. The pillage succeeded, and for the next 500 years Caesarea was little more than some impressive old buildings slowly being covered by sand.

In the 1700s Ahmed Jezzar Pasha, Ottoman governor of the province, sent his workmen to Caesarea to reclaim much of its Carrara marble, columns of decorative stone, and finely carved capitals for use in the reconstruction and beautification of his provincial capital at Acre (Akko), north of Haifa.

In 1884 Muslim colonists from Bosnia (which was soon to become part of Christian Yugoslavia) arrived in Caesarea and attempted to found a fishing village. Malaria and the shifting sands convinced them to head inland and become farmers instead. An Arab village survived here through much of our century, though. It was abandoned in 1948.

Caesarea's modern history begins in 1940, when Kibbutz Sedot Yam was founded. During the first decade of the kibbutz, its members discovered the unexpected richness of Caesarea's archeological remains. A full campaign of restoration followed, and today the city is one of Israel's most impressive sites.

ORIENTATION: The remains of Caesarea (Qesari or Qesarya, in Hebrew) are spread along a three-kilometer (two-mile) stretch of Mediterranean beach. At the southern end is Kibbutz Sedot Yam and the bungalow complex called Kayit V'Shayit (see below). North of the bungalows is the Roman theater, part of the national park, and half a kilometer north of that is the entrance to the walled Crusader city. Just inland from the Crusader city entrance is a small snack restaurant and a shady parking lot. Be sure to wander behind the restaurant for a look at the ruins of a Byzantine street (described below). Finally, about a kilometer north of the city, a 10- or 15-minute walk along the beach, is the impressive Roman aqueduct.

TOURING THE RUINS: You'll arrive at either the Roman theater or the Crusader city, which are in fact right next to one another, though the entrance gates are half a kilometer apart. Entry to both the theater and the Crusader city is on the same ticket, which costs NIS2 ($1.35) for an adult, half price for a child. Hours are 8 a.m. to 4 p.m. daily, to 3 p.m. on Friday and eves of holidays.

You can get a map showing the details of all the various eras of construction at this site, both on land and out in the water—the cities and harbors of Straton's Tower, of Herod, the Romans, the Byzantines, and the Crusaders. I recommend that you do this, since it will give you a much better idea of the scope of the place. The excavations you see are only a very small part of what's actually there, waiting to be discovered.

I'll assume you're going to see the ruins from south to north, starting with the theater.

The Roman Theater

The theater represents a direct link to the time of Jesus and Pontius Pilate, which is when it was constructed. Capable of seating 5,000 spectators, the theater has been restored (1959–1970) to its former glory. You may be lucky enough to visit when a summer concert or performance is planned, and sit on the warm, pale limestone seats with the Mediterranean as a backdrop. You should test out the acoustics by sitting in the stands and listening for someone on the stage to speak or clap hands.

The Crusader City

You enter the Crusader city on a bridge across the deep moat, then through a great gatehouse with Gothic vaulting. Emerging from the gatehouse, you find yourself in the fortified town, which was large, but it covered a mere fraction of the great Herodian/Roman city. Sites within the fortified town are marked by signs in Hebrew and English, which make a self-guiding tour. Especially noteworthy are the foundations of the Crusader Church of St. Paul (1100s), down toward the sea, near the little Turkish minaret (1800s). The citadel, next to the group of shops and restaurants, was badly damaged by an earthquake in 1837, as was most of the Crusader city.

The Port of Sebastos

Looking from the Crusader city out into the sea, you see a quay extending out. This arm formed a part of the Crusader port—but that's only a small part of its story.

King Herod's harbor at Caesarea, completed in 10 B.C. and named Sebastos, extended at least three times as far out into the sea as what you see today. It curved around to the right, where a separate northern breakwater extended out to meet it roughly where the northern Crusader fortification walls meet the sea. It was not just a breakwater, but a wide platform, with room for large quantities of cargo, housing for sailors, a lighthouse, gigantic Colossi statues, and two large towers guarding the entrance gates to the harbor, which were situated on the harbor's northern side. The harbor could be closed off by a chain stretched between the two towers, preventing ships from entering; it was large and protected enough to permit ships to winter over, a significant asset in terms of commerce, permitting the departure of ships laden with cargo from the East first thing in the spring, as soon as winter ended.

Herod's harbor was one of the largest harbors of the Roman world, mentioned by historian Josephus Flavius as being an especially amazing feat of technology because it was totally man-made, built without benefit of geographical features such as a bay or cove. Historians searching for the harbor did not find it until 1960, when a combination of aerial photography and underwater archeological explorations revealed the ruins sunken offshore.

One reason that today we don't see more evidence than we do of this fantastic port structure has to do with the presence of two geological fault lines just off the coast—one just beyond the quay you see, the other about twice as far out, both running below the Herodian port. Historians and archeologists believe that the large harbor structure, the ruins of which are now submerged underwater, probably sank vertically downward shortly after its construction—by the 3rd century A.D. at the latest—perhaps in response to an earthquake. It probably sank by about 5 to 6 meters (16 to 20 feet); with sea level today being about 4 to 5 meters (13 to 16 feet) higher than it was in Herod's time, the result is that the ruins are submerged today about 9 meters (30 feet) underwater.

The excavation of the underwater ruins is an important international project, one of the major endeavors of the Center for Maritime Studies at Haifa University. There's a **diving center** at the site of the ancient harbor (tel. 06-361-441), where you can get a map of the site, complete with directions for a self-guided diving tour of the ruins, with an abbreviated version for snorkelers.

The Byzantine Street

Fifty yards east of the Crusader city entrance, behind the little snackshop, is the Byzantine Street, or **Street of Statues,** actually part of a forum. The statues are of an emperor and other dignitaries. Much of the stone for construction of the forum was taken from earlier buildings, as was the custom. The Byzantine Street was discovered and excavated by kibbutzniks from Sedot Yam in the 1950s.

The Hippodrome

Head east from either the Byzantine Street or the theater to reach the ruined hippodrome, in the fields between the two access roads. Measuring 80 by

320 yards, the hippodrome could seat upward of 20,000 people. Some of the monuments in the hippodrome may have been brought from Aswan in Egypt—remember, expense was no object when Herod built for Caesar!

Jewish Quarter and Roman Aqueduct

Caesarea's **Jewish Quarter** is outside the walls of the Crusader city, near the beach directly north. The community that flourished here during Roman times was well within the boundaries, and the walls, of Herod's city.

The great **aqueduct** north of the Jewish Quarter is almost nine kilometers (six miles) in length, though most of it has been buried by the shifting sands. There was an earlier aqueduct here, but the present construction dates from the A.D. 100s. The southern part of the aqueduct is exposed to view, and you must see it.

LIFE ON A KIBBUTZ: The **Caesarea Shore Resort** sounds like one of those posh places for internationals. Well, people from all over the world do frequent it, but it's not all posh. It is pleasant, casual, and beautiful in its own way. And the people who operate it are friendly, warm, and conscientious. It's also known as **Kayit V'shayit Ltd.** (Sedot Yam 38805; tel. 06-362-928 or 361-161), and road signs will direct you until you arrive in the large parking lot facing a small snack-bar that fronts the main dining room. If you want to stop just for a meal or snack, you're better off in the dining room.

If you'd like to stay overnight or longer, there's a range of facilities that includes a Guest House, where $26 per person covers bed and breakfast in a room with private shower. There's also full camping regalia here—with showers and guards, the works. Without staying over, you can enjoy beach fun, tennis courts, and showers for a modest charge. Those who sleep here have nightly entertainment to boot. The resort is open from May 1 to November 1, and there's a $4 off-season discount in May and October.

HEADING NORTH: Heading northward from Caesarea, we come across Zich-ron Yaakov, Dor, Athlit, and Ein Hod.

Zichron Yaakov

In the hills north of Caesarea, Zichron Yaakov has the distinction of being one of the first towns to be settled in Israel, founded in 1882. Of interest here are the wine cellars (they'll give you a tour and some wine afterward), and the **Roth-schild Family Tomb** set in handsome gardens. And right near the wine cellar, stop in to see the **Aaronson Museum;** it commemorates the days during World War I when the Aaronson family worked at an experimental farm at Athlit and supplied the British with intelligence information.

Opposite Zichron Yaakov is **Kibbutz Maagan Michael,** whose beautiful carp ponds at the edge of the sea also serve as a bird sanctuary. Depending on the season, birdwatchers can find herons, cranes, and storks. This kibbutz pro-duces plastic products, and is also a livestock center with herds of Brahmin-type cows and in-residence Israeli cowboys.

Dor

On the highway skirting the beach, road signs announce **Nahsholim,** a kib-butz located on one of Israel's most beautiful bathing beaches: **Dor Beach.** A wide expanse of sandy beach, it is beautified by natural lagoons. Looming near-by is **Tel Dor,** a mound containing the remains of the ancient city that was inhab-ited since Bronze Age times, by Phoenicians, Israelites, Greeks, and Romans. The ruins of a massive Greco-Roman temple dedicated to Zeus (Jupiter) add drama to the site. Farther to the north at modern Dor is a picturesque area of caves eroded by the sea to form a natural tunnel at the water's edge.

Here, too, is another kibbutz-operated vacation hotel, the 66-room **Nah-sholim Kibbutz Hotel** (Carmel Beach 20815; tel. 06-390-924 or 399-533). About an hour's drive from Tel Aviv, and easily reached via local buses or sheruts, it's a great place to spend the day, or several days. The islets around the beach make for sheltered and warm swimming, even during the winter or storm seasons, and the recreation facilities cover almost everything you can think of. Rates are $23 to $32.25 single, $34.50 to $50.50 double. There are antiquities around this recreation village, and it's a good base for sightseeing tours. Meals are available in the air-conditioned dining room.

Athlit

A short drive northward along the coast brings you to the ruins of a castle from Crusader times—the last Crusader fortress, in fact, to fall to the Arabs, in A.D. 1291. In the ruins, archeologists have also discovered relics and pottery from the Persian-Hellenistic and Phoenician periods. They might have been able to find more, but the earthquake in 1837 caused the Turkish ruler, Ibrahim Pasha, to remove much of Athlit's crumbled masonry and send it to Acre and Jaffa for reconstructing damaged buildings. Unfortunately, you can't go into the Athlit castle for a closer look, because it's smack in the heart of a security zone of the Israeli navy. (The military base you see at Athlit was originally built by the British as an internment camp for immigrants who illegally entered the country.)

Ein Hod

Inland, and almost directly across from Athlit, is the artists' village of Ein Hod. Road signs will point the way for drivers, and from 10 a.m. to 5:30 p.m. there's Egged bus service all the way up the mountainside to this famous colony. You can also take bus 921 to the Ein Hod roadway that intersects with the older, more inland Tel Aviv–Haifa highway, and hitchhike up the mountainside from there. (True hikers will find the ten-minute, half-mile trek a simple one.) Regardless of how you get up there, do make the trip.

Built over an abandoned Arab village, Ein Hod ("Well of Beauty") is the world-famous Israeli artists' colony, operated along certain cooperative lines: the village members have their own council of elders; the handyman is employed by the entire community; the gallery takes a much smaller percentage on sales than do other galleries; the workshops are shared; and the proceeds from the amphitheater's shows (summer weekends only) are used for the welfare of the village.

Under the guidance of the village's former mukhtar (headman), Marcel Yanko, the sculptors, painters, and potters rebuilt an old village according to their own specifications in 1953. They sawed, hammered, and plastered, planted gardens, patched leaky ceilings, installed plumbing, and turned a mosque and storehouse into a café and workshop. With help from the Tourist Office, the Haifa Municipality, and private donations, they now have a large gallery, several workshops, and an outdoor theater.

It's a picturesque place, tranquil and rugged looking, with a view of sloping olive groves and the broad Mediterranean that can inspire even the nonartistic. Crumbling archways and Moorish vaults are left as relics of the past.

Ein Hod's **restaurant** (tel. 04-942-016) displays brightly colored murals by some of its artist-members in an otherwise simple but roomy place. Moderately priced, it offers typical Israeli fare. A reduction of 25% is available to students.

The restaurant is particularly popular on Friday nights, when it serves a traditional Sabbath meal, including homemade gefilte fish and tcholent.

The **Ein Hod gallery** (tel. 04-942-029) carries a good selection of the village's work—silver jewelry, lots of ceramics, lithographs, etchings, oil paintings, watercolors, tapestries and shawls, sculpture, and woodwork. Most of Ein Hod's 200 full-time residents are craftspeople. They'll box your purchases and mail them to you wherever you live.

Admission to the gallery is by a small donation for adults. Its hours are 9:30 a.m. to 5 p.m. (on Friday till 4 p.m.) every day of the week, but it's closed Yom Kippur and Israeli Independence Day.

The **Janco-Dada Museum** (tel. 04-942-350) is open Sunday through Friday from 9:30 a.m. to 4 p.m., on Saturday until 5 p.m.

A three-hour tour to Ein Hod leaves Haifa daily except Friday at 9:30 a.m. It includes a drive through the Carmel mountain range, visits to Haifa University and the Druze market of Daliat El-Karmel, and visits to art galleries, artists' studios, etc. Contact **Mitspa Tours,** 1 Nordau St. (Haifa 33122; tel. 04-644-889).

Continue driving along the road that runs through Ein Hod, and you'll reach the delightful resort of **Nir Etzion.** It's run by the kibbutz of the same name. The kibbutz offers 74 rooms at $28.75 to $39 single, $36.75 to $57.50 double; kosher meals conducted in a religious, warm, friendly atmosphere; and transportation to nearby Dor Beach. It's also near Mount Carmel woods. The address is Nir Etzion Kibbutz Hotel, Carmel Beach 30808 (tel. 04-842-542).

ON TO ACRE: Not far from Athlit, you enter the outskirts of Haifa, and you'll notice signs for the lovely **Carmel Beach** (Hof Ha-Carmel), where for a small fee you can sun and shower afterward. But if you happen to be broke, backtrack half a kilometer to the **Municipal Beach,** which is free, including shower. The **Bat Galim Beach,** at Haifa's northernmost point, is free too.

SKIRTING HAIFA: Keeping the emphasis of this chapter on the smaller resort towns, kibbutzim, and archeological sites that line Israel's Mediterranean coast, we're going to skip right past Haifa. You no doubt will want to stop in this lovely city for several days. Such a city deserves a chapter unto itself, and gets it—turn to Chapter VI, then come back here to continue your ramblings northward along the coast.

NORTH FROM HAIFA: Independence Road in Haifa port runs northward out of the city past a heavily industrial area. At a crossroads called the "checkpost," bear left, following the signs, over the railroad tracks and you'll be on the northern coastal road to Acre and Nahariya. This latter road is also heavy with industry, and it's an industry you won't miss, because the smell of a sprawling chemical and fertilizer company overpowers the entire area.

The road to Acre and Nahariya passes through the Haifa suburbs of **Kiryat Motzkin** and **Kiryat Bialik,** both German-Jewish settlements. Kiryat Bialik is famous for an ambush the Hagana staged there in March of 1948, when an Arab munitions convoy was blown up and nearly took Kiryat Bialik with it. The ambush averted the invasion of Haifa.

7. Acre (Akko)

Acre (or Akko, or Acco), with its romantic minarets, massive city sea walls, and palm trees framed against the sky, has a long, startlingly eventful history.

It was first mentioned by name in the chronicles of Pharaoh Thutmoses III, about 3,500 years ago. It was a leading Phoenician port, and although it was allotted to the tribe of Asher, the tribe was never able to conquer it (Judges 1:31). The town is mentioned as part of David's kingdom, and was given by Solomon to Hiram, king of Tyre, in return for his help in building the temple.

Alexander the Great made his conquest of Acre in 332 B.C., and later, in 280 B.C., it was captured by the Ptolemies, and renamed Ptolemais. This is the name it holds in the New Testament when mentioned in passing as a stopping place of St. Paul (Acts 21:7). Julius Caesar stayed here too, in 48 B.C.

Jews had been living in Acre in relative peace with the other local inhabitants ever since the time of its allocation to the tribe of Asher, but during the Bar Kokhba revolt a large number of Jews were slaughtered by the Romans. Nevertheless, remnants of the Jewish population continued to live here.

When the Arabs conquered Ptolemais in A.D. 636, the town reverted to its former name of Acre, by which it was known until it was taken in 1104 by the Crusaders, who renamed it St. Jean d'Acre. It was the seat of Crusader government in the region, and the Crusaders did a lot of building here, including an entire underground city, which you still can visit today.

The Crusaders held Acre until the 13th century, except for a four-year period after the battle of Hittin in 1187; but the armies of Saladin lost the city again to the forces of Richard the Lion-Hearted, and it remained in Crusader hands until captured by the Mamelukes in the 13th century. The fall of Acre ensured the doom of the Crusader dominion in the Holy Land.

The Mamelukes sacked the town, and it lost its former importance. But Bedouin Sheik Daher el-Omar conquered the town in 1749, and began a serious rebuilding program. His plans came to a sudden end when he was murdered in 1775 by Ahmed Jezzar Pasha.

It was under the impetus of El-Jezzar that the town was given most of its important rebuilding. Structures from El-Jezzar's rule still standing today include the Jezzar Pasha Mosque, the Khan El-Umdan, the Turkish bathhouse now housing the Municipal Museum, the massive stone walls, and the aqueduct to the north.

Acre's decline as a major port was sealed by the advent of the steamship and other modern naval technology, with shipping activities gradually transferred to the larger port at Haifa, across the bay. Haifa remains today Israel's primary port.

Acre became famous again in this century as the scene of the largest prison break in history when, on May 4, 1947, 251 prisoners were freed from Acre Fortress as the result of a daring escape plot executed by Jewish underground fighters. The Citadel is today a museum, known as the Museum of the Heroes, where you can see historical memorabilia from this part of Israel's history, as well as the cell where Bahaullah, founder of the Baha'i religion, spent 2 years in the 1860s.

GETTING TO ACRE: From Haifa's Egged bus station, buses 361, 461, and 501 go north to Acre (Akko) before turning east and heading for Safed (Zefat) in Galilee. Buses 251 and 271 leave the Haifa bus station every ten minutes, bound for Acre. After your visit to Acre, if you plan on heading north to Nahariya, you'll have to hop a no. 271 Haifa–Acre–Nahariya bus.

ORIENTATION: Today Acre is actually in two distinct parts. There's the modern city of Acre, home to about 30,000 souls, a number of large industrial plants (including Steel City) and immigrant housing projects. Then there's the Old City, still surrounded by high, thick stone walls on all sides, situated on the tip of land jutting out into the sea, forming the protected Bay of Acre. It's the Old City that holds the charm and interest for tourists.

Coming into town by car, you can simply head for the minarets in the Old City. Arriving by bus, here's what to do: walk out of the bus station, turn left, and walk one long block to the traffic lights on Ben-Ami Street. Turn right (west) onto Ben-Ami and walk four long blocks to Haim Weizman Street. Turn left onto Weizman and you'll see the walls of the ancient Turkish fortress about two blocks ahead. Soon you'll see the minaret and dome of the Jezzar Pasha Mosque.

Don't want to walk? City buses nos. 1, 2, 61, 62, 63, and 65 all make stops at the entrance to the Old City.

Directly across from the Mosque of Jezzar Pasha is the **Tourist Information Office** (tel. 04-910-251), open from 8:30 a.m. to 4 p.m. Sunday through Thursday, closing early on Friday. Here you can ask any questions you may have, and also here—or next door, at the entrance to the Subterranean Crusader City— you can buy a large, wonderfully detailed map of the entire city of Acre for only NIS1 (65¢).

A Note to Women: Women unaccompanied by men attract a lot of attention around Acre. Even a pair of young ladies, or several together, may be surprised at the amount of attention they generate. Your best bet, especially after dark, is to find a trusty male or two with whom to share the stroll around Acre. A couple, or a pair of couples, or a group, of tourists is such a common sight in Acre that it arouses little notice.

WHERE TO STAY: There's only one place to stay in the Old City itself, and that's at the **Acre Youth Hostel** (P.O. Box 1090; tel. 04-911-982), at the tip of the Old City, down by the lighthouse. It's got 120 beds, with family rooms or dorm rooms available, and a shared guests' kitchen in case you want to do your own cooking. Prices are the same regular IYHA rates of $5.50 per night for those with an International Youth Hostel card, $6.50 without the card; you can pay $2 less if you prefer to prepare your own breakfast. There's a 10 p.m. curfew here, but no lock-out during the day, so you can come and go as you wish. It's an interesting old stone building, with a nice lobby upstairs, complete with marble and stone floor, high arched ceiling and windows, with a view of the sea wall and Haifa across the bay. Why all the luxury? Because this is the building that was once the palace of the local Ottoman governors, that's why.

If you're not up for staying in the youth hostel, there are some fine hotel choices just a short ride from Old Acre.

The three-star **Argaman Motel** (P.O. Box 153, Acre Beach 24101; tel. 04-916-691) is on the south side of Acre, at the intersection of the main northbound road and its branch into town. Situated as it is, this hotel has one of the most beautiful beachfront views in Israel—with Haifa on a point to the south, and on the northern tip of the wide arc of the bay, the ancient walled city of Old Acre. The Argaman is built right on the beach, with 75 spacious double rooms, all with wall-to-wall carpet, air conditioning and heat, private balcony, telephone, and immaculate tub and shower. Prices are $30 single, $40 double all year, for bed and breakfast, with a 10% discount for stays longer than one week. During high season (July, August, and Jewish holidays), half board may be required, bringing the price up to $40 single, $60 double; but with the hotel's reputation for culinary excellence, this should not present too much of a deterrent.

Next door is the four-star **Palm Beach Hotel and Country Club** (P.O. Box 2192, Acre Beach 24101; tel. 04-912-891 or 912-892), a 140-room luxury tower whose rooms have every convenience. Prices here are $45 single, $60 double in high season (July, August, and Jewish holidays), dropping to $30 single, $40 double from November through February. Midseason rates are $33 single, $45 double. The largest benefit of staying here, in addition to the wonderful beach and view, is the free use of the country club and other facilities (see "What to Do" for country club details). While there's a chance that nonguests may be able to attend the country club when it's not too busy, the only way to guarantee the privilege is to be a guest at the hotel or to become a country club member. Besides the country club, there are also a piano bar, a discothèque, a self-service restaurant, and an evening terrace café on the premises.

Both the Argaman Motel and the Palm Beach Hotel are located about a 25-minute walk around the bay from the southern gate of Acre's Old City. You can also hop a bus into town.

Another short drive from Acre, this time to the north, is **Nes Ammim** (Mobile Post Ashrat 25225; tel. 04-922-566), a 200-member Christian village organized in 1963 for the purpose of bringing Jews and Christians into closer contact. You can stay at the Nes Ammim Guesthouse for $35 single, $46 double, bed and breakfast, in one of 48 double rooms with private bath and tub. While here, you can enjoy the swimming pool, bar, botanical gardens, and get a free tour of the community. If you're not staying here but are interested in the community, call ahead and arrange for a tour. To get to Nes Ammim by car, drive northward along the highway until you see the signs pointing eastward to Nes Ammim and Regba; turn here and go 4 km (2 miles) inland. Coming by bus is a bit more of a challenge, but it can easily be arranged; call ahead and they'll tell you the best way to do it.

WHERE TO DINE: You'll have no trouble finding a good place for lunch, except if you want kosher food—there's not much of it in Acre.

Among the most convenient and easy to find of Acre's eateries is the **Monte Carlo Restaurant** (tel. 04-916-173), right at the very southern end of Weizmann Street, on Saladin Street between the Ahmed Jezzar Pasha mosque and the Suq El-Abiad market. Open every day from 11 a.m. till at least midnight, the Monte Carlo has the standard mix of European and Middle Eastern dishes, courteous service, and pleasant surroundings. A three-course lunch can cost as little as NIS12 ($8) here, though you may find yourself digging in and spending a bit more.

Another good choice is the clean and pleasant **Oudeh Brothers Restaurant,** in the Old City market area (tel. 04-912-013), with four large, airy dining rooms and a large patio. Open daily from 9 a.m. to midnight, it offers a 25-salad mezza, lamb shishlik with rice and salad, meat with hummus, pickles, and pita, and lots of seafood. Turkish coffee is on the house if you've ordered a meal. A complete meal with soft drink will cost about NIS12 ($8) to NIS22.50 ($15).

One of Acre's best-known eateries is **Abu Christo,** near the Old Port (tel. 04-910-065), where your meal is enhanced by a waterfront view. It's particularly nice in good weather, when you can sit out on the terrace under reed shades. Choices include steak with french fries, fish and chips, and shrimp with tartar sauce for NIS12 ($8) to NIS22.50 ($15). Full bar. Open daily from 9 a.m. to midnight in summer, closing around 5 to 8 p.m. in winter.

A sea view is also one of the attractions at **Ptolemais Restaurant,** in the fisherman's quay, very near the aforementioned Abu Christo (tel. 04-916-112). Open daily from 7 a.m. to 1 a.m. in summer, till around 8 p.m. in winter, it dishes up terrific fish entrees and meat meals like beef with hummus at prices about the same as at the Abu Christo. Watermelon makes a refreshing dessert. Students get a 10% reduction. Here, too, there's a full bar, and you can sit either inside or out on the waterfront patio, with the boats in the harbor bobbing up and down just a few feet away.

Down by the lighthouse, the **Migdal Or,** 11/325 Ha-Hagana St. (tel. 04-

917-640), is open daily from 9 a.m. to midnight, dishing up Middle Eastern food and fish, with full meals of meat or fish priced from NIS12 ($8) to NIS22.50 ($15). Full bar here too.

For medium-priced Jewish food, try **Han Asultan,** in the Burj building opposite the Franciscan monastery. Open daily from 11 a.m. to 4 a.m., it's a combination restaurant, pub, and (on Friday and Saturday nights) a nightclub—with a striptease show, no less! The food here is reasonably priced—the most expensive thing on the menu is steak with pepper and tchina for NIS12 ($8)—and there's fish, of course, as well. The decor here is dramatic, with bright-red tablecloths in the high-arched, Crusader-style stone building.

Up on the roof there's a nightclub called **The Burj,** open every night except Sunday from May to October on the rooftop terrace. And next door there's the **Burj Tea House,** serving wine and cheese in the combination pub and art gallery.

The **Argaman Restaurant and Cafeteria,** at the Argaman Motel at the Argaman beach just south of town (tel. 04-916-691), is noted for delicious food, the Hungarian goulash being the specialty of the house. In the self-service cafeteria line you can get it for NIS6 ($4) with one supplement (potatoes, for instance); add another NIS1.50 ($1) for each salad course you choose. Over in the sitdown restaurant, NIS15 ($10) includes a full meal with appetizers, soup, salad, main course with supplement, and dessert.

Next door is the **Palm Beach Self-Service Restaurant** (tel. 04-912-892 or 912-895), open every day from 8 a.m. to 5 p.m. In the summer it's open again every evening from 8:30 p.m. until 1 a.m. with live music and an outdoor café. Prices here are excellent—you can get a meat, rice, and vegetable meal for NIS7 ($4.65), a hamburger or hot dog with fries for a little less.

WHAT TO SEE: Allow yourself a half day to wander through Old Acre's medieval streets. The best place to start your tour is at the Mosque of Ahmed Jezzar Pasha. Right across the street from Jezzar's mosque is the marvelous Subterranean Crusader City, and just a few steps farther is the Municipal Museum, housed in Ahmed Jezzar Pasha's Turkish bath. Next you'll wander through the pleasant and colorful market streets, past El-Zeituneh Mosque to the Khan El-Umdan caravanserai, marked by a tall segmented tower.

Just beyond is the port, a good place to stop for lunch (see "Where to Dine," above). Here you can also hire a boat to take you on a sea tour of the city walls (about $2.50 per person).

In Venezia Square (Ha-Dayagim in Hebrew), facing the port, is the Sinan Pasha Mosque, and behind it the Khan El-Faranj caravanserai. Yet another khan, named El-Shwarda, is a short distance to the northeast. From Khan El-Shwarda it's only a few steps back to the Ahmed Jezzar Pasha Mosque.

Finally, you'll want to visit the Museum of Heroism and El-Jazzar's Wall on Ha-Hagana Street.

There's no missing the Old City of Acre, with its high walls, spiking minarets, and jumble of medieval streets. Follow Weizman Street south, through the walls of El-Jezzar, and keep an eye out for the bulbous dome and high minaret of the Jezzar Pasha Mosque (or Mosque of El-Jezzar). Once you've found the mosque, you're ready to poke around the fascinating *Arabian Nights* streets of Old Acre.

Mosque of Ahmed Jezzar Pasha

Ahmed Jezzar Pasha was the Ottoman Turkish governor of Acre during the momentous times of the late 1700s. Napoleon had invaded Egypt, and the English joined the Ottomans in trying to drive him out. Jezzar Pasha, thinking Napoleon an easy enemy to defeat, set out confidently for Gaza with his forces, but Napoleon's French legions drove him right back to Acre. The battle raged around Acre's walls, with English ships adding a bombardment. The French were forced ultimately to withdraw, but Jezzar Pasha's troubles were far from over. Internal unrest, and the jealousy of other semi-independent Ottoman governors in the region, kept Ahmed Jezzar busy just trying to hold his district together. A few years later Jezzar was called upon by Istanbul to march into Arabia and try to put down the revolt of the ultra-religious Wahhabi movement.

These constant battles to keep the peace finally wore out the pasha, and he died in Acre in 1804. Despite his great ability as a governor, the tumultuous times helped to brand him as a stern administrator. His nickname, El-Jezzar ("The Butcher"), didn't help matters, even though it came from his days as a military leader in Egypt. There, having to revenge the murder of an Ottoman general by Bedouin, he put to death the number of insurgents that tribal justice demanded. The Ottoman governor of Egypt quipped that he was a "camel butcher," and the name stuck.

For all of his sternness, Ahmed Jezzar clearly loved Acre and did a lot to beautify it, building fountains, a covered market, a Turkish bath, and the harmonious mosque that bears his name.

Among the pasha's most ambitious building projects was his mosque complex, built in 1781, an excellent example of classic Ottoman Turkish architecture and social welfare. Every great man in the empire wanted to endow a mosque in his own name, an act which not only added to his glory on earth but also made lots of points for him in heaven. The mosque proper was only the centerpiece of the complex. Around it might be built all sorts of other charitable institutions: a hospital, insane asylum, orphanage, soup kitchen for the poor, theological seminary, library, ablutions fountain, Turkish bath (so the faithful could bathe before Friday prayers), fountains, and mausolea for the mosque's founder and relatives. Often shops were built into the walls of the mosque complex, and the rent from the shops provided money for the maintenance of the mosque. Though the greatest of these complexes were built in Istanbul, the Ottoman capital, the one in Acre gives you a good idea of the harmonious Ottoman architecture (rooted in Byzantine and Persian), and how the mosque complex worked.

As you approach the mosque area, El-Jezzar Street turns right off Weizman Street. The mosque entrance is a few steps along El-Jezzar Street on the left. Before you mount the stairs to the mosque courtyard, notice the ornate little building to the right of the stairs. It's a sebil, or cold-drinks stand, from which pure, refreshing drinking water, sometimes mixed with fruit syrups, was distributed to all and sundry—another of the mosque complex's services. Note especially the fine tile fragments mounted above the little grilled windows just beneath the sebil's dome. Tilemaking was an Ottoman specialty.

Up the stairs, you enter the mosque courtyard. A guard will sell you a ticket for NIS1 (65¢). Just inside the entry, mounted on a pedestal, is a marble disc bearing the tughra, or monogram, of the Ottoman sultan. The graceful loops and swirls actually spell out an entire phrase in Turkish: the sultan's name, his father's name, and the legend "ever victorious."

The arcade around the courtyard can be used for prayers during the hot days of summer, as can the arcaded porch at the front of the mosque. The shadirvan, or ablutions fountain, opposite the mosque entry, is used for the ritual cleansing of face, neck, hands, and feet five times a day before prayers.

You must slip off your shoes before entering the mosque proper. This is not a religious rule, but a hygienic one: worshippers kneel on the carpets during prayer, and want to keep them clean.

Inside, you'll notice the mihrab, or prayer niche, which indicates the direction of Mecca, toward which worshippers must face when they pray. The galleries to the right and left of the entrance are reserved for women, the main area of the floor for men. The mimber, a sort of pulpit, is that separate structure with a curtained entry, stairs, and a little steeple.

Around to the right is a mausoleum and a small graveyard which hold the tombs of Ahmed Jezzar Pasha and his successor, Suleiman Pasha, and members of their families. It's all so still, peaceful, and serene now that it's impossible to imagine what passions and alarums swirled through this place almost two centuries ago.

The mosque is in use by Acre's Muslim population, so when it's in service for prayer (five times a day), you must wait until the prayers are over to enter the mosque (about 20 minutes).

Subterranean Crusader City

Virtually across the street from the Mosque of Ahmed Jezzar Pasha is the Subterranean Crusader City. Enter the cool darkness and you'll find a tourism information kiosk. You can buy a city map here, and also a single ticket for NIS2.50 ($1.65) for adults, NIS2 ($1.35) for children, good for both the Crusader city and the Municipal Museum in the nearby Turkish bath.

The Crusaders built their fortress atop what was left of the Roman city. In Ottoman times the cavernous chambers were used as a caravanserai until Napoleon's attack. In preparation for the defense of his city, Ahmed Jezzar Pasha ordered the walls heightened, and the Crusader rooms partially filled in with sand and dirt, the better to support the walls. Much of the dirt has been removed now, allowing a fairly good look at where the Crusaders lived, worked, dined, and prayed in their city of St-Jean-d'Acre in the late 1100s.

When you buy your ticket, you're in a hall constructed by the Crusaders (bottom) and the Ottomans (top). You pass into another hall that once held an illegal (in Muslim times) wine press, a Middle Eastern bootlegging operation! Next comes the courtyard, where the 125-foot-high walls of Acre Citadel loom above. The Citadel, used by the British as a prison during the Mandate, now houses the Museum of Heroism (see below).

Beyond the courtyard, through a huge Ottoman gate, are the Knights' Halls, once occupied by the Knights Hospitallers of St. John. The original entry to the halls is buried several yards beneath the present one. In the ceiling of the hall, a patch of concrete marks the spot where Jewish underground members, imprisoned by the British in the Citadel (directly above the hall) attempted to break out. It was these men who discovered the Knights' Halls, though it didn't help them much. As they had no idea what to expect if they crawled through the darkness, they disguised their discovery and waited for the mass escape, which came later.

Back through the courtyard, you now head for the Grand Maneir, or center of government in the Crusader city. Past it, through a narrow passage, is the Crypt, so named only because of its present depth; it was actually the knights' refectory, or dining hall. Beyond the refectory is a longer tunnel leading to the Post (El-Posta), a series of rooms and a courtyard similar to a caravanserai, the precise use of which is not known. Over the centuries it was no doubt used for many things.

Municipal Museum (Turkish Bath)

Down at the end of El-Jezzar Street, just around the corner, is the Municipal Museum. Your Subterranean Crusader City ticket will admit you here. The building is the Hammam El-Basha, built by Ahmed Jezzar Pasha as part of his mosque complex in the 1780s. The museum exhibits are interesting, but the building itself is fantastic.

The first few small rooms hold collections of artifacts from Acre's last 2,000 years. Beyond them you walk along a passage (with a garden through the grill-work on your right) to the folklore exhibit. Here, in what was no doubt a build-ing adjoining the bath, are mannequins dressed in Ottoman garb, arranged in various scenes of everyday life. Ottoman rule of Palestine lasted from 1516 to 1917. Note especially the pretty tilework.

Follow the passage onward from the folklore exhibit. Yes! That unlikely looking passage does actually go somewhere; don't backtrack.

Now you're entering the bath proper. Turkish baths were built on the Roman plan, with three distinct rooms. The first was the entry and dressing room, the next was the tepidarium (Roman name), with warm steam, and the last was the caldarium, with hot steam. The hot room was always the most or-nate.

As you walk through the first two rooms, note the tiny glass skylights in the domes. The third room, the one for hot steam, is rich in marble, fancy stone, and mosaic work. In the center is a circular platform for steam bathing. The heat source was beneath it. Some Turkish baths have a small swimming pool here instead. Four private steam cubicles occupy the four points of the compass.

The exhibits here, mostly enlarged copies of drawings, lithographs, and en-gravings, give you a look at Acre during the Napoleonic wars.

When you're finished your explorations, a guard will let you out a door just off the hot steam room. Turn right, then right again, and you'll repass the muse-um entrance on your way into Acre's bazaars.

In the Bazaars

Acre's "formal" market is the Suq El-Abiad, just east of the Mosque of Ahmed Jezzar Pasha. But numerous streets within Old Acre serve as shopping areas for fruits and vegetables, condiments, meat and fish, and various house-hold needs. Make your way south through the city, toward the port. If you need a point of reference, ask a local to point you toward the Khan El-Umdan.

Khan El-Umdan

Before you reach this Ottoman caravanserai, you'll know where it is. Atop its northern wall is a staged tower, like a campanile. The khan (dating from 1785) is much older than its tower, which was built as a clock tower in 1906 to celebrate the 30th year of the reign of Sultan Abdul Hamid II. El-Umdan means "The Pillars," and when you enter this vast colonnaded court you'll know how it got its name. Its builder was—you guessed it—the same Ahmed Jezzar Pasha, another of his harmonious works in the public service. This one served com-merce: a caravanserai was a combination warehouse, office building, banking center, stable, and factory. It was built on the site of a Crusader monastery of the Dominican order. Now the building is deserted, but as you stroll around the courtyard or sit at the well near the center, it's easy to imagine all the many activities that have gone on here.

The Port

Just to the east of Khan El-Umdan is Venice Square (Ha-Dayagim), and the Sinan Pasha Mosque. The port is to the southeast. Once the busiest port on the coast, with the advent of steamships the title was taken by the more modern port at Haifa, which you can see across the bay. Though galleons and galleasses no longer ride at anchor here, you'll still see industrious fishermen at work. Many boatmen will be glad to take you on a cruise around Old Acre. Settle on a price in advance (about $1 to $2.50 per person), and get a boat that will not take all day to ferry you around the point and back.

Here by the port are the Abu Christo and Ptolemais restaurants, mentioned above. Ptolemais, by the way, was what the Greeks called Acre in ancient times.

Other Khans and Mosques

Up behind the port, take a look at two more caravanserais. The **Khan El-Faranj** (or Afranj), the Inn of the Europeans ("Franks"), is a few steps north of the Sinian Pasha mosque. The Oudeh Brothers Restaurant, mentioned above, has a patio dining area in the khan's courtyard. This complex began life in 1729 as a Franciscan convent, but some of the building was apparently rented to French and Italian merchants.

Northeast of the Khan El-Faranj is the **Khan El-Shwarda,** right next to a tower in the city walls called Burj Es-Sultan. The Burj is famous because it is the only construction actually built by the Crusaders that remains intact; all the rest have been ruined, or extensively modified in rebuilding. At the tower's base is one of Napoleon's cannons, cast in Liège, just before Napoleon's battle here, and captured by the Ottoman and English forces.

Walk up Marco Polo Street to your next stop. Marco Polo, by the way, was one of several famous visitors to Acre in medieval times; another was King Richard the Lion-Hearted.

The Khan El-Shwarda, at the northern end of Marco Polo Street, occupies the site of a convent of the nuns of St. Clare which ceased to operate when the Crusader city fell in 1291. There's not a lot to look at today.

The **Mosque A-Ramal** (or El-Ramel), the former "Sand Mosque," was built in 1704–1705. You'll find it on Marco Polo Street. A Crusader inscription was found on the southeast wall of this mosque, which today forms part of the back wall of a nearby shop, the fourth shop on the left from the mosque entrance. The Latin inscription, which the shopkeeper will uncover for visitors, reads, "Oh, men who pass along this street, in charity I beg you to pray for my soul—Master Ebuli Fazli, builder of the church." The mosque is now used as a scout house, and it's open daily from 4 to 6 p.m. (admission free).

The Lighthouse

An old lighthouse, still in use, stands atop the Crusader fortification of Burj Es-Sanjak, on the extreme southwest point of land at Acre. From here you get a marvelous view, both north and south.

Just north of the lighthouse, you'll notice a large space in the sea wall. This stretch of the wall was destroyed during the heavy earthquake of 1837, the same earthquake that destroyed several cities in the mountains east of here, leveling them.

Museum of Heroism

The museum is in the Citadel of Acre, reached by walking north from the lighthouse on Ha-Hagana Street, which runs along beside the sea wall. (You can also come here directly from El-Jezzar Mosque, if you want to stop by here early in the day. To do so, walk down El-Jezzar Street and continue in as straight a line as possible to Ha-Hagana Street, which skirts the city's western sea walls. When you reach the sea, turn right and soon you'll see the entrance to the museum on the right-hand side.)

The museum is open every day from 9 a.m. to 4 p.m. (on Friday until noon). Entrance is NIS3 ($2) for adults, NIS2 ($1.35) for children and students. For an extra NIS3 ($2) you can buy a book telling the whole story of the famous prison escape that took place here.

This complex of buildings was used as a prison in Ottoman and British

Mandate times, but is now a mental hospital. Part of the prison has been set aside in honor of the Jewish underground fighters imprisoned here by the British. With the help of Irgun forces, over 200 prisoners staged a mass escape in May 1947. If you saw the movie *Exodus*, that was the break-out and this was the prison. Among the exhibits are the entrance to the escape tunnel, and displays of materials bearing witness to British repression of Zionist activity during the Mandate.

Not all prisoners were lucky enough to escape, however. Eight Irgun fighters were hanged here in the ten years before Israel's independence. You can visit the death chamber, called the Hanging Room, complete with noose.

Inmates here included no less than Zeev Jabotinsky and Dov Gruner, among other leaders of Zionism and Israel's independence movement.

Before the Mandate, the prison's most famous inmate was Bahaullah (1817–1892), founder of the Baha'i faith. He was exiled from his native Persia in the 1860s, first to Istanbul, later to Acre. As he had proclaimed himself the Promised One, a prophet in the rank of Moses, Jesus, and Mohammed, the Ottoman authorities imprisoned him here, later transferring him to house arrest in a villa just north of Acre (see below).

Walls of El-Jezzar

Ahmed Jezzar Pasha had on his hands the most serious threat Acre had faced since Crusader times. Menaced by Napoleon's mighty fleet and forces, he built an elaborate system of defenses around his city. To appreciate the work, turn right as you come out of the Museum of Heroism onto Ha-Hagana Street and walk a few steps north. You'll see the double system of walls with a moat in between. Jutting into the sea is an Ottoman defensive tower called the Burj El-Kuraim. You're now standing at the northwestern corner of the walled city. Walk along the walls eastward (inland) and you'll pass the Citadel, the Burj El-Hazineh ("Treasury Tower"), and cross Weizman Street to the Burj El-Komander, the strongest point in the walls. The land wall system continues southward from here all the way to the beach.

At the entrance to the Old City on Weizman Street, near the Walls of El-Jezzar, is a sunken children's playground bordered by the **Dahar El-Omer Walls.** Dahar El-Omer (or Daher El-Amar) was the sheik who captured Acre from the Mamelukes, who had taken it from the Crusaders in the 13th century. The Mamelukes had done some damage to the town, but were not able completely to destroy the massive stone fortifications. When Dahar El-Omer took over, he set about rebuilding the city walls.

Bahji

The Baha'i faith is an exemplary one. Baha'i followers believe that God is manifested to men and women through prophets such as Abraham, Moses, Jesus, and Mohammed, as well as the Bab (Bahaullah's predecessor) and Bahaullah himself. The Baha'i faith proclaims that all religions are one, that men and women are equal, that the world should be at peace, and that education should be universal. Baha'i followers are encouraged to live simply and to dedicate themselves to helping their fellow men and women. They are looking forward to a day when there will be a single world government and one world language.

The Baha'i faith grew out of the revelation of the Bab, a Persian Shi'ite Muslim teacher and mystic who flourished from 1844 to 1850, when he was executed by the Persian shah for insurrection and radical teachings. In 1863, Mirza Husein Ali Nuri, one of the Bab's disciples, proclaimed himself Bahaullah, the Promised One, whose coming had been foretold by the Bab. Bahaullah was exiled by the Persian government, in cooperation with the Ottoman leaders, to Baghdad, Constantinople, Adrianople, and finally to Acre, where he arrived in August 1868. He and several of his followers were imprisoned for 2½ years at the Acre Citadel. The authorities later put him under house arrest, and he was eventually brought to Bahji, where he remained until his death in 1892. He is buried here in a peaceful tomb surrounded by magnificent gardens. To Baha'is, this is the most holy place on earth.

Despite their peaceful intentions, Baha'is are still persecuted, especially in Iran, where the faith was born, but where the Shi'ite Muslims in authority today look upon them as blasphemers and heretics.

You can visit the shrine at Bahji ("Delight"), where Bahaullah lived, died, and is buried, on Friday, Saturday, and Sunday only, from 9 a.m. to noon. The house's beautiful gardens are open to visitors every day, from 9 a.m. to 4 p.m. Catch a no. 271 bus heading north toward Nahariya, and make sure it stops at Bahji.

Going north from Acre, you'll see an impressive gilded gate on the right-hand side of the road after about two kilometers. This gate is not open to the public. Go past it until you are almost three kilometers from Acre, and you'll see a sign, "Shamerat." Get off the bus, turn right here, and go another three-tenths of a kilometer to the visitors' gate.

The Ottoman-Victorian house holds some memorabilia of Bahaullah, and the lush gardens are a real treat, similar in richness and peacefulness to those at the Baha'i Shrine in Haifa.

WHAT TO DO: The favorite local spot for swimming is the **Argaman Beach,** just south of town by the Argaman Motel. This is one of Israel's most beautiful Mediterranean beaches, with the view of Haifa on one end of the bay, the old sea walls of Acre on the other. Lifeguards are here in summer.

The **Palm Beach Hotel and Country Club** (tel. 04-912-891 or 912-895) is here on Argaman Beach—and a fine country club it is too, with an outdoor Olympic-size swimming pool plus a heated indoor pool, tennis, volleyball, basketball and squash courts, Ping-Pong tables, health club, Finnish sauna, massage by appointment (for an extra fee), private beach with lounge chairs and shades, grassy terrace . . . and so on. Although the country club is reserved for members and hotel guests, tourists are usually welcome for a day-use fee in the nonpeak seasons. Call ahead to make a reservation and ask the price.

NIGHTLIFE: As for the nightlife around Acre—well, one of the most enjoyable evening activities is the same as in the daytime, namely, **strolling around** through the tiny *Arabian Nights* streets, past the old khans and the minarets towering above you framed by moonlight and stars, gazing from the old port out across the bay toward the sparkling lights of Haifa, seeing Acre's little lighthouse on duty . . . it's all just too romantic. On a quiet night, moonlight shining in, you can stand in the courtyard of Khan El-Umdan and imagine all the people, animals, activities, and human dramas that have passed through here. The colonnaded courtyard, the well, the tower overhead, still fairly ring with their voices and footsteps. Another interesting moonlight walk is around the city's sea walls. Exotic Arabic music fills the air day and night all around Old Acre, and I've rarely enjoyed a moonlight walk more.

In your evening stroll around Acre you'll notice several places for the exercise of the favorite evening indoor sport—no, not *that* one! I'm talking about **billiards.** All around Old Acre, light and music pour out into the streets from the open doors of billiard parlors, and you're welcome to come in and shoot a few games.

You can sip a beer or cocktail at one of the waterfront restaurants, at the Burj's rooftop nightclub during the warm months, or at the other Burj meeting places (see "Where to Dine" for details on all of these). But if you're ready for a real live striptease act, head for the Burj's **Han A-Sultan** restaurant and night-club on a Friday or Saturday evening, open until 4 a.m. Everyone is welcome.

The **discothèque** at the Palm Beach Hotel and Country Club (tel. 04-912-892 or 912-895) is also open to everyone, with music and dancing and the first drink all included in the NIS7.50 ($5) cover charge. It's open every night of the week in summer months, on Friday only in winter.

Also here at the Palm Beach is the outdoor **Pundak Café**, open in summer-time only, from 8:30 p.m. to 1 a.m., with live music out on the terrace, food and drinks.

NORTH TO NAHARIYA: Several kilometers north of Bahji is another sort of memorial, not nearly so peaceful. This one is in **Kibbutz Lohame Ha-Geta'ot** ("Fighters of the Ghettos"), founded by fighters and survivors of ghettos in Po-land, Germany, and Lithuania. Pictures and documents, models and maps pre-sent the life and culture of Jewish communities in Europe before their destruc-tion, and outline the suffering and resistance of ghetto dwellers. There is also an extremely moving exhibition of paintings and drawings done by the children of the camps—bits of realistic, fantasy-world horror tales set down on scraps of paper, recording the life of a child in a ghetto. Admission to the memorial is free. Open daily from 9 a.m. to 4 p.m., on Saturday from 10 a.m. to 4 p.m.

Right next to the kibbutz and museum is another sight. Paralleling the road, on the east, is a handsome **aqueduct** built by Ahmed Jezzar Pasha in 1780 over one the Romans left. The aqueduct originally supplied Acre with water from the Galilee's springs. Its ruins are beautifully picturesque, with many arch-ways framing sabra plants.

8. From Nahariya to the Border

NAHARIYA: Founded by German Jews in the mid-1930s, Nahariya is a popular summer resort with Israelis, but foreigners are catching on. On the Lag b'Omer holiday in the spring, which is the only day a Jew can marry during the six weeks between the Passover and Shavuoth holidays, Nahariya is packed with honey-mooners. Maybe there's a connection between Nahariya's honeymoon attrac-tions and the fact that on its beach archeologists dug up a Canaanite fertility goddess. It's a nice thought.

This holiday town has an unusual main street: a stream runs down the mid-dle of it. Horsecarts clop-clop along the thoroughfare and will take you around town; settle on a price before you start out.

Orientation

Nahariya is a small city of some 30,000 souls, and so it's pretty easy to find your way around.

The Central Bus Station and the railway station are just off the main high-way on **Ha-Ga'aton Boulevard,** Nahariya's main stem. Before leavng the pre-cincts of the bus station, drop by the **Tourist Information Office** on Ha-Ga'aton to pick up a map of the town. Here's how to find it: When you leave the Central Bus Station, turn to your left and walk down about half a block on Ha-Ga'aton. On the left you'll see a small square, and at the far end of the square, a seven-story edifice with flags waving in front. This is the Municipal Building, and it's here you'll find the Tourist Information Office (tel. 04-922-121), open Sunday through Thursday from 9 a.m. to 1 p.m. and 4 to 7 p.m., on Friday from 9 a.m. to 4 p.m.; closed Saturday.

Head down Ha-Ga'aton and you'll be going due west, to the sea. Don't worry about the weight of your bags as you must lug them only about five blocks to get to a hotel.

Hotels

Most of Nahariya's hotels are located, quite logically, at the western end of Ha-Ga'aton Boulevard near Galei-Galil Beach. Here's how I'll help you find them. Walking down Ha-Ga'aton, all but one of my recommended hostelries are on side streets going right (north) off Ha-Ga'aton, so I'll start on the main stem and then describe the lodging possibilities on each side street as we pass it. By the way, all the hotels except two—the Yarden and Erna House—have kosher kitchens.

On Ha-Ga'aton Boulevard: The **Hotel Astar,** 27 Ha-Ga'aton Blvd. (Nahariya 22444; tel. 04-923-431), is not far from the bus station, on the left-hand (south) side of the street. It's got three stars and 26 rooms, all with tubs in the bathrooms, telephones, heat and air conditioning, and most of the rooms have balconies. Singles go for $28 and doubles run $35 most of the year, rising to $35 single and $46 double in high season, and reducing to $23 single and $28 double November through February. A nice little Swiss-style dairy/vegetarian café serves as the hotel's dining room; it's the Lachmi Coffee Shop, open six days a week from 7 a.m. to 8:30 p.m., on Friday until 4 p.m.

On Weizman Street: About three blocks west of the bus and train stations along Ha-Ga'aton, turn right onto Weizman Street and just there on your right will be the **Hotel Rosenblatt,** at 59 Weizman St. (P.O. Box 91, Nahariya 22100; tel. 04-923-469). The two-star, 35-room Rosenblatt is quite attractive from the outside, with lots of greenery and a good, central location. The rooms are air-conditioned, centrally heated, and equipped with showers (only three rooms have tubs). Prices are $19 single, $24 double, going up to $22 single and $33 double in high season.

On Jabotinsky Street: Next street off Ha-Ga'aton is Jabotinsky Street, running parallel to the beach but one block inland. Here you will come to several hotels and little pensions.

Right at the corner of Ha-Ga'aton, at 1 Jabotinsky St., is the **Motel Arieli** (tel. 04-921-076), a converted house with a nice garden, only a block from the beach. Exotic plants, friendly management: this is one of those plain-but-sympathetic places in which a room with shower costs $12.75 single, $25.25 double in season, with use of the kitchen included. Reductions of about 20% are offered off-season, and anyone presenting a copy of this book is entitled to a 10% reduction anytime.

Walking north along Jabotinsky, you'll spot houses with little signs out front: "Rooms to Let." These **house pensions** may have only one or two rooms, with or without private facilities. You can check with the **Tourist Office** (tel. 04-922-121) for what's available, or you can wander along Jabotinsky and nearby streets to see what turns up. For instance, there are pensions at no. 7 Jabotinsky (the "Netzer"; tel. 04-920-466) and no. 12 Jabotinsky (tel. 04-921-049), and quite a few more as you walk along. Prices hover around $10 per person, depending on season and facilities.

Soon you'll come to the rather posh, three-star **Hotel Eden,** 48 Ha-Meyasdim St. (tel. 04-923-246 or 923-247), at the corner of Jabotinsky and Ha-Meyasdim Streets. The Eden has 50 rooms, all but four of them with a tub in the private bath, radio, telephone, with air conditioning and heat throughout, and room service. The swimming pool (open in warm season only) hosts diving classes; all day long, in high season, a variety of programs are offered, including aerobics, dancing, sports, nightclub entertainment, children's programs, and so on, designed to make the hotel a complete vacation center. The disco bar is open every night in summer, Thursday through Sunday in winter. The nighclub, open from 9 p.m. until 2 a.m., offers a nightly show for NIS12 ($8), which includes the first drink. Prices here are not bad for all this activity: $28 single, $42 double in high season; $20 single, $26 double from November through February; and $25 single, $32 double the rest of the year.

Directly across from the Eden, on the opposite corner, is the **Hotel Yarden,** 48 Ha-Meyasdim St. (Nahariya 22383; tel. 04-922-966 or 927-105). Since it's a new hotel it hasn't yet been graded, but I'd say it rates about three stars. It has 23 rooms, all with air conditioning and heat, radio, telephone, wall-to-wall carpeting, private bath with shower (four rooms with tub), and room service too. The Yarden is open from April through November only. Prices are $16 single, $22 double, except during July and August when they rise to $24 single, $30 double.

The **Kalman Hotel,** 27 Jabotinsky St. (tel. 04-920-355), has two stars, 20 rooms with bath or shower, air conditioning, and heating. All but four rooms have large balconies, and there's a swimming pool too. This is a pleasant, family hotel, run by the family who lives here on the premises. Prices are listed at $16 single, $27 double in high season, and $14 single, $22 double the rest of the year, for bed and breakfast; however, you may likely find prices reduced further in low season, down to $10 per person, single or double; there are also student and other discounts.

The neat and well-kept **Erna House,** 29 Jabotinsky St. (tel. 04-920-170), right next door to the Kalman, is a converted house with the look of a solid, comfortable little hotel. Since adding a new building in front, it has 18 rooms, with private toilet and shower, air conditioning and heat, carpeting, telephone, and a TV in your room if you request one, at no extra charge. This is another family-run enterprise, rating one star, and priced at $15 single, $22 to $26 double most of the year, rising to $18 single, $30 double during high season.

Keep on walking along Jabotinsky and you'll come to the **Hotel Silberman,** 48 Jabotinsky St. (tel. 04-925-809 or 920-094), near the corner of Max Steinmetz Street. It's a very simple, but clean, two-star establishment, with 16 rooms, each with private toilet and shower. Common areas include a bar and TV room in addition to the pleasant dining room. Prices, including breakfast, are $15 single, $25 double in winter; $20 single, $30 double in high season.

On Ha-Ma'apilim Street: The road that goes north at the end of Ha-Ga'aton and skirts the beach is named Ha-Ma'apilim Street, and this is where you'll discover Nahariya's greatest concentration of hotels.

Only a short block north of Ha-Ga'aton Boulevard is the **Panorama Hotel,** 6 Ha-Ma'apilim St. (P.O. Box 84, Nahariya 22100; tel. 04-920-555), with 30 air-conditioned rooms, half with tubs and half with showers. The two-story hotel is modern, attractive, and neat as a pin with wall-to-wall carpeting inside, sea views from most of the rooms, and a nice rooftop terrace. The rooms rent for $24 single, $30 double for most of the year, raising to $32 single, $49 double in high season.

Look inland from Ha-Ma'apilim Street at this point and you can spot the **Hotel Frank,** just back from Ha-Ma'apilim across a vacant lot at 4 Ha-Aliyah St.

(P.O. Box 58, Nahariya 22381; tel. 04-920-278 or 920-279). With three-star amenities and 50 guest rooms, the Frank's prices are $23 single, $28 to $30 double November through February; $29 single, $32 to $37 double most of the year; and $42 single, $53 to $58 double during high season, when this price includes the half-board minimum. (On Passover and Succoth, add another 15% to these high-season rates.) You'll get shower- or tub-equipped bathrooms, telephones, air conditioning, and heating—plus a bonus of very friendly service. In the past, all the rooms had balconies. On the land side, they still do; but on the sea side, the balcony space has been used to enlarge the rooms, making a sitting area with nice windows—so the rooms are bigger and you still can see the sea.

Back on Ha-Ma'apilim, another block north will bring you to the large and, for Nahariya, imposing structure which is our next choice.

The three-star **Pallas Athene Hotel**, 28 Ha-Ma'apilim St. (P.O. Box 335; tel. 04-922-381 or 922-382), has many things going for it, including all the three-star amenities—heat, air conditioning, carpeting, private bath with tub, radio, TV lobby, and so on. But then there's more: piano bar, sauna, TV in your room on request, children's playroom, health club facilities, and best of all, a rooftop swimming pool and a rooftop terrace with lawn furniture—and what a view! You can see all the way up to the Lebanese border at Rosh Ha-Niqra, and all the way down to Haifa. Views are what this place is all about: all the rooms have nice sea views, with windows jutting out at an angle from the sides of the building, and even the dining room is built to maximize the sea view, with its high ceiling and floor-to-ceiling windows. Prices here are $29 single, $37 double most of the year, going up to $32 single, $49 double in high season, and down to $23 single, $30 double November through February.

By the way, you'll also see some of those "rooms to let" signs here along Ha-Ma'apilim Street.

On Ha-Meyasdim Street: Parallel to Ha-Ga'aton and one block north of it is Ha-Meyasdim Street, which you may already have spotted in your hotel search.

The **Hotel Kari Laufer**, 31 Ha-Meyasdim St. (tel. 04-920-130), is an older, 28-room hotel, well kept up and looking just like a large family pension in Germany or Austria. Accommodations, therefore, are plain but sympathetic, with toilets, showers, and air conditioning in most cases. Prices are $21 single, $32 double most of the year; $26 single, $39 double in high season. The first thing you'll notice here are the carefully tended gardens all around, and the large trees and hundreds of flowers make it an exceptionally nice place to sit outside and enjoy the salty sea breezes. You can see the sea from here (in fact, the Laufer is located just opposite the entrance to the public beach), and whether you get a room with a sea or a garden view, you'll enjoy the large balcony veranda off your room.

A Hostel: The official IYHA Youth Hostel is not right in Nahariya, it's up the coast a bit at Akhziv (see that section for details). If you're looking for a youth hostel here in town, try the private one at 6 Wolfson Street. There's no sign, but it's there in the two-story building at that address, not far from the bus station. Here's how to find it: When you exit the bus station onto Ha-Ga'aton Boulevard, cross Ha-Ga'aton, walk to your right (heading east) about one block, and you'll come to Wolfson. Turn left, walk down Wolfson about a block or so, and you'll see no. 6 on your right-hand side.

Restaurants

Nahariya is not exactly what you'd call a gourmet's mecca. It's too small to support the variety of cuisines and establishments to be found in, say, Netanya.

And many vacation visitors to this superbly tranquil and orderly town have their meals at their hotels, taking advantage of half-board or full-board plans.

Still, it's fun to go out for a bite. First place to go is along **Ha-Ga'aton Boulevard,** with its bistros, sidewalk cafés, and two commercial plazas which hold many possibilities for light meals and snacks.

The plazas are named **Ha-Banim Square** (Kikar Ha-Banim) and **Ha-Iriya Square** (Kikar Ha-Iriya), and they're right across Ha-Ga'aton from one another, at the intersection with Herzl Street, half a block west of the bus station. Each square has a cinema, lots of shops, other services, and some indoor-outdoor eateries such as the **Pizzeria Capri** (tel. 04-920-100) in Ha-Banim Square (the one on the north side of Ha-Ga'aton). Stop and pick up an individual pizza and a soft drink, pay about NIS3 ($2) to NIS5 ($3.35), and enjoy the comings and goings of people in the square as you consume it. Open Sunday through Thursday from 9 a.m. to 1:30 p.m. and 4 p.m. to midnight, on Friday to 2 p.m., and on Saturday from 4 p.m. to midnight.

Want a true restaurant? In a town of self-service cafés, there is in fact a reasonably priced restaurant, the **Donau Restaurant,** 32 Ha-Ga'aton Blvd. (tel. 04-928-699). Simple but sympathetic, this "Rumanian Grill" has tables outdoors on the sidewalk, indoors in a small bistro-like air-conditioned dining room, and in summer, on a garden patio out back. Rumanian dishes are the order of the day here: the specialties of the house are Rumanian-style meats barbecued over coals; a giant weinerschnitzel so large it fills the entire plate, with a plate of fries and a salad on the side; for NIS10 ($6.65); and a Rumanian chorba soup, a hearty stew made of lamb meat and vegetables, for NIS4 ($2.65) to NIS6 ($4). A large, full supper, with wine, tip, and everything included, may run about NIS15 ($10) to NIS23 ($15.35), depending on the main course ordered. In summer, the restaurant is open from 10 a.m. to 1 a.m.; in winter, from 11 a.m. to 11 p.m. By the way, in addition to the delicious food and friendly atmosphere, one of my favorite attractions here is Coco, a gray parrot born in Brazil, which can converse with you in English, Hebrew, or Rumanian, take your pick. They say that Coco's kind of parrot lives 200 years, so if you visit the restaurant 150 years from now, Coco should still be here.

Across the street from the Donau, at 33 Ha-Ga'aton, you'll see several **Penguin** restaurants, all of them open seven days a week. Actually, one is a restaurant, one is a café specializing in ice cream, desserts, and light snacks, and in between is a third place with a much different style: El Gaucho, an Argentinian grill restaurant.

El Gaucho (tel. 04-928-635) specializes in grilled meat—and lots of it—cooked over the coals right there behind the many cuts of fresh meat on display for all to see. The decor here is massive Spanish-colonial style, with lots of special touches like cowhide, a South American pan flute, and horns on the walls. You can sit inside, or out in back on the palapa-covered patio. It's not only the decor that is imported: the chefs, also, are brought from South America, as is much of the meat. Most of the meat served here is veal, but while you can get a half-chicken dinner for as little as NIS8 ($5.35) or steak for NIS10 ($6.65), the house specialty is the mixed grill, a giant repast for two (or even more) people, for NIS26 ($17.35). All meat dinners are served with bread and butter, baked potato with butter and sour cream, vegetables, salad, dessert, and the special Chimichuri meat sauce that's so delicious you'll be sopping it up with the bread. Every meat order means 700 grams of meat—that's over a pound and a half! For the price, the good food, and the atmosphere, you can't beat this place. In the summer you may find live, authentic South American music in the evenings, if you happen to be here at the right time. Open from noon to 4 p.m. and 6 p.m. to midnight, every day.

The **Penguin Restaurant** (tel. 04-920-027) also has both inside and outside restaurants; it's a great place to come for good, inexpensive general fare. You'll find spaghetti or lasagne, fish, or fried chicken with potato and salad for NIS6 ($4), or an omelet for NIS4 ($2.65)—or you can just stop in for a beer, an espresso, or a glass of fresh-squeezed juice. Your waiter, in keeping with the restaurant's namesake animal, will serve you in black and white. Open daily from 11 a.m. to midnight.

To find out about the tempting **Penguin Ice Cream Café,** look a little further down, under "cafes."

The **Chinese Inn Restaurant,** 28 Ha-Ga'aton St. (tel. 04-923-709), is easy to spot from Nahariya's main street. But to enter this second-floor eatery you must go around to the back of the building and up the stairs. There's an extensive à la carte menu, plus various combination menus for two, three, or four people. The six-course combo for two people is NIS37 ($24.65). A lunch special for NIS12.50 ($8.35) includes soup, eggroll, fried rice, choice of main dish, and choice of dessert. There's a nice Chinese decor with lots of wood and crimson; try to get a table overlooking the street. The Chinese Inn is open from noon to 3 p.m. and again from 7 p.m. to midnight, every day of the year except one—Chinese New Year.

One of Nahariya's newer and better restaurants is the **Singapore Chinese Restaurant,** at Ha-Meyasdim and Jabotinsky (tel. 04-929-209), across from the Yarden and Eden Hotels. It's big, fancy-ish, full of atmosphere, and open for both lunch and dinner. You'll have to spend a bit extra to dine here, though: if you get one of the fixed combination dinners from the menu, for two to six people, you'll spend about NIS20 ($13.35) per person; but if you want to enjoy a surprisingly large selection of dishes, then order from the 110-item menu. The Singapore is run by people from Singapore, hence the name, and you can try a number of Singapore specialties, including Singapore chicken, Singapore oven roast duck, a Singapore Sling cocktail, or Singapore ice cream with Chinese fruits, coconut, raisins, and a fruit garnish, for dessert. The restaurant is open seven days a week, from noon until 3 p.m. and again from 7 p.m. to midnight; closed on Chinese New Year and on major Jewish holidays.

As in other cities, the eatery at the **Egged Bus Station** is recommended for low-priced fare. Open early for breakfast, until around 4 p.m.; closed Saturday. Clean and pleasant, and kosher.

Cafés

For the yummiest cakes and pastries in town, check out the **Contidoria Har'el,** 20 Ha-Ga'aton Blvd. (tel. 04-927-655). Here you can watch the passing scene from a sidewalk café with umbrella tables or sit cozily within while enjoying rich cream cakes, fruit tortes, almond pies, etc., for NIS1.20 (80¢) and espresso for NIS1.50 ($1). The baguettes, those long, skinny French breads, are baked here continually throughout the day, so you can always stop by and get one that's still warm and fresh from the oven; a sandwich will cost NIS3 ($2). Open Sunday to Thursday from 6 a.m. to midnight in summer (to 10 p.m. in winter), on Friday until 4 p.m., and on Saturday after 6 p.m.

A favorite among Nahariya café-sitters is the **Hollandische Konditorei,** at 31 Ha-Ga'aton (tel. 04-922-502). It's as pleasant as its rosy-cheeked proprietress, with small tables out front and a few inside. Rich cakes and pastries, often covered or filled with chocolate and cream, are served every day from 6 a.m. until 2 or 3 a.m. in summer, to 10 p.m. or midnight in winter. Abandon your diet, all who enter here!

At the **Penguin Café,** 33 Ha-Ga'aton (tel. 04-928-635), the portions of ice cream are simply enormous, and relatively cheap (for what you get) at NIS3 ($2) to NIS7.50 ($5). The menu lists only four types of dishes: ice cream (banana splits, milkshakes, fruit cocktail, etc.), blintzes, pancakes, and beverages. Nothing is over $5, most items are considerably less. The Penguin, with its convenient outdoor Ha-Ga'aton location, is a favorite with just about everyone in Nahariya, both young and old. You can sit at a sidewalk table, or enjoy the old-fashioned ice-cream-parlor decor inside. Open from 7:30 a.m. to midnight (or later), seven days a week.

For Picnic Supplies

Look for the big **Supersol supermarket** at the intersection of Ha-Ga'aton and Herzl, near the twin squares of Ha-Banim and Ha-Iriya, across the street from the Central Bus Station. Cold meats or cheeses, prepared foods, and deli items are all on the shelves. Beverages too.

WHAT TO SEE AND DO: One of the best possibilities is to get married here on

Lag b'Omer, and stay over for at least three days so that you can be entertained every day by the municipality and enjoy a discount on facilities and services. If you're already married, you're out of luck, because bigamy in Israel is considered a major crime—although even married folks do get some discounts at this time of year.

The main beach, **Galei-Galil,** has won prizes for cleanliness and safety. It offers (in addition, of course, to the Mediterranean Sea) an Olympic-size outdoor pool, a heated, glass-enclosed indoor pool open all year round, a children's pool, dressing rooms, playgrounds for children, and restaurants. At the marina breakwater you'll see people fishing off the rocks, and you can rent a sailboat if you like, or go skindiving. Tennis, basketball, and volleyball courts are other attractions, as is the big water slide just on the north side of the beach. There's a small fee of about NIS3 ($2) for adults, NIS1.50 ($1) for children, to use the beach facilities.

If you just want to take a dip in the Mediterranean, you can go about two blocks south to the free **Municipal Beach,** which doesn't cost a cent, not even for the lifeguard standing watch.

The view from both of these beaches is lovely. On a clear day—and most of them are—you can see all the way from Rosh Ha-Niqra at the Lebanese border to the north, and to Haifa in the south.

If you'd like to go **horseback riding,** call Bakal's Riding School (tel. 04-920-534) to make an appointment.

For a nice **hike** every Saturday, you can contact the Friends of Nature (Hovevei Hateva), 36 Ha-Ga'aton Blvd (tel. 04-920-246 or 921-923).

If you're interested in **meeting the locals,** contact the Tourist Information Office in the Municipal building, Ha-Iriya Square (tel. 04-922-121); they can arrange it. The local chapters of the Rotary, Lions, Soroptimists, and Freemasons also extend a warm welcome to international members; contact the Tourist Information Office for meeting times and places.

Nahariya's claim to ancient fame is the ruin of a **Canaanite temple** accidentally discovered on Ha-Ma'apilim Street, a few yards up from the Municipal Beach in 1947. Experts believe it to be a temple dedicated to the Canaanite goddess of the sea, Asherah (or Astarte) dating from about 1500 B.C. Not much to see here, but you can hang around and pick up ancient vibrations for a few minutes before pushing on to the next sight, which actually contains some objects worth examining.

In the seven-story Municipality Building, on Ha-Iriya Square, is Nahariya's **Municipal Museum,** with several separate museum departments arranged on the fifth, sixth, and seventh floors of the building. The fifth floor houses an art exhibit. The sixth floor, in addition to an interesting malacology collection (that's shells), displays many artifacts, exhibits, and historical tales from the area around Nahariya (Israel's entire north coast), with its fascinating history dating all the way back to the Stone Age. It's definitely worth stopping in here to get a quick education about the area you're visiting. Up on the seventh floor are two more museum departments: one showing the history of the town of Nahariya, and the other a Museum of German Jews, which, in addition to cultural memorabilia, displays photographs and writings of Sigmund Freud, Alfred Adler, Erich Fromm, Albert Einstein, Robert Oppenheimer (creator of the atom bomb, with Einstein), Oscar Hammerstein, artist Max Liebermann, Henry Kissinger, and U.S. Supreme Court Justice Felix Frankfurter, to name just a few.

The Municipal Museum is open Sunday through Friday from 10 a.m. to noon, plus Sunday and Wednesday afternoons from 4 to 6 p.m. Admission is that loveliest of all prices—it's free.

NORTH OF NAHARIYA: Heading north along the main road, after 4 km (2½ miles) you'll see the road to **Akhziv Beach,** on the left (west). It's another kilometer down to the beach proper, where you'll find a parking lot, changing rooms, shelters and snack stands, as well as freshwater showers. There's a charge for admission at busy times.

Heading north again, a kilometer past the Akhziv Beach road you'll pass the parking lot and entrance to Akhziv National Park, with its Garden Restaurant, amid the restored ruins of a seaside village.

Akhziv is actually a very old settlement, with foundations in the Bronze Age and a history of settlement through Iron Age, Roman, and Byzantine times. It was in existence at the time Joshua assigned the tribes of Israel to their various territories; it is mentioned in the Bible as a Canaanite town which the tribe of Asher, to whom it was allotted, was never able to conquer (Judges 1:31). The Crusaders built a fort here. You can visit the Nahariya Municipal Museum's archeological exhibits to see the wealth of artifacts recovered here, and learn about the long and varied history of the town.

During the summer you may have to pay NIS1.50 ($1) admission to **Akhziv National Park,** but most of the time you can just wander through the gates and up the hill through the lovely gardens. It's a beautiful spot for a picnic. The park is open every day of the year: from 8 a.m. to 5 p.m. April through September, until 4 p.m. October through March, closing one hour earlier on Friday and on holiday eves.

At the far end of the parking lot is the entrance to Club Méditerranée's Nahariya vacation resort.

In more recent history, Akhziv was an Arab village; the village was deserted in 1948, but that was not the end of Akhziv's history. In 1952 Eli Avivi arrived, got government permission to settle, and promptly declared the "independence" of Akhzivland, which is just north of the park boundary. The ramshackle Arab house that is Akhzivland's main structure houses not only Mr. Avivi's living quarters, but also his personal museum of artifacts found on and near Akhzivland (remember, its history goes back to the Bronze Age!). You can visit the museum anytime for less than a dollar admission, and if you have your sleeping bag, you can also avail yourself of the opportunity to plunk down here, for a small fee, in the youth hostel section of Akhzivland (which may amount to little more than a space on the lawn).

Food and Lodging

Another half kilometer northward brings you to **Camping Akhziv** (Akhziv 25220; tel. 04-921-792), where you'll pay about $5 per person for camping with all facilities. Little bamboo bungalows are also available for rent for $35 in August, more like around $13 the rest of the year, for up to four people; small trailers, with room for up to four people, rent for $14. There are also eight mobile homes, with air conditioning and full kitchen, each holding up to ten people.

If a youth hostel is what you're looking for, the **Yad Le-Yad Youth Hostel** (P.O. Box 169, Nahariya; tel. 04-921-343) is just a little way north of Camping Akhziv. The hostel has 350 beds, arranged in two-, four-, and six-bed rooms, plus 21 bamboo bungalows housing four people. There's a TV room, basketball court, and visitors' kitchen available, and it's in a prime location just across the road from the beach. Rates are $6.30 for a room for IYHA members, $5 for a bungalow, about $1 more for nonmembers. Hostel guests are given discount tickets to many attractions nearby, including the caves at Rosh Ha-Niqra, the diving club at nearby Camping Akhziv, and the Akhziv National Park. The hostel is open all day, with no lock-out times or curfews.

Just a few steps north of the youth hostel is the **Wimpy Cafeteria/ Restaurant,** open seven days a week, from 6 a.m. to 3 a.m. in summer, until 9 p.m. in winter, with a casual atmosphere and an assortment of snacks.

Akhziv Bridge

The town of Akhziv, from which this area takes its name, has a history going back to biblical times. Yet the name is most often remembered in connection with a tragic, heroic event that took place here on the night of June 17, 1946. Attempting to cut British rail communications with neighboring Arab states, a Hagana demolition team was destroying railroad bridges along this line. (You can still see the right-of-way, and even some rails, from the disused line.) At the Akhziv bridge, however, they were spotted by a British sentry, who fired a flare in order to get a better look. The flare ignited the team's explosives. The bridge was blown, but not one man survived. The 14 who perished are commemorated by a large black metal monument across the road from the youth hostel.

Gesher Haziv

This settlement, named after the incident at the bridge, was founded in 1949 by a group of Americans and Israelis. They began with tents, upset kibbutz tradition by keeping the children in the parents' home, and now have a handsome settlement on a hill overlooking their fertile fields by the sea.

The kibbutz has a diving center on the shore, and a kibbutz guesthouse (tel. 04-927-711) with 48 comfy rooms with private baths (and tubs), priced at $36 to $40 single, $48 to $56 double, breakfast and service included. Guests have access to seaside diving center facilities at discount prices. You can dine in the kosher restaurant whether or not you stay at the guest house.

ROSH HA-NIQRA: This is a location on the border with Lebanon, astride a tall cliff overlooking the sea. On a clear day, standing atop the cliff, you can see the coastline as far as Haifa. Beneath the cliffs are grottoes carved out by the sea, reachable via cable car. Operating from 8:30 a.m. to 4 p.m. (till 5 or even 7 p.m. in summer), on Friday till 3 p.m., the cable car ride costs about NIS5.25 ($3.50) for adults, NIS3.75 ($2.50) for children and students. You can walk out into the caves and passages and see the pools of water lapping the rocks. To see the artifacts that have been recovered from these caves, visit the Municipal Museum in Nahariya.

To reach Rosh Ha-Niqra, take the bus from Nahariya, running several times a day; sherut service is also available, from right in front of the Nahariya central bus station, on Ha-Ga'aton Boulevard.

You can dine at a reasonably priced self-service restaurant on top of the cliff called **Mitzpe Rosh Ha-Niqra.** The view is terrific. Open the same hours as the cable car.

HAIFA

MOST HAIFA RESIDENTS feel sorry for anyone who doesn't live there. After visiting Haifa, you may well agree. Some compare the town, beautifully situated on a hill overlooking a broad bay, to San Francisco and Naples . . . and it's hard to be more complimentary than that.

Israel's third-largest city (population 250,000; 30% are Christians and Muslims), and the capital of the north, Haifa is like a triple-decker sandwich—the raucous **port area** being the first tier; the business district (**Hadar**), higher up, being the second; the enchanting **Carmel** district, nestled even higher on the upper pine slopes, constituting the third.

A QUICK HISTORY: Almost every square foot of Israel has been populated since earliest ages, and Haifa is no exception. The prophet Elijah knew this territory well—from the top of Mount Carmel he won a major victory over 450 priests of Baal (I Kings 18:19–40) during the reign of King Ahab and his notorious wife, Jezebel. Also in biblical times, the Phoenician harbor center of Zalemona thrived here, with predominantly Greek settlers, and the Jewish agricultural village of Sycaminos (sometimes called Shikmona) clung to the northwestern peak of Mount Carmel (3rd-century Talmudic literature mentions both towns).

The Crusaders called the area Caife, Cayphe, and sometimes Caiphas—which suggests the modern town's name might stem from Caiaphas, the name of Jerusalem's high priest during the days of Jesus.

Once a center of glass and cochineal-purple industries, Haifa was destroyed when the Arabs reconquered the area, and it virtually slept until the late 19th century when Jewish idealists moved into the area. Even with a population of 10,000 at the beginning of the 20th century, the city as we know it today scarcely existed: the huge port area was still a tangled marsh, with Bedouin encamped on nearby sand dunes. In the Carmel hills above the city, shepherds brought their flocks to graze.

Haifa got its first shot in the arm in 1905, when the Haifa–Damascus Railway was built. The Balfour Declaration and British occupation boosted it some more, as did a 1919 railway link to Egypt. But the real kick-off came when the

British built its modern harbor—an arduous enterprise begun in 1929 and completed in 1934. Thereupon Haifa began its transformation into the vital trading and communications center it is today, taking on major importance as a shipping base, naval center, and terminal point for oil pipelines. For some reason, the ancient engineers of Caesarea, Athlit, Akhziv, and Acre—the most historic ports along Israel's coast—had never foreseen the advantages of building a major harbor at this point on the Mediterranean coast, naturally sheltered by the Carmel mountains.

One visionary, however, did realize the future role of Haifa. In 1898, when he sailed past the spot that was to become modern Haifa, he foresaw that "huge liners rode at anchor" and at "the top of the mountain there were thousands of white homes and the mountain itself was crowned with imposing villas. . . . A beautiful city had been built close to the deep blue sea. . . ." He saw "a serpentine road to Mount Carmel." The visionary was Theodor Herzl, father of Zionism, who recorded these prophesies in his book, *Old New Land*. Miraculously, the city developed precisely along the lines he predicted.

The vision of the Zionist leader was a reality for hundreds of thousands of immigrants, whose first glimpse of the Promised Land came as they crowded the rails, their ships drawing through the morning haze, with Haifa looming up on the Carmel hills before them. The port below, the Baha'i dome shining in the lower hills, and the mountain clustered with forests and houses, was like the sight of heaven for the tides of homeless, scarred refugees who fled here after the war.

On April 21, 1948, Haifa became the first major city controlled by Jews after the end of the British Mandate and the U.N. Partition decision in 1947. Although Haifa's previous growth had already spurred development of residential areas such as Bat Galim, Hadar Ha-Carmel, Neveh-Shaanan, and even Herzlia, the new wave of immigration (more than 100,000) gave rise to others: Ramot Ramez, Kiryat Elizer, Neveh Yosef, and Kiryat Shprinzak. Haifa Bay, east of the port, became the "backbone" of the country's heavy industries, with oil refineries and associated industries, foundries, glass factories, fertilizer and chemical industries, cement works, textile manufacturing, and yards for shipbuilding and repair in preponderance. Plans are now in progress to convert the areas southwest of the port into Israel's own "Riviera." (The beaches are already excellent.)

1. Finding Your Way Around Haifa

Israelis say that Tel Aviv is the place for fun, Jerusalem for learning, and Haifa for work. Haifa does have a brisk workingman's flavor about it, although the residents bristle when one implies that the town is just a "bourgeois workers' village"—a favorite taunt of Tel Avivans.

Of all its graces, Haifa is richest in panoramic views. For purposes of orientation, you might think of Haifa as a city built on three levels. Whether you come by ship, bus, or train, you will arrive on the first or the port level of the city. The second level, **Hadar Ha-Carmel,** meaning "Glory of the Carmel," is referred to simply as the **Hadar.** This is the business section. At the top of the hills is the **Carmel** district, a patchwork of verdant residential neighborhoods with its own small but busy commercial center called Central Carmel, numerous hotels and pensions, restaurants, small museums, and two of Haifa's brightest cultural beacons: Haifa Auditorium and Bet Rothschild (the James de Rothschild Cultural Center).

ARRIVING IN HAIFA: The city's transportation center is at its northernmost tip, in the district called **Bat Galim,** about 2 km (1½ miles) northwest of the downtown port area. Right next to one another in Bat Galim are the **Egged Bus Terminal** and the **New Central Railway Station.** From here, you'll have to take a city bus to either of my recommended hotel districts, in Hadar or Central Carmel. For Hadar, catch a no. 10 or 12; for Central Carmel and the top of the mountain, you want a no. 3, 22, or 24.

Coming by sea? Your ship will dock right in the port at the **Maritime Passenger Terminal,** and from there it's only a short walk to the Paris Square (Kikar Paris) station of the Carmelit subway which climbs the mountain to Hadar and Central Carmel. Read on.

Should you get off the train at the **Old Railway Station** in Plumer Square, you've got a somewhat longer walk to the Paris Square Carmelit subway station.

Because Haifa is built all the way up the side of a mountain, many of its main streets are sinuous switchbacks, curving and recurving to accommodate the steep slopes of Mount Carmel. The streets are always and forever bewildering, and you will find yourself lost repeatedly. If Haifa weren't so pleasant and beautiful, this would be a chore; instead, each time you get lost will yield new discoveries.

About the only straight road in Haifa is the one that climbs the slopes of Carmel underground: the Carmelit.

THE CARMELIT: The Carmelit (the subway) is a fast and efficient means of getting up and down Haifa's various levels. Its terminal station is located on Jaffa Road, a few blocks north of the port entrance and not far from the old (Mercaz) railway station. If you have trouble finding it, just ask anyone, "Eyfo ha'Carmelit?"—"Where is the Carmelit?"—and you'll be pointed in the right direction. The port area stop is called **Paris Station,** in honor of its French builders.

Pulled on a long cable up and down the steep hill, the Carmelit resembles a sort of scale-model Métro, with only 1,800 yards of tunnel. It's picturesque, yes —and it also happens to offer the best means of getting from the port to Hadar and Carmel. There are six stops in all. Here's a list of them, starting from the bottom of the mountain and going up to the top:

1. Place de Paris (lower terminus, port area)
2. Solel Boneh (Hassan Shukri Street)
3. Ha-Nevi'im (Hadar business district, tourist office)
4. Massada (Massada Street)
5. Eliezer Golomb (Eliezer Golomb Street)
6. Gan Ha-Em (Central Carmel business district, upper terminus)

The Carmelit is much quicker and cheaper than a bus or sherut (trains run every ten minutes).

Transport Fares and Hours

Bus fares are charged according to destination. In Haifa, some buses run on Saturday, except for the hours between 6 p.m. on Friday night and 9 a.m. on Saturday morning. Bus fares are by distance traveled, so you must tell the driver where you're going. The Carmelit operates daily from 5:30 a.m. to midnight and does not run from an hour before sundown on Friday to sundown on Saturday. And taxis can always be found.

Note: You may check your bags in Bat Galim at Egged's baggage checking department before heading out to find a hotel.

TOURIST INFORMATION: Haifa is virtually paved with tourist information offices, and you should have no trouble connecting with one in short order upon your arrival. There's a Municipal Tourist Office in the Egged Bus Terminal, 170 Jaffa Rd. in Bat Galim (tel. 04-512-208), open Sunday through Thursday from 9 a.m. to 4 p.m., on Friday from 8 a.m. to 1 p.m.; closed Saturday.

The main **Israel Government Tourist Office (I.G.T.O.)** location is at 20 Herzl St., near the intersection with Balfour (tel. 04-666-521 or 666-522), open Sunday through Thursday from 8:30 a.m. to 5 p.m., on Friday until 2 p.m.; closed Saturday. Here you can obtain the monthly calendar "Events in Haifa and the Northern Region," plus any other info you might need. To get here, take the Carmelit to the Ha-Nevi'im stop, walk up Herzl Street 100 yards, and it'll be on your right.

The Municipality of Haifa maintains several **information booths** around town:

In Hadar: 23 Ha-Nevi'im St. (tel. 04-663-056), open Sunday through Thursday from 8 a.m. to 7 p.m., on Friday till 1 p.m.

In City Hall: 14 Hassan Shukri St. (tel. 04-645-359), open Sunday through Thursday from 8 a.m. to 1:30 p.m., on Friday till 1 p.m. (Carmelit stop: Solel Boneh).

In Central Carmel: 119 Ha-Nassi Blvd. (tel. 04-383-683), open Sunday through Thursday from 9 a.m. to 1 p.m., on Friday from 8 a.m. to 1 p.m. (facing the Gan Ha-Em / Central Carmel Carmelit stop).

All are closed on Saturday.

Also check the 24-hour **telephone hotline** "What's On in Haifa" (tel. 04-640-840), a recording by the Haifa Tourism Development Association telling about events going on around the area. This organization also puts out a monthly poster, "Special Events in Haifa," listing many events of interest; look for it in the bus station, in hotels, in all the Tourist Information Offices, and in other places around town.

USEFUL FACTS: Haifa is different from Tel Aviv and Jerusalem, so check these facts to smooth your way.

Bookstores and Newsstands: There are **Steimatzky** branches at 82 Ha-Atzma'ut St. (tel. 04-663-501), 16 Herzl St. in Bet Ha-Kranot (tel. 04-665-042), 130 Ha-Nassi Ave. (tel. 04-388-765), and in the Central Bus Station (tel. 04-538-056).

Buses: Haifa's municipal buses operate from 5 a.m. to 11:30 p.m. Sunday through Thursday; on Friday, bus service halts around 4:30 p.m.; there is limited Saturday service from 9 a.m. to midnight. For information, call 04-515-221.

Consulates: The **United States Consular Agent** in Haifa is James Sassower Ltd., 37 Ha-Atzma'ut St. (tel. 04-669-042 or 672-176), down in the port area near the Palmer Gate / Khayat Street intersection.

Medical Services: Dial 101 for Magen David Adom **first aid** services, or 102 for an **emergency** hospital admission. For the mobile intensive-care unit, the number is 04-512-233. The **National Poison Control Center** (tel. 04-529-205) is at Rambam Hospital, on call 24 hours a day.

Post Office: Haifa's Central Post Office is at 19 Ha-Palyam St.

STUDENTS IN HAIFA: The **Israel Students Tourist Association (ISSTA)** has an office in Hadar at 28 Nordau St. (tel. 04-660-411 or 669-139). It's open Sunday through Friday from 8:30 a.m. to 1 p.m., plus 4 to 6 p.m. on Sunday, Monday, Tuesday, and Thursday; closed Saturday. Anyone is welcome to come here, not only students, although students will find particularly favorable budget rates. You can ask here for information not only about Haifa, but also about air and boat transportation to other parts of the world (you can buy your tickets here), renting a car, tours around Israel and Egypt, hotels, and many other travel agency services. Also pick up the booklet "International Student Travel Guide," telling about student travel deals in many countries.

TRANSPORTATION TO BEN-GURION AIRPORT: El Al airline has an early baggage check-in service in Haifa, as well as in Tel Aviv and Jerusalem. In Haifa, it's been located at the El Al office, 80 Ha-Atzma'ut Road (tel. 04-641-166), at the corner of Khayat Street, but it's scheduled to move. If you want to use this service, call ahead to be sure of the current location.

El Al now offers another service in Haifa: daily early-morning **bus** transportation to Ben-Gurion Airport, available to anyone, not only to El Al's customers. The bus leaves the Egged central bus station daily at 3:30 a.m., stopping at many hotels along the way, with its final departure from the Dan Carmel Hotel at 4:15 a.m. It will pick you up anywhere along its route if you call in advance to request it. You can purchase tickets in advance from the El Al office, travel agents, or hotels (but not directly from the bus driver) for NIS11.50 ($7.50). For further information or to reserve a ticket, phone El Al's office (tel. 04-670-170).

Another transportation service to Ben-Gurion Airport is **Melia** (tel. 04-384-667 or 384-669); call for current info.

2. Where to Stay

Hadar holds a few very reasonable hotels and pensions, and staying in Hadar puts you right at the center of everything. But Central Carmel is much nicer, really—more trees, more quiet, more views. And with the Carmelit, you're only minutes away from the other parts of the city.

HOTELS IN HADAR: First thing to get straight is that there are hotels on two different streets with very similar names. Herzl Street branches off from Ha-Nevi'im near the Ha-Nevi'im Carmelit station. Herzlia Street is a bit farther up the hill on Ha-Nevi'im Street, and it branches off to the north, the opposite direction from Herzl Street. Now that you've got your bearings, you're ready to set out in search of Haifa's good, clean, inexpensive rooms.

An inexpensive hotel in the Hadar region is the **Nesher,** 53 Herzl St., corner of Yehiel Street behind Barclays Bank (Haifa 33504; tel. 04-640-644). The two-star, 15-room hotel is like a pension—the reception is two flights up—with prices the same all year round, at $15 to $20 single, $28 to $32 double, breakfast and service included. Students get a 10% reduction. The pastel-painted rooms have running water, ten have showers, and all are heated and air-conditioned. Toilets are in the hall.

Another Hadar hotel is the **Talpiot,** 61 Herzl St., corner of Arlosoroff (Haifa 33504; tel. 04-673-753), with 24 rooms, all heated (nine air-conditioned), over half with private shower, and two with bath and toilet facilities. Students receive a 15% reduction from November to February. In all, the Talpiot is much like the Nesher, and not far from it, although at the Talpiot you need only walk up one flight to get to the reception desk. Rates at the Talpiot also remain constant all year, at $16 single, $24 double.

Should you want a real hotel rather than a pension, be prepared to pay more—but you'll get more. The three-star **Hotel Carmelia,** 35 Herzlia St. at the corner of Zionism (Ha-Ziyonut) Avenue (tel. 04-521-278 or 521-279), is only a few minutes' walk from the Ha-Nevi'im Carmelit station and the center of Hadar. Well kept, large (50 rooms), and modernized, the high-ceilinged rooms all have air conditioning and heat, well-maintained tub or shower bathrooms, telephones, a pleasing modern decor, and an elevator to serve them. Most

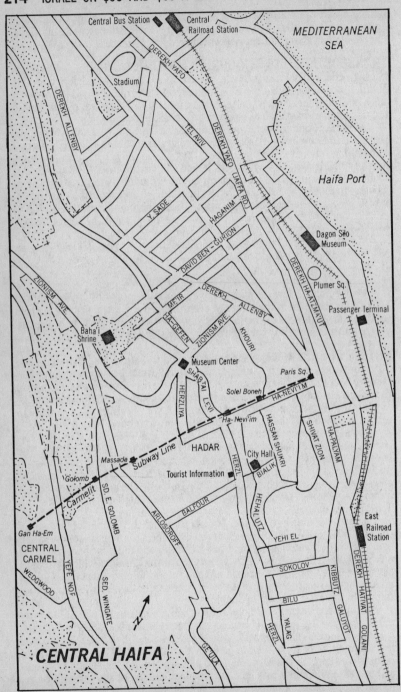

CENTRAL HAIFA

rooms also have little balconies with partial views of the city and harbor, but there are also some "quiet rooms" on the inside of the hotel, with no balconies (and no street noise). The hotel bar has a dance every Friday night with '60s music; there's also an adjoining tennis court, open from 9 a.m. to 2 p.m., and a pleasant streetfront patio with flowers. Prices are the same all year: $32 single, $46 double, with reductions if you stay longer than one or two nights.

A Hostel in Hadar

The **Bethel Tourist Hostel,** 40 Ha-Gefen St. (Haifa 35053; tel. 04-521-110), near the intersection with Ben-Gurion Boulevard, is operated by friendly, hospitable Americans. There are seven clean and bright separate-sex bunk rooms, 75 beds in all. The charge for a bunk is always kept around $4. Rules are the standard hostel type: you must be up and out by 9 a.m., in by 10 p.m.; registration for bunks is from 5 to 9 p.m. only (4 to 7:30 p.m. on Friday), but you can drop off your luggage at any time during the day; the common room and gardens remain open for use all day long, with basketball, volleyball, table tennis, and swings. During busy periods a maximum stay of three days may be involved. The price for a bunk does not include meals, but a snackbar on the premises can provide simple, low-cost breakfasts (and on Friday only, supper), or you can buy supplies at nearby shops. To get to the hostel, take a no. 8 or 22 bus from the Central (Egged) Bus Station, or a no. 10 or 12 from the port area, and tell the driver you want to get off at Ha-Gefen Street. After you alight, walk west up the hill on Ha-Gefen; the hostel is on the right-hand side. Remember: Registration for bunks is in the evening only.

By the way, Haifa's other youth hostel is on the south side of Mount Carmel (see below).

HOTELS IN CENTRAL CARMEL: Up here on top of Mount Carmel, when you climb the stairs out of the Gan Ha-Em Carmelit station you'll come above ground on busy Ha-Nassi Boulevard. Walk southwest (up the slope) and in short order you'll arrive at the main intersection of Central Carmel, Ha-Nassi, and Sea Road (Derekh Ha-Yam).

If you arrive in Central Carmel by city bus no. 22, look for this same intersection to use as a reference point.

The beautiful verdure of Carmel even surrounds this business district, and the large Gan Ha-Em park is just west of the Carmelit station. Besides the various expensive hotels placed atop Mount Carmel for the benefit of the view, a little searching can uncover comfortable but cheaper accommodations. I'll give explicit directions on how to reach every hotel recommended below, because the winding streets can be difficult and exasperating to negotiate until you've got your bearings.

I can't help beginning with my favorite hotel in all Haifa, the three-star **Hotel Dvir,** 124 Yefe Nof St., also called Panorama Road (Haifa 34454; tel. 04-389-131). All but 4 of the Dvir's 39 rooms come with tubs in the bathrooms; each one has a telephone, TV, clock-radio, heat and air conditioning, wall-to-wall carpet, and lovely decor. Ten of the rooms have an incredibly beautiful view of the city, the harbor, and across Haifa Bay to Acre and the mountains beyond. These rooms all have the entire view wall made of glass, and a nice balcony; get one of these if you can. But even more significant than the view is the service. The Dvir is run as a hotel training school for the Dan hotel chain, and the young people who serve you here are out to get good marks both from you and from their supervisors—the service is tops. Year-round prices, considering the service and the view, are reasonable: $30.50 single, $48 for one person in a double room, $53 for two in a double, including a fine breakfast. To get to the Dvir, come out of the Carmelit station, turn left and cross busy Ha-Nassi Boulevard, and then look for Shar Ha-Levanon Street; walk the short block to the end of Shar Ha-Levanon, turn right, and you're on Panorama (Yefe Nof) Road. Look for the Dvir just a block or two down.

For the next hotel, if you're walking from the Carmelit station, go southwest along Ha-Nassi, past the Haifa Auditorium (on your right). Past Haifa Auditorium, Ha-Nassi Boulevard becomes Moriah Avenue. Continue walking along Moriah, and four blocks beyond Haifa Auditorium you'll come to a little narrow street named Ha-Mayim, on the right. Go down Ha-Mayim, and you'll come to the **Hotel Vered Ha-Carmel** (tel. 04-389-236 or 389-238), on the left-hand side. (You can also take bus 21, 23, 28 or 37, and get off at the Moriah Street stop, which is the second one after Central Carmel.) The official address is 1 Heinrich Heine Square, Haifa 34485. The location is quiet, shady, and cool; the hotel has been modernized and redecorated. All 22 rooms now remind one of a well-run pension in, say, Austria, with white walls, blond wood, telephone, clock-radio, color TV, air conditioning, central heat, tiny toilet, and shower stalls; a few rooms have small patios. The hotel is surrounded with pretty garden terraces. Prices? Not too bad. In winter, singles cost $29, doubles with two beds are $35, and doubles with one double bed are $44. Prices in high season are about 10% higher. If you take one of the few rooms that have a shared shower in the hall, you pay 10% less, anytime.

A Guesthouse/Hotel and a Hospice

Hotel Beth Shalom Carmel, 110 Ha-Nassi Blvd. (P.O. Box 6208, Haifa 31060; tel. 04-337-481 or 337-482), is a German Protestant guesthouse, open to all comers, with 30 rooms. All are clean and airy, and equipped with phones, air conditioning, heating, private bath (tub and shower), and toilet. The rates all year round are $26 single, $38 double; breakfast is included, and the minimum stay is three nights. To find Beth Shalom, start from the Gan Ha-Em Carmelit station and walk northwest on Ha-Nassi, down the slope, past Gan Ha-Em park; you'll see the hotel just past the park, on the same (left) side of the street.

St. Maximo's Hospice, 3 Megiddo St. (P.O. Box 6008, Haifa 31060; tel. 04-381-274 or 381-989), is close to Carmel's center of action, but it seems like a peaceful haven. Megiddo Street would run right into Ha-Nassi Boulevard if it went straight through, but it's been blocked off to traffic, putting the hospice at the end of a tree-lined cul-de-sac, only a two-minute walk from the Carmelit station on Ha-Nassi. It's an old stone building entered through a shady courtyard with large trees, behind a stone wall protecting it from the street. Although the building is full of old-world charm, inside it's been renovated, and sports 25 rooms with private toilet, tub and shower, wall-to-wall carpet, and heat—no air conditioning needed here, with the thick stone walls and so many trees. There's color TV in the sitting room. Prices are $23 single, $36 double, including breakfast, all year round. To find St. Maximo's, go straight across Ha-Nassi Boulevard from the Carmelit station and go up the stairs between the two banks. Walk straight ahead (you'll be on Megiddo Street) and the first thing you'll see on your left will be a long stone wall with lots of large trees behind it. Only a tiny sign right beside the gate tells you that this is St. Maximo's.

The Big Splurge

If you want to try one of Carmel's expensive luxury hotels, it will set your budget back a bit, but it should be a most enjoyable experience. Of the four- and five-star hotels on Ha-Nassi Boulevard, my choice would be the **Nof Hotel,** 101

Ha-Nassi Blvd. (Haifa 34642; tel. 04-388-731), which I think affords the most luxury for the money. You'll find magnificent panoramic views in all 100 rooms, luxury decor and accommodations, and excellent kosher food in the hotel dining room, the rooftop garden café, and at the renowned penthouse Chinese restaurant (I've listed this separately under "Where to Eat"). Best of all, if you come with this book in hand and stay at least three nights, you'll get a 15% discount, bringing the price per night to $41 single, $60 double in the winter (mid-November through February), or $48 single, $70 double the rest of the year.

A Hospice in the Port Area

St. Charles German Hospice (tel. 04-523-705) is right on one of the port area's major thoroughfares, at 105 Derekh Yafo. But it's a quiet place, set back from the street in a large, stone-walled, 120-year-old complex of gardens and stone buildings. The hospice is run by the sisters of the Carmelite order, but it's open to all travelers. Rooms are simple, two or three beds to a room, with high ceilings, spare and practical furnishings, and running water in a sink in each room, with ample toilet, bath, and shower facilities down the hall, and a nice sitting room too. Prices are $14 per person with breakfast, $10 without breakfast; you're welcome to use the kitchen to prepare meals, and to relax in the large garden. Cheaper accommodations can be had downstairs in dorm rooms; $6.60 a night, no meal included.

THE YOUTH HOSTEL: Haifa's IYHA Youth Hostel is the **Carmel Hostel** (tel. 04-531-944 or 532-536; "Hof Ha-Carmel Mobile Post," Haifa 30862, is the mail address). With 350 beds, the Carmel Hostel has dormitory rooms, bungalows, and eight family rooms, each with private toilet, shower, and balcony overlooking the Mediterranean. In fact, from this hillside location, everywhere you go you can see the Mediterranean, with a nice public lifeguard-protected beach just a 20-minute walk down the hill. You're also not more than a 5-minute walk from tennis, squash, and lawn bowling courts, a pizzeria, and a Chinese restaurant/pub, and a 20-minute bus ride from downtown Haifa. Video movies are shown every evening in the recreation room. All three meals are served (kosher), with dairy meals priced at $2.10, meat meals at $3.50. The hostel is open all day long, so you can come and go as you please; no curfew, either! It's located in Hof Ha-Carmel, on the coast south of Haifa on the main highway. Bus 43 goes right to the gate, every hour from the Central Bus Station; no. 45 will drop you on the shore road. Ask to be let off at the Israel Tennis Center. You'll see the hostel complex, up the hill behind the tennis center, amid fragrant cypress trees. The walk up the hill will take about 15 minutes.

Another IYHA Youth Hostel near Haifa is the one at **Kiryat Tivon,** 12-A Zeid St. (tel. 04-931-482), a 20-minute, 14-km (8½ mile) ride on bus 75 from Haifa's Central Bus Station. Facilities include 100 beds, family rooms, and kitchens for visitors' use.

A bit farther away is the **Young Judea Youth Hostel,** Kefar Maccabi Post (tel. 04-442-976), in Ramat Yohanan, 30 minutes from Haifa by bus. To get there, you can take bus 63 from Haifa to Kiryat Ata (leaving every ten minutes), and from there take the bus to Kibbutz Ramat Yohanan. There's also a bus direct from Haifa's Central Bus Station, bus 66, but it leaves only three times a day, at 6 a.m., 1:20 p.m., and 5 p.m. Once you're there, you'll find 130 beds, family rooms, kitchen facilities, and swimming too. No lockout or curfew here.

Since all the above hostels are part of the IYHA (the Israel Youth Hostels Association), prices are the same for all: $5 for members under 18, $5.50 over

18, $1 extra for nonmembers. All prices include breakfast, hot showers, and clean sheets.

3. Where to Eat

Haifa can cater to every culinary taste and pocketbook. The eateries are everywhere, escalating in price and geographic levels from the falafel stands adjacent to the port area to the Dan Carmel Grill Room overlooking the Mediterranean from one of Israel's most scenic spots.

We'll start our explorations in Hadar, where you can find just about anything. From there we'll climb up Mount Carmel to Central Carmel, with its small but varied selection of restaurants. Finally, we'll explore the streets, markets, and back alleys of the downtown port area in search of tasty, inexpensive meals. A note on eateries in the bus and train stations is at the end of the downtown port section.

IN HADAR: Start your restaurant search, as usual, from the Ha-Nevi'im Carmelit station at the intersection of Ha-Nevi'im Street and Shabtai Levi/Herzl Streets, right in the heart of Hadar. By the way, this hub is also named Masaryk Square (Kikar Masaryk).

For General Fare

First we'll look at a few restaurants that serve up varied meals—good places for that inexpensive meal when you're not particularly interested in being adventurous.

Walking out of Masaryk Square on Herzl Street, a couple of blocks up you'll come to one of Haifa's most popular restaurants: **Matamim,** 24 Herzl St. (tel. 04-665-171). The sign is in Hebrew only, but you can look for the displays of fresh food in the windows on either side of the glass door, and the many happy customers inside. The food here is good quality, traditional Jewish home-style food, glatt kosher; the decor is artistic, the atmosphere pleasant and busy; and the prices are surprisingly low. Put it all together and you can see why the place is so popular. A full roast beef supper, including dessert and coffee, is NIS11 ($7.35), less if you order chicken, and there's a wide variety of Jewish specialties. How about some ptcha (jellied leg), for NIS2.50 ($1.65)? Or you can come in for just a bowl of soup—seven kinds, priced from NIS1.60 ($1.05) to NIS2.50 ($1.65)—a beer or wine, or coffee and dessert. Matamim is open from 10 a.m. to 10 p.m., on Friday until 2 p.m.; closed Saturday.

Standing at the corner of Herzl Street and Shemaryahu Levin Street, you can see a large, three-story department store, **Hamashbir Lazarchan,** just a little to one side, at the corner of Shemaryahu Levin and a tiny back street called Yona Street. Unlike most American department stores, this one has a supermarket too—it's down on the basement floor. Up on the third floor there's a busy self-service cafeteria, where you can get a sandwich, coffee, and dessert all for NIS4.40 ($2.95). Hot dishes are served here too, also nicely priced. It's open daily from 8:30 a.m. to 7 p.m.; closed for the Sabbath.

Ha-Nevi'im Street has some nice choices for a quick, informal meal. One good open-air eatery is **Bis-Bo,** 25 Ha-Nevi'im St. (tel. 04-668-010), a tiny place with a few counter tables, a sandwich bar, and a friendly atmosphere. Calling itself an "American-style deli," it serves up American delicacies like a double hot dog for NIS2 ($1.35), a long list of various hamburgers and cheeseburgers for NIS2.10 ($1.40) to NIS4 ($2.65), French fries for NIS1.50 ($1), big sandwiches for NIS1.20 (80¢) to NIS3.50 ($2.35), and a cup of hot soup for only NIS1 (65¢). It's open from 8:30 a.m. to 9:30 p.m., closing early Friday and opening after sunset on Saturday.

Nearby is **Milky Pinky,** 28 Ha-Nevi'im St. (tel. 04-664-166), a block up from Masaryk Square. You'll know it when you see all the pink, and the outdoor tables. It has a variety of quick food items such as pancakes, blintzes, pizza, and ice cream, and an omelet breakfast special priced at NIS3 ($2). Open from 8 a.m. to midnight, on Friday until 2 p.m., on Saturday after sunset.

For Arabic Cuisine

Located as it is on the edge of Galilee, with its large number of Arabic citizens (who are Israelis), Haifa can claim some very fine Arabic restaurants, in all price ranges. Here are my Hadar favorites. First, two inexpensive Arabic eateries. Then, some more high-class Arabian restaurants.

For Middle Eastern fare, two good choices are **Diab Bros. Restaurant,** 6 Herzlia St. (tel. 04-660-342), offering chicken, kebab, or shishlik with rice, and open from 7 a.m. to midnight seven days a week; and the **Elihu Restaurant,** also at 6 Herzlia St. (open from 8 a.m. to midnight, closing for the Sabbath), offering the same basic Middle Eastern fare. Nothing fancy here, but good food at decent prices—about NIS15 ($10) for a full meal. From Masaryk Square, go up Ha-Nevi'im toward Mount Carmel, and take the first right—that's Herzlia. The restaurants are on the right just around that corner.

Walking down Ha-Nevi'im from Masaryk Square, toward the port, will reveal two fancier places. The second street on the left holds the **Restaurant 1001 Nights,** 3 Daniel St. (although you probably won't find a street sign; tel. 04-663-704). Pleasant, darkish, and not overdecorated, Restaurant 1001 Nights is the place to try *siniya,* baked ground meat with tchina and pine nuts; or eggplant stuffed with ground lamb, shishlik (that's shish kebab) served with french fries and vegetables, or perhaps lamb cutlets. A full meal here runs about NIS15 ($10). Open seven days a week from 7:30 a.m. until midnight (or even later, depending on the crowd).

Pricier, and a bit more fancy, is the **Peer Amram Brothers Restaurant,** on the third street to the left off Ha-Nevi'im down from Masaryk Square, at 1 Atlit St. (tel. 04-665-707). Prices here are fully double those of the aforementioned 1001 Nights, but there are some fancier selections here too, such as baked lamb, or a mixed grill with lamb and beef. A full meal of either of these, with a choice among 25 different salads, wine, coffee, and dessert, will run about NIS45 ($30 —knock off NIS14, $9.35, if you decide against the wine), but these are the house specialties, the most expensive dinners; anything else will be less. This award-winning restaurant has been 25 years in the same location, and you'll find it there still, open daily from 8 a.m. to 11 p.m.; being a kosher establishment, it closes early on Friday, opening again on Saturday evening after the Sabbath.

For a tasty Arabic meal in elegant surroundings, try **Mattar Restaurant,** 5 Yona St. (tel. 04-668-150), located beside the large department store, Hamashbir Lazarchan, near the corner of Herzl and Shemaryahu Levin Streets. Signs will direct you around to the right side of the building, where you enter and go up a flight of stairs to the second floor, where you see a large crystal chandelier hanging in the window. The decor here is simple but elegant, and there's a varied menu of good Arabic food. You can order meats (pork, veal, lamb, beef, chicken, and liver, to name a few) roasted, fried, or cooked on the Oriental grill; a full supper may run about NIS20 ($13.35). Hours are 10 a.m. to midnight, seven days a week.

Other Ethnic Fare

Many people have observed that Haifa is much like San Francisco, and when you enter the **Chinatown Restaurant/Café,** at 1 Haim (or Hayyim, or Weizman) Street (tel. 04-641-877), if you've been to San Francisco, you'll think this is a case of déjà vu. The building even has one of those bay windows so characteristic of San Francisco architecture, with an ambience and decor reminiscent of everybody's favorite city as well, and an outdoor garden patio. There's an extensive à la carte menu, and a special five-course lunch for NIS8.50 ($5.65), served from noon until 5 p.m. on Friday and Saturday nights you'll find live music after 10:30 p.m. If you want Chinese food to go, you can get that here too. Open seven days, from noon to midnight.

For kosher Moroccan food, and Middle Eastern food as well, there's **Ba-Ly,** 3 Ha-Nevi'im St. (tel. 04-645-242). House specialties are couscous, roasted calf, or brains à la Morocco, at NIS10 ($6.65) for a full meal, or the King's Plate of lamb, at NIS14 ($9.35). The kitchen sits between the air-conditioned dining room and the Moroccan bar on the other side, sending out tempting smells. The restaurant is open from 8 a.m. to 10 p.m., closing for the Sabbath.

And for a good Italian meal, or even just a slice of pizza to go, try **Pizzeria Rimini,** 20 Ha-Nevi'im St. (tel. 04-640-201). The Rimini's name and its appearance from the street are deceptive—it's a lot more of a restaurant than meets the eye at first glance. From the sidewalk it looks like your usual little pizza joint selling a slice to take away for NIS1.20 (80¢). A further glance reveals tables inside, but look again—you haven't seen the half of it yet. Go through this tiny dining area and up the stairs to the rear, and on the second floor you'll find a spacious, nicely decorated dining room, with music, lots of windows overlooking the street, air conditioning, and a friendly ambience. When you see the menu, you'll be surprised again: it contains not only pizza, for NIS4.50 ($3) to NIS8.50 ($5.65), but other Italian specialties as well, and even not-so-Italian meals like steak. There's a beer and wine list, and you can have a full, rich Italian dinner for about NIS15 ($10), wine, dessert, and tip included. Hours are 8 a.m. to midnight, seven days a week. By the way, take a look at the wall as you enter, and you'll see it's practically wallpapered with awards for excellence in the restaurant field, winning awards year after year.

An excellent choice for Rumanian fare is **Leon & Ioji Gratar Romanesc,** 31 Ha-Nevi'im St., near the corner of Emek Ha-Zetim (tel. 04-538-073). No more than a hole-in-the-wall on the east side of Ha-Nevi'im as you climb toward Carmel, Leon and Ioji's is a Rumanian gourmet's find. A few sidewalk tables, room for only five tables inside, a bottle-stocked bar, glass cases filled with toothsome goodies—that's all there is. Start by ordering "hok" (hock, a slightly sweet Rhine-type wine), and the waiter will bring a bottle of the light white wine and a bottle of soda water. Mix two-thirds to three-quarters of a glass of wine with one-third to one-quarter of a glass of soda—that's the Rumanian way. A real chow-down for two comes to a surprisingly low NIS13 ($8.65) to NIS15 ($10) per person. It's unbeatable. Leon & Ioji's is open from 8 a.m. to midnight every day except Friday, when it closes at 3 p.m.

Vegetarian Meals

Hearty home-cooking—vegetarian only—is featured at **Ha-Tzimhonia,** 30 Herzl St. (no phone), a bright and functional-looking restaurant that is always jam-packed with hungry locals at lunch. For less than NIS8 ($5.35) you can have a soup, fish, and vegetable lunch or supper; add a bit more if you want dessert. À la carte, a Swedish plate (cold salads) or cooked vegetable plate is NIS2.50 ($1.60). Open from 9 a.m. to 8 p.m.; closed on Friday from 1:30 p.m. until Sunday morning. By the way, Ha-Tzimhonia's name on the sign is in Hebrew only —look instead for "Vegetarian Restaurant—Dairy Farm Food." The restaurant is near the corner of Yoffe (Hillel) Street, a steps-street lined with flower stalls and snackshops.

The Falafel Center of the World

Now it's about time I pointed out Haifa's unique street corner, a falafel-fresser's vision of heaven. Shortly after noon, when the large Israeli breakfast has just begun to wear off, you'll notice a mob of people at the corner of Ha-Nevi'im and Hehalutz Streets, just a block north down the hill from Masaryk Square. Shops here do a booming business in falafel sandwiches prepared at lightning speed by experienced cooks. They stuff the essentials in the flat bread pouch, then hand it to you for the final embellishment, which you dip out of dozens of bowls set before you: tomatoes, olives, pickled beets, hot peppers, turnip and radish slices, lemon slices, shredded cabbage, tchina sauce, etc., ad infinitum. Prices are an all-time low—only about NIS1.40 (95¢). Watch to see what others are paying. These guys work on a low-margin, high-volume basis, and at Falafel Corner the munching is audible even over the pounding traffic! Don't miss it. This is Haifa for real.

Coffee and Art

This area harbors several fascinating, and fattening, coffeehouses where prices are low because you serve yourself, entertainment is cheap because it's your own conversation, and the bonus is free art shows by contemporary Israeli painters and sketchers.

For afternoon tea or a light meal, try the **Ritz Self-Service Conditoria,** 5 Haim St. (also called Hayyim, or Weizman, Street), near Nordau Street (tel. 04-662-520). An old-world sort of place, the Ritz attends to your visual as well as gustatory pleasures—there are magazines and newspapers in full supply, and there is an art gallery on the premises. The food is excellent. Sandwiches of egg or cheese, snacks such as Russian eggs, pancakes, soup, blintzes, ice cream, cakes, strudels, tortes, etc., are all available. Figure to pay about NIS4 ($2.65) for coffee and strudel. Open from 6 a.m. to 10 p.m., seven days a week.

At the air-conditioned **Beiteinu,** 29 Jerusalem St. (tel. 04-668-059), self-service is the order of the day. Salads, goulash, moussaka, gefilte fish, stuffed vegetables, schnitzel, roast beef, or liver—all served with mashed potatoes and salad—are all on the menu, but you can just as well drop in only for coffee and cake. The Beiteinu, on Jerusalem Street between Haim and Menahem Streets, is actually the cafeteria in the William Green Cultural Center, and you can tour the art exhibits before or after you have your coffee. Open daily from 11 a.m. to 8 p.m., except for Saturday when it's open from 11 a.m. until 2:30 p.m.

Sweets

If you have a sweet tooth, Hadar has many little sweet shops to tempt you.

Pinat Hatzaut (no phone), on the corner of Ha-Nevi'im and Hehalutz Streets, specializes in those Turkish pastries dripping with honey and nuts, and whatever variety is your special favorite, you'll probably find it here, with extra-large sizes of all kinds priced at only 90 agorot (60¢). There are also donuts, bagels, huge pretzels, and other treats. Open daily from 4 a.m. to midnight, closing Friday afternoon and all day Saturday.

Just a little way up from this corner, on the other side of Hehalutz Street, there's a large sweet shop selling a wide variety of chocolates and candies; a little farther up, a shop specializing in cookies; another with hot nuts and seeds; another with fresh-squeezed orange, grapefruit, and carrot juice, and so on. This little street is not only the falafel center of the world, it's also a sweet-lover's paradise.

Over on Herzl Street, near the corner of Shemaryahu Levin Street, look for **Contidory Ha'uga,** 14 Herzl St. (tel. 04-665-288), a bakery doing a lively business in every kind of baked goods, from simple rolls, bread, donuts, and cookies, up to the most artistic refrigerated confections of chocolate and whipped cream. You can get a cup of cappuccino here too, and enjoy it with a sweet, but you'll have to stand up along the coffee counter—the place is so busy, they've taken out the chairs to make room for all the customers. Hours are 8 a.m. to 8 p.m., on Friday to 3 p.m.; closed Saturday.

IN CENTRAL CARMEL: At the top of Mount Carmel, let's start our restaurant-going at the Gan Ha-Em Carmelit station on Ha-Nassi Boulevard.

Arriving by Carmelit, you come above ground on the Gan Ha-Em side of Ha-Nassi Boulevard. On the opposite side of the street, next to the entrance to the Carmelit, is a row of shops and banks fronting on the little park. Many set out sidewalk tables to catch customers, who sit there to catch sunshine.

Directly across from the Carmelit station, **The Bank,** 119 Ha-Nassi Blvd. (tel. 04-389-623), is a bright, clean, artsy restaurant on the inside, with modern art on the walls and white wicker furniture, but you can equally enjoy sitting at the sidewalk tables and watching the activity around Central Carmel. The Bank is great for light meals—pancakes, blintzes, sandwiches, salads, crêpes, cake, and cappuccino, or many kinds of ice-cream confections. Prices aren't bad, either. Open from 8 a.m. to 1 a.m., seven days a week.

Up behind here is **Krips Contidoria,** also at 119 Ha-Nassi Blvd. (tel. 04-381-717), a sweets shop with pastries, cookies, cakes, and cheesecakes too—but wait until you see the Krips chocolates! Chocolate animals of all sizes greet you at the door, with rabbits, for instance, from three inches to almost three *feet* tall! Or you could try out a life-size chocolate basketball, or special selections like cognac marzipan or truffles. You can get a cup of coffee and enjoy a pastry at one of the tables inside or out on the sidewalk. Hours are 8:30 a.m. to 8 p.m., on Friday until 2 p.m.; closed Saturday.

Head up Ha-Nassi Boulevard a few doors to no. 125 and you'll find **The Pub** (tel. 04-381-082), a popular restaurant/pub with lots of wooden tables inside as well as out on the sidewalk, modern music, and a youthful, lively atmosphere. Several kinds of draft beer come for NIS5.50 ($3.65) the liter, with cocktails also served, as well as snacks and light meals, pancakes, desserts, and ice cream. The food here costs several shekels more than at other places nearby—a cheeseburger, for example, costs NIS9 ($6)—but it's a fun place to come for a beer, with olives on the house. Open every day from 9 a.m. to 3 a.m.

Two doors up, also at 125 Ha-Nassi Blvd., **Sami Barekas** (tel. 04-389-435) is another good choice for a light snack, with good prices and snacks like poppy-seed rolls, bagels, boiled eggs, milkshakes, and Turkish sweets, in addition to the several kinds of barekas (broikas). Here again, sit inside or out on the sidewalk. Open from 6 a.m. to 9 p.m., on Friday until noon, and on Saturday after the Sabbath.

Central Carmel has its own incarnation of the **MacDavid** hamburger-stand chain at 131 Ha-Nassi Blvd. (no phone). Like the MacDavids in Tel Aviv, this one serves up convincingly delicious burgers, fries, and Cokes, with the bonus that, on a hot day, one can order a frosty bottle of beer (try that in a McDonald's!). The top-class burger, with fries and beer, will run NIS7 ($4.65) or so, but a simple hamburger and a soft drink will only cost half that amount. MacDavid is on Ha-Nassi between Wedgwood and Rabbi Elhanan Streets, open daily from 9 a.m. to 1 a.m. daily.

Very near MacDavid, right at the busy intersection of Ha-Nassi Boulevard and Wedgwood Street, is **Bagel Nosh,** 135 Ha-Nassi Blvd. (tel. 04-385-293). You'll recognize it by its sidewalk patio tables behind a little picket fence; it's pleasant indoors too, with a cozy decor of dark wooden furniture. The specialty of the house is bagels (of course), with 20 different spreads to choose from, also lox, salads, soup, omelets, desserts, ice cream, and assorted coffees, wines, beers, and milkshakes. Prices aren't bad, and it's a fun place to come for a snack and some good conversation over a "nosh plate"—bagel, butter, and salad, plus your choice of five spreads and salads for NIS7.30 ($4.85), or nine for NIS12 ($8). The breakfast special is a great deal too: omelet, vegetables, salad, bagel, butter, marmalade, cheese-spread ball, juice, plus tea or coffee, all for NIS4.60 ($3.05), served until 11:30 a.m. Hours are seven days a week from 8 a.m. to midnight, later on Friday and Saturday nights.

Now we'll cross Ha-Nassi Boulevard for some nice eateries on the other side of the boulevard. All the places I'm mentioning are within a short walk up the hill from the Carmelit station. Again, we'll start from there and walk up.

The **Chin Lung Chinese Restaurant,** 126 Ha-Nassi Blvd., near the corner of Sea Road (Derekh Ha-Yam; tel. 04-381-308), will stump you at first as there seems to be no restaurant at all behind the sign and posted menu. But go down the adjoining steps and you'll discover a nice cellar dining room with an interesting, folksy Chinese decor, done in gold and crimson, with gold tablecloths and fresh flowers. The food is mostly Szechuan style, which can be spicy but needn't be if you don't like hot food. There are 50 items to choose from here; best bargains, as always, are the set meals. Choose from among the set meals for two people and you'll pay about NIS15 ($10) per person; one of these meals is vegetarian. Beer, wine, and cocktails are served. The Chin Lung is open every day of the week, from 11:30 a.m. to 3 p.m. and again from 6:30 p.m. until midnight.

Peer Pizza Via Veneto, 130 Ha-Nassi Blvd. (tel. 04-382-333), at the corner of Mahanayim Street just before the gas station, used to be called the Peer Café-Restaurant. It still serves many Central Carmel residents as a favorite place for coffee and the morning paper. But at lunch and dinnertime the crowd calls for pizza, 14 varieties of it, and other Italian staples like spaghetti, cannelloni, and lasagne. A main-course pizza or pasta at the Peer runs about NIS5 ($3.35) to NIS8 ($5.35), which is quite moderate, as our budget goes. There's also a daily set-menu lunch and dinner special, which for NIS9 ($6) includes soup, salad, potatoes, a meat main dish (different every day), fruit salad, and coffee. Drop in anytime, from 7 a.m. to 1 a.m. in summer, 8 a.m. to midnight during the rest of the year.

Rothschild Center, on Ha-Nassi Boulevard beside the Haifa Auditorium, has a nice **self-service cafeteria** (tel. 04-387-877), open seven days a week from 9 a.m. to midnight, where you can see the wide array of soups, salads, main courses (fish, meat, or vegetarian), and desserts all laid out before you as you come down the line. It's a pleasant place, and popular too, with tables both inside and out, and prices especially low: you can get breakfast for NIS3 ($2), or a dinner or lunch of soup, a whole fish, rice, and vegetable, plus beverage, for about NIS10 ($6.65) maximum.

As Ha-Nassi Boulevard heads up past Haifa Auditorium, the street name changes to Moriah. The first right turn, a block past the auditorium, is Ha-Broshim Street. The **Restaurant Gan Rimon** (tel. 04-381-392) is at 10 Ha-Broshim, 1½ blocks from Moriah on the right-hand side. It's a quiet, shady, peaceable place to retreat from the bustle of the city for a set lunch. In fact, lunch is the only meal served. Yours might be assorted hors d'oeuvres or soup, braised beef or turkey, with potatoes and salad, and pudding or ice cream for dessert. The price, with tip, will be NIS8.50 ($5.65) for a meat course with potatoes and salad, or NIS12 ($8) for the entire set-menu lunch from hors d'oeuvres to dessert (there's a choice among three main courses); you may also choose to order from the à la carte menu. Dine inside or out under the trees on the shady patio. Remember: lunch only (closed Saturday).

In a moment I'll mention some restaurants along Ha-Nassi Boulevard and Panorama (Yefe Nof) Street that are much more elegant, and have that spectacular Panorama view—and are costlier too. But there's one place here along the "view side" of Ha-Nassi Boulevard where you can have your cake (no pun intended) and eat it too, enjoying the gorgeous view while remaining within your budget. That's at **Panorama Center,** beside the Dan Panorama Hotel. It's a modern enclosed center with several pleasant eating places, with everything from an inexpensive fast-burger counter to a dairy café and a fancy grill restaurant (all are kosher).

My recommendation here is the **Viennese Gallery** (tel. 04-352-222), on the loft balcony above the dairy self-service Café Carmel. The view is incredible from up here, and the distinctive architecture does everything to maximize the view, with a curved, two-story, 100% window wall. Unlike the café below, where you can order a full meal from the à la carte menu from NIS8 ($5.35) to NIS18 ($12), the Viennese Gallery serves mostly desserts and coffees; but although the surroundings are so fancy, prices really are quite low. You can get a gorgeous Viennese pastry with a whole pot of freshly brewed tea or coffee for NIS3.20 ($2.15), or for NIS2.50 ($1.65), the "Viennese Fantasy," a combination of as many flavors of ice cream and as many toppings as you like—you select the combinations. You'll find it open from 10 a.m. to midnight, seven days a week.

Elegant Dinners

For not too much money, you can escape the normal café-restaurant life one night and have a fine dinner in one of Haifa's better hotels and restaurants. Here are some tips.

The dining room of the **Hotel Dvir,** 124 Yefe Nof St. (tel. 04-389-131), has a set-menu, fixed-price dinner each evening except Friday for about NIS21 ($14) plus VAT (if you pay in shekels), tip, and whatever beverage you order. Sound like a lot? It's not, for what you get. Very friendly, attentive service, a dining room with a glass wall overlooking the twinkling lights of Haifa harbor, and a repast that might run like this: potage Parmentier, a mushroom omelet, roast chicken or roast lamb with ratatouille and potatoes, a salad, and "Charlotte d'Eve" for dessert. You can save money by paying in dollars or with a dollar-account credit card, and by ordering a less expensive beverage.

One of the very nicest places for an afternoon meal—and a sun and a swim —is the **Dan Carmel Hotel,** 87 Ha-Nassi Blvd. (tel. 04-386-211). Surprisingly, you can do all this relatively economically; a whole day at the swimming pool, open during the warm months, is just a few dollars for an adult, even less for a child (more on Saturday), and that includes hot showers, private deck chairs, sporting and health-club facilities, access to the adjoining gardens, and of course the pool. As for food, the poolside coffeeshop serves fish and dairy dishes, salads, cakes, and soft drinks. Prices are fair, but still geared to five-star-hotel standards; you are paying not only for the food, but for the spectacular scenery and luxury services. Buses 22 and 23 will take you to the Dan Carmel.

In another part of the Dan Carmel Hotel is a restaurant that you won't believe the first time you walk into it. It's called **Le Rondo,** and you'll see why it was named "Round" the minute you come in. Perched high above the spectacular Panorama view, the restaurant is almost completely round, with a high domed ceiling, walls completely done in glass, elegantly set tables all around the sides, and a five-star buffet laid out on a huge round table in the middle of the room. A pianist entertains on the baby grand every evening throughout the dinner hours, from 7:30 to 10:30 p.m. (Friday evening excepted). Buffet lunch is served from 12:30 to 2:30 p.m., for NIS23 ($15.35) per person, and one of the traditional specialties of the hotel is the famous Saturday Sabbath lunch buffet, for NIS25 ($16.65).

Nearby, in the **Nof Hotel,** 101 Ha-Nassi Blvd. (tel. 04-388-731), up on the penthouse floor there's a well-known **Chinese Restaurant**—and it's kosher. NIS21 ($14) to NIS27 ($18) will get you a full supper or lunch, any day from noon to 3 p.m. and again from 7 p.m. to midnight; closed Friday evening and Saturday afternoon, reopening after the Sabbath.

Another fine Chinese restaurant (but not kosher) is the **Panorama Chinese Restaurant,** 120 Panorama (Yefe Nof) St. (tel. 04-382-979), near the Dvir Hotel. You'll see the 108-item à la carte menu posted down by the sidewalk, and even if you decide to have one of the ample fixed-menu meals, priced at NIS10 ($6.65) or NIS18 ($12) per person, you'll still probably take a while to decide what to choose for a main course among all the Chinese specialties of chicken, beef, or pork prepared with things like sweet-and-sour or spicy sauce, vegetables, nuts, pineapple, ginger, spring onion, green peppers, and so on. While considering your choice, climb the long flight of stairs up from the road to the crimson-decorated dining room perched way up on the hill, with that wonderful view. It's open every day, from noon until midnight.

Our final elegant restaurant selections do not have that panoramic view, located as they are right at the heart of Central Carmel, across from the Carmelit station. But their special cuisine and rich decor still make them fine choices. You'll find them one above the other, at 119 Ha-Nassi Blvd.

First, there's **La Trattoria Chez Edy** (tel. 04-382-020), specializing in gourmet French and Italian meals, and Tunisian couscous. The Italian choices are the least expensive, with eight pasta meals priced at NIS8 ($5.35) to NIS10 ($6.65), or 14 pizza selections from NIS5.50 ($3.65) to NIS11 ($7.35). The French meals, costing more like NIS25 ($16.65), are known for their fine gourmet sauces. If you like couscous, choose couscous tunisien (meat and meatball) for NIS16.50 ($11), or royal couscous (meat, meatball, spicy sausage, and chicken) for NIS21 ($14). There's also an extensive wine and dessert list from which to choose. Open seven days from noon to midnight; it's recommended to call for reservations.

Upstairs, **Caty's House** (tel. 04-389-618) is a small glatt kosher restaurant also serving couscous and French cuisine. The specialty here is bouillabaisse Marseilles, which for NIS26 ($17.35) is a complete meal. Another specialty here is fish; you might want to try, for example, a meal of St. Peter's fish from the Sea of Galilee, with mushrooms and garlic sauce, for NIS20 ($13.35). Open Saturday to Thursday from 4 p.m. to midnight.

An Exceptional Bargain

For an exceptionally low-cost meal—in exceptional surroundings—take bus 24 or 37 from Central Carmel to the campus of the **University of Haifa.** The bus ride will cost some shekels, but the view from the campus—situated, as one person said, "at the top of the world"—is worth a million. On the campus you can have breakfast, lunch, dinner, or a snack at any of the several kosher cafés. You don't have to be a student—guests of all ages are welcome—but you do pay student prices: three-course meals for around NIS5 ($3.35), and they're generous ones (soup, chicken, beef, or shishlik, vegetables, and dessert). These three-course menus are served from 11:30 a.m. till 3 p.m. in the main building's Golden Cafeteria. There's also a dairy cafeteria, open from 8:30 a.m. to 3:30 p.m., which is even less expensive: for a lunch of salad, a hot pita sandwich, and coffee, you'll pay NIS3 ($2) at the very most, with a sweet roll or cheese sandwich for only NIS1 (65¢). Down in the Terrace Building is another, similar cafeteria, and also a student coffeehouse/pub open from 10 a.m. until 2 a.m. every day, with a free disco dance every Thursday night from 10 p.m. on. The Multi-Purpose Building has some nice cafés too.

Similar food bargains are to be found at the campus of **Technion City,** at the many student-priced cafeterias around the campus and at Bet Student, the Technion's Student Association house.

RESTAURANTS DOWN BY THE PORT: Down along the waterfront is the guts of the city of Haifa: the raucous, bustling port, the warehouses and ships' chandlers, the Customs brokers and truckers and trainmen. A healthy sense of everyday work and business fills the district, and all is no-nonsense, purposeful activity.

It's doubtful that you'll spend a lot of time sightseeing down here, but you'll want to come down and have a look, and when you do that you should also avail yourself of the opportunity to lunch or dine in one of the port's many good Arabic restaurants or market eateries.

Many of the most interesting restaurants are right near the port end of the Carmelit subway line, at Paris Square (Kikar Paris), so we'll start here. If you're not coming by Carmelit, find Paris Square where Jaffa Road (Derekh Yafo) changes names and becomes Ha-Palyam Street, at the intersection with Khatib and Eliya Streets.

Near Paris Square

After you exit from the Carmelit station in Paris Square, walk around to your right. Behind the station and across the street are a few Arabic restaurants, all in a row. All the way to the left is **Abu Yusuf,** 1 Ha-Meginim St. (tel. 04-663-723). The sign is in Hebrew and Arabic only, but if you peek through the door there's no mistaking it: big windows, high arches, bare tables filled with Arab and Druze workmen, and the general atmosphere of a railway station without the trains. The food tends toward the Lebanese, with kubbeh, hummus with meat, grilled heart (delicious!), roast chicken. Have kubbeh (or kibbeh), hummus, eggplant salad, fool beans, and a shot ("jot") of anise-flavored arak brandy, and two people will pay about NIS9 ($6) to NIS12 ($8) each. Abu Yusuf offers fresh fish and grilled lamb dishes too, and has won awards several years in a row. Open every day from 7 a.m. to midnight, except Friday, when it closes at 4 p.m.

On the other corner of the row, over at the right, is the **Salah Brothers Restaurant,** 5 Ha-Meginim St. (tel. 04-640-763). That's what it says in Hebrew on the arched yellow neon sign over the door, but if you don't read Hebrew, look for the word "Queen's," which is actually not the name of the restaurant but the name of a drink it serves. Either way, you'll probably smell the delicious aromas wafting out into the street. Prices are similar at all of these Arabic restaurants; you can get a full meal from the à la carte menu, from the soup and salad to the after-dinner coffee and dessert, for NIS15 ($10) to NIS23 ($15.35), depending on the main dish you order, from chicken to grilled lamb. Open from 7:30 a.m. to 2 a.m. seven days a week.

Restaurant Zvi, 3 Ha-Meginim St. (tel. 04-668-596), is located between the two aforementioned restaurants. It has a bit wider variety than the other two, specializing in seafood, European, Middle Eastern, and Yiddish cuisines. Lobster, shrimp, and calamari all come for NIS7 ($4.65) to NIS11 ($7.35) on the à la carte menu; there's also a special tourist menu, which for NIS12 ($8) offers soup or salad; choice of steak, schnitzel, kebab, or chicken; soda or beer; and coffee or tea. Open every day from 11 a.m. to 11 p.m.

My favorite feature of all the above restaurants is that when you come in the door, you're greeted by a huge salad bar, with at least 16 (or more) kinds of colorful and tasty salads to choose from—take your pick, mix them up as much as you like. I love the challenge of trying to taste a tiny bite of every one.

In the Market

Let's venture into the throbbing produce market now to find some eateries favored by people who work here. Go out the door of the Paris Carmelit station, then left and almost immediately right onto Eliyahu Ha-Navi Street, Eliya Street for short. **Naim's** is on the left, the first restaurant on the street at no. 6 Eliyahu Ha-Navi (tel. 04-640-309). Steaming bowls of vegetable soup, meat baked with okra, roast lamb or veal, even duck with rice—all send their tempting smells out from this tiny place, not to mention the exotic smells of grilling hearts, kidneys, and lamb testicles. You can pop in just for a steaming bowl of soup, for NIS3 ($2), or a full meal of soup, salad, meat main dish, coffee, and dessert for about NIS15 ($10). Not much atmosphere—or even elbow room—just good food. Open every day from 6:30 a.m. until 9 p.m.

A couple of doors down from Naim's, on the corner of a little passageway leading into the market, is another enormously popular place, **Restaurant Abu Hani** (no phone). If you're here around lunchtime (or anytime, actually), you're likely to find it packed with people, and since it's a small place with only a few chairs inside, many of the munchers will be standing around inside or out on the sidewalk. The attraction here again is delicious food at a good price. You can get a hot shishlik sandwich for NIS3.50 ($2.35), a falafel for NIS1.20 (80¢), and a soda pop for NIS1 (65¢). Open daily from 8 a.m. to 4 p.m., closing for the Sabbath.

You'll see many falafel and snack stands all around the **market district.** If you feel like getting some picnic fixings, fresh fruits, vegetables, fish, meats, or anything else at great prices, just wander around the narrow market streets and you'll probably find what you're looking for. To get there, go down the little passageway to one side of the Abu Hani restaurant mentioned above; you can also enter from Jaffa (Yafo) or Ha-Atzma'ut Roads. Once you're there, you'll know you're in the right spot, as you squeeze among the crowds of people buying and bargaining in the tiny alleyways. It's a pleasure and an adventure to buy your groceries here.

A Fancier Place

About four blocks northwest of Paris Square along Jaffa Road (Derekh Yafo) brings you to Ha-Bankim Street. Up this short street on the left at no. 7 is the **Shmulik and Dany Restaurant** (tel. 04-514-411). Deservedly popular for its first-class traditional home-style Jewish cuisine, Shmulik and Dany's walls display awards for excellence and glowing newspaper reviews, along with Shmulik's collection of Israeli art. The bright, bold colors of the modern decor are quite a change from the bare market eateries, and yet this is not really an expensive place. For NIS15 ($10) you can feast on soup or something such as stuffed cabbage, then a Viennese schnitzel, or roast beef, or roast chicken breast with mushrooms, plus a soft drink. The renowned roast duck is a bit—but only a bit—costlier. Shmulik and Dany is open for lunch only, every day but Saturday, from 11:30 a.m. to 4 p.m. When you arrive here, you'll see the sign, but no restaurant; walk up the stairs to the second floor and you'll know you're there when you see all the happy eaters.

Another place, fancier still, is **Me & Me,** 17 Ben-Gurion Blvd. (tel. 04-522-093), right at the corner of Ben-Gurion and Ha-Meginim. This is a classy restaurant and bar that will break your budget—a full supper of, let's say, filet mignon or chateaubriand, including wine and all, will come to NIS60 ($40) or NIS70

($46.65) for a couple—but you might like to come for a drink at the bar and enjoy the ambience, the pianist on the baby grand, or the dinner-dancing on Friday nights. Open every day from 11 a.m. to midnight, on Friday till 2 a.m.

For Dessert

The **Exodus Conditoria,** 31 Ha-Atzma'ut Rd. (tel. 04-669-072), is just the place for a light breakfast, afternoon tea, or dessert after lunch. The glass cases are crammed with delicious croissants, chocolate cakes, pastries, strudels, cream cakes, and the like. Coffee and tea are served, prices are fatteningly low (that is, you're tempted to go for another serving), and hours are 8 a.m. to 7 p.m., except Friday when they close at 2 p.m., and Saturday when they're closed all day. Note that this is a *conditoria,* not a cafeteria, so it's a pastry shop. Coffee and pastry won't cost more than $2.50. The Exodus is down the street from the American Consular Agency, on Ha-Atzma'ut near the intersection with Eliyahu Ha-Navi Street (that's the vegetable and fruit market street).

Another good bakery in the downtown area is **Hershko Melekh,** which, although the address is 21 Asfor St. (no phone), can be found by walking down Ha-Meginim Street until you're directly across from the Italian church; by this time you will smell the bread baking, and you can just follow your nose to find it (the sign outside is in Hebrew only). This is not so much a sweets shop as it is a bakery for bagels, rolls, pretzels with onions and spices, or pizza. Prices here are good, and you stand an excellent chance of walking in to find something coming piping hot out of the oven—couldn't be any fresher than that. Another plus is that, no matter when you come, you're sure to find it open—it's baking away 24 hours a day. This, too, is a popular place with locals in the know.

IN THE BUS AND TRAIN STATIONS: Right in the Egged Bus Station in Bat Galim is the **Egged Restaurant,** not the most romantic place to dine, but just right for a cheap, filling meal before or after a long bus journey. There's a full set-price menu for lunch, with soup, chicken or meat course, vegetable, and dessert. Open from 7 a.m. to 4 p.m.; closed Saturday.

Over in the Bat Galim railway station is **Olamei Hod,** a cheerful and air-conditioned restaurant with tables covered in colorful prints and flowers in vases. Try it for set-price breakfasts or lunches. Open from 5 a.m. to 7 p.m., closing early on Friday and all day Saturday.

IN BAT GALIM: Bat Galim means "Daughter of the Waves" in Hebrew, and you'll know how it got its name when you stroll along its beachfront promenade and see the turquoise waves crashing along the rocks. Although Bat Galim is really a residential suburb, you might find yourself coming here for a dip at one of its beaches or at the public pool, a stroll along the waterfront promenade, or a good time at one of its nice restaurants, pubs, or discos. And if you take a ride on the aerial cable car going between the beach and Mount Carmel, at the lower terminal you'll be right at the end of Bat Galim. The restaurants I'll mention are all within about a five-minute walk from there.

If you're not reaching Bat Galim from the cable-car terminal, you can easily walk over from the main bus or train stations—Bat Galim is located behind the stations. If you're at the Central Bus Station and want to walk, go through the underground tunnel which connects it to the train station; when you come out of the train station, you'll be in Bat Galim. You can also take buses 40, 41, 42, and 44, which go from the bus station to the cable-car terminal; or if you're driving, come across at Hel Ha-Yam, the main boulevard running just east of the bus station.

All the places listed below are within a short distance of one another, on or near Bat Galim Avenue, a short divided boulevard leading directly to the sea, and the waterfront promenade right in front of it. Let's say you're standing at the intersection where Bat Galim Avenue meets the promenade; I'll give you directions from there.

Note: All these restaurants are open seven days a week.

The first place you'll notice is the **Pagoda Chinese Restaurant,** 1 Bat Galim Ave. (tel. 04-524-585), right there on the corner. In a converted seaside house, the Pagoda sports the Chinese lamps, crimson this-and-that, and fresh flowers you might expect. It's owned and operated by the same friendly family that runs the Chin Lung Restaurant on Ha-Nassi Boulevard in Central Carmel (see above), so you know the service will be fine and the food equally so; also, that the food will be Szechuan style. There's no fixed menu here, only à la carte, but there's a wide selection and the prices aren't too high. You can get a full four-course meal, with tea, for around NIS15 ($10) or so, but you can always just pop in for a plate of chow mein too, and pay much less. It's open from noon to 3 p.m. for lunch, and again from 7 p.m. to midnight.

Just across on the other corner you'll see **Misadag** (tel. 04-524-441). This agreeably rustic fish and seafood restaurant is more expensive, but it also has food that you won't find elsewhere, with salt- or freshwater fish prepared in the styles of Provence, Paris, Tunisia, and Italy, to name a few, and an equal number of tempting shrimp and seafood dishes. House specialties are fish in sour cream and garlic sauce, and shrimp with cucumbers, mushrooms, and almonds. You can get filet mignon, if you like, as well. Prices for a full meal, including wine, dessert, and all the trimmings, can run about NIS35 ($23.35) to NIS40 ($26.65), about NIS10 ($6.65) less if you forgo the wine. Open daily from noon to 4 p.m. and 7 p.m. to midnight.

A couple of doors down, at 2 Bat Galim Ave., is a much different kind of place. It's called **Chipsbopo** (no phone), and you'll recognize it by the colorful landscape painted up over the wide doorway, the wooden tables both inside and out, and the friendly pub atmosphere. This is the place to come if you're looking for a simple, inexpensive bite to eat: a hamburger or hot dog, with fries and a salad, costs NIS4 ($2.65). You can get a liter of draft beer for NIS5 ($3.35), or half a liter for half the price. It's open daily from 10 a.m. to midnight.

For another elegant fish and seafood restaurant, go one block inland to the **Dolphin,** 13 Bat Galim Ave. (tel. 04-523-837). Here again, prices are higher but so is the quality: an entire meal of soup, Greek salad, shrimp, vegetables, bread, dessert, coffee, and wine, runs about NIS30 ($20). Open daily from noon to midnight, except for Friday when it closes briefly between 4 and 6:30 p.m.

Back down on the promenade near our corner starting point, just a few doors north of the Pagoda, there's an excellent restaurant called **Shipodi Ha-Tikva,** 19 Pinhas Margolin St., at the corner of Avdimi Street (tel. 04-535-205), and although the sign is in Hebrew only, you can't miss it, with its brick fountain and cast-iron railings. If you like to see what you're getting before you order it, this is the place for you. You can serve yourself from the abundant and colorful salad bar, filling your plate with as many of the 18 varieties of salads as you can squeeze onto it for only NIS4 ($2.65). Beside the salad bar is a refrigerated case with meats on display, most already on the skewer and ready to pop onto the charcoal grill; choose from all kinds of lamb, chicken, beef, and veal. Have a baklava or chocolate mousse with a cup of coffee for dessert, and the entire full, rich meal will cost about NIS15 ($10). There's a full bar here too, with beer on tap. You'll enjoy the clean dining room, the view of the promenade, and the air conditioning in summer, heat in winter. Open daily from noon to 1 a.m.

Walking the other way now, up along the promenade toward the cable-car terminal, on your left you'll pass a black-and-white pub/piano bar with an archway over the door. Though you won't be able to read the sign unless you read Hebrew, you'll know it's **Panass Boded** (tel. 04-534-978) by the entertainment listings posted out front. If you're walking by in the daytime though, you'll find it closed; this is a nightspot, open from about 7 p.m. until about 4 a.m. seven days a week.

By now you'll have noticed an interesting structure just a little way out into the sea—an old passenger ship which has been converted into a restaurant, bar, terrace café, and disco dance floor. It's called **Hasfinah** (tel. 04-539-000), and to reach it you walk out a short gangplank to the little stone-and-sand island constructed especially for the boat to sit on. None of the food here is cheap, but it's not too expensive either, and it's worth an extra shekel to enjoy the unique surroundings. The menu lists a variety of light meals, including omelets, blintzes, soups, and salads; one set "promotional menu" of soup or salad, fish and chips, beer or soft drink, and coffee, all for NIS15 ($10); and an assortment of ice-cream dishes and desserts. The café by day becomes a different place by night: from about 9 p.m. on, there's music and dancing. A cover charge of NIS10 ($6.65), including the first drink, is charged only on Friday nights, when it's a popular discothèque with the young folks; other nights, the music varies. Open daily from 9 a.m. to 2 a.m.

Keep on along the promenade and soon you'll come to the lower cable-car terminal, from which you can ascend to Stella Maris up on Mount Carmel. Both the lower and upper terminals have nice restaurants and bars.

4. What to Do and See

I'll group the major sights according to the three main sections of the city. But before setting out, you would be well advised to check with the **Haifa Municipality Information Offices**, the **Israel Government Tourist Office (I.G.T.O.)**, and the 24-hour **tourist information hotline**, "What's On in Haifa" (tel. 04-640-840), for additional information.

Many of Haifa's museums are open free of charge on Saturday (Haifa Museum is an exception), so you might want to schedule your museum visits for that day; other days, you can get a 72-hour pass good at all the municipally run museums for NIS3 ($2); check the museum section for details.

HAIFA TOURS: For a free 2½-hour guided walking tour of Central Carmel (atop the mountain), get up, have breakfast, and be at the signposted meeting point by 10 a.m. any Saturday morning. The meeting point, marked by a sign, is on Panorama Road (Yefe Nof) at the intersection with Shar Ha-Levanon; Ha-Levanon is the little street that meets Ha-Nassi right behind the Gan Ha-Em Carmelit station. Ha-Nassi curves and heads northwest behind the Carmelit station. Don't curve with it, keep going straight—that's Shar Ha-Levanon, and Panorama Road (Yefe Nof) is a short block down. To come by bus, you can take bus 23 from Ha-Nevi'im Street, or bus 21 from Herzl Street, both in Hadar; they both run on Saturday (note that the Carmelit subway does not).

Mitspa Tours, 1 Nordau St. (tel. 04-674-341 or 674-342), is a local company offering two tours, priced at NIS15 ($10) each, to take you around the environs of Haifa. There's the "Five Religions" tour, visiting religious sites in and near Haifa, and another tour covering many places nearby. Call for details.

Some of the large tour companies also offer tours which include Haifa; you can check with them directly for info.

SIGHTSEEING IN HAIFA: Those preliminary notes out of the way, I now introduce you to Haifa, Israel's major port, world center of the Baha'i faith, cultural and commercial capital of Galilee and the north.

In Hadar

As I've noted before, Hadar Ha-Carmel is the business section of Haifa, located halfway between the lower (port) town and the Central Carmel residential section.

Herzl Street—Main Street of Haifa: You'll want to stroll here just to catch the bustling flavor of this busy shopping street. All manner of things are available for refreshment on Herzl Street. During the season, entrepreneurs set up big vats of boiling water and sell you fresh ears of corn wrapped in their husks. Other exotica for the palate: falafel, carrot juice, watermelons, inexpensive fruit punch, and plain soda (gazoz)—a wide choice of snacks to sustain yourself while window shopping.

At 20 Herzl St. you'll find the **Israel Government Tourist Office,** a storehouse of information on hotels, tour possibilities, and special events. They also publish a pamphlet telling you what's doing the week you're in Israel. Take one, and you may discover some special concert or art exhibit that you hadn't heard about. Also be sure to ask about new sights and sites, data, and entertainment in and around the Haifa area. I.G.T.O. is open from 8:30 a.m. to 5 p.m. daily except Friday, when it closes at 2 p.m. Closed on Saturday, of course.

Old Technion: Turn right on Balfour, walk up the hill more or less behind the Tourist Office, and you'll find the entrance to the Old Technion campus, on the right, still very much in use. (The new, modern Technion campus, in Carmel, will be discussed later.) This old campus no longer houses students and classes, all of which have been moved up to the Technion City campus in Carmel.

The Old Technion campus is being developed as a museum site, home of the **Technoda—the National Museum of Science and Technology** (tel. 04-671-372). The approach to exhibits here is definitely an active one: they're working models, designed to stimulate the curiosity of young people in particular, but actually of interest to all ages. Exhibits include such common devices as the car, elevator, toilet, solar water heater, and airplane, showing how all these things do what they do; more sophisticated, but equally easy to understand, exhibits include demonstrations of laser technology and mathematical principles. Plans are in the works for a space gallery, including a planetarium, and you'll likely find other attractions as well by the time you arrive.

Technoda museum hours are Monday, Wednesday, and Thursday from 9 a.m. to 5 p.m., on Tuesday to 7 p.m., on Friday to 1 p.m., and on Saturday from 10 a.m. to 2 p.m.; closed Sunday. Admission is NIS4 ($2.65) for adults, NIS3 ($2) for children, students, soldiers, or seniors, or NIS10 ($6.65) per family. All of the Hadar buses (nos. 18, 19, 21, 28, 37, 42, and 50) come nearby.

Both old and new Technion comprise Israel's equivalent of M.I.T., offering courses in all phases of engineering—chemical, industrial, agricultural, electrical, mechanical, civil—as well as in architecture, town planning, nuclear science, aeronautics, electronics, and metallurgy. The faculty totals in excess of 1,500 persons.

The original Technion building looks like an ancient Turkish palace, and there's a very good reason for that. In 1913 a group of German benefactors, non-Zionist Jews who were running schools in Palestine, decided to establish a training ground for Jewish engineers who would work for the sultan of Turkey, then ruler of Palestine. (The Germans built all sorts of things for the Turks in the Middle East—hospitals, roads, mosques, factories—and when countries were

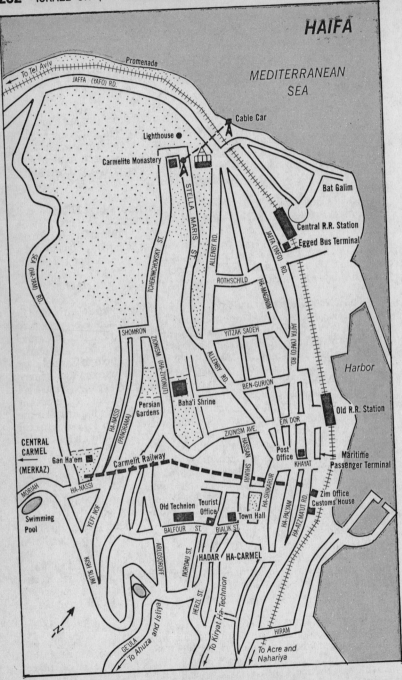

choosing sides in the First World War, Turkey naturally sided with Germany, the architects and engineers of the Ottoman Empire. But Turkey picked the losing side, and lost the entire Middle East when the League of Nations gave England the Mandate for the previously Turkish-occupied Palestine.) The handsome *Arabian Nights* palace, now the Technion building, was constructed —but never put to use—by the German group.

What happened was a language problem. The German donors insisted that German, the classic language of science and technology, be the language of instruction. But the Jewish engineering students, ardent Zionists, insisted that Hebrew be the language of instruction. As a result, the students refused to attend classes, and the staff walked out: a complete stalemate—and then the war came. The abandoned Technion became first a delousing station, then a meat slaughterhouse, a hospital, and a target for artillery shells. In 1925 the school was renovated, and more buildings were constructed; ultimately the eight acres of midtown campus became hemmed in by Haifa's growing business and residential district, which didn't permit the campus to expand any further in Hadar. Hence, the "new" Technion City in Carmel.

Baha'i Shrine: Haifa's most impressive sightseeing attraction is the splendid **Baha'i Shrine and Gardens,** reached from Zionism (Ha-Ziyonut) Avenue (take bus 22 from the port, or bus 23 or 25 from Hadar). Haifa is international headquarters for the Baha'i faith, which began in Persia in the mid-19th century in a bloodbath of persecution.

The Baha'i leaders were exiled to the Ottoman Empire in 1863, and much of the Baha'i doctrine was then formulated in the Holy Land. The immaculate, majestic Baha'i gardens—with their stone peacocks and eagles, and delicately manicured cypress trees—are a restful, aesthetic memorial to the founders of this faith. Baha'i leaders claim some 4 million adherents all over the world, with fast-growing numbers in newly developed countries. In the States, there's a white-domed nine-sided Baha'i Temple on the shores of Lake Michigan, at Wilmette, just outside Chicago.

Baha'is believe in the brotherhood of all men, a common world language, and the unity of all religions. They see the leaders of the different religions—Christ, Buddha, Mohammed, Moses—as messengers of God, sent at different times in history with doctrines varying to fit changing social needs, but all preaching substantially the same message. The most recent of these heavenly teachers, according to Baha'is, was Bahaullah. He was exiled by the Turkish authorities to Acre, wrote his doctrines there, and died a peaceful death in Bahji House (which you should visit) just north of Acre.

In the Haifa Gardens, the huge domed shrine entombs the remains of the Bab, the Bahaullah's herald. It is open to visitors from 9 a.m. to noon daily; you must remove your shoes before entering. The tomb is a sight to see—with ornamental goldwork and flowers in almost every nook and cranny. The Bab's remains, incidentally, were hidden for years after he died a martyr's death in front of a firing squad. Eventually, however, his followers secretly carried his remains to the Holy Land. The gardens are open until 5 p.m. Admission is free.

On a higher hilltop stands the Corinthian-style **Baha'i International Archives** building, modeled after the Parthenon, and the **Universal House of Justice,** with 58 marble columns and hanging gardens behind. These are business buildings, not open to tourists. They, and the shrine of the tomb of the Bab, all face toward Acre, the burial place of Bahaullah.

All the beautiful grounds that you see were planned by Shoghi Effendi, the late Guardian of the Faith. In addition to curious tourists, you'll see pilgrims who have come from all parts of the world to pay homage to the first leaders of this universal faith. (Incidentally, at the entrance to the shrine you will be given a pamphlet providing further details on Baha'i history and doctrine).

Mitzpoor Ha-Shalom (Peace View Park): The grounds of the Baha'i Gardens are split by Zionism Avenue. Farther up the hill on Zionism Avenue is the lovely Mitzpoor Ha-Shalom (Peace View Park), also called the **Ursula Malbin Sculpture Garden,** at the corner of Shnayim Be-November Street. Amid trees, flowers, and sloping lawns are 18 bronze sculptures by Ursula Malbin of men, women, children, and animals at play. The view from here is magnificent—on a clear day you can see all of Haifa's port area, Haifa Bay, Akko, Nahariya, and up to Rosh Ha-Niqra at the Lebanese border, plus the mountains all around. Entrance is free.

Central Carmel

Carmel means "Vineyard of the Lord"—from the two Hebrew words, "Kerem-El"—and this merging of the religious and agricultural is most appropriate in view of the fact that a great religious trial once took place on this fertile hilltop chain: the confrontation of the vengeful prophet Elijah with the idolators of Baal (I Kings 17–18).

You'd never know there was anything but utter tranquility up here, because the range is an area of gentle breezes and wooded ravines, its sloping hills dotted with white homes. Each of Carmel's houses has a spritely little garden, and almost every one of them has a view of the Mediterranean. To Carmel residents, the sight of a flaming orange sun dipping into the sea at six o'clock is almost commonplace. The pace here is leisurely, the air clear, the skies blue and sunny, the view magnificent. You can readily see why the citizens of Carmel are so chauvinistic about their neighborhood.

Haifa also boasts Israel's largest **national park**—25,000 acres of pine, eucalyptus, and cypress forest. It encompasses a large area of the Carmel mountain range, and contains many points of interest that are well marked and easily reachable. And, of course, it also has picnic areas, playgrounds, a restaurant, etc. Take bus 37 to get to it.

Technion City: Technion—the Israel Institute of Technology—is Israel's version of M.I.T. Its 300-acre campus in the Carmel hills is one of Israel's major showplaces. Begun in 1954, it now consists of 50 buildings, including 12 dormitories, a wind-tunnel laboratory, and the Churchill Auditorium. All in all, it's a most impressive university complex, and the view of the city, the bay, the coastline clear to Lebanon, and the snow-topped Syrian mountains is simply superb. Most important, the reputation of the school has grown so rapidly that, like many of the world's leading scientific institutions, it attracts students from many foreign countries—you'll see them strolling on the campus.

Since so many people from all over the world come to see and to seek information about the Technion, the **Coler-California Visitor Center** (tel. 04-210-664 or 210-668) has been established to introduce the campus to visitors, and it's really worth a visit. You'll be greeted by a real live robot when you come in. There's a free 25-minute film shown at 9 a.m., 11 a.m., and 1 p.m., showing the different kinds of modern technology being practiced, researched, and taught here. You'll also receive a pamphlet and map of the campus, which you can use to take your own self-guided tour. Both the visitor center and the student-priced cafeteria downstairs (highly recommendable for a good budget lunch) are open Sunday through Thursday from 8 a.m. to 2 p.m., on Friday until noon; closed Saturday. Admission is always free.

Many entertainment activities are held every evening (except Monday) at

Bet Student, the Technion's Student House (tel. 04-234-148). Call during the daytime for info on folk, disco, and '60s dancing, films, and other activities. You can also stop in at Bet Student's pub, cafeteria, or restaurant, to have a good meal at student prices, NIS4.50 ($3) or less.

To reach the Technion, take bus 17 from the Central Bus Station, bus 31 from Central Carmel, or bus 19 from Hadar at Daniel Street, next to the Armon Cinema on Ha-Nevi'im Street just down from Masaryk Square.

University of Haifa: On the road from Haifa to the nearby Druze village of Daliat-el-Carmel you'll see the buildings and tower of the University of Haifa, a sprawling, somewhat sensational educational center. Designed by world-famous architect Niemeier, the university began operation in 1963, under the joint auspices of the City of Haifa and the Hebrew University. At that time, the students numbered 650, now 9,000 (regular and extension), and today the university offers Bachelor of Arts programs in some 31 departments as well as Masters of Art, Ph.D.'s, and other graduate programs.

Covering fully 200 acres, the campus is well worth a visit. The view is magnificent as are the architecture and the art. From the 30th (top) floor of the tower, which you can visit anytime, you get an incredible view of practically the entire north of Israel, on a clear day.

There's a surprising amount of art everywhere you look around the campus; all the university's public spaces were designed by the Department of Fine Arts, and it shows. Especially notable are the large murals located in the university lobby.

The campus's several art galleries are not to be missed. Up on the tower's 30th floor, the **Oscar Ghez Gallery** houses a moving memorial collection of works by artists who perished in the Holocaust, compiled by Mr. Ghez over a 30-year period. In the main part of the university, the **University of Haifa Gallery** and the **Regina Helm Sculpture Gallery** display important works by Israeli and foreign artists.

The **Reuben and Edith Hecht Museum of the Archeology of the Land of Israel** is one of Israel's best-planned museums, with a large number of exhibits, complete with interesting and informative explanations, on all aspects of Israel's archeological heritage.

The art galleries, and the museum, are open Sunday through Thursday from 10 a.m. until 1 p.m. The galleries are also open on Tuesday until 4 p.m.; the museum has Tuesday-afternoon hours from 4 to 6 p.m., and Saturday hours from 10 a.m. to 1 p.m.

Free guided tours of the museum and the campus are available, but you must call in advance to reserve a spot. Museum tours are held Sunday through Thursday at noon, on Tuesday at 5 p.m., and on Saturday at 11:30 a.m.; call 04-240-577 to make the arrangements. Tours of the entire campus are held every day at noon; call the university information numbers (tel. 04-246-445, 240-098, or 255-478) to sign up.

If you want a bite to eat, you can get a great bargain at any of the kosher student cafeterias around campus. There's a meat cafeteria, a dairy cafeteria, a pub, and several snackbars; you'll find more details on these under restaurants in the section called "An Exceptional Bargain"—and they really are.

The Haifa University Students Association sponsors many activities throughout the week, including movies, disco, folk dancing, and more. Call the Students Association (tel. 04-240-513 or 240-519) during office hours, 8 a.m. to 3 p.m., for information on these and other activities.

Regular bus and sherut service connects the university with many parts of Haifa; from downtown, take bus 24 or 37.

Stella Maris: Ha-Nassi Boulevard and Tchernichovsky Street go northwest to the Stella Maris French Carmelite church, monastery, and hospice (P.O. Box 9047; tel. 04-523-460). Situated on Stella Maris Road, across the street from the Old Lighthouse, with a magnificent view of the sea, the monastery served as a hospital for Napoleon's soldiers during his unsuccessful siege of Acre in 1799. The pyramid in front of the church entryway stands as a memorial to these soldiers, bearing the inscription "How are the mighty fallen in battle," from King David's lamentation over Saul and Jonathan (II Samuel 1).

The church, open daily from 8:30 a.m. to 1:30 p.m. and again from 3 to 6 p.m., is a beautiful structure, with Italian marble so brightly and vividly patterned that visitors sometimes mistakenly think the walls have been painted. Colorful paintings on the dome, done by Bro. Luigi Poggi (1924–1928), a lay brother of the Carmelite order, depict episodes from the Old Testament, the most dramatic being the scene of Elijah swept up in a chariot of fire; also notable is the statue of the Virgin Mary, carved from Cedar of Lebanon. The cave situated below the altar, which you can walk down into, is believed to have been inhabited by Elijah.

Be sure to visit the rooms to the right of the entryway, where you'll find a charming Nativity scene, a museum with artifacts from the Byzantine church occupying this same spot before the Carmelites built here, and other historical finds, and a small souvenir shop.

One of the brown-robed monks will gladly give you a free pamphlet with information about the history of this site, and of the Carmelite order, dating back to the arrival of the Crusaders on this mountain in the late 12th century. They will answer any questions you may have, and guide you around to point out the various interesting details of the church—for example, the many little votive candles burning on the altar above the cave, each representing a Carmelite community in another country (the United States has its candle up on the left).

Masses are said in English every morning at 6:30 a.m., and on Sunday at 7 and 9 a.m. Modest dress is required to enter the church.

Residential Districts: Most of Haifa's middle- and upper-middle-class residents live in five main areas of Carmel: Neve Shanaan Ramat Ramez, the Merkaz section, Ahuza, French Carmel, and Danya.

Neve Shanaan is a typical Israeli *shikun*, a housing project, complete with stereotyped apartments, play areas for children, and a small shopping center. The living quarters in these buildings are fairly small, but very light and airy, with a balcony patio for each one of them. You reach Neve Shanaan by winding upward, climbing in the direction of the new Technion. The road is serpentine, and foot by foot you'll find yourself mounting higher and higher over the city of Haifa. (Bus 15, 16, 17, 18, or 19.)

Merkaz is central Carmel, last stop on the Carmelit. It's the smallest of the three large shopping areas in Haifa, and you'll find here banks and shops, a supermarket and outdoor café, a zoo, a Rothschild community house, Haifa Auditorium, the new Panorama Center, several museums and parks, and a main square with a road branching off into four different directions on Carmel. (All the 20 buses, plus 30, 31, 37, 91, and 92.)

Ahuza is the last stop on the Haifa bus line (21, 22, 23, 24, 28, 37), and it's the swanky, northernmost part of town. Many homes here are villa-size, each strategically built on the side of a hill with a view.

French Carmel is a middle-class residential area above the lighthouse and Carmelite Monastery. (Buses 25, 30, 31.)

Danya is a relatively new, exclusive neighborhood skirting the top of Carmel. New villas are rising all the time here, some architecturally startling. (Bus 39.)

An Arabic community is also located on Carmel—**Kababir,** with about 700 people, a fine view, and a lovely new mosque (the round white building). (Bus 34.)

In the Port

Theodore Herzl wrote, "If there is a will, it will not be a dream." For thousands of refugees who had the will to make their way to the Promised Land, arrival at the port of Haifa was a dream come true.

Independence Road (Rehov Ha-Atzma'ut): This is the main street in the port area. The seaward side of the street is thickly clustered with rather battered four-story buildings, each housing a shop on its street level and business offices above. Across the street is an assortment of cafés, a post office, a police station, and a few other shops.

Nearby, on Jaffa Road, is the old railway station, still functioning; the main terminal is to the northwest in Bat Galim.

Next to the old Mercaz railroad station is the **Dagon Grain Silo,** and a unique silo it is. At the entrance facing Kikar Plumer, you'll find a fascinating little museum known as the **Archeological Museum of Grain Handling in Israel.** On display are earthen storage jars, striking mosaic murals, and various exhibits showing the development of one of man's oldest industries—the cultivation, handling, storage, and distribution of grain. There are even some grains of wheat here over 4,000 years old—as well as fertility statues and flint grain sickles. The exhibit traces the course of history in this land from 12,000 B.C., the Middle Stone Age, down through the Copper and Bronze Ages, the periods of the Patriarchs, Prophets, Maccabees, Byzantines, etc.

It's a free exhibit, and there's a free tour of the plant itself daily (except Saturday) at 10:30 a.m.; telephone 04-664-221 for reservations. The public is admitted only at the time of the tour, or by appointment. Every visitor receives a table of the archeological periods of history, which reminds you that Moses lived during the Bronze Age, 1300–1200 B.C., and that David was king of Israel in 1000 B.C., during the Iron Age. The table is a handy little reference, especially valuable when you go poking around some of the ancient sites in Galilee and the Negev. Buses 10, 12, and 22 will bring you here.

It's from this port area that you'll be leaving (or arriving) if you come or go from Israel by ship. (Check the first chapter of this book for information on ships serving Israel.)

Jaffa Road (Derekh Yafo): The street behind Independence Avenue (Rehov Ha-Atzma'ut), running roughly parallel to it, is Jaffa Road, where you can buy many of your souvenirs at prices considerably cheaper than elsewhere. But it takes some window shopping. This is an unusually inexpensive area, off the tourist path, where you'll see the residents of the lower town doing their shopping. The finjan coffee sets and brass trays, as well as the Middle Eastern–style earrings available here, undercut by several shekels the going prices in the fancier-looking shops.

Farther along Jaffa Road, past the bus and train stations, west in the direction of Tel Aviv, the road changes names, becoming Sederot Ha-Hagana (Hagana Boulevard). Driving along here, you'll see a large ship on the left-hand side of the road. The vessel *Af-Al-Pi* ("Nevertheless"), is a memorial commemorating all the ships that defied the British blockade to smuggle immigrants into Israel. This clandestine immigration movement—called "Aliya Beth"—is one of the most harrowing phases of Israeli history. Refugees from the Nazi plague and escapees from DP camps were packed onto these illegal ships, and many succeeded in making it undetected past British ships guarding Israel's Mediterranean coastline. Others, however, were not so fortunate. The *Struma* waited endlessly at sea for some country to accept the 765 refugees aboard until at last it sank. Others, like the *Patria*, went down in Haifa harbor, with hundreds killed; still others, like the *Exodus*, ran the British blockade only to have its passengers shipped to a Cyprus detention camp, or, pathetically enough, returned to a detention area in Germany, the nightmare from which the survivors had just come. The *Af-Al-Pi* is now the **Clandestine Immigration and Naval Museum.** Nearby, on Allenby Road, is the Maritime Museum (see below for details). Buses 43, 44, and 45.

The Aerial Cable Car: Directly across the road from the *Af-Al-Pi*, and even more noticeable from the highway, is the lower terminal of the Haifa Aerial Cable Car (tel. 04-510-509), on your right-hand side beside the sea. It rides through the air from the beach at the western end of Bat Galim up to the tip of Mount Carmel, the site of the Old Lighthouse and Stella Maris. The round aerial cars, imported from Austria, are equipped with recorded messages about what you're seeing as you go up and down (flip the switch to choose English or Hebrew). Round trips cost NIS3.50 ($2.35) for adults, NIS2.50 ($1.65) for children; you can ride daily from 9 a.m. to 11 p.m. in winter, until midnight in summer (closed for the Sabbath, from Friday before sunset until Saturday after sunset). For NIS1 (65¢) less, you can ride one way and take the bus from there. (Buses serving the cable car are Carmel buses 26, 28, and 31 to the top terminal, buses 40, 41, 42, and 44 to the bottom terminal.)

Both the top and bottom terminals have lovely restaurants and bars, designed with the beautiful views in mind.

In the bottom terminal's downstairs hall, an artist's exhibit is held every Saturday, with a different artist featured every week.

If you want to cross from the lower cable-car terminal over to visit the *Af-Al-Pi*, at this writing it's a bit of a risky business, even though they're so close to one another. Many people do it though, and there is a crosswalk with a traffic light here at the intersection, which you should use if you're crossing the busy highway. But as yet, to get from the lower terminal up to the highway, you must go through a hole in the fence on either side of the railroad tracks. This situation will probably be remedied someday (possibly by the time you're reading this). Until then, if you don't want to cross the tracks this way, you must take a bus to the Central Bus Station and transfer to another bus to come back to the *Af-Al-Pi*. If you're driving, this doesn't take very long to do, but by bus. . . . You can see why so many people come through the hole in the fence instead.

Elijah's Cave: From the *Af-Al-Pi*, it's just a short walk up to Elijah's Cave (tel. 04-527-430), nestled at the base of steep Cape Carmel, below the Stella Maris lighthouse and the Carmelite Monastery. Tradition has it that Elijah hid here when fleeing the wrath of King Ahab and his wife, Jezebel; it's also the site where Elijah established his school upon his return from exile, thus earning the name "School of the Prophets," where Elisha, among others, studied. The cave is also said to be a place where the Holy Family found shelter for a night on their return from Egypt.

The cave is holy to Jews, Christians, Muslims, and Druze, all of whom venerate the prophet Elijah. Pilgrimages and huge dramatic ceremonies are held at this cave many times each year.

Elijah's Cave is open in summer Sunday through Thursday from 8 a.m. to 6 p.m., in winter until 5 p.m.; Friday hours are 8 a.m. to 1 p.m. all year round; closed Saturday and holidays. Head coverings are available at the entrance to the cave. No entrance fee, but donations are accepted. Buses 43, 44, and 45 let you off at the highway nearby.

Museums, Institutes, Galleries, and So Forth

Haifa is rich in fascinating museums of many kinds. You can visit the museums for little or no money—costs at most of the museums are so low they're not worth mentioning, almost always no more than a dollar or two, if that. And most museums that are open on Saturday are free to the public on that day. Haifa Museum is an exception to this rule. But you can get a good deal on the Haifa Museum in another way, by buying a single 72-hour pass for NIS3 ($2), which admits you to the entire Haifa Museum complex, the Tikotin Museum of Japanese Art, and the National Maritime Museum.

The **Haifa Museum** complex at 26 Shabtai Levi St. (tel. 04-523-255), not far from the Carmelit subway's Ha-Nevi'im station in Hadar, contains several museums of interest. The **Museum of Ancient Art** displays archeological collections of Mediterranean cultures from the beginning of history until the Islamic conquest in the 7th century. Outstanding collections of Greco-Roman culture, Coptic art, painted portraits from Fayyum, coins of Caesarea and Acre, terracottas of all periods, and finds from the Haifa area. The **Museum of Modern Art** has a collection of paintings and sculpture by Israeli artists as well as prints by Israeli and foreign artists. A library and slide collection is open to the public. Lectures, art films, and slide presentations are held in the evenings. The **Museum of Music and Ethnology** has displays of ancient Jewish origin plus African, Asian, and American Indian tribal art. The Folktale Archives contains about 10,000 tales, most in Hebrew but with English summaries. There are also displays of musical instruments in their proper ethnic settings, giving you some insight into who used the instruments, when, and how—a very fine way to run a museum! Hours are 10 a.m. to 1 p.m. daily except Friday; on Tuesday, Thursday, and Saturday there are extra hours, from 6 to 9 p.m. Buses 10, 12, 22, and 28.

For a look at the **Reuben and Edith Hecht Museum of the Archeology of the Land of Israel** (tel. 04-240-577), containing thousands of unique archeological items illustrating the theme of "The People of Israel in the Land of Israel," head for the Main Building at Haifa University. (Turn to the section on Haifa University, above, for information on this and the several noteworthy art galleries around the campus.) Free admission. Buses 24 and 37.

Haifa's **Railway Museum** (tel. 04-531-211) is in the old Haifa East railway station opposite 40 Hativat Golani Ave. in the port area. Two 1950s-vintage diesel locomotives, several cabooses, a club car built in 1922, and a passenger coach dating from 1893 are the major exhibits, but there are also displays of photographs, timetables, tickets, and other memorabilia going all the way back to the railroad's construction in Ottoman times (1882). Admission is free; hours are 10 a.m. to 1 p.m.; closed Friday and Saturday. Buses 17, 42, and 93.

The **Tikotin Museum of Japanese Art,** 89 Ha-Nassi Blvd., north of the commercial district in Central Carmel (tel. 04-383-554), has examples of almost all kinds of Japanese art and crafts, along with a library of 2,000 books. Hours on Saturday and holidays (when admission is free) are 10 a.m. to 2 p.m.; Sunday through Thursday it's open from 10 a.m. to 5 p.m.; closed on Friday. Buses 22 and 23, and Carmelit subway (Gan Ha-Em station).

Grouped together at 124 Ha-Tishbi St., on the northwest edge of Gan Ha-Em park in Central Carmel, are the **Museum of Prehistory** (tel. 04-337-833), the **Zoo,** (tel. 04-337-886), and the **Biological Institute.** The first of these maintains a permanent exhibit of fossils and artifacts from the Carmel region. Each of the others, in its own way, features the animal life of the country, with particular attention paid the fish indigenous to Israel's waters and the fauna of the Carmel region. Visiting hours for the museums are 8 a.m. to 2 p.m. Sunday through Thursday, and 10 a.m. to 2 p.m. on Saturday; closed Friday. Zoo hours are Sunday through Thursday from 8 a.m. to 4 p.m., on Friday until 1 p.m., on Saturday from 9 a.m. to 4 p.m. In July and August, hours are extended to 6 p.m. (still closing at 1 p.m. on Friday). A fee of NIS6 ($4) admits you to the zoo, and an additional 50 agorot (35¢) admits you to the museums. Buses 22, 23, and 31, and the Carmelit subway (Central Carmel stop).

The **National Maritime Museum,** 198 Allenby Rd., just up the street from the *Af-Al-Pi* near Bat Galim (tel. 04-536-622), encompasses 5,000 years of seafaring in the Mediterranean and the Red Sea. Hours: Sunday through Thursday from 10 a.m. to 4 p.m., on Saturday and holidays to 1 p.m.; closed Friday. Small fee, except on Saturday and holidays, when it's free. Buses 3, 5, 43, 44, and 45.

The **Clandestine Immigration and Naval Museum,** 204 Allenby Rd. (tel. 04-536-249), next door to the Maritime Museum and opposite Elijah's Cave, details the story of illegal immigration during the British Mandate period. The *Af-Al-Pi* is on the grounds here. Open Sunday and Tuesday from 9 a.m. to 4 p.m., on Monday, Wednesday, and Thursday to 3 p.m., on Friday and holiday eves until 1 p.m.; closed Saturday. Small fee. Buses 3, 5, 43, 44, and 45.

The **Israel Edible Oil Museum** (tel. 04-670-491) is found in the Shemen Oil Factory in the industrial section of Haifa. Many interesting items connected with the oil industry in Israel, from 2,000 years ago up to the present, are housed in the original old stone factory building. Hours are Sunday through Thursday from 9 a.m. to noon; closed Friday and Saturday. Bus 2.

The **Mané Katz Museum,** 89 Yefe Nof (Panorama Road) near the Dan Hotel in Central Carmel (tel. 04-383-482), houses his works and collection—drawings, aquarelles, gouaches, oil paintings, sculpture, and Judaica. Open daily except Friday from 10 a.m. to 1 p.m. and 4 to 6 p.m., on Saturday from 10 a.m. to 1 p.m. Free admission. Buses 22, 23, and 31, and Carmelit subway (Central Carmel stop).

The **Chagall Artists' House,** 24 Zionism Ave. at Herzlia (tel. 04-522-355), exhibits the works of contemporary Israeli artists. Open from 10 a.m. to 1 p.m. and 4 to 6 p.m. Sunday through Thursday, 10 a.m. to 1 p.m. on Saturday, closed Friday.

And then there is the **Rothschild Community House** (Bet Rothschild) in Central Carmel near Haifa Auditorium at 142 Ha-Nassi Blvd. (tel. 04-382-749 or 383-424), which always has something of interest for tourists. Call to see what's up. Interesting too are the lectures at **Bet Ha-Gefen** (tel. 04-525-252), the **Arab-Jewish Community Center,** on Ha-Gefen Street opposite the Chagall Artists' House.

SPORTS IN HAIFA: Ha-Poel and Maccabi are two sports leagues in Israel. By contacting either of these—or the Haifa Municipality or the local I.G.T.O.—you'll get the latest data on where you can play tennis, do gym exercises and workouts, or take in sports events as a spectator.

A 15-minute ride south of downtown Haifa, in the Kefar Zamir suburb, are the **Haifa Tennis Center** (tel. 04-522-721 or 532-014), the **Haifa Squash Center** (tel. 04-539-160), and the **Haifa Lawn Bowling Club** (tel. 04-387-487); all have regular hours, and you're welcome to come and play—but you must call in advance to reserve a court. Buses 43, 45, and 3a.

For horseback riding, call the **Carmel Riding Center** (tel. 04-842-730) at

Ein Hod, 20 minutes to the south of Haifa, which offers riding excursions with a magnificent view of Carmel National Park and the sea.

Haifa is well stocked in the water-sports department, and you'll have many excellent low-cost swimming pools and beaches from which to choose. The **Carmel Beach (Hof Ha-Carmel)** can be reached by bus 3 or 45 from Shapiro Street. . . . **Hof Shaket,** a pay beach in the harbor area of Bat Galim, is open with a lifeguard all year round, and can be reached via bus 40, 41, or 42. . . . **Bat Galim** swimming pool and sea beach is on the opposite side of the small Bat Galim promontory. There are also tennis courts here, and adjoining the beach, a sandy stretch known as the **Municipal Beach,** and this—budgeteers note—is free to all comers. . . . In the Central Carmel section you'll find the **Maccabi** swimming pool on Bikkurim Street (tel. 04-80100), heated in winter, and serviced by bus 21, 22, or 23 and by the Carmelit (rates double in winter). . . . Open the usual May to October season, the **Ha-Poel** swimming pool is on Ha-Poel Street. . . . There's also a public beach at **Kiryat Haim,** a Haifa suburb; take bus 51. . . . South of town, heading toward Tel Aviv, are a number of other nice public beaches, including **Hof Zamir** and **Hof Dado.** . . . Don't forget the pool at the **Dan Carmel Hotel,** for a whole day's worth of pool, shower, and sporting privileges (for details, see the restaurant section, above). Finally, you'll find several wonderful swimming areas outside Haifa, at **Akhziv, Tantura,** and **Caesarea**—all described in the preceding chapter.

5. Haifa By Night

Haifa is certainly not Tel Aviv, or even Jerusalem, when it comes to nightlife, but there are possibilities. Check in the *Jerusalem Post,* which despite its name is a national paper covering events and cultural offerings, movies, and whatnot throughout all Israel. The Friday-morning edition includes the indispensable weekly calendar of happenings, some of which are in Haifa. Better yet, call the 24-hour **telephone hotline** for "What's On in Haifa" (tel. 04-640-840), and check with any of the Tourist Information Offices, to find out about special events happening around town.

The **James de Rothschild Cultural and Community Center,** Bet Rothschild, next to Haifa Auditorium at 142 Ha-Nassi Blvd. (tel. 04-382-749 or 380-489), always has something going on: a dance, exhibit, or concert. Haifa's **Cinémathèque** (tel. 04-383-424) is housed in the same building, showing a wide variety of films (up to three different movies every day, many in English), including special-interest art film screenings; call for info. Right next door is the huge, blocky **Haifa Auditorium** (tel. 04-380-013), Haifa's largest concert hall, where you can find symphony, opera, the Israel Philharmonic, dance concerts, and many other cultural events and big happenings; there's also usually an interesting art display in the lobby, which you can see anytime for free, from 4 to 7 p.m. (except Friday). The Rothschild Center and Haifa Auditorium are just a short stroll south of the Central Carmel commercial district, where Ha-Nassi Boulevard becomes Moriah Avenue.

Around the far side of the Rothschild Center is **Martef Esser** ("Cellar Ten"), once a Rothschild wine cellar. It's now run by and for students, open Friday evenings from 9 or 10 p.m. on with live music of many kinds (jazz, classical, and more), and a nice wicker coffeehouse/bar atmosphere. There's a NIS5 ($3.35) cover charge for the music on Friday nights.

Lots of shows are offered at the **Haifa Municipal Theater** (tel. 04-670-956), in Hadar where Pevsner, Yehoshua, and Trumpeldor Streets meet. Play performances are sometimes in Hebrew, sometimes in English, and sometimes both, in simultaneous translation.

Looking for a club, a place to hang out, listen to music, have a drink, and dance? You'll find many nice places in every district of town. The **Haifa Tourism Development Association,** 10 Ahad Ha-Am St. (tel. 04-671-645), has compiled a list of recommendable spots; call for info.

Most of the better-class hotels have nice bars, and the one at the **Hotel Carmelia,** 35 Herzlia St. in Hadar (tel. 04-521-278 or 521-279), has a dance with '60s music every Friday night. **Palache's Pub,** at the Dan Carmel Hotel, 87 Ha-Nassi Blvd. in Central Carmel (tel. 04-386-211), Haifa's most high-class five-star establishment, also has a bar with dancing.

Many of Haifa's restaurants also have bars with evening entertainment; see "Where to Eat" for details. Both the upper and lower terminals of the **Aerial Cable Car,** too, are enjoyable places to stop on an evening out, with restaurants, bars, and dancing; you can ride the cable car until 11 p.m. most of the year, until midnight in summer.

If it's **disco** dancing you're in the mood for, you'll find it in Haifa. In the downtown port area, try the **London Pride,** 85 Ha-Atzma'ut Rd. (tel. 04-663-839), a disco, pub, and bar. Up in the Carmel district, there are more disco choices. **Fever,** on the Gan Ha-Em Promenade (no phone), is a favorite with teenagers. There's also **Sunset,** 124 Ha-Nassi Blvd. (tel. 04-256-928); and at 120 Panorama (Yefe Nof) Road, near the Hotel Dvir, you'll find **Club 120** (tel. 04-382-979), a private disco club (but tourists are welcome), rocking on Saturday nights and packed with young Haifans out for a good time.

The Student Associations at the **Technion** and at **Haifa University** have entertainment of one kind or another going on almost every night. Look under the universities, mentioned previously in this chapter, for details.

Folk dancing classes meet Monday and Thursday at 8:30 p.m. at Bet Rothschild (see above), and on other days at the universities; call for info.

The **Bridge Club** meets at Bet Rothschild every Sunday and Wednesday at 8:15 p.m., and every Tuesday at Bet Goldblum, nearby at 124 Ha-Nassi Blvd. (tel. 04-382-104).

6. Excursions from Your Haifa Base

Many of the villages outside Haifa are among the most interesting attractions in Israel. We'll visit three of them: **Daliat-el-Carmel, Isfiya,** and **Muhraka.**

DALIAT-EL-CARMEL AND ISFIYA: These sister Druze villages are located 15 minutes from the Ahuza section of Carmel. If you're driving, just ask for the road to Daliat-el-Carmel ("Eyfo ha-derekh l'Dalia?") By bus (92 or 93), the trip takes half an hour from the central station, and it's a splendid drive along the uppermost rim of Carmel. The Mediterranean is way down below you, and so is the entire city, the port, and the industrial area. Bring your camera.

As mentioned, these villages are inhabited in the main by Druze, Arabic-speaking (and appearing) people who are, however, not Muslims. Theirs is a rather secretive religion; they draw heavily on the Bible and venerate such personages as Jethro (father-in-law of Moses). The Druze were loyal to Israel during the 1948 war, and several of their brigades are highly respected detachments in the Israeli army. The Druze gravitate toward big swarthy mustaches, and due to "genetic influence" (Romans, Crusaders, and British) several centuries back, many of them are blond. Druze children and young women are well known for their beauty.

They are an industrious people, and you'll see that their terraced hillsides are meticulously cared for and, as a result, very fertile. The houses are also square and box-like in the Arabic style—and many are new, built by Druze construction experts. Outside their own villages, the Druze find employment on kibbutzim as electricians, builders, carpenters, and mechanics; in the extreme north and south of the country, many Druze are border policemen—and you'll never find a tougher, more uncompromising lot when it comes to that kind of work. Their hospitality, though, is legendary.

In both villages, you can buy quite extraordinary souvenirs and hand-crafted items, new or antique, at moderate prices. (Markets will be closed on Friday, the Druze Sabbath day.)

There are several cafés in both villages well worth stopping into for a drink, just to observe the local citizenry. As you'll soon see, the conservative Eastern European Jew and his boisterous sabra son aren't the only ones in Israel to be affected by the generation gap, Israeli style: in these Druze villages, you'll see only older men in flowing gowns and headdresses, while the younger men wear Western-style clothes.

Should you become friendly with a Druze while you're in Israel, try to get yourself invited into the village when there's a wedding. It's a happy, spectacular, all-day affair, marked by intriguing customs and foods that you'll never forget.

Isfiya is the first village you'll reach from Haifa; Daliat-el-Carmel is a very short ride farther.

Various tours go to these villages (check with Tourist Information for details), but you can also go to the villages on your own. There's a sherut service which leaves Haifa during the evening from 6 p.m. to 6 a.m., departing from Hadar at the corner of Shmaryahu Levin and Herzl Streets. Between 6 a.m. and 6 p.m., the sherut service is downtown at the corner of Ha-Atzma'ut Road and Eliahu Ha-Navi Street, near Kikar Paris. The sherut takes 25 minutes to reach Daliat-el-Carmel.

Overnight in Isfiya? The **Stella Carmel Hospice** (P.O. Box 7045, Haifa 31070; tel. 04-222-692) charges $17 per person, bed and breakfast, for simple but pleasant accommodations in the Main House rooms. Other bed-and-breakfast accommodations are available in dormitory rooms ($7 per person), in Portakabin rooms ($12 per person), and in Annex rooms with private bath ($21 per person). Lunch and dinner are available as well.

MUHRAKA: Half a mile south of Daliat-el-Carmel is a road on the left side of the main road. Its destination is not posted, but it meanders and climbs to the monastery at Muhraka, the place where Elijah defeated the prophets of Baal (take inter-urban bus 92). You'll see a dramatic stone statue of Elijah, sword raised to heaven, and a lovely Carmelite monastery, open daily from 8 a.m. to noon and again from 1 to 5 p.m. (on Friday until noon only). The view from here is unsurpassed.

OTHER DESTINATIONS: Haifa proves to be an excellent place to park your bags while scouting out other attractions around Israel, for in Israel nothing's really that far away. And while Haifa's not exactly in the middle of the country, it does happen to be quite close to some of the more popular sights. The nearer places include Ein Hod, Caesarea, Acre, and other locations described in the previous chapter. It's also quite a simple matter to cover Bet Shearim, the Yizreel Valley, Nazareth, and parts of Galilee from Haifa. For specifics about transportation and prices, your best bet is to visit the I.G.T.O.

Aside from I.G.T.O., the following companies have all sorts of tour plans for your consideration: **Egged Tours,** 4 Nordau St. (tel. 04-643-131); **United Tours,** 5 Nordau St. (tel. 04-668-886); **Carmel Touring,** 126 Ha-Nassi Blvd. (tel. 04-382-277); **Mitspa Tours,** 1 Nordau St. (tel. 04-644-889).

Chapter VII

GALILEE

1. Nazareth and the Yizreel Valley
2. Tiberias and the Sea of Galilee
3. Safed (Zefat)
4. Upper Galilee and the Golan Heights
5. South of Galilee: The Jordan Valley

ROUGHLY SPEAKING, everything to the north and east of Haifa is known as "the Galilee" (Ha-Galil)—Israel's lushest region. Every springtime the residents of Haifa pour out into Galilee to experience anew that sense of wonder at the return of foliage to the valleys and slopes, and to marvel again at the pioneer perseverance of the oldtime settlers of Galilee farm communities (kibbutzim) who lived in tents, risked malaria, and fought off Arab attacks to cultivate this land.

Beginning in March a vast blanket of green covers Galilee and seems almost to inundate the watchtowers, settlements, and stone Arab villages of the region. One Haifa Galilee-lover told me: "In March, Galilee is so green that it hurts your eyes." Everywhere you see farms whose fields are carefully tilled patterns of orange groves, rich vegetation, vineyards, and fruit orchards.

In biblical times, according to Josephus, some 204 towns in these hills supported about 15,000 residents each, giving Galilee a dense 3 million population. Today this fertile countryside is the site of the majority of Israel's collective farms, but it is also home for most of Israel's longtime Arab residents, and it is in their sleepy little villages that you can still witness the classical rhythm and character of biblical days.

It was only natural, of course, that this fertile region should have been the first in Israel to have been developed. Initially it was to the shores of the Sea of Galilee, in the Jordan Valley and around the Emek Yizreel (Valley of Jezreel, usually just called the Emek) that the early Zionist pioneers came with their dreams of a socialist utopia, founded on principles of agricultural toil. Then, in the '20s and '30s, they took their bucolic Marxism into Galilee's plains and forests. They established Israel's front line of defense, sweating out malaria attacks and returning the fire of Arab snipers. They considered it a luxury when they changed from tents to modest little houses, but as they prospered so did Israel itself grow. Babies born in these settlements grew into hardy young farmers, their playfields not the ghettos of Russia and Poland that their parents had known, but rather the grassy meadows and fruit fields of their settlement. During the War of Independence in 1948 several Galilee settlements shook under the fury of invading Arab armies, but most held out, farming and fighting at the same time. In at least one case, the tenacity of the settlers under fire prevented a massive breakthrough that could have caused the fall of Haifa. War memorials throughout Galilee tell you about these times.

Aside from the Galilee–Jerusalem road skirting the Jordan River, there are two good central routes for entering Galilee: one is from Haifa to Acre and east to Safed, then down to the Sea of Galilee. The other is due east from Haifa to Nazareth and straight across to Tiberias. We'll follow one route and then the other—and then a third, an offshoot of the Haifa–Nazareth road which will detour down through the Jordan Valley and land us south of the Sea of Galilee.

1. Nazareth and the Yizreel Valley

The ride from Haifa to Nazareth takes just an hour (it's 25 miles), leaving the port city via Ha-Atzma'ut Road and then heading inland over the four-lane highway that runs along the foot of the Carmel range. On the left is the **Valley of Zebulon,** hidden behind the likes of oil refineries, soap factories, and cement works.

After the industrial zone, the landscape undergoes a change in character. You begin to see farm settlements, the most important of which are **Yagur** and **Allonim.** Yagur is one of the country's oldest kibbutzim, founded in 1922. You then start climbing into the foothills of the Lower Galilee, and soon, about 35 or 40 minutes out of Haifa, you'll see an observation signpost on your right. Be sure to stop, because this is one of the loveliest views in Israel.

THE YIZREEL VALLEY: From this point, the Yizreel Valley (commonly called the Emek, "Valley") spreads out below. The largest and most fertile valley in Israel, the Emek lies between the Galilee mountains to the north and the Samaria range to the south, and it houses some of Israel's oldest and best-known settlements—**Mishmar Ha-Emek, Hazorea, Givat Oz, Ginegar,** and the giant moshav, **Nahalal.** From the height on the Nazareth road, the valley has the appearance of being the most cultivated, fertile place in all the world. The rich, dark soil is crisscrossed in checkerboard patterns of fruit trees, vineyards, and green vegetable fields. It is a breathtaking quilt of colors, some blocks golden with wheat, some black with heavy cultivation, others orange with brilliant flowers.

But it wasn't always this way. About 60 years ago this was a breeding swamp of malaria. In the early 1920s the Keren Kayemet (Jewish National Fund) launched its biggest land reclamation project; slowly but surely, each and every square foot of swampland was drained and every mosquito killed. Russian, German, and Polish settlers filled the new settlements. The cultivation of the Emek soon became one of Israel's heroic, adventurous tales, rhapsodized in dozens of romantic songs in which the tilling of soil and the smell of roses are common lyrics.

But as you look at this splendid fertility, remember also that this was one of the bloodiest battlefields in history. Here the Egyptians shed blood 4,000 years ago, as did the Canaanites, the Mongols, the Greeks, the Romans, and the Crusaders in later centuries. From Mount Tabor, overlooking the Emek's northeast corner, the prophetess Deborah launched her famous attack against the Canaanite armies. And several years later, Gideon's forces swooped down from Mount Gilboa on the Midianites and slaughtered the plundering Bedouin tribe.

But it was also on this fertile plain that the Israelite tribe suffered one of its most calamitous national defeats—when King Saul and his sons, including Jonathan, died during a clash with the Philistines. It is with regard to this battle that the Book of Samuel records David's immortal lament:

The beauty of Israel is slain upon the high places:
How are the mighty fallen!
Tell it not in Gath,
Publish it not in the streets of Ashkelon:
Lest the daughters of the Philistines rejoice,
Lest the daughters of the uncircumcised triumph.

Ye mountains of Gilboa,
Let there be no dew, neither there be rain, upon you, nor fields of
    offerings:
For there the shield of the mighty is vilely cast away,
The shield of Saul, as though he had not been annointed with oil.
From the blood of the slain, from the fat of the mighty,
The bow of Jonathan turned not back,
And the sword of Saul returned not empty.

Saul and Jonathan were lovely and pleasant in their lives,
And in their death they were not divided:
They were swifter than eagles,
They were stronger than lions.
Yet daughters of Israel, weep over Saul,
Who clothed you in scarlet, with other delights,
Who put on ornaments of gold upon your apparel.
How are the mighty fallen,
And the weapons of war perished! [II Samuel 1]

In postbiblical years the Turks fought here, and Napoleon battled at its
edges. In 1918 General Allenby defeated the Turkish forces on the Emek, and
here, too, Israel's armies in 1948 overwhelmed the Arabs.

It is an irony of history that the Emek region, which has known every conceivable type of war and human misery, today flourishes in such splendor.

Bet Shearim

Somewhat reminiscent of the Sanhedrian Tombs in Jerusalem, the **Bet
Shearim Burial Caves** are located 20 km (12 miles) from Haifa, on the main road
that heads toward Afula (which is the main town of the Jordan Valley).

In 2nd-century Israel Bet Shearim was the home of Israel's Supreme
Court, the Sanhedrin, as well as headquarters of the famous Rabbi Yehuda Ha-
Nassi, compiler of the Mishnah. Many learned and famous Jews were laid to rest
in the cemetery of the town, a tranquil grove of cypress and olive trees. Over the
centuries, however, the tombs were destroyed and the caves looted. Earth and
rock covered the catacombs as if they had never existed. But finally they were
unearthed, first in 1936, and then fully explored after the War of Independence.

The entire site here is particularly well tended: parking lot, washroom facilities, and outdoor café.

Enter the spooky burial chambers through an opening in the rock or a
stone door. Inside the cool chambers are sarcophagi carved with rams' horns
and lions' heads, or a menorah, in some ancient time. Catacomb 20 is the most
formidable unearthed so far from the point of view of legible inscriptions, carvings, and interesting relics, but archeologists claim that only a fraction of the
original effects remain; over the centuries tomb robbers have looted the almost
200 sarcophagi.

The excavations and museum are open daily April through September from 8 a.m. to 5 p.m., on Friday until 3 p.m.; October to March hours are 8 a.m. to 4 p.m., on Friday until 3 p.m. For information, telephone 04-931-643.

Megiddo (Armageddon)

Back on the road, you pass **Hazorea** and **Mishmar Ha-Emek,** two old and large kibbutzim, and then you come to Megiddo, about 35 km (22 miles) southeast of Haifa, the leading fortress overlooking the Emek, and the site of countless battles through the centuries. Due to its strategic position on the major route leading from Egypt to Syria and Mesopotamia, this location has always been much coveted, much attacked, and much fortified. Archeologists have uncovered the remains of cities of fully 20 distinct historical periods here on this tel, dating from 4000 to 400 B.C., and it is frequently mentioned in biblical and other ancient texts.

In the Bible, the name is mentioned mostly in connection with war. In the Old Testament, you'll find it mentioned in a number of places: I Kings 4:7, 8, and 12; I Kings 9:15; II Kings 9:27; II Kings 23:29, 30; II Chronicles 35:22; Joshua 17:11; Joshua 12:7, 21; Judges 1:27; Judges 5:19; and Zechariah 12:11. In the New Testament, the book of Revelations names Armageddon (a corruption of the Hebrew *Har Megiddo*—Mount Megiddo) as the place where the last great battle will be fought when the forces of good triumph over the forces of evil: "For they are the spirits of devils, working miracles, which go forth unto the kings of the earth and of the whole world, to gather them to the battle of that great day of God Almighty. . . . And he gathered them together into a place called in the Hebrew tongue Armageddon" (Revelations 16:14, 18).

It's interesting to note that Megiddo has been a place of battle not only in historic times, but continuing right down into our own century. General Allenby launched his attack against the Turks from the Megiddo Pass in 1917, and in 1948 the Israeli forces also used the fortress site as a base of operations against the entrenched Arab armies.

As you enter Megiddo today, now a national park, there is a **museum** with detailed information about the excavation, the artifacts found there, the biblical and historical references relating to its past, and a model of the site as it now exists. Many more artifacts discovered here have been removed, and may now be found in the Jerusalem Antiquities Museum and the Rockefeller Museum.

You can **walk among the ruins** of many fascinating structures here, including a palace from the time of King Solomon, and King Ahab's "Chariot City" and stables with a capacity of almost 500 horses. There is also a large grain silo from the reign of Jeroboam Ben Joash, king of Israel in the 8th century B.C., and a building from the time of King David (1006–970 B.C.). On strata way down below the later buildings, you can see excavated ruins of temples 5,000 and 6,000 years old, constructed during the Chalcolithic period.

Perhaps most amazing of all is the **water tunnel** dating from the reign of King Ahab in the 9th century B.C. You enter it by walking 183 steps (120 feet) down into a large pit in the earth, whereupon you can walk along the tunnel extending 215 feet to a spring located outside the city, which was camouflaged by a wall covered with earth, designed to assure a constant supply of fresh water to the city even when it was under seige.

Of course, Megiddo had imposing city walls. Today you can see remnants of the walls, and also the city gates and guarded entranceways, as they existed during many eras; some of the most impressive are those built during the time of King Solomon. The observation points afford a spectacular view of the huge valley below, clearly showing the route the armies and travelers took.

To get to Megiddo by bus, take bus 302 from Haifa, which leaves Haifa's Central Bus Station several times in the morning and returns from Megiddo sev-

GALILEE AND GOLAN

eral times in the afternoon. Megiddo is open daily from 8 a.m. to 4 p.m., except for the water tunnel, which closes at 3:30 p.m. Admission is NIS2.30 ($1.55) for adults, 50 agorot (35¢) for children.

Afula

After leaving Megiddo, the road swings across the Emek to Afula, a town in the center of the valley that serves as the administrative and commercial headquarters of the Emek. The road to Afula follows a historic route, although road signs announce only communal settlements. Through the centuries flocks of pilgrims have traveled along this path on mules, horses, and camels to reach the waters of the River Jordan.

Afula itself, though, is a fairly recent phenomenon. It was settled in about 1920, mostly by American Jews. Today the palm trees they planted back then tower over Afula's main street, a boulevard which leads to the circular flowering park that's more or less the center of town. The large yellow concrete building, straight ahead and slightly to the right, was the British Mandate Police Headquarters.

You can get a good kosher East European meal at the **San Remo Coffee Restaurant,** Kikar Ha-Atzma'ut (tel. 06-522-458), an air-conditioned and very clean eatery. A full three-course meal is NIS12 ($8); there's a self-service section as well. Alcoholic beverages are served. Open from 7:30 a.m. to 7 p.m., closed from Friday at 3 p.m. until Sunday morning. By the way, the restaurant is pretty well hidden by trees, so look for the square with the sculpture of three intertwined circles—that's Kikar Ha-Atzma'ut. Then look for the parking lot near the sculpture. The restaurant is right off the parking lot, behind an enormous tree.

NAZARETH, PAST AND PRESENT: This biblical town, where Jesus grew up, clings to the inside of a vast bowl, its mud and limestone houses tiered like the seats of an amphitheater. Today the city houses Israel's largest Arab community outside Jerusalem—over 50,000, half of them Christian, half Muslim—and shares with Jerusalem its position as headquarters of the Christian mission movement in Israel, with over 40 churches, convents, monasteries, orphanages, and private parochial schools. In fact, Nazareth's very name is used by Arabs and Israelis to designate Christians, just as Jesus was also known as the Nazarene. In Arabic, Christians are called "Nasara," and in Hebrew "Notzrim."

Despite the fact that Jesus grew up here, Nazareth was only a tiny hamlet in biblical times, scarcely recorded on maps or mentioned in historical works. For the real flavor of what the village must have been like, turn into the narrow alleys that wind up and back into the terraced limestone ridges, and wander through the old **Arab Market** with its narrow cobbled streets.

An important thing to keep in mind is that Nazareth is virtually locked solid on Sunday, wide open on Saturday.

Orientation and Information

Nazareth lies on the main road from Haifa to Tiberias, and from Tel Aviv to Tiberias—it's a transportation hub. As you approach Nazareth from Haifa, the road is a series of hairpin turns up through the King George V Forest, planted by Keren Kayemet (the Jewish National Fund) over 40 years ago. Now it's wonderfully lush and shady.

After the 40-km (26-mile) trip from Haifa, you come over the hill and enter Nazareth on **Paul VI Street,** the town's main stem. Note that Nazareth has a "bypass," a road that circles the town—hence the confusing signs which point in opposite directions for the same destination.

One of these destinations is **Nazareth Elit** (or Nazorat Ilit), the new, modern, mostly Jewish suburb to the north, which is actually a separate municipality. You'll pass by it on your way to Tiberias.

Down Paul VI Street and into the center of Nazareth, you follow the signs to the **Basilica of the Annunciation,** Nazareth's principal religious monument which is just off Paul VI Street on Casa Nova Street. Use the basilica's huge cupola, topped by a beacon, as your landmark in Nazareth. Most everything you'll need is within sight, even within a few steps, of the basilica.

Casa Nova Street is the approach to the basilica, and on it you'll find restaurants and cafés, hotels and hospices, and also the **Tourist Information Office** (tel. 06-573-003), on the left-hand side. Unlike the I.G.T.O. offices in most of Israel, which observe the Jewish Sabbath and are closed on Saturday, this one is open Monday through Friday from 8 a.m. to 5 p.m., on Saturday to 2 p.m.; closed Sunday.

The **Central Bus Station** in Nazareth is off Paul VI Street just east of Casa Nova Street, a few steps from the Basilica of the Annunciation.

Accommodations

There are three three-star hotels, and several Christian hospices in Nazareth, and some in each category are suitable for our pocketbooks. Prices for accommodations in Nazareth remain the same all year round. **Hotel Galilee,** a three-star establishment on Paul VI Street five minutes' walk south of the basilica (tel. 06-571-311), has 90 rooms, all with private toilets and showers (four of the rooms have tubs as well), air conditioning and heat, plus a bar and coffeeshop on the premises. Rates, including continental breakfast, are $25 single, $40 double. Big, modern, pleasant, recommendable.

The **Nazareth Hotel** (P.O. Box 291, Nazareth 16000; tel. 06-577-777 or 554-502) is a three-star hotel that's somewhat out of the center of things—on Paul VI Street just past the turn to Haifa. It has 88 rooms, all with balconies, private baths and toilets, phones, air conditioning, and heat. Facilities include an Oriental bar and restaurant on the main floor, a TV lounge, and parking in front of the hotel. Single rooms cost $31, and doubles run $40.

The three-star, 92-room **Grand New Hotel,** St. Joseph Street at the ring road (tel. 06-573-020 or 573-325), is a modern establishment with accommodations that offer good views. Rooms have air conditioning, heating, toilets, phones, and baths with tubs. Guests pay $32 single, $42 double.

The **Casa Nova Pilgrims House** (tel. 06-571-367) is right across the street from the Basilica of the Annunciation. It was built in 1896 by American Franciscans, and is still run by the Franciscans for religious pilgrims. Much in demand, it is patronized mostly by organized groups, mostly for stays longer than one night, and may be booked up to a year in advance; however, sometimes an individual or two slips between the cracks, so it's worth at least a try to stay here, with your best luck being if you reserve as far ahead of time as possible. The hospice has been completely renovated and now has 62 rooms, with per-person rates at $17 for half board, $19 full board (no bed-and-breakfast rates). Highly recommended.

The **Convent of the Sisters of Nazareth,** just half a block up from the Casa Nova on Casa Nova Street (tel. 06-554-304), provide 25 beds (50 in summer) for young people in immaculate dormitories, separate for men and women. Facilities include hot showers, a large living-dining room, and a kitchen where you can prepare meals. You pay $3 a night for a bed. Be aware that there's no heating in the winter. Register as soon as possible after 4 p.m.

Two other religious hospices are located a bit more distant from the center of town, and you may need a map to find them.

The **Frères de Batharram Monastery** (tel. 06-570-046), to the west of the town's central district, offers hospice accommodations for 50 people, with two or three in each room. Prices are $10 per person, no meals.

On the very outskirts of town, to the north, is the hospice of the **Franciscan Sisters of Mary** (tel. 06-554-071), with half-board rates of $15 per person (no bed-and-breakfast rates here).

Restaurants

The **Astoria Restaurant,** on Casa Nova Street right at the intersection with Paul VI Street (tel. 06-577-965), is open daily—including Sunday—from 8 a.m. to 10 p.m. Reasonably priced Middle Eastern fare is featured here. Clean and airy, a full and interesting menu, and incongruous full-wall photomurals of the Rhine Valley—complete with castle—characterize the Astoria. No fewer than two dozen lamb dishes are listed on the menu, plus chicken and a fine selection of salads. Two salads, a grilled-meat main course, hot flat bread, pickles, a soft drink, service, and tip will run about NIS11 ($7.35) to NIS16 ($10.65), but don't be put off. You can eat for much less money if you like.

Save room for dessert, however. On Casa Nova Street is a Middle Eastern sweet-fancier's vision of the pearly gates. Up on the left-hand side of Casa Nova Street, just before it meets the basilica, is **Abu-Diab Mahroum's Sweets** (tel. 06-571-802 or 576-022). The shop windows are filled with the most agonizingly tempting delicacies: baklava, Turkish Delight (maajoun) with nuts, Esh el-Bulbul ("Hummingbird's Nest," a shredded-wheat bird's nest filled with nuts and laced with honey), or burma, a roll of shredded wheat stuffed with pistachios and soaked in honey or syrup. The shop is always full of local people who've dropped in to pick up a box of dessert, and the lightning-fingered clerks deftly stuff the boxes in what seems to be no time at all. Have a portion and a cup of Turkish coffee for about NIS4 ($2.65), depending on which sweet you order, or buy some by the gram or kilo to take out. Mahroum's is open from 7 a.m. to 9 p.m. every day.

By the way, since I first recommended Mahroum's Sweets in this book some years ago, several other confectioners' shops have opened on Casa Nova Street, each calling itself—you guessed it—Mahroum's Sweets! The others may be fine, but I still prefer the original, right near the Basilica of the Annunciation.

Want to find picnic fixings? Wander up into the market, which you enter off Casa Nova Street. All the shops you need are in this fascinating, exotic Middle Eastern bazaar.

Sights and Sites of Nazareth

There are three occupations for tourists in Nazareth: shopping in the market, visiting the holy Christian shrines, and taking a glance at the new Jewish quarter.

The Market: The market streets, entered via Casa Nova, are narrow, crowded, and highly exotic. Remember that the deeper you get into the market, the smaller the shops become and the lower the prices. One of the first things to note is the trench running dead center of the street, and one of the first precautions is to stay out of it as much as possible—it's the donkey trail. Snaking upward, the narrow roadway is lined with tin-roofed shops that give you a good idea where the expression "hole-in-the-wall" originated. In these shops you'll see everything from plows and ram's horns to cakes, leather goods, chandeliers, plastic buckets, and fine jewelry. Daily necessities are displayed side by side with antiques from Turkish times that sell for thousands of shekels. You can buy a finjan coffee set here or, if you want to play Lawrence of Arabia, a kefiya, the

Arab headdress. One shop, deep in the market, carries narghilis (bubble pipes). One reliable shop is the **Mazzawi Bazaar.** If you're a coin collector, try the tiny shop of **Amin,** where you'll find quite an assortment of coins and prices. Whatever you buy, be sure to shop around, and whatever you do, bargain over everything.

Religious Edifices: The **Basilica of the Annunciation** is located on Casa Nova Street, on the spot where, according to Christian tradition, the angel Gabriel appeared before Mary, saying: "Hail Mary, full of grace, the Lord is with thee, blessed art thou among women. . . . Behold, thou shalt conceive in thy womb, and bring forth a son, and shall call his name Jesus" (Luke 1). The present Basilica of the Annunciation, a new and boldly beautiful monument completed in 1966, was built over earlier structures dating from 1730 to 1877.

The very earliest church was built over a cave, the one in which Mary sat when Gabriel spoke to her. You can still see the cave—or grotto, actually. As you enter the basilica, you'll be on the ground (or cave) level, which is in fact the church's crypt. After you've toured the crypt, walk back to the entrance and you'll see steps up to the nave.

Modern, bold, daring—and effective—are the words that come to mind when one is confronted with the basilica's architecture. So many of the Christian shrines in Israel were built in the styles of earlier ages that it's refreshing to explore a modern work done in a modern style that's highly successful. Around the nave, on the walls, are murals contributed by countries and peoples throughout the world, done in "national" styles by the national craftspeople. Each is a masterwork in itself, but several stand out from the rest. On the left (north) wall, the Japanese mural of the Madonna and Child is excellently harmonious, and Mary's kimono-like robe is made entirely of Japanese seed pearls! The mural from the United States, on the right (south) wall, seems harsh, discordant, and excessively bold at first. But it is directly opposite the basilica's north-side door, and is meant to be viewed as one enters that doorway—go over to the doorway and try it. From here, the mural is still daring, but it works. The Madonna and Child is the theme of the murals because, of course, this was the site of the Annunciation to Mary.

The basilica is open daily: summer hours are 8 to 11:45 a.m. and again from 2 to 5:45 p.m.; in winter it's 9 to 11:45 a.m. and 2 to 4:45 p.m. (Many of the churches in Nazareth observe these same hours, closing for the "noontime siesta" during the middle of the day.)

The Basilica of the Annunciation is the major religious sight in Nazareth, but others are close by. Walk out the north-side door to reach them.

The **Church of St. Joseph** is 100 yards away, constructed on the site thought to be occupied by Joseph's carpentry workshop. From the sanctuary, stairways on either side go down to another floor below, where you can see old stone construction, an ancient water cistern, and a mosaic floor dating from the Byzantine period. Hours are the same as at the Basilica of the Annunciation, above.

On the main street in the bazaar is the Greek Catholic **Synagogue Church** which Jesus frequented: "And He came to Nazareth, where He had been brought up; and, as His custom was, He went into the synagogue on the Sabbath day, and stood up for to read" (Luke 4:16). Farther along the road is the **Franciscan Mensa Christi Church,** believed to occupy the spot where Christ dined with his disciples after the Resurrection.

Mary's Well, with its source inside the **Greek Orthodox Church of the Annunciation,** is another holy site for Christians visiting Nazareth. This church was built at the end of the 17th century over the remains of three former churches. Go down Casa Nova Street to Paul VI Street, turn left, then go up two blocks, and veer off on the street to the left of the public fountain; the church is about one short block up this street, straight ahead. It's open daily from 8 a.m. to 5 p.m. all year round (all day through with no lunchtime break). As you enter the church, you'll see a colorful mural on the archway above the stone staircase leading down to the well, showing the angel Gabriel coming to Mary and announcing in six languages, "Hail, thou that are highly favored, the Lord is with thee: blessed art thou among women." Look up and you'll see that the entire ceiling is covered with brightly colored murals depicting scenes from the Bible. There's really a lot of lively action going on up there! Proceed through the archway before you and you'll come to the well itself, touching in its simplicity—a small, perpetually flowing spring, and beside it, a round stone well where you can lower a metal cup to bring up water.

The **Basilica of Jesus the Adolescent,** maintained by the French Salesian Order, is one of the handsomest churches in Nazareth, built in 1918 but in a 13th-century style, with pillars composed of clusters of slender columns rising upward to the vaulted roof. There's a lovely marble statue of Jesus the Adolescent by the sculptor Bognio. You'll find plenty of present-day young people here too, since the large building to the left of the church is used as a school. It's located high on a hill north of the center of town—a bit of a climb, but well worth the effort, both for the church itself and for the sweeping vista of the town and the surrounding landscape.

Our Lady of Fright Chapel, sometimes called the Tremore, is built on a lofty wooded hill south of the center opposite the Galilee Hotel. It's in a quietly rustic location, built on the spot where Mary watched while the people of Nazareth attempted to throw Jesus over a cliff—the Precipice, or Lord's Leap rock, a quarter of a mile away (see Luke 4:29).

Although Nazareth is famous as a Christian city, half its population is Muslim, and the town hosts some lovely Muslim structures. The beautiful and modern **Al-Salam Mosque** is in the eastern quarter of town, just a short block from Paul VI Street. Started in 1960, it was completed five years later. Its platform resembles the Taj Mahal in India. In the southern part of the city is the new **Al-Huda Mosque.**

And finally, a little over six miles southeast of Nazareth, **Mount Tabor** (at 1,800 feet above sea level the tallest of the Lower Galilee Mountains) merits a visit. At the summit stands the **Basilica of the Transfiguration,** which, according to Christian tradition, marks where Jesus was transfigured in the presence of three of his disciples. Also on the mount is the Church of Elias, built in 1911 by the Greek Orthodox community. On a clear day, you can see the Sea of Galilee, Mount Hermon, the Mediterranean Sea, and the Emek from here. Mount Tabor is accessible from Nazareth by Egged bus or taxi.

The Jewish Quarter: Nazareth's 25,000 or so Jewish residents live in Upper Nazareth (Nazorat Ilit), a new part of town on a ridge to the northeast of the city. Construction was begun here in 1957, largely in connection with the establishment of several factories in the area, including a huge textile plant, an auto plant, and light industries producing biscuits, chocolate, and rugs.

2. Tiberias and the Sea of Galilee

Five main roads lead to Tiberias and the Sea of Galilee: from Safed, from the Jordan Valley, via Mount Tabor, and from Nazareth. Then, too, there's the shortcut from Afula to Tiberias. But the usual favorite is the road from Nazareth, if only for that dip in the road and that sudden unfolding of the mountains when the Sea of Galilee is suddenly spread down below you—truly one of Israel's most enchanting and rewarding spectacles.

It happens best on a clear day, about five miles from Tiberias. You have been on winding mountain roads, going up and down from dale to dell. Arab villages are sprawled on the hillsides, their stone houses packed onto the slopes, their arches and walls dotting the landscape. You'll also have passed the famous sabra cactuses, thickly clustered at the road's edge, those monstrous prickly pear plants with their dangerous spiked arms and little orange fruits.

Then you round a bend and there it is—the Sea of Galilee, a tranquil lake in a pastoral valley almost too lovely to believe. As you get closer, you see how alive the landscape around the lake becomes, how the descending slopes are carpeted with green, with the almost make-believe white settlements nestled comfortably along the grassy hills that roll down to the lake. There is a smell of heaven in this lovely scene, and you can almost hear the shepherd's flute.

This is the lake where the miracles of the New Testament occurred. On its shores, Jesus preached to the crowds and fed them by multiplying the bread and fish. Here he restored the sick and maimed to health. Today, on the waters where Jesus once walked, speedboats zoom past in utter disregard of the sea's oldtime magic, and waterskiers skim effortlessly along the surface of the lake.

Don't be startled by the names given to this body of water. In olden times, the Arabic and Aramaic poets called it the Bride, the Handmaiden of the Hills, and the Silver Woman. The ancient Hebrews called it the Lute in honor of the soothing harp-like sounds of its waves, and because of the form of the lake which is roughly lute-shaped. Today, Israelis still call the Sea of Galilee "lute"—in Hebrew "Kinnor," or **Kinneret,** as it is popularly known. According to one lexicographer, an ancient sage has written: "God created the seven seas, but the Kinneret is His pride and joy."

Some 700 feet below sea level, the Sea of Galilee is only 13 miles long, from the place where the Jordan flows in at the north to where it empties out in the south. Its entire breadth and length is within Israeli territory, except that at some points along its northern and eastern reaches, the shoreline was, before the 1967 war, Syrian territory and is now within the Israeli-occupied Golan Heights.

Abundant in fish, Kinneret's waters are a vast reservoir of sardine, mullet, catfish, and the unusual combfish. They are the same fish once caught by the Disciples, and they are hauled in in nets today in the same manner. However, the boats have changed, the white-sailed fishing vessels of biblical times giving way to the kibbutzniks' diesel-powered craft, equipped with sonar devices for hunting out shoals of fish.

Tiberias is the tourist center for the Galilee and Golan regions, making an excellent base for explorations of these nearby areas as well as Lake Kinneret. Its climate makes it a tourist center all year round, although the busiest time is in the summer months, especially July and August. In the winter Tiberias' unique location enables you to go snow skiing on Mount Hermon (1½ hours' drive, 9,000 feet above sea level) in the morning, and be waterskiing back on Lake Kinneret (700 feet below sea level) in the afternoon—and in the evening, dining on anything from a 65¢ falafel to a $25 supper at one of Israel's most acclaimed restaurants, or enjoying a dance on a night-sailing ferry. In about an hour you can drive from Tiberias to the Golan Heights, the Lebanese border, Safed, Nazareth, the Yizreel Valley, or down through the Jordan Valley to the south, as well as to any place on the Sea of Galilee, or you can simply stay put and enjoy the pleasures of Tiberias itself. For all these reasons, despite its small size, Tiberias has become the major tourist center for its region.

A BIT OF HISTORY: The ancient town of Tiberias, built in A.D. 18 by Herod Antipas (son of Herod the Great) in honor of the Roman emperor Tiberias, is today one of Israel's leading winter resorts. That doesn't mean, however, that its shoreline architecture resembles the plush and palatial pleasure domes of the Riviera. On the contrary. Although the waterfront at Tiberias has large, beautiful hotels and modern bathing beaches, there are also the Arabesque domes of the mineral water bathhouses, the scars of archeological digs, and the tombs of the great rabbinical sages.

After the Temple of Jerusalem was destroyed, Tiberias became the great Jewish center in the Holy Land. It was here the famous Mishnah was completed in A.D. 200 at the direction of Rabbi Yehuda Ha-Nassi, "Judah the Prince." The Jerusalem Talmud was compiled in this town in A.D. 400, and the vowel and punctuation grammar was introduced into the Hebrew language by the learned men of Tiberias. Mystics, academicians, and men with supposedly magic powers populated Tiberias, breathing into the city a power and knowledge still held in reverence by many throughout Israel and the world today.

This towering scholarship, unfortunately, declined in the years that followed, due to the many battles fought here by the Arabs, Crusaders, and Turks. Tiberias must have reached a low ebb during the Middle Ages, because an Arab historian, El Makdase, recorded around A.D. 1000 that residents of the town languidly and wastefully passed each year by doing nothing more than dancing, feasting, playing the flute, running about naked, and swatting flies. So heavy were the flies, and so famous a reputation had Tiberias acquired, that one sage wrote: "Beelzebub, the Lord of the Flies, holds his court in Tiberias."

Efforts were made by pashas and scholars in the 18th and 19th centuries to restore some of the city's former potency, but such plans were doomed in 1837 by an earthquake, which reduced much of Tiberias to rubble. This year in Tiberias you can still see a few remains of those early times during your sightseeing. But you'll have to hunt out these old sights in Tiberias, because to most people the town is simply a resort and a good base of operations for excursions around the Sea of Galilee.

A GEOLOGICAL NOTE: The location here is also distinctive in a geological sense, and knowing something about this will enable you better to appreciate the landscape you'll see, as well as many of the older buildings.

Stand anywhere around the shore of the Sea of Galilee and you'll notice that on the eastern side are cliffs, dropping sharply down to the lake below; in fact, you can stand at the Sea of Galilee, 700 feet below sea level, and look up toward the north and see Mount Hermon towering above you, 9,000 feet above sea level.

The reason for this is that you are standing on one of the earth's major geological fault lines, the **Syrian/African Rift** (or break, or fault). For this reason the entire area, geologically speaking, is known as the "Valley of the Rift." The fault line begins in southern Turkey / northern Syria, extends southward through Israel (from north to south, through the Hula Valley, the Sea of Galilee, the Jordan Valley, the Dead Sea, down to Eilat), and all the way to Lake Victoria in Malawi, Africa. Relative to one another, the east side is moving north, the west side (where you are if you're standing by the lake) is moving south.

It's due to this geological movement that the mountains and valleys here are shaped the way they are, and it's also the reason for the earthquakes and volcanic eruptions which have occurred here over the centuries, and the mineral hot springs bubbling up from the ground around the shores of Lake Kinneret and the Dead Sea. The volcanic activity has been a while in the past, but you can see evidence of it in the older buildings and in Tiberias' Old City Wall, whose large black stone bricks are made from volcanic rock, called black basalt.

As for earthquakes, the largest major one in modern times occurred on January 1, 1837, and it was a zinger, demolishing most of the towns in the area, including Tiberias and Safed. But don't worry: geologists who measure the tensions in the earth are not expecting another major earthquake here for many years, probably not until the next century, so don't expect an earthquake to shake up your visit.

Another interesting feature of the Syrian/African Rift is that it forms a highway for bird migration. Two of Israel's major wildlife reserves—Hula Valley in the north, Hai Bar in the south—serve as stopping-off points for the birds on their long journey, and are popular with birdwatchers and nature lovers.

ORIENTATION: Tiberias (or Teverya; pop. 35,000) spreads out along the Kinneret shore and climbs the hillside to the west. The very center of Tiberias is **Kikar Ha-Atzma'ut,** or Independence Square, in the Old City. Surrounding Ha-Atzma'ut Square is historical Tiberias, the city of the rabbis, the early Christians, and the later Turkish governors.

The **Central Bus Station** (tel. 06-791-080 or 791-081) is barely two blocks inland from Ha-Atzma'ut Square along Yarden Street. Unless your bags are filled with bricks, you should be able to walk to any hotel in the Old City.

The **Tourist Information Office** is also just off Ha-Atzma'ut Square at 8 Elhadeff St. (tel. 06-720-992), up the hill a bit on the right-hand side. Hours are 8 a.m. to 5 p.m. Sunday through Thursday, to 2 p.m. on Friday; closed Saturday. You can find friendly help here with any question or need you may have. In an active tourist center like Tiberias, new attractions often pop up, so it's a good idea to check here for what's current at the time you're in town.

Another resource for travelers is the **Voluntary Tourist Service,** with kindly volunteers at all the major hotel lobbies, waiting to answer your questions. You'll find them there in the evenings, Sunday through Thursday from 6 to 8:30 p.m., holidays excepted. (If you want further information about this program, you can call the head office in Tel Aviv at 03-222-459, or ask at the Tourist Information Office.)

Tiberias's main street changes names as it winds through the city. As it descends from the mountains to the lake it's called **Ha-Nitzahon Road;** in the residential district of Kiryat Shmuel up on the hillside it becomes **Yehuda Ha-Nassi Street,** and as it descends to approach the Old City its name changes to **Elhadeff** (or El-Hadeff or Alhadif) **Street.** After passing Ha-Atzma'ut Square it becomes **Ha-Banim Street,** and this name serves it all the way to the southern limits of the city.

Northwest of the Old City, up on the hill which overlooks downtown, is the large residential district of **Kiryat Shmuel,** which has lots of moderately priced hotels.

South of the Old City about 1½ km (one mile) is the section called **Hammat,** or **Tiberias Hot Springs.** Ruins of an ancient synagogue and town, a national park, a museum, and the Tomb of Rabbi Meir Baal Haness are located near the springs.

North of the Old City, Gdud Barak Road skirts the water's edge and several beaches on its way to **Magdala** (where Mary Magdalene came from), **Tabgha** (where the miracle of the loaves and fishes took place), **Mount of Beatitudes** (where Jesus preached the Sermon on the Mount), and **Capernaum** (Kefar Nahum).

GETTING AROUND: You can **rent a bicycle** at Gal-Cal Rent A Bike (tel. 06-736-278) in the Central Bus Station, at NIS10 ($6.65) for 24 hours, with hourly and half-day rates also available. While you're here, you might also ask about renting a rubber boat, a mask and snorkel, or camping gear. Hours are Sunday through Thursday from 9 a.m. to 6:30 p.m. (on Tuesday and Friday to 2:30 p.m.); closed Saturday. (Since it's closed Saturday, if you come in to rent something on a Friday, you get to keep it until Sunday for no extra charge.)

You can **rent a car** at any of five different major rent-a-car companies with offices in Tiberias, many of them found in the block of Elhadeff Street north of Ha-Yarden Street, the block where the Tourist Information Office is located. In alphabetical order, here's a listing of their telephone numbers: **Avis** (tel. 06-790-898 or 790-199), **Budget** (tel. 06-792-393), **Eldan** (tel. 06-792-233), **Europcar** (tel. 06-721-158), **Hertz** (tel. 06-791-822 or 792-950). Check to see which is offering the best prices at the time you're there—it pays to shop around.

ACCOMMODATIONS IN TIBERIAS:

Due to its significance as a center for tourism, vacationing, and pilgrimage, Tiberias has a number of suitable accommodations of many kinds, from youth hostels to five-star hotels, with a few religious institutions as well. I've tried to sort out the choices for you, making it easy to see at a glance the variety of accommodations available. First, I'll list hotel choices in the various areas of town, then the alternatives to hotels—private rooms, hostels, hospices, and a few more selections that are out of town (but not too far). With all the variety, you should be able to find something which ideally suits your taste and pocketbook.

Practically every hotel in Tiberias has a kosher kitchen; several hotels not only control carefully the *kashrut* of their kitchens, but see to it that an atmosphere of orthodoxy prevails in their establishments. Strictly observant Jews find these the perfect bases for a Tiberias vacation. Two of these, in the Kiryat Shmuel area, are not only kosher but glatt kosher, have synagogues on the premises, and are enjoyable places to stay: the Ron Hotel and the Ariston (see the details under the descriptions of these hotels).

Downtown Budget Hotels

In the downtown and beachfront areas you can find five-star hotels that charge over $100 per night—but you don't need to spend that much to have an enjoyable stay downtown. Although most of the moderately priced three-star hotels in Tiberias are up on the hill in the Kiryat Shmuel district, you can find a few possibilities downtown too. And don't neglect to check out the private rooms, hostels, and hospices downtown either. Just because it's a hostel or a hospice, don't automatically assume that that means a big dormitory room with a crowd of screaming youngsters, or that you have to be a monk to stay there. Not at all! To get a room to yourself, ask if "family rooms" are available. You may pay a dollar or two extra, but you still may find it less expensive than a hotel, and equally suitable.

However, as for hotels, a couple of nice possibilities do exist. One especially pleasant place is **Hotel Toledo** (tel. 06-721-649 and 791-229), offering 24 clean, simple, but attractive rooms with private tub and shower, air conditioning and heat, and friendly management. Prices, including breakfast, are $22 single, $30 double. The street it's on may be called Ha-Perahim, or Ha-Rab Bibass, or maybe even Yehuda Ha-Levi Yarkon (street names have been changing quite a bit in this town), but in any case, follow these simple directions and you won't have any trouble finding it: walk down the stairs and out the front door of the Egged bus station, across the lawn to the street, and turn right. Take the next right onto Ha-Rab Bibass Street, and the hotel is a half block up on the right-hand side.

The spartan but functional **Panorama Hotel**, 19 Ha-Galil St. (tel. 06-720-963), about three blocks south of Ha-Atzma'ut Square, has 35 rooms with private shower and toilet, air conditioning (but no heat), a TV lounge, and a nice outdoor terrace with a view of the lake. The rooms on the lake side of the building have that nice view too. Prices here are definitely a good deal, at $7 single, $12 double, or in August, $12 and $20 respectively. These prices do not include breakfast, but there's a restaurant downstairs where you can eat for about $1 to $2.

Also on Ha-Galil Street, at no. 4, is the **Hotel Polonia** (tel. 06-720-007), with 25 rooms and prices at $15 single, $30 double all year, breakfast included.

Downtown Hostels and Hospices

Tiberias's downtown area boasts a number of nice hostels and hospices, which are an excellent choice for the budget traveler.

Top on the list of recommendable spots is the **Yoseph Meyouhas Youth Hostel** (P.O. Box 81; tel. 06-721-775 or 790-350). It's sparkling clean, well run, centrally located; it's in an attractive, historical building; and on the Youth Hostel network, it's noted for its good food. With 240 beds, you can usually find a room here; but as it's a popular place, you might want to reserve in advance or check in early, if you come during peak seasons. Prices here are the same as at all official IYHA hostels: $5.50 for members over 18, $5 under 18, $1 more for non-members, breakfast included. You can get a family room (that means a room to yourself) for $1 extra per person, and air conditioning for 65¢ per day in hot weather. Dinner is an especially good deal: for $3.60 you get soup, salad, cooked vegetables, rice or potatoes, bread and butter, and beverages; for another $1.50 you can get meat too. Either way, you'll get more food than you can eat, and it will probably be delicious. Meyouhas is easy to find—it's the huge black basalt building, clearly marked, on the corner of Ha-Yarden and Ha-Banim Streets, two of Tiberias's principal streets, just a block up from the lake. The building is closed up tight from 9 a.m. to 3:30 p.m. (that means everybody out, office closed), but you can check in anytime after 3:30 p.m.; curfew is at midnight or 1 a.m.

Another nice spot, but more expensive, is the **Church of Scotland Hospice** (P.O. Box 104, Tiberias 14100; tel. 06-790-144 or 790-145), just behind the Meyouhas Youth Hostel. The hospice, built 100 years ago as a Scottish missionary hospital, has several buildings made from those black basalt stones distinctive of the region. The hospice welcomes all visitors, and prices are $23 single, $38 double, for a simple room with full private facilities. Registration is from 7:45 a.m. to 12:30 p.m. (to noon on Saturday), and again from 4 to 6:30 p.m.

Along the lakeside promenade you'll find the **Franciscan Hospice** (P.O. Box 179, Tiberias 14101; tel. 06-720-516), run by the Terra Santa Franciscan Church. It's in a historic stone building built by the Franciscans in 1900, in a complex that also includes an elegantly simple church whose altar is all that remains of the 12th century Crusader church. Accommodations are simple, with ten high-ceilinged rooms, three or four beds to a room. Since it's hostel style, you may be sharing a room with other people, in addition to sharing toilets, solar-heated showers, and a kitchen where you can prepare your own meals. No curfews here; you can come and go as you wish. There's an outdoor terrace, with a lovely closeup view of the entire lake. The price is $5 per person, not including breakfast year round.

The **Castle Hostel** (P.O. Box 169, Tiberias 14101; tel. 06-721-175) is a little farther down on the waterfront promenade, in a historic black basalt building that does indeed look like a castle. It has 108 beds (an average of six beds in each room); separate or mixed sexes, as you prefer. Prices are $7 to $9 per person in summer, including breakfast, but quite a bit lower (around $4 per person, no breakfast) in winter. There's a cafeteria here in the evening, and a nice terrace overlooking the lake. The hostel closes between 9:30 a.m. and 4 p.m.; curfew is at 11 p.m. (at midnight on Friday and Saturday), so if you're coming to check in, plan around these times.

Two other hostels which young people may like are just around the corner from one another, also in the downtown area.

Maman Hostel (tel. 06-792-986) is on Atzmon Street (no number), near where it intersects with Ha-Shiloah Street; just walk out of the bus station, go across the little grassy area and turn to your right (you'll be on Ha-Shiloah Street), walk up two blocks, and you'll see it. There's a friendly and relaxed atmosphere here for young international travelers, with about 50 beds available in eight-bed dormitory rooms ($3.35 per person), a double room for two ($5 per person), or downstairs, a private room with its own bathroom and kitchen, going for $16.60 a night (that's the price for the room, not per person). Mixed or single-sex rooms, as you prefer. If you want breakfast it's an extra $2, but you also are welcome to use the hostelers' kitchen to prepare your own meals. There's a pub in the evening on the outdoor balcony terrace, and air conditioning too, during hot weather. Maman is open all day, with no curfew, and you can even rent a bicycle here.

Walk down the hill from here—or walk up from Ha-Galil Street—and on Tavor Street (no number, but you can't miss it) you'll see the 60-bed **Nahum Hostel** (tel. 06-721-505). One of the nicest things about this place is its rooftop outdoor evening pub, with a fine view of the lake and video music as well. There's a shared kitchen, air conditioning, and bicycles for rent, plus you can come and go anytime. Prices are $3.35 per person in a dorm room, $6.60 per person in a double room, or $16.50 ($8.25 per person) for a double room with its own private toilet and shower.

In Kiryat Shmuel

Kiryat Shmuel is a nice residential and hotel district up on the hill overlooking Tiberias and the Sea of Galilee. All the hotels I'll mention here are clean, modern, recommendable, and with three-star facilities (except for a couple of exceptions, which I'll note). Three stars means private bathroom (usually with tub as well as shower; ask to make sure you get a room with a tub if you want one), air conditioning and heat, telephone and radio in the rooms, carpeting, TV room, usually a bar in addition to a nice dining room, plus private parking facilities. All these hotels have kosher dining rooms, and two, the Ron and the Ariston, are glatt kosher. Being up on a hill, almost all have at least some rooms with enjoyable, or even spectacular, views. Again, if you want a room with a view facing the Sea of Galilee, specify it when you book your room.

You may want to take a taxi to get up to Kiryat Shmuel if you're arriving in Tiberias by bus, for it's about a half-kilometer away from downtown, and that half-kilometer is all uphill. Once you've got your bearings, you can use the city bus with ease; or if you're spry, the 20-minute walk up and down the hill into downtown Tiberias will give you some healthy exercise.

The first hotel you'll come to as you head up Elhadeff Street toward Kiryat Shmuel is the **Continental Hotel** (P.O. Box 102; tel. 06-720-018 or 791-870), right on the corner of Elhadeff and Tabur Ha-Aretz Streets. You'll find it a pleasant, friendly place, with rooms prices at about $22 single, $40 double all year round. Half the rooms have balconies, with a nice lake view.

Farther up Elhadeff Street, where Elhadeff intersects Yehuda Ha-Nassi Street, is the 84-room **Galilee Hotel** (tel. 06-791-166 or 791-168). Prices here vary throughout the year, ranging from $27 single, $36 double in low season (June, and November through January, at this hotel), to $35 single, $52 double in August and for the Jewish holidays. You can get a suite by adding $5 per person.

As soon as it crosses Yehuda Ha-Nassi, Elhadeff Street becomes Ohel Yaakov Street, and it's at this intersection, right between the Galilee and the Eden hotels in either side, that you'll find the **Peer Hotel,** 2 Ohel Yaakov St. (P.O. Box 625; tel. 06-791-641 or 791-642), with 70 rooms. A special feature here is the disco bar and nightclub, open to all comers with no cover charge. Prices are $29 single, $40 double for most of the year, with reductions of a few dollars at certain times.

Right next door, there's the modernly decorated, 82-room **Hotel Eden,** 4 Ohel Yaakov St. (P.O. Box 565; tel. 06-790-070 or 722-461). The new disco, Club Eden, open every Friday and Saturday night plus one additional evening during the week, is a popular place, and though it costs $6.50 (including first drink) for outsiders, it's free admission for hotel guests. Prices at the Eden are $25 single, $37 double most of the year; $35 and $49 respectively during high season.

Hotel Astoria, 13 Ohel Yaakov St. (tel. 06-722-351 or 722-352), another fine choice, has 56 rooms, some with balconies, and all the other three-star amenities. Here you'll pay varying rates for high, low, and regular seasons, ranging from $20 to $30 single, $30 to $42 double, depending on the time of year.

The 72-room **Hotel Tiberias,** 19 Ohel Yaakov St. (P.O. Box 550, Tiberias 14223; tel. 06-792-270), is a friendly, family-operated, newly renovated three-star hotel, with a guest book containing favorable comments from visitors from all over the world. The heated swimming pool is covered in winter so that it can be used all year round; other special features include sauna, whirlpool baths, exercise room, weight room, video room, card room, pub, and a disco/piano bar for guests only. Professional massage by appointment ($10). Considering all these extras, prices here are reasonable at $28 single, $39 double (add $6 per person in high season). In addition to the hotel entertainment, you also get discounts to many tourist sites around the lake. (Not listed as kosher.)

Go down the hill to the end of Herzl Boulevard and you'll come to the 75-room **Hotel Ariston,** 19 Herzl Blvd. (tel. 06-722-002 or 790-244). Prices here remain the same all year, at $25 single, $40 double. You'll probably get a room with a balcony and a spectacular view of the lake; be sure to ask for one. Glatt kosher; synagogue here too.

A fine choice is the **Ron Hotel,** 12 Ahad Ha-Am St. (Tiberias 14222; tel. 06-790-829 or 790-760). Not to be confused with the Hotel Ron Beach or the Hotel Ram, the 54-room Ron is a wonderfully pleasant place, with a congenial atmosphere and marvelous lake views, due to its position perched on a hill. Be sure you ask for a room with a view. Prices remain the same all year, with singles going for $25 to $30, doubles for $37 to $44. Glatt kosher, with a synagogue on the premises.

Next to the Ron, at 14 Ahad Ha-Am St., is the four-star **Golan Hotel** (P.O. Box 555, Tiberias 14222; tel. 06-791-901 or 791-904), a fancy establishment with 78 rooms, all with magnificent views, and a swimming pool too, used during the warm season. Prices here are a bit higher, but not by that much, really: low-season rates are $32 single, $44 double, and regular rates are $37 single, $52 double. High season here is on holidays only, when rates go up to $43 single, $64 double—so why not come when it's not so expensive? It's quite a nice place, with an outdoor cafeteria and garden, and an intimate bar with dancing.

Just across the street from the Hotel Ron, you'll see the back door to the small, two-star **Hotel Sara,** 7 Zeidel St. (tel. 06-720-826). (Of course, you're welcome to come in the front door too, which faces Hayim Park.) Actually, it used to be called the Hotel Sara; by the time you read this book, maybe the signs will have been changed to reflect the new name: **Ganei Shmuel.** At this writing, in addition to the name change, a lot of refurbishing is going on in the small, 17-room hotel; all the rooms have private toilet and shower, one with tub, some with fan only, some with heat and air conditioning, and more improvements on the way. Rates are $15 per person with breakfast, $10 without the meal, single or double; $5 more in high season.

Another simple, two-star choice is the **Hotel Arnon,** 28 Ha-Shomer St. (tel. 06-720-181), with 20 rooms, all with private toilet and shower (two with tub), and air conditioning. Prices are the same all year: $18 single, $32 double, except for Jewish holidays, when they go up 25%.

Finally, look toward Ha-Nassi Street of an evening and you'll see the red neon lights announcing the **Hotel Daphne** (P.O. Box 502; tel. 06-792-261 or 792-263) towering above you. Located near the intersection of Ha-Nassi and Ussishkin Streets, the three-star Daphne has two buildings, for a total of 73 modern rooms, some with lake view. Prices here remain the same all year: $23 to $27 single, $35 to $40 double, including free transportation to the Tiberias Hot Springs, and discounts on Kinneret sailings and many other tourist activities.

On the Beach

North of town along Gdud Barak Road toward Magdala and Capernaum are several beachfront hotels. To stay here is to stretch our budget a bit—but not really all that much.

The **Quiet Beach Hotel** (P.O. Box 175, Tiberias 14101; tel 06-721-441 or 720-602) is perhaps the best, a new building with 73 rooms, each with balcony, phone, radio, air conditioning, wall-to-wall carpeting, and private bath. The hotel has pretty lawns, a swimming pool (though it's right on the lakeshore), sailboats, and waterskiing. Rates are very reasonable in autumn, winter, and spring: $32 single, $46 double; from July 15 through August, prices rise substantially.

The **Ron Beach Hotel** (P.O. Box 173, Tiberias 14101; tel 06-791-350) has all the conveniences, a restaurant noted for its lake fish, and prices of $37 single, $53 double, breakfast and service included, in season. You get reductions at other times.

South of the center is another place you might want to consider.

All the way down past the Hot Springs is the **Ganei Menora Hotel** (P.O. Box 99; tel. 06-792-769 or 792-770), also called the Menora Gardens. With 73 rooms and a country club-like setting, the Ganei Menora makes up for its distance from the center of the action. It's superbly quiet here, with lots of trees and flowers, and guest rooms in all sorts of buildings, large and small: a main building (with kosher dining room), bungalows, and motel-type units. Some of the rooms in the main building have balconies and wonderful views of the lake; all come with radio, air conditioning, and telephone. Prices are $25 single, $37 double all year round, except for Jewish holidays when they rise to $28 single, $40 double. The Ganei Menora is popular with retired people, who value its peaceful, quiet location.

Rooms in Private Homes

As in many parts of Israel, people rent out rooms in their homes and apartments. In Tiberias, several families have done this so successfully that they've been able to remodel the house to accommodate guests, and now these places are about the equivalent of two-star hotels, with private entrances and your own key—so you can come and go as you wish, without worrying about disturbing the family.

The **Cohen House,** 4 Dona Gracia St. (tel. 06-721-608), is in a convenient location about a five-minute walk from downtown, yet out of the way enough to be far removed from the hubbub and noise of the city center. It has four double rooms, plus one apartment which is good for larger groups or longer stays. The double rooms share a kitchen and a small garden, but each has its own private bath with shower. It's quiet and peaceful here, not far from the lake. Prices for one night are $10 single, $16 double; for two or three nights you'll pay $8 single, $14 double; and there are further reductions for stays of a week or more. Prices remain the same all year; in high season or on Jewish holidays, you should definitely reserve in advance. The price of the room does not include breakfast, but there's a supermarket nearby and you can save money by being able to use the kitchen to prepare your own meals.

Up in Kiryat Shmuel are a couple of other fine choices.

At **Bet Habler,** 16 Rachel St., Kiryat Shmuel (tel. 06-721-746), the ten guest rooms are very simple: the only private facilities are your room, clean but simply furnished, and a sink with hot and cold running water, plus air conditioning and heat. However, there are ample shared facilities, including toilets, showers, and large bathtubs, a kitchen for your use, and a large TV/sitting room. Prices for rooms (no meals served here) are $10 per person per night, single or double, remaining the same all year.

A little farther out, but highly recommended, **Bet Berger,** 27 Naiberg St., Kiryat Shmuel (P.O. Box 535; tel. 06-720-850), has clean rooms, all with private shower, refrigerator, air conditioner, and heating. There's a cozy living/sitting/TV room downstairs, and fully equipped kitchens on each floor for guest use. Some of the bedrooms have terraces. Prices are $12 single, $18 double in winter, rising to $18 single, $25 double in August; no breakfast.

There are many more of these rooms in private homes. The best way to get into the market is to ask at the **Tourist Office,** 8 Elhadeff St. off Ha-Atzma'ut Square (tel. 06-720-992). And don't forget **Homtel** (tel. 03-289-141), which, although its main office is in Tel Aviv, can assist you in renting private rooms and apartments in any part of Israel.

Kibbutzim

Probably the most fascination can be found in a kibbutz guesthouse, and the nearest one to Tiberias—only a six-minute ride from downtown—is the **Nof Ginossar Guest House,** (Post Kibbutz Ginossar 14980; tel. 06-792-161 or 792-164). There is regular bus service, but for someone with a rented car, this is the perfect place to stay in Tiberias. Prices are very splurgy for us, but it is rated four stars, is right next to the sea, and has its own museum, tennis courts, beach and gardens, with kayaks, sailboarding, sailboats, and fishing poles for rent. The atmosphere is quiet, bucolic, and unhurried. The second-floor dining room (kosher) has a fine view of the Sea of Galilee, as do the rooms. There are 170 rooms in all, with either private bath or shower, air conditioning, and central heating. The guesthouse conducts a regular series of kibbutz tours and lectures with slides of kibbutz life. Rates for bed and breakfast are $38 single, $51 double for most of the year, a few dollars more or less during particularly high- or low-season times.

West of Tiberias, in what is known as Lower Galilee, is the **Lavi Guest House** (Lower Galilee Post 15267; tel. 06-799-450). Buses travel to Lavi direct from Tiberias and the ride takes only 15 minutes. This is a religious kibbutz with a great swimming pool and comfortable accommodations plus lecturers on kibbutz life. Rates for bed and breakfast—once again on the splurgy side for us (three star)—range from $35 to $39 single, $46 to $55 double. There is a minimum weekend rate of one full board plus one half board, and Holy Day prices are considerably higher.

Also, don't forget the many guests facilities at **Kibbutz Ein Gev,** on the eastern shore of the Sea of Galilee (described below).

Accommodations Around the Lake

Several nice possibilities exist for staying around the lake, especially if you enjoy camping. (By the way, if you need camping gear, you can rent it from **Gal-Cal Rent A Bike,** tel. 06-736-278, located in the Tiberias Central Bus Station; they also rent rubber boats, masks and snorkels, and bicycles.)

Here are a few especially enjoyable camping spots: On the south side of the lake, **Ma-Agon** (tel. 06-751-172 or 751-360) and **Ha-On** (tel. 06-757-555 or 757-557); then heading up around the east side of the lake, there's camping (and other guest facilities as well) at **Kibbutz Ein Gev** (tel. 06-763-750), and a little farther north, at **Ha-Golan Beach** (tel. 06-763-750), near the Luna Gal Water Amusement Park.

You can consult the **Tourist Information Office** in Tiberias (tel. 06-720-992) for information on other camping areas in the vicinity—there are many!

Three miles to the west of Tiberias, just off the road leading to Nazareth, **Kefar Hittim Camping** (Mobile Post Lower Galilee 15280; tel. 06-795-921 or 795-962) has 50 "chalets" overlooking a lovely hillside and the Sea of Galilee below. Each chalet holds up to four people, and has all its own facilities, including bathroom, kitchen, two bedrooms, and a large living/dining room, with air conditioning and heat, renting for $23 per night single, $34 double most of the year, higher in July and August, up to $58 double. There's camping here too, of course, and also a horse and pony ranch where you can go riding.

Back on the east side of the lake, the **Ramot Resort Hotel** (Mobile Post Ramat Ha-Golan 12490; tel. 06-763-760 or 763-636) has a deluxe, 80-room, air-conditioned hotel perched on the hillside overlooking the lake, with bed-and-breakfast prices of $38 single, $53 double in low season; $55 single, $88 double in high season. There are also 46 two-bedroom wooden cabins here, with kitchenettes, balconies, and showers, where prices are $5 less (no breakfast). There's a full recreation program, with swimming pool, horseback riding, archery, and organized trips.

Finally, there are two International Youth Hostels located near the lake, one to the north of Tiberias and one to the south.

Some 12 km (7¼ miles) to the north of Tiberias, at Kare Deshe, there's the **Yoram Youth Hostel** (Korazim Mobile Post; tel. 06-720-601), with 180 beds, family rooms, kitchen facilities available, and air conditioning. It's usually open all day, with no lock-out times. To get here from Tiberias, take the bus toward Kiryat Shmona or Safed and tell the driver where you're going; he'll let you off about an 800-yard walk from the hostel.

Then there's the **Taiber Youth Hostel** (P.O. Box 232, Tiberias; tel. 06-750-050), at Poria, 4 km (2½ miles) to the south of Tiberias. It has 140 beds, family rooms, and a hostelers' kitchen, and is usually open all day long. As of this writing, there is no bus coming to this hostel, and it's often reserved for large groups who come with their own bus. Call for current information before you come.

Both of these hostels have the same rates as at all the IYHA-affiliated hostels in Israel: $5.50 members, $6.50 for nonmembers, 50¢ less for those under 18, includes bed and breakfast, clean sheets, and hot showers.

RESTAURANTS IN TIBERIAS: Tiberias has a variety of restaurants, cafés, and snackshops to fit every taste and budget. Be aware, this is a small town, and so you won't find anywhere near the excitement and variety of Jerusalem, Tel Aviv, or Haifa; still, for a town of its size, Tiberias has a number of possibilities. Most eateries are open seven days a week; if a restaurant named here is closed for the Sabbath, I've mentioned it. Remember, too, that your hotel probably has arrangements for lunch and supper, and you may want to take advantage of these as well.

As luck would have it, the dining possibilities in Tiberias are nicely grouped in a few sections of town. Here they are, beginning with full restaurants, going on to cafés and light-lunch places, and ending up with the inevitable falefel stands.

Waterfront Restaurants

The speciality in Tiberias is the St. Peter's fish, so called because it is the very fish that swam in the Sea of Galilee when Christ called Peter away from his nets to follow him and become a "fisher of men." It's a white fish that is indigenous to the Sea of Galilee and its taste resembles bass. (The Waldorf Astoria has been importing it for some years, because of its subtle, very special taste.)

The best place to search out a good portion of St. Peter's fish, or even shish kebab for that matter, is down along the waterfront promenade in the Old City. You can get there by walking down Ha-Yarden Street until you reach the lake. Or just look for the minaret of the Great Mosque (there's only one), and pass by the mosque, heading for the shore. This is Old Tiberias, a municipal redevelopment project in which ancient crumbling buildings are being restored and new amenities—such as the waterfront promenade—are being added.

Three of the attractive waterfront restaurants have the same management, the same menu, the same prices, and the same delicious food. These are the **Nof Kinneret** (tel. 06-720-310), the **Galei Gil** (tel. 06-720-699), and the **Roast on Fire** (tel. 06-720-310). The decor is different in each restaurant, so stroll along and see which you like the best; but if the weather is fine, you'll likely want to eat at one of the promenade tables right down by the water's edge. Plan to spend about NIS15 ($10) for a large (over a pound) serving of St. Peter's fish, french fries, salad, and pita bread; if you add wine, coffee, and dessert besides, it will come to about NIS24 ($16). All three restaurants offer the fish fried, charcoal grilled, or in a special sauce, and there are lots of other choices too, such as steak, chicken, veal, or liver, all for about NIS12 ($8) the full meal. Hours are 8:30 a.m. to midnight seven days a week—but during the busiest tourist season, in summer, they may be open longer, even 24 hours.

Café Hayam Eli Abadi (tel. 06-720-048) is another restaurant along the promenade with the same type of food, the same prices, and the same hours as the restaurants above.

Karamba Vegetarian Restaurant/Bar (tel. 06-791-546) is a very different kind of place, and very attractive and enjoyable too, with its tropical decor and wicker furniture both indoors and out on the patio. It has different menus for winter and summer, offering hearty hot dishes in winter, such as vegetable pie topped with cheese for NIS8 ($5.35), with light meals, fruit dishes, and salads— like the Karamba salad, with assorted vegetables, cheese, nuts, raisins, and yogurt dressing, for NIS7 ($4.65)—emphasized more in summer. It's also a tropical bar and after-hours spot, with nice music, open in summer from 10 a.m. to 5 a.m., in winter from 5 p.m. to 6 a.m.

Near the Mosque

Near the waterfront promenade, you'll see the minaret of the Great Mosque rising above the surrounding buildings. This historic edifice is now incongruously located right in the middle of a modern commercial center. Head for the mosque, walk around among the many shops, restaurants, cafés, and pubs, and you're sure to find some spot that catches your fancy. Almost every place has tables both indoors and out on the walkway too. There's a lot of variety here, so I'll just give you a few examples.

For pizza, try **Pizza Pinate** (tel. 06-792-204), where the pizzas are tasty, good-sized, and nicely priced: the most expensive pizza in the house, the full combination, costs NIS6 ($4). Open from 8 a.m. to midnight most of the year, 24 hours in July and August.

Right beside the Great Mosque, you'll find the **Crimson Flower Chinese Restaurant** (tel. 06-790-221), a small, clean restaurant with attractive decor and good service. The Cantonese menu lists the usual chicken, pork, beef, and duck dishes, with a full meal going for NIS10 ($6.65) to NIS15 ($10). Open seven days, noon to 3 p.m. and 6 p.m. to midnight.

Bistro Tal Pub/Restaurant (tel. 06-790-941) is actually more of a pub, but it's not a bad place to catch a table outside; order turkey, kebab, or a hamburger, which with salad and fries will come to NIS10 ($6.65); one of seven kinds of beer; and sit and watch the world go by. Open from 11 a.m. until midnight or 2 a.m.

Next door is the **Dolphin Fish Restaurant** (tel. 06-790-958), with a menu and prices similar to the fish restaurants down on the waterfront. Open from 10 a.m. to 11 p.m.

For espresso, cappuccino, and excellent baked goods and pastries, try the **Contidoria Yatsek** and **Kapulsky,** two bakeries right next to one another. At either place, a pastry and cappuccino at a sidewalk table will cost about NIS3 ($2), but beware: they both do a lively business in baked goods to go, and it's not easy to resist the temptation to come away with a whole bag of delicious goodies. They're open from 8 a.m. to 10 p.m.

Downtown Restaurants

Ha-Kishon Street is a tiny, one-block-long passage intersecting with Ha-Banim Street about two blocks south of Ha-Yarden Street. Walk along this tiny street and take your pick of nice restaurants, including **Gan Esther, Avi's Tea House, Little Tiberias,** and other places where full meals are priced at NIS10 ($6.65) to NIS18 ($12). Though Ha-Kishon Street is best in the evening, most places are open at lunchtime as well.

On Ha-Galil Street, in the three blocks heading south from Ha-Yarden Street, are a number of inexpensive restaurants, snackshops, pubs, falafel strands, and so on. One nice, kosher, family-style place, specializing in Middle Eastern food, is the **Guy Restaurant** (tel. 06-721-973), on Ha-Galil about one block south of Ha-Yarden, in a small white building set back a bit from the street. House specialties include eggplant, artichokes, tomatoes, or other vegetables stuffed with rice or rice with meat, and pastry stuffed with nuts, all priced between NIS4 ($2.65) and NIS5.50 ($3.65). Main meat courses, with french fries and salad, pita bread, and pickles, run NIS8 ($5.35) to NIS18 ($12). Hours are noon to midnight, closing before sunset Friday, reopening after sunset on Saturday.

Just a little farther south, still on Ha-Galil Street, is the **Abu Shkara Yemeni Restaurant** (tel. 06-792-103 or 790-560), with delicious Yemeni and Oriental food on an à la carte menu. Open from 9 a.m. to 11 p.m. seven days a week.

Don't neglect the restaurant at the **Egged Bus Station**—it may be the least expensive place in town to get a hot and wholesome meal. For example, meat with two side dishes costs NIS3.40 ($2.25); a hamburger on a roll goes for half that amount. You can get a beer for another NIS1 (65¢). It's open from 7 a.m. to

10:30 a.m., 11 a.m. to 2:30 p.m., and 3:30 p.m. to 7 p.m., closing early Friday and all day Saturday for the Sabbath; it's kosher.

North of Downtown

Tiberias has two restaurants which, although not more than about a ten-minute walk from downtown, are a bit tucked away, out of the main rush. It's well worth the walk to visit them, as both have great atmosphere, nice decor, and delicious food.

The Lamb and the Goose Pub/Restaurant (tel. 06-790-242) is on Dona Gracia Street (no number), near the old castle. It has an old-world European flavor, cozy and comfortable, with dark wooden furniture, a high wood-beamed ceiling, gentle lighting, nice music, and people talking. Since it's both a pub and a restaurant, you're welcome to come in just for a shot or a draft, but the food is a treat. Among the many house specialties are various goose and lamb dishes, including such rarities as grilled goose liver, goose shishlik, and young lamb shishlik or ribs, with prices ranging from NIS10 ($6.65) to NIS20 ($13.35) for a three-course meal. Tourists who mention the name of any hostel or hotel get a 10% discount. Open from noon to 1 a.m., closing at 4 p.m. on Friday and re-opening on Saturday after the Sabbath.

The final restaurant I'll mention is the most famous restaurant in Tiberias —**The House** (tel. 06-720-226 or 792-353), a Chinese-Thai restaurant with a wide array of exotic, expertly prepared dishes. You can really go to town here ordering gourmet dishes from the à la carte menu at NIS15 ($10) to NIS30 ($20) for a complete meal, or you can get the six-course meal for two people for a total tab of NIS37.50 ($25). While it's not cheap, this may be one of the best restaurants for the price anywhere in Israel. The decor is lovely, with the sound of the waterfall and fountain at the entrance wafting up to the dining rooms above, all beautifully decorated. There's also a congenial bar/lounge, complete with fireplace for chilly evenings, on the ground floor. The House is open daily from 1 to 3 p.m. and 6 p.m. to midnight, except on Saturday when it remains open straight through from 1 p.m. to midnight. From downtown Tiberias, go north on Gdud Barak Road, the one heading north out of town toward Safed; after a few minutes' walk, you'll see the House, marked by signs, up above on your left.

For Falafel

By now you have seen enough of Tiberias to know that Ha-Yarden Street next to Shimon Park is "Falafel Row" in this city. The line-up starts right outside Ha-Atzma'ut Square and stretches up toward the bus staion, little stands tended by Mama, Papa, or Sis. Quality can vary, so can fixings, so stroll along and see what sort of falafel sandwiches are coming over the counter before you stop to buy. The price, at my last munch, was only NIS1 (65¢).

Picnic Supplies

You might want to pick up fixings for a picnic, or for meals you can cook yourself if you stay in one of the places where you can use the kitchen facilities. Of course, there are many shops of all kinds downtown, but if you want to go to one place that has everything, head for the **supermarket** right in front of the Great Mosque, with a wide selection, and a deli department too. It's open Sunday through Thursday from 7 a.m. until 6:45 p.m., on Friday until 1:45 p.m., and on Saturday evening from 7 to 9:30 p.m.

WHAT TO SEE AND DO: Tiberias is a small town, but it offers a great number of sights and activities.

Guided Tours

Every Saturday morning at 10 a.m., a free two-hour walking tour of Old Tiberias leaves from the lobby of the Plaza Hotel, down by the lake.

With Tiberias as a starting point, you can take guided tours of both the Golan Heights and the Sea of Galilee. Check the sections on those areas for details.

In addition to the large tour companies, a variety of private guides are also available. You may want to inquire at your hotel or youth hostel at the major hotels, or at the Tourist Information Office, about excursions going by limousine (sherut) or taxi. Prices are competitive, and so can be quite reasonable, and you may enjoy the change from a large bus, besides seeing out-of-the-way places you wouldn't otherwise get to see.

Main Street, Tiberias

Galilee (Ha-Galil) Street, the main shopping street, runs outside the old wall. You can see remains of the former rampart that enclosed the city, as well as a few old mosques in ruins at the wall's edge. Walk along the street running perpendicular to Galilee Street down toward the sea; on your left is a small war memorial, and on your right the Bank Leumi, with a sculptured frieze on its outer wall.

View from the Water's Edge

Down along the waterfront promenade you'll find the most popular gathering spot in Tiberias, with a magnificent view across the lake. If you arrive in summer, chances are there will be children here leaping off the rampart into the water, and then climbing back up the old steps for another foray. Off on the left, 100 yards away, are the huge, castle-like remains of a **Crusader fort** (now the Castle Inn), jutting up in basalt stone from the water. Directly across the lake is a green patch, Kibbutz Ein Gev, and a few other brave settlements which for years endured periodic shelling from the Syrian heights. To the left is towering **Mount Hermon,** which perpetually wears a snow-laced peak. From the foothills pour the waters that form the sources of the Jordan River. The mountains in the distance, opposite you, are part of the **Golan Heights,** pink and desolate. (See the end of this chapter for description of a Golan trip.)

Tombs of the Rabbis

Located off Yohanen Ben-Zakkai Street is **Rambam's (Maimonides')** **Tomb,** one of the principal reminders that Tiberias was once the central congregating spot of the learned. Rabbi Moses Ben-Maimon, known as Maimonides, or Rambam, was the greatest Jewish theologian of the Middle Ages. A Sephardic Jew, born in Cordova, Spain, he was an Aristotelian philosopher, a humanistic physician, and a leading scientist and astronomer. His principal work was *The Guide for the Perplexed.* The famous philosopher, who died in 1204, is now honored by a newly restored and beautified mausoleum and gardens. Nearby is the tomb of **Rabbi Yochanon Ben-Zakkai,** founder of the Yavne Academy, and on a hillside just west of town is the memorial to **Rabbi Akiva.** This great sage compiled the commentaries of the Mishnah before the Romans tortured him to death at Caesarea in A.D. 150 for his role in aiding the Bar Kokhba revolt. The tomb of **Rabbi Meir Baal Haness,** located on the hill above the Hot Springs, is considered one of Israel's holiest sites. Rabbi Meir, called the "Miracle-Worker" and the "Light-Giver," is remembered in a white building that has two tombs. The Sephardic tomb, with the shallow dome, was built around 1873 and contains the actual grave, close to the interior western wall of the synagogue; the building with the steeper dome is the Ashkenazi synagogue, erected about 1900.

Huge bonfires are lit at his tomb by the Orthodox four days before the Lag b'Omer holiday in the spring.

All the tombs are open daily between 8 a.m. and 4 p.m. (or possibly later in summer—but to be on the safe side, get there by 4 p.m.).

Terra Sancta Church

Down on Tiberias' lakeside promenade, squeezed in among the fish restaurants and inconspicuously set back from the shore, stands Terra Sancta, a church and monastery of the Franciscans, that order of brown-robed monks founded in 1270 by St. Francis of Assisi, with the three knots of their corded belts symbolizing their vows of poverty, chastity, and obedience. Another name for the church is St. Peter's Parish Church.

By either name, the church is an interesting place. The first church was constructed here by the Crusaders around A.D. 1100. After the Muslims conquered Tiberias in 1187, the church was converted to a mosque; around the middle of the 17th century, the Franciscans began coming here each year from Nazareth to celebrate the Feast of St. Peter, paying a price to the Muslims for the use of the site. Later on in the same century the Franciscans obtained the site for themselves.

The present church still contains part of the original Crusader church, but only a part—the apse (altar), which, on the outside, is shaped like the bow of a boat, coming to a point. In the old days the waters of the Sea of Galilee used to lap at the foot of this symbolic prow of the ship of the church.

The rest of the present church was built by the Franciscans in 1848, with the façade dating from 1870. The church's façade is identical to that of the Franciscan church in Assisi, where the order began, with red stone imported from Assisi. In the courtyard facing the church is a white stone monument built by the Polish in 1945, dedicated to Our Lady of Czestochova, and a bronze statue of St. Peter, a copy of the statue in St. Peter's Basilica in Rome.

You can visit the church daily from 8 to 11:45 a.m. and 3 to 5:30 p.m. Masses are said weekdays at 7 a.m., on Sunday and holidays at 8:30 and 11 a.m.

There's a hospice here as well; see above for details.

While you're here, if you're interested in churches, you might want to also walk to the historic **Greek Orthodox church** located just a little farther to the south along the waterfront, or the **Church of Scotland** a little to the north. Both of these are no more than a block or two from Terra Sancta.

The Hot Springs of Tiberias and Ruins of Hammat

Famous for their curative powers for over 3,000 years, the thermal baths a mile south of Tiberias are heavily frequented by visitors and Israelis. Pharmacies in Israel keep well-stocked supplies of mineral salts from these Tiberias springs, and many an Israeli swears by their therapeutic effects.

The hot waters contain high amounts of sulfuric, muriatic, and calcium salts, and over the centuries they've reportedly cured such ailments as rheumatism, arthritis, and gynecological disorders. They are probably the earliest-known thermal baths in the world, noted by Josephus, Pliny, church historians, and many Arabic writers. Some biblical commentators have surmised that at these baths Christ cured the sick and maimed, and others place their origin at the time of Noah, when the insides of the earth were turned upward by the Flood. In Israel, there's a legend that Solomon entered into a conspiracy with demons to heal his kingdom's ailing people at this site, tricking them into perpetually stoking the fires in the earth below to heat up the water.

Some of the baths look like swimming pools, others like Turkish baths, complete with domes, vaulted ceilings, and marble columns. The largest is the

Ibrahim Pasha pool, where inside a huge stone lion guards the clientele. Arabic legend says that a barren woman need only sit on this lion after bathing and her wish for conception will come true.

Several medical treatments are available, including physiotherapy, therapeutic massage, inhalation, mud baths, and so on. To gain a true appreciation of the waters and the variety of ills they are used to cure, check out the **Lehman Museum** next to the springs (more on this in a minute).

All the springs at the seafront are operated by **Tiberias Hot Springs Company Ltd.** (tel. 06-791-967 or 791-968), which offers baths and treatments in both old and new buildings. There's an inexpensive restaurant on the premises. Egged buses nos. 2 and 5 pass the springs.

Hours of operation are somewhat different in the various pools. Hours for pools in the old building are the same as for the physiotherapy treatments in the new building, that is, Sunday through Friday from 7 a.m. to 1 p.m. The thermal pools at the **Young Tiberias Hot Springs** (this is the large indoor/outdoor pool for swimming) are open the same days from 8 a.m. to 8 p.m., plus Saturday from 8:30 a.m. to 7:45 p.m. A ticket for use of all the pools costs NIS13 ($8.65) for adults, NIS8 ($5.35) for children aged 3 to 12, with rental of a bathing suit and bathrobe (bring your own, or else be prepared to rent one) an extra NIS2 ($1.35). Pool plus massage costs a total of NIS30 ($20).

While you're visiting the springs, plan to spend a little time exploring the ancient ruins of **Hammat,** a city built on this site well before the founding of Tiberias in the 1st century A.D. Hammat and Tiberias existed side by side for millennia as "twin cities." Now a national park, you can gain entrance to the ruins seven days a week from 8 a.m. to 4 p.m. for the small fee of NIS1.10 (75¢) for adults, 50 agorot (35¢) for children.

This ancient town contains some of the most magnificent mosaic work you'll see in Israel: the floor of the synagogue (4th century A.D.), with colorful mosaic depictions of the zodiac circle, four women representing the seasons of the year, and the sun-god Helios riding on a chariot through the heavens, plus various Jewish symbols as well, including the Ark of the Covenant. Also in the park is the **Ernest Lehman Museum,** giving detailed information about the history of the area and the curative powers of the hot springs.

Up the hill from the baths is the Tomb of Rabbi Meir Baal Haness, a disciple of Rabbi Akiva, and one of the great sages who helped to compile the Mishnah in the 2nd century A.D. (see details under "Tombs of the Rabbis," above.)

Boat Rides on the Lake

A **ferry** goes between Tiberias on the west side of the Kinneret and Kibbutz Ein Gev on the east side, seven days a week, departing from Tiberias' waterfront promenade at 10:30 a.m., arriving at Ein Gev 45 minutes later. After spending an hour at Ein Gev, it departs for Tiberias at 12:15 p.m., arriving at 1 p.m. The round trip costs NIS6 ($4).

Many people take this opportunity to try out the excellent restaurant at Kibbutz Ein Gev, or just to stroll around the kibbutz. If you like, you can plan to take the ferry only one way, and take bus 18 or 21 back to Tiberias. Buses go between Tiberias and Ein Gev about every two hours.

If you happen to be here in July or August, you'll find the ferry runs more frequently, with three or four boats every day. For information, contact the **Kinneret Sailing Company** at the waterfront office (tel. 06-721-831 or 720-248 in Tiberias, 06-758-007 in Ein Gev).

The **Lido Kinneret Sailing Co.** (tel. 06-720-226 or 721-538) operates a daily ferry between Tiberias and Capernaum; call for details on this, as well as on waterskiing and sailboard rental.

Both of the above sailing companies offer **evening cruises** at various times of the year, especially in summer, some with dancing on board; call for info, or ask at the Tourist Information Office, where you can also get the latest scoop on all the **water sports** offered on and around the lake, including waterskiing, water parachuting, sailboarding, giant water slides, kayak trips, and more.

Cultural Events

The sleepy quality of Tiberias is really deceptive, because there's much going on—and I'm not merely alluding to thermal cures or rock 'n' roll along the shore. Here are some examples:

The **Ein Gev Music Festival** takes place in spring during Passover week.

Israeli folkdance and song festivals are organized along the waterfront in summer; the I.G.T.O. will supply particulars.

The **Succoth Swimathon** across the Kinneret (three miles). Everyone is welcome to join, but bring a medical certificate attesting to the fact that you are not overly drownable. Contact the Jordan Valley Regional Council, Mobile Post, or the Ha-Poel Sports Organization, 8 Ha-Arba'ah St., Tel Aviv (tel. 03-260-181).

There are summertime shows and performances at the **Samakh Amphitheater** on the southern tip of the Sea of Galilee by local and foreign entertainers.

Special activities are organized for groups and include lectures and slide shows on the geographical, historical, and archeological aspects of the region. These shows are given, usually upon request, by the I.G.T.O. regional director.

Art Galleries

One pleasant section of Tiberias, near the bustle of downtown but seeming somehow removed from it, is an area specializing in art galleries. You'll find one gallery in the old Crusader Castle on Dona Gracia Street, and many others nearby. A few of the galleries also have enjoyable cafés; the Mazal is to be recommended highly, but many of the others are very nice too. This tiny artists' area is located between Elhadeff and Dona Gracia Streets, in the couple of blocks extending northward from Ha-Yarden Street.

Beaches

The **Blue Beach** charges a few dollars for the use of its lake facilities. The price includes a beach chair.

The **Quiet Beach** fees include all the swimming facilities. Open from 8 a.m. to 6 or 7 p.m.

The **Ganei Hammat Swimming Beach,** opposite the Ganei Hammat Hotel, near the Tiberias Hot Springs, is open daily from 9 a.m. to 5 p.m. It offers deck chairs, showers, and a snack kiosk.

The **Valley Beach** near the Galei Kinneret Hotel has a fine waterfront and all the requisite facilities. There's also a nearby Wimpy and the Valley Beach Restaurant. There's a charge for entrance and use of facilities May to September; the rest of the year it's free.

Sironit Beach is open from 8 a.m. to 5 p.m., April through October. There's also a **municipal beach** south of Sironit Beach, open from 9 a.m. to 5 p.m.

Other popular beaches include **Ron Beach, Shells Beach, Lido Beach,** and **Gay Beach.**

Horseback Riding

Outside of town, but not really that far away, you can rent a horse for trail riding in the Galilee; call **Vered Ha-Galil** (tel. 06-935-785) or **Kefar Hittim Horse and Pony Ranch** (tel. 06-795-921 or 795-922).

NIGHTLIFE IN TIBERIAS: Being a holiday resort, Tiberias is busy with things to do at night. Folklore events are often scheduled at some of Tiberias' hotels, and everyone is welcome to attend. For full details, contact the **Tourist Information Office** on Elhadeff Street next to Ha-Atzma'ut Square.

The many nice pubs and cafés, bars and restaurants open until the wee hours around Tiberias make it easy to spend a pleasant evening.

A good place for a quiet drink is the bar of the **Galei Kinneret Hotel,** at the southern end of the Old City on the beach. While you're imbibing, glance at the exhibition of books that have mentioned the hotel. You'll find the works of Leon Uris, James D. McDonald, Taylor Caldwell, and Edwin Samuel.

For pubs, try the **Big Ben,** a popular British-style pub located along the southern side of the complex built around the Great Mosque (just look for the minaret near the lake). It's open daily from 9 a.m. to 4 a.m.

Another nice pub in the same complex is **Bistro Tal;** it's a restaurant and a pub too.

Then there's **The Lamb and the Goose,** also a restaurant/pub (see "Restaurants," above).

Up behind the Lamb and the Goose, in the area between Elhadeff and Dona Gracia Streets, are several gallery/cafés, tasteful, romantic places to spend an evening or a quiet afternoon. One of the nicest of these is the **Mazal Gallery/Café,** located on F. E. Hoofein Street (signs posted on Elhadeff Street direct you to the spot). You may find the Mazal open from June through October only; if you like an artistic café atmosphere, check to find out, because this is one of the town's nicest spots. But there are several others here in the same neighborhood, so stroll around and see which ones you like the best.

Want to go out dancing? There are many possibilities around Tiberias—and even out on the water.

Discothèques abound. The most unusual, I'm sure, is the summer disco dancing on the Sea of Galilee, on the boat operated by the Kinneret Sailing Co.; call 06-721-831, or stop by its office at the waterfront promenade, for info

For regular landlubbers, but still right down beside the water, there's the **Castle Inn Discothèque and Bar,** near the southern end of the lakeside promenade. There's a NIS5 ($3.35) entrance fee, NIS4 ($2.65) for Castle Inn Youth Hostel guests. You'll find it open every night in summer from 9 p.m. to 2 a.m.; on Friday and Saturday only during the winter.

The **Blue Beach Discothèque and Bar,** a little north of town, is open weekends in winter, more often in summer.

Up in Kiryat Shmuel, check out the modern **Eden Club** disco at the Eden Hotel (see my hotel recommendations for info).

And speaking of the Eden, don't forget that many, in fact most, of the hotels (and even the youth hostels) around town have nice bars and pubs where you can relax in the evening and enjoy a drink and conversation with fellow travelers.

Also at the hotel, I'll admit that one of my favorite late-evening pastimes after a long, active day is to watch the **late-night movie** (in English) on TV. The movies are sometimes very good, often the top box-office hits you may have missed when they first came around. The films usually come on around 10 or 10:30 p.m.; check the newspaper for listings.

CIRCLING THE SEA OF GALILEE: It's time to take a tour around the Sea of Galilee, heading north to begin a circle which will bring us back to Tiberias—and then we'll head on into the Upper Galilee region.

As of this writing, there is no regular bus route which completely circles the lake. I expect there will be such a route in operation soon, perhaps even by the time you arrive. In the meantime you'll have to go by tour bus, bicycle, or boat (for boats to Ein Gev, see above). Buses 18 and 21 go south from Tiberias around the lake to Ein Gev, leaving every two hours or so. For Capernaum and other sites to the north, take bus 841, leaving Tiberias every 40 minutes. In summer, there is boat service from Lido Beach to Capernaum.

Tours

The one way to get all the way around the Sea of Galilee by bus is to take the **"Minus 200" tour,** offered by Egged Tours (tel. 06-720-474) at Tiberias' Central Bus Station. Check for details about how the tour works. At this writing, the price is $5 for one day, or $8 for two days (as you prefer), with the bus circling the lake several times a day and allowing you to get off and on again at many of the major points of interest all around the lake, meeting up with the bus again as it makes another trip around. When you go with this tour, you get discount coupons for admission to the sites, and for any meals you may buy at several restaurants along the way.

Magdala and Migdal

Two miles north of Tiberias along the lakeside road, you'll come to the old village of **Magdala,** the birthplace of Mary Magdalene. There's not much left to see nowadays, but it's a lovely area, with tall eucalyptus trees and vegetation abundantly beautiful. The town was right down by the water's edge. Up on the hill just to the south of old Magdala, along the far (west) side of the highway, you can still see the sarcophagi (stone coffins) carved out of the rocks, in the place that was Magdala's cemetery.

The modern town of **Migdal,** founded in this century, is about one mile to the north of the site of ancient Magdala.

Kibbutz Ginossar

A little farther on, you'll find yourself in a lush valley with many banana trees. These are part of the agriculture of Kibbutz Ginossar (tel. 06-792-161), and the valley is the Ginossar Valley. The kibbutz museum has an old boat preserved from Jesus' time, and you're welcome to come in and see it. You'll see the kibbutz entrance clearly marked from the road. Kibbutz Ginossar has a nice guesthouse too (see my accommodations recommendations, above, for details).

Tabgha

Getting to Tabgha, where Jesus miraculously multiplied the loaves and fishes, you proceed northward along the shoreline from Migdal, passing **Minya,** a 7th-century Arabian palace that is one of the Muslim world's most ancient and holy prayer sites. It's open every day from 8 a.m. to 4 p.m.

At Tabgha, you'll find the beautifully restored Benedictine monastery and the **Church of the Multiplication of the Loaves and Fish** (tel. 06-721-061), whose basilica floor is one of the best-preserved mosaic representations in all of Israel. In one scene it depicts a basket filled with loaves of bread, with two fishes standing upright. The larger mosaic, however, is a vivid and colorful tapestry of all the birds that once thrived in this area: swans, cranes, ducks, wild geese, and storks.

Be sure to read the fascinating history of this church posted just inside the entrance, in the church's courtyard. Beginning in the year A.D. 28 (still during Jesus' lifetime), the Judeo-Christians of nearby Capernaum (Kefar Nahum) venerated a large rock, upon which Jesus is said to have placed the bread and fish when he fed the 5,000 (Mark 6:30–44). The rock was used as the altar in a church erected over the spot in around the year A.D. 350.

After many changes, invasions, and finally destruction, the ancient church ruins, hidden for 1,300 years, were excavated, and the mosaics discovered. The present church was built in 1980–1982, a reconstruction of the Byzantine-era edifice, built upon the same foundation.

The church is open daily from 8:30 a.m. to 5 p.m.; modest dress is required to enter. Admission is free, but donations are accepted. There's also a good bookstore and souvenir shop on the premises.

Just east of the Multiplication Church is the **Heptapegon** ("Seven Springs" in Greek), also called the **Church of the Primacy of St. Peter,** or **Mensa Christi.** To reach it, you must leave the Multiplication Church, return to the highway, turn right, and climb the hill to a separate entrance. This Greek Orthodox church is open daily from 8 a.m. to 5 p.m.; modest dress is required, and admission is free.

It was here on the shores of Galilee that Jesus is said (John 21) to have appeared to his disciples after his crucifixion and resurrection. Peter and the others were in a boat on the lake, fishing, but with no luck. When Jesus appeared, he told them to cast their nets again. They did, and couldn't haul in the nets because they were so full of fish. As the disciples sat with their master having dinner, Jesus is said to have conferred the leadership of the movement on Peter as first among the disciples. The theory of Peter's primacy, and the tradition of that primacy's being passed from one generation of disciples to the next, is the basis for the legitimacy of the Roman pontiff as leader of Christendom.

The church, of black basalt, dates only from the middle of our century, though it rests on the foundations of earlier churches. Within is a flat rock called Mensa Christi, "Christ's Table," as this was where Jesus dined that evening with his disciples. Outside the church, you can still see the stone steps said to be where Jesus stood when he appeared, calling to the disciples; on the beach are seven large stones, which may once have supported a little fishing wharf.

If it's early in the day and the sun is not too hot, you can easily walk to nearby Capernaum (three kilometers, or about two miles) and perhaps, if you're in decent shape, to the Mount of Beatitudes.

Mount of the Beatitudes

Just beyond Tabgha, on a high hill, is the famous Mount of the Beatitudes, now the site of an Italian convent. Here, Jesus preached the Sermon on the Mount.

There are many good views of the Sea of Galilee and its surroundings, but the vista from here is probably the best. One odd fact about this church is the inscription on the sanctuary, which informs you that the entire project was built by Mussolini in the 15th year of his rule in 1937.

Capernaum (Kefar Nahum)

"And they went into Capernaum; and straightaway on the sabbath day, He entered into the synagogue, and taught" (Mark 1:21). On this site where Christ preached are now an excavated synagogue, a Franciscan monastery, and other excavations spanning six centuries, including an unusual octagonal church and several houses of the period, an ancient olive press, and a 2nd-century marble milestone on the Via Maris ("Coastal Road"), the Roman route that stretched from Egypt to Lebanon. An extension, to Damascus, branched off from the coast at Caesarea, passing near Mount Tabor and over to the Sea of Galilee, where it went around the west side of the lake and up through Capernaum, continuing on toward Qasrin, in the Golan Heights, and onward to Damascus. (It's interesting to note that the road we've been following north from Tiberias to Capernaum still follows this same path, the old Via Maris road.)

In those days, Capernaum was a border town between the kingdoms of Antipas and Philippas, a large town for its time, with a population of about 5,000. It's thought that the size of the town, and the significance of its location, were among the reasons why Jesus may have chosen this site for his ministry. The New Testament holds reference to a prophecy of Elias in this matter as well (Matt. 4:13–16).

Capernaum was the hometown of Peter the fisherman, and at least four other of Jesus' original followers, the place where Jesus began to gather his disciples around him, saying, "Follow me, and I will make you fishers of men" (Matt. 4:19). Many of the things Jesus did took place right here. You can read about Capernaum in the New Testament at Matt. 4:12–16, 8:5, 9:1, and 17:24; Mark 2:1; Luke 7:1–5; and John 6:17. Also see Matt. 11:23–24 and Luke 10:15.

Capernaum's synagogue is a splendid Roman-like affair, with tall columns, marble steps, and shattered statuary, and numerous symbols from those times: carved seven-branched menorahs, stars of David, palm branches, and rams' horns. It's not the actual synagogue in which Christ taught, since it dates from around the 2nd or 3rd century A.D., but it may stand on the same site, its doorway facing south toward Jerusalem. The excavations of basalt stone in the garden lead down toward the sea, where you can still glimpse the remains of a small-boat basin with steps leading to the water. There is a small admission fee; the site is open daily from 8:30 a.m. to 4:15 p.m.

Horseback Riding

There's an honest-to-goodness dude ranch, **Vered Ha-Galil,** in Upper Galilee (tel. 06-935-785). At the Korazim-Almagor crossroad between Tiberias and Rosh Pinna, 3½ km (2¼ miles) past the turnoff to the Mount of the Beatitudes, it is easily reached by car or bus. And whether you arrive in a limousine or attached to a backpack, you'll be welcomed just the same by owner Yehuda Avni, a Chicago boy who came to fight in the late 1940s, stayed on to give kibbutz life a whirl, finally dreamed up this place, and settled down for good. Yehuda and his wife, Yonah (fantastic cook!), run a relaxed and informal place, calm and serene. Aside from the rustic accommodations and American-style cooking, horseback riding is the big attraction here, for beginners as well as skillful riders.

Yehuda offers trail rides by the hour, day, or week, into the hills or down toward the Sea of Galilee. Up into the hills means Safed, Tel Hai, across kibbutz fields, along wadis (dried-up creek beds), over slopes strewn with black basalt rock, and through Arab villages. One of the best rides stops at an Arab village. Trips heading downward stop at the Mount of the Beatitudes, Migdal, Tabgha, and Capernaum, and usually there's a break when you tie up your horse under a eucalyptus tree and go for a swim in the Sea of Galilee. Other planned tours last several days, exploring places such as Nazareth, and combining camping or hotel overnights to Gilboa, Mount Tabor, around the Sea of Galilee, and into the Golan Heights, with Arab meals and scenic extremes.

Yehuda tends to wax poetic about his rides: "When a tiny black speck in the distance becomes a Bedouin tent where you're welcome to dismount and have coffee; when a winding trail suddenly opens up into the fertile valley of Ginossar; when you're riding through the vineyards along the ridge overlooking the sky-blue Sea of Galilee and you suddenly understand why the Sermon on the Mount was given here . . . well, then you know you're visiting Galilee as it should be visited, on horseback."

Horseback riding will cost you the following: $9 an hour, $25 for half a day on the trail, $42 for an entire day with lunch. All rides are accompanied by guides.

In addition to the stables, Vered Ha-Galil has rooms for changing and showers, an outdoor grill, picnic tables, a rustic restaurant, and a bar and grill. There are also accommodations for 28 people in beautiful double-roomed stone cottages that look like Swiss chalets. I have been here often, and I recommend it highly. Cost per night per person varies from $22 to $35 single, $37 to $60 for a couple, breakfast included. The higher-priced accommodations are cottages that can sleep up to two children as well, for an additional charge. Backpackers can sack out in the bunkhouse for about $13 per night, breakfast included. If you're really low on bucks, ask permission to sleep on the lawn.

The restaurant is certainly one of the best in Israel, and for the American palate it's a dream. A meal consisting of real chicken-in-the-basket, lemon meringue pie, and old-fashioned Yankee coffee costs $11.

When Avni first began, the whole proposition of horseback riding was in its infancy (except with the Bedouin, of course). Now there is a steady proliferation of stables—about 70 of them—mostly in kibbutzim.

For further information about horseback riding, write to the Secretary, **Israel Horse Society,** c/o Ministry of Agriculture, Galil Ma'aravi, Doar Na Ashrat, Israel.

In 1966 a bunch of amateur horse-lovers—from the moshavim and kibbutzim, from the cities, even from Bedouin encampments—got together for a fun-and-games competition called the **Sussiyada.** It's now an annual thing and most popular. Check with the I.G.T.O. for where/when details, but it's usually held in Afula.

Korazim

Just beyond Vered Ha-Galil are the ruins of Korazim (Chorazin), a flourishing Jewish town in Roman times. A large, 2nd-century synagogue of black basalt has been excavated, as well as streets, houses, and ritual baths attached to the synagogue, which was apparently destroyed by earthquake in the 3rd century and never rebuilt.

Korazim is mentioned in the New Testament as a town which was rebuked by Jesus. "Woe unto thee, Chorazin! woe unto thee, Bethsaida! for if the mighty works, which were done in you, had been done in Tyre and Sidon, they would have repented long ago in sackcloth and ashes" (Matt. 11:21; Luke 10:13).

The Eastern Shore

Coming around the northern end of the lake, you come to a junction from which Hwy. 87 heads up into the Golan Heights to its new "capital," the town of Qasrin, covered later on in this chapter.

Southward, down the eastern shore of the lake, you'll pass **Ha-Golan Beach and camping area,** the newest on the lake. Not far away is the **Ramot Holiday Village.** Several kilometers farther south is another junction, and another new road heading up into Golan.

Luna Gal

Passing around the northern part of the lake, where the Jordan River enters the lake, we come to Luna Gal (tel. 06-763-750), the largest water-amusement park in Israel, in fact, they say, the largest in the world outside the United States. It hosts a wide array of attractions and activities including water-skiing, pedalboats, kayak tours of the Jordan River, sailboarding, water parachuting, and more. There's an entrance fee, which isn't small, but it's worth it for what you get. You may find it open during the warmest months only, from around April to October or so; call for the latest details, or check with the Tourist Information Office in Tiberias. From Tiberias, you can take bus 22.

Kursi

Here on the eastern shore lies Kursi, in the "country of the Gergesenes" (or Gadarenes), where Jesus met two men "possessed with devils, coming out of the tombs, exceeding fierce, so that no man might pass by that way" (Matt. 8:28). Jesus cast the demons out of the men and into a herd of swine, causing the whole herd to race headlong into the Sea of Galilee and drown (Matt. 8:28–34; Luke 8:26–39).

For many years, speculation existed about the location of Kursi (also called Gergasa) and the church believed to have been built there, but it was not until after the Six-Day War, when Israel claimed the territory, that a bulldozer clearing the way for a new road uncovered the ruins of a Byzantine church complex, complete with a monastery dating from the 5th to 7th centuries. Most remarkable among the discoveries was the underground crypt, where more than 30 skeletons were found, all of middle-aged men, except for one child.

Ein Gev

About two-thirds of the way south along the lake's eastern shore brings you to **Kibbutz Ein Gev.** Nestled between the hills of Golan and the lakefront, Ein Gev was founded in 1937 by German and Czechoslovakian pioneers. These days Ein Gev boasts a 5,000-seat **auditorium,** which in recent years has presented some of the world's greatest musicians at its twice-yearly music festivals; Pablo Casals, Rudolf Serkin, Isaac Stern, and many other virtuosos have appeared here. On the hillsides around the auditorium are tiers of vineyards, and elsewhere on the grounds are a banana plantation and date groves. Fishing is another flourishing industry here.

Not far from the auditorium, in a handsome garden, is a bronze statue of Hanna Orloff depicting a woman holding a child aloft. The inscription is from Nehemiah: "For the builders, every one had his sword girded by his side, and so builded."

This settlement bore the brunt of heavy attacks in the 1948 war, and its tempting position at the foothills, below heavy Syrian military emplacements, made it a perennial target. Rarely, however, was anyone here injured from those battles, perhaps as a result of an endless maze of slit trenches throughout the grounds, as well as concrete shelters dug into the earth.

Attractions at Ein Gev today include a pretty **lakeside restaurant,** with a well-deserved reputation for excellence, where a set meal based on, say, St. Peter's fish (natch!) will cost about NIS15 ($10). It's open every day of the week from 10 a.m. to 4 p.m., except Friday when it closes at 2:30 p.m.

The kibbutz also has accommodations at the **Ein Gev Holiday Village** (tel. 06-758-027), about a mile south of the kibbutz proper. There are campsites with space for a camper or tent, costing $6.60 for one person or $8.50 for two, with prices an extra $3.80 per person in summer (July and August) and on Holy Days. There are also about 100 cabins, sleeping up to six people, each with its own bathroom, kitchen, air conditioning, and heat. Rates for most of the year are $18.25 single, $27.20 double, no meals included; higher at high-season times. (There's a mini-market nearby for groceries.) Call or write for reservations at busy times, when you may have to pay for four beds, minimum; if so, plan to come with family or friends.

It's easy to get to Ein Gev from Tiberias, by bus 18 or 21, tour bus (Egged's "Minus-200" tour), or ferry.

Farther south along the lake are two more campsites, those at **Ha-On** (tel. 06-751-144) and **Ma'agan** (tel. 06-751-360). Ma'agan is very near the junction for the road to the hot-spring resort of Hammat Gader. (Ask at the Tourism Information Office in Tiberias for info on other campsites around the lake and in the vicinity; there are many to choose from.)

Hanyon Ha-On Ostrich Farm

That's right, an ostrich farm! Located on the southeast corner of the lake, this is the largest ostrich-breeding farm in the world, outside of South Africa. You can see the entire life cycle of the rare bird here, from the time the chick pops out of the egg all the way through to its mating rituals (in season). There's an entrance fee; you can check with Tiberias' Tourist Information Office for further details.

Hammat Gader

The hot springs of Hammat Gader (tel. 06-751-039), east of the southern tip of the Sea of Galilee, are a favorite Israeli spa and vacation spot. Nestled in the valley of the Yarmuk River, this dramatic site has been occupied for almost 4,500 years. You won't be disappointed by a side trip to the springs. Pack your bathing suit, then catch bus 26 from Tiberias. Hammat Gader is 21 km (12½ miles) southeast of the city. If you're driving, it's 8.5 km (about 5 miles) east of the junction with the highway that rings the lake.

As you wind down the steep road into the Yarmuk Valley, you'll pass several sentry and guard posts. That's Jordan on the other side of the valley, the steep hillside dotted with fertile farms and orchards.

The elaborate complex of Hammat Gader offers something for everybody: there are hot sulfur springs and baths for medical therapy, beauty treatments, serious swimming, and just plain splashing and playing; there is an alligator zoo in a jungle setting (you stroll through on rustic elevated walkways, safe from the expansive jaws and hefty appetites of the frightening denizens); the ruins of the Roman spa city are extensive and significant, and several important parts (the baths, the theater) have been beautifully restored; for the kids, the park has rides and bumper cars. Of course there are showers and changing rooms, bar and restaurant. You must also know that admission to the grounds costs NIS7.50 ($5) for adults, NIS6.25 ($4.15) for children, a significant sum if you're taking the whole family, but a sum well spent. When you buy a ticket to Hammat Gader, incidentally, it entitles you to a 10% reduction in price to visits to the Ha-On Ostrich Farm and the Luna Gal Amusement Park.

Most of the park is self-explanatory, with signs in English as well as Hebrew. At present the Roman ruins are set up as a self-guiding tour (you can also ask at the park office for information about guided tours of the park, which are available).

The Roman city here was first constructed in the A.D. 200s, restored and beautified in the 600s, and destroyed by an earthquake in the 900s. A later "ruin," a disused mosque of late but very handsome design, dominates the site with its graceful minaret. The spa was known as El-Hamma to the Arabs and Turks. Now the mosque is forlorn and empty, disfigured by graffiti.

Come to Hammat Gader on a weekday if you can. On Saturday it can be very crowded and busy.

Speaking of busy, you'll notice that, among the hot, warm, and cold pools —the hottest being the water inside the covered section, cooling off as it gets farther away outside—there's probably a crowd gathering down at the far end of the warm-water pool. Make it a point to sit here, with the warm mineral water crashing down onto your back from the waterfall made as the water leaves the pool and heads down the valley. You may find it one of the most exhilarating back massages you've ever had.

You'll find Hammat Gader open seven days a week, from 8 a.m. until 4 p.m., except for Friday and holiday eves, when it closes at 1 p.m. From November through February it closes a bit earlier, at 3:30 p.m. (still 1 p.m. on Friday). These are the hours for the closing of the ticket offices; you may remain on the site one hour beyond these times.

From Hammat Gader, as you're climbing back up out of the valley toward the lake, look at the park from above and you'll see that only some of the watery ponds are the ones you saw with crocodiles. The other ponds are used for raising shrimp.

Back on the lakeshore road once again, turn and head west. You'll pass the entrance to Ma'agan on your right, then the junction with the highway heading south to Bet Shean and the Jordan Valley. Just after the junction, the road turns northward, heading for Tiberias, right by Kibbutz Degania.

Degania

Degania is the country's very first kibbutz, founded in 1909 by Russian pioneers. Without any real experience in farming, this handful of self-made peasants left city jobs to fight malarial swamps and Arab bands.

Much of the philosophical basis of kibbutz life was first formulated in this Jordan Valley settlement by its leaders, A.D. Gordon, a salt-of-the-earth thinker who was one of the most influential men in Israel's modern history. Gordon believed that a return to the soil and the honesty of manual work were the ingredients for creating a new spirit in man. He wielded a pick himself right till the day of his death at the age of 74—although he never, because of some abstruse matter of principle, joined the kibbutz as a member. On Degania's grounds a natural history museum, **Bet Gordon** (tel. 06-750-040), contains a rich library and exhibition of the area's flora and fauna.

Degania grew so quickly that its citizens soon branched out to other settlements. The father of Moshe Dayan, famous patched-eye commander of the Sinai Campaign, left Degania to help establish **Nahalal**, Israel's largest moshav settlement. Eventually, too, some of the younger Degania settlers established their own kibbutz right next door, and called it simply **Degania B.**

If you get confused as to which is which, **Degania A** is the settlement with the tank at the gate—a reminder of the battle the settlers waged against Syrian tanks in 1948 (the members fought them off with Molotov cocktails). It also has a fairly ancient look about it. In contrast to some of Degania A's old yellow stucco buildings, Degania B exudes a newer air.

Degania A and B have about 450 settlers each, and both settlements are prosperous, successful ventures, their beauty enhanced by subtropical plants and towering palm trees.

Hof Tsemah

Near Kibbutz Degania, there's another water amusement park, Hof Tsemah. Although it's not as large as Luna Gal, it's still a very enjoyable place, with a carnival atmosphere, a wide sandy beach, sunbathing areas, grassy picnic grounds, a buffet, and rental of water-sports equipment including kayaks, pedalboats, and other amusements. Like Luna Gal, Hof Tsemah may be open only in season; check with the Tourism Office in Tiberias for current information.

A Dip in the River Jordan

Kibbutz Kinneret, just west of Degania, has established a spot where Christian pilgrims can immerse themselves in the waters of Jordan in safety and tranquility. The **Baptismal Spot,** called **Yardenit,** is 200 yards west of the lake-shore highway (follow the signs), shaded by lofty trees. The river flows by very peacefully, but its currents can be dangerous, so no swimming is allowed. Snack and souvenir stands provide refreshment, sustenance, and amusement. No charge for the baptismal dip.

From Tiberias and the Sea of Galilee, our next destination is the ancient and mystical city of Safed (Zefat, Zfat, Tsfat, Tzfat, etc.), an hour due north of Tiberias and less than two hours due east of Nahariya.

3. Safed (Zefat)

Skirting the Yermak, Israel's lofty mountain range (3,000 feet), you finally climb up into Safed (pronounced "Tsfaht" in Hebrew), Israel's highest town with an elevation of 2,790 feet. This quiet city is built on three slopes and looks down onto a beautiful panorama of villages and tiered hillsides. Safed's name comes from a Hebrew root word (*tsafeh*) meaning to scan, or look—in other words, a lookout. It's easy to see how it got its name when you see the wide vista that the town commands.

Safed's history began in A.D. 66, during the time of the Second Temple, when Josephus Flavius started building atop the Citadel mountaintop. The Crusaders built a fortress up on this peak in 1140, and it's the ruins of that fortress (the Citadel) that can still be seen today.

In 1188 Safed was conquered by the Muslims, went back into Crusader hands in 1240, but was conquered again 20 years later, this time by the Mamelukes. During the 16th century the Ottoman Turks chose the strategic location of Safed for the provincial capital, and it became the primary government, economic, and spiritual center for the entire region.

It was during this flowering age that the persecuted Sephardic Jews from Spain came here. Having escaped the horrors of the Inquisition, these Jewish intellectuals launched into a complex and mystical interpretation of the Old Testament called Cabala (Cabbalah, Kabala, Kabalah, Kabbalah, etc.). The town became a great center of learning, with a score of synagogues and universities. During this period of intellectual mysticism the first printing press in the East was introduced here, and in 1578 the first Hebrew book was printed, a commentary on the scroll of Esther. The back streets of the city, winding and cobbled, and resounding with the chant of prayers, are still frankly medieval.

In 1837 the entire town was leveled by a powerful earthquake. It was rebuilt, but not to its former size or glory.

Two developments have occurred to make modern Safed (pop. 18,000) especially attractive to visitors. First, it has become a resort town with many hotels, and second, it now plays host to an artists' colony which flourishes right down the street from the row of synagogues. Perhaps it was Safed's mysticism, coupled with its picturesque lanes and scenic location, that prompted that substantial flock of painters, sculptors, and ceramicists to settle here. However, there is no mystery about Safed's magnificent location, its high and cool atmosphere, and its dramatic landscape. The city, not very mystically, is also a favorite summer resort for Israelis who yearn to escape from the heat of the plains to the crispness of Galilee's heights.

GETTING THERE: Bus 459 will take you from Tiberias to Safed. From Haifa, a bus from the central station or a sherut will take you to Safed, via the northern coast road that parallels the Mediterranean until Acre, where a right turn leads directly into the lower Galilee hills. Buses 361, 461, and 501 operate from 5:15 a.m. to 9 p.m. You can also come on bus 981 from Tel Aviv, bus 964 from Jerusalem, or bus 367 from Nahariya.

ORIENTATION: Safed is built on hilltops. The main part of town is compactly clustered atop one hill. South Safed occupies another hilltop to the south, and Canaan perches on a hillside across the valley to the east.

Although you may find occasion to go to Mount Canaan (a few hotels are there), you'll spend most of your time in the center of Safed. **Jerusalem Street** (Rehov Yerushalayim) is a circular street which girdles the hill, passing through the commercial street, the **Artists' Quarter** and residential sections, before beginning its circle again. At a healthy stride, you can walk the circle of Jerusalem Street in about 15 minutes, and once you're finished you will have seen an awful lot of Safed.

The **Egged Bus Station** (tel. 06-931-122 or 931-123) is at the lowest point on Jerusalem Street's circle through town, where Jerusalem Street intersects with **Derekh Jabotinsky.** Walk up to Jerusalem Street from the bus station and go right, and after 400 yards you will come to the **Tourist Information Office,** 23 Jerusalem St. (tel. 06-930-633), on the left-hand side, open from 8 a.m. to 1 p.m. and 4 to 7 p.m. daily, to 1 p.m. on Friday; closed Saturday. But if you come up from the bus station and go left, you'll be headed the short way into the commercial district. In any case, once you find Jerusalem Street you can't, simply *can't,* get lost in Safed.

Another feature that makes Safed supremely easy to get around in: Virtually all city buses go from the center to the hotels on Mount Canaan. Buses 1, 1/3, 1/4, and 3 all go there.

ACCOMMODATIONS IN SAFED: Several possibilities exist for accommodations in Safed: hotels right in town and on Mount Canaan nearby, a youth hostel, and rooms in private homes.

The prime season for tourism in Safed is July and August, when the cool mountain air makes a refreshing change from the baking temperatures of the plains. In the winter Safed is one of the chilliest places in Israel, especially at night. The thermometer in Safed can easily read a good 20° cooler than at Tiberias, only an hour's drive away, and it can get windy too—so be sure to bring along some warm clothing.

Due to the climatic conditions here, you'll find that prices will be higher in the busy season (July, August, and the major Jewish holidays), lower at other times. Don't be deterred by the seasons, winter or summer, but do be aware of the differences: in summer you'll find the town humming with tourists, activities of all kinds, and higher prices; in winter you'll find prices will be lower, there'll be plenty of rooms available in every category, and you'll be able to enjoy the quiet, peace, and mystery that is Safed.

If you're coming in winter, you may find that some of these hotel choices may be closed. Don't worry; you won't have any difficulty finding plenty of open rooms available.

All the hotel dining rooms are kosher.

On and Off Jerusalem Street

The first hotel you'll come to on Jerusalem Street if you're coming up from the bus station is **Hotel Beit Yossef,** 2 Jerusalem St. (P.O. Box 407; tel. 06-930-012 or 931-141). You'll see a large sign out front announcing "Tours of Safed begin here." Built a century ago to house a Scottish missionary hospital, it was converted to a hotel in March 1986 by two enterprising American immigrants who met while studying to become tour guides. There are 85 rooms around the 17 acres of wooded grounds, with accommodations ranging from $10 per person per night in the hostel section to $14 per person in the three-star building; add about $3 to these room-only rates if you're getting bed-and-breakfast. Prices remain the same all year. In addition to the hotel facilities, during the summer there are lots of interesting programs, including classes, guided tours, and hikes to nature and Christian archeological sites. Daily walking tours of Safed leave from the sign in front of the hotel.

Between nos. 14 and 16 Jerusalem Street is a little walkway, called Rehov Javitz (Javitz Street). Find it, and it will lead you to the **Carmel Hotel,** 8 Javitz St. (Safed 13208; tel. 06-930-053). Housed in a delightful old building that's been modernized, the Carmel's 14 rooms are very plain but clean and nice, with twin beds and shower (toilets are down the hall). All the rooms have nice views. Prices here are $15 single, $30 double, all year round (but if you're coming during high season, call ahead to be sure).

As you walk down Javitz Street, you'll see several signs advertising rooms to let, plus some other interesting places.

Walk up the slope along Jerusalem Street, and at about 24 Jerusalem St., on the left, look for a little passage called Rehov Ridbaz (Ridbaz Street). Down Ridbaz are three fine hotel choices.

The three-star **Hotel Tel Aviv** (tel. 06-972-555 or 972-382), also called the **Berinson House,** has 38 rooms in a fine old stone building, each with bathroom and tub, air conditioning, and telephone; rooms are wonderfully quiet, some with balcony, all with a magnificent view of the Sea of Galilee and/or Mount Meiron. Prices are $27 single, $38 double in low season; $35 single, $53 double in high season, which, at this hotel, is reckoned to include September as well—and watch out for the Jewish holidays, when 20% more is added to the high-season rates.

Also down Ridbaz Street is the considerably cheaper **Hotel Hadar** (tel. 06-930-068), with only two stars and 20 rooms, each one with shower. In August you must take full board with your room, and this adds about $12 per person to the price. During other summer months, you pay $31 single, $46 double; during spring and fall the price is $20 single, $25 double; and in the winter it goes down to a low $17 single, $20 double, breakfast and service included.

Right across the path from the Hadar is the **Hotel Ha-Galil** (not to be confused with the Hotel Nof Ha-Galil on Mount Canaan). The Ha-Galil is similar to the Hadar in price and appointments.

The **Hotel Friedman,** Israel Bek (or Beck, or Bak) Street (tel. 06-930-036), has two stars and 30 very clean rooms. An extra bonus is the fine collection of artwork from Safed and many other places—you'll feel like you're in an art gallery as you walk around the halls. There's a nice, homey atmosphere. A large terrace provides an unforgettable view of the surroundings. There's a 10% to 15% reduction for students except in the summer. For normal mortals, the price for a room is $10 per person for bed only, $3.50 extra for breakfast, although you're welcome to prepare your own in the shared guests' kitchen (open all the time). Families or groups will enjoy the big family rooms with up to five beds. The Friedman is open April 1 to December 1 only.

The **Central Hotel,** 37 Jerusalem St. (P.O. Box 64, Safed 13000; tel. 06-972-666), has 60 rooms, three stars, and some fine examples of local art. Rooms have air conditioning and heating, wall-to-wall carpet, toilets, and baths or showers. A patio one floor above street level is a pleasant feature. Prices are listed at $47 single, $78 double in high season; $34 single, $52 double in low season; but during the really slow months you may find them as low as $25 single, $28 double.

The pleasant, moderate-sized **Hotel Yair,** 59 Jerusalem St. (tel. 06-930-245 or 930-655) manages to be modern and folksy at the same time. All of the 36 rooms come with tubs in the bathrooms, and many come with little balconies and wonderful views of the valley and Mount Canaan. The lobby is up one flight, the rooms up yet another, and there is no elevator. You'll like it here. Charges are $25.25 single, $33.25 double in most months, substantially less from mid-November through February. During the winter it may be closed if business is slow. In July and August and on Jewish holidays, add about 20% to the prices quoted.

For a Splurge

The favorite inn in Safed is the four-star **Rimon Inn** (P.O. Box 1011, Safed 13110; tel. 06-930-665 or 930-666), in the Artists' Colony, a five-minute walk from the center of town. Prices here, of course, are higher: in the dead of winter you'll pay $35 single, $40 double; spring or fall prices are $46 single, $58 double; and in high season there's a minimum half-board requirement, bringing the prices up to $71 single, $95 double. But it's a lovely place. In addition to all the usual four-star luxuries, you'll find acres of gardens and wooded areas, swimming pool, over half the rooms with large balconies, beautiful views, extra touches like a guitarist in the bar on weekends, and some interesting history as well. Part of the main building derives from the 17th-century Turkish period, when it served as a khan (inn) and a post office. The dining room, for example, was originally the stable, and you still can see where the horses were tied.

On Mount Canaan

A 34-room, three-star establishment is the **Nof Ha-Galil Hotel,** on Mount Canaan (tel. 06-931-595 or 971-666). Rates begin at $20 single, $40 double off-season, rising to $35 single, $52 double in high season, with a 10% reduction for the third person in the room. Their rooms have heating, phones, baths, and toilets; a warm, family atmosphere prevails.

Other three-star hotels on Mount Canaan with similar prices and facilities are the **Hotel David** (tel. 06-930-062 or 971-662) and **Hotel Pisgah** (tel. 06-930-105 or 970-044).

The Youth Hostel

Bet Benjamin, or Bet Benyamin (P.O. Box 1139; tel. 06-931-086), has 118 beds, heating in all the rooms, hot showers, and the normal low IYHA official rates of $5.50 for members, $6.50 for nonmembers, bed and breakfast included. The hostel is located in south Safed on the corner of Ha-Nassi and Lohamei Ha-Getaot Streets, not far from the intersection of Ha-Nassi and Weizmann. Take bus 6 or 7 to get here. While you're here, be sure to see the lovely statue in the park adjoining the hostel.

When it's not being used for seminars, the **Ascent Institute** also acts as a hostel, charging $4 to $7 per night—and if you need to, you may be able to work for your keep. This may be an especially interesting place to stay from June through September, when there are free lectures every day, refreshments served, a Jewish drop-in center, and a lot going on. **Beit Yossef** (see it under "Hotels") also mixes programs with hostel and hotel facilities.

The IYHA official hostel has a lot of competition for clientele here in Safed. By poking around town a little—or even by being approached at the bus station as you arrive in Safed—you can probably find a hostel that will be less expensive. Just be wary and make sure of what you're getting for the price.

Cheaper is not always better! When you go to any IYHA official hostel, you know the price in advance, and you know you'll get a nice, clean room, a hot shower, and an adequate breakfast. If you go for the private hostel, check before you pay to be sure your accommodations will be up to the standard you're hoping for.

Rooms in Private Homes

You might also check with the local tourist authorities, or at the bus station, about the possibility of renting a room in a private home. Prices range from $5 upward, without meals. Or ask at the homes where you see a sign "Room for Rent." You're sure to see them as you make your rounds looking at hotels.

SAFED'S RESTAURANTS: The first thing you'll notice about Safed is its multitude of sandwich, snack, and falafel shops ranging the length of Jerusalem Street, open day and night—except for the Sabbath, from before sunset Friday until after sunset Saturday, when the whole town is closed up tight. Stroll along, see what's available, and take your pick.

For a real sit-down restaurant, try **Ha-Mifgash** (which means "meeting place" in Hebrew), right on the main street in the center of town, at 75 Jerusalem St. (tel. 06-930-510 or 974-734). There are fully four different parts to this restaurant. The first thing you'll see is the self-service falafel counter in front. Inside, there's the main dining room, with mouthwatering aromas drifting out from the kitchen. Over to the left side is another room, which was a large water cistern in the previous century. And downstairs from this, there's a wine cellar stocked with over 3,000 bottles of Israeli wine, with a multitude of choices from every part of the country. The restaurant's owner is glad to assist in your wine selection to accompany your meal; there's wine tasting here too. The specialties of the house are stuffed zucchini or pepper for NIS4 ($2.65), moussaka (eggplant stuffed with meat) for NIS5 ($3.35), and the baked lamb, which comes as a full meal for NIS16 ($10.65). Other meat meals are priced at NIS10 ($6.65) to NIS12 ($8), and all include soup, salad, potatoes, bread, and dessert. There's a choice of eight different soups, plus a soup of the day. Portions here are large. Students and soldiers get a 10% discount. Open daily from 9 a.m. to 11 p.m. (to midnight in summer), on Friday till 4 p.m., on Saturday after the Sabbath. Kosher.

By the time you read this, there will likely be a big new **commercial center** across Jerusalem Street from the Restaurant Ha-Mifgash, with a large cafeteria, various restaurants, a cinema, and more.

A good place to come for coffee and a light snack is Safed's version of the **Sami Barekas** chain, right beside the new commercial center mentioned above. While Sami Barekas anywhere is not exactly a gourmet heaven, this particular one is notable for its lovely view, making it a most enjoyable place to stop for coffee and one of several kinds of barekas, donuts, and other snacks.

The **Restaurant Pinati**, 81 Jerusalem St. (tel. 06-930-855), is just a few steps down the hill from Ha-Mifgash. Plain but clean and friendly, the Pinati will serve you full meals of grilled, baked, or goulash meats, which with salad, potatoes, rice, and cooked vegetables, go for NIS11 ($7.35) to NIS16.50 ($11); the specialties are veal or lamb, fresh from the oven. If you're feeling adventurous, you might try the unusual lung goulash. You can also help yourself to the salad bar for NIS5.50 ($3.65). This is the one restaurant in Safed that's open on the Sabbath; hours every day are 9 a.m. until 1 or 2 a.m.

The tidy **Café Mercaz**, right next to the Central Hotel and beside Safed's main post office, is a clean, cheery place with sidewalk tables, light meals, and tempting pastries. Take your morning coffee break or afternoon tea here. A cup of something hot and a plate of something fattening (but delicious!) will cost about NIS3.50 ($2.35).

A nice vegetarian restaurant, **Hiseddet Ha-Kikar,** is open on the square in the old Jewish Quarter, serving a good vegetarian menu emphasizing fish and salads.

Then there's the old standby, the self-service cafeteria at the **Egged central bus station,** where you can get a good kosher lunch or dinner for NIS4.50 ($3) to NIS6 ($4). It's open daily from 6 a.m. to 3 p.m. and again from 4 to 7 p.m., closing early on Friday and all day on Saturday in observance of the Sabbath.

WHAT TO SEE AND DO IN SAFED: Attractive and appealing though it is,
Safed is also somewhat secretive. There is much to see, but a traveler unfamiliar with the city's crooked streets and unimpressive doorways will pass right by most of the sights worth seeing. I'll do my best to help you uncover the secrets of Safed, starting with its fascinating Cabalistic synagogues. But first, consider getting some local help—by taking a guided tour.

Tours
In the past, two of the major tour companies—Egged and Galilee—had organized tours leaving daily in summer, beginning in Safed and roaming around the Galilee region. As of this writing, these tours are cancelled, and the gap has been filled by a number of local enterprises, all run by licensed guides who live in Safed and love the town.

For **daily walking tours** of Safed's Old City, go to the big sign announcing "Tours of Safed begin here," just at the entrance to the Hotel Beit Yossef, at 2 Jerusalem St., opposite City Hall (tel. 06-930-012 or 931-141). In summer the tours leave at 9:30 a.m., 1 p.m., and again at 4 p.m.; in winter, daily at 9:30 a.m. only. For $5 you get an informative two-hour walking tour of Old Safed that will introduce you to many of the sights in town, and much of the fascinating history.

Also through the Beit Yossef Hotel, **IsraHai Tours and Seminars** runs a variety of interesting tours and programs, as does the **Ascent Institute.**

Seminars and working trips go to many nature reserves in the Galilee area; contact **Bet Sefer Sadeh** (tel. 06-989-072) for info.

Cabalist Synagogues
The Cabala is an esoteric system for interpreting the Scriptures. Cabalists believed that the system originated with Abraham, and was handed down by word of mouth from ancient times. Historians of religion dispute this, however, saying that Cabalism arose only in the 600s and was a thriving belief until the 1700s.

In the Cabalistic system, every single symbol in holy writ has deep significance—each letter, number, and even accent in the holy books actually says a lot more than it appears to say. If you know the Cabalistic system of interpretation, they say, you can learn these hidden meanings. In addition, the names of God have mystical powers in themselves, and can be used to ward off evil and to perform miracles.

Cabalism was, in a way, a reaction to the heavy formalism of rabbinical Judaism. It allowed for more latitude in the interpretation of holy writ, and gained great popularity in the 1100s. The most significant Cabalist text is the Zohar, a mystical commentary on the Pentateuch (the first five books of the Old

Testament). Now that you're in on the secret (more or less), you should wander around where some of the greatest Cabalistic scholars lived, prayed, and worked.

It's not easy to say exactly where these Cabalist synagogues are, because the religious quarter has few street names, and the streets are really a collection of alleyways and courtyards. Ask for "kiryat batei knesset," the synagogue section.

Among the most famous old synagogues here is that named for **Rabbi Joseph Caro,** who lived and worked here in the 1500s. Very near it is another, named in honor of **Rabbi Moses Alsheikh.** Just a few steps away is the synagogue of **Rabbi Isaac Abuhav,** a sage of the 1400s, which contains an ancient Torah scroll said to have been written by the rabbi himself. Nearby is another, dedicated to **Rabbi Yosef Bena'a.** The latter is also called Ha-Lavan ("The White").

The synagogue quarter has two houses of worship dedicated to **Rabbi Isaac Louria,** who was called "Ha-Ari." Although Ha-Ari lived, studied, and taught in Safed for only 2½ years at the end of his life (he died here at the age of 38), the fruits of his work were so profound that they ended up changing the face of Judaism forever. The fortress-like Sephardic synagogue, graced by fine carved-wood doors, is built where the rabbi actually studied and prayed, down at the edge of the cemetery. The Ashkenazi one is closer to Jerusalem Street, at a spot where the rabbi is said to have come in order to welcome the Sabbath. The original building, constructed after Rabbi Louria's death, was destroyed by an earthquake in 1852 and later restored. Its Ark, done in the 1800s, is especially fine.

It's in touring these synagogues that you'll find some of the richest benefits of coming with an official guide. Every nook and cranny has a story connected with it—including not a small number of supernatural occurrences.

Cemetery

At the end of the synagogue area is a cemetery containing the tombs of many famous Cabala leaders; they're the ones you see with the sky-blue coloring, the many rocks upon them placed as symbols of love, respect, and remembrance. Here, too, is a military cemetery containing the resting places of soldiers who fell in all the wars, and nearby is yet a third cemetery containing the graves of Israelis who served with the underground Stern Gang and Irgun forces. Buried here are members of these groups executed by the British in Acre prison, including Dov Gruner, one of the best known of the outlawed fighters.

Cave of Shem and Eber

Another holy site is the Cave of Shem and Eber (or Ever), the son and grandson of Noah. This cave, located just off Ha-Palmach Street near where the Ha-Palmach stone overpass crosses Jerusalem Street, is said to be the place where Shem and Eber lived, studied, and were buried. Legend also has it that Jacob spent 14 years here studying before he went to the house of Laban, and that here he immersed himself in a ritual purifying bath before he wrestled with the angel. Today there is a synagogue opposite the cave; if the cave is locked, you can ask the caretaker of the synagogue and he will open it for you.

Oleh Ha-Gardom

Going down the hill from Jerusalem Street, in the area between the synagogues and the Artists' Quarter, is a straight stairway: Oleh Ha-Gardom. Stand at the top of this stairway, where it intersects with Jerusalem Street, and you're within sight of a lot of Safed's 20th-century historical landmarks.

Oleh Ha-Gardom was the dividing line between Safed's Jewish and Arab Quarters until 1948; that's why all the synagogues are clustered on the right-hand side, as you're facing down the stairway. The present Artists' Colony is in what used to be the Arab section. Look up toward the Citadel and you'll see a remnant of strained times: there's a small opening in the fortress there for a direct line of machine-gun fire pointing straight down the stairway, placed by the British to keep an uneasy peace between the two communities.

The day the British withdrew, at the end of the British Mandate in May 1948, the Arab and Jewish factions went to war. Look at the walls of the old police station and you'll see it's pocked with bullet holes from the fighting.

As you're standing here at the intersection of Jerusalem Street and Oleh Ha-Gardom, look down Jerusalem Street a little way and you'll see a war memorial, with a tablet telling the details of how the fighting favored first the Arabs, then the Jews. Poised on a stone mount, there's a Davidka ("little David"), one of those homemade Jewish mortars that, although not too accurate or damaging, made a terrific noise and gave the impression of being much more dangerous than it actually was.

Citadel

At the top of the hill, in the beautiful hilltop park, are the ruins of a Crusader fortress from which you can enjoy a fine view of Mount Meiron, Mount Tabor, the Sea of Galilee, and a scattering of tiny hill villages and settlements. This site, the highest in Safed, was once the scene of a 1st-century Galilean stronghold and a 12th-century Crusaders' lookout post. Here again, the Israelis had to push the Arabs back from the heights—sustaining heavy losses—and a war memorial commemorates the event.

Museums

Safed, for such a small town, has a number of interesting museums.

The **Museum of Printing Art,** in the Artists' Quarter at the corner of Arieh Merzer and Arieh Alwail Streets, has many notable exhibits. It's no accident that this museum was established in Safed—Safed was the site of the first Hebrew press in Israel, which was set up in 1576 and published Israel's first Hebrew book a year later. Here you can see a copy of the first newspaper printed in Israel (1863); a copy of the *Palestine Post* of May 16, 1948, announcing the birth of the State of Israel; a centuries-old Cabala printed here in Safed; pictures of the Gutenberg Bible and of Gutenberg himself, and his shop in 1455; examples of modern Israeli graphics; and many other things. The museum is open Sunday through Thursday from 10 a.m. to noon and again from 4 to 6 p.m., on Friday and Saturday from 10 a.m. to noon. Free admission.

Habad (or Chabad) House, on Ha-Maginim Street between Maginim Square (Kikar Maginim) and the Oleh Ha-Gardom steps, is a museum of Jewish history, with changing exhibitions of special interest to young people. Open Sunday through Thursday from 9 a.m. to 4 p.m.

Down the hill, in south Safed, you'll find **Hameiri House** (P.O. Box 1028; tel. 06-971-307), the **Museum and Institute for the Heritage of Safed.** It's housed in a historic 16th-century edifice, the restoration of which was done over a 27-year period completed in 1985. Artifacts and documents portray the history of Safed's Jewish community over the centuries, its struggles and survival. It's open Sunday through Friday from 9 a.m. to 2 p.m., and can also open up on Saturday for groups, with advance notice. Admission is NIS2.50 ($1.65) for adults, NIS1.50 ($1) for children.

Art in Safed

Safed, as I mentioned earlier, is host to a thriving colony of artists of all kinds. For the most part, these are not your starving-in-a-garret types; rather, they are some of Israel's finest, with work exhibited in museums, galleries, and private places throughout Israel, Europe, and North America. They live in Safed for the artistic and inspirational atmosphere of this birthplace of Jewish mysticism.

To get to the **Artists' Colony,** you can just ask anybody in town for directions; walking up Jerusalem Street, you'll see signs pointing the way—it's the whole area down the hill from Jerusalem Street between the Oleh Ha-Gardon stairway facing the police station and the stone overpass which crosses Jerusalem Street. It's only a few steps down from Jerusalem Street, with picturesque houses, tiny streets, manicured gardens, and displays of art outdoors in summertime. Many artists have galleries set up in their homes, where you can meet the artist as well as see the varied creations. All of the galleries are open in summer, which is Safed's busy time of year. In the winter many of them may be closed. But don't despair: if you come during the winter, you can still examine art from over 60 of Safed's artists at the General Exhibition.

The **General Exhibition** is the one place in the Artists' Quarter where the work of Safed's many artists can be seen all in one place. Housing the creations of artists working in all mediums from paint to ceramics to silk, the gallery is open all year round, with hours Sunday through Thursday from 9 a.m. to 6 p.m., on Friday to 2 p.m., and on Saturday from 10 a.m. to 2 p.m.

Another distinctive gallery is the **Ethiopian Folk Art Center** (tel. 06-974-835), just off the Oleh Ha-Gardom stairway at the edge of the Artists' Quarter. Many of the Ethiopian Jews who have immigrated to Israel have been resettled in Safed. The Folk Art Center, founded in 1985, displays all kinds of beautiful and distinctive Ethiopian art, including embroidery and weaving, ceramics, basketry, sculpture, clothing, and more. Proceeds from the sale of these items go directly to the workers who make them—an important means of income, and pride, to the newly adapting community of Ethiopian Jews. The center is open Sunday through Thursday from 9 a.m. to 6 p.m., on Friday until 1 p.m.; closed Saturday.

The **Ora Gallery** (tel. 06-974-910), just a little farther down the same street, is another unique gallery, specializing in Hassidic art. You'll find unusual pieces here, mostly paintings, with symbolism based on the Cabala. Summer hours are 9 a.m. to 6:30 p.m. Sunday through Thursday, until 1 p.m. on Friday; closed Saturday. In the winter it closes earlier—at 4 p.m. in good weather, or 1 p.m. in bad weather, with Friday and Saturday hours remaining the same.

On the other side of the Artists' Quarter you'll find the **Ziffer Garden,** a sculpture garden with many of Ziffer's statues, and a gallery off to one side showing Ziffer's development from realistic to abstract art. Summer gallery hours are Sunday through Thursday from 9 a.m. to 1 p.m. and again from 4 to 6 p.m., on Friday to 1 p.m., on Saturday from 10 a.m. to 1 p.m.

The **Israel Bible Museum** (tel. 06-973-472) will surprise you if you're expecting it to be like your usual museum. Dedicated in 1985, the museum (previously the home of the Turkish governor in Safed) is full of inspirational, dramatic art pieces by contemporary artist Phillip Ratner. At the Israel Bible Museum, he has taken his life's inspiration, the Bible, and made it the focus of some very moving creations. "My art is my love song as David's was the Psalm," he says, and it shows. March through November, the Israel Bible Museum is open Sunday through Thursday from 10 a.m. to 4 p.m., on Friday and Saturday from 10 a.m. to 2 p.m. If you come December through February, you'll find it open Sunday through Friday from 10 a.m. to 2 p.m.; closed Saturday. Admission is always free. To find it, look for the sign on the opposite side of the street from 14 Jerusalem St., and climb the stairs going up. You'll ascend through a beautiful garden with a lovely view of Mount Meiron in the distance. Or you can enter from the other side, walking down from Derekh Hativat Yiftah, the road that circles the Citadel.

All the art exhibitions around Safed are good places to think about acquiring good, inexpensive gifts and souvenirs. Many of the artists and exhibitions have both large and small reproductions of their work available. The prices vary, but many are fairly inexpensive, and they're an interesting reminder of Safed.

One final exhibit to see: For a look at the chocolate-maker's art, stop by the **Vered Ha-Galil Chocolate Factory** (tel. 06-973-805) for a tour and a taste. It's not far from the heated swimming pool in Safed's industrial section.

Sports

As you turn into town, in a hollow to the right of the road, near the Central Bus Station, is **Emek Hatchelet Swimming Pool,** which has been around since 1959. The area is beautifully landscaped, with small gardens and a tiny bridge flanked by lounge chairs, tables, and big colorful umbrellas. There are two pools here (one for children), game tables under thatched sun shelters, a completely equipped children's playground, plus a mini-golf course. Aside from showers and dressing rooms, facilities include a restaurant serving everything from ice cream to a full steak-and-chips meal. It's open daily from June through part of September, from roughly 9 a.m. to 5 p.m. Several days a week the last couple of hours in the afternoon are reserved for men-only or women-only swims. Entrance fees are NIS3 ($2) for adults, NIS2 ($1.35) for children.

The **Heated Swimming Pool** (tel. 06-974-294) is open all year. In summer, hours are Sunday through Thursday from 10 a.m. to 10 p.m., on Friday until 5 p.m., on Saturday until 6 p.m. In winter it's open Sunday through Thursday from noon to 10 p.m., on Friday from 10 a.m. to 3 p.m., and on Saturday from 10 a.m. to 4 p.m. Take bus 6 to the industrial part of Safed.

Ask at the Tourist Information Office for details about the new **Sports Center,** with tennis and basketball courts and more, and a capacity of 600 people. It's covered, and heated in winter. For more information about **tennis courts,** also call 06-971-222.

Plant a Tree

Just outside the highway entrance to Safed is a Keren Kayemet Le-Israel (Jewish National Fund) **Tree Planting Center.** It's in a historic location: in the 16th century Joseph Caro wrote here, and in our present century it was the scene of heroic Jewish struggles against the British. Palmach soldiers built a fortress here during the British Mandate, which the British destroyed, only to have it built again. The restored fortress was opened to the public in 1971, containing an exhibition of documents, press cuttings, and photographs relating to the site.

Here at this site, the Jewish National Fund has established the **Biriya Forest.** You are welcome to come and contribute to the ongoing history of the land by planting a tree with your own hands. It is a lovely place for your very own tree. It costs about $7. Hours are Sunday through Thursday from 8 a.m. to 2 p.m., on Friday until 12:30 p.m. For further information you can ask at the Safed Tourist Information Office, or you can contact a Jewish National Fund Office, with information on various foresting and tree-planting centers throughout Israel. In Jerusalem, call 02-635-261 or 635-213; in Tel Aviv, it's 03-234-449.

CULTURAL EVENTS AND NIGHTLIFE: Summer is the time for most of Safed's musical events. About eight **chamber music concerts** are held throughout the year, mostly in the summer, as well as a summer musical workshop, at the

Wolfson Community Center, on Ha-Palmach Street near the market. For **piano concerts,** check out Hemdat Yamim (tel. 06-989-085) on the Acre–Safed highway, which usually has concerts every Monday and Saturday evening during the summer.

By the time you read this, the new **Igal Alom Theater** should be open on Jerusalem Street, with everything from Shakespeare to ballet and popular folk dancing. It's named after the man who was the liberator of Safed in the 1948 war.

For that other kind of dancing, ask at the Tourist Office to find out what **discothèques** are happening around town. Usually you'll find them open around three times a week or so in summer, and on Saturday nights during the winter. One example is the **Citadel Bar,** located up at the top of the Citadel hill; it's open all day, serving as a pub, coffeehouse, social club, and meeting place for a game of cards or the like; at night it's a bar and disco.

Then there's the **Pub Carmel,** easy to find by walking down Javitz Street from Jerusalem Street (it's the one between 14 and 16 Jerusalem St.), past the Carmel Hotel until you get to the end of the street—only about one long block off Jerusalem Street. It's an attractive dark-wood pub, with walls of that hewn stone so characteristic of Safed's architecture. You'll find it open every night in summer, on Friday and Saturday nights the rest of the year, from about 9 p.m. to 3 a.m.

Don't forget the nightly **free lectures** offered at Ascent Institute during the summer, along with refreshments and a friendly drop-in center. And if you'll be in town on a Friday evening, ask at Ascent, or also at the Tourism Office, about arranging for some friendly **Sabbath hospitality** (call by Thursday).

A SIDE TRIP TO MEIRON: Five miles west of Safed lies the town of Meiron, a holy place for religious Jews for 1,700 years. Like Safed, Meiron is an extremely religious town, having had a continuously Jewish population for nearly 18 centuries. When Jerusalem fell to the Romans in the 2nd century, the Israeli tribes took to the high grounds near here, settling in isolated areas too remote for their persecutors' vigilance. One early Meiron inhabitant, a 2nd-century Talmudist named Shimon Bar Yochai, continued to defy the Romans and was ultimately forced to hide in a cave in Peqiin, outside Meiron. There, according to legend, he wrote the Zohar, the *Book of Splendor,* which is the bible of the mystical Cabalist sect.

Meiron is the scene of considerable pageantry during the holiday of Lag b'Omer, which occurs in the spring just 3½ weeks after Passover. Thousands of Orthodox Jews pour into Safed from all over the country. There follows a torchlight parade with singing and dancing as the column of black-gowned zealots hike to Meiron. There they burn candles on top of **Rabbi Shimon's Tomb** and light a great bonfire into which some, overcome by emotion, throw their clothes. The festivities go on all night. In the morning 3-year-old boys are given their first haircuts, and the cut hair is thrown into the fire.

In this devoutly religious town there still exists an ancient synagogue from the 2nd century, as well as Rabbi Shimon's tomb, and a rock called the **Messiah's Chair.** Reputedly, on the day the Messiah arrives, he will sit right here while Elijah blows the trumpet to announce his coming.

Picnic tables are scattered along the roadside between here and Safed—bring a sandwich. An excellent base for seeing Galilee is the **Moshav Meiron Guest House** (tel. 06-739-361), a 12-minute drive from Safed. It is a complex of individual, steep-roofed, multicolored cottages which provide family facilities and sleeping accommodations for six—two on the ground floor and four in an attic room. Total cost is about $55 per day and this includes cooking facilities, bedding, kitchenware, etc. The moshav itself was founded in 1949 and is home to Hungarian and Rumanian immigrants. A good place to visit and truly inexpensive when you're sharing costs.

Sasa and the Biram Synagogue

On the northern foothills of Mount Meiron is **Kibbutz Sasa,** a settlement started by a group of Americans and Canadians in 1949 in a deliberately chosen region where the pioneers hoped to test their convictions. This settlement has more than its share of artists and university degree-holders, who built their settlement atop a hill 3,000 feet high and persevered despite many problems, including a polio epidemic that tragically took many lives and threatened to break the morale of the settlers. Sasa is called an "American" kibbutz, and consequently VIP guests are often brought here by the government to be shown what one group of American expatriates accomplished in Israel.

Just two miles away is **Biram,** the oldest and best-preserved synagogue in Israel, its grounds housing—according to legend—the grave of Queen Esther.

ON THE ROAD TO ROSH PINNA: The **Seaview Vegetarian Hotel** (P.O. Box 27, Rosh Pinna 12000; tel. 06-937-103 or 937-104), located along the road between Rosh Pinna and Safed, is a peaceful oasis for vegetarians and naturists, with a lovely view of the Sea of Galilee below. Finnish sauna, whirlpool bath, swimming pool (open May to October), gymnasium, solarium terrace, library, social games, card room, and video movies are all included in the daily rate. For an extra fee, you can also get a massage or participate in a yoga group. There are 25 acres of lovely hillsides to explore, plus excursions to the Galilee on request. The 22 double rooms all have color TV, air conditioning, radio, and telephone, and go for $30 single, $50 double during the low tourism season, with bed and breakfast. Half-board and full-board arrangements can be made for an extra $5 per meal. Rates during high season (July, August, and Jewish holidays) jump to $41 single, $73 double, with extra meals proportionately more expensive too.

The real deal here is the good vegetarian dining. Organically grown fruits and vegetables are served from the kosher kitchen, following precisely the rules of vegetarians and naturists. Even if you're not staying as a guest, you are still welcome to come and eat. The dining room is open seven days a week, from 7 to 8:30 a.m., 1 to 2:30 p.m., and again from 7 to 8 p.m.

4. Upper Galilee and the Golan Heights

Leaving Tiberias or Safed, the main highway heads due north toward Kiryat Shmona and Metulla. North of Kiryat Shmona, roads head west/south along the Lebanese border back toward Safed, and east to Hurshat Tal National Park, Baniyas Waterfall, and the Mount Hermon Ski Center in the Golan Heights.

The Golan Heights holds few major "destinations" for the casual tourist except the ski center. Nature buffs and campers will find more attractions here, in the many nature reserves and national parks. Nonetheless, you really should see the area, for its historical significance, its landscape, and its many unusual sites.

The way I highly recommend seeing the Golan is by a one-day guided tour. Several are available, leaving from Tiberias. It takes all day to see the Golan, and by the end of that day you'll have seen most of the places of interest and learned a good deal about the history of the area, both ancient and modern. For the average visitor, this will be enough. And for anyone wishing to spend more time and delve into the riches of the Golan in more depth, it will be a good general introduction to the region. After you've seen the whole area, you can always go back to the places you like the most, with more understanding about them than if you'd just gone on your own, or go back to explore other places you missed.

A one-day tour of the Golan Heights will cost you $15 to $22, depending on which tour you choose, and there are several to choose from.

The two major touring companies in Tiberias, **Egged** and **Galilee,** each offer Golan tours for the same price, $22, going to about the same places. (It's tour no. 101 with either company.) The Egged tours go at 8:30 a.m. on Tuesday, Thursday, and Saturday, leaving from the Tiberias Central Bus Station; you can also arrange to be picked up at your hotel for no extra charge. You should reserve in advance; contact the Egged Tours office in the Central Bus Station (tel. 06-720-474 or 791-080). The Galilee tours leave at 9 a.m. on Tuesday and Saturday; contact the Galilee office, 10 Ha-Yarden St. (tel. 06-720-550 or 720-330), to reserve.

A third option, especially popular with younger people and the youth hostel set, is to see the Golan with **Shoshan Oded** (tel. 06-721-812), who picks up tourists from all the Tiberias youth hostels every morning (call in advance to reserve your space, or reserve through any hostel). His price, $15, is a bit less than the official bus-company tours, and it must be noted that he is a taxi driver, not an official government-licensed tour guide. However, he knows the Golan region like the back of his hand, and the real attraction is his sparkling personality and lively banter as he drives the seven-seat sherut taxi all throughout the Golan to take you around. He has become so popular that, often, more taxis must be added to accommodate all the riders, and if so, it's a good idea to try to ride in the car that he himself is driving. Everyone who goes with him finds him delightful.

Yet another option is to check with Tiberias's major hotels, many of which will have information about private guided tours.

If you want to start out from somewhere other than Tiberias, Egged and Galilee offer tours leaving from Haifa, Tel Aviv, and Jerusalem; check their information booklets, or call, for details.

WHERE TO STAY: Upper Galilee and Golan are not paved with hotels, as you might imagine. There is one four-star hotel in Kiryat Shmona, a youth hostel in nearby Tel Hai, and another youth hostel in Rosh Pinna. Kiryat Shmona is the hub of this area, and thus the most desirable place to stay, especially if you're traveling by bus. Metulla, rather a dead-end up on the Lebanese border, has several good moderately priced hotels, but not much to do. There is one accommodation near the Mount Hermon Ski Center.

Then there are the kibbutz inns and guesthouses. Ha-Goshrim and Sha'ar Yashuv are very convenient, being east of Kiryat Shmona, next to the Hurshat Tal park, on the road to Baniyas and the Mount Hermon Ski Center. Kefar Giladi is between Kiryat Shmona and Metulla. Kefar Blum is southwest of Kiryat Shmona. Ayalet Ha-Shahar is the farthest south of these, closer to Rosh Pinna, on the main road north to Kiryat Shmona.

Descriptions of these accommodations are given below in the appropriate places along the routes. But before you head into Upper Galilee and Golan, it'd be good to do some telephoning and get an idea of how busy these hostelries will be. You don't want to be left without a bed. If you don't phone, take an early bus from Tiberias or Safed and head straight for your chosen hostelry to make sure you can pin down a place to stay. Once you've done that, you're at your leisure to wander.

INTO UPPER GALILEE: From Tiberias, you can catch a bus going northward as far as **Metulla,** Israel's most northerly town—and you'll find that the ride passes fascinating sights. (Depending on the season, you might have to change buses at Kiryat Shmona.)

The trip begins along the western shore of the lake, goes through the valley of **Ginossar** and past Capernaum. Alongside the names of Kinneret, Galilee, and Tiberias, Ginossar must also take its place as a biblical name for the Sea of Galilee.

Soon you'll pass the turn-off for **Rosh Pinna** ("corner stone" in Hebrew), an undistinguished-looking, pleasant small town, the oldest modern town in all of Galilee, founded in 1882 by Rumanian Jewish immigrants. It now boasts Galilee's major airport. Just outside Rosh Pinna is the only memorial in the country to a member of the underground extremist army. Dedicated to Shmuel Ben Josef, the first Jew hanged by the British in Palestine, this simple but striking monument looks from a distance like an arm thrust upward at the sky, its fist shaking in defiance at the heavens.

There's a 100-bed youth hostel at Rosh Pinna, known as **Nature Friends** (tel. 06-737-086), with family rooms, central heating, and kitchen facilities available for your use. Prices are the same as at all the IYHA hostels: $5.50 with membership card, $6.50 without the card, breakfast included.

Farther along the main road is the turnoff to **Mishmar Ha-Yarden,** Galilee's oldest moshav, established around the turn of the century, and one of the few settlements overrun and destroyed by the Arabs during the 1948 siege. Beyond the settlement, crossing the Jordan into Golan, is the bridge called **Benot Yaakov,** "Daughters of Jacob," believed to be the place where Jacob crossed the river on his return from Mesopotamia. The bridge is also on the ancient caravan route from Damascus to Egypt, part of the Via Maris.

Tel Hazor and Ayelet Ha-Shahar

On the left (west) side of the road is **Tel Hazor,** a prehistoric mound which serves as yet another reminder of this land's incredibly long history. The artifacts discovered here are in a nearby museum. Read on.

A short distance past the tel (mound), on the east side of the road, is **Kibbutz Ayelet Ha-Shahar** (Upper Galilee 12200; tel. 06-932-611 or 932-666), with its luxurious four-star guesthouse—really a major hotel for Upper Galilee travelers. All 144 rooms have private baths (most with tubs), radios, and telephones, plus central heat. The swimming pool is open in warm weather, the gardens all the time. Prices are not low, though: one person pays $40 and two pay $62 for room with breakfast. There's an off-season reduction of 10% to 20%.

At the entrance to Kibbutz Ayelet Ha-Shahar you'll see the **Hazor Museum** (tel. 06-737-313). It has exhibits from 21 different archeological strata spanning 2,500 years, from the early Bronze Age to the Hellenistic period in the 2nd century B.C. (By the way, the kibbutz is one of Israel's handsomest—same goes for its guesthouse.)

The Hula Valley

The best view of this beautiful reclaimed swampland is from the **Nebi Yusha** fortress just off the main road, on the **Hill of the 28.** A memorial in front of the British Taggart Fort recalls the time when these Hagana soldiers climbed the hill from Hula in the dead of night and fought to gain this strategic point. The odds were against them as they weathered a rain of machine-gun fire and grenades from the windows of the fort. When efforts to dynamite the building failed, because of the concrete-reinforced base, the group's commander plunged into a suicidal mission. He strapped the dynamite to his back, ignited it, and threw himself at a weak point in the wall, sacrificing himself for the objective. In all, 28 fighters died in taking this hilltop strongpoint, and today birds nest in the many shell holes on the walls of the fort.

Beyond the memorial plaques is an observation point where the view of the Hula Valley down below is nothing short of magnificent.

This breathtaking area, which stretches in both directions as far as the eye can see, was once a vast marshland teeming with wildlife. It was considered the smallest of the three lakes fed by the Jordan—the Sea of Galilee and the Dead Sea are the other two. To Israelis who remember it in its marshland state, the Hula was a lovely place—a home for water buffalo and wild boar, a place abundant in exotic birds and wildflowers. Species of cranes and storks would migrate here, coming and going from as far away as Russia, Scandinavia, and India. To those who knew its thickets of papyrus, its dragonflies and kingfishers, and its tropical water lilies (some claim it looked a little like the shores of the Nile), the Hula was a bit of paradise. The Arabs had legends about the Hula's charms, where spirits walked in the evening mist luring young people into the mysterious marsh.

After years of wrangling with neighboring governments—as well as with the French and British—the Israelis got the chance to drain the Hula marshes after they achieved independence. The country needed every drop of water and every square foot of fertile land. So bulldozers and dredges changed the Hula, reclaiming its wild beauty into a mammoth checkerboard of rich fields. But in one small section a wildlife preserve lingered, a vestige of the Hula's past.

The project took seven years, from 1950 to 1957. Control over the Hula's waters was also a necessary phase of the Lowdermilk and other Jordan River diversion plans, which bring water to the barren southern reaches of Israel.

However, the project cost the area in terms of an upset ecosystem, and in 1970 a reconstruction project was launched. Today the **Hula Nature Reserve,** 15 km (9 miles) south of Kiryat Shmona and 3 km (1½ miles) east of the highway, is again alive with gray herons, cormorants, ducks, wild boar, jamoos (water buffalo), and other former inhabitants that died or went elsewhere when the swamps were drained. Open daily from 8 a.m. to 4 p.m., on Friday till 3 p.m. Admission costs NIS2 ($1.35) for adults, half that for kids. Free guided tours take place Saturday, Sunday, Tuesday, and Thursday from 9:30 a.m. to 1 p.m.

Heading north again, you'll pass the turnoff (to the right, east) toward **Kefar Blum** (Upper Galilee 12150; tel. 06-943-666), a kibbutz with a three-star guesthouse. The 59 rooms here all have central heating and telephones; there's a swimming pool too. Fishing, birdwatching, and jogging are prime kibbutz activities. For the rooms, guests pay $31 to $33.25 single, $43.75 to $48.25 double.

KIRYAT SHMONA: This is the "big town" in Upper Galilee (pop. 18,000), with a wide main boulevard, carefully laid-out residential districts, a busy bus station, and a fascinating monument to the turbulent past: three old army tanks, painted in bright basic colors, next to a gas station on the left side of the road as you enter from the south.

Where to Stay and Eat

The town's prime hostelry is without doubt the **Hotel North** (also called **Ha-Tzafon**—"north" in Hebrew; P.O. Box 319, Kiryat Shmona 10200; tel. 06-944-702 or 944-707). With 90 rooms and four stars, it's a bit out of our budget range, but you should know about it as hotels are so scarce in this part of the country. Radios and phones in the rooms, an elevator, dining room, restaurant and cafeteria/pizzeria, a bar/discothèque open nightly from 9 p.m. to 2 a.m., and TV lounge (programs from Syria and Lebanon, plus video films), car-rental agency in the lobby, swimming pool, and prices at $46 single, $58 double (add

$10 in high season). You'll spot the six-story hotel from the bus station, which is right across the street, or from your vehicle passing through town.

If you don't mind staying out of town, you can head for **Kibbutz Kefar Giladi** (Upper Galilee 12210; tel. 06-941-414), halfway to Metulla. The three-star, 155-room guesthouse offers tidy rooms, virtually all with bathtubs, at prices of $34.50 single, $50.50 double. For that price, of course, you'll enjoy not only the room and the pool, but also a glimpse of kibbutz life.

As for dining, the dining room in the **Hotel North** is the fancy choice in town, with kosher five-course lunches and dinners served from 12:30 to 2:30 p.m. and 7 to 8:30 p.m., at NIS15 ($10) per meal, open every day. The hotel's cafeteria/pizzeria, open nightly (except Friday) from 7 p.m. to 1 a.m., serves 12 kinds of pizza for NIS6 ($4) to NIS10 ($6.65), sandwiches for NIS2.25 ($1.50).

If you can do with something less elegant, sample the variety of **open-air eating establishments** on the little street facing the bus station, and on the main highway immediately north of the hotel. You'll see many tables set up with awnings on the sidewalk terraces. Several restaurants offer pita specialties that you can stuff yourself from the large selection of fixings all laid out buffet style, with a base of falafel, hamburger, shwarma, shishlik, or steak, priced from NIS1.50 ($1) to NIS5 ($3.35) depending on which you choose. You'll also find pizza, pastries, ice cream, espresso, and other snacks at low prices due to the large number of young soldiers who use Kiryat Shmona's bus station as the transfer point to outposts in Israel's northern region.

For a good hot indoor meal, the small, pleasant self-service restaurant at the **Egged bus station** offers breakfast or dinner for about NIS2 ($1.35), a hearty hot lunch for NIS5 ($3.35). Open from 5:15 to 10:15 a.m., 11:15 a.m. to 4 p.m., and 4:30 to 7 p.m., closing early Friday and all day Saturday; it's kosher.

The Youth Hostel: Kiryat Shmona's youth hostel is actually at **Tel Hai** (Upper Galilee Mobile Post; tel. 06-940-043.) There are 200 beds here, family rooms and communal kitchen (you provide your own plates and pots). You can take the northbound bus heading for Metulla and it will drop you right at the front door of the hostel; if you're driving, follow the orange signs leading to Kibbutz Kefar Giladi, and you'll come to the hostel about 300 yards up from the highway on Tel Hai road, 2½ km (1½ miles) north of Kiryat Shmona.

HEADING NORTH: From Kiryat Shmona, you can head north past Kefar Giladi and Tel Hai to Metulla, then backtrack to Kiryat Shmona before heading east, to Golan.

Tel Hai and Trumpeldor

Heading north from Kiryat Shmona, you might now begin thinking about Joseph Trumpeldor, in whose memory this town was founded. Kiryat Shmona means "Town of the Eight" and that refers to Trumpeldor's group of six men and two women who died at nearby **Tel Hai** defending their settlement from Arab attackers in 1920. It was also the scene of one of the worst terrorist attacks.

In another few miles you come to the monument to Trumpeldor at Tel Hai, a statue of a lion at the edge of a cliff, his head thrown back and mouth open, bellowing his strength at the skies. Rarely do foreign visitors hear about Trumpeldor, and to an Israeli this is shocking. For Trumpeldor is the Israeli Nathan Hale, a model of courage and heroism who continues to fire the spirit of the nation's youth. He was born in Russia in 1880, served in the czar's army, lost an arm, and was decorated for gallantry by the empress of Russia. Then, as an ambitious Zionist leader, he came to Palestine in 1912, and with his self-styled Zion Mule Corps, fought with the British in the disastrous Gallipoli campaign. After the war he became a leader of Russia's pioneer agricultural youth movement and settled at the Tel Hai kibbutz. It was here that Trumpeldor fought off marauding Arab bands with the other settlers, until one day when a particularly heavy attack came and the one-armed Trumpeldor refused to leave the settlement. In a furious last-ditch stand, he and seven comrades were killed on the kibbutz grounds.

The grave of this national hero, beneath the roaring lion, is inscribed with his last words: "It is good to die for our country." The Jews got their own country 28 years after he uttered those words.

Metulla

This is as far north as you can go in Israel proper. Founded in 1896 by a Rothschild grant, the town is a pretty, pine-scented oasis where farming, fruit-growing, and apiculture (the cultivating of bees) are vigorously pursued by the residents of this village at the Lebanese border. During the rainy season you can see an Israeli waterfall in action here, cascading down from the Tanur Pass into the Iyon River.

Where to Stay and Eat: A quiet little town, with a lot of soldiers and considerable military action because of its proximity to the Lebanese border, Metulla does boast several good lodging places, among them the two-star **Hotel-Pension Arazim** (Metulla 10292; tel. 06-944-144 or 944-145), where everything gleams with love and polish, and the food, service, and accommodations are old-worldish in style and quality. It has 40 rooms, all with toilet, bath and/or shower, plus a bar, gift shop, private swimming pool, and tennis courts. The food's kosher and there's central heating. Bed-and-breakfast rates are $22 single, $44 double; a little more in high season, possibly much lower in the winter off-season. Students get a 10% reduction during July and August and 20% in winter.

There's also the two-star **Ha-Mavri Hotel** (Metulla 10292; tel. 06-940-150), just a few doors down from the Arazim, with 18 rooms, all with shower and toilet. Some rooms have a balcony and view of Lebanon, which can also be seen from the airy dining room. Singles are $23 and doubles run $32 in regular season, but in winter the prices may go down to as low as $10 per person.

An excellent choice is the **Sheleg Ha-Levanon Hotel** (P.O. Box 13, Metulla 10292; tel. 06-944-015 or 944-017), with 40 rooms, all equipped with phones, private baths and showers, toilets, and clock-radios. You can rent a TV by day, although there's a color set in the lounge. Tennis courts, two swimming pools (one for children), a piano in the lobby, a handsome bar/dining room, and a garden patio are other amenities. High-season rates are $25 to $32 single, $50 double, with low-season rates listed as $21 to $28 single, $42 double—but here, too, actual winter rates may be much lower, just as at the other hotels. Various discounts apply here as well: students, or travelers who come with a copy of this book in hand, get a 15% reduction in price, plus free admission to the Nahal Iyon Nature Reserve.

As for dining, in addition to the two hotel restaurants and coffeeshops already mentioned, at the end of the road are two casual, comfortable restaurants.

Right on the corner you'll see the **Galily Peak Self-Service Restaurant and Bar** (tel. 06-941-023), open and airy, where you can get steak and fries for NIS10 ($6.65), hamburger and fries for NIS7 ($4.65), soup for NIS3 ($2), or a wide variety of bar selections. Open seven days a week from 7:30 a.m. to 9:30 p.m.

Behind here, in the large white building, you'll see signs pointing to the **Metulla Restaurant** (no phone). Up on the second floor, almost literally overhanging the Lebanese border, with glass walls all around, a terrace outdoors for summer and a cheerful wood-burning stove for winter, you'll find it friendly, comfortable, and clean, serving basic Lebanese and European dishes. Open seven days from 1 p.m. to midnight.

What to See: Metulla became a bustling place during the Israeli invasion of Lebanon, but now that the troops are withdrawn it looks as though it will settle back into its picturesque torpor. This is as it should be, for Metulla, with its tawny limestone buildings accented by dark wood, cypress and evergreen trees, is the Israeli equivalent of a Swiss mountain village—tidy, tranquil, in tune with nature. All the same, there are those bomb shelters here and there throughout the town, reminding you that this is the Middle East, not Switzerland.

Metulla has a tiny **museum,** which you will see as you wander around town. As for nature, that's what there is to see here. Right down by the Lebanese border is the **Nahal Iyon Picnic Ground,** shaded by tall eucalyptus trees and furnished with picnic tables and campgrounds. Past the picnic ground, a rough road skirts the Lebanese border, heading east and south to the **Nahal Iyon** (or Ayoun) **Nature Reserve** that runs along the entire east side of Metulla, along the Iyon Stream, between Metulla and the Lebanese border. You can drive or walk into the reserve from here; admission is NIS2.20 ($1.45) for adults, half price for children. It's open daily from 8 a.m. to 4 p.m., until 3 p.m. on Friday.

Ha-Tanur, the **Tanur Waterfall,** is here in the Iyon Nature Reserve, 2 km (1¼ miles) south of Metulla. To get to the waterfall, you can come down through the nature reserve, or you can take any bus, or walk downhill out of town toward Kiryat Shmona, and after two kilometers turn left (east) and walk down into the valley another 400 yards. After the 20-minute walk, you'll wander into a bit of paradise. In all but the driest months of summer the waterfall will be crashing merrily, filling cool, tempting pools at its base. All of this is shaded by great trees which have grown up in appreciation of the abundant waters. It's one of Israel's loveliest spots.

The Tanur Waterfall is part of the Nahal Iyon Nature Reserve, so you pay NIS2.20 ($1.45) for admission to the park.

About a kilometer (half a mile) west of Metulla you can visit the **Good Fence,** the border crossing between Israel and Lebanon. The fence got its name in 1976 when a Lebanese child was brought across into Israel to receive medical care, and the name stuck. Today Lebanese cross the border daily to work in Israel. As you stand on the Israeli side, look around you and consider the inscription on stone plaques in English, Hebrew, and Arabic: ". . . and they shall beat their swords into plowshares and their spears into pruning hooks. Nation shall not lift up sword against nation, neither shall they learn war any more" (Isaiah 2:4).

If you have a car, or if you don't mind a bit of a hike, you might want to go up to **Lookout Mountain,** the peak about one kilometer (about half a mile) west of Metulla, for a bird's-eye view of the surrounding area.

HEADING EAST: If you decide to head east from Kiryat Shmona, you'll find lots to see and do. Along the road to Mount Hermon—that snow-capped peak you've probably already noticed—are two kibbutz guesthouses, a beautiful national park, hot springs, a crusader fortress, and a ski center.

For transport, you might want to consider taking a guided tour, or banding together with some other travelers to hire a taxi for the day. (They may be able to help you with this at the Hotel North.) Otherwise, getting around Golan can take more time than you want to spend.

Buses? You can hop a no. 25, 26, or 36 to get to Hurshat Tal, Tel Dan, and

Baniyas, on the edge of the heights. For a trip deep into Golan, catch a no. 55 to Qasrin, unofficial "capital" of the region.

Hurshat Tal and Kibbutz Inns

Only five kilometers (three miles) from Kiryat Shmona lies **Hurshat Tal National Park,** famous for its ancient oak trees, some of which may date from the time of Jesus and the Second Temple. Somehow these hoary survivors escaped the ravages of disease, woodcutters, and modern development, and stand as yet another testimony to the antiquity of this legendary land. The Dan River, a tributary of the Jordan, passes down this valley, collecting in a series of artificial lakes and ponds, where you can swim. That, and picnicking, are the two prime activities. There's a camping site too. The park is open from 8 a.m. to 4 p.m. daily, for a small admission fee.

Right next door to Hurshat Tal is **Kibbutz Ha-Gosherim,** founded by Turkish Jews in 1948. The kibbutz inn (tel. 06-945-231) boasts three stars, 121 rooms with private bath (tubs), a kosher dining room, and a swimming pool—a very good base for exploration of Upper Galilee and the Golan. You pay $31 to $40.25 single, $43.75 to $57.50 double, to stay here.

There's a guesthouse in **Moshav Sha'ar Yashuv,** called **Hotel Gan** (Moshav Sha'ar Yashuv, Mobile Post, Upper Galilee 12240; tel. 06-941-768). Near Kiryat Shmona, it is perfectly situated for trips to the Golan and Baniyas, and only one kilometer from Hurshat Tal, the beautiful national park. Bed and breakfast for a single occupant in a double room costs $18, $28 for a double, during low season. High-season rates are $23 and $36, respectively. Add 10% to these rates during Passover, Independence Day, Shavuoth, Rosh Hashannah, Succoth, and Hanukkah. Students get a 10% reduction. Dinner is $8. There is both heating and air conditioning, and it is a very lovely place.

Tel Dan

By now you may have picked up that "tel" means a prehistoric mound which was once a settlement, and also that Israel is full of such mounds. The one at Tel Dan, 9 km (about 5½ miles) east of Kiryat Shmona and then three kilometers north, was a thriving Canaanite community when Joshua led the conquering Israelites here over 3,000 years ago. In fact Dan was the northern limit of the Promised Land (the southern limit was Beersheba). Today the ruins are protected in the **Tel Dan Nature Reserve.** Many cold-water springs gush right up from the ground here, forming the Dan River, one of the three principal sources of the Jordan River. Due to the abundance of springs, the area is lush with greenery.

Another interesting ruin here in the nature reserve, reconstructed by the National Parks authority, is a 700-year-old Arabic stone flour mill, run by waterpower, with a 2,000-year-old pistachio tree nearby. Walking trails and picnic areas make this a surprisingly pleasant place to stop for a while. It's open seven days a week from 8 a.m. to 4 p.m., until 3 p.m. on Friday. Admission is NIS2.25 ($1.50) for adults, half price for children. It's easy to come by bus: just get off at Kibbutz Dan and it's a 15-minute walk. Buses run between Kibbutz Dan and Kiryat Shmona about every two hours.

In the nearby **Kibbutz Dan** is a nature museum, Bet Ussishkin (tel. 06-941-704), with exhibits covering the flora, fauna, geology, topography, and history of the region. Hours are 8:30 a.m. to 3:30 p.m., on Friday until 2 p.m.; closed Saturday. There's a NIS2 ($1.35) admission fee for adults, NIS1.50 ($1) for children.

ONWARD TO GOLAN: Past Kibbutz Dan, you're into the Golan Heights. Your first stop will be Baniyas Waterfall, but before you get there, you might like to know something about this region, still open to dispute between Syria and Israel.

Recent History

A trip through the Golan Heights is a lesson in contemporary history. This is where the June 1967 war really started when, two months earlier on April 7, the Syrians bombarded Ein Gev from their positions on the hills above the eastern shore of the Sea of Galilee.

Israel served notice on Syria that it would stand for no more. Syria appealed to Egypt and Iraq, claiming that an Israeli invasion was imminent. Egypt called for war, turned out the U.N. from Gaza and the Straits of Tiran, and massed its armies on the Israeli border.

What happened that May—the torturous waiting, the failure of diplomacy —is familiar to everyone interested in Israel. Equally familiar is the morning of June 5, when the Israeli Air Force destroyed the combined air forces of three Arab countries. All that week, however, Syria continued to rain fire on the settlements around the Sea of Galilee. Israeli planes, tanks, and paratroopers were spread thin fighting on the Egyptian, West Bank, and Jerusalem fronts.

Syria did not attack—only a probe here and there, at Tel Dan, at Sha'ar Yashuv—and continued shelling the farms and fields . . . until Friday, June 9. On that day the Israeli army could spare the armor and men necessary; elsewhere, the war had been won. Only the Golan remained, and it was taken quickly, if painfully.

After the Six-Day War, Israel embarked on a careful and selective policy of settling the Golan with kibbutzim and moshavim. Then, in 1973, the Yom Kippur War broke out, and the surprise Syrian attack nearly drove the Israeli forces back behind the original armistice line. Settlement after settlement fell as the initial onslaught caught Israel completely unprepared. It took about a week for Israel to take the offensive again, and the Syrian forces were not only pushed out of the region, but a salient (later returned) was cut into Syria itself. After the fighting, Kuneitra, the ruined principal city of the area, was returned to Syria.

A Warning

When touring the Golan area, do not go exploring for shell fragments or souvenirs in the hills near the bunkers. Estimates range from 100,000 to 1,000,000 for the number of mines Syria planted in this area over the last 20 years. It may be 10 or 20 years before the Israeli army finishes minesweeping the area. It must be done inch by inch, and since many of the mines are the plastic kind not detectable by metal-seeking devices, laboriously slow probes and earthturning machines must be used. En route you will see a couple of places where the tour buses stop to give visitors a look at the bunkers. Two million visitors (mostly Israeli) have been there before you—so you can be sure it's safe. The barbed-wire fences that line much of the road, and the triangular yellow-and-red Hebrew signs on them, all mean the same thing: *mine field*.

Baniyas

Just after Tel Dan you will cross into what was, till June 10, 1967, the impregnable fortress—Golan.

First stop is the **Baniyas Waterfall**, less than a mile inside the zone, 15 km (9½ miles) from Kiryat Shmona, and less than one kilometer off the main road. Beyond the parking lot a path winds downward to the biggest waterfall in these parts. (There's an equally big one at Metulla, but it cascades only in winter).

Baniyas is one of the principal sources of the Jordan River. Head down to the stream for a look at the waters rushing along clear and cold through an area of deep-green growth. You should remember that these clear, fast-running waters have begun several hundred feet higher on the Hermon slopes, and that the destination, after dropping into the Jordan River, is the Sea of Galilee. Jordan ("Yared Dan") means "descending from Dan," and the river, whose origins are right here, picks up again south of the Sea of Galilee for a twisting, turning run of 70 miles before emptying into the Dead Sea and becoming a stagnant, oily mixture.

Back on the highway, one kilometer east of the falls you turn left, then left again into the parking lot of the Baniyas springs. This ancient site has been all fixed up by the National Parks Authority. It's open from 8 a.m. to 4 p.m. daily, on Friday until 2 p.m. Admission costs NIS2.25 ($1.50) per adult, half price for children.

The prime attractions at Baniyas are the pure, cold springs that burst from the earth beneath a sheer rock wall and rush downward to Baniyas Waterfall, thence into the Jordan. The waters originate on the slopes of Mount Hermon.

Springs and grottoes are always fascinating places. In ancient times the Canaanites, and later the Greeks, built shrines and temples here. The Greek name Paneas (after Pan, the god of fertility) was modified in Arabic to Baniyas as Arabic has no "p" sound. Though an earthquake collapsed the impressive grotto of the Greeks, you can still see little shrines carved into the rock face, most dating from Hellenistic times.

Under the Romans, the settlement here was named Caesarea Philippi after Philip, son of Herod, who followed in the ancients' ways and also built a temple.

Baniyas figures in the New Testament as the place where Jesus designated Peter as the "rock" (Petrus) upon which the Church would be built.

The Crusaders held Baniyas for a number of years, taking care to fortify the nearby hilltop with what is now **Nimrod Castle.** Later Christians built a chapel to St. George on the hillside at Baniyas. Muslims converted the chapel into a shrine dedicated to El-Khader (the prophet Elijah). The shrine is still there, on the hillside. A steep path leads up to it. Don't go up to visit the shrine (it's closed most of the time); go up for the view.

So for several thousand years, to a dozen peoples and a half dozen religions, Baniyas has been a holy place.

Today it's a nature spot, a swimming spot (if you can stand the icy waters), a picnic spot, or a place for a meal or snack.

From Baniyas, you'll want to make a loop which mounts the slopes of Hermon past Nimrod Castle and Neve Ativ to the Mount Hermon Ski Center, then down through the Druze villages of Majdal Shams and Masada. You'll finally come down to the main road again and start heading south to Kuneitra and Qasrin.

Nimrod Castle

Follow the road signs to **Kalaat Namrud,** Nimrod Castle. It's worth going out of your way to see Nimrod for two reasons. First, it offers a spectacular view, and second, it's the biggest, best-preserved Crusader castle in these parts, in much better shape then those at Montfort and Belvoir.

As you come around under the wall of the castle you'll see the narrow vertical slits in the wall where archers were once stationed. From the high ground within the castle your eyes have a feast. To the left is the zigzagging cleft of Baniyas rift. In a lush, green pocket farther on you see Tel Dan kibbutz, then a series of carp ponds, Kiryat Shmona on the hills beyond, and the rectangles of brown and green of the Hula Valley extending southward for miles and miles.

Behind the castle to the north sits **Mount Hermon,** white-maned in winter months, snow-streaked in the spring and summer. This slope and pinnacles of Mount Hermon, 6,500 feet, are within Israel's borders.

Inside Nimrod you'll see many deep holes, water-filled cisterns 30 feet deep. Very little was damaged here during the Six-Day War, although its position dominating the area made it a strategic spot, and indeed a Syrian observation post/mortar position was attacked here. One version has it that only one 500-pound bomb was dropped on Nimrod—no one wanted to wreck such a pretty castle. Strafing attacks routed the Syrians, and the Israelis turned it into an artillery-spotter post of their own. As you can see from up here, whoever controlled Nimrod, in by-gone days as well as today, controlled the traffic from Lebanon to Tiberias and the Jordan Valley.

Nimrod Castle is now a national park, open daily from 8 a.m. to 4 p.m., till 2 p.m. on Friday. Admission costs NIS2.25 ($1.50) for adults, half that price for children.

Skiing in Golan

The snow season in Israel usually begins in December or January and lasts until about mid-April. It is advisable to ski on weekdays when the slopes are less crowded.

The **Mount Hermon Ski Center** (tel. 067-40121) lies high on the slopes of Mount Hermon. Roads up to the site are subject to blockage by heavy snow, so check on conditions in advance by telephone, radio report, or newspaper. On Saturday in ski season, the hotels in this region, the roads, and the parking lot fill up early and quickly: you should plan to get there earlier and quicker. Also, on Saturday and holidays a special traffic pattern is in effect for the narrow roads in this region: you must approach the resort via Masada and Majdal Shams only; you exit via Neve Ativ. Of course, if you're catching a bus from Kiryat Shmona, you needn't worry about any of this. Those driving should just follow the flow of Saturday traffic.

The parking lot (800 cars, and jammed full on a snowy Saturday) is below the ski center. You'll be stopped on the road before you reach it, and you'll pay an entrance fee of NIS6 ($4) to the site. From the parking lot, shuttlebuses run you up to the base station.

You can enjoy the snow whether you're a skier or not, for one lift caters exclusively to nonskiers. It will take you on the ride (almost a mile) to the 6,630-foot summit, where there's an observation point and cafeteria. A separate lift takes skiers to the summit starting point for downhill runs. Cost for a round trip on the nonskiers' lift is NIS10 ($6.65) per adult, about 60% of that price for a child.

As for the slopes, there are four runs from the upper station, the longest being about a mile and a half, meant for average to fairly good skiers. Learners can use the short chair lift, a 1,300-foot trip to a height of 885 feet above the base station. Gentle slopes at the bottom of the hill are good for first runs and for children.

Picnic tables and a snackbar at the base station provide sustenance. There's also a ski school and an equipment rental shop. Most Israelis rent equipment rather than own it, which is yet another reason why you should arrive early if you plan to ski on Saturday. You don't want to find that all the equipment has been rented out. Plan on spending about $40 to $50 per person for a day on the slopes: admission and lift fees, equipment rental, and a snack for lunch.

The ski center is open daily from 8:30 a.m. to 3:30 p.m., weather and security conditions permitting. You must admit, it's a pretty unique addition to a vacation trip: skiing in the Golan Heights!

Majdal Shams and Masada

These Druze villages on the slopes of Mount Hermon are inhabited by the fiercely independent people whose religion is still something of a mystery to outsiders. They are farmers for the most part, and don't mind tilling the steep, rocky ground so long as they are left in peace. Since the birth of the Druze religion almost 1,000 years ago, those in authority have usually found it convenient to do just that. The Ottomans, for instance, gave the Druze considerable autonomy. It just wasn't worth the time and expense to conquer them.

The Druze religion is an offshoot of Islam, but very different from either of the major branches, Sunni and Shi'i. Here are some of the secrets: It all starts with the Fatimids, an Islamic dynasty which grew powerful in the 900s. The Fatimids conquered most of North Africa and parts of the Mediterranean, even taking Genoa for a time. Among their caliphs (leaders with both religious and secular powers) was one Hakim (996–1021), the sixth of the Fatimid line, who in the year 1020 proclaimed himself to be the reincarnation of God. As you can imagine, many people disagreed with him on this, and he was assassinated within a year. But his claim was believed and supported in Syria and Lebanon, especially among the people who would come to be called Druze. Thus the foundation of the Druze faith is that Hakim was and is God, that he did not die (because God can't die), but rather is in hiding and will reappear to rule the world when the time is ripe.

Between the two villages, on the road, is the small volcanic-crater lake of Birkhet Ram, now used as a reservoir. The **Birkhet Ram Restaurant** offers a place to stop and buy a meal. Do it if you're at all hungry, as there are few such restaurants in Golan. It's open from 8 a.m. to 6 p.m. There's a falafel stand and snackshop here as well.

Toward Kuneitra

After the slow, bouncing ride back from Hermon to the main road, the way becomes clear, flat, and well paved. Heading toward Kuneitra, you pass villages of a type you haven't seen before, in which houses are made of the monotonous black basalt rock of this region. Where the roofs are tiled red on these black homes, the villages are Circassian ("Cheerkhasi" in Hebrew). The Circassians reached this part of the world via southern Russia, the Caucasus, and Iran.

A new road circumvents Kuneitra. There's a mound though, near the United Nations base, which is worth visiting. You can look out into the ruined city and across into the wide, barren plain that leads to Damascus.

Nearby is **Kibbutz Merom Ha-Golan,** a commune of youngsters tending fields and orchards and representing countries from all over the world. There are similar settlements all over the Heights, and they are really worth visiting, spanning the spectrum from religion to irreligion and from socialism to quasi-free enterprise. The two denominators they all have in common are dedication and youth. If you're over 30 on the Golan, you're going to feel very old indeed.

Most of the kibbutzim and moshavim don't mind visitors, but they are really not equipped to entertain, and the members are frequently too busy to interrupt their labors. Still, if you need a helping hand, you'll get one.

Kuneitra (or Quneitra) was the chief Syrian city in Golan before the war. Now it is largely deserted, just another landmark ghost town created by politics and war.

Qasrin

The new (1977) Israeli "capital" of Golan is the town of Qasrin (Kazrin, Katzirin, etc.), right smack in the center of Golan, founded on the site of a 2ndto 3rd-century town of the same name. Qasrin is the administrative hub, a town of new apartments, offices, schools, factories, and a few shops. Bus service is from Kiryat Shmona (take no. 55).

A few unlikely contrasts here serve as strong reminders of the town's strategic position, both geographically and in the flow of recent history. It's a nice suburban-looking town, but it's completely surrounded by barbed wire. You'll see bomb shelters surrounded by beautiful rose gardens; the shelters are now used as neighborhood recreation centers, clubhouses, music halls, and so forth.

Qasrin is known for its sweet, natural mineral water, bottled and exported to the rest of the country.

Qasrin is where you'll find the **Golan Archeological Museum** (P.O. Box 30, Qasrin, Golan Heights 12900; tel. 06-961-350), which, while small, is modern, light, well planned, and really worth a visit for its many informative exhibits relating the extensive human history of this area. One of my favorite exhibits is out in the garden, a reconstruction of a dolmen, using the original stones just as they were found—the dolmen is that Stonehenge-like structure unique to this area, placed by man in the 4th millennium B.C. (remember that Abraham was here in 1700 B.C.; these were much earlier). Hours are Sunday through Thursday from 9 a.m. to 2 p.m., on Friday until 1 p.m., on Saturday from 10 a.m. to 2 p.m. Admission is NIS1.50 ($1) for adults, NIS1 (65¢) for children, or NIS4 ($2.65) for the whole family.

Qasrin is useful to you as a place to pick up some groceries or snacks, have a slice of pizza and a cold drink, or find emergency services. There are also several sites of interest nearby.

The **Ya'ar Yehudiya Nature Reserve,** stretching from Qasrin to the shores of the Sea of Galilee, is famous for its ancient oaks, forested valleys, and waterfalls. Within the reserve are several waterfalls (especially at Mapal Gamla) and rivers.

Another site worth seeing is **Berekhat Ha-Meshushim,** a pool amid natural hexagonally shaped columns. The columns were formed when mineral-rich molten rock cooled slowly, taking on the crystalline structure. Also in Ya'ar Yehudiya are several ancient dolmens (huge monoliths), the use and provenance of which is still something of a mystery. The dolmens are not far from Gamla (see below).

Just outside Qasrin to the southeast along the main road are the ruins of a synagogue dating from the A.D. 100s and 200s. Not much farther away (another 12 km, or 7 miles, southeast) near Zomet Daliyot is a much more impressive site named **Gamla,** where Jewish residents battled Roman legionnaires in A.D. 68. This was the same revolt during which Jerusalem and the Second Temple were destroyed (A.D. 70), and the Zealots of Masada committed mass suicide rather than fall into Roman hands (A.D. 73). The story of the battle at Gamla is chillingly similar to that of Masada.

The well-fortified town of Gamla was first conquered by Jewish forces under Alexander Yannai in 90 B.C. Its name came from the site: a hill that looks like the hump of a camel (*gamal*).

Shortly after the revolt against Rome broke out in 66, Gamla filled with Jewish refugees fleeing Roman control. The inhabitants held their own against the Romans for a while, even inflicting heavy casualties on the Romans in the battles. But the resources of Rome were almost limitless, and when those of Gamla gave out, the people here—all 9,000—chose death before subjugation, flinging themselves off the cliff.

From Qasrin, you can leave Golan by heading north and west toward Ayalet Ha-Shahar, or by heading southwest, to the Sea of Galilee.

5. South of Galilee: The Jordan Valley

The Sea of Galilee is the River Jordan's reservoir, and the lake's water level is carefully controlled so that the fertile bottomland of the Jordan Valley gets the maximum benefit. In the winter rainy season, Israeli planes often seed the clouds above the lake to fill this reservoir to the brim before the summery dry period begins.

The Jordan is not so much a mighty river as a mighty important one. No broad Mississippi or Danube or Rhine, the Jordan is little more than a desert stream, but its life-giving waters are crucial to the agriculture of the area. It has brought fertile silt down from the Sea of Galilee for so many centuries that its valley is one of the most bounteous farming regions in the country.

The fastest way south to Jerusalem is right along the river to Jericho (Yeriho), and thence up into the Judean hills. An alternative route is via Afula in the Yizreel Valley (see section 1 of this chapter), then south through the West Bank towns of Nablus, Shechem, and Ramallah (see Chapter III, section 4).

If you're coming south along the lakeshore from Tiberias, see that section for a description of the lake entrance to the valley and of the first major town, Degania. Below, I'll tell you what it's like to approach the valley from Afula.

FROM AFULA TO BET SHEAN: Southeast of Afula, you'll pass **Kibbutz Yizreel.** Once an ancient Arab town, Yizreel was described by Edward Wilson in an 1889 travel account in the *Century Illustrated Magazine:* "Its location is central, and its position as a military stronghold admirable. The Arabs call their town Zerin [Yizreel]. Their houses are dreadfully humble and comfortless, and all the wealth of the town seems to have been used for the preservation of the ancient tower, which stands among the houses."

The road then skirts the slopes of Mount Gilboa, where the tragedy of Saul (described previously) occurred. A farm collective on Gilboa's slopes defies the curse Samuel put upon this land. There is also a road running right to the top of the mountain, where there is a view of everything—the Galilee mountains, the Emek, the Mediterranean, Jordan.

On the left of the road is a string of communal settlements—**Ein Harod, Tel Yosef, Bet Ha-Shita.** A large, well-developed settlement, founded in 1921, Ein Harod has a population of nearly 2,000 settlers. It boasts a hostel, amphitheater, a culture hall where many ideological conferences are held, an archeological and natural history museum, and an art gallery which has had exhibitions of Chagall, Hanna Orloff, Milich, and the American artist Selma Gubin.

The Approach to the Valley

Just after Ein Harod, the road sign points to **Heftziba** and **Bet Alpha,** both communal settlements. Kibbutz Bet Alpha was one of the early Jordan Valley settlements, founded in 1922 by pioneers from Poland and Galicia who cleared the swamps. During one of their swamp-draining operations, a remnant of a synagogue was uncovered, and experts from the Hebrew University attested it was a 6th-century B.C. find. Financed by Temple Emmanu-El of New York City, excavation produced what is one of the most impressive ancient synagogues uncovered in Israel. Highly ornamental and somewhat Oriental in motif, the **Bet Alpha Synagogue** has an elaborate mosaic floor divided into three panels: the first depicting Abraham's sacrifice of Isaac, the second a Zodiac wheel, and the third a pastiche of religious ornaments.

Sachne, Israel's largest natural swimming pool, lies in Gan Ha-Shlosha park (admission NIS3, $2), a cool scenic nook just beyond Bet Alpha kibbutz. With its waterfall and splendid framework of tall trees and distant mountains, it is a favorite picnic site for Israeli families.

Right down the road is **Kibbutz Nir David** and nearby in Gan Ha-Shlosha park is the **Museum of Regional and Mediterranean Archeology** (tel. 06-583-045), an interesting exhibition that attempts to place ancient Palestine within the framework of Mediterranean civilization. Statuary, pottery, metalwork, jewelry, and coins displayed here range from Neolithic to the Mameluke eras, the finds themselves being products of Corinth, Cyprus, Persia, Egypt, and elsewhere, from the Pillars of Hercules to the Jordan River. Hours are 8 a.m. to 2 p.m. (to 1 p.m. on Friday, 10 a.m. to 1 p.m. on Saturday); admission is NIS2.25 ($1.50).

Bet Shean

The weather grows a bit warmer as you approach the pass at Bet Shean, and the altitude, or lack of it, plummets to 300 feet below sea level. The rocky hillsides are harsh, and aglow with a burnt-orange color; indeed, in the dry seasons the slopes seem almost feverish in their hot desolation. But don't be deceived. This is a highly fertile area, despite the low rainfall (12 inches annually). Springs and streams flowing down from Mount Gilboa have been directed toward the Jordan Valley's fields, and the fertile soil here supports thousands of acres of wheat, vegetables, banana groves, and cotton fields.

Bet Shean is another pass which, like Megiddo, has had a long succession of militaristic rulers, situated as it is on the great caravan route from Damascus to Egypt. On a high hill called Tel Bet Shean, archeologists have cut into layer upon layer of civilization, every 20 feet representing a culture and a few hundred years.

All the way down they uncovered five separate strata of Canaanite and Egyptian civilizations, with altars and ruins of the Ramses II period. From 1200 B.C. they discovered Hebrew ceramics, the type used around the time King Saul's body was hung by the Philistines on the Bet Shean wall. Then came a Scythian period when the Greeks named the town Scythopolis, and in a higher slice the layers of dirt and rock revealed fragments from Roman times. Some 70 feet into the "tel" (Hebrew for an archeological mound or hill), parties dug up a 7th-century Byzantine town with a sizable quantity of mosaics and delicate columns. Closer to the top they uncovered the remains of Crusader castles from the Middle Ages. And still higher up, the jugs and farm tools of the Arab and Turkish settlers of the last five centuries. The **Bet Shean Museum,** containing an interesting collection from this area, is open every weekday.

Elsewhere at Bet Shean you'll see the **Roman Theater,** which is the best-preserved Roman theater in Israel. This playhouse has 15 tiers of white limestone in nearly perfect condition, and several more tiers of crumbling black basalt. And scattered on the floor—like a mammoth jigsaw puzzle—is a collection of broken columns and fragments of statues, all waiting to be fitted together. Estimates are that 8,000 people can be seated here.

THE JORDAN VALLEY: Once you head south from Bet Shean, you are solidly in the Jordan Valley. The fertile abundance of the land becomes immediately apparent. You see the emerald-green splashes of farm settlements in the distance, and soon you come to them, with their straight, carefully planted rows of beautiful fruit trees. That slick, luxuriant vegetation is particularly apparent in the Bet Shean Valley, entrance to the Jordan Valley. One ancient sage has written: "If Israel is Paradise, then the Bet Shean Valley is the gate to Paradise."

You are now in subtropical country—notice the profusion of date palm trees, banana groves, and orchards of pomegranate. Colorful mango trees and grapefruit orchards are also a dominant theme, interrupted only by neat blue rectangles of carp-breeding ponds. But this area, for all its richly fertile appearance now, took a heavy toll on the lives of early settlers.

Incidentally, if you're looking for the River Jordan and can't seem to find it, don't be discouraged. The reason it's hard to locate is that it often dwindles down to a mere trickling stream, winding capriciously inside a great rift in the earth. There are only a few places where it looks like it's supposed to—lush and green, with myrtle and reeds.

THE DEAD SEA AND THE NEGEV

IF YOU HAVE the usual preconception of what a desert is like—sand, nothing but sand—you're in for a surprise. The Negev is not a desert in that sense at all. In Hebrew the word of Israel's southern region is *midbar,* meaning wilderness, which is precisely what the Negev is. There are expanses of sand in the Arava region just north of Eilat, but for the most part the Negev is a great triangular swath of boulders, pebbles, wind-sculpted mountains, eroded landscape, Bedouin encampments, and brave, lonely settlements. The people of the region are different—they have to be. The Negev could easily be regarded as a sort of Israeli Siberia, and yet the contrary is true. The taming of the desert is the prime challenge of the idealistic, and perhaps the greatest single achievement of the people of Israel.

Just a few decades ago the mighty Negev reached high into the north and lapped at the settlements of Rishon-le-Zion and Gedera. Now the Negev has been pummeled and forced backward. Traveling down south you'll see no desert traces at all until reaching Beersheba, and then, to your amazement, you'll discern that the formidable wilderness has been rolled back even beyond that city. Where vultures and scorpions once reigned, winter crops and early vegetables are grown. Inch by inch a dead land is being reclaimed, and if there is ever peace in the region, the most arid of lands will be taught to bloom again.

In this chapter we'll explore all of Israel's vast southern territory, as well as the Egyptian Sinai peninsula.

RECENT HISTORY: One of the Negev's earliest and most energetic advocates was a man named Amiram Ovrotsky, whose achievements represent far more to Israel than the expansion of tourism. Like so many Israeli youngsters, Ovrotsky fell in love with the desert at an early age. During his army service he spent long months in the Negev, checking out biblical references in the region, learning the secrets of Bedouin survivability, and classifying flora and fauna.

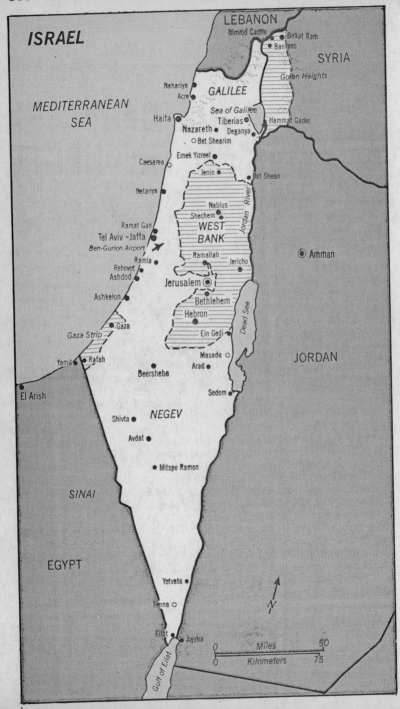

ISRAEL

LEBANON
Nimrod Castle
Birkat Ram
Baniyas
SYRIA

MEDITERRANEAN
SEA

Nahariya
Acre
GALILEE
Golan Heights

Haifa
Sea of Galilee
Tiberias
Hammat Gader

Nazareth
Deganya
Bet Shearim

Emek Yizreel
Caesarea
Jenin
Bet Shean

Netanya

Ramat Gan
Tel Aviv –Jaffa
Ben-Gurion Airport
Nablus
Shechem
WEST
BANK

Ramla
Ramallah
Jericho
Amman

Rehovot
Ashdod
Jerusalem

Ashkelon
Bethlehem

Hebron

Gaza Strip
Gaza
Ein Gedi

Dead Sea

Yamit
Rafah
Masada
Arad
JORDAN

El Arish
Beersheba
Sodom

Shivta
NEGEV

Avdat

SINAI
Mitspe Ramon

EGYPT

Yotvata

Timna

Eilat
Aqaba
Miles
50

Kilometers
75

Gulf of Eilat

Jordan River

After the army he joined the Ministry of Agriculture and became obsessed by a single idea—proving that the most inhospitable of all Negev regions, the area around Sodom, could be made to sustain human life again. He extracted a parcel of salt-choked land from the ministry for his private experiments, and labored at night to wash out the chemicals, working with his hands because he had no tools. After months of arduous effort, he proved a point. He began to scratch life out of the bleached, somnolent land.

Every previous study of the region, most conducted by the British, had indicated that the salinity in the soil was such that no successful farming could be embarked upon. Ovrotsky's achievement was therefore regarded as a fluke by his colleagues, and the experiment was deemed completed. So he quit the ministry, bought a tent, and proceeded to work the land by himself. The sun almost killed him. Lack of water was a constant peril. The only real food he obtained were the scraps and leftovers that the nearby Dead Sea Works employees left for him. It was an uphill struggle, but slowly he began to change the face of the soil. The dominant color became green.

Youngsters began appearing from all over the country. Somehow they'd heard about his work. They would simply arrive, unfurl sleeping bags, and begin working. No questions were asked. Payment was impossible. Some came for a month. Others stayed for years.

Sleep was a premium because of the constant vigil necessary against Arab marauders from across the hills in Jordan. A gun was like a third arm. And despite all the difficulties, the landscape continued to change. Winter vegetables were produced in abundance. Onions and tomatoes were successfully grown on land once certified as dead. Cattle were imported from Africa.

Ovrotsky no longer has anything to do with the settlement he founded and called Neot Ha-Kikar, but the living testament to his belief exists in the form of a neat moshav located in one of the Negev's most desolate regions.

Most people arrive in Israel with limited itineraries. There's so much to see, and so little time to do it in. A strong tendency exists to scrap the Negev in favor of the most conventional sites. I can only say that it is a pity to do so. The Negev is as much Israel as is Tel Aviv. The historical artifacts of the wilderness are as intrinsic to Jewish history as the more settled regions in the far north. Flying over the area, on the way to Eilat, will give you a general appreciation of the region, but to really understand what Israel is about you have to smell the desert, wipe the sand out of your eyes, and tread the paths of the Hebrew nomads.

GETTING THERE:
You can go to Beersheba by bus or sherut from Jerusalem or Tel Aviv, running several times per hour. The trip takes about two hours. The sherut service is operated by **Yael Daroma**, whose terminals are at 44 Yavne St., Tel Aviv (tel. 03-622-555), 2 Lunz St., Jerusalem (tel. 02-226-985), and 195 K.K. Le-Israel St., Beersheba.

The company also has a service to Eilat (a 5½-hour trip) four times a day (three times on Friday). Seats should be booked in advance. There is one bus a day from Eilat to Sharm-el-Sheikh.

SOME PRACTICAL ADVICE ON DESERT TRAVELING:
A preliminary caution: Between April and October the desert is awfully hot. You'll discover this when you get to Beersheba, and if you think it's warm there, wait till you see what the areas of the Dead Sea and Eilat have for you in the way of dry air that feels as if it had been pumped in from a blast furnace.

Be prepared for the heat, but don't let it scare you off. During the six or seven really hot desert months, simply follow these rules:

Always wear a hat when out in the sun.

Drink plenty of liquids—as much and as often as possible. You needn't bring your own; the supply is plentiful.

Get an early start on your day.

Stay out of the sun between noon and 3 p.m.

Don't cram your schedule. Go slow.

Eat sparingly—of fruit, dairy products, and seafood.

Dress as comfortably and lightly as possible.

Take salt pills, if you find they help you.

Be judicious about sunbathing (sun poisoning here is Israel's major tourist malady).

Bring insect repellent.

1. South to Beersheba

Beersheba is our jumping-off point. From here it's only an hour to Sodom and the Dead Sea, four hours by bus to Eilat. Increasingly, tourists use this ancient biblical town as their base of operations for excursions into the desert.

Only a few years ago this town of 130,000 was the "Dodge City" of Israel. It had an unruly Wild West flavor about it, and only the toughest and most adventurous types came here to work and live. Today the town is growing up, and that old spirit is dwindling somewhat in the face of housing developments and municipal buildings in the new part of town. It is the capital of the Negev.

Still, when your car or bus is an hour out of Tel Aviv on the way to Beersheba, you'll know you're entering a different kind of Israel. The face of the countryside changes; hills disappear and green fields turn dustier and drier; housing projects give way to occasional black tents in the fields near the side of the road; the metal of the car burns you as you rest your arm on the window.

Beersheba is another of the ancient cities of Judah. The Bible contains two versions of the story of the town's origin. The first tells of a covenant made between Abraham and Abimelech over a well that Abraham had dug in the desert here (Genesis 21:25–33). The second story also involves a well, dug by the servants of Isaac, who gave the well and the town its name: "And he called it Shebah: therefore the name of the city is Beer-sheba unto this day" (Genesis 26:32, 33). The phrase "from Dan to Beersheba" appears repeatedly throughout the Bible; Dan stood at the northern boundary of the Israelites' territory, Beersheba at the southern end.

Beersheba has also been a watering place and trading post for thousands of postbiblical years. It was always a center of desert traffic, located as it is on the northern fringe of the Negev. It has been—and still is—the refueling and supply terminus for those hardy souls who venture into the desert.

THE BEDOUIN MARKET: Be sure to be in Beersheba on a Thursday. That's market day for the Bedouin tribes who come in from the desert to buy and sell in the colorful marketplace. You can't miss what's happening. Lean, sun-seared Arabs in long gowns are bartering over sacks of flour and coffee, holding conferences on the exchange for hand-woven rugs and baskets.

Besides watching the Bedouins go through their weekly shopping, you can yourself pick up some (sometimes questionable) bargains on Thursday—in particular, clothes, spices, sheared wool in sacks, copper and brass coffee sets with shining, decorated trays, those lethal-looking long knives, woodcarvings, fancy Arabian saddles, bubble pipes, and all manner of rugs and baskets. If the mood hits you, you can also climb aboard a camel in this market and be photographed atop him. Don't be perturbed, incidentally, by his protesting spits and snorts.

It's not his resentment of tourists that he's emitting, but simply his own accompanying music for standing up and sitting down.

Most of the marketeering here goes on between 6 a.m. and noon near the municipal marketplace, on the southeastern edge of town, in an area set aside for this purpose.

Plans are now in the works for the construction of several permanent shops at the Bedouin market site, so that the arts and crafts can be displayed all the time, not only on Thursday. A motel is in the planning stages here as well. Perhaps these developments will be carried out by the time you visit Beersheba; you can ask at the I.G.T.O. for current details.

ORIENTATION: As a desert stopping-place, Beersheba has been around for thousands of years. But as a town, its history dates only from its founding by the Turks in 1907. You can follow its development and its growth to a frontier metropolis of 130,000 souls in the town's museum (described further on). But what worries us now is to get around the city.

A small section of Beersheba is laid out on the street-grid plan. That's the original Turkish town, and it's still the commercial "downtown" of Beersheba, with many of the important shops and businesses, budget and moderately priced hotels and restaurants.

Herzl Street is the major downtown north-south thoroughfare. Main streets east and west are **Ha-Atzma'ut (Independence) Street** and **Keren Kayemet Le-Israel (K.K. Le-Israel) Street,** which has been made into a pedestrian mall along several blocks. Right where Herzl and Ha-Atzma'ut intersect is the old Turkish city hall, the Allenby Garden (a park); and behind the Turkish city hall is the Great Mosque, now the Negev Museum.

The rest of modern Beersheba sprawls northward from the old downtown section. But the famous Bedouin market site is next to the municipal market, on the southeastern edge of downtown.

The **Central Bus Station** is not far from downtown, a few blocks northeast off Ha-Nessi'im Boulevard. A new railway station is being constructed near the Central Bus Station, but at present there is no rail service to Beersheba. A train will be running again, however, when the planned railway heading south to Eilat is put into operation.

The Beersheba office of the **Israel Government Tourist Office** (tel. 057-36001) is located directly across the street from the Central Bus Station, on Ben-Zvi Street in the Ein Gedi building. It's open Sunday through Thursday from 8 a.m. to 6 p.m., on Friday until 1 p.m. (closed Saturday), with every kind of information you could want about Beersheba, and about many places nearby too.

You'll want to see some of new and modern Beersheba, but for your daily needs such as rooms, meals, information, and incidentals, you must first be able to find your way around the old downtown section. Luckily, it's small, and after 20 minutes' wandering you should feel right at home.

All the shops and businesses in Beersheba close down between 1 and 4 p.m., reopening from 4 to 7 p.m. This afternoon siesta during the hottest part of the day makes a lot of sense in the desert climate of Beersheba.

ACCOMMODATIONS: As I've said, Beersheba has spruced itself up considerably, offering tourists a variety of clean, air-conditioned accommodations. In the budget category, the best bets are the following:

Budget Hotels

Top on the list is **Hotel Zohar,** 3 Shazar Blvd. (tel. 057-77335 or 77336), near the New City Hall, 2 km (about 1¼ miles) from the Old City. It's a highly recommendable, three-star establishment worth the outlay, comparing favorably with many first-class hotels in service and amenities. Its 64 rooms have bathtub and shower, telephone, carpeting, radio, and air conditioning. Prices remain the same all year, at $18 single, $30 double, including a hearty Israeli breakfast. There's an outdoor terrace restaurant, coffeeshop, and a bar with a very interesting wall, the creation of a Yemenite sculptor. A lovely park is right across the street.

Once no less than a sheik's harem, the **Ha-Negev**, 26 Ha-Atzma'ut St., at Trumpeldor (tel. 057-77026), is now a kosher and air-conditioned two-star hotel. The old building is about 200 years old and has nine large rooms. The new building has 21 rooms, most with showers and air conditioners. In the old building, you can get a room with or without breakfast; some of the rooms have air conditioning, private toilet and shower; others have no air conditioning and shared bathroom facilities. Prices here are $11 to $15, single or double, and $17 triple, without breakfast, or a few dollars more if breakfast is included. In the new building prices are $18 to $21 single, $27 to $32 double, depending on whether you order breakfast.

The **Arava Hotel**, at 37 Ha-Histadrut St. (Beersheba 84212; tel. 057-78792), near Keren Kayemet ("K.K. Le-Israel") Street, is centrally located just one block from the police station. A tiny TV room behind the lobby is fixed up comfortably with chairs, a table, and a sofa. The Arava has 27 simply furnished rooms, two with private bath, the rest with private shower, and all are air-conditioned. Singles cost $17.25 to $19.50, and doubles run $28.75, breakfast included. By the way, the reception desk and hotel are one flight up.

Finally, there's the two-star **Hotel Aviv**, 48 Mordei Ha-Getaot St. (tel. 057-77335). The 22 rooms here all have small balconies, telephone, wall-to-wall carpeting, and private bath or shower. You can get a TV in your room free on request. Bed-and-breakfast rates are $17 single, $23 double, from November through February; $23 single, $30 double, the rest of the year. On presentation of this book, you'll receive a 10% discount on these prices, anytime.

A Guesthouse and Youth Hostel

A few blocks from the Great Mosque are two lodging choices you'll want to consider: the youth hostel named **Bet Yatziv** and **Bet Sadot Valev**, the guesthouse, both with the same address and telephone number: 79 Ha-Atzma'ut St. (tel. 057-77444). These hostelries are located on beautiful, park-like shady grounds, with a large swimming pool open during the warm season. To find them, get to the important intersection of Herzl and Ha-Atzma'ut Streets in the Old City, very near the Great Mosque (look for the minaret). Walk southwest along the park which harbors the Great Mosque. After two long blocks (400 yards) you'll cross Hativat Ha-Negev Street, and soon you'll come to Bet Yatziv —there's a big sign.

The guesthouse has 70 simply furnished rooms with private baths and evaporative air conditioners for $16 single, $22 double, with bed and breakfast. The 100-bed youth hostel has some family rooms, and charges standard IYHA rates of $6.50 for IYHA members, $7.50 for nonmembers.

RESTAURANTS: Beersheba has never had a stunning culinary reputation, but the dining situation is starting to improve, with several nice little restaurants, cafés, and pubs around town. Beersheba also has a large number of quick-service counter restaurants, particularly on the blocks of Keren Kayemet Le-Israel Street that have been turned into a pedestrian mall; the inevitable plate of shishlik and french fries isn't bad, and it's quite filling too. If it's a true restaurant you're in the mood for, try some of the places below.

Perhaps Beersheba's most elegant and tasty restaurant (outside the big hotels) is the **Jade Palace Chinese Restaurant,** at 79 Ha-Histadrut St. (tel. 057-75375), at the corner of Yair Street right in the old downtown section, open from noon to 3:30 p.m. and 7 p.m. to midnight daily, Sabbath included. High-backed chairs, tablecloths, wine goblets, and the requisite Chinese lamps make it a very pleasant place to dine, and a welcome change from the normal Beersheba cuisine. An 89-item à la carte menu features many varieties of duck, pork, beef, chicken, fish, and seafood; set-menu lunches are priced at NIS15 ($10), 7- to 11-item set-menu dinners at NIS25 ($16.65) per person for two people. You can get Chinese food-to-go here too.

Israel's crêpe-and-blintz madness was destined to hit Beersheba, and it has. Drop in at **Palachinta,** 98 Ha-Histadrut, corner of Yair (tel. 057-329-663), for a plateful of dinner or dessert crêpes. The small whitewashed dining room is in a fine old limestone Turkish building, marked simply by a sign that reads "Crêpes." Inside, it has a cozy coffeehouse atmosphere, intimate and artsy in a comfortable sort of way. A few more tables are placed out on the sidewalk. Blintzes and crêpes are priced from NIS8 ($5.35) to NIS11 ($7.35); coffees, cocktails, and desserts are also served. Open Sunday to Thursday from 8 a.m. to 2 p.m. and 4 p.m. to midnight, on Friday to 3 p.m., and on Saturday after the Sabbath from 6:30 p.m. until 1 or 2 a.m. Palachinta is at the same intersection as the aforementioned Chinese restaurant.

Pitput ("To Chat"), 122 Herzl St. (tel. 057-37708), is a pleasant pink-and-white café for light meals like sandwiches, omelets, soups and salads, desserts, and coffee. You can get a sliced cold duck, roast beef, or turkey sandwich with potatoes and salad for NIS5 ($3.35). Open Sunday through Thursday from 10 a.m. to midnight, on Friday from 9 a.m. to 3 p.m., on Saturday from 7 p.m. to midnight.

For European dining, there's the kosher **Ha-Mirpesset** ("The Balcony"), 45 Herzl St., at the corner of Ha-Palmach Street (tel. 057-37788). You'll see a large corner balcony terrace out front, a bar and several attractive dining rooms inside. A full meal here, from soup to dessert, with a selection from the wine list, will run you about NIS20 ($13.35) to NIS25 ($16.65). Choose from dishes like baked lamb, roast beef, stuffed Cornish game hens, and meats and fishes hot from the charcoal grill. Open from 11 a.m. to midnight, on Friday until 4 p.m., and on Saturday after the Sabbath from about 6:30 p.m. on.

A little farther down Herzl Street, **Ilie Steak Restaurant,** 21 Herzl St. (tel. 057-78685), is nothing fancy to look at (although it does boast an interesting full-wall mural of a black-and-white photograph of camels walking in the desert), but what it lacks in decor it makes up for in good, fresh food. Many meats and fishes are on display in the refrigerator case; house specialties are Rumanian kebab and sirloin filet steak, grilled over charcoal. Add salad, french fries, a beer or soda, and tip, and you'll pay NIS16 ($10.65) to NIS24 ($16), depending on the meat you choose. Open Sunday through Thursday from noon to midnight, on Friday to 4 p.m.; closed Saturday.

Near the aforementioned Ilie Restaurant, between Herzl, Ha-Histadrut, Ha-Avot, and Smilansky Streets, is a nice park called Gan Ha-Nassi, with a small, inconspicuous-looking building at the corner of the park where Smilansky and Ha-Histadrut Streets meet, and that's where you'll find **Bet Ha-Fuul** (no phone), serving up a hearty lunch of Egyptian fuul beans with sauce and a boiled egg, assorted salads, and several fresh, thick rounds of pita bread, all for NIS4 ($2.65); add another NIS1 (65¢) for a soft drink or a beer. If you prefer a huge serving of hummus as a main course, you'll pay NIS3 ($2) and still get all the salads and bread. Again, not much in the decor department, but popular with the locals for its good food. Bet Ha-Fuul is open from 7 a.m. until 3 p.m.;

closed Saturday. Outside, a falafel counter, open daily until around 8 or 10 p.m., serves up a fine falafel for NIS1.20 (80¢).

Bet Limon, 18 Ha-Histadrut St. (tel. 057-71095 or 35861), is a yellow-and-white kosher restaurant a few doors down, facing the park. It gets its name from the large lemon tree growing right in the center of the restaurant's spacious dining room. The sweet aroma is intoxicatingly lovely, filling the entire place—three separate dining rooms, in decreasing sizes—especially during the months from April to June, when the tree is in full bloom. Lemons come all year; try the fresh lemonade made from the special house recipe. Specialties here are Tunisian couscous, and roast lamb with mushrooms and wine sauce; with a platter of ten salads, and all the accompaniments, a full meal comes to about NIS25 ($16.65). Open from 10 a.m. to midnight; closing Friday at 4 p.m., reopening Saturday at 6:30 p.m., after the Sabbath.

About a block away, **Restaurant Bar Sheba,** 30 Kefar Ha-Darom St. (tel. 057-77191), is a small European-style restaurant/pub with dark wooden tables inside and on the patio out back, and a menu of meats, soups, salads, pancakes, desserts, and other foods prepared in European style. Meat with any of a variety of sauces (Stroganoff, hollandaise, Russian, or Hungarian) comes for about NIS15 ($10) for the full meal. Hours are 10:30 a.m. to 2 a.m. seven days a week.

In a different part of town, near the New City Hall and more or less across the street from the Hotel Zohar, **Café Rowal** (tel. 057-38309) is located downstairs in the Hever Community Center–Beersheba Theater building. It's worth going out of your way to visit this charming café: it's a lovely place, with a ceiling two stories high, dozens of hanging plants, wicker furniture, and tasteful art all around. It features delicious cakes, especially the Black Forest cake—but you'll have a hard time deciding which one to choose from among all the chocolate, marzipan, cheese, and other varieties. With a cappuccino, it will set you back about NIS5 ($3.35); there's also a nice menu of salads, blintzes, quiche, soups, juices, ice cream and other desserts, plus beer and wine, from which to choose. The café is popular with the after-theater crowd, but it's a pleasant place to visit anytime—open daily from 9 a.m. to 1 a.m., on Friday to 3 p.m. and again from 9 p.m. on, and on Saturday from 7 p.m. on.

And finally, as always, you'll find a clean and reasonably priced restaurant in the **Egged bus station** (tel. 057-76604), a large, cafeteria-style operation that's always mobbed at lunch. In the meat section (open daily from 8 a.m. to 4 p.m.; closed Saturday) a lunch of, let's say, a quarter chicken, beans and rice, salad, and a soft drink, comes in at just under NIS5 ($3.35). The dairy section is open daily from 6 a.m. to 7 p.m., closing for the Sabbath; like all the Egged restaurants, it's kosher.

SEEING THE SIGHTS: I've already told you about the city's Bedouin market place, and after you've immersed yourself in the profusion of exotic sights and smells in that area, the second place to go in Beersheba is the **Negev Museum** in the turn-of-the-century Turkish mosque, located on Ha-Atzma'ut Street (tel. 057-39105), in a pleasant little park in the center of the old city. Just look for the minaret, and you'll have no trouble finding the museum at the corner of Ha-Atzma'ut and Herzl Streets. The museum is open on Sunday and Monday from 8 a.m. to 2 p.m., on Tuesday and Friday to 1 p.m., on Wednesday and Thursday to 4 p.m., and on Saturday from 10 a.m. to 1 p.m. Admission is NIS1.50 ($1) for adults, half price for children.

As you approach the mosque, note the graceful *tughra* (the Ottoman sultan's monogram) in a medallion over the main door. Old photographs, mounted in moveable display frames in the main exhibition room, give one a fascinating glimpse back into Beersheba's early days as a municipality. When the Turks founded the modern city in 1907, the mosque and the Town Hall and the railway station were all there was. Pashas and provincial governors, staff officers in ancient motorcars, early settlers are all revealed in the photos.

But that's just the city's history. Other displays go far, far back to the Stone Age, Chalcolithic, Canaanite (Bronze Age), Israelite (Iron Age) through Byzantine periods. The Negev was densely populated during the Byzantine period, especially between Beersheba and Gaza; many excavations have been made, and here in the museum you'll find displays and information about several. A model of Tel Beersheba from the Chalcolithic period (3500 B.C.) shows how the people lived, in underground cities and houses, with room temperature at about 77°F all year round in the blistering desert heat. Sixth-century mosaics from the church of Kissufim in the western Negev show colorful depictions of desert scenes: a man on a horse fighting a leopard (native to this region); a wolf hunting a hare and a gazelle; a young man leading a camel by a rope; lions, birds, and more, with inscriptions in Greek.

Yad Labanim (tel. 057-37744), right across the square from City Hall, is dedicated to the memory of Beersheba soldiers fallen in battle. Photographs and documents illustrate how the liberation war was fought here. The memorial museum is open Sunday through Thursday from 9 a.m. to 1 p.m. Free admission.

Several miles outside of town, but well worth a visit, the **Museum of Bedouin Culture** (tel. 057-961-597) houses a fine collection, the result of many years of work among the Bedouin peoples of both the Negev and the Sinai. Ample explanation is given so that the displays are not only interesting to see but highly informative as well, describing the different customs and way of life of Bedouin tribes in the Negev and the Sinai, and also the Jbaliyya (Jebaliya) tribe which has been associated for centuries with the Santa Katerina Monastery on Mount Sinai. The museum is open Saturday through Thursday from 9 a.m. to 3 p.m., on Friday until noon; there's a small admission fee. To get here, drive north from Beersheba on the road to Tel Aviv; after 24 km (14½ miles) you'll see a sign pointing to Lahav, or Kibbutz Lahav, and the Joe Alon Center. Turn right here, go another 7 km (4¼ miles) until you see the sign directing you up the hill to the Joe Alon Regional and Folklore Center; the Bedouin Museum is part of this center. As you're heading up the hill, you'll be going through part of the Jewish National Fund forest; this is a nice, shady place to stop for a picnic. Unfortunately, there's no bus service to the museum.

Another fascinating display of Bedouin culture can be found at the **"Man in the Desert" Museum** (tel. 057-73308 or 70303), at Tel Sheba, the Bedouin community just outside of town, showing how the Bedouin people have adapted to survival in this not-so-hospitable climate. Open daily.

Abraham's Well

Abraham's Well is located at the southern end of Keren Kayemet Le-Israel Street, at the intersection of Derekh Hevron, down by the riverbed. Two large round stone walls, one open, the other covered by an arched stone roof, are surrounded by a stone courtyard, some desert date palm trees, and a wooden water wheel for drawing up the water. The wells are no longer in use, but you can still see the water far down below.

It may have been here that Abraham watered his large flocks, and he settled a dispute with Abimelech over rights to the water almost 5,000 years ago (Gen. 21:25–34). Scholars still cannot decide whether "Beer-Sheba" means "Well of the Covenant" (that is, the truce between Abraham and Abimelech) or "Well of the Seven," for the seven ewe lambs that Abraham gave Abimelech as a peace offering.

Monument to the Negev Fighters (Andarta)

Of all Israel's war memorials, this one—completed in 1969—is possibly the most original, certainly the most evocative. It's located on the northeastern edge of the city, just off the road that leads to Hebron, and commemorates the brigade that captured the Negev during the 1948 War of Independence. The memorial, consisting of 18 symbolic sections, flows like a fantastic cement garden over the summit of raw windy hill. Here the entire Negev campaign has been reduced to its essentials: a concrete tent wall, a bunker, a hill crisscrossed by communications trenches, a pipeline, nine war maps engraved in the floor of the square. Over, through, and around these structures you can climb and walk, thus becoming part of the desert action. You can climb to the top of the tall cement tower—representing the watch and water towers that were shelled on the Negev settlements—and look out across the desert's vast sandy expanse; you can file singly through the inclined walls of the Pass that lead into the Memorial Dome, and enter the symbolic Bunker.

This is the most famous work of one of Israel's most famous artists, Danny Caravan; people come from great distances not only out of interest to see the memorial to the war, but also to see the masterwork of this famous artist.

You can get to the monument easily in a private car or taxi. If you want to go by bus, take bus 55, going to Tel Sheba several times a day, or bus 388 heading for Arad. Ask the driver to let you off near Andarta; from where you alight, it's about a 15-minute, half-mile walk up the hill to the memorial.

Ben-Gurion University of the Negev

Not to be missed is the Ben-Gurion University of the Negev. Its faculties include the humanities, social, technical, natural and health sciences, and a medical school. Many of the more than two dozen departments emphasize the development of the Negev. The imaginative architecture combines the awareness of climatic conditions and the practical needs of the students and teachers. Tours can be arranged in advance through the Public Relations Department (tel. 057-664-444 or 664-111 or 61238). Visiting students might want to try the **Gimmel** disco, open nightly except Friday when the action moves to the Library Building on the new campus. Foreign students can also take an ulpan here for credit.

The **Research and Development Authority** of the university (tel. 057-78382 or 78383), in the new town, is a unique establishment and altogether necessary in Israel. It investigates such matters as artificial rainmaking, the exploitation of solar energy, desalinization of water, and the general chemical and biological conditions relating to the growth and maintenance of life in a desert climate.

Then there's also the **Herbert Cashvan Large Animal Center** (tel. 057-690-514), with an equine center specializing in the development, breeding, and veterinary medicine of Arabian horses. Research is also being done with camels, with attention focused on development of the camel as a source for meat and milk, among other things.

And Elsewhere

If you have the time, there are several other spots to see in Beersheba. The **cemetery** on Ha-Atzma'ut Street at the entrance to the town is for the British soldiers who died taking Beersheba from the Turks in 1917. Beersheba, incidentally, was the first city in Palestine to fall to the British in that war.

The old **railway station** on Tuviyahu Street is worth a look. It was along the Beersheba line that ran to Egypt that Lawrence of Arabia played his train-blowing tricks. Of course, that was the Turkish line dismantled by General Allenby. It ran along the western side of town.

Also worth a visit is **Tel Sheba,** a village of homes constructed for the usually nomadic Bedouin. Some keep tents nearby, perhaps in case four walls become a bit too much, but those who have chosen to live there seem to like it. Much thought indeed went into the feasibility of this project—on the parts of builders and future residents alike. A Visitor's Center (tel. 057-73308 or 30100) has been set up here, with an interesting museum called "Man in the Desert," showing how the Bedouin people have survived in the desert environment; there's also a gift shop carrying local Bedouin handcrafts, an outdoor covered cafeteria, a restaurant set up in a Bedouin tent, and even a camel, in case you want to ride. From the Central Bus Station, take bus 55, running several times each day.

The digs of many seasons have unearthed an ancient Israelite city at **Tel Beer Sheba**—in fact, many layers of civilization. The city walls and gates have been uncovered. A dominant feature of the city is a circular street with rows of buildings on both sides. A deep well was found right outside the city gates and the city's central canalization project was discovered. A huge ashlar four-horned altar was found and reconstructed. It is now exhibited in the Negev Museum, mentioned above.

Other archeological sites near Beersheba are **Dimona, Shivta,** and **Mamshit** (Kurnub). You can inquire at the I.G.T.O. or at the Negev Museum for details on these. There's also **Kadesh-Barnea,** well represented in the Negev Museum.

Sightseeing Tours

It is possible, while in Beersheba, to visit a **Bedouin encampment** and to join in a Bedouin-style dinner. Group tours to the encampment are organized by **Mr. A. Zakai** in his tour office at 75 Hehalutz St. (tel. 057-77477), on the corner of Ha-Atzma'ut. Drop in or phone ahead and see if you can hitch along with one of these groups. If so, the cost will be anywhere from $12 for the "short visit," which consists of a chat with the sheik over coffee or tea, camel ride, and Bedouin music, to about $20 for the full "sunset visit" with Bedouin dinner, which includes the above, and a typical rice, mutton, and fruit meal, eaten with the fingers or in pita. These prices include transportation to and from Beersheba, and can be higher if there are fewer than 25 people in the group. It might be wise to phone ahead before reaching Beersheba to find out when the next group is going out. Office hours are from 8:30 a.m. to 1 p.m., and again from 4 to 6 p.m. every afternoon except for Wednesday and Friday; closed Saturday.

SWIMMING: This you'll definitely want to do here—I guarantee it. There is a pool for youths near an area called **Shechunat Aleph** (tel. 057-38723), open from 8 a.m. to 6 p.m. Bus 3 passes it. Another pool is near the university. Use bus 4 or 5. Both are open from May to September. Entrance fees at both pools are reasonable.

In addition, there are two pools at the **Country Club** (tel. 057-33444), one for children and the other for adults. A roof is under construction for winter use. Open from 7 a.m. to 6 p.m. from May to September for the uncovered pools. Friday afternoons and Saturdays are reserved for members only. The club also has tennis courts. It's located a little distance from downtown, going out Tuviyahu Boulevard, just past Lon Grove, on the left. There's bus service in summer only.

The four-star **Desert Inn** (tel. 057-74931 or 74934), located out the same way but just *before* Lon Grove, also on the left, has a pool as well.

And in the Old City, the **Bet Yatziv Youth Hostel** and **Bet Sadot Valev Guest House** (tel. 057-77444) have a large swimming pool out behind the hostel. You'll find them at 79 Ha-Atzma'ut Street, about three blocks northwest of Herzl Street, past the Turkish mosque.

PARKS: In Beersheba's hot, dry climate, there are several beautiful parks full of trees, playgrounds, and picnic facilities, making lush, shady oases in the desert. Sitting among the trees, having a nice picnic, or watching children playing in the playgrounds, you'll feel a peaceful quiet.

Several parks are especially recommendable. **Pa'Amon Ha-Cherut Park** is located just across the riverbed from Abraham's Well, at the south side of the Old City. A much larger park, **Lon Grove,** is on the western outskirts of the city, near the country club and the Desert Inn; go out Tuviyahu Boulevard, the road heading to Ashkelon and Gaza, and you'll see it on your left as you're almost out of town. Yet another nice park is **Gan Moshe,** located between City Hall and the Beersheba Theater, across Shazar Street from the Zohar Hotel. All of these are very pleasant places; take a look at the map and you'll see several more parks, large and small, dotted around town.

NIGHTLIFE: At **Mandy's Discothèque,** 57 Hadassah St. (tel. 057-35609 or 33719), the entrance fee of NIS15 ($10) per couple includes one drink each; every subsequent drink is NIS2.50 ($1.65), and olives and cheese are on the house. Generally, you dance to recorded music, but occasionally there's live entertainment. Students get a discount. Open nightly from 9:30 p.m. to 3 a.m.

Artsy types tend to congregate at the **Shva Tea House–Restaurant,** 29 Smilansky St. (tel. 057-71454), in the Artists' Quarter. Walls hung with interesting weavings, and various other art objects here and there, set the mood for conversation, cocktails, perhaps a light supper. Toasted sandwiches, spaghetti several different ways, even a hefty steak for a hefty price can be ordered here, but you can just sit with a cup of coffee, a beer, a glass of wine, or an aromatic herbal tea (lots of these) for as long as you like. (As of this writing, Shva was temporarily closed, but it should be reopened by the time you arrive.)

In Beersheba you can visit art galleries at night, and the I.G.T.O. can direct you to many of them. Most are along Smilansky Street; of special note is the **Liraz Art Gallery,** 25 Smilansky St. (tel. 057-37963 or 39087), situated in a turn-of-the-century colonnaded Turkish house surrounded by a high stone wall. Changing exhibits of Israeli art are shown along with permanent antique exhibits. Open from 9 a.m. to 1 p.m. and 5 p.m. to midnight; closed Friday night. (When I last visited the Liraz, it was temporarily closed, but expecting to reopen in April 1988.)

Beersheba also has a number of cozy pubs, many of them found in a small area on the southern side of Old Town. At 18 Ha-Avot St. (tel. 057-33318) there's **Chaplin Pub/Coffeehouse,** a small place in another of those old, charming, whitewashed Turkish limestone buildings. Posters of Charles Chaplin and Marilyn Monroe deck the walls, and every Thursday evening there's a '30s dance, with many people coming in costume (you are welcome in costume or not). Light meals like pizza, salads, desserts, and coffees are served, in addition to a full bar selection. Open seven days a week from 9 p.m. to 2 a.m.

Around the corner are a number of other nice pubs, open roughly the same hours; you can stroll around of an evening, hear the music, and see the gentle lights flooding out into the street from the open doors. One of these is the **Simta Coffee Theater,** which sometimes features Israeli folksongs, sometimes jazz or country music. All of these pubs are tucked away on **Shloshet Bnei Ha-Od Street** between Ha-Avot and Smilansky Streets.

Several of the places I mentioned as restaurants have nice bars and pubs too.

For **folk dancing,** there are several opportunities in town. Saturday nights, starting at 8 p.m., there's dancing at Ben-Gurion University; on Thursday, dancing is held at Makiv Gimel High School, on Mivtza Yoav Street in the Shechuna Bet district (take bus 12). Tuesday evenings, there's dancing at **Skateland** (tel. 057-35186 or 31809); the rest of the time, as you'd imagine, Skateland is for skating, and various other kinds of family entertainment. Skateland is found in the south part of the city; go out Keren Kayemet Le-Israel Street, past Abraham's Well and the riverbed, and keep on going about one kilometer; you'll see Skateland on the left. By the way, right across the street from Skateland is **Montana**—a good place for an ice cream.

Films are shown every day at the university; call 057-39943 for info.

Beersheba is justifiably proud of its **Chamber Orchestra** (tel. 057-76019). Tickets are by subscription—but you may be lucky enough to buy a ticket before the performance at the box office or from someone who is unable to go. The concerts start promptly at 8:30 p.m. when the doors shut tight. Ask at the I.G.T.O. when the next concert will be held. Concerts are also given at the **S. Rubin Music Conservatory** (tel. 057-31616). The **Beersheba Theater** performs at Bet Ha-Am, in the Hever Community Center, the large white building in Gan Moshe, the park between City Hall and the Zohar Hotel. Performances are usually in Hebrew only. Check *This Week in the South* for current programs, or call 057-73478.

Meeting the Israelis can be arranged at the **Government Tourist Office** (tel. 057-36001).

2. Ein Gedi and Masada

It's about 50 km (30 miles) from Jericho to Ein Gedi along the shore of the Dead Sea, and another 15 km (10 miles) from Ein Gedi to Masada. Your adventure into the Negev can start from Jerusalem in one of two ways: south through Bethlehem and Hebron to Beersheba (see Chapter III, "The West Bank"), or via Ein Gedi and Masada. Whichever route you choose, don't fail to see Masada, and to consider a dip in the Dead Sea at Ein Gedi.

The road from Jerusalem along the Dead Sea coast passes Qumran, where the momentous discovery of the Dead Sea scrolls took place. For details, see Chapter III.

EIN GEDI: Right on the shores of the Dead Sea is the fertile kibbutz of Ein Gedi. Nearby are waterfalls (about which more below), a phenomenon that you would hardly expect in the midst of a desert. There are sulfur springs and ruins; it is, in all, a rich and rewarding area.

Lodgings and Meals

Ein Gedi is not a full-fledged resort. There are no hotels as such. But Kibbutz Ein Gedi (Mobile Post Dead Sea 86980), has a very popular guesthouse and a youth hostel, and the Ein Gedi Camping Village has trailers you can rent. Above all, reserve your bed in advance. Beds are scarce, and in great demand.

The kibbutz has the **Ein Gedi Guesthouse** and buses arrive from all the principal cities on regular schedules. The office is open from 8 a.m. to 8 p.m. (tel. 057-84757), and the kiosk opens twice daily. Each day the kibbutz provides transportation to and from the sulfur springs establishment, as well as the nearby beach area. Room and full board costs $59.50 single, $89 double—a bit splurgy, but it does include breakfast, lunch (dinner is $8), snacks, movies, slides and lectures, the sulfur baths, and transportation to them and the beach daily. Guests clean their own rooms, however. All 103 rooms are air-conditioned and have shower and TV; because of high occupancy, it's a good idea to book well in advance.

There's also a self-service restaurant called **Pundak Ein Gedi** at the Ein Gedi Camping Village. Air-conditioned, it seats 140 people and serves breakfast, lunch, and "tea" (until 4:30 p.m.). Prices are quite reasonable, with main courses for NIS5 ($3.35) to NIS8 ($5.35). As for the **Ein Gedi Camping Village** (Mobile Post Dead Sea 86980; tel. 057-84342), it has 40 travel trailers and 23 motel-style rooms which it rents for $30 single, $44.75 double, service—but not breakfast—included.

About five kilometers south of Ein Gedi proper is **Hamme Mazor** (tel. 057-84813), also called Ein Gedi Sulfur Springs, a modern building in which you can take the mineral-rich spring waters on the shores of the Dead Sea, or have a meal. Admission to the spa costs NIS10 ($6.65) for adults. Facilities here include indoor warm and hot mineral pools for men, for women, and for mixed bathing—six pools in all. There's a fish and dairy restaurant downstairs that will do nicely for lunch—about NIS7 ($4.65) to NIS10 ($6.65). The spa has its own Dead Sea swimming beach, and plenty of the famous Dead Sea black mud to smear on your skin. Come and take the cure any day of the week from 7 a.m. to 5 p.m. Any bus to Ein Gedi will drop you here; try bus 486 or 487 from Jerusalem.

A 200-bed youth hostel, **Bet Sara** (Mobile Post Dead Sea 86980; tel. 057-84165), is located just off the main road, about one mile north of the kibbutz. Very clean and well run, Bet Sara offers a fantastic view of the sea and mountains. Highly recommended. Near Ein Gedi, Roman ruins, and an excavation of a 3rd-century A.D. synagogue, it's 1,250 feet below sea level in a verdant oasis with sweet-water pools. Well kept and homey, it has air-conditioned family accommodations, and basic rates of $3.50 for a bed if you have a hostel card, $4.50 if you don't; $2 for breakfast, $4 for supper. The hostel has its own swimming place in the Dead Sea. To get there, you take a bus from Beersheba via Arad, or from Jerusalem.

What to See and Do

Ein Gedi has been an oasis in the desert for thousands of years. The Song of Solomon rhapsodized it thus: "My beloved is unto me as a cluster of camphire from the vineyards of Ein Gedi." A place of fertility, Ein Gedi was settled in 1949 by a group of pioneers who planted it with cotton, grapes, vegetables, and flowers. The kibbutz planners built their houses where there was absolutely nothing. With seeming magic, they created beautiful locations affording them stunning views of the entire dramatic area and the wild, foaming **Ein David Gorge,** where the water drops from a height of nearly 300 feet.

You can reach **David's Spring** (the Ein Gedi waterfall and natural pools) from the kibbutz grounds, but it's a more direct route if you enter from the main road across from the Ha-Ashalim Camping Ground.

You'll spot a large parking lot, at the back of which is a small kiosk equipped, even in this arid wilderness, with a gleaming espresso machine, plus cold drinks and snacks, of course. It's open daily from 9 a.m. to 4 or 5 p.m. From here you simply follow the trail and the signposts, winding through tall pines and palm trees up and into the desert hills. You proceed between slits in the rock formations, under canopies of papyrus reeds, and, after about ten minutes of steady climbing, you'll hear the wonderful sound of rushing water. In another five minutes, your appetite whetted, you arrive at what is surely one of the wonders of the world—the Ein Gedi waterfalls, hidden in an oasis of luxuriant green vegetation that hangs clustered around in a canyon wall. Tumbling down out of the heights, the falls represent the happiest sight you'll see in this blistering-hot region. Nature has conveniently etched pools at the foot of the falls, with water so cool you'll never want to leave.

The falls are within the **Ein Gedi Nature Reserve,** open from 8 a.m. to 3:30 or 4 p.m.; rates are according to the standard national parks tariff. No food is allowed on the grounds—conservation and ecology are of prime importance here.

Near Ein Gedi are the **ruins** of ancient Ein Gedi, one of Israel's most important archeological sites. A mosaic synagogue floor from the 2nd or 3rd century has been excavated, along with remains of a small pool and ancient buildings. Byzantine remains have also been found here, and on a nearby cliff is part of a sanctuary dating from about 4,000 B.C.

Across the Dead Sea to the far left are the Moab Mountains, where Moses was buried, and Gad, Rueben, and half the Mannasseh Tribe settled after helping Joshua claim the rest of the Promised Land. To the right it seems the sea ends, but it's simply a strip of peninsula from the Jordanian side, and this is about the middle of the Dead Sea. It's called Ha-Loshon ("The Tongue"). The water here is over 1,000 feet deep, but from the other side of the peninsula to Sodom it's only about 15 feet deep.

MASADA: Every Israeli schoolchild has made the climb to Masada. It is a national tradition to have made the ascent at least once—for Masada is the scene of one of the most heroic and tragic incidents in Jewish history. Here a small garrison defied the might of the powerful Roman army. The story, as Flavius Josephus recorded it, is worth retelling. Few people ever heard of it before they came to Israel until the 1981 week-long television spectacular and the book based on it.

The fabulous King Herod had built a magnificent palace and fortress atop this mountain sometime around A.D. 40. He furnished the luxurious place with every known comfort and laid in storehouses of food and arms, protecting the entire establishment with an impregnable fortress. In succeeding years a small Roman garrison occupied the mount. However, during the Jewish revolt against the Romans in A.D. 66, an army of Jewish fighters suddenly attacked the garrison and took over the fortress. They lived off the vast storehouses of food and had more than enough arms with which to defend themselves. The weapons were even put to use in raids on Jerusalem.

Finally, in A.D. 70, two years after the fall of Jerusalem, the Romans became so incensed with the Masada situation that they decided to lay siege to the rebellious base of operations and put an end to all Jewish resistance. After a year's worth of siege engines, flaming torches, rock bombardments, and battering rams, the Masada fortress was still in Jewish hands. But with 10,000 Roman troops camped on the hillside and daily bombardments smashing at the walls, it became only a question of time until the 900 heroic defenders would succumb.

One brutal attack spelled the end: The flaming torches at the fort's wall were whipped by a wind into the midst of the defenders, and the garrison's ramparts came crashing down. The Romans, seeing that Masada was practically defenseless now, decided to wait until dawn before they would conquer it triumphantly in their own good time.

But that night the 900 men, women, and children who inhabited Masada held a strange meeting. Their leader, Eliezer Ben-Yair, persuaded them to accept death bravely, on their own terms, and not to die as slaves of the Romans, or be butchered by them. So that evening nearly 2,000 years ago, one of history's greatest mass suicides occurred. Ten men were chosen executioners, and they carried out their distasteful mission on the families who willingly lay down together. Then one man killed the other nine and ran himself through on his own sword. Two women and five children survived, hiding in one of the caves. The Romans, who had expected to fight their way in, were doubly astonished at the lack of resistance and at the "calm courage of their resolution . . . and utter contempt of death." So, Flavius Josephus wrote, ended the Jewish resistance in Palestine.

The Excavation Site

Masada excavations have unearthed perhaps the most exciting ruins in the entire country. Indeed, much of the historical information about the Masada episode is now authenticated as a result. Climbing paths from both the Dead Sea side and the Arab side can bring the visitor up to the top of the Masada mountain, which remains a symbol of courage, and one that has long moved scholars, laymen, and soldiers to make the ascent.

Professor Yadin, who led the exploration, finds it difficult to say which were the most important finds among the walls, houses, straw bags, plaits of hair, pottery shards, stone vessels, cosmetic items, cooking utensils, the synagogue, the scrolls—all invaluable for providing information about the Second Temple Period. But among the most intriguing finds are the ritual baths (mikves), the ostraca that might have been the very lots cast by the defenders in their final moments, and the Roman siege engines.

Getting Up There

You've got two choices—climb or ride. If you climb, especially in the summer months, be sure to start literally at the crack of dawn. The gathering heat reaches murderously enervating proportions by the middle of the day. Climbers are frantically urged by the National Parks Authority to please—please—wear a good shade hat and drink as much as you can hold before starting up (again, for those who didn't catch it previously, this is because your head will fry without a hat, and you lose much more body moisture than you'd ever believe in this heat that evaporates it before it's noticeable).

Climbers have two choices of where they'll begin their ascent of this mountain: the route from the Dead Sea side, or the one from the mountain side, accessible via Arad. The route from where you are now, the Dead Sea side, is fondly called the **Snake Path.** Why? Well, the path does indeed snake up the mountain in steep, hairpin curves. As for actual snakes—I suppose it's easier for a reptile to get up the mountain via this path than it is for a biped, but I've never seen any trying. Depending on your age and vitality, your surefootedness, stamina, wind, and general muscle tone and fitness, the trip up will require from half an hour to an hour. Getting down takes every bit as long and is equally awkward. Snake Path opens at 7:30 a.m. and closes at 3:30 p.m., and you must start down by then just to get to the bottom before dark. The same hours apply to the path up the other side. The mountain-side path is called **The Battery,** after a battery the Romans built there. Getting to the top via that route takes only 15 to 30 minutes, and many little old ladies do it frequently, not to mention younger folk.

In my opinion, tourists should get a reward for scaling Masada—but just the opposite is true—it costs money! The opportunity to brave Snake Path costs a dollar or two for adults, much less for students or children up to age 18. Buses stop at both places, operating regularly between Masada and key cities.

It costs $5 or so, round trip, to ride up via cable car and be deposited about 75 steps from the fortress top. Students and youngsters get a reduction. Each bright-yellow car holds 40 people and delivers them, via wire and electricity, in three minutes flat—hardly time to say "My, what a lovely view." The cable-car launching structure is large and modern, built by a Swiss firm with lots of mountain-sidling experience. Cable cars operate from 8 a.m. to 4 p.m., on Friday and eves of holidays from 8 a.m. to 2 p.m. (also operates on Saturday).

Meals and Accommodations

The **Isaac H. Taylor Youth Hostel** (Mobile Post Dead Sea; tel. 057-84349) at Masada has 130 beds in a dormitory configuration. It's air-conditioned, and has a hostelers' kitchen. Beds cost $4.50 to $5.75 per night. Reserve in advance, if you can, for the next closest bed is 42 km away, in Arad.

You'll see a sign which reads "Guest House" on one of the buildings down the hill from the cable-car station. The dark little makeshift rooms used to be rented to tourists, but are no longer. What you will find here are restaurants. **Herod's Hall** is the full restaurant with waiter service, **Elazar** is the self-service cafeteria, and there's also a shady little terrace with a snackbar. Take your pick. By the way, if you're burdened with luggage when you reach Masada, you can have it secured in one of those former guest rooms for a charge of 75¢.

3. Arad, Neve Zohar, and Sodom

The modern desert town of Arad is not a mirage, but rather a well-planned town located on the site of an ancient Israelite settlement—a concrete testimonial to the continuity of Jewish history. Located about 30 miles east of Beersheba, it is regularly served by buses and sheruts. Arad is the logical place to stay if you're coming east from Beersheba, or if the youth hostel at Masada is full up, which often happens. Although there are several new hotels at Neve Zohar, and more abuilding, they are pretty expensive, and meant for those coming to take the curative waters.

Here's what you'll encounter along the road if you drive over, or take the bus, from Beersheba.

ON THE ROAD: As soon as you leave Beersheba, you'll see clusters of Bedouin tents and flocks—and houses, for today the Bedouin are settling down more and more (perhaps because the government of Israel is making sure they have a fixed water supply, so they need no longer roam the land in search of it).

At the first major intersection not far from Beersheba you're presented with a choice: Shall it be straight on to Hebron, or a right turn for Arad and the Dead Sea? Since we've been to Hebron already (Chapter III), we'll take the turn and watch the Bedouin, who work and live near the highway. A bit farther on you'll begin to see Bedouin villages—the Abu-Rabiya tribe has four such settlements between Beersheba and Arad, all fairly close together. Some of the villages consist of shacks, others of tents; some are quite large, others may be nothing more than three houses and five tents. Another thing to note is that the Bedouin here do a lot of farming, growing mostly wheat, but also other grains, and fruits and vegetables, most of which they sell in the Beersheba markets. And while you're busy noting things, note that there is a great deal of experimental agricultural work being done along this road: sisal is grown without irrigation; tamarisk, eucalyptus, and other trees are planted in small areas, their growth watched carefully by scientists who are planning to cultivate even more of Israel's desert.

THE TOWN OF ARAD: When the road starts snaking around tight curves, you'll know you're just about in Arad. Driving into Arad is like entering almost any small American city: there are wide highways with overhanging lights, high-

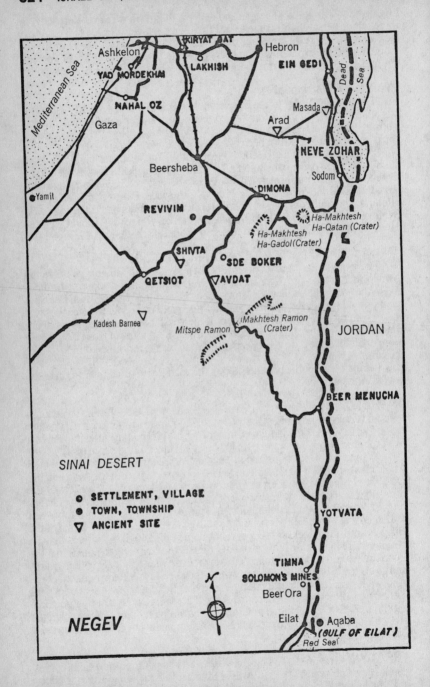

rise apartments everywhere, and a busy shopping mall (they call it *merkaz* here).

One of the interesting things about Arad is that it's a planned city, begun in 1961, and mapped out for efficiency to meet the rigid desert restrictions in the most comfortable manner. It's some 2,000 feet above sea level and its ultra-dry climate is considered a blessing to sufferers of asthma and similar troubles. Each year it grows more popular as a vacation place for singles, couples, and families; by staying here, a tourist can get quite a realistic picture of Israeli life.

Orientation and Information

As Arad is a small town of only some 13,000 souls (but growing), finding your way around it is simplicity itself. No doubt you will come into town from the main highway via **Hebron Street.** The third cross-street is **El'azar Ben-Yair,** and at this corner—Hebron and Ben-Yair—is the town's principal commercial center. The post office is at this corner, and right next to it is the **Tourist Information Office** (tel. 057-958-958 or 958-144). Follow the signs to find the office (on foot) in the commercial center. It's open Sunday through Thursday from 9 a.m. to noon and 4 to 7 p.m., on Friday from 9 a.m. to noon; closed Saturday. By the way, bus schedules are posted in the tourist office window.

Once you've reached the commercial center you've just about got Arad figured out. Go east on Ben-Yair for a kilometer or two; the street's name will change to Moav Street, and you'll be in the hotel area. Go only three blocks east from the post office on Ben-Yair, turn right (south) on Ha-Palmach Street, and you'll be headed for the youth hostel.

Accommodations

Basically, you have three choices in Arad. You can put up in a hotel in the hotel area, or one of the smaller, more modest hotels downtown, or in the downtown youth hostel. Sometimes you can rent a room in a private home. Check with the tourist office for information on these.

The Youth Hostel: Arad's modern hostel is named the **Bet Blau-Weiss** (P.O. Box 34; tel. 057-957-150), named for a Central European Zionist youth movement. The Blau-Weiss ("Blue and White") has 130 beds, a kitchen for your use, family rooms, central heating, and swimming facilities. Price per person per night is $5 to $6.30, depending on your age. The Blau-Weiss is down Ha-Palmach Street, just past Atad Street, on the left.

Downtown Hotels: About the only real hotel downtown is the two-star **Arad Hotel,** 6 Ha-Palmach St., between Yehuda and Atad Street (P.O. Box 8, Arad 80750; tel. 057-957-272 or 957-040), near the center of town next to the municipality. Singles are $21.75; doubles run $35.75. The hotel has a tiny "pocket garden" full of roses and cactuses, not to mention a rather astounding sculpture of a bearded sage cut from a six-foot driftwood branch which is planted like a tree. This is not a luxury hotel, but it is clean and comfortable. Students, incidentally, get a discount simply by not paying the 15% service charge. The dining room is pleasant and not expensive. All of the 51 rooms are air-conditioned and capable of sleeping up to five people; all are heated and equipped with private shower and toilet.

In the Hotel Area: Now for the normal hotels, arranged in their own park-like setting on Moav Street away from the center of town, served by municipal bus.

The **Nof Arad Hotel** (P.O. Box 80, Arad 80750; tel. 057-957-056 or 957-057) has three stars and 165 rooms, some in cabins and the rest in the hotel itself. The cabins are cement structures containing four rooms, each with air conditioning, telephone, shower, and toilet. Off-season rates (mid-November to the end of February) are $24.25 to $26.50 single, $32.25 to $36.75 double; high-season rates are about $2.30 per person higher. Rooms in the hotel's new (1984) wing are more luxuriously furnished and cost about $5 per person more. The hotel features a fully equipped clinic for the climatic treatment of asthma. There is a swimming pool here, and the self-service breakfasts are good, particularly the fresh, hotel-baked rolls. Recommended.

Across the street from the Nof Arad is another three-star hotel, the **Margoa Arad Hotel** (P.O. Box 20, Arad 80750; tel. 057-957-014 or 957-191). It has 165 rooms and two different price scales—one for the hotel itself and the other for the semi-detached cottages. Single occupancy in the rooms is $38; double occupancy costs $55.25. There's a large swimming pool here, open from the spring (Passover) to the late fall (Succoth). Entertainment is sometimes available during that same interval.

Finally, the **Hotel Masada** (P.O. Box 62, Arad 80750; tel. 057-957-140 or 957-260) is rated at four stars but sees fit at present—to draw customers, no doubt—to charge three-star rates. Its 104 rooms are all air-conditioned, bathtub-equipped, centrally heated, radio- and telephone-equipped, served by an elevator, and priced at $40.25 single, $57.50 double in the high season. Off-season (mid-November through February, except the holiday period), rates go down $4.60 per person.

Rooms in Private Homes: It is also possible to rent a room in a private home. Folks are very friendly in Arad; you can ask most anyone on the street, and if they can't help you, they'll probably have a friend who will. And since Arad is such a friendly place, it's a good spot to **Meet the Israeli.** Ask at the Tourist Information Office or call 057-958-144.

Restaurants

If you're looking for a gourmet experience, Arad is not the place. But wholesome food is available, and I'll cite a few eateries that I've discovered in the town.

The Polish-owned **Galit Restaurant,** 37-7 Ben-Yair St. (tel. 057-90793), a few doors down from the post office and the tourist office, in the Commercial Center, has just six tables covered with red and white cloths. You might begin your meal with a bowl of kreplach soup, salad, or gefilte fish. Among the main courses are goulash, roast chicken, and roast duck; you'll pay about NIS11 ($7.35) for a full three-course meal here. Open Sunday to Thursday from noon to 9 p.m., on Friday from noon to 3 p.m., and on Saturday from noon to 4 p.m.

Right next door to the Galit is the perfect place for dessert or afternoon tea, the **Ugit Pastry Shop** (tel. 057-958-311). You can't miss its display case filled with tempting Central European–style goodies. Coffee and tea are served.

The Commercial Center has various other snack and light-meal establishments serving pizza by the slice or by the pie, and sandwiches and falafel. For a piece of pizza or a falafel, plus a cool Maccabee beer, expect to pay around NIS5 ($3.35).

Arad Activities

Most people come to Arad's high, dry location for relief of asthma rather than for sightseeing. However, you should take the trouble to get to the viewpoint down at the far eastern end of Ben-Yair/Moav Street near the Hotel Masada. At the road's end, a path begins, heading out to a modern sculpture on the promontory. The view of the spare landscape, the haunting silence, and the wildflowers (in spring) provide a happy memory of your visit here.

Shopping has been centralized to a great degree in Arad and most everything can be found at the **Shopping Center.** Food, clothing, cosmetics, stationery, banks, a hairdresser, pharmacy, even a photography store.

The **Abir Riding School** can be found in the Industrial Area. Telephone 057-94147 for details.

Many activities take place at the **Matnas Cultural Center** opposite the Tourist Information Office. Youngsters meet on Friday night, the Chess Club and Melave Malka meet on Saturday night, the Bridge Club meets on Monday night, and there's folk dancing Tuesday night.

Tel Arad

Some four miles west of Arad is Tel Arad, a partially reconstructed 5,000-year-old Canaanite town with a 3,000-year-old Israeli fort. It's open Sunday to Thursday from 8 a.m. to 4 p.m. October to March; until 5 p.m. the rest of the year, closing an hour earlier, respectively, on Friday and holiday eves. Entrance fee is minimal.

TO NEVE ZOHAR AND SODOM: If you're traveling during Israel's seven dry months, be sure to get an early start. The atmosphere becomes hot and sultry by noon, and a weird kind of languid breathless heat, in which nothing stirs, settles over the entire area.

On the Road

The ride from Arad to the Dead Sea (just 45 minutes) is almost all downhill, and the word "steep" is hardly adequate. From Arad's heights, where the land is all a chalky sandy color, the wilderness to the west turns increasingly darker, changing to tans and then deeper shades of brown. During the 28.5-km (17-mile) trip, the scenery will doubtless hold your attention. You'll pass through the **Rosh Zohar** fields of large underground reservoirs of natural gas. Don't miss an observation point to the left, **Mezad Zohar;** you won't know its uniqueness till you're out of the car, leaning against the rail of the sun-shelter and looking out and down. Here are remains of a Roman fortress, down in the valley that served as the major roadway from the Dead Sea up until the day the highway you've been plying was opened. (These desert valleys, or wadis, were carved out over the centuries by the fast fierce floods of sudden rains.) A second observation point is a bit farther down, this one with a huge map so that you can identify what you're looking at. Then the road really swings down and you finally have before you a vista of the Dead Sea and part of the Judean wilderness beyond it.

Should you be coming directly from Beersheba (by bus, sherut, or private car), you'll drive just over an hour, and you can take the road through another of those desert development towns, **Dimona.** The most famous of Israel's hastily constructed boom towns, Dimona was the subject of considerable controversy, because at one time many thought it was inhuman and impossible to expect people to live and work in such a climate. However, the handful of tents that started the town in 1955 soon became a thriving community of 22,500 people living in stone houses—a town complete with movies, cultural centers, textile and phosphate plants, even an atomic reactor.

Three miles farther, on the right, is a deserted stone blockhouse, a former police station on a high hill which stands on the site of an ancient Byzantine town **(Memphis).** Nearby, in a deep gorge, are three dams dating from the 6th century A.D., in which ancient engineers were able to store enough water to keep the residents supplied even during the dry season.

Memphis is one of the many ancient desert cities under close scrutiny by Israel's modern scientists, who are convinced that many of these classical methods of desert-living are still applicable in today's planning for cities in the Negev.

Beyond a Roman fort called **Tamar** (20 km, 12 miles, farther on), the road starts to descend rapidly. Abruptly, around a turn, you are confronted with one of Israel's most amazing sights—and certainly the most bizarre—the Dead Sea. It lies there, 3,000 feet below you, in a heavy haze. Around it the mountains of Moab and Edom are lifeless and parched.

Soon you pass the sea-level sign, all the time descending lower and lower through the Arava plain, passing potash and bromide factories along the way. Signs commemorate the workers who were ambushed constructing this road in 1951, and the actual opening of the roads to Sodom in 1953. Then, with the dust churning up behind you, the car pulls to a stop: You are at the edge of the Dead Sea, the lowest point on earth, 1,300 feet below sea level. (Death Valley in California, America's lowest point, is only 282 feet below sea level.)

Half of the 48-mile Dead Sea is in Israel's territory (about 100 square miles of it), but even working with that little area the technicians find that they can scarcely deal fast enough with the vast reservoir of chemicals being constantly removed from the sea. This water is 25% solids, of which 7% is salt, and that's the saltiest water on earth, six times as salty as the water in the ocean. Each day, tons of chlorides, bromides, and sulfides are removed for processing and export. No fish can live in these miles of mineral-rich liquid.

The Dead Sea

From Arad to the Dead Sea, as I said, is about a 45-minute ride. The main highway intersects a road paralleling the coast. Turn right for Sodom and the Dead Sea Works, and for the highway to Eilat. We'll take the left turn to Ein Bokek, Masada, and Ein Gedi (this road goes all the way to Jerusalem).

Just before the intersection, you can fill up on gasoline and such at a large modern filling station on your left, and from here you can catch sight of the **Neve Zohar Camping Site** (tel. 057-84306). Trees shade the area. There are kitchens with stoves, a place to buy food, a restaurant with moderate prices, a first-aid station, petrol pump, picnic area, post box, hot showers, parking lot, bus station . . . everything!

Also at Neve Zohar you will find the **Bet Hayotzer** museum, which houses an exhibition of the Dead Sea industries. It is free and open daily from 9 a.m. to 12:30 p.m. and again from 1:30 to 5 p.m.

Just across the road from the camping site is an excellent place to take your dip in the Dead Sea, an experience that will prove difficult to forget. But first listen to a few words of caution: Wear sandals and a hat—the sandals protect your feet against sharp stones, and the hat prevents your head from sizzling. And be sure to keep the water out of your eyes—it burns! The water has a very bitter, oily taste should you accidentally get a mouthful, but it's almost impossible to accidentally go under; you float on the Dead Sea even if you don't know how to float, so high is the water's density. Afterward you may opt to rinse off with a shower (some say the waters of the Dead Sea give them an "unpleasantly creepy feeling"; others love it), or leave the film of mineral residue on your body till bedtime, as the Israelis do. They say it's healthy and good for the skin. They go equally wild over the black mud scooped from the sea bed, smearing it all over themselves, especially anyplace that hurts or stings. It's supposed to be good for muscle and joint problems, and many physicians do in fact recommend Dead Sea soaks.

Israelis (Europeans too) also go for mineral water baths in a big way. If you want to give this sort of thing a try, go up the road to **Zohar Springs** *(Hamei Zohar)*, and immerse yourself in the naturally hot waters that have even more minerals per gram than the Dead Sea. If you're not so hot on this activity, stop by anyway, if only for a snack at the restaurant next door and a superb view of the Dead Sea and the surrounding wilderness mountains.

Zohar Springs

Unlike the waters of Ein Gedi's spa, those at nearby Zohar Springs (tel. 057-84261) can be very helpful for skin diseases like psoriasis. These were Cleopatra's favorite waters for her beauty needs, and today the waters are said to be cleansing for skin and scalp, improving skin texture and even smoothing wrinkles. Experts came out here about 20 years ago, investigated the waters, had them analyzed by Hadassah experts, and found that the waters contained the highest mineral content of any waters in the world: 300 grams per liter. "Also, in the baths here," they explain, "you take 10% to 14% more oxygen than in any other water in the world, and that's more purifying. Tired and nervous people come here for a week and it changes their lives. They calm down, get quieter and more settled."

People with doctors' notes can take advantage of a weight-loss program devised by the local medical team—but the current management prefers to emphasize the strictly curative powers of Zohar Springs. The young professional behind the desk said that the experts here will cater the treatment baths according to what complaints you have—spine, joint, bone, or muscle problems, etc. If you want the whole spa treatment, though, you'll have to have a medical okay. For an on-the-spot check up, there is a resident physician. You can skip all this by bringing along a note from your own doctor certifying that your blood pressure can stand the stimulation of the waters.

This is quite a luxurious place. It is equipped with a central air-conditioning system, excellent facilities in the sulfur baths and pools, mud baths, vibration and electro-galvanized baths, underwater massages, and cosmetic treatments. The baths are open every day of the week from 7 a.m. to 3 p.m. At both of the above spas it's advisable to check your valuables.

Accommodations and Meals

The Dead Sea area is fast becoming an important tourist resort; the following is worth looking into.

The already-mentioned **Neve Zohar Camping Site and Restaurant** (tel. 057-84306) looks fine and is inexpensive. Bungalows sleep two people. The restaurant is very reasonably priced, but if you care to do your own cooking the adjoining grocery is well stocked. The camping ground facilities are open all year.

Most of the luxury hotels are near Ein Bokek, a few kilometers north of Zohar Springs. The first you'll come to is the **Moriah Dead Sea** (tel. 057-84221) with five stars and double-room prices, in season, over $150 (half board). About 2.5 km (1½ miles) north of the Moriah are some four-star hotels, the **Moriah Gardens** (tel. 057-84351), the **Galei Zohar** (tel. 057-84311), and the **Ein Bokek** (tel. 057-84331). Prices for double rooms here are about $70.

Of Ein Bokek's hotels, only the 160-room **Tsell Harim** (tel. 057-84121) comes anywhere near our budget range. Bed-and-breakfast here goes for $35.75 to $38 single, $41.50 to $46 double.

SODOM: Retrace your drive along the shore, back to whichever highway (Arad or Beersheba) brought you to the sea-hugging road. Only don't turn there, just keep going and you'll be in Sodom in no time (ten kilometers, or six miles). Bear in mind that today's Sodom (1,300 feet below sea level) is no real town as such, just factories and equipment. Once there was a café, a youth hostel, a pension-like hostel. Once it was possible to cool off in the famous Sodom cave, with its twisting labyrinth of shining salt walls, gleaming stalactites, and the broad chamber with a funneled chimney-like opening at the top. But that's been closed as a safety precaution. Today about all you can do here is look around at one of the most tortured-looking areas you're ever likely to see. Nearby, however, is **Moshav Neot Ha-Kikar**—proof that even the most arid and desolate desert land can be reclaimed.

The calm, oily sea is on one side, bizarre, agonizing mountain slopes on the other. Clumps of white foam, a solid brine, cling to the dried shrubs and clumps of whitened stone. There is a noxious smell of sulfur in the air, and some of the trees next to the sea are petrified, with crystals of gypsum and bitumen hanging from them in weird shapes.

The wicked city of Sodom, lowest inhabited place on earth, is no more. The famous citadel of degeneracy is now one big hot potash concession. Here the road that runs along the Dead Sea shore is bordered on the left by a wall of solid salt. (Taste it if you don't believe me.) Reportedly, one of the pillars along the bordering wall is of the curious woman who looked back. The legendary pillar—which does suggest such a shape—stands above the entrance to the Sodom cave. According to the biblical story, angels were going to save Mr. and Mrs. Lot and family, and in telling them to run for it, they also admonished them not to look back. Mrs. Lot's curiosity is mummified in perpetuity in the pillar of salt.

The fire and brimstone that hit Sodom and Gomorrah was probably a Tertiary-era volcano that shattered this area, according to scientific evidence. In any event, a recent proposal for constructing a desert-like gambling casino here —along Las Vegas lines—drew a wrathful protest from religious leaders. Their objection? The city was destroyed once for its wickedness; don't tempt history to repeat itself.

4. Into the Negev

The Talmudic scholars say that Negev means "dry," and Old Testament experts claim it means "south." Both are correct—in literal terms. A vast waste-land of almost 4,000 square miles, this desert is Israel's future—for population expansion, for chemical industries, for farming. Studies have proved that one-fifth of the desert area can be used for some form of agriculture or other, and looking at the bleak, dry landscape, even this seems a high figure.

Some deserts can be boring, just hot and dry. Not the Negev. This region is a constantly varying landscape of red, black, and yellow, accented by valleys, deep craters, and burnt-brown mountains.

Craggy limestone walls, mounds of sandstone, red and even green dunes of sand are everywhere strewn with great blocks of black volcanic silex. Saw-toothed mountain ridges, abruptly hollowed out by the wild gorges left from the Great Middle Eastern Earthquake, starkly point back to the day when these mountains just fell down and this desert opened its granite jaws to everything living on top of it—truly awesome.

Now you've got a choice. You can head toward the Jordanian border and take the highway from Sodom to Eilat; it's much faster, but there's only stark, indigenous scenery to see. Or you can go to Beersheba and take the older and much slower road through the heart of the Negev to reach the port of Eilat on the Red Sea. If you choose the latter, there are five major points of interest along this fascinating road: Shivta, the Sde Boker settlement, Bedouin tribes,

Mitspe Ramon, and the scenery, as well as a number of archeological sites and digs, the best known and most accessible being Avdat.

The trip to Shivta, a 6th-century Byzantine commercial city, is best done by bus tour or private car. You can try to hitch it, but don't do this in extremely hot weather, and start early in the day.

SHIVTA:
The Nabateans built a way station here in the 1st century B.C., but Shivta (or Subeita) became rich and famous during the time of Justinian the Great (500s), when Byzantine wealth and power were at their height. Caravans laden with pilgrims and merchandise made their way between Egypt and Anatolia, between the Red Sea and the Mediterranean, and many stopped at Shivta. Besides this commercial wealth, Shivta's ingenious citizens built an elaborate irrigation system that allowed them to farm the barren soil.

But Shivta's location on major trade routes proved its undoing when the Arab armies, inspired by Islam, burst out of Arabia on their way to world conquest. The easily accessible city was overrun, and the trade routes slowly changed, but though Shivta survived as an Arab town for a number of centuries, by the 1100s it was a ghost town.

Shivta is about 50 km (30 miles) southwest of Beersheba, off the Nizzana road. If you don't have a car, you can catch a bus toward Nizzana (no. 44) and get off at the "Horvot Shivta" stop. A road leads south into the desert through a military zone, and Shivta is 8½ km (5 miles) along this road.

It's easy to get lost in the military zone, and important not to, so here are explicit directions: from the highway, the Shivta road is two-lane and paved for the first 2½ km (1½ miles). It then narrows, and after another kilometer you pass a road, on the left, to the military installation. After passing this road, it's another five kilometers (three miles) over a rough, curvy one-lane road to Shivta. There are few signs.

Before the birth of archeology around 1800, people in need of construction materials had always looked with favor on deserted ruins. An ancient city might contain all sorts of cut stone ready to build with. The ruins of Shivta remained in fairly good condition throughout the centuries because they were too far away from newer building sites to make pillage economical. So what we have here is a city of the 500s, as intact as history has left anywhere.

Restoration work began in 1958. Buildings include three churches, a mosque, a caravanserai, and houses. Signs identify the principal buildings, and tell you something about them.

Shivta is an impressive site, but not absolutely essential to your Israeli sojourn. If you have a car, don't miss it. If you're on foot, spend your time at Avdat—unless you have lots of time. By the way, there are no facilities whatsoever at Shivta. It's in the middle of nowhere.

SDE BOKER:
Some 50 km (30 miles) due south of Beersheba, where the only things you see are sand and parched mountains in every direction, you suddenly come to a farm settlement. Green orchards and blossoming vegetable fields seem to have miraculously sprung from the desert soil here. This is the famous Ben-Gurion kibbutz, Sde Boker. The settlement was begun in May 1952, at the prime minister's instigation, when the country was first encouraging settlers to populate the Negev. His words, "If the State does not put an end to the desert, the desert may put an end to the State," provided an inspiration. He provided an example by becoming a member of this kibbutz in 1953; he lived and worked here till his death in 1973, at the age of 87. He and his wife, Paula, are buried here, and many of his books and papers may be seen in the **Paula and David Ben-Gurion Hut** (tel. 057-80124). Visiting hours are Sunday to Thursday from

8:30 a.m. to 3:30 p.m., on Friday, Saturday, holidays, and holiday eves from 9 a.m. to 1 p.m. Groups are asked to phone 057-85124 in advance.

Over the years Sde Boker began to thrive, as did several other young settlements in the Negev peopled by a hardy and tough desert breed of Israeli. A campus of the Ben-Gurion University of the Negev has been established at Sde Boker. A modern library, housing the **Ben-Gurion Institute and Archives,** and containing 750,000 documents associated with Israel's first chief of state, is located here. The institute also serves as a center for the study of desert areas.

BEDOUIN TRIBES: After leaving Sde Boker, you are *really* in the desert. The black-tented Bedouin camps grow sparser as you proceed farther south; whatever the natural growth of grass and fruit in the Negev, it is all in the northern part, so even the perennial wanderers do most of their wandering in the northern desert regions.

Roughly 32,000 Bedouin roam Israel's deserts and hills, an estimated 27,000 in the Negev, 5,000 in the Galilee mountains. Until recently they haven't respected border lines very much—as is their inherited perogative—but Israel has been campaigning to entice them with the benefits of civilization in the modern land of the Bible. Clinics and hospitals give their babies free service, the government has provided them with land to till and develop, and some have settled down to become desert construction workers.

AVDAT: Ten kilometers south of the Paula and David Ben-Gurion Hut (13 km, 8 miles, from Sde Boker) is the national parks archeological site of Avdat (or Avedat). This was a city of the Nabateans, the same desert people who built a magnificent city at Petra, now in Jordan, which was their capital.

Avdat was carved out of the forbidding desert during the 2nd century B.C. (100 to 199 B.C.). Ingenious engineers reclaimed the soil, made provisions for water, and made the desert bloom. After their migration from the deserts of Arabia, the Nabateans no doubt looked upon the Negev as fertile.

Besides the Nabatean ruins, you can see Roman and Byzantine construction. A booklet, on sale at the site, explains it all.

There's lots to see here, and Avdat's site atop a hill gives you a commanding view of the vast desert. Avdat, restored with U.S. government funds, is administered by the national parks department, and charges its standard rates for admission; it is open every day.

MITSPE RAMON: At Mitspe Ramon, a clay-mining town where you'll pause for a drink, you'll find a view that will make you rub your eyes in disbelief. It's a combination of the Grand Canyon and the surface of the moon—a fantasy of orange and black patterns, in shapes at once flat, twisting, and massive—that defies description. Should you get a late start on your trip south—and it's not advisable to drive this narrow road by night—your one solace is seeing this view by sunset. Then the enormous panorama, which resembles my notion of what the earth's surface looked like 50 million years ago, becomes drenched with a reddish pastel hue.

Just in case you'd like to stay overnight, there's the modern, clean **Bet Noam Youth Hostel** (tel. 057-88443), with 160 beds, family accommodations, hot showers, cooking facilities, and a café and supply store.

Incidentally, the region is now accessible by plane as well. Shahaf (tel. 03-452-735 in Tel Aviv, 059-74508 in Eilat) has regular air service to Mitspe Ramon.

KADESH-BARNEA: Scholars have come up with three different versions of the route they believe Moses took as he led the Jewish people out of Egypt and into the Promised Land. But all three versions converge at Kadesh-Barnea, located about 40 km (24 miles) to the east of Mitspe Ramon.

Kadesh-Barnea served as a center for the confederation of tribes that wandered in the Negev and the Sinai during the time of Abraham; it was also called Enmishpat at that time (Genesis 14:1–11). But most of the biblical references to it are connected with the time of the Israelites' sojourn in the desert under Moses. The Bible says they "abode in Kadesh many days" (Deut. 1:46); it was from Kadesh that Moses sent 12 men to spy out the land of Canaan (Numbers 13:26), and messengers to the king of Edom to request passage through his territory (Numbers 20:14). It was also at Kadesh that Moses smote the rock and got water (Numbers 20:11), and here that his sister, Miriam, died and was buried (Numbers 20:1).

For generations, controversy prevailed as to the location of the biblical Kadesh; early in this century, a general consensus emerged, identifying the site with Tel el-Qudeirat, located in the fertile valley watered by the spring of Ain el-Qudeirat.

Ten seasons of excavation have unearthed three fortresses built one atop the other, guarding the southern border of the kingdom of Judea, the earliest dating from the early 10th century B.C., the latest existing up until it met its fate at the time of the destruction of the First Temple (586 B.C.). Numerous examples of pottery and ostraca (tablet writings) have also been found here, but no traces of the followers of Moses. This is logical, since the nomadic character of the society under Moses left little trace in the landscape. But although we see no evidence of their passing, it is very moving to stand here and look around at the scenes where the great biblical stories took place.

Kadesh-Barnea is well represented at the Negev Museum in Beersheba, and also in the Rockefeller Center Museum in Jerusalem.

INSIDE THE NEGEV: This petrified desert world, with temperatures ranging from 125°F during the day to 50° in the winter dawn, has been somewhat tamed by the 235-km (140-mile) road, well banked but a bit narrow, running from Beersheba to Eilat on the Red Sea. Unseen from this main road are the majority of the desert's agricultural settlements and mining works, as well as Nahal (Noar Ha-Lootzi Lo'hem or Pioneering Fighting Youth) military pioneering villages.

If you're going by sherut or driving by yourself, stop the car at some uninhabited spot and listen to the almost frightening stillness of a world where nothing seems to stir.

Equally mysterious in the Negev are the secondary roads leading off the main route—cryptic paths winding their way into the flatlands and beyond the dunes, seemingly without purpose, but actually ending up in an agricultural collective. Also unseen, except for an occasionally patrolled pumping station, is the vast network of cement water conduits based in part on the Jordan River diversion project, which brings life to these desert outposts.

At the end of the road: the port of Eilat on the Red Sea.

5. Eilat

This city at the southern tip of the Negev vies with Tiberias as the country's leading winter tourist resort. Eilat's chief claims to fame for the tourist are fine beaches and sunshine about 360 days out of the year. But with 20,000 inhabitants who have an average age of 26 years, Eilat is actually a combination military outpost–vacation center–shipping port. The city's first-class hotel area is less than a mile from the Jordanian border. Easily viewed across the bay, dazzling in a haze of desert sand, and partly shaded by rings of date palm trees, is the Jordanian port city of Aqaba, population 20,000. Some 20 km (12 miles) south of Aqaba begins Saudi Arabia. To the west are the mountains of Sinai.

IN KING SOLOMON'S TIME: It was from the port of Eilat that Solomon sent and received his ships from the land of Ophir, laden with gold, wood, and ivory. Israeli shipping rights on the Red Sea, opened by virtue of the Sinai campaign, and again during the Six-Day War, make the port of Eilat a bustling place which employs a large number of the residents. Although the harbor doesn't look like much, it is one of the most classical ports in all history. "And King Solomon built a navy of ships in Ezion-geber, which is beside Eloth on the shore of the Red Sea" (I Kings 9:26). Hiram, Solomon's famous admiral friend (he was king of Tyre), brought to Eilat his spices and gold from the land of Ophir, and it is even thought by some that the Queen of Sheba landed at Eilat when she came to Jerusalem to see Solomon and "commune with him all that was in her heart."

THE SPECIAL PEOPLE OF EILAT: Here you'll find all kinds of folks, from young men who are grimy, tough, and ready for anything, to young housewives wheeling the many baby carriages you see in this town. But Eilat definitely has a youthful, adventurous flavor, a rare freedom of spirit that seems to move the entire population. The cocky, happy-go-lucky attitude of Eilat's population is really a very necessary factor. Without it, they probably couldn't persevere over the indescribably hot summertime days. Israelis who had begun to find the north too confining and cramped have moved down here for the challenge; so too have a few who practice yoga, pluck guitar strings, and who, in general, were displeased with "the people up north"—for whom they have little hope. This is an individualist's town, and it's also a town for making money.

ORIENTATION: There are four easily distinguishable areas in Eilat: the town itself, built on gentle hills rolling down toward the sea; **Coral Beach,** about 6 km (3½ miles) from town on the western shore of the harbor; **Taba,** a disputed (with Egypt) strip of sand south of Coral Beach; and **North Beach,** a ten-minute walk from the center of town on the eastern shore of the harbor. This latter is where the major beach activity is concentrated, where you'll find the best accommodations, and where the public beach is located. This is also the site of an elaborate marina system which started with the building of a horseshoe-shaped lagoon, cutting several hundred yards inland in back of the "hotel row" section. Around this lagoon, in which you can swim, are hotels, motels, and a caravan camp. It's a masterful plan, worked out by teams of marine surveyors and architects; as a result of it, more and more tourists can enjoy Eilat—the languid days, the bountiful sun, the red-tinted green waters, the calm of the midday sloth, the dusty hills, the cool desert breezes of night.

The best way to pilot yourself around Eilat is to step into the tiny **Israel Government Tourist Office** (tel. 059-72268), in the Commercial Center, directly across Hatmarim Boulevard from the Egged Bus Station, and pick up a free English-language map on which everything is clearly marked out for you. While you're here, be sure to pick up a copy of the pamphlet "Events in Eilat," telling all the events coming up for the month you're here. Bus schedules and schedules of events in the region are posted in the office window, so you can inform yourself even when the office is closed. Hours are Sunday through Thursday from 8 a.m. to 6 p.m., on Friday and eves of holidays to 1 p.m.; closed Saturday and holidays.

The **Eilat Municipal Tourist Information Office** (tel. 059-74233) is another helpful resource; it's located downstairs and around to the rear of the Neptune

Hotel on North Beach. It's open Sunday through Thursday from 8 a.m. to 1 p.m. and again from 2 to 8 p.m., on Friday until 4 p.m., and on Saturday after the Sabbath from 6 until 8 p.m.

TRANSPORTATION: Several daily Arkia flights (tel. 059-76102) link Eilat with points north and south, and sheruts and Egged buses ply the route from Eilat to Beersheba, Sodom, Tel Aviv, and Jerusalem each day. To get around Eilat, there are local buses and taxis. All hotels have bus schedules (in Hebrew).

If you arrive by bus, you will be planted squarely in the center of town on the main street—**Hatmarim** (or **Ha-Temarim**) **Boulevard.** From there, any hotel in town is within walking distance, as are the North Beach hotels if your luggage is light; local city buses 1 and 2 go from the Central Bus Station to the North Beach area, around the lagoon, and down as far as the Jordanian border. Better take a taxi, or city bus 15, if you're heading out to Coral Beach. You can also leave your luggage at the bus station while you go in search of accommodations.

If you arrive at Eilat's little downtown airport, you will be right at the bottom of the hill, where Hatmarim Boulevard meets Ha-Arava Road (the road north to Beersheba). It will be only a ten-minute walk or less to almost any of our Hatmarim Boulevard hotels, or to the hotels on the North Beach.

All the local city buses (1, 2, and 15) run every 20 to 30 minutes or so, from early morning until about 7 or 8 p.m. They run seven days a week, stopping early on Friday (about 3 or 4 p.m.) in observation of the Sabbath.

The downtown airport can receive only small aircraft such as Arkia's De-Havilland Dash 7s. Larger planes, such as jumbo jets, land at Ouvda airport some 60 km (37 miles) north of Eilat. During the season from October through April, many charter jets come in from Europe, as Eilat is a favorite sunny winter resort for Europeans; at times during this period, you'll feel like you're in summertime Sweden, France, or some other country as you walk around Eilat and look at the passersby. The bus ride from Ouvda to town can take an hour, but highway improvements currently under way should cut that time somewhat.

KEEPING COOL IN EILAT: This is tricky, but it can definitely be done if you don't overbake, if you cover your body and head, and if you drink great quantities of liquid.

The winter is another and far better story. The thick dusty heat is gone, and the air is cool and dry, the sun out continuously, the water warm enough for swimming almost every day.

In the summer, most service establishments in town—hotels, motels, and the moderately priced restaurants—are air-conditioned. In some of the older homes you will still see the Eilat version of air conditioners, which are called "desert coolers." Based on the simple idea of injecting droplets of water in front of a fan, instead of dehumidifying (with an air conditioner) an already dehumidified place, the desert coolers keep indoor Eilat at a comfortable temperature.

During summer, the outdoor afternoon heat exceeds 110°F—they call it 45° Celsius, if that makes it seem better—and it's best to stay in the shade for the three hours between noon and 3 p.m. Severe cases of sunpoisoning are the comeuppance for those who don't heed the precaution. The warm breezes abate at night. Increasingly, Israelis are opting for summer vacations in Eilat. No reason why you shouldn't.

Once again, drink lots and lots of liquids here—winter or summer, whether you feel thirsty or not. The climate here is deceptive; the heat is so dry that even in winter when you don't feel so hot, or even when you're in the shade, the air is parching the liquid out of your body. The sweat dries almost in the same instant it reaches your skin, so you're not aware that you're sweating, or that you're becoming dehydrated.

One of the first symptoms of dehydration is a feeling of extreme fatigue for no apparent reason; if you drink water, you'll start to feel better almost immediately. Another symptom is headache; if you've been sitting down and suddenly get dizzy upon standing up, that's another sign. Water is the best thing to drink. Doctors recommend that during the heat of summer, you can drink three liters (15 glasses) of water every day, and that's not too much. You may feel like a water bottle sloshing around, but believe me, it's better than dehydration.

By the way, you can drink the water in Eilat—thanks to the large desalinization plant. Prior to 1965 many a sightseer had his stay in Eilat ruined by a bad case of "tourist trots" caused largely by the heavy amounts of magnesium in Eilat's water.

ACCOMMODATIONS: There is never really a low tourism season in this popular resort town, except for maybe the months of May and June. From October to the end of April, charter flights bring European tourists escaping the cold European winters; at various times the town may be filled up with Scandinavians, French, or other nationalities. During the Israeli holiday season of July and August the town is full of Israeli vacationers, with some stray summer tourists lingering up until the European charter season begins again in October. In the past, Eilat's high season was considered to be in the relatively cooler winter season; with the prevalence of air conditioning, and the development of the town for tourism, it's now becoming a popular spot all year round.

Since the change is a gradual one, many hotels have developed their own systems for determining when to charge high- and low-season rates. You can generally count on paying high-season rates during July, August, and the Jewish and Christian holidays; many places also charge high-season rates during the October-to-April period, but some do not. I'll give you the high- and low-season rates; bear in mind that the times when each are charged can fluctuate from place to place.

At all of the hotels I'll mention, the kitchens are kosher.

Winter in Eilat is delightful, with warm days and plenty of sun; evenings can be warm, once in a while, but often a chilly wind comes in off the desert when the sun goes down, so be sure to have some warm clothes along with you. Despite the heat, Eilat is a wonderful sea resort even during the summer—if you observe the basic precautions about desert traveling. The Red Sea water is cool and refreshing during the hot part of the summer, when the Mediterranean is about the temperature of a lukewarm bathtub. The sea is calm too, and you can get in some waterskiing, sailboarding, water parachuting, kayaking, and other water sports.

We'll start our hotel explorations right on the main stem, Hatmarim Boulevard, beginning at the bottom of the hill near the airport and the road to Beersheba. As we climb the slope, we'll come to the Egged Bus Station, and look at a few hotels up past here in this central area of town. Then we'll scour the fairly elegant North Beach area for some moderately priced finds. After that, I'll tell you about a couple of affordable hotels on Coral Beach, several miles south of town, and about the various hostels, rooms in private homes, and rental apartments that are available as alternatives to the hotels.

On Hatmarim Boulevard

Start right at the bottom of the hill, near the Shalom Shopping Center and the airport. Walking up, you'll see our hotels all ranged on the left-hand side of the street.

The three-star **Etzion Hotel** (P.O. Box 979, Eilat 88000; tel. 059-74131 or 74132), is on Hatmarim near the bottom of the hill. It has 97 air-conditioned rooms, most with tubs in the private baths. There's a large dining room, sauna, swimming pool, snackbar, and nightclub with nightly programs of music, singing, etc.; video movies too. Rates are $32 to $36 single, $44 to $52 double; if you stay for seven nights, you pay for five, except in high season. Special discount prices may be in effect at certain times; students always get a 10% discount.

The **Red Sea Hotel**, Hatmarim Boulevard (P.O. Box 277, Eilat 88000; tel. 059-72171 or 72172), two stars, is next to the tourism office. Here you'll find 40 rooms (including six large ones suitable for families), all with toilet, shower, telephone intercom, air conditioning and wall-to-wall carpeting. Singles pay $19 to $29; and doubles pay $30 to $43, depending on the time of year. There's a small swimming pool. Students get a 10% discount, and any guest gets the seventh night's stay for free.

The 31-room, air-conditioned **Eilat Center Hotel** (P.O. Box 414, Eilat 88103; tel. 059-73176, 73177, or 73178) is on Hatmarim directly opposite the bus station. It is actually a studio apartment rental place which rates three stars. Each room has wall-to-wall carpeting, sofa, kitchenette, small refrigerator, cutlery (pots and pans are limited to first come, first grab), and private bath and shower. There's also a TV room. Including continental breakfast, single room price is $23 to $29, $40 double in low season; and $36 to $42 single, $64 double in high season; prices are between these figures for most of the year. If you prefer a no-breakfast plan, you'll pay $2.50 per person less. Students get a 10% reduction. You can borrow a mask and snorkel for no extra charge; there's a Ping-Pong table too. You're going to think I've misled you, as the Center Hotel doesn't really look like a hotel. But, sure enough, it's there, right at the back of the plaza with the post office and a cinema. The reception desk is a little kiosk.

On Ha-Negev Boulevard

Walk up the hill just a bit farther on Hatmarim Boulevard and turn right just after the Hamashbir Lazarchan department store. Now you're on Hativat Ha-Negev Boulevard. A short way down on the left-hand side is our next choice.

A very pleasant hotel, set in a garden, is the small, one-star **Dekel (or Ha-Dekel) Hotel,** Hativat Ha-Negev Boulevard (P.O. Box 525; tel. 059-73191). Accommodations are modest but clean. Showers and toilets, and desert coolers to keep out the heat, have been installed in the 17 rooms, and the gardens around the hotel are beautiful: palm trees, bougainvillea, and other flowers blooming in the desert. Prices are a bargain: $21 to $24 single, $29 to $33 double, continental breakfast and service included. Add $2 per person more on Jewish holidays and Christmas. Rooms come with up to four beds. The Dekel is more or less behind the Egged Bus Station, so if you come by bus you can simply trot around to the back, down the hill, and spot the hotel.

Near Elot Street

Two nice, new choices have opened up farther up the hill into town (but still not more than a ten-minute walk from the bus station).

Tower Apartments, in the Tzofit Elite (Mor) Center at the corner of Elot and Anafa Streets (P.O. Box 2007, Eilat 88104; tel. 059-75136 or 75139), offers 38 studio apartments and eight suites, each with two large family rooms holding from two to six people. All come with fully equipped kitchenette, bathroom with tub, telephone, air conditioning, and balcony with chairs and a nice view. Prices include room cleaning and daily towel changes; bed-and-breakfast rates are $23 single, $35 double most of the year; a few dollars less during May and June, and a few dollars more during July, August, and holidays.

The two-star **Melony Club Hotel**, 6 Los Angeles St. (P.O. Box 520, Eilat 88000; tel. 059-73181 or 73185), is another fine choice, with 18 double or single rooms, plus another 18 family rooms for four or five people, each with kitchenette, toilet and shower, air conditioning, telephone, and a good view. There's a swimming pool with lounge chairs all around, a television and video room in the lobby, and a lovely rooftop pub with a fine view of the Gulf of Eilat. Bed-and-breakfast prices remain the same all year: $26 single, $41 double, except for holidays when they go up 20%.

Near the New Tourist Center

The New Tourist Center, right across (west of) the main highway from North Beach at the corner of Derekh Ha-Arava and Derekh Yotam, is a useful landmark and a prime nightlife area for Eilat's younger crowd. The location is supremely convenient.

Just to the rear of the New Tourist Center is the three-star **Edomit Hotel** (P.O. Box 425, Eilat 88105; tel. 059-79511 or 79514), eight stories tall, whose 85 rooms all command a nice sea view, and come with heat and air conditioning, radio and telephone, and a color TV room. Prices remain the same most of the year, at $39 single, $53 double, going up only during holidays, when a supplementary charge of $8 per room is added. A dairy dinner is available for an extra $7. The Edomit has single, double, triple, or quadruple rooms, and family plans too.

Behind the New Tourist Center, up the hill and off Yotam Boulevard, is the two-star **Adi Hotel** (P.O. Box 4100, Eilat 88000; tel. 059-76151 or 76153), a newish, modern place with 32 rooms. It's fairly well hidden, so look for the red-and-white "ADI" sign, which is on the wall of the hotel, about 50 yards west up the hill behind the New Tourist Center in the Zofit (or Tzofit) Tahtit section of town. When you get to the hotel, you'll find a small and congenial building faced with nubbly stucco, with a shady front patio and air-conditioned guest rooms, all with private baths (tubs) and telephones. Some rooms have balconies with a Red Sea view. Prices are $32.25 single, $41.50 double, but readers of this book get special reduced prices of $20 single, $30 double, except for Jewish and Christian holidays, when rates rise to $35 single, $46 double. These prices are for people arriving at the hotel; rates may be higher if you're reserving in advance, so be sure to clarify the price you'll pay at the time you reserve your room. The Adi's location is great: quiet, with views, yet walking distance to the beach.

On North Beach

By looking down from the town on the glimmering lights of North Beach and the Lagoon, you wouldn't think it was a budget-hotel area. Well, most of it is definitely not. Four-star hotels abound, and prices soar in this choice location. But search carefully and you can find rooms easily within our budget.

The two-star **Dalia Hotel** (tel. 059-75127), near the elegant Galei Eilat Hotel, has 52 air-conditioned rooms, all with toilet and private bath or shower, telephone, and radio. Rates in this prime location are $28 single, $46 double. Students get a 10% discount during May and June. Downstairs is the Copacabana nightclub, one of the most popular in town, with '60s dance music from 9:30 until 11:30 p.m., when the cabaret show begins, which may include juglers, acrobatics, singers, and even a striptease show (male or female). Hotel guests get a 20% price reduction at the Copacabana. There's also a swimming pool, and the Red Sea and North Beach are just a minute away.

The **Bel Hotel** (P.O. Box 897; tel. 059-76121 or 76123), behind the Moriah

Hotel, has two stars, 84 rooms, and a pleasant ambience. It's a three-minute walk from the sea. All rooms have private bath with tub, toilet, air conditioning, phone, and a terrace. There's a dining room and bar on the premises. Bed-and-breakfast rates, including an Israeli breakfast, are $23 single, $36 double, going up to $33 single, $46 double during high season (which at this hotel is calculated to be about half the year).

Two new three-star hotels are located over behind the lagoon, both within our budget range.

The **Americana Hotel** (P.O. Box 27, Eilat 88000; tel. 059-75176 or 75179) has a young, active holiday atmosphere, and a policy of doing everything possible to give its guests an enjoyable vacation so that they'll return again. Its 106 rooms are situated around a large swimming pool/terrace with one huge pool and another, smaller one for children; 40 rooms have private balconies, 26 have private kitchenettes, and all come with wall-to-wall carpet, bath and shower, air conditioning and heat, radio, and telephone. Video films are shown daily in the TV room; volleyball, basketball, water-sports bookings, billiards, darts, and table tennis are all available. The Americana disco is the most popular one in town with young folks from around ages 18 to 22; it's open nightly from 10 p.m. until 2 a.m., and while there's a NIS10 ($6.65) admission charge for outsiders, it's free for hotel guests. There is also a candlelight dinner with live piano music every night during the high season. Prices are $46 single, $64 double during much of the year, with a significant price rise during holidays, dropping to $42 single, $53 double in the low season.

Nearby is the **Moon Valley Hotel** (P.O. Box 1135, Eilat 88000; tel. 059-75111 or 75118), with 196 air-conditioned rooms with tub and shower, spread out in one-story buildings arranged around a large swimming pool; billiards, video movies, and other entertainment are in the lobby. Here, too, there's a nightclub and a disco, open nightly from 10:30 p.m. on, with no cover charge. Prices are $35 single, $46 double most of the year, rising to $40 single, $53 double during high season.

The **Queen of Sheba** (P.O. Box 196; tel. 059-72121 or 72126), located right on the beach, is the least expensive of the four-star hotels in North Beach, with low-season rates at $35 single, $46 double; regular-season prices of $40 single, $69 double; and high-season rates up out of our price range at $52 single, $75 double. The 92-room hotel has every luxury you can think of.

Also right on the beach, but farther down toward the Jordanian border, is the **Blue Sky Caravan Holiday Village** (P.O. Box 621, Eilat 88105; tel. 059-73953 or 73954). It's a collection of 64 small travel trailers, set in their own park. Each trailer (or "caravan," the British word) has a bathroom with toilet, shower, kitchenette, desert cooler, and two or more beds. The beach is only steps from your door. The standard Israeli breakfast is included in the rates. Blue Sky's rates are good, and even better when you consider that you get your own kitchenette: $20 single, $25 double, all in. Add 20% for holiday periods.

Nearby is the **Sun Bay Camping and Holiday Village**, North Beach (tel. 059-73105 or 73106), virtually on the Jordanian border. All but 10 of the 63 bungalows have air conditioning; about a third have their own private toilet and shower. Prices, which do not include breakfast, remain the same all year: $20 single, $25 double ($27 on weekends and holidays). The bungalows that have no air conditioning and share a public shower are cheaper, priced at $7 per person (up to four in a room). Students get a 10% discount. You can also rent camping sites for $3.50 per person, but you must provide your own tent. A restaurant and food store are on the premises. The bungalows at Sun Bay are clean, with colored curtains and bedspreads, facilities throughout are quite good, and the beach is especially beautiful.

On Coral Beach

Catch a no. 15 bus along Hatmarim Boulevard or Ha-Arava Road to get to Coral Beach, for a swim or to bed down at the **Caravan Sun Club Hotel** (tel. 059-73145 or 73146). The Caravan operates as a two-star hotel, although its facilities and its 108-room size seem to qualify it for more stellar recognition. Forty of the rooms have bathrooms with tubs; the rest come with showers. All are air-conditioned, with their own private terraces with tables and chairs, facing onto lawns in this rambling, comfortable, informal hotel. On the swimming pool terrace are a bar, cafeteria, billiards, table tennis, and all in all a very pleasant ambience; the hotel also has its own facilities for skindiving, sailboarding, boating, sailing, horse riding, and bicycling, plus desert safaris, a candlelight bar, a discothèque, and a children's playground. Rates for most of the year are $27 single, $36 double; during August and holidays, it's $35 single, $46 double. The Red Sea Sport Club (tel. 059-76985) is housed on one side of the hotel, with rentals and lessons on many sports.

The **Coral Sea Hotel** (tel. 059-79555), while so new it has not yet been graded, rates about three or four stars, and is a fine place to stay if you can get a room there; since it's so nice for the price, it's often booked up half a year in advance, but it's well worth a try. Many extra touches here, including a large swimming pool and smaller children's pool, whirlpool bath, snackbar and Bedouin tent (with camel and all) by the pool, volleyball, aerobics and pool games, video movies daily, evening entertainment with piano and singing from 6 to 9 p.m., and a nightclub with a show nightly at 10 p.m. (no cover charge). The 144 rooms in the six-story tower all have nice sea views, air conditioning, bathtubs, and every comfort. Prices for all this are $34 single, $46 double all year, except for holidays when rates are 20% higher. This hotel is just across from Eilat's Club Méditerranée.

At the other end of the spectrum, **Coral Beach Camping** ("Almog" Beach in Hebrew; tel. 059-71911 or 79272), right across from the Coral Beach Nature Reserve, has Caroline bungalows with two to five beds, renting for $11 single, $13 double, and $5 per child. These rates include hot showers but no breakfast; no cooking facilities here, but there's a snackbar, and a market nearby. You can also pitch your own tent, paying $2.50 per adult, $2 per child.

Yigal's Camping (P.O. Box 994, Eilat; tel. 059-76461), located directly across from the Underwater Aquarium/Observatory, also rents bungalows, each with its own shower and toilet. Prices are $11 single, $17 double, $22 triple.

Hostels

Eilat's **IYHA Youth Hostel** (P.O. Box 152; tel. 059-72358) is just south of the New Tourist Center, at the southern limits of Eilat. A long flight of steps leads up the hill to the modern hostel, which boasts 160 beds in air-conditioned dormitories, dining room, and beach nearby. The office is open for registration from 7 to 10 a.m. and 4 to 11 p.m.; there's a lockout period during the day between 9 a.m. and 4 p.m., but no evening curfew. Prices are standard: $6.50 for IYHA members, $7.50 for nonmembers. A landmark: Look for the Red Rock Hotel on the North Beach, then look west (inland) to spot the hostel. Due to Eilat's popularity with young people, the official youth hostel is often full; when it nears the full-up point, IYHA members are given preference.

Luckily, Eilat is a town of many hostels. Most of them are located near the bus station. When you come into town, if you're carrying a backpack, you'll likely be met as you alight from the bus by runners for various hostels, asking if you need a room. Although many of the hostels are more or less the same, you should check several, and be sure to see the accommodations you'll get, before you pay. Some of the private hostels have four to six beds in each room; some have 20 or more. Some have a private toilet and shower in the room; others have a communal shower down the hall. Prices vary by a few shekels, roughly NIS8 ($5.35) to NIS12 ($8) per person per night.

Of the hostels right across the street from the bus station, the **Red Mountain Hostel,** 137/2 Hativat Ha-Negev St. (Eilat 88000; tel. 059-74936), is clean, with an average of six people per room, private toilet, sink and shower in every room, a nice patio terrace out front, and a pub/TV room with good music and video movies. Prices are NIS10 ($6.65) during the week, NIS12 ($8) on weekends; on weekends, you must book for both Friday and Saturday nights. Mixed or single-sex rooms, as you prefer.

There are many other hostels nearby from which to choose. You can leave your bags at the bus station baggage-check counter and walk around to visit several, since they're all so close.

Camping

Eilat and the areas surrounding it are lovely for camping, with the warm weather, placid sea, and beautiful beaches. Campers from many countries can be found around Eilat. Several camping and holiday villages offer bungalows or trailers for rent, in addition to space for tents. Since they do provide a roof over your head, I've put them in the hotel section, in all the appropriate areas of town.

Several other campgrounds offer places where you can put down a tent, especially along the strip of coast south of Eilat heading toward Taba, at the Egyptian border.

Many people prefer not to pay at an organized campground, but rather to put up their tents along the beach for free. This is common and acceptable in Eilat and the environs; in fact, south of town, and also east toward the Jordanian border, it became such a common practice that the municipality of Eilat has now set up bathroom facilities with showers and plenty of drinkable water for the use of these campers. You can pitch your tent anywhere; one favorite spot is at **Taba Beach,** beside the Egyptian border; another is on **North Beach** right beside the Jordanian border. In general, Taba is preferred by a younger, more hip crowd, and North Beach by families and older, more sedate types. At North Beach (in front of Sun Bay Camping) you can pull your car right up to the sandy beach, and it's not a bad idea to tie your tent to your car, or otherwise nail it down—the desert winds can be very strong. The view from this beach is especially lovely, with the mountains of Jordan on one side, of Israel and Egypt on the other, and a straight view down the finger of water forming the Gulf of Eilat.

At either of these public sites, or any others, you must, of course, use normal common sense as relates to thievery and safety, just as you would need to do anywhere in the world.

Rooms and Apartments

Another option in Eilat is to rent a room in someone's home, or if you prefer, a whole apartment. You can ask at the **I.G.T.O.** (tel. 059-72268), across from the bus station, or at the **Eilat Municipal Tourist Information Office** (tel. 059-74233), near the Neptune Hotel on North Beach, for recommendations on agencies and individuals from whom to rent; be aware that, while you'll see several rental agencies around Eilat, it's best to use these established tourism offices for referral, since there have been complaints from people using other sources. Prices for a two-bedroom apartment (holding four people or more) are about $30 (up to $50) per day during most of the year, $50 to $80 per day during high season (July, August, and holidays). Especially for a group of people, this is one of the best ways to economize in Eilat.

RESTAURANTS: As you might expect in a burgeoning resort community, Eilat has a plentiful supply of places where one can get a hamburger, falafel, plate of spaghetti, or omelet. But good, true restaurants are more difficult to come by. They exist, though, and I'll lead you to them while mentioning the better snack and light-meal establishments.

For ease of orientation, I've grouped my restaurant recommendations under five headings corresponding with the five places you're most likely to find yourself during a stay in Eilat.

Near Hatmarim Boulevard

Ascending the slope of Hatmarim Boulevard from the airport, the left-hand side of the street is virtually paved with little cafés, sidewalk snackshops, quick-service restaurants, and eateries of every type. It's impossible to choose from among them as prices, owners, staff, policies, and menus seem to change several times even during the same winter tourist season. Suffice it to say that you should have no trouble locating your desired light lunch here, indoors in air-conditioned comfort or outdoors at a shady patio table. Take a tip from me though: beware of places with lots and lots of empty tables, especially at meal-times.

Hatmarim does hold some real restaurants, though, all of them up above the Egged Bus Station and the intersection with Hativat Ha-Negev Street. And the farther up you go, the better (or cheaper) they become—once you leave the press of the crowd, prices go down.

Yemenite specialties and Arabic food are served at the kosher **Ha-Kerem ("Spitzer") Restaurant,** Eilat Street, corner of Hatmarim (tel. 059-74577). Meatballs with chips, salad, or rice are offered, as are the likes of cow stomach or lungs, grilled or roast beef, chicken cutlets, and goulash. Any of these come with rice, salad, or chips for only NIS3.50 ($2.35), and a glass of arak (anise brandy) is another NIS1.20 (80¢). It's open Sunday through Thursday from noon to 3 p.m. and again from 6 to 9:30 p.m., closing on Friday at 3 p.m., re-opening Saturday evening after the Sabbath. The decor here is very plain, almost stark, except for the family photographs of the elaborate Yemenite costumes worn on special occasions; but the food is delicious.

Another fine, inexpensive choice in this area is **Pundak Habira,** on Almogim Street a couple of blocks down the hill from Hatmarim Boulevard (no street address or phone). It's another of those popular-with-the-locals places, patronized not for its fancy decor (nonexistent here) but for its large portions of tasty food. Choose from many meat dishes—goulash, roast chicken or beef, liver, meatballs, pork steak, stuffed cabbage or peppers, etc.—and an equally wide selection of hearty soups and salads, and the whole meal of soup, salad, bread, main course, and a beer will come in at around NIS9 ($6); you can easily eat here for under $5 by choosing from the à la carte menu. Pundak Habira is open for lunch only, from noon until 3 p.m., every day except Friday and Saturday.

Then, of course, there's the restaurant in the **Egged Bus Station,** at the corner of Hatmarim and Hativat Ha-Negev, which, as in so many places in Israel, may be the least glamorous restaurant in town, but also the one at which you can get the most good, wholesome food for the money. Sunday through Friday it's open for breakfast from 7 to 10 a.m. and for lunch between 11:30 a.m. to 3 p.m. (closed Saturday). You can get a hearty lunch here—soup, salad, a main course of chicken or fish (for example), vegetables, bread, and juice—all for NIS5 ($3.35).

From downtown Eilat it's only a short taxi ride to the **El Gaucho Argentinian Grill Restaurant** (tel. 059-71009), on Derekh Ha-Arava at the entrance to

Eilat, open daily from noon until 1 a.m. Here you'll find authentic South American cuisine, decor, music, and even South American chefs in gaucho outfits—and great food at a great price. Huge portions of fresh beef, veal, and chicken are served up with all the deluxe trimmings, including the special authentic chimichurra sauce; a full, large meal will cost about NIS12 ($8), all included.

In the Shalom Center

The big shopping-and-eating complex at the foot of Hatmarim across from the airport is called the Shalom Center. Within it are several places to get a bite, including the **Pancake House** (tel. 059-73692), open from 8 a.m. to midnight daily, on Saturday from 10 a.m. to midnight. Many tables have a view of the airport (?) and North Beach, there's a bar/lunch counter, and the menu (in English) lists pancakes priced from NIS3 ($2) for a simple, plain pancake to NIS9 ($6) for the "Sundae." Note that these are thick American-style pancakes, not thin crêpes. Despite its name, the Pancake House has a full list of restaurant dishes as well, including roast beef, goulash, steak, chicken, and burgers. Prices for these more substantial items are in the same range as for pancakes. You might like to try the other house specialty: Mexican chili, which for NIS6 ($4) comes with salad and chips or rice.

In the New Tourist Center

Eilat has various building "complexes," as you have already noticed on Hatmarim Boulevard. One such commercial complex, known as the New Tourist Center, is right at the intersection of Ha-Arava Road (the north-south highway) and Yotam Road, at the western limits of North Beach. The New Tourist Center is not handsome as buildings go—its jumble of signs, shops, and stairways is a riot of colors, shapes, and styles, especially at night—but it serves Eilat's purposes. It serves ours too. North Beach is not far away, and the New Tourist Center harbors all sorts of eateries for famished beachniks.

In past editions of this book I've recommended various restaurants and eateries in the complex. But these days ownership and standards are changing so fast that it's impossible to know which places will remain good from season to season. Best idea is to look upon Hatmarim Boulevard as the street for restaurants, and the New Tourist Center as the place for beach snacks and light fare.

Near North Beach

My favorite spot on North Beach is **Rhapsody in White** (tel. 059-74646), the restaurant/bar out on the east end of the marina, floating in the bay. On one side is a large water slide, on the other a lovely indoor/outdoor restaurant and bar, with a gorgeous view, pleasant music—all in all a most enjoyable place. You can come for a full meal, a light meal (pizza, omelet, chef's salad, etc.), or simply a drink or a cup of coffee, and sit over the water to enjoy the beautiful scene. There's a nightly dinner special, at a bargain price; you might find fresh Red Sea fish with soup, salad and chips for NIS12 ($8). If you come during the evening, you'll see how fresh this fish really is: a fisherman in a little boat fishes right off the side of the floating restaurant deck, catching fish attracted to the lights of the restaurant shining into the water. I've sat here of an evening with the water lapping just a few feet from my table and watched larger fish chasing smaller ones, seen foot-long squid feeding on the small Red Sea fish—only to see the fisherman come by and catch the squid, to be used as calamari in the restaurant. There is live dancing music at least three times a week, nightly in summer, and a full bar. Open daily from 9 a.m. until at least 10 p.m., until 2 a.m. or even later when it's busy.

Various burger, falafel, and pizza shacks are set up around the main North

Beach area, but there's also one very enjoyable, budget-priced restaurant. It's the **Oasis Restaurant** (tel. 059-72414), right at the western end of the footbridge across the lagoon channel (the huge Queen of Sheba Hotel is on the other, east, side of the footbridge). Low, squat, decked with stuffed fish, nets, and other nautical paraphernalia, with dining either indoors or out on the covered patio, the Oasis is just that— a low-budget, fun place in a high-price desert. The mood here is extremely informal, offbeat, and friendly, a big contrast to the polish and politeness of the surrounding hotels. Portions tend toward the huge and hearty (the grilled chicken portion is half a chicken). A full dinner of fresh fish or chicken, liver or sausages, with salad platter, potatoes, and a jug of wine, including tip, will cost around NIS16 ($10.65), all in. Open every day from 1 p.m. to midnight.

All the way at the other end of North Beach, down by the Jordanian border between Aqaba and Eilat, is **The Last Stop** (tel. 059-75798), a nice, informal kosher restaurant with a menu special that's a very good deal: for NIS10 ($6.65) you get all you can eat of fresh fish and a number of fresh salads, plus all the wine you can drink, up to an entire bottle of wine for each person. You're served at your red-tableclothed, candlelit table. Also on the menu are steak, chicken, hamburgers, and so on, priced from NIS7 ($4.65) to NIS10 ($6.65), and other light meals and salads. It's open from noon to 11 p.m., closing on Friday at 4 p.m. and reopening on Saturday after the Sabbath at around 7 p.m. There's a stage here for live music and space for dancing; when a special show is being staged, it's put on after the 11 p.m. closing time, and is advertised in the local bulletins.

On Coral Beach

Just across from the Tour Yam glass-bottom-boat marina is a row of many ethnic restaurants—French, Moroccan, steak, barbecue, and so on. But set off to itself is a place I enjoy immensely: **The Fisherman's House** (tel. 059-79830), a large, very informal self-service, all-you-can-eat restaurant with lots of long tables indoors and also on the terrace out front. This is a great place to come for a casual meal when you're really hungry, as you can keep on returning to the self-service line for more servings of about six kinds of fish cooked in different ways (baked, fried, in sauce, etc.), savory rice, baked potatoes, cooked vegetables, and several kinds of fresh salads—all for only NIS8.80 ($5.85). Children up to age 10 eat for half price. For the same price, you can also get meat or chicken from the grill, but only one big serving—and still get all you can eat of everything else. Desserts and drinks cost extra; with ice cream and espresso after your meal, your bill will come to about NIS12 ($8). It's open from noon to midnight seven days a week.

Right across the street, beside Tours Yam, is a more elegant fish restaurant, **The Last Refuge** (tel. 059-72437), with an attractive nautical decor, tables inside or out on the seaside terrace, and generous portions of fish and seafood, with a full dinner coming for about NIS22 ($14.65) to NIS28 ($18.65). Open seven days, from noon to 3:30 p.m. and again from 6 p.m. to midnight.

Down the road about 200 yards, across from the Coral Beach Nature Reserve, is another more expensive fish and seafood restaurant, **La Barracuda** (tel. 059-73442 or 74080), with an accent on French cuisine. Quality is high here; you choose the fish you want from a large platter, and also choose any way of preparing it, including grilled, fried, etc., and a choice of six gourmet French sauces. There's also lobster, shark soup, a full bar, French desserts, and a most enjoyable decor. Prices for fish, chips, and salad run NIS20 ($13.35); a full extravaganza meal with soup, appetizer, wine, dessert, coffee, and tip comes to about NIS25 ($16.65) to NIS40 ($26.65). Open from 1 to 4 p.m. and 6 p.m. to midnight seven days a week.

With awards for excellence lining its entrance walls, **Mandy's Chinese Restaurant** (tel. 059-72238), above the Aqua Sport complex on the beach across from the Club Med, serves Szechuan and Cantonese specialties. Eggrolls, sweet-and-sour pork or fish, spareribs, and a number of Thai dishes (chicken with lemon and mint, for instance) are on the 108-item menu. It's a fairly elegant place, with the usual indoor air-conditioned dining room or outdoor sea-breeze-swept patio. Prices reflect the elegance and the quality of the cuisine, and the set-price menu is NIS17 ($11.35) for the menu for two persons, although soup and main course ordered à la carte will be a good deal less. Mandy's is open from noon to 3 p.m. and 6:30 p.m. to midnight, seven days a week.

TOURS AND SIGHTS: Eilat offers a wealth of activities to investigate before you go plummeting into the wide expanses of Sinai. If you wish to join up with a tour, consult section 6 in this chapter for most of the required information—Sinai and Eilat are usually considered one great tour arena, and nearly all the major operators cited either include Eilat in their itineraries or use the city as the jumping-off point.

Boat Cruises, Boats for Hire, Snorkeling, Scuba-diving, Etc.

You can hire boats 24 hours a day at the North Beach marina and lagoon—boats for waterskiing, water parachuting, sailboats, fishing boats, paddleboats, motor sea-cycles, sailboards, kayaks, and motorboats are all available.

The best-equipped firm for snorkeling and scuba-diving is **Aqua Sport,** also called the **International Red Sea Diving Center** (P.O. Box 300; tel. 059-72788). Right across the highway from the Caravan Sun Club Hotel on Coral Beach, the Aqua Sport center can fulfill your needs for mask, fins, and snorkel, wet suits, weightbelts, depth gauges, buoyancy compensators, cylinders, etc. Diving lessons (in English), diving tours (half or full day), even three-day camping/diving safaris are on the program. A six-day diving course ($150) leads to international-ly recognized two-star diver certification; with six days' bed-and-breakfast at the divers' hostel, the cost comes to $220. Many other programs are offered as well, including rental and lessons in sailboarding. Bed-and-breakfast at the Aqua Sport hostel is $10 per day in double or quadruple rooms. Aqua Sport also has a program of week-long summer camps for kids ages 10 to 15 during July and August; parents can leave the kids and go off for a week, and the kids are exposed to a world of underwater and maritime activities and fun. Also operating through Aqua Sport is the **David Pilosof School of Underwater Photography,** with half-day to 14-day programs on underwater video and still photography. In the evening, there's a pub, underwater video films, and occasional live entertainment, dancing, etc. Aqua Sport is open every day from 8:30 a.m. until 2:30 a.m.

Red Sea Sport Club, located at the Caravan Sun Club Hotel (tel. 059-76985), is another diving center near Coral Beach. It offers facilities similar to those at Aqua Sport, plus other activities including sailing and boating, deep-sea fishing, night cruises, desert safaris, horseback riding, canoes and paddle-boats, waterskiing, and bicycle rental, in addition to its diving and sailboarding programs. It's open daily from 8:30 a.m. until 4:30 p.m. in winter, until 6 p.m. in summer.

On North Beach, there's **Lucky Divers** (tel. 059-75749), located downstairs in the Moriah Hotel, facing the beach. It also offers rental of diving equipment and a number of organized diving programs.

All of the above places offer introductory dives for people who have never dived before and want to try it out. It costs about $30 for an hour-long, one-to-one session with a diving instructor, who spends about half an hour giving you the instruction you need to go down and another half hour with you 18 to 20 feet below the water, out in the Red Sea coral reefs. This is a great way to get a short introduction to diving before committing yourself to a full six-day program.

And in the etc. category, there's **Raffi Pipson's** polygon-shaped place on the shore across from the Caravan Sun Club Hotel (tel. 059-72909). Here you can loll on the beach, skindive, snack, shower, surf, sunbathe, and swim. Raffi is a licensed underwater and desert guide. For nonswimmers he provides air mattresses, snorkels, masks, and fins to explore the wonders of Coral Beach—$9 for the works. Swimmers can rent the equipment without the mattress. He also rents kayaks and flatboats. Daytime activities are on from 7 or 8 a.m. until sunset. At night there's a disco from 10:30 p.m. until. . . .

Glass-Bottom Boats

Leaving from the jetty just north of Coral Beach, or from North Beach near the Neptune Hotel, these boats offer a wonderful view of a fairytale marine world. You putt-putt out into the bay, and through the glass below you see the beginnings of tall mounds of coral on the fluted, pale-green sandy floor. Then the waters turn a deeper green, the mounds of coral grow higher and thicker, and soon clusters of rainbow-colored fish are darting under your eyes—brilliantly blue fish, long-finned purple fish, pink blowfish, yellow and red striped fish. It's like looking into a giant, complex aquarium in Technicolor and Cinemascope, and the sight you see is that of a new world of mountains and soft plains, of sea creatures darting this way and that, slithering into crevices to escape marauding sand sharks and frolicking on the slopes of coral mountains. You can't help being hypnotized by this silent, dream-like world. Two companies that operate out of the North Beach marina, near the Neptune Hotel, are **Tour Yam Ltd.** (tel. 059-75353), and **Israel Yam** (tel. 059-77925). Israel Yam operates daily 1½-hour glass-bottom-boat trips leaving North Beach several times throughout the day, for $4.50 per person. Tour Yam's glass-bottom boats leave from its wharf just north of Coral Beach (tel. 059-72111 or 72436), every hour on the hour between 10 a.m. and 3 p.m. for a 50-minute trip down by the Coral Beach Nature Reserve and the Underwater Observatory/Aquarium. Cost is $4.

Sailboat Cruises

Several sailboats will take you on a full-day (10 a.m. to 5 p.m.) excursion to Taba, on the Egyptian border, or to Coral Island and the Fjord, two points of interest along the Egyptian Sinai coast south of Eilat. If you go to the Egyptian coast, you can't land (you won't have a visa, and there's no Customs post on the beach!), but you can swim from the boat, snorkel, relax in the sun on board, and have a lunch which is included in the cost of the cruise. For a bit more money, you can take your turn waterskiing or sailboarding. You can choose either full-day or half-day trips. Cost for all day is about $15, lunch included (several of the boats have kosher kitchens); prices start at around $6 for a simple sail. You can just walk along the marina in front of the North Beach lagoon any day and take a look at all the boats to choose from, seeing which appeal to you; you can also reserve in advance (not a bad idea to make sure you get a space) at most travel agencies, at the marina, or at large hotel desks.

Coral World Underwater Observatory and Aquarium

Located just south of Coral Beach, this unusual installation is genuinely fascinating. The complex consists of three one-story buildings on the beach with distinctive rounded roofs, and the observatory, which has been sunk into position 100 yards out to sea in that part of the coral reef known as the Japanese Gardens. A pier binds the observatory to the coast. Of the three buildings, two are the Maritime Museum and Aquarium (P.O. Box 829, Eilat; tel. 059-76666), with fascinating collections of live fish—some of which glow in the dark! The aquarium is built on the "fish roundabout" plan: you stand in the middle, and the fish swim around you in a huge circular tank. The third building is a pleasant snackbar-café. There are also large outdoor observation pools—one for big sharks, another for sea turtles and rays. The tower of the observatory rises out of the sea to a height of 20 feet; inside, a spiral staircase of 42 steps leads down to the observatory itself. Since the water in the gulf is generally crystal clear, observation of the magnificent fish and coral life is unparalleled. It's like scuba-diving without the cost, danger, or inconvenience!

The best time to visit the observatory (open from 8:30 a.m. to 4:30 p.m., until 3 p.m. on Friday) is between noon and 3 p.m. Admission for an adult is NIS9 ($6), and NIS5 ($3.35) for children ages 5 to 16. The Eilat local city bus 15 comes this way every half hour.

Swimming in the Red Sea

You have a choice of swimming spots in Eilat: either use the sand beach in front of the **Moriah Hotel** as far as the Sun Bay Caravan on one side, or Coral Beach, which is a short drive around the curve of the bay. The beach near the Moriah Hotel rents waterskis and boats, but make sure you know where you're going, because you don't have to ski very far to get into both Jordanian—and hot—water. My preference, though, is **Coral Beach.** It's quiet, inundated with coral and fish, and always less crowded. And at Coral Beach you can swim underwater (by all means get a snorkel) and see the shimmering emerald waters and the bed of red coral stone. Hundreds of underwater prowlers have picked the floor of the sea clean around here, but if you're lucky, you may still find some interesting shells. At both beach areas there are cafés and shaded structures designed to keep you cool.

Although the waters around Eilat are safe, always take the elementary precautions of not going out too far alone, keeping in mind that depth is deceptive where the water is so clear, and understanding that the numerous sharks sharing the sea with you are not particularly hungry for you. You'd better know, too, that the corals and shells are protected by law; it is *strictly forbidden* to remove them from the water or to collect them from the beaches.

Coral Beach Nature Reserve

The Coral Beach Nature Reserve (tel. 059-73988) is located just down the coast south of Eilat; you can take city bus 15 from downtown Eilat, running half-hourly, and be at Coral Beach in about 15 or 20 minutes. It's a beautiful place, developed and set aside by the Israel Nature Reserves Authority for its wonderful natural coral reefs teeming with colorful, exotic sea fishes of every description. When you go in, you get a flyer pointing out a number of underwater trails; for NIS6 ($4) you can rent a snorkel, mask and fins, or you can bring your own, or your diving gear. You can also make arrangements here for an introductory dive; for about NIS47 ($31.35), you can have a one-to-one session with a diving instructor, who will take you down and introduce you to what it feels like to dive, with about half an hour to give you the instruction you'll need, and another half an hour several meters down below the water in the coral reefs. You can buy an illustrated book here for NIS5.50 ($3.65) telling about all the various fish, wildlife, and coral living here in the sea.

An important warning: Be very sure to wear some sort of foot covering every time you enter the water here, as the coral can cut your feet, and there are many spiny, stinging sea urchins living in the coral, not to mention rockfish, rays, and other animals that won't bother you unless you step on them—but if you do step on one with your bare feet, you'll certainly wish you hadn't.

The nature reserve and beach is open every day of the year except Yom Kippur, from 8 a.m. to 5 p.m.; there's a fee of NIS3.50 ($2.35) for adults, NIS1.70 ($1.15) for children ages 5 to 17, and NIS1 (65¢) for Eilat residents.

Birdwatching in Eilat

Eilat is one of the best places on earth for birdwatching, due to its prime location on the migration path for birds going between Europe and Africa. Migration times are twice a year: from September through November the birds head south to Africa, and from March through May they head back north to Europe. During spring 1986, more than a million raptors of about 30 different species were counted in the Eilat area; over 400 species of song birds, sea birds, and waterfowl have been recorded. The migration of large birds of prey, especially steppe eagles in the autumn, is especially impressive.

Eilat's **Birdwatching Center** (P.O. Box 774, Eilat; tel. 059-77236 or 71506), with an office in the King Solomon Palace Hotel, is a storehouse for information and activities relating to birdwatching around Eilat. It conducts guided birdwatching tours daily between February 15 and May 30, from 8 to 10 a.m., for a fee of $3; for an extra $1, you can rent a pair of binoculars to use on the hike. Between February 15 and May 15 a general spring census of birds is conducted, and you can participate in this, if you like, and also visit the bird-banding station during the morning hours on most days of the week. Similar activities take place again in the fall. Lectures, nature films, literature, and background material are also offered.

If you're planning a trip to be in Eilat at the best time for birdwatching, try to come during the middle of either the spring or fall seasons. Some of the bird species start out early, some go later, so at the beginning and end of the seasons you'll only see some of the species. During the middle time the species overlap, and you'll see more different kinds.

Israel Palace Museum

The Israel Palace Museum (P.O. Box 167, Eilat 88101; tel. 059-74658), located next to the Caesar Hotel in North Beach, is a unique and moving exhibition of an unusual form of art, made especially poignant by the story of the woman who created it.

The artist, Magda Watts, was born in 1929 in Nyiregyhaza, a town 150 miles from Budapest, Hungary. Throughout her childhood, she enjoyed making dolls. In 1944 the Nazis invaded Hungary and Magda was deported to the concentration camp at Auschwitz, and later to Nurenberg, together with the rest of her family. Consoling herself, she made a doll of bits of cloth. Her mother and two of her sisters went to the gas chambers; her father and brother died of hunger. But when the Nazis saw the doll that Magda had made, they sent her to work in a doll factory, to make dolls for the Nazis. It was probably this work that saved her life; but after the experience of being forced to make the dolls under such circumstances, after Magda got out of the camps she never made another doll for 39 years.

She moved to Israel in 1951 and worked in other art media for many years. In 1983, after a visit to her birthplace and the scenes of her past, she returned to Israel in a deep depression—and for the first time since the war, began making dolls again, in a monumental project of psychological and spiritual catharsis.

The result is what you see on display at this museum: over 1,000 dolls, set up in 54 separate dramatic scenes, showing the history of the Jewish people from Adam and Eve down to the present. The Holocaust scene is in there, and knowing the life of the artist fills this scene with special meaning; but it's only one episode in a long story of a people through generations. The entire collection was designed and executed by Magda herself, including all the painted scenes, the clothing, and everything else. All the dolls are handmade; they are beautiful not for their extravagance as fine art, but rather more for their simplicity and the profound story they tell of the Jewish people, and of the artist Magda Watts and our capacity to heal ourselves.

The museum is open in winter Saturday through Thursday from 9 a.m. to noon and again from 4 to 8 p.m., on Friday and holiday eves from 9 a.m. to 1 p.m. Summer hours are the same, except that the afternoon hours are 6 to 10 p.m. Admission is $4.50 for adults, $2.50 for children.

King Solomon's Pillars

One of the favorite excursions from Eilat is to the **Timna Valley National Park,** 27 km (17 miles) north of Eilat. Tour buses make the trip daily. It's not really practical by public transport unless it's January or February, you allow a very full day, and you don't mind walking miles and miles.

Driving in a private car, head north, pass the Timna Mines (on your left, west), and then in a few kilometers you'll see a sign "Ammude Shelomo," and another saying "Biqe'at Timna." Turn left onto the road indicated, and head west toward the striking, jagged black hills.

Several kilometers in from the highway is the main gate, where you'll pay an admission fee of NIS3 ($2) for adults, NIS2.40 ($1.60) for students, NIS1.50 ($1) for children; hours are 8 a.m. to 4 p.m. daily. Once in the preserve, you follow the road 3½ km to a right turn for the ancient Egyptian copper mines, another kilometer along. The mines consist of sandstone arches, underground mining shafts, and galleries. About three kilometers from the mines, along another side road, is a parking area from which you make the short walk to see a wall face carved with figures in chariots. All these twists and turns are marked clearly by signs.

Along the roads you will have noticed "The Mushroom," a curious rock formation with a huge boulder resting on a column of sandstone, the result of erosion.

But the most striking formation in the preserve is undoubtedly **Solomon's Pillars.** Go back to the main road of the preserve and head east for several kilometers. The pillars, a series of sandstone fins jutting out of a rock face, are at the end of the road. Climb into the fins along a path with steps to see some Egyptian rock carvings, and then down the steps on the other side to the site of a small temple dedicated to the Egyptian goddess Hathor. Not much left of the temple, alas.

The spare, clean air of the desert, the hot sun, the quiet of the preserve are sure to make a lasting impression. You can get information on hiking trails from the staff at the main gate.

The development of Timna Valley National Park has become a major project of the Jewish National Fund of America. A recreational lake and Visitors Center are being built in the Nechushtan Recreation Area not far from Solomon's Pillars and the Sphinx. When completed, the lake will provide facilities for swimming, boating, and fishing.

Hai Bar Wildlife Reserve

The **Hai Bar National Biblical Wildlife Reserve,** all 8,000 acres' worth, is 40 km (24 miles) north of Eilat. Its purpose is to save rare and endangered desert

animals mentioned in the Bible, as well as other rare desert animals of western
Asia and northern Africa, breeding them for eventual release into the wild.
Among the 450 animals found here are the Nubian ibex, the Dorcas gazelle, the
Persian onager, the scimitar-horned oryx, the addax antelope, and the Arabian
gazelle, as well as wolves, hyenas, foxes, desert cats, leopards, cheetahs, wild
donkeys, lots of ostriches, and many species of snakes, lizards, and even preda-
tory birds. Many of these animals are nocturnal, due to the blistering desert
heat, but some example of each nocturnal species is kept in a large area so that it
can be observed. You can ride around the reserve in your car (closed vehicles
only) and observe the animals at close range.

Open from 8:30 a.m. to 1:30 p.m. daily; entrance fee is NIS3 ($2) for
adults, NIS2 ($1.35) for children. The tour takes about two hours, and it's best
to avoid the hot afternoon in summer. If you have no car, take a guided tour
from town.

You'll notice that the Hai Bar Reserve has many trees, signifying that water
is lying below the arid desert. This area is known as the Yotvata Oasis, and it is
believed that this was one of the places where Moses stopped as he brought the
Children of Israel up out of Egypt.

EILAT NIGHTLIFE: Sure enough, in this sun-and-fun resort the crowds move
from beach to bar, disco, or club after the sun goes down. The Israel Government Tourist Office's weekly bulletin, "Events in Eilat," available for free at the
Tourist Office on Hatmarim Boulevard (across the street from the bus station),
will let you know what's happening where.

Several of the **major hotels** have nightclubs, piano bars, and discos. These
are some of the liveliest places in town, patronized by international tourists, Israelis, and native Eilatis alike. The **New Tourist Center** also has a lot going on in
the evening, with several pubs and indoor/outdoor cafés humming with activity.

Various **Israeli folklore evenings** are sponsored by the big hotels, usually
beginning about 9:30 p.m. several nights a week. Music for dancing, or a disco,
often follows the performance. The fee ($5 to $7) includes first drink, or perhaps
wine and cheese.

Movies

The **Cinemathèque Club** screens films in English at the Philip Murray Cultural Center, at the corner of Hatmarim Boulevard and Hativat Ha-Negev.
Regular starting time seems to be around 9 p.m.; admission is charged.

The major hotels often show films as well. Check the Tourist Office's bulletin "Events in Eilat" for details.

ONWARD TO SINAI: Sinai has been returned to Egyptian control, and the
Egyptian-Israeli border is now just south of Coral Beach. But by the terms of
the Egyptian-Israeli peace treaty, Sinai is open to Israeli and foreign tourists
coming from Eilat. Though there are now border formalities to complete as part
of a Sinai excursion, you shouldn't let a few dollars in fees and a few minutes in
time deter you at all. Sinai is spellbinding, and you won't want to miss it.

6. Into Sinai (Egypt)

Personally, I would be suspicious of any travel writer who claimed to know
Sinai. Sinai—that vast, triangular, nearly barren peninsula that is 3½ times larger than Israel and has an indigenous population that would fit into the small
corners of any of Israel's major cities—is simply too strange to grasp. A

wretched acacia tree, by virtue of its even more wretched surroundings, becomes a thing of wonderment. The harsh, stone cliffs in the center of the region are awesome, but the long coastal strip is soft and undulatory. The bogs east of the Suez Canal transform the striking reflections of the sun into a perpetual mirage of blue water. Armies come and go, but only the Bedouin remain rooted to the area.

"We have known many strangers," a sheik from the el-Muzzeina tribe once told me. "There were the Turks and the English, the Egyptians and the Israelis. They are like the sand. The wind blows them into a monument. And then the wind destroys them. Only the Bedouin remain."

RECENT HISTORY: Sinai was vacated by the Turks after their World War I defeat at the hands of England. Under British occupation the region was politically joined with Egypt to the west. During the 1948 War of Liberation, Israeli forces penetrated the area, but withdrew immediately after an armistice was signed in 1949. Then, in 1956, the Suez Campaign erupted, the Egyptian forces were pulverized, and the entire peninsula was occupied until American pressure forced a quick and reluctant Israeli retreat. The same story repeated itself in 1967, but the Israeli army remained this time. A road was paved from Eilat to Sharm El-Sheikh, excursions were introduced into the area, tours were conducted to the lonely, majestic Santa Katerina Monastery in the mountainous center of the region, and a strong Israeli imprint was embossed on the desert. The Yom Kippur War produced new convulsions, and Israel withdrew from the entire area adjacent to the canal and from the oil fields of Abu Rudeis.

The peace treaty between Israel and Egypt states that tourist exchanges will be encouraged to continue. Indeed, the tours to the Santa Katerina Monastery, in Egyptian territory, operate almost daily without a hitch, in a spirit of friendly and mutual cooperation.

THREE WAYS TO SEE SINAI: Depending on your schedule, your budget, and your personal interests, you'll choose one of three ways to see Sinai: by bus on your own, by overland guided tour, or by air excursion. (Note: You cannot drive a rental car from Israel into Sinai.) Here are details.

By Bus

A Sinai trip by public bus is only for the hardy and adventurous who have time on their hands. Here's what you do: any day at noon (no later!), be waiting at a no. 15 bus stop along the main highway south. The no. 15 Egged bus will pick you up and take you past Coral Beach to the border station. It will take you about 1½ hours to complete all the formalities, have your passport stamped, and pay the $5 Sinai Travel Tax (in lieu of an Egyptian visa). The Travel Tax allows you to stay in Sinai (and Sinai only) for up to seven days. If you want to go to Cairo or elsewhere in Egypt, you must obtain the standard Egyptian visa (a more elaborate and costly procedure). Once done with Customs and Immigration formalities, you buy your Egyptian bus ticket. One bus per day leaves the border station for Sharm El-Sheikh at the southern tip of Sinai, departing at 2 p.m. The return bus, also the only one each day, departs Sharm El-Sheikh each morning, arriving at the border station around 1 p.m.

By the way, you can now travel between Cairo and Santa Katerina, Nuweiba, or Sharm El-Sheikh by luxury toilet-equipped buses. Two buses a day leave the Sinai Terminal in Cairo's Abbasia Square. The 7 a.m. bus from Cairo goes to Santa Katerina (1 p.m.), then on to Nuweiba, Taba, and the Israeli border station near Eilat. The 9 a.m. bus from Cairo goes to Santa Katerina, then south to the divers' paradises of Dahab and Sharm El-Sheikh, arriving at 7 p.m.

If you have camping gear, you'll find it very handy during a Sinai adventure as accommodations are few, far between, and basic.

By Overland Tour

A combination of safari, camping trip, nature outing, and sheer adventure is the best way to describe a Sinai overland trek. Various organizations operate treks and tours in Land Rovers, command cars, and open trucks which head into the desert and up into the mountains. You make camp each night and share expedition duties and chores.

Of the outfits running treks, most interesting is **Neot Ha-Kikar Desert Tours.** The Neot Ha-Kikar people seem to thrive in barren places, so Sinai is a natural for them. A four-day Sinai trek costs about $220; a five-day trek is about $275. They have offices in most cities, but the main office is at 36 Keren Ha-Yesod St., Jerusalem 92149 (tel. 02-699-385).

Other companies, such as **Arkia Airlines** and **Johnny Desert Tours,** run various trips at comparable prices. Any travel agent can book space on any of these tours for you.

Too rough? The big tour agencies (**United Tours** and **Egged,** especially) operate one- and two-day trips into Sinai, including a run down the coast to Sharm El-Sheikh and the climb up to Mount Sinai and the Santa Katerina Monastery. These are more expensive, but more comfortable, than treks.

By Air Excursion

Arkia (tel. 059-76102 or 76103), with offices in the New Tourist Center, still flies from Eilat into Sinai. The tour takes a full morning and early afternoon. You fly over Sinai—what a view!—and land near Santa Katerina, where you pass Customs. Then you are bused (about a half hour) to the monastery and Mount Sinai. Return to Eilat is in time for a late lunch. The price is about $200, which includes lunch and also $20 worth of Egyptian taxes and fees.

These tours are operated from Tel Aviv and Jerusalem as well. Other itineraries, including Sharm El-Sheikh, are offered too. Check with Arkia, the only firm that runs such tours.

TRAVEL TIPS: There are a few basic axioms to understand before embarking on a desert trip. The climate is extreme and varies from coast to mountains. Coastal temperatures in the summer soar to over 100° Fahrenheit during the day, cooling off pleasantly in the evening. It's a bit cooler in the mountains during the day, and even the summer evenings can be cool. Winters are another proposition, though. Along the coast, days can be warm enough for January bathing and nights mild enough to take a sleeping bag out to the beach. The mountains, however, can be bitterly cold at night. The winds are savage, and I've seen more than one stream turn into ice. So whatever you do, and whenever you do it, dress accordingly, keeping in mind that a warm sweater and a bathing suit are not mutually contradictory in Sinai.

The geography of the region is inhospitable, but the people are not. The Bedouin can be marvelously friendly.

Caution

I don't know how many of you have ever experienced a flash flood in the desert, but it's an awesome sight—and a dangerous phenomenon. If you're wadi-hiking in the winter and you hear a thunderous rumble, scramble for the high ground as quickly as possible. The water rushes down from the mountains, carrying with it everything in its path, and then vanishes as quickly as it appeared.

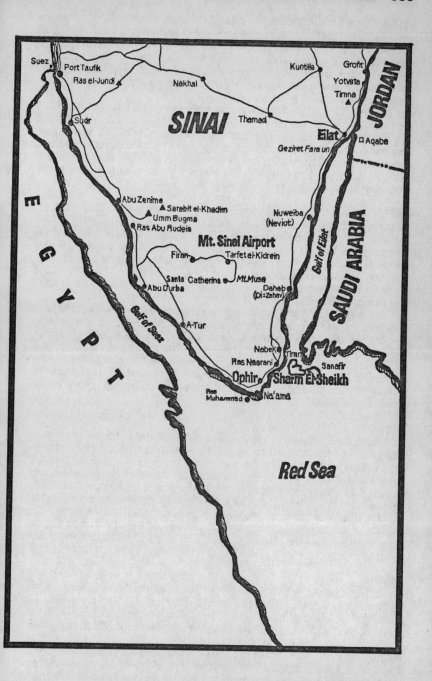

Scuba-diving and Snorkeling

The whole region from Eilat southward is a diver's paradise. A strip of coral runs all along the coastline and the fish life is unbelievably profuse. One reason cited for the name of the Red Sea: "When a perfect calm meets the setting sun, its light reflected from the red mountains of Edom and Median in Jordan and Saudi Arabia, the deep steel-blue water turns a crimson shade, making it, indeed, a red sea."

Corals sting and cut. There is a spiny rock fish that is highly poisonous to the touch. If you step on a sea anemone, you'll wish you hadn't. I've heard of only two fish-bite incidents in the history of the region, but if you're spearing, keep your piscatorial catch on a free-flowing string a distance from you—blood attracts sharks and barracudas, and there are plenty of them (usually sated and docile) in the area. Nor will the water protect you from sunburn, so, as the Arabs say, "Shwaya, shwaya"—go easy.

FROM EILAT TO SHARM EL-SHEIKH: As you begin your journey, you pass the center of Eilat, the port and the marine center, Coral Beach and the Taba border station, and in a short time you find yourself sandwiched squarely between rugged, bare mountains on your right and the blue-green coral sea on your left. Within about 15 minutes you'll be approaching a fairytale island, complete with a ruined Crusader fortress that the Christians called Isle de Gris and the Mamelukes dubbed el-Karrie. This is **Coral Island** and is accessible by small boat or amphibian. Try not to miss it because it really is impressive.

Three miles south of Coral Island is another traditional favorite, the **Fjord,** so named because it does indeed resemble the beautiful fjords of Scandinavian countries. A deep blue bay with a border of white beach, it is almost totally enclosed by harsh, angular, high red rock formations. This is a good spot for sunning, swimming, skindiving, and such; actually, the entire Red Sea coastline of Sinai is a mecca for water-sports enthusiasts. From Eilat to Ras Muhammad (south of Ophira), you'll find what's been called (by experts) the greatest coral activity in the world.

Nuweiba

After the Fjord, you continue southward to the oasis of Nuweiba, a flourishing strip of land, complete with palm trees and soft breezes. There's a camping area here, where tourists can stay for minimal costs, and a moderately priced refreshment stand as well. In the oasis area you'll also see the ruins of an old fortress, built during the Ottoman Empire, where caravans stopped during their journeys along the coast. Even today, Bedouin tarry to spend the night within the crumbling walls of its enormous courtyard, and you'll easily find traces of their frequent visits here, as well as in some of the small ruins surrounding the old edifice. Nuweiba has a holiday village, with air-conditioned rooms at three-star Eilat prices.

Dahab

If Nuweiba delights you, just wait till you reach the oasis of Dahab, much farther south along the shore. This spot has been called Sinai's most beautiful scene by travelers who know the entire peninsula quite well. Sprinkled with the crude houses, and shelters of a thriving, friendly Bedouin village, lush with palms and dunes, shell-strewn sands and warm waters, Dahab indeed revels in nature's bounty. Overnights here can be a real treat. Your guide probably will take care to direct your eyes, as the sun begins to set, to the color play between nearby mountains, the sea, and the large oasis. When I was last in Dahab, most of our group slept under the stars, cushioned by blankets or sleeping bags laid out on the sands, the surf lulling them to sleep. If you do the same, you'll perhaps understand why moon worship was prevalent in this area in ages gone by. (Although there's no conclusive proof, certain experts go so far as to link the name of Sinai with Sin, the Mesopotamian moon god.) Sun worship was big around here too, and you'll have no doubt why when you see that desert sun and feel its powers. (If comfort holds more appeal than rustic romance, Dahab has a hotel-restaurant with comfortable—though not luxurious—double rooms priced at about $25.)

Sharm El-Sheikh

Down here at the southern tip of Sinai, Na'ama Bay is the snorkelers' and divers' paradise. Among the facilities ranged along Na'ama Bay is the **Aquamarine Hotel,** and its International Diving Club. The hotel is among the town's better places to stay, at $30 double, breakfast and dinner included. In the town of Sharm El-Sheikh proper there's a youth hostel as well.

SANTA KATERINA AND MOUNT SINAI: If you're not into snorkeling or
scuba-diving, Sinai's main attraction is its namesake, high in the peninsula's jagged mountains.

Most of us think of Sinai as a flat, sand-filled desert when in fact it is mostly mountains. The highest peak, Jebel Musa (Mount Moses) is almost 7,500 feet. The sprawling and ancient compound of Santa Katerina Monastery, over a mile high (and thus cool in winter), is right next to the peak that the Greek Orthodox believe to be **Mount Sinai,** where Moses received the Ten Commandments. Nearby is **Mount Horeb,** the site of **Elijah's Cave,** and a church erected in honor of his journey there. Yoram Tsafrir, a Hebrew University archeologist, has written that the mountains' ". . . diversity of form and color . . . height and steepness lend an impressive power to the landscape, inspiring religious feeling . . . the overwhelming might of the Sinai landscape . . . providing . . . a tangible demonstration of the ephemeral quality and insignificance of Man against the timelessness of primordial creation."

On the subject of monasticism at Mount Sinai, Tsafrir writes that the ". . . distinctive feature of early monasticism in Sinai lies in the firm belief in the Mount of the Lord and in the mystic tendency to become one with the surrounding mountains."

The devout pilgrim Etheria visited this area around A.D. 400, and her writings tell of seeing these mounts, as well as the **Burning Bush** (more about this later). She visited the monks in the area and was shown where the **Golden Calf** stood on **Mount Aaron (Jebel Haroun);** the **Valley of Repose,** where the Children of Israel camped, plus **Monastery Stream (Wadi El-Deir),** where, another tradition says, the Tablets of the Law were hurled down by Moses. She described two churches, and scholars now say the one at the base of the peak was probably built by a 4th-century Syrian monk, Julianus Sabas, while the one adjacent to the Burning Bush site was probably the earliest part of Santa Katerina, even though some people insist on attributing it to Constantine's mother, Helena.

Under constant attack from Saracens (a term describing all Arab tribes of the area until the Middle Ages), the monks needed defensive fortifications, especially since their lifestyle proscribed violence. Thus Justinian, in the Byzantine era, built the walls you'll find surrounding the monastery now. At that time, it seems, the enclosure was relatively empty, including little more than the church and a hostel, which were very famous throughout the Christian world. The monastery was a caravanserai and rest stop for pilgrims, even as it is today, and one of the more important monasteries through religious history. After the Muslim conquest in the Middle Ages, a mosque was built over the ruins of the hostel, and the mosque still exists, squatting among the tightly squeezed buildings that now fill the compound's space.

Accommodations

Yes, you can stay at Santa Katerina, if there is a room available. The 22-room **Hotel Al-Salam** charges $65 double, breakfast and dinner included.

The alternative is the monastery's hostel, which charges $13 per person per night, without meals.

Seeing the Sights

Today's tourist or pilgrim will probably be most interested in two of the buildings: the one that houses the **library,** and the **church.** In the library is a vast collection of icons, many representing the priceless few to escape 8th- and 9th-century iconoclasts; and something on the order of 3,300 manuscripts, some executed by monks through the centuries, but most brought as gifts by pilgrims since the days of the 12th century. This virtual treasure trove is regarded by scholars as the second-greatest religious library in the world, the Vatican being the first. Not for nothing have the monks of Santa Katerina ardently guarded their possessions through the centuries. Since 1967 everyone has had free access to the monastery, and scholars have been running in and out, exclaiming over what they've found. What has attracted most attention of late is something called the *Psalterium Sinaiticum,* the oldest-known Slavic translation of the Book of Psalms, in Glagolitic script, dating from the 11th century and rated as exceedingly important. Tourists are not allowed to wander through the library at will, but there are many glass-enclosed icons and documents to see here.

The **Church of the Burning Bush** (sometimes called a chapel, sometimes a cathedral with nine chapels), although small, is filled to the brim with gilt and paint, carved wood and enormous brass lamps, paintings and art treasures in great abundance. Some say that the church is the oldest structure in the monastery compound; others say it dates "only" from the Middle Ages. But there is no question that its most significant treasure is a huge mosaic, executed shortly after the building was completed, and said to be one of the earliest and most beautiful in the Middle East. Within recent years the mosaic has been restored and cleaned by a team of Americans.

About Saint Catherine: By now some of you might be wondering who Saint Catherine (Santa Katerina) was, and why there's a monastery in her name in the middle of the desert. Most stories about her agree that she was a wealthy and noble Egyptian who converted to Christianity, then went about converting others. It seems that when she chided the converted king (Maximinus) about his rather un-Christian morals, she was tortured to death, her body subsequently disappearing. Some time later, a monk in this vicinity dreamed of finding a great treasure atop the highest peak of Sinai. He promptly scaled the mountain and there he found the remains of Catherine. On the spot he built a memorial chapel, and her bones were taken down to the monastery to be enclosed in a golden chest buried in the church. Saint Catherine became a favorite in Europe during the Middle Ages, which had much to do with the constant flow of pilgrims to this site.

The Skull House: Although you can't see Saint Catherine's bones, you will be able to see the bones of some 1,500 monks who've died in the monastery. These are carefully arranged by type of bone (leg bones with leg bones, skulls with skulls) in the Skull House in the gardens outside the enclosure. Only one skeleton is intact, and this one is now preserved inside a glass case in the middle of the rather creepy crypt. It's St. Stephen, still dressed, seated. Until very recently St. Stephen's remains sat before the door of the building, guarding the bones within from all harm. (This bone preservation may seem strange to you, but experts say it's a common desert monastic practice, reflective of the lack of burial space in the rocky terrain.)

The Burning Bush: More to see at the monastery: A raspberry plant behind the chapel which monks point out as the Burning Bush, itself is overshadowed by a tree called Aaron's Rod. That tree produces whitish papery pods, roughly crescent-shaped, that the monks here consider the "almonds" that grew overnight, according to the Bible; they consider as well the tree's long branches the source of the rod that became a snake and then a rod again. You can also see three entrance gates to the monastery. According to a booklet produced by the monks, the original gate "has been closed for centuries without any reason." Another gate was opened for the visit of an archbishop about 100 years ago and subsequently closed again. The one you'll enter is quite old. There's another way of getting into the compound, but nobody uses it much any more—a basket hoisted up by muscle power.

The Local People: Most of the people you'll see hereabouts are either monks or Bedouin, the latter performing the physical tasks about the monastery and its nearby gardens and plantations. These Bedouin are of the Jebaliyeh tribe, and it is thought they were originally brought here from Rumania by Justinian to guard the monastery. As time passed and various conquerors claimed the land, the tribe converted to Islam, and they are Muslims to this day. Despite their own religious beliefs, however, they are fiercely proud of having been chosen as protectors of this holy Christian site. You'll see their village of stone houses nearby.

Chapter IX

DETAILS, DETAILS!

An Alphabetical Directory of Useful Facts on Everything from Airlines to Youth Hostels

NOTHING IS MORE FRUSTRATING than having to search for that bit of information you know is there but can't find. My solution to that common travel problem is a directory of useful facts, all in alphabetical order, cross-referenced, and keyed to other chapters of this book which might have even more information on a given topic. No matter what your question, a quick riffle through the pages of this chapter should turn up the answer to it.

AIRLINES AND AIRPORTS: Israel has one world-class airport, **Ben-Gurion International Airport,** in Lod outside Tel Aviv, served by **El Al** and many other international carriers. Smaller internal airports at Tel Aviv, Jerusalem, Rosh Pinna, and Eilat are served by **Arkia Israel Inland Airlines.**

From Jerusalem, a sherut will stop by and pick you up from your hotel—no matter which one, no matter what time of the day or night—if you make prior arrangements. Your hotel will usually do this for you.

El Al has a special airport **check-in service** at their office in Jerusalem, 12 Hillel St. (tel. 02-233-333). Every evening (except Friday) for several hours after the normal close of business, the office stays open and actually checks passengers in for flights the next day. For instance, if your flight is scheduled to leave at 8 a.m., you'd be required to get to Ben-Gurion Airport at least three hours before flight time, or at 5 a.m. This means getting up, washed, dressed, and ready to board a sherut at 4 a.m.! But if you go to the Hillel Street office between 6:45 and 11 p.m. the night before, they'll check you in, check your baggage through, accept your payment of the airport exit tax, and give you your boarding pass right on the spot. Then you need only get to the airport 1¼ hours before flight time. You can order that sherut for about 6 a.m., your heavy bags will already be transported to the airport and onto the plane by El Al, and you can proceed directly to Passport Control.

A similar service is available in Tel Aviv at the El Al town terminal (tel. 03-216-262 or 216-263), by the Central Railway Station in north Tel Aviv. Advance check-in is from 4 p.m. to midnight every day but Friday and holidays. Also in Haifa at the El Al office, 80 Ha-Atzma'ut St. (tel. 04-641-166), corner of Khayat, in the port area only a block from the Paris Square Carmelit terminus. Haifa early check-in operates each evening except Friday from 6:30 to 10 p.m. (Note: As of this writing, the office is scheduled to move to a new location, and may well have moved by the time you arrive. Call and check.)

ARCHEOLOGICAL DIGS: You can volunteer to work at an archeological dig if you are 18 or older, prepared to stay for at least two weeks, and physically fit and capable of doing strenuous work in a hot climate. You will have to pay your own fare to and from Israel. Most excavations take place between June and October, but there are off-season digs. Lectures are given at some sites, and some offer academic credits for the work. If you'd like to join a dig, contact the Department of Antiquities and Museums, **Ministry of Education and Culture,** Rockefeller Museum, Jerusalem 91911 (tel. 02-278-603). It's best to inquire as far in advance as possible.

BANKS: See "Money," below.

BOOKSTORES: With such a multilingual population, Israel's cities are well supplied with bookstores and kiosks vending foreign-language books and periodicals. The most efficient and accessible distributor of foreign-language books (including lots in English) is **Steimatzky's**—just ask at your hotel for the address of the Steimatzky's agent.

BUSES: The bus systems, both in cities and in the countryside, are excellent. You'll see bus stops in the most unlikely places—in the desert, or by a Bedouin encampment, for instance. More details in Chapter I, Section 5, "Arrival, and Travel Within Israel."

CAMPING: Beautiful, interesting sites, and serviceable facilities mark Israel's camping sites. And at these fresh-air places you're not restricted to tents, but can choose to live in a hut or caravan, complete with electricity. Modern showers and conveniences are always nearby, and kiosks supplement or provide all your food needs. There's usually good transportation to each location.

You can avoid paying VAT if you pay in foreign currency. There's a minimum three-day charge on Rosh Hashannah and Shavuoth. Rates at other than the above-indicated times are lower.

Some camping sites offer mobile homes—fully furnished units with a living room, two bedrooms, kitchen, bath, and toilet. These can accommodate up to six people. Bed linens are supplied, as well as kitchen utensils.

Package deals including airport transfers, auto rentals, etc., are available. Contact the **Israel "Chalets" and Camping Union,** P.O. Box 53, Nahariya 22100 (tel. 04-925-392), for rates, literature, and further information.

Here's an example of costs: adults with their own tent pay $2.80 to $4.50 per night to camp; children are charged between $1.20 and $2.30. A bed in a campground bungalow, sheets and electricity included, costs $7 to $9. To rent a small mobile home or cabin sleeping four costs $29 to $70 total, depending on the campground, the services provided, the season, etc.

By the way, you'll be glad to know that containers of propane and butane gas are readily available in Israel, and many of them have American-style fittings, so you can use your Stateside stove or lantern in Israel. French "Camping Gaz" tanks are also available.

Here's a list of Israel's campsites, by major tourist destination, in alphabetical order:

Ashkelon

Ashkelon is owned by Ashkelon Regional Council and the National Parks Authority (P.O. Box 5052; tel. 051-36777). Near Yad Mordechai, it's on the Mediterranean, open year round, and has all possible facilities.

Caesarea

Neveh-Yam is owned by Neveh-Yam Kibbutz, Mobile Post, Hof Ha-Carmel (tel. 04-942-240), and is near Caesarea, Athlit, Elijah's Cave, Ein Hod, Mount Carmel, and it's right on the Mediterranean. Open all year (you can stay in winter, but there are no provisions), it offers the works and a playground.

Eilat

Eilat is owned by Y'elim, Mobile Post, Eilat (tel. 059-74362). It's within easy reach of King Solomon's Pillars, the underwater world of the Red Sea, and of course the desert. Open year round, it has a provisions store, playground, and trailers for rent.

Ein Gedi

Ein Gedi, under the management of Production and Development, Mobile Post, Dead Sea (tel. 057-84342), is situated about 3½ miles from the famous sulfur springs in Ein Gedi. Open year round, it consists of 20 mobile homes, tent sites, and rows of four-bedded rooms with air conditioning, hot water, and kitchenettes with refrigerators. A self-service restaurant is nearby.

Haifa

Moshav Dor Recreation Village, Mobile Post, Hof Ha-Carmel, on the coast about ten miles south of Haifa at Moshav Dor (tel. 06-399-018), has campsites, bungalows, and prefab "igloos" for rent, plus swimming, boating, refrigerated lockers, and flush toilets. Advance reservations are recommended.

Jerusalem

Bet Zayit, owned by Moshav Bet Zayit, Mobile Post, Harei-Yehuda (tel. 02-537-717), is situated about four miles west of Jerusalem near Kibbutz Kiryat Anavim and Kibbutz Ma'ale Ha-Hamisha. Open all year. There are bungalows for rent, a playground for children, a swimming pool, restaurant, and provisions store, plus refrigerator boxes and cooking gas containers.

Mevo Betar Moshav, Mobile Post, Ha-Ela (tel. 02-912-474), is 11 miles southwest of Jerusalem. There are tents, bungalows, and mobile homes, as well as a swimming pool and a place to buy groceries.

Ramat Rachel, owned by Kibbutz Ramat Rachel, P.O. Box 98, Jerusalem (tel. 02-715-712), is about 1½ miles from the center of Jerusalem. No caravans or tents here—just bungalows. There's a swimming pool, a restaurant, and a place to buy groceries.

Kiryat Shmona

See "Upper Galilee."

Nahariya

Akhziv, owned by Sulam Tzor Regional Council, Mobile Post, Western Galilee (tel. 04-921-792), is a few miles north of Nahariya and is open April through October or November. One of the better-equipped sites, it has fishing, swimming, diving, a playground, and a kosher self-service restaurant. In addition to regular camping facilities, there are ten mobile homes.

Tiberias

Ein Gev campsite is owned by Kibbutz Ein Gev, Post Ein Gev (tel. 06-758-027). Near Tiberias, Hammat Gader, Sea of Galilee, Tabgha, Mount of the Beatitudes, and Capernaum, it is open all year. Ein Gev has straw bungalows, mobile homes, an area for pitching tents, and caravans—all on an excellent beach. And the nearby kibbutz has one of the area's finest restaurants.

Ha-On, owned by T.H.M. Co., Ltd., Ha-On, Mobile Post, Jordan Valley (tel. 06-757-555), is near Ein Gev's location and is open April through October. Here there are bungalows, a restaurant, and swimming, as well as the usual facilities.

Kefar Hittim, Post Tiberias (tel. 06-795-921). Two miles from Tiberias and owned by Moshav Hittim, it is an easy distance from all the sites on and near the Sea of Galilee. Open from April to October it is well equipped—close to a swimming pool, outdoor cinema, and playground.

Ma'agan, owned by the kibbutz of the same name, Mobile Post, Jordan Valley (tel. 06-751-360), is in the same area as Ein Gev, and has a restaurant, a sandy beach, and refrigerators. Open April to November, Ma'agan has mobile homes.

Upper Galilee

Tal, owned by the Upper Galilee Regional Council and the National Parks Authority, P.O. Box 464, Kiryat Shmona (tel. 06-940-400). Near Tiberias and Kibbutz Ha-Gosherim, it's a good spot for seeing Galilee, Safed, Baniyas, the Jordan River, and Mount Hermon. Open all year round (although a bit wet, cold, and dreary in winter), it accommodates cars and trailers, has tents and cabins, and a restaurant, plus cooking facilities, refrigerators, and sinks. There are hot and cold showers, telephones, gas pumps, a children's playground, and a provisions store. Campers here can swim and fish.

CAR RENTALS: See Chapter I, Section 5, "Arrival, and Travel Within Israel."

CHILDREN: See Chapter I, Section 1, "Before You Leave Home," for tips and information on traveling with children in Israel.

CLIMATE: The range of average temperatures (average low and average high) in Israel, stated in terms of Fahrenheit degrees, follows:

	Jan.	March	May	July	Sept.	Nov.
Jerusalem	45–57	52–66	61–80	67–83	66–82	54–66
Tel Aviv	48–66	55–71	60–79	71–87	70–83	55–75
Haifa	51–62	55–70	62–76	71–83	72–83	59–70
Tiberias	54–69	57–79	68–92	77–98	72–96	62–77
Eilat	52–72	67–75	73–97	80–105	80–100	59–82

Actually, Israel uses the Celsius system, which, because the numbers are smaller, often deceives Americans into thinking that it doesn't get all that hot in Israel.

If you're a scientifically minded type who wants to know that exact Fahrenheit equivalent, multiply the Celsius reading by 9, then divide by 5, and add 32 degrees. But when you get Celsius temperatures over 40° forget about converting—just stay out of the sun.

The Israeli seasons are somewhat different from those in America and Western Europe. To start with, the Israeli winter doesn't normally involve snow —although there are occasional flurries every couple of years in Jerusalem and Upper Galilee, and Mount Hermon on the Golan Heights is snow-covered. Winter in Israel starts with some showers in October, and continues through a time of periodic heavy rainfalls from November to March. In most parts of the country you need sweaters and medium-weight coats during the winter. Swimming is out in the Mediterranean during this time, except during occasional heat waves, although you can definitely swim in Eilat and the Dead Sea in the winter.

From March to September, it seldom rains at all. Nevertheless, at the beginning of March the entire country seems to turn green; in the months that follow, the heat gathers intensity, reaching its peak in July and August, when the only relatively cold spots are Jerusalem and the high mountains around Safed (where you'll sometimes need a sweater in the evenings). The landscape is dry and parched by late August, but by September the temperatures are falling off a bit. The October rains are the herald of a new winter's arrival.

Generally, Israel's Mediterranean climate is somewhat similar to that of southern California: days of brilliant sunshine, intense summer heat, breezy nights, the coastal winds of winter. However, California doesn't know about the hot and dry easterly winds that often plague Israel at the beginning and end of the summer, usually May and September. These are the easterlies, the *khamseen,* from the Arabic word meaning "fifty," since the wind was traditionally believed to blow for 50 days a year. Thankfully, it doesn't.

CONSULATES: See "Embassies," below.

CRIME: In general, Israel is a pretty safe place, and you might find yourself feeling safer here than at home. But this doesn't mean you can ignore simple, commonsense precautions. Don't leave valuables lying around your hotel room when you're not in it. Don't leave valuables on view in a rental car. Watch out for pickpockets in crowded buses and markets. Be especially careful in the narrow streets of Jerusalem's Old City bazaar, where watches are regularly lifted right off wrists, bracelets disappear, and necklaces are snatched almost without your knowing it. Remember also that resort towns, with their large populations of cash- and camera-carrying tourists, are always prime turf for rip-off artists.

Muggings are rare, but they do occur. When you notice conditions good for muggers, such as dark streets, out-of-the-way places, etc., don't say to yourself "It can't happen here." It probably won't, but be safe rather than sorry.

Alas, women must take more precautions than men, as elsewhere in the world, but your home-country precautions will suffice.

CUSTOMS DUTIES AND PROCEDURES: You can bring $150 worth of tax-free gifts into the country. You can also bring in 250 cigarettes, one bottle (four-fifths quart) of liquor, and a reasonable amount of film. When you leave you can convert up to $3,000 back into foreign currency at the airport, so keep your bank receipts.

DENTISTS: See "Medical Care," below.

DOCTORS: See "Medical Care," below.

DRUGS AND DRUGSTORES: See "Medical Care," below.

ELECTRICITY: The electric current used in Israel is 220 volts A.C., 50 cycles. If you bring an electric shaver, iron, or radio, you can buy an inexpensive transformer in Israel to convert the current to the American voltage cycle. Or you can buy 220-volt equipment at special shops in New York that can be directly used in Israel.

Sockets (or "power points," to our British readers) usually take special Israeli three-prong plugs. If your appliance has two prongs on its plug, you can buy an adapter in Israel quite easily and cheaply.

EMBASSIES AND CONSULATES: Israel's official capital is Jerusalem, but certain countries do not recognize this position. Until an international conference works out details to everyone's satisfaction (don't hold your breath), some embassies remain in Tel Aviv while others are now in Jerusalem. No matter. For a traveler's needs, a consulate is what's required, and both cities have those.

For information on visas, see "Visas," below.

Remember that embassies and consulates tend to observe the national and religious holidays of both countries—of Israel and of the embassy country. But embassies normally operate on the Monday through Friday work week; closed Saturday and Sunday. Often, there's a break for lunch from 1 to 2 p.m.

Canada

Embassy **in Tel Aviv** at 220 Ha-Yarkon St. (tel. 03-228-122).

United Kingdom

Embassy **in Tel Aviv** at 192 Ha-Yarkon St. (tel. 03-249-171); consulate-general **in East Jerusalem's** Sheikh Jarrah section on Mount of Olives Road (Derekh Har Ha-Zetim; tel. 02-282-481); consulate **in West Jerusalem** near the Khan, the Railway Station, and St. Andrew's Church, on Ha-Rakevet Street (tel. 02-717-724).

United States

Embassy **in Tel Aviv** at 71 Ha-Yarkon St. (tel. 03-654-338). Two consulate buildings in Jerusalem: **in West Jerusalem** at 18 Agron St. (tel. 02-234-271); **in East Jerusalem** at the intersection of Nablus Road (Derekh Shechem) and Pikud Ha-Merkaz Street. The East Jerusalem post has the consular section, which is what you want (same phone number). The United States has a consular agent **in Haifa,** who handles mostly maritime matters, but will be glad to advise tourists on problems such as finding a doctor. The agent is James Sassower Ltd., 37 Ha-Atzma'ut St. (tel. 04-669-042 or 672-176), down in the port area near the Palmer Gate / Khayat Street intersection.

HITCHHIKING: Hitchhiking in Israel is called *tremping,* and the method of solicitation is unique. Forget about sticking your thumb out. The procedure here consists of holding your arm out stiffly to your side with the forefinger pointed toward the ground as if notifying the driver precisely where to stop.

Women should hitch only when absolutely necessary, and must take the normal and necessary precautions as incidents can and do happen here like anywhere else in the world. Don't hitch alone. Take rides only in cars with mixed company, though two women might take a ride with a single male driver. Don't hitch at night, or in lonely out-of-the-way spots (don't accept rides that will drop you at a bus stop somewhere in the middle of the Negev, but rather wait for a ride going to a town or to your destination).

Be sure, by the way, to wear a hat while you're out hitching. The sun beats down awfully hard while you're waiting for a car to stop.

HOLIDAYS, PUBLIC AND RELIGIOUS: Israel is certainly the world's most confusing place when it comes to holidays. Jews stop work at midafternoon on Friday; Muslims, at sundown on Thursday; Christians, all day Sunday. In Tel Aviv, no buses run on Saturday until sundown; in Jerusalem, buses run in only half the city on Saturday; in Haifa, there's partial bus service on Saturday.

Some shops open just as others are closing for a holiday. Lots of religious holidays are "moveable feasts," which change dates each year. The entire Muslim religious "Hijri" calendar starts 11 days earlier each year—it's a lunar calendar.

How to keep your wits amid all these openings and closings? Read carefully the following information.

The Sabbath in Israel

The Bible states that the seventh day is one of rest—a time when no fires are lit, no money handled, no business transacted, and so forth. So that's the way it is in most of Israel, where the Sabbath is celebrated on Saturday. By 2 or 3 o'clock on a Friday afternoon (the Israeli Sabbath begins at sundown), most shops have closed for the day, buses and trains stop running an hour later, and the movie houses are closed at night with the exception of a few maverick movie theaters in Tel Aviv. Then, on Saturday, almost all shops are closed (except a few cafés plus Arab or Christian establishments), and nearly all transportation stops (only Haifa has bus service at this time, and only taxis or small sherut companies ply in or between cities). Most admission-free museums ordinarily open for part of the Sabbath; entrance tickets, when required, must be bought in advance. Many strictly kosher restaurants follow this same no-money-handling rule, accepting only advance prepaid orders for Sabbath meals, which will often be served cold (cooked in advance). Also, do watch for signs in restaurants or hotel dining rooms asking you not to smoke on the Sabbath, so as not to offend some Orthodox guests.

If you want to drive on Saturday, it's up to you. About the only people who'll try to stop you are the ultra-religious Jews, such as those in Jerusalem's Mea Shearim section. There they tend to get rather heated about those who break their particular interpretation of the Sabbath. However, if you steer clear of such areas, you'll find that many Israelis do indeed take to the roads on Saturday—going on picnics, to the beaches, to visit friends and family. Almost all gas stations are open on the Sabbath. Precise Sabbath commencement information is available from local newspapers.

Israelis work six days a week, and as most everything is shut down on Friday nights, they make Saturday nights their stay-up-late-and-have-a-party time. By sundown transportation services resume, and movie houses begin selling tickets for evening shows. By dark, all entertainment places are usually packed full, including the many sidewalk cafés in all cities. Come Sunday morning, all these folks return to work again, waiting for another Saturday night to roll around.

Israel's Unusual Calendar(s)

If awards were given for "daily" confusion, or for having the maximum number of holidays a year, Israel would probably win them all. First, the country "officially" operates on two separate systems for determining day, month, and year. The Jewish Calendar (charted from Creation, which they date as some 5,740-odd years ago) and the Gregorian Calendar (a Christian system named for Pope Gregory XIII, and used in most countries, including the U.S.). Recognized, but "unofficial," are even more dating systems—such as the Julian (Julius Caesar) Calendar, which runs 13 days behind the Gregorian; or the Muslim Era, dating from A.D. 622, when the Prophet Mohammed hied from Mecca to

Medina. Not only do these calendars disagree about the date, but also about whether time is measured by sun, moon, or a combination, and when the year should start and end. (I've never calculated how many New Year celebrations occur each year in Israel, but I do know of at least three Christmases.)

Holidays

Israeli holidays will affect your visit in several important ways. First, hotels and campsites will fill to capacity and rates will rise by as much as 20%. Next, transportation and restaurant service may be curtailed or completely suspended, and places of entertainment may be closed. On the other hand, a holiday is a special occasion, and you won't want to miss the special events that may take place.

Here's a general guide to when Jewish festivals occur. Keep in mind that a festival that generally falls in March, say, may sometime fall on a late date in February or early in April. Note also that not all holidays are subject to Sabbath-like prohibitions and closings. Holidays on which things do close down are indicated by an asterisk(*).

January-February

The Israeli Arbor Day, **Tu b'Shevat,** comes in January or February, with thousands of schoolchildren singing, dancing, and traipsing off to plant trees all over the country.

March

Early March ushers in the Feast of Lots, **Purim,** remembering the time (5th century B.C.) when Queen Esther saved her people in Persia. This is an exciting time (so too the food) when folks dress up in fancy costumes, have parties, parade in the streets, give gifts, and generally make merry.

April

Early April is often the time when *Pesach (Passover) rolls around. No bread, beer, or other foods containing leavening are obtainable for seven days (eight days outside Israel), and hotel and restaurant meals may cost more because of the culinary complexities. During the days just before the holidays, housewives furiously clean their kitchens, and houses in general, to render them spotless and free of any stray bits of leavening. The first night of the holiday is devoted to a **seder,** a family meal and ritual recalling the Exodus of the ancient Israelites from Egypt. Many hotels and restaurants have special seders for tourists (the tourist office can direct you). The first and last days of this holiday are Sabbath-like affairs, which means the country more or less closes down.

Two weeks after the end of Pesach comes **Israel Independence Day,** with speeches and parades.

May-June

*Shavuoth, or Pentecost, is the harvest celebration which occurs in May or June. A joyous time, it is a special favorite of agricultural settlements. It is often marked by plays, entertainment, and children dressed in white, wearing floral crowns. Since it also recalls the receipt of the Ten Commandments, plus the bringing of the "first fruits" to the Temple, it is observed as a religious holiday.

Lag b'Omer, ending 33 days of mourning, is the chief happy celebration for the Hasidim, who leave Jerusalem and other cities at this time to sing and dance around bonfires at the Meiron tomb of the mystical Rabbi Shimon Bar Yochai, in Galilee. Children around the country also sing, dance, and light bonfires.

July-August
The fast day of **Tisha b'Av,** in July or August, is a time set aside to remember the destruction of the First (587 B.C.) and Second (A.D. 70) Temples. Entertainment facilities are closed.

September-October
*Rosh Hashannah,** the Jewish New Year, is the start of the High Holy Days. Since the Jewish calendar starts in September or October, that's when the new year falls. It is a two-day religious festival, not an occasion for revels but rather for solemn contemplation and prayer.

A week later, the High Holy Days culminate in *Yom Kippur,** the Day of Atonement, most solemn of Jewish holidays. Observant Jews spend nearly the whole day in synagogue. Places of worship are crowded, but the large synagogues reserve seats for tourists, and some of the larger hotels organize their own services. Yom Kippur is a fast day, but hotel dining rooms serve guests who wish to eat. Everything comes to a standstill. There is no vehicular traffic, beaches and swimming pools are deserted, restaurants, cafés, and entertainment places are closed, and even television and radio stations suspend broadcasting.

Five days after Yom Kippur comes *Succoth,** a seven-day period for recalling how Moses and the Children of Israel dwelled in "booths" as they left Egypt to wander in the desert. Observant families have meals and services in specially built, highly decorated yet simple huts, located outside in gardens or on balconies. Succoth is also a harvest festival (the Feast of the Tabernacles) and thus a kibbutz favorite. On the first day of Succoth, Sabbath-like restrictions are observed. It culminates with *Simhat Torah,** when Jews rejoice that they have the Torah (the Law); street festivities in Jerusalem and Tel Aviv mark this day. On Simhat Torah, cantors read the final verses of the Torah (the first five books of the Bible), and then start again at its beginning.

December
Hanukkah, which falls in December, celebrates the victory of the Maccabees over Syrian-Greeks and the consequent rededication of the Temple in 164 B.C. The menorah, the symbol of this holiday, is lit nightly for the eight nights of the festival.

HOSPITALS: See "Medical Care," below.

HOURS OF OPERATION: Perhaps the most complex subject in all of Israel, even thornier than the Arab-Israeli debate, is the subject of when things are open and when they're closed. There simply is no standard. You go to the bank, you find it's closed on Wednesday afternoons; or that the post office is closed Saturday, although its telegraph window is open; or that the Church of Mary Magdalene in the Garden of Gethsemane is open only two days a week. I've given hours of operation whenever possible in the text of this book. See also specific sections on "Mail" and "Money," etc., below, but here's an idea of when various institutions—post office, banks, and the like—are in operation.

The **banks** are usually open from 8:30 a.m. to 12:30 p.m. and 4 to 5:30 p.m. —except on Monday and Wednesday, when they're closed all afternoon. On Friday, the hours are 8:30 a.m. to noon.

Some **shops** keep to a schedule of 8 a.m. to 1 p.m. and 4 to 7 p.m. Sunday through Thursday; they generally close for the Sabbath by 2 or 3 p.m. (in winter, later in summer) on Friday and don't reopen until Sunday morning.

You can visit **government offices** on weekdays, usually from 7:30 or 8 a.m. Some offices are closed to the public on Friday, and all are closed on Saturday; they are open during summer weekdays till 1 or 3 p.m.; in winter months they remain open until 2 or 4 p.m.

In Bethlehem, Nazareth, Ramallah, and other Muslim or Christian cities, the **Israel Government Tourist Offices** are open on Saturday and closed Sunday. Otherwise, the I.G.T.O. doors are open from 8 a.m. to 6 p.m. daily during the summer, till 5 p.m. during the winter. On Friday they close at 3 p.m. in summer, at 2 or 3 p.m. in winter.

HUNTING:
The really serious hunters in Israel are the Arabs and Druze, the latter being particularly obsessed by the sport. There is game in the country— duck, hare, partridge, porcupine, wild boar, quail, and even a few wildcats in the Negev—and there are a couple of hunting clubs, like the **Israel Hunters Association** in Tel Aviv and the **Partridge Club** in Haifa. The season runs from September until the end of January and is sometimes extended until March; additional details are available through the I.G.T.O. You must check with the Israeli consul and apply for your license *before* you come.

INFORMATION FOR TOURISTS:
The Ministry of Tourism maintains information offices both in Israel and abroad. The international offices are located in the following cities:

Canada: In **Toronto,** at 180 Bloor St. West, Toronto, Ontario, M5S 2V6 (tel. 416/964-3784).

United Kingdom: In **London,** it's the Israel Government Tourist Office, 18 Great Marlborough St., London W1V 1AF (tel. 01/434-3651).

United States: Offices in these cities: **Chicago**—5 S. Wabash Ave., Chicago, IL 60603 (tel. 312/782-4306); **Houston**—4151 Southwest Freeway, Houston, TX 77027 (tel. 713/850-9341); **Los Angeles**—6380 Wilshire Blvd., Los Angeles, CA 90048 (tel. 213/658-7462); **Miami**—420 Lincoln Road Bldg., Miami Beach, FL 33139 (tel. 305/673-6862); **New York**—Empire State Bldg., 350 Fifth Ave., 19th Floor, New York, NY 10118 (tel. 212/560-0650).

In addition, there are Israel Government Tourist Offices in Amsterdam, Copenhagen, Frankfurt, Hamburg, Johannesburg, Madrid, Paris, Milan, Stockholm, Vienna, and Zurich.

Also, you'll find lots of I.G.T.O. branches in Israeli cities, working alongside the local municipal tourist authorities.

They exist for one purpose only: to serve the tourist. Located in almost every city and nearly all major sightseeing destinations, they can provide you with details and advice concerning hotels, tours, events of current interest, shopping, almost any other matters which concern you, including dealing with complaints against those bearing their emblems. Branches are open from 8 a.m.

to 6 p.m., on Friday until 3 p.m. The following listing gives addresses, area codes, and telephone numbers of the I.G.T.O. offices in Israel. The Haifa Port facilities, incidentally, are open only when passenger ships dock.

Jerusalem	24 King George V Ave.	Tel. 02-237-311
	Jaffa Gate	Tel. 02-282-295 or 282-296
Tel Aviv	7 Mendele St.	Tel. 03-223-266 or 223-267
Haifa	18 Herzl St.	Tel. 04-666-521, 666-522, or 666-523
	Haifa Port, Shed 12	Tel. 04-663-988
Ben-Gurion Airport	Main Hall	Tel. 03-971-485
Tiberias	8 Elhadeff St.	Tel. 06-720-992
Beersheba	Nordau Street	Tel. 057-36001
Eilat	New Commercial Center	Tel. 059-72268
Safed	Municipality Building	Tel. 06-930-633
Bat Yam	Ben-Gurion Road	Tel. 03-889-766
Nazareth	Casa Nova Street	Tel. 06-573-003
Ashkelon	Afridar Commercial Center	Tel. 051-32412
Arad	Commercial Center	Tel. 057-98144
Bethlehem	Manger Square	Tel. 02-742591
Netanya	Ha-Atzma'ut Square	Tel. 053-27286
Nahariya	Egged Bus Station	Tel. 04-922-121

Each year the I.G.T.O. comes up with new and exciting events and plans (check with the I.G.T.O. each place you go), and also repeats some favorite events each season:

Meet the Israelis

The I.G.T.O. sponsors a program whereby you can meet Israelis in their homes and share a cup of tea with the family. The idea is to bring together people of similar interests and backgrounds. If, for example, you're an architect and want to talk shop with an Israeli architect, you need only apply to the I.G.T.O., which will set it up for you.

Plant a Tree

To many people, Israel was first associated with the act of dropping coins into a rectangular blue-and-white box. There were thousands of such boxes and the coins went toward planting trees in Israel. As a result of all those coins, as well as other donations and the labor of many workmen, the **Keren Kayemet Le-Israel** (Jewish National Fund) has planted about 160 million trees in Israel.

Once in Israel, however, you *can* plant a tree—and with your own hands—and feel some connection with the physical development and beauty of the country. This emotional outlet for sightseers was established by the Jewish National Fund. It costs $7 a tree, and the J.N.F. will tell you how it's done. Check with the Keren Kayemet directly: in Jerusalem, at the head office, King George V Avenue and Keren Kayemet Street (tel. 02-241-781); in Tel Aviv, 96 Ha-Yarkon St. (tel. 03-234-449), opposite the Dan Hotel. In New York, the address is 42 E. 69th St., New York, NY 10021 (tel. 212/879-9300).

Discounts

Alone, or in cooperation with other organizations, the I.G.T.O. has arranged some very nice special discounts for tourists in Israel. Instead of paying to enter each archeological site or national park, you can buy a ticket at the office of the **National Parks Authority,** 4 Rav Alluf M. Makleff St., Ha-Kirya, Tel Aviv (tel. 03-252-281). It will get you into all 33 sites and parks during any two-week period. The special rate is for adults of 18 or over. Children or students pay for entry in each national park or site.

Volunteer Tourist Service (V.T.S.)

If you happen to spot someone wearing a badge imprinted with "V.T.S.," you know immediately he or she is your friend—a member of Israel's Volunteer Tourist Service. You'll find these helpful volunteers at the Arrivals Hall of Ben-Gurion Airport from 2 to 9 p.m., and at major hotels in Eilat, Haifa, Jerusalem, Tel Aviv, and Tiberias from about 6 to 8:30 p.m. They are ready to offer assistance in locating friends or relatives, arranging home hospitality, answering any questions, etc. V.T.S. has offices in Tel Aviv at 7 Mendele St. (tel. 03-222-459); in Jerusalem at Jaffa Gate (tel. 02-288-140); in Haifa at 10 Ahad Ha-Am St., Hadar (tel. 04-671-645); in Eilat (tel. 059-72344); in Tiberias (tel. 06-795-072); and in Nahariya (tel. 04-920-135). These offices are open from 8:30 a.m. to 1 p.m., daily except Saturday and Jewish holidays.

KIBBUTZIM: See the Appendix, following this chapter.

LANGUAGE: English is Israel's major international language. Street and road signs are in English, Hebrew, and Arabic. English will suffice in virtually every shop, restaurant, and hotel in the three major cities, as well as most other places. If, however, you chance to encounter a storekeeper who speaks only Russian, Polish, Yiddish, or one of the 17 or so other relatively common languages, just look for his 12-year-old son, who's studying English in school.

If you find yourself groping for another language, try French, German, or Yiddish. Most Israelis with Slavic origins know French, and most of the Israelis of North African birth—the thousands and thousands who come from Morocco, Algeria, and Tunisia—also speak fluent French.

But Hebrew is the national language, followed by Arabic. You can use the glossary at the back of this book as a crutch, and you'll find that your stabs at speaking Hebrew will be warmly appreciated. For predominantly Arab areas, I've added an Arabic glossary too.

A Note About English Spellings

You will doubtless notice when traveling in Israel, or just reading about it (in this book as well as any other), that the English spellings of Hebrew or Arabic place names is haphazard, to say the least. That's because the Hebrew and Arabic alphabets are different from the English alphabet and transliterating the Hebrew or Arabic characters into English characters does get a bit hairy. Thus you see a town like Netanya spelled "Natanya" or "Natania." Or Eilat, "Elath," or Ashkelon, "Ashqelon." And on and on. The basic rule to follow is: if it sounds the same as the place you're looking for, it is the same—forget about the exact spelling.

Language Schools

Should you plan an extended visit to Israel, you should know that a good many kibbutzim operate language schools called **ulpanim** which are based on the principle of working for your education, room, and board. In exchange for half a day of Hebrew-language classroom instruction, you work the other half day in a job assigned by the kibbutz—in the fields, kitchen, or wherever you are needed.

The **Jewish Agency**—here in America, abroad, and in Israel—makes the arrangements for you. Classes are mixed, and your classmates may be Argentinian, Polish, Rumanian, Moroccan, Persian, and Russian.

The three big cities have ulpanim where you just pay a low fee and don't have to work for your keep. These are five-month courses, very reasonably priced. If you're interested, apply to the Jewish Agency, either in your own country, or in Israel. In America, their main office is at 27 W. 20th St., New York, NY 10011 (tel. 212/255-1338).

As far as students are concerned, the following Israeli institutions offer accredited summer courses in the Hebrew language which can earn from 6 to 12 credits: **Hebrew University**, Mount Scopus, Jerusalem (tel. 02-273-602); **Tel Aviv University**, Ramat Aviv (tel. 03-420-111); **Bar Ilan University**, Ramat Gan (tel. 03-752-103); **Haifa University** (tel. 04-254-111); and **Ben-Gurion University**, Beersheba (tel. 057-71241).

LAUNDRY AND DRY CLEANING: Both are surprisingly expensive in Israel, and both can be even more expensive if you have to pay for "express" service. You can save a bit of money by going to the laundry/dry cleaner's yourself rather than having the hotel do it. But the cost will still surprise you: $6 to $7 to have a pair of blue jeans washed and pressed! Thank heavens for drip-dry clothes.

MAIL: Post offices and mailboxes in Israel are identified by a blue sign bearing a white leaping deer. English-style red letter boxes are also used. You can buy stamps at shops and newsstands bearing a similar sign.

The main post offices in the large cities are usually open from 7 a.m. until 7 p.m. Sunday through Thursday. Hours for smaller, branch post offices are 8 a.m. to 12:30 p.m. and 3:30 to 6 p.m. All post offices are open on Friday and eves of holidays from 7 a.m. to 1 p.m. All are closed Saturday.

Post offices have current postal-rate schedules, printed in English and Hebrew, on their bulletin boards.

By the way, post offices in Israel are also the points from which you send telegrams or Telexes, and the post office also operates the telephone system. See below under "Telephone, Telegraph, Telex."

When you're looking for a mailbox ("letterbox"), note that in some cities there are two kinds. Those painted red are for mail to points outside the city and the country; those painted yellow are for mail within the city only. At this writing, these special yellow intracity boxes are found only in Jerusalem and Tel Aviv, as an experiment. You, as a visitor, will no doubt use the only the red boxes.

Here are some addresses of post offices which you'll find convenient:

Jerusalem—The main post office is at 23 Jaffa Rd. not far from the intersection with Shlomzion Ha-Malka Street. East Jerusalem had its own main post office, which is now a branch, opposite Herod's Gate at the corner of Saladin Ibn Sina, and Sultan Suleiman Streets.

In the Old City, the post office is a few steps from Jaffa Gate, up past the Citadel of David and next to the gate of the Christ Church Anglican Hospice.

A branch in West Jerusalem is on Keren Kayemet Street near the corner with King George V, and the Jewish Agency.

Tel Aviv—The main post office is at 132 Allenby Rd. There are branches on Ha-Yarkon Street at Trumpeldor, at 3 Mendele St. between Ha-Yarkon and Ben-Yehuda (next to the Hotel Adiv), and just off Dizengoff Square on Zaman-hof Street.

Haifa—Haifa's main post office is a short stroll from the Paris Square Carmelit station, on Ha-Palyam Street near the Shikmona Park, in the port area.

You should know that it can take two weeks or more for a letter to travel between Israel and the North American continent, and that's airmail.

MEDICAL CARE:
Want the address of a good doctor who speaks your language, or a similarly qualified dentist? Contact your embassy or consulate. They keep lists of such professionals who have been used successfully by staffers and visitors in the past. They don't make any claims or guarantees—this is strictly a goodwill service on their part.

Remember also that on weekends and holidays, the consulate always has a duty officer on call if a real emergency arises.

Israeli cities are well organized to care for medical emergencies. **Magen David Adom** ("Red Shield of David") is the Jewish equivalent of the Red Cross. They provide ambulance and first-aid service in virtually every city and town. At their clinics in major cities, you can get emergency medical or dental treatment on the Sabbath or at other times when normal practitioners are unavailable. For Magen David Adom **emergency service** in Jerusalem, Haifa, Tel Aviv, and most other parts of the country, dial 101. For emergencies requiring **hospitalization**, dial 102.

The Magen David Adom clinic in Jerusalem is in Romema, near the Central Bus Station.

There are **rape crisis centers** in Jerusalem (tel. 02-245-554), in Tel Aviv (tel. 03-234-819), and in Haifa (tel. 04-382-611).

Most telephone operators and police personnel speak English and will assist you in finding any special help you may need, if not helping you themselves. Hopefully, you'll never need emergency assistance.

You might, however, need or want something for sunburn or minor physical discomforts, in which case you'd look for one of the many **pharmacies,** or chemist shops, in all towns and cities. In Israel, unlike in the States, pharmacists are allowed to advise about medicines and medications, and can sell you many items that would require a prescription in the U.S. In fact, unless the medicine you require is in the addictive-drug category, you can buy it by simply asking in most pharmacies.

If you need a pill at night, Friday afternoon, or on Saturday, when drugstores are closed, don't panic: check the *Jerusalem Post* or the door of the nearest pharmacy for a list of pharmacies on round-the-clock emergency duty in your area.

MONEY:
The Israeli unit of currency is the **New Israeli Shekel,** abbreviated "NIS." The shekel is divided into 100 *agorot* (singular: *agora*). The shekel replaced the lira in March 1980, and that "old" shekel was replaced by the New Shekel in August 1985. You probably won't come across any of the old shekel notes or coins. If you do, keep in mind that 1,000 old shekels equal one New Shekel.

Though the New Shekel is now fairly stable, and hyperinflation seems to be in the past, the Israeli currency is still a bit shaky and subject to devaluation. In

January 1987, the New Shekel was devalued from NIS1.50 to about NIS1.61 for $1 U.S.

Exchange Facilities

In most cases, you will want to exchange your foreign currency at **banks**. They usually give the best rate of exchange. **Hotels** will change money for you as well, and their rates might be good, but you should check hotel rates. Sometimes they are not as good as the banks' rates.

In Jerusalem, Bethlehem, and West Bank towns you should take notice of a special money-saving possibility. East Jerusalem's Arab **moneychangers,** clustered in and around Damascus Gate, are not just some romantic leftover from the Middle Ages. These calculator-equipped entrepreneurs are operating in complete legality and with modern efficiency. Usually, their rates of exchange are a good deal better than the banks, and you save even more money because the moneychangers do not charge a service fee as every bank does. If a moneychanger says he'll give you NIS1.68 for a dollar, that's what you'll get, not NIS1.68 minus a 10-agorot service fee. In general, you make out better at a moneychanger's.

As for banks, it can really pay to "shop around" for a bank with a low service fee. Some banks charge over a dollar to change any traveler's check, no matter what denomination. In my experience, the Israel Discount Bank, with lots of branches, has a fairly low service fee. Whichever bank you go to, inquire about the fee *before* you change money!

Bank hours differ, but most banks are open from 8:30 a.m. to 12:30 p.m. and 4 to 5:30 p.m. on Sunday, Tuesday, and Thursday. On Monday, Wednesday, and Friday, hours are 8:30 a.m. to noon; closed Saturday. Jerusalem's moneychangers are open long hours straight through the day; the Muslim and Christian moneychangers work on Saturday, and the Muslims work on Sunday too.

Traveler's Checks and Credit Cards

No trouble using either of these modern types of money. Traveler's checks in major hard currencies are accepted at all banks and moneychangers. Always take your passport when changing checks.

Personal checks are sometimes accepted, but you can never depend on it. Ask the merchant before you assume you can pay with a personal check.

The major credit cards—American Express, MasterCard, VISA, Access, Eurocard, etc.—are accepted at all hotels except the very smallest, at many restaurants and shops, and for cash advances at banks. Some banks accept one card, but not the other, of the two major bank cards (MasterCard and VISA). Try the local branch of Bank Leumi le-Israel and the Israel Discount Bank for VISA; for MasterCard, try a Bank Hapoalim or United Mizrachi branch.

NEWSPAPERS AND MAGAZINES: Your indispensible source of news, entertainment, and information in Israel is the highly acclaimed daily newspaper named the *Jerusalem Post.* It is available throughout the country on the morning of the date of publication (by mid-morning in Eilat). The *Post* will tell you about concerts in Haifa, movies in Safed, and events throughout the world. If you can't find it in the business section of the town you're in, or at a newspaper kiosk, try the big tourist hotel—it's sure to have it.

The Friday-morning edition of the *Post* carries the weekly magazine section filled with features, entertainment notices, and radio and television listings.

You pay a bit more for this larger edition. On Monday, the *Post* includes an insert bearing "The Week in Review" section from the *New York Times*'s Sunday edition. By the way, the *Post* does not appear on Saturday.

The big hotels also stock various foreign newspapers and periodicals. *Time, Newsweek,* and the *International Herald-Tribune* are not hard to find.

Want to see what the Palestinians have to say? Pick up a copy of *Jerusalem Al-Fajr,* an English-language Palestinian weekly paper published in East Jerusalem and on sale in East Jerusalem and West Bank cities.

PHOTOGRAPHY: The variety of colors, landscapes, dwellings, and peoples make Israel a shutterbug's paradise. Fortunately, all sorts of film can be bought almost anywhere in the country, to refuel cameras of folks who find they just can't snap the pictures fast enough. However, as film is more expensive in Israel than in the U.S., budgeteers will probably prefer to bring extra rolls with them. As for developing, Israel is geared to process color and black-and-white, but most tourists mail or tote exposed film home for that. Since the sun's so bright, and reflections tend to get glaring, many "pro" photographers use special filters to soften such effects. If you're really a photography fanatic, I suggest you investigate this, and other special photographic conditions in Israel, before leaving home—a Stateside Israeli Government Tourist Office or Israeli Consulate can guide your research, and there are several books about it. Aside from that, there are only three restrictions on picture-taking in Israel: certain military areas, which are plainly marked in several languages as no-photo territories; aerial photography over inland routes without special permission; and certain people, who use their own sign language (usually hands over face) to let you know they don't want to be photographed. Most of the time such people are simply following a religious interpretation linking photos to "graven images," although sometimes they are actually afraid that a photo can capture or control some of their personal essence or soul.

POLICE: Each city and town has its own municipal force, and the army keeps a vigil throughout the country. In the major cities, in an **emergency,** dial 100.

POST OFFICE: See "Mail," above.

RADIO AND TELEVISION: I always carry a little portable radio when I travel, and Israel is a real radio-listener's paradise. Signals come in from all the countries of the Eastern Mediterranean, and often from Europe as well. The Voice of America, with a relay station on the Greek island of Rhodes, and the BBC's World Service are both accessible on the AM (middle-wave) dial.

Kol Israel ("The Voice of Israel") broadcasts news bulletins in English on 576 or 1170 kHz at 7 a.m., and 1, 5, and 8 p.m. On FM, the English bulletins are at those times and also at 10 p.m. and 12:30 a.m. on 88.2 MHz. News in French follows these English programs. There's even a schedule of bulletins in Easy Hebrew for those learning the language.

The **Voice of Peace,** broadcasting from "somewhere in the Mediterranean," has programming 24 hours a day at 1540 kHz on the AM (medium-wave) band, and also on FM.

Also, you can hear news broadcasts in English from Cairo and Amman at various times throughout the day.

Israeli television has converted to color, so you can now enjoy all those old movies (most in English, with Hebrew subtitles) in lifelike hues. Jordanian television broadcasting from Amman is easily picked up in Jerusalem and some other cities. There's always a news bulletin in English, and many familiar American or European programs.

SHOPPING: See the Appendix, following this chapter, for a Shopping Guide.

SPORTS: If you're a doer rather than a watcher, you'll find it possible to combine sporting activities with much of your sightseeing. The summer is terrific for water sports in seas, lakes, springs, and pools. Skindiving enthusiasts can flipper through what's often called the world's greatest underwater scenery in the Red Sea at Eilat. Fully stocked sporting centers flourish around those areas, where all equipment, as well as underwater guides and instructors, can be hired. Above-water sports—skiing, boating, surfing, swimming—also thrive around Eilat, plus all along Israel's strip of golden Mediterranean beach, at the Sea of Galilee, and in the many public or hotel pools scattered all over the land.

Basketball runs a close second to soccer as the nation's most popular sport; games are frequent, and I.G.T.O. and ticket offices can provide the when/where details.

Cycling

Ever consider seeing Israel on two wheels? The **Israel Cyclists Touring Club** (P.O. Box 339, Kefar Saba 44102; tel. 052-23716) promotes guided tours between March and October. Generally, the tours are 8, 9, or 14 days, and packages include accommodations, meals, a guide, bus transportation when necessary, entrance fees to sights on the itinerary, and insurance. Contact the I.C.T.C. for further information.

Also check with the **Jerusalem Cyclists' Club** (P.O. Box 7281, Jerusalem; tel. 02-248-238). They rent out bicycles by the day, and offer low-priced tours with hostel accommodations.

STUDENTS IN ISRAEL: The discounts offered to students traveling in Israel are unequalled anywhere else in the world. Students are treated royally, via an elaborate program of reductions that lower the tab in youth hostels and hotels, on buses and trains, even in swimming pools, restaurants, and sundry places of entertainment. Your passports for these savings are, first, the **International Student Identity Card** (available in the U.S. from the Council on International Educational Exchange, William Sloane House, 354 W. 34th St., New York, NY 10001; tel. 212/695-0291—you must present proof of full-time student status; write for information) and the **International Youth Hostel Card** (available in the U.S. from American Youth Hostels, Inc., P.O. Box 37613, Washington, DC 20013; tel. 202/783-6161).

Information and assistance on student, youth, and budget travel to Israel (and other destinations, for that matter), is available from any office of **Council Travel Services,** the travel division of the Council on International Educational Exchange. Council Travel's New York office is at 35 W. 8th St., New York, NY 10011 (tel. 212/254-2525). There are also offices in Amherst, Austin, Boston, Cambridge, Chicago, Dallas, Los Angeles, Minneapolis, Portland (Oregon), Providence, San Diego, San Francisco, and Seattle. Be sure to ask for the council's free Student Travel Catalog.

The ISSTA

When you arrive in Israel, make your first stop at the **Israel Students Travel Association (ISSTA),** which offers a never-tiring helping hand to students and does an excellent job of looking after visiting young people. ISSTA offices in Israel are at 109 Ben-Yehuda St., Tel Aviv 63401 (tel. 03-244-376 or 247-164); 5

Eliashar St., Jerusalem 94236 (tel. 02-225-258); and 28 Nordau St., Haifa 33124 (tel. 04-660-411). Hours are usually 9 a.m. to 1 p.m. and 3 to 6 p.m.; offices close on Wednesday and Friday at 1 p.m., and all day Saturday.

If you've arrived in Israel equipped with the aforementioned student and hostel cards, then you can go directly, without any further ado, to the central train and bus stations in any of the three major cities to receive discounts on their routes throughout the country.

And should a student really need someone to talk to, he or she can call one of Israel's many colleges or universities and ask for the **Foreign Student Advisor.**

In each chapter I've listed the student facilities available in each particular area. Incidentally, students should always show student cards when requesting reductions. This tack might work even in cases where an establishment is not advertising student discounts.

The ISSTA's staff is composed of young people, specialists in the field of student and youth travel. Here the student is treated as a first-class client and is offered a wide variety of special services, planned and developed by people who fully understand the student's needs and problems. ISSTA accommodates students (bring proof) from the start to finish of their stay in Israel with:

1. Special inland tours at very inexpensive prices.
2. Volunteer work groups in kibbutzim (volunteers only accepted if they register abroad in advance).
3. Reservations in inexpensive hotels, university dormitories, and vacation centers for the youth/student.
4. Special student charter flights between Israel and almost any point in Europe, also the Far East and Africa. European flights are guaranteed by the operator.

Most of these services are operated throughout the year, the main ISSTA seasons being winter (November through March), spring (April through June), summer (July through September), and autumn (October).

Tours Within Israel

The ISSTA operates tours within Israel ranging from four to seven days; they're open to individual as well as group booking. The tour price includes bed-and-breakfast accommodations, entrance fees, a tour bus, and a government-licensed guide. Prices range from $130 for four days to $230 for a seven-day excursion covering the entire country.

Charter Flights from Europe

The ISSTA operates, on a year-round basis, special charter flights between Europe and Israel for students and scholars. The seat you buy is confirmed—you are *not* a standby. These flights are jointly operated with various national student travel bureaus in Europe and form an extensive network of flights between Israel and Europe. All aircraft used are jets, and all flights are on non-IATA carriers such as Arkia and Dan-Air. These flights are priced specially for students and offer discounts of 40% to 70% off the regular fare. From mid-April to mid-September, you can fly to Israel from London, Paris, Rome, Athens, Zurich, Amsterdam, Copenhagen, Madrid, Barcelona, Dublin, Stockholm, Helsinki, Oslo, Munich, Düsseldorf, the Far East, Africa, and vice versa, and can also time your flights in conjunction with flights to or from the U.S. The rest of the year you can fly from Athens, London, Zurich, and Copenhagen.

Members of students' families—husband or wife and children—are now allowed to fly to and from Israel on student charter flights, at the same rates and subject to the same conditions as the student in the family.

TAXIS: Each municipality sets fares, and issues a chart quoting current fares. But in all cases, it's good to agree on an amount before you get in the cab, as many cabbies ignore the meters. That avoids any unpleasantness at the end—and there is often unpleasantness.

When looking for a sherut, always ask before climbing in to see that it truly is a sherut. Otherwise, a gloating driver may whisk you to your destination at taxi rates. Having trouble finding a taxi on the Sabbath? Go to a big hotel entrance. They're there!

TELEPHONES, TELEGRAPH, TELEX: All these services are operated by the post office in Israel. I'll take them one by one:

Telephones

To save money, try making all your calls from public telephones—which can be found in street booths, in hotels, in many restaurants and most public places, as well as in all post offices. You'll need special tokens to operate most phones, and I suggest you stock up at a post office, where you must ask for *asimonim* (singular: *asimon)*, currently priced at 20 agorot (13¢) apiece. A public telephone **local call** requires one token for unlimited time; many hotel and restaurant phones are connected to time-tallying meters. For a **zonal call,** the charges mount according to distance, duration, and time of day. A long-distance—interzonal—call requires an area code plus number, and also costs according to distance, duration, and time of day. Long-distance calls are expensive. Have a pocketful of tokens, and keep loading them in as they drop, or you'll be cut off. If you can't find a number in the English telephone directory, dial 14 for **Information,** although you'll be charged for it, unless the number is not listed. For information on **international direct dialing,** phone 195. The cheapest time to call overseas is from 1 a.m. to 7 a.m. (that's 6 p.m. to 1 a.m. E.S.T. in the States).

For the time, dial 15; for weather, dial 03-625-231. Dialing 100 reaches the police, and 101 gets first aid. Dialing 14 will let you know the hours when the **Sabbath** and/or Jewish **holidays** start and end (this information can also be found in the newspapers). **Airport arrivals** can be checked by dialing 03-614-656 and **departures** at 03-971-461.

How to Dial: Except when making local calls, Israel's phone system requires an area code before the actual number. Tel Aviv and the airport are 03; Jerusalem is 02; Haifa, 04; and Netanya, 053. Other codes are easily obtainable from the map in the phone book. I've included the area code with every phone number given in this book.

For example, let's say you want to call the Ministry of Tourism in Jerusalem (tel. 02-241-281). From a phone in or near Jerusalem you dial "241-281," but from Tel Aviv or Haifa or any other Israeli city or town you dial "02-241-281." When you call from another country to a number in Israel, you do not dial that initial "0" (zero). So from New York, London, or Timbuctoo, you dial up an international line, then you dial Israel's country code (972), Jerusalem's area (or city) code (2), then the local number (241-281), like this: 972-2-241-281.

Some special public telephones in Jerusalem and Tel Aviv can be used to place international collect ("reverse-charge") calls. You can dial from Israel to other countries, even collect, but you'll end up paying a surcharge in any case.

Telegraph

Sending a telegram is always easy in Israel. Most hotels will accept them; big-city post offices often have late-hour counters from which you can send a wire. In Jerusalem, the counter at the main post office at 23 Jaffa Rd. stays open 24 hours a day. In Tel Aviv, a similar service is provided at the Telegraph Office on Mikveh Israel (Miqwe Yisra'el) Street: go down Allenby Road to Yehuda Ha-Levi Street, turn left and immediately bear right onto Mikveh Israel Street.

Telex

The post office will send a Telex for you from most of its major post offices. Unlike a telegram, the addressee must have Telex service (a Telex machine in the office), but if your addressee does have Telex, you can send a message much more cheaply than if you sent him a telegram. Telex offices have the directories, so you can even look up the addressee's name and number if you don't know it already.

TIME DIFFERENCES: Israel operates on the same time all year long, with no change to Daylight Saving Time in summer. The basic time difference between New York and Jerusalem is seven hours: when it's 5 a.m. in New York, it's already noon in Jerusalem. During Daylight Saving Time, the time difference comes down to six hours: when it's 6 a.m. in New York, it's noon in Jerusalem.

TIPPING: It used to be that no one tipped in Israel. The social consciousness and idealism of the early days has worn off somewhat now, however. In the more expensive tourist spots—hotels, restaurants, clubs—tip as you would at home, 10% or 15%, unless the menu states that a service charge is included. In more modest places, do as the Israelis do: leave the small change. The person waiting on you may pick up your offering with indifference. That's probably because he or she didn't really expect a tip, rather than because the tip was too small.

You needn't tip taxi or sherut drivers unless they've performed some special service. But you should always offer a tip to a guide or caretaker (self-appointed or otherwise) who actually does help you to see some holy site or ancient ruin. If there is no admission fee, and if a man or boy comes running to unlock the gate for you, he deserves a small tip. But when he offers you a guided tour, or simply begins to guide you, you can say no. By saying nothing, you encourage misunderstanding. By saying yes, you've made a contract, and you should proceed to agree on a price.

Tip about 10% at the barber's or hairdresser's, part to the person who washes your hair, part to the one who cuts it.

Cinema or theater ushers don't expect tips. But a hat or coat checker and a lavatory attendant does—a few coins will do unless a price is posted.

When staying in a hotel room for the better part of a week or more, the housekeeping staff deserves a tip. When you first go to your room, the bellboy should get a tip.

TOILETS: Israeli cities and touristic sights are well provided with public toilets. Look for signs to the "W.C.," or "OO," or look for the various male-female symbols: pipe and fan, man and woman silhouettes, etc.

VISAS: They're given free to U.S. citizens, without prior application, when they enter Israel and show valid U.S. passports. Good for three months, the tourist visa can be extended for another three consecutive months at any office of the Ministry of the Interior. To work, study, or settle in Israel, you need the proper permit before arrival. If you plan to visit Arab countries, ask for a separate visa (if your passport is stamped by the Israelis, that stamp will close most Arab-world doors). Americans need no smallpox certificate unless they've spent the 14 days immediately prior to entering Israel in a country where there's been a recent smallpox outbreak (the same applies for Europeans or Canadians).

WATER: Drink lots and lots of it to prevent dehydration during the hot, dry Israeli summer. Tap water is drinkable throughout Israel, although you may prefer to buy the tastier bottled water available in pharmacies and grocery stores. In a café, ask for "soda" and you'll receive a bottle of plain, bubbly soda water.

WEIGHTS AND MEASURES: I've already discussed the conversion of Celsius readings into Fahrenheit under "Climate," above, and there are several other measuring units using the metric system that you'll want to understand.

Metric measure	American measure
1 liter	1.0567 liquid quarts
0.9463 liter	1 liquid quart
3.7853 liters	1 U.S. gallon
4.546 liters	1 Imperial (U.K.) gallon
1 kilogram (kg)	2.2046 pounds
453.6 grams (0.4536 kg)	1 pound
1 centimeter	0.3937 inch
2.54 centimeters	1 inch
1 meter	39.37 inches
30.48 centimeters, or 0.3048 meter	1 foot
1 kilometer (km)	0.621 miles
1.6093 km	1 mile

Here are some conversion tricks: think of a half kilogram (500 grams) as slightly over a pound; of a liter as just over a quart; for distance, take the number of kilometers, divide by 10 and multiply by 6 to get mileage. Thus if the distance to a city is 150 km, divide by ten (15) and multiply by six (15 × 6) to get miles: 90 miles. When you're buying gasoline, 40 liters equals 10.57 gallons.

You may notice that when tracts of land are described, they are measured in dunams. A dunam is roughly a quarter of an acre.

YOUTH HOSTELS: Age is no barrier, nor is membership, when you want to stay at one of Israel's 32 comfortable and well-scattered hostels. They offer real rock-bottom prices and friendly welcomes to all. Clean, well tended, usually modern, and with kosher kitchens, they're highly thought of in these parts, even if some of them enforce the youth hostel hours strictly: arrive by 5 p.m., lights out by 11 p.m., quiet till 6 a.m., checkout by 7 or 8 a.m., and offices closed between 9 a.m. and 5 p.m. Usually the maximum stay at any given hostel is three days, but this can be extended with the manager's approval.

Only hostels bearing the triangular sign are authorized by the Israel Youth Hostels Association. It is advisable to book in advance.

Having a youth hostel membership card does give you certain advantages —like better rates at the hostels, plus discounts at some restaurants, national parks, historical sites, museums, and on buses and trains. In Jerusalem the **Israel Youth Hostels Association** is located at 3 Dorot Rishonim St. (P.O. Box 1075, Jerusalem 91009; tel. 02-222-073 or 221-648). The Tel Aviv address is 32 B'nei Dan St. (P.O. Box 22078; tel. 03-455-042). You're welcome to write here for detailed membership data, and for information on present offerings of the **Youth Travel Bureau.** You can also check your hometown for a branch of the association, or write for data to American Youth Hostels, Inc., National Campus, Delaplane, VA 22025.

Prices at hostels vary slightly for members and nonmembers. In the self-service kitchens, there's a fee to cover gas used for cooking, per person, per meal. Most hostels provide cooking utensils only; you bring along your own plates, cups, cutlery, and towels.

Note: Not all youth hostels take foreign currency, and it's a good idea to check availability of space (especially in summer months) before arriving.

The Israel Youth Hostels Association also has 14-, 21-, and 28-day bargain-priced tours; inquire at the Jerusalem office.

PRACTICAL MATTERS

1. Living and Working on a Kibbutz
2. A Shopping Guide
3. Menu Translations and Restaurant Tips
4. A Hebrew and Arabic Glossary

DOING THINGS the Israeli way—that's the subject of this Appendix, which was written to help you explore a kibbutz, buy a souvenir, order a meal, or greet the locals in their own lingo.

1. Living and Working on a Kibbutz

At some point in your visit, you'll undoubtedly want to stay on an Israeli kibbutz. A kibbutz (in the plural, kibbutzim) is Israel's unique version of the collective farm, and it's been the mechanism whereby the greater part of the country's territory was first cultivated and developed. If you are simply touring Israel and want to spend a day or two in a rustic, kibbutz atmosphere, then you can take a room in one of the many modern kibbutz guesthouses. If you're young, healthy, and have at least a month to spare, you can earn your keep on a kibbutz as a volunteer worker. Or if you want to learn Hebrew and can spend six months at the course, you can attend a kibbutz language school, going to classes for half a day and working for your board and room the other half. Anyway you choose to do it, seeing kibbutz life firsthand is a stimulating, thought-provoking experience.

The kibbutz is, of course, a major conversational topic of tourists in Israel, largely because its accomplishments, ideals, and unconventional living patterns have been spread far and wide and romanticized in fiction. A friend of mine in the Israeli foreign ministry, who often chaperones visiting guests to various kibbutzim, once remarked that few people are passive to the kibbutz idea: "They are either all for it or violently against it."

Try to keep an open mind during your visit. The kibbutz movement is a complex subject which has been dissected, analyzed, laughed at, misunderstood, and reevaluated every year for the past few decades. Although all kibbutzim are basically similar, each has individualities, and the only way you can properly understand what a particular kibbutz is all about is to live on it; even then you must have a knowledge of the underlying ideology and machinery guiding the community in order to understand properly all that you see.

If you go to a kibbutz, here's some background information to keep in mind:

THE KIBBUTZ MOVEMENT: This strange new world of collective farm ownership had its origins in the beginnings of the 20th century, when pioneers from Eastern Europe envisioned the kibbutz ("group") as the instrument of colonization for the national rebirth of the Jewish homeland. Its early establishment involved a socialist-Zionist dream, as well as a reaction against the slow-footed orthodoxy of European Jewry. The early pioneer ideologists saw the collective as a utopian vanguard of social and economic equality based on free choice and democratic principles.

Down through the years, however, the role of the kibbutz has undergone drastic and evolutionary processes. From its first role of resettling and reclaiming the land, it moved immediately into the forefront of the country's defense, and was a key factor in the protection and absorption of new immigrants. When it finally was freed from do-or-die crisis, the kibbutz had an opportunity to examine itself, to look within and analyze this segment of people that had never totaled more than one-fourth of the country's Jewish population. Subtle, and not so subtle, changes began to be noticed. Ideological problems notwithstanding, the kibbutz continued to increase output, adding factories and new industries even though it already produced one-third of Israel's total agricultural products and 8% of the nation's gross national product. In all, kibbutzniks have had a profound effect on their countrymen. For example, 10% of the Knesset (Israel's parliament) is composed of kibbutzniks.

The simplest way to define kibbutz ideology is to quote the kibbutznik's motto: "To everyone according to his needs, and from everyone according to his abilities." The underlying principles of any kibbutz are social and economic equality, collective responsibility for the needs of the membership, and communal ownership of the means of production, with the corresponding elimination of private property. On an individual level, this means that each member has no need for money of his own. His work is primarily determined by the needs of the commune, and his children, in most settlements, are raised by experts.

In addition to the ideological conviction behind this pattern of life, it arose also out of the necessity of conditions in early Israel. It was obvious to the settlers of the '20s and '30s that the character of the land was such that it could be most successfully cultivated by group effort, not only because of geography, but because of the military needs of the times—self-defense of the country by citizen soldiers, farmers, and watchmen, who would surely have perished outside the strength of the group. And once within the group, it was felt, the individual would be subordinated to the greater goals of the collective. A kibbutz is work-oriented, and people are judged by their work ability. It is a society in which a person must prove himself or herself as a worker, since the society stands or falls on the success of its physical laborers. Because of the nonphysical labor background of the members, it was necessary to establish a new criterion of achievement. A tremendous emphasis—a glorification even—was placed on the idea of manual labor, and in many instances "work" itself became elevated to a mystical, holy ideal.

STAY AND PAY: Although the kibbutz guesthouses are popular with tourists nowadays, time was when they catered strictly to Israelis. The whole idea of such places was born during World War II, a time when food was scarce and the agricultural kibbutz communities had better food and fruits, and more of both, than the town workers. So it became a custom for kibbutzniks to invite town friends to visit, eat, and relax whenever they could—which wasn't often, as town businessmen and factory workers didn't even get an annual leave then. But in 1945 annual vacations were instituted, and the first actual guesthouse opened to give city people a week of peaceful, rural rest. The peace and quiet still appeal to kibbutz guests. Today the kibbutz guesthouses enjoy high ratings among hotels, and seem to offer at least as many or more comforts for holiday guests. One thing's certain, the service is always better—maybe because the kibbutzniks who are serving aren't hired help—they're either volunteers or members who live on the kibbutz, and the visitors are like guests in their home.

Today numerous kibbutzim have built accommodations for tourists on their premises. They all have good dining rooms, and most of them have swimming pools or beaches. Spending a few days in a kibbutz is a restful affair and certainly a splendid educational experience. In addition, you don't have those diesel-chugging noises outside your window, as you often do in the city hotels. Here you are out of doors most of the time in a refreshing, relaxed setting.

As kibbutzniks are well aware of the outsider's curiosity, they frequently sponsor lectures, hold question-and-answer sessions, and take you touring on the kibbutz grounds. Feel free to ask any questions you wish.

Kibbutz Hotels, 90 Ben-Yehuda St. (P.O. Box 3193, Tel Aviv 61031; tel. 03-246-161), publishes a small booklet listing all the guesthouses, with prices, amenities, and a map. You can pick up this booklet at any I.G.T.O. or write to the association. In the U.S., you can get information from Kibbutz Hotels' representative, TOAM U.S.A. Corporation, Suite 620, 60 E. 42nd St., New York, NY 10165 (tel. 212/697-5116).

Starting in Upper Galilee, we'll stop at each of the guesthouses and I'll offer some comments.

Upper Galilee

Some of the country's best kibbutz guesthouses are located in northern Galilee, where they make excellent jumping-off points for trips in the upper and western reaches of that lush area, as well as to the Golan Heights.

One of the handsomest (although expensive, by kibbutz standards) is **Ayelet Ha-Shahar,** Upper Galilee 12200 (tel. 06-932-611), which is a veritable paradise surrounded by beautiful gardens; every conceivable type of flower seems to be blooming on your front lawn. In addition to the gardens, the kibbutz sports a first-rate kosher restaurant, a public relations officer for sightseers, a fine swimming pool, an artists' gallery, and *duty-free* gift shops—all of them branches of reputable Israeli firms. The 124 rooms, all with private shower or bath, are air-conditioned in summer, centrally heated in winter. Sounds fancy for a kibbutz, but a kibbutz it is—one of the oldest in the country (founded in 1915 by Russian pioneers), and so proud of the kibbutz ideal that it runs regular lectures (French and English) on kibbutz life. Ayelet Ha-Shahar is north of Safed, a 45-minute bus ride from Tiberias. The fine Hazor Museum is here, and the kibbutz can arrange connections for tours of nearby Hazor excavations.

In the extreme northeastern corner of the Galilee is another guest-accepting kibbutz, **Ha-Goshrim,** Upper Galilee 12225 (tel. 06-945-231), whose grounds are interlaced with running streams that form the sources of the Jordan River. Tall eucalyptus trees offer afternoon shade while you sit and watch the swift cold water rush by at your feet. In addition, you have a swimming pool, tennis court, and nearby fishing. You're close to the Hula Nature Reserve and Mount Hermon. A special Ha-Goshrim feature is a modernistic concert hall and dining room, where you can enjoy the tranquility of this pastoral setting in a little patio café, comfortably shaded by mulberry trees and drenched with the rich sweet smell of the figs that grow nearby. All of the rooms have private toilet, bath, and shower. Food served here is kosher.

A personal favorite of mine is **Kefar Blum** guesthouse, Upper Galilee (tel. 06-943-666), 45 minutes north of Tiberias and 10 minutes southeast of Kiryat Shmona. This is a warmhearted, friendly kibbutz, settled mainly by English-speaking people (American, English), and it doesn't take much time to get on first-name terms with the staff at the guesthouse. The rooms are situated in two double-decker, motel-style buildings facing out on a lawn with deck chairs and backed by pine trees. The hills of Galilee ring the kibbutz and the Jordan River runs by it. This kibbutz has tennis courts and one of the finest swimming pools in the country, Olympic size and used by Israel's Olympic swimming team for workouts. The view of the distant hills from the pool is magnificent. You're free to wander at will through the kibbutz grounds, the orchards, and along the river (you can fish here). If you want to tour the kibbutz, someone can usually be found to guide you. The food at the guesthouse is kosher and excellent, and the hospitality couldn't be more cordial.

Farther north, ten minutes above Kiryat Shmona and an hour's drive from Tiberias, is **Kefar Giladi,** Upper Galilee 12210 (tel. 06-941-414). Here, too, there are comfortable accommodations, heating in winter, air conditioning in summer, tennis courts, basketball courts, a terrific library with books in many languages, a swimming pool, and lovely rustic surroundings. All the rooms have private toilet and bath or shower. Kosher food; three stars.

Near Tiberias

In Lower Galilee, close to Tiberias and the Kinneret, there are three guesthouses. Directly on the Sea of Galilee is **Nof Ginossar**, Lake Kinneret (tel. 06-792-161). The two-wing hotel, five minutes north of Tiberias, provides air-conditioned rooms with phone and bath or shower. Fishing and swimming are the principal pastimes for guests at Nof Ginossar. Four stars; kosher food.

About 15 minutes south of Tiberias is **Kibbutz Lavi,** Lower Galilee 15267 (tel. 06-799-450), and it's best to telephone and confirm a room before traveling out here—not just because the guesthouse is popular, but because once you arrive to find all 54 rooms taken, you'll have a difficult time finding another place to stay. The rooms are scattered along flowered walkways atop a mountain that offers breathtaking views. The constant breezes here make air conditioning unnecessary, even on hot days, but most rooms are air-conditioned nonetheless, and centrally heated for cool nights. Each has private bath or shower, a coffee-making unit, and a sofa that converts into a third bed. The kibbutz has a large and attractive swimming pool, and guests are treated to frequent films and lectures. Lavi is an Orthodox religious kibbutz, but guests are relatively free from restrictions. You may dress and do as you please—but please respect the Sabbath (don't smoke publicly, etc.). The kibbutz synagogue is situated beautifully on a carpet of greenery, and services are held there each morning and evening. The dining room is airy and neat, and anyone is welcome to stop in for refreshments or full meals. You can buy postcards, shaving cream, paperback books, and such at Lavi's souvenir shop. The majority at Lavi work mainly at agricultural tasks (the topsoil had to be imported to this bare mountain). A secondary industry is the making of synagogue furniture; in fact, the kibbutz has become the main supplier of such throughout Israel. You are welcome to visit the workshops. You may also take a look at the Holstein dairy cows, or sit and watch TV in the wood-paneled guest lounge/bar. There is bus service to and from this three-star guesthouse.

On the Mediterranean Shore

Five kibbutzim with guesthouses are located directly on the shores of the Mediterranean, spaced from just above Herzlia in the south to just above Nahariya in the north. All of these boast excellent beaches.

On the northern Mediterranean coast, 40 minutes north of Haifa and close to Lebanon, stands **Kibbutz Gesher Haziv,** Western Galilee 22815 (tel. 04-927-711), founded in 1949 by a group of Americans and Israelis. You wouldn't suspect, judging from the present evidences of prosperity, that the members started out living in tents! At any rate, this kibbutz is situated on a high hill with a wonderful view of the sea below. It has a swimming pool, not to mention access to one of the best beaches in the country, at Akhziv. Built in 1962, the motel cabins are modern and bright. The majority of the rooms are air-conditioned, and all are heated in winter. Gesher Haziv accepts Diners Club cards, which always strikes me as a pretty remarkable inroad on kibbutz ideology. Kosher kitchen; three stars.

One of the kibbutz members here—the principal of the high school—wrote a fine account of the Israeli collective system, called *Life in a Kibbutz.* The book is on sale in the office, and it goes a long way toward helping a sightseer understand this radically different kind of society. You'll also be interested to know that Gesher Haziv was an experimental kibbutz, since it challenged the normal kibbutz practice of having children live in separate quarters from their parents, and was one of the first to start a new trend by insisting that the children live at home.

Working south down the seaboard, we come to **Bet Hava,** Shavei Zion Post 25227 (tel. 04-922-391), just five minutes from Acre and 25 minutes north of Haifa. The beach is a big attraction here, as is the swimming pool. Kosher kitchen; air conditioning; three stars.

A bit south and sharing the same stretch of golden beach is **Nahsholim Holiday Village,** Kibbutz Hof Dor, Post Hof Ha-Carmel (tel. 06-390-924). This kibbutz operates both a guesthouse and a vacation village. Rooms have showers and are directly on the beach; dancing and Israeli folk evenings are often featured. Nonkosher kitchen.

Close to the historically fascinating ruins at Caesarea, and on the beautiful Caesarea beach, is **Kayit Veshayit,** Sedot Yam 38805 (tel. 06-362-928 or 361-161). Another vacation village, this one is within easy reach of all Caesarea's attractions: Roman ruins, beach with water-sports equipment, 18-hole golf course, nonkosher kitchen. Music and drama festivals take place nearby in summer.

Shefayim, Mediterranean Coast 60990 (tel. 052-70171), is a beachside guesthouse above Herzlia, about 20 minutes north of Tel Aviv. All rooms have private showers and air conditioning at this large place, which features all sorts of sports on the beach and grounds as well as occasional entertainment. Kosher kitchen; three stars.

Inland—South of Haifa

Located on Mount Carmel, a 20-minute drive from Haifa, the **Bet Oren** guesthouse, Mount Carmel 30004 (tel. 04-222-111), has rooms with bath or shower, plus an impressive swimming pool. This is an excellent base for touring the Haifa area and Lower Galilee, and it offers a breathtaking view of the Mediterranean coast. Three stars; kitchen.

Nir Etzion, Carmel Beach 30808 (tel. 04-942-541), has neither private beach nor swimming pool but does take guests on daily jaunts to nearby Tantura Beach, one of the loveliest in Israel. Situated above the artists' village of Ein

Hod, it is charmingly rustic and comfortable; all rooms with shower. Kosher kitchen; three stars; synagogue on premises.

Inland—South of Tel Aviv

This kibbutz lies off the road that runs south from Rehovot. Ultra-Orthodox **Hafetz Haim,** Gedera 76817 (tel. 055-93888), is well situated for touring and has its own private whirlpool and swimming pool. Each room has a bath or shower, air conditioning, and central heating. This is a three-star place.

Near Jerusalem

There are three guesthouses in the Judean Hills hereabouts, all within 15 to 20 minutes of Jerusalem. **Kiryat Anavim,** Judean Hills 90833 (tel. 02-348-999), accommodates its guests in houses built along a hillside. Most have private bath or shower, but some share facilities; all have air conditioning, heating, and phone. Activities include swimming in the private pool, occasional dances and special programs. Kosher kitchen; three stars.

At **Ma'ale Ha-Hamisha,** Judean Hills 90835 (tel. 02-342-591), 12 km (7½ miles) from Jerusalem, all rooms have private bath or shower. The grounds here are lovely, and there's a swimming pool and entertainment for guests. Kosher kitchen; three stars.

Shoresh, Judean Hills 90860 (tel. 02-341-171), makes an equally good base for seeing Jerusalem and the West Bank. All rooms with private shower; swimming pool and sports facilities; kosher kitchen; three stars.

Neve Ilan, Judean Hills 90850 (tel. 02-341-244), offers fully furnished five-room cottages with all amenities. A mini-market and laundromat are on the premises. The 80-room, three-star guesthouse is very comfy, with wall-to-wall carpeting, central air conditioning and heating, twin beds and a fold-out couch, radios, and private baths. There's even a heated swimming pool, covered in winter, plus tennis, basketball, and volleyball courts. Neve Ilan is 15 km (9 miles) west of Jerusalem on the road to Tel Aviv, 35 km (21 miles) southeast of Ben-Gurion Airport. Prices for the accommodations are well within the budget of this book.

Finally, don't forget the aforementioned three-star **Ein Gedi,** Dead Sea 86980 (tel. 057-84342; see Chapter VIII); and **Mizpe Rachel,** at the Ramat Rachel Kibbutz, Jerusalem 90900 (tel. 02-715-712).

STAY AND WORK: If you have the time, this is the best way to experience kibbutz life—and awfully cheap as well. I know of no other country in the world where the traveler who is low on funds can arrange to work for his keep in an invigorating outdoor atmosphere, and be assured of clean quarters and good food. Many young people who come to Israel for the first time get to know the country in depth this way—working for a while at a kibbutz in the north and then heading south to work in another neck of the woods—almost without spending a dime for the entire trip. All you need is a cooperative spirit and the willingness to work hard six to eight hours a day, six days a week, wherever the kibbutz might need you—from the apple orchards, to the fish ponds, to the dishwashing sinks in the kitchen.

In exchange for that work, you're given your bed, clean sheets, normal room amenities, and three big meals a day—the fuel for your inner fires. You will also be given work clothes, some personal items, and pocket money—a few dollars a month. It is recommended that you bring along your own toiletries and work clothes at the start. Hospitalization insurance costs several dollars and is mandatory.

The kibbutzniks, incidentally, are happy to have you, especially at harvest time when they need extra hands. You'll labor beside them, dine with them, share in the kibbutz activities with them, and be invited to their rooms for tea. You may learn a little Hebrew and make some life-long friends. In all likelihood you'll meet people like yourself from all over the world. You'll gain an incomparable insight into kibbutz life this way, and you'll also perspire a lot and get a few more muscles.

There are certain requirements for working on a kibbutz. You must be between 18 and 32 and healthy (they prefer that you bring along a medical certificate). You must plan a minimum stay of one or two months, as required. Although you can request to be placed on a particular kibbutz—and this request will be honored if possible—you will be placed where needed and given whatever work the kibbutz needs to get done. This means that you have to be willing to shovel manure if asked, scrub dishes, or spend your days in the fields. Remember that the kibbutz is a work-oriented society, and you are accepted in direct ratio to your willingness and ability to work. In September, October, and March through June there are places on many kibbutzim. Be sure to register far in advance if you plan to be there in July or August, when Israel's youth movements are out on the kibbutzim.

To apply for work on a kibbutz, you *must* go through the Jewish Agency. Write ahead, giving the date of your arrival, and they will make all arrangements.

The address is **Kibbutz Aliya Desk,** Jewish Agency, 27 W. 20th St., New York, NY 10011 (tel. 212/255-1338). In Tel Aviv their address is 12 Kaplan St. (tel. 03-258-311, extension 14, 20, or 24). The Tel Aviv office is open from 7:30 a.m. to 3 p.m., on Tuesday until 2 p.m., on Friday until noon.

You can also work in a **moshav,** which differs from a kibbutz in that land is owned by each individual family and worked for profit by each. Production, distribution, etc., is collectively planned. Most moshavim are agricultural, and since they are smaller than kibbutzim, and based more on family units, more contact is made between volunteers and hosts. You can easily be placed on moshavim most of the year, although it's difficult in summer. You get work clothes, a place to sleep, food, and pocket money—something like $30 to $50 a month. If you want to work in one, contact the Jewish Agency Volunteer Department in Tel Aviv or New York at the above addresses.

If you just want a day's look at kibbutz life, two kibbutzim near Jerusalem are set up to offer you just that.

Kibbutz Tzora (tel. 02-916-913), 30 km (18 miles) from Jerusalem, will give you its "Taste of Kibutz Life" tour from 8 a.m. to 2 p.m. any day but Saturday (or holidays). Call for details and reservations.

Kibbutz Ramat Rachel (tel. 02-717-621), just south of Jerusalem, will give you a free tour any Sunday. Tours are conducted in English, German, Hebrew, and Afrikaans. Again, you must call for details and reservations.

2. A Shopping Guide

Any hard-core shopper will adore plying his or her skills in the flea markets and local shops or stalls—where buying becomes a real art, involving sharp-eyed scouting and recognition of an item's value, plus a near-ceremonious bargaining rite. Many people don't know, though, that Israel is a land of modern discount and department stores, diamond and fur marts, and a souvenir wonderland of gold as well as gilt. Some disappointed travelers come home saying that goods in Israel are expensive—they're the folks who didn't know what to look for or where to go. In this section I'll give you a rundown of particular types of bargains and goods found only in Israel; then I'll give you a few useful shopping tips.

Without too much looking, you'll easily find most any item you could ever imagine buying. Products from around the world abound in Israel's shops. What is of more interest to us here, and what are the real "finds," are those items that are uniquely Israeli—made in Israel by Israelis, be they kibbutzniks, individual craftsmen, large manufacturers, or Bedouin. The descriptions in this section are of goods tourists seem to fancy most, and I'll try to tell you how to recognize their quality.

DISCOUNTS: Another important tip—if you're buying certain items—is to look for shops that display a red certificate of recommendation by the Ministry of Tourism. Here, you'll get a reduction on prices of particular items when you pay in foreign currency. Included in the discounted list are jewelry, clothing, giftware, rugs, and footwear. And a larger reduction is given in some other stores selling leather goods, if these items are delivered to the airport and can be qualified as "duty-free" purchases. However, do know that all shops that give discounts usually charge a good bit more for the merchandise to begin with, and frequently you can get better buys by shopping around. In any event, I suggest you price items in more than one place before buying anything anywhere.

Tourists paying in foreign currency can get a refund of Israel's hefty Value Added Tax (VAT) on single purchases of more than $50 when they leave the country with the purchased items. Here's what you do: when you buy that big-ticket coat, or jewelry item, etc., ask the shopkeeper to give you a "VAT Refund Form." Then, when the time comes for you to leave Israel, get to the airport in plenty of time and submit your refund form to a bank branch. You get your money on the spot.

BARGAINING: When you shop in markets and stalls, you should understand that you're deep in Arab culture, where bargaining is an accepted way of life. You'll find a friendly haggle over price is part of the shopping ritual. And in the Old City of Jerusalem, the bargaining game becomes quite a sport, much like a poker bluff. You pretend a passing interest in an item. The shopkeeper makes you an offer. You give him a look of displeasure and note that you are interested, yes, but not at *that* price. What is your best price, you ask? He gives you a price about 10% lower than the first. Then you offer him 50% of the first price. Impossible, he tells you. And so is your best price, you tell him. Given five minutes of this backing and filling, you'll probably hit a price about 20% to 30% lower than the original price. This approach only works if the item is costly enough to start with. Only a few shopkeepers will bother with all that ritual arguing over a few dollars' purchase. Should you be interested in two items at the same shop, you'll generally get a better price. It takes practice at this sort of thing. Also, don't let your heart get set on something and find yourself forced to meet a high price. You can usually find that same item elsewhere, and try the bargaining game with someone else.

And although the general rules of the game outlined above are accepted in Jerusalem's Old City market, remember there are great individual differences. Some shopkeepers just won't budge more than a dollar or two, no matter how wily you think you are. They are the merchants who feel that eventually they can get the higher prices, and they might just as well hold out for them. They have learned that the world contains an inexhaustible supply of shoppers who manage to make their way into the bazaar.

SPECIAL SHOPS: Located in all key cities are two stores that you should visit without fail. They are **Maskit** and **WIZO,** and both of them carry native crafts, everything from jewelry, pottery, fabrics, embroidery, and clothing, to glassware and religious articles. All merchandise is of the highest quality and workmanship. You will find clothing, for instance, that is not only elegant and high fashion but also anticipates future trends.

It is not only the merchandise that makes these places special. Supported by the Ministry of Labor, the Maskit shops are the outlets for the Maskit home industries program, which provides work for immigrant women. Workers are supplied with materials and trained by expert instructors. They earn money as they learn new skills. WIZO is sponsored by the Women's International Zionist Organization. Its items are handmade by the needy and profits go right back to help others.

Neither Maskit nor WIZO is what you'd call "cheap." Neither is the quality. And you would pay twice as much for the same items back home, since both organizations export to the States—to Neiman-Marcus and its ilk.

SHOPPING HOURS: Some stores in Israel are closed Tuesday afternoon all year round. In some places they're also closed Wednesday afternoon in July and August. Department stores are usually open from 9 a.m. to 7 p.m. Sunday to Thursday, closing early on Friday. Stores in Jerusalem's Old City are open on Saturday, as are stores in East Jerusalem.

HAND-STITCHERY AND WOVEN CRAFTS: Today's shopper in Israel seems to share the current international mania for anything hand-stitched or woven— and in Israel such work is about the hottest of all market items. It's produced in varying quality by Yemenite, Bedouin, Arab, and Druze craftspeople. All of it tends to be expensive by Israeli standards, but much of it is quite low or reasonably priced by U.S. standards.

Most of the Yemenite work is done with fine threads, frequently metallic silver or gold, and always with great care, delicacy, and finesse in both stitches and patterns. Items produced by Bedouin, Arab, and Druze are quite different from Yemenite work, but similar to each other—generally in bright colors, and sewn with thick threads that are often handmade from sheep or goat fleece. The patterns are usually bold, in keeping with the rougher textures of fabrics and yarns. Whereas Yemenite work customarily decorates fine gowns of silky fabrics, elaborate religious items and garb, beautiful linens, blouses, shirts, dresses, and children's outfits, you'll find Bedouin stitchery covering small pouch-purses that swing from the hip; cotton, heavy wool, or velvet dresses of red, black or dark hues; elaborate men's vests, jackets, and shirts; and small "picture pieces" for use as rugs or hangings.

For quality, the Yemenite stitchery is outstanding, consisting usually of sturdy fabrics and colorfast threads, easily washed or cleaned and lasting for years. When you buy the work of the Bedouin, Arab, and Druze, you should be more careful. Much of the most gorgeous stuff is stitched into ancient, rotting, or dirty cloth; some of the vivid, fabulous colors will run if washed or cleaned. The former have learned more about public demand, and the latter are learning fast. Much of the Yemenite work is done by standards for factories and marketing outfits; most of the Bedouin, Arab, and Druze work is individually produced according to ancient ways. However, there are shops and cooperatives now selling top-quality work of both types; if you buy at these shops you'll pay slightly more, but you will get better value.

The woven work is usually a safe and good buy, no matter where you get it. But when you buy it, the farther you are from its origin, the more it'll cost. This means your best buys will be in the Druze villages near Haifa, the Beersheba Bedouin Market (every Thursday morning—the earlier the better), the Old City in Jerusalem, and in the predominantly Arab towns such as Nazareth, Bethlehem, Hebron, Acre, and so forth. Where the woven work abounds, you'll also find good selections of stitchery. As for the Yemenite work, although some say there's more in Jerusalem than elsewhere, I have found it abundant everywhere, and at rather standard prices. By the way, if you look at some of the woven items with a total disregard for their actual purposes, you'll often see things you can use effectively in ways the craftsman never dreamed of. For example, some of the donkey and camel harnesses and saddles can make belts, trims, wall hangings, and so forth.

Since the whole stitchery bit has become so overwhelmingly popular, some clever folks have begun imitating it in mass-produced machine-stitched items. Today these are much more abundant than the handwork, and much less costly. Many times these products are excellent buys, but I've been often disappointed by the poor quality of the fabrics and threads. My advice is to be careful where you buy them. At shops like **Maskit, Batsheva, WIZO,** etc., the machine or handwork is more expensive but totally reliable. Also excellent in every respect is the **Elder Craftsman's Shop** (open from 9 a.m. to 1 p.m. and 4 to 6 p.m.), and the **Work Center** (open from 8 a.m. to noon), 14 Shivtei Israel St., in Jerusalem (tel. 02-287-831). They sell handcrafted articles made by the elderly and disabled from almost every ethnic group in the country. The excellent work has won many prizes for the craftspeople.

JEWELRY AND ORNATE METALWORK:
It's everywhere, all kinds, from cheap to expensive, mass-produced to one-of-a-kind. But if you want the best buys in fine diamonds, gems, and jewelry of internationally recognized top quality, try the **Diamond Mart** in Haifa. Also, scout the fine jewelry stores in each key city and I.G.T.O.-recommended **Tourist Discount Center.** You can really make dazzling buys of fine jewelry in Israel.

Israel is also famous for its Yemenite jewelry—another fine and delicate art produced by these craftsmen. Usually it's characterized by fine filigree work with thin wires of metal intricately joined and meshed to create almost-solid designs. The metal is ordinarily silver, sometimes hand-dipped gold. Whether plain metal or stone-studded, the work is quite ornate and leans toward the ceremonial and quite dressy—not sporty. Probably the best-known pieces are the earrings with one or several drop levels, executed of metal or set with stones or tiny bangles. There are also large quantities of necklaces, bracelets, rings, cufflinks, and pins, as well as numerous small items for display or religious use, including birds, boxes, dishes, ritual herb and spice holders, filigree cases or covers for cigarette lighters, compacts, Torahs and Bibles, etc.

Growing greatly in popularity is the Bedouin, Arab, and Druze jewelry. Unlike the Yemenite work, these pieces are usually heavy or massive and roughly executed. Sometimes the metal is silver, but often it's tin or copper; most of the stones are roughly cut or shaped shards from desert mines, semiprecious bits highly valued here since the time of Cleopatra. This jewelry often incorporates coins—old and new, fake and real, large and small—pierced to dangle, often pounded and stone-studded, and usually very worn. These are often supplemented with roughly cut and tooled bits of metal, usually in triangles and diamond shapes. Another interesting item used in jewelry here is the clove bud; cloves frequently are strung into patterns with tiny beads and a dangling coin or two, because the women who make them find the aroma quite pleasing to themselves and their men.

Some of the items are very, very old, as is much of the Yemenite work you can buy, but there are so many good copies being turned out today, it's almost impossible to tell the ancient from the new. I thought I had it solved when I learned which types of chains and engravings were done in different times—later I learned that virtually every style is being hand-copied today. So I began looking for what would strike my fancy, rather than what was supposed to be valuable. The one thing I can pass on—for your protection—concerns some of the stones. Amber is a great favorite in such jewelry, and fake amber is common. Either of two simple tests will spot a fake immediately—the rub or the burn. Fake amber, when rubbed briskly against your clothing, will gather enough electricity to pull at paper or hair if immediately placed near either. And since fake amber is plastic, it burns easily when touched with the lit end of a cigarette. Another, even more expensive stone, is called atik, which means old. It is usually roughly cut, then polished, and made into beads of about a quarter-inch diameter; the color is a marbled combination of red and beige-white streaks. Try the burn treatment on this too, should you have any doubts. Both stones appear in necklaces, earrings, rings, and bracelets as well as in strings, and they are occasionally set into knives, small objects, etc. They can also be bought single for your own settings.

A popular style of jewelry and small objects is the interesting Persian miniature work that's found in large quantities nowadays, especially in Jerusalem. The jewelry takes the form of bracelets, brooches, pendants, cufflinks, tie bars, rings, and such, and is made of small pieces of ivory, bone, ceramic, or plastic, delicately hand-painted with figures, flora, and fauna. The colors are usually bright, and the prices vary according to the finesse of the painting rather than the material employed, or even the age. Most often the pieces are square or oblong, but sometimes they're cut as circles, ovals, triangles, hearts, or intricate designs. Aside from the jewelry, you can also buy miniature paintings. Then, too, the hand-painted Persian work is available in fine porcelain and ceramics, fashioned into thin cigarette holders, small pipes, many small boxes, and jewelry items, as well as large pieces such as hanging lamps. It really is beautiful work. Other items to look for in shops that have this type of ware are small inlaid metal statues, usually of birds, made of brass, copper, or chased silver, and set with aqua and coral semiprecious stones. These small objets d'art would sell for at least double the price if bought Stateside. In Israel, you'll find them mostly in Jerusalem, and in Middle Eastern shops and stalls throughout the country. The least expensive I saw were at the Beersheba Bedouin Market, although they certainly didn't originate there.

In either traditional or modern styles, shoppers will find a plethora of religious jewelry throughout the Holy Land—in metals, woods, ivory, real and fake, elaborate and simple, expensive and very, very cheaply priced, and in designs for every religion.

Modern jewelry, made by Israeli craftspeople, is also to be found everywhere in Israel. Some of it is mass-produced and quite inexpensive; there's also an excellent selection of special designs and one-of-a-kind pieces. The modern jewelry makers work in all sorts of media—metals, ceramics, stones, seeds, leather, you name it. And most of the modern work is clearly influenced by the more ancient jewelry of the land, which gives it a special character. You'll often see bits of ancient glass embedded in a new necklace or bracelet, age-old symbols etched into new pins or earrings, modern adaptations of ornaments thousands of years old.

OLIVEWOOD: Some of the most beautiful and unique items you can buy here are made of olivewood. Whether it's intricately carved or simply smoothed, it remains a richly veined light wood, very decorative. And it's used to make souvenirs for all budgets, from $1 to $100 or more. Some of the most popular items are the necklaces and belts fashioned largely from polished olive pits or small carved beads. Many vases, jugs, bowls, and such are easily found and very well priced, and the carvings range from highly styled to primitive. Many people buy the carved figures of biblical characters or the sets of Nativity scenes, but the bestselling item is probably the camel. Then there are rings, earrings, bookmarks, letter openers, buttons, bead curtains, desk sets, whatever. Although works of olivewood are available everywhere, the best buys are in the Arab Christian shops in Jerusalem, Bethlehem, and Nazareth.

COPPER AND BRASS: Most of these items are difficult to transport. However if you are flying for the United States *directly* from Israel, you may be able to take a large piece with you.

Don't, incidentally, buy copper and brassware in a shop on the main streets of any of the cities if you want to pay a realistic price. Instead, look for these pieces in the Flea Market in Jaffa, in Acre, in Jerusalem's Mea Shearim, or Nazareth. And if you find something that you *must* have (don't let the shopkeeper know this), switch immediately to an attitude of detachment; it will start the process of bargaining in your favor.

One of the ways to tell if a copper vessel is good or not is by its weight. The heavier the object, the greater the amount of copper in it. If the piece is black and dirty, you can scrape it and see the copper underneath. And when you're back home, you can clean it yourself with fine sandpaper, steel wool, and a great deal of patience. The large trays make beautiful cocktail tables, and can also be hung on your living room wall as an ornament.

EILAT STONES: "And King Solomon gave unto the Queen of Sheba all her desire, whatsoever she asked . . ." (I Kings 10:13). The Old Testament doesn't say which gifts Solomon gave to his royal guest; possibly some were those green stones from his mines—pendants and brooches of turquoise green streaked with malachite and shades of blue, pink, and purple.

A beautiful aquamarine to dark-blue color, these stones are sold all over Israel—either as stones, or as pendants, and set in either modern or traditional settings. The best place to purchase them is of course in Eilat itself, where they are mined, and where the selection is enormous and the prices the lowest in the country. Go to the factory where the stones are cut, polished, and set, and you will have a wonderful time trying to decide which one of these stones you want —since each has a slightly different design and color scheme.

POTTERY: Here again is a craft available in contemporary or ancient styles, with the contemporary work seen everywhere, varying fantastically, and priced in every range. The ancient-style work generally comes from the Arab, Bedouin, and Druze villages, and is always priced much lower there. Paints, glazes, texture, sizes, quality, and craftsmanship vary greatly, but you're certain to find something that pleases you. Probably the most outstanding work comes from Hebron, where craftspeople sell their wares in their own little shops.

Besides the Eilat stones mentioned above, a new product has appeared here—the clay from King Solomon's copper mines at Timna is made into pottery. The clay contains iron and copper, and after the pottery is fired the finished product resembles metal. When it is glazed with a transparent glazing and fired, the blue-green color of the copper appears and looks like malachite stone. A workshop where one can witness the whole production process is situated on Ha-Arava Road, near the Sonol and Delek gas stations. It's called **Eilat Art Centre.**

KNITWEAR: Israel is as famous for its knitwear as for its fur products, and its knits are sold throughout the world. There are several shops and manufacturers specializing in fine knits; **Iwanir, Aled, Maskit,** and **WIZO** are among those where the quality is always superb. You'll see shirts, suits, dresses, slacks, ensembles, coats—and although these are often high-priced for Israelis, they do remain one of the foreign bargain shopper's best local buys.

LEATHER AND FURS: Israel is unbelievably furry for so hot a climate. In this land you'll find fabulous furs and leathers for prices that would seem absurd back home. For elegant, well-tailored, fine-quality, and personally fitted coats and such, you can save many dollars—even hundreds of dollars—depending on your selection. If suede is your favorite, or leather, you'll find great buys in suits, coats, jackets, slacks, bags, baubles, and trinkets—from the finest quality to medium and low, with prices varying accordingly. All key cities sell these goods and they're also exported around the world. The styles are all you'd want them to be, from traditional to avant-garde. Gloves and small leather items are also good buys in Israel, and available everywhere, as are luggage pieces.

Products of sheep or goat skins are much lower in price—also in quality. Although the small skins, throw rugs, hangings, jackets, and hassocks sell very well, you'll also find slippers, hats, gloves, suitcases, boxes, bags, and so forth, all in these skins that are treated according to ancient customs. I do suggest you take a good whiff of these items before buying, because sometimes they do reek, and it's almost impossible to remove or hide the odor. Also, the sheepskins are usually a bit higher, for their durability is supposed to be greater. You'll see most of these items in the Arab markets and stalls of Jerusalem's Old City, Nazareth, Acre, Bethlehem, and Hebron. Prices are best in Hebron and other West Bank areas, as most such work comes from there. The very best buys will be at various factories scattered through the West Bank areas.

GLASSWARE: Plenty of glassware in Israel, and the two most distinctive types are either contemporary or Hebron. The contemporary glassware is made in factories and by individual artists and often simulates the looks of ancient Israelite work. This stuff is beautiful indeed, but it's costly and hard to ship or take home because of breakage. I've seen excellent tiny copies of ancient vessels, handmade, that make good collection pieces, and even hold miniature flower arrangements (you can buy dried flowers to take home with you, if you're interested).

Hebron glass almost always comes from one of five factories (small shops, really) operated in Hebron by members of one family. The most popular shade is blue with a bit of green in it, but it's also made in dusty yellows and golds, greens, purples, silvers, and clear shades. Vases come in all shapes and sizes, and there are mugs, beads, ornaments for camel and donkey saddles (these make great napkin holders), and pendants about the size of a half-dollar that are quite eye-catching when strung with raw leather and hung around the neck. Impressed with many religious and simple designs, they're cheap and make interesting, appreciated gifts. Although the Hebron glass is sold throughout Israel, it's naturally much less expensive when you buy it in Hebron—and the selection's better there as well.

You'll also find many places that carry authentic ancient glass pieces, from hundreds to thousands of years old—they are of course high in price, but not as high as you'd think.

BASKETWARE: Gay baskets, trays, and pots of all shapes and sizes can be bought in the Druze villages near Haifa or in the markets of Nazareth, the West Bank, the Old City of Jerusalem, Beersheba, Acre, and many city shops as well. All of these items are light and durable, make wonderful decorative pieces for your home, and will be easy to transport. The color schemes of the heavy-woven baskets and trays are unusually animated—reds, blues, greens, oranges, purples, all mixed and expertly woven together, making them one of the best folk crafts in Israel. Some are made of rushes, some of raffia . . . some of porcupine quills!

3. Menu Translations and Restaurant Tips

For most travelers, Israeli foods are an altogether novel experience. With the country's population swelled by immigrants from 70 countries, it is only natural that a rather diverse cuisine should have developed through the years.

I can group the cooking into three main types: **European** (which means Polish, French, German, Viennese, and Hungarian), **dairy-vegetarian** (including the traditional Jewish dishes), and **Arabic or Middle Eastern.** Nearly all hotels and a good number of restaurants are kosher.

Breakfast is likely to be the most startling meal of the day. Time was when the hardy settlement workers had to pack away a 5 a.m. feast sufficient for the next seven hours in the fields. Tourists may not have quite so arduous a day ahead of them, but Israeli hotels do serve up overwhelming breakfasts. Many hotels have buffet tables laden with fresh vegetables, various cheeses, boiled eggs, olives, herring, sardines, etc., with coffee and rolls in accompaniment.

Lunch and dinner vary according to taste and pocketbook, often accentuating dairy products and vegetables. Israeli meat is plentiful, but substandard compared with American cuts. Poultry, however, is good and evident everywhere.

Here's a description of the more common local foods:

Pita: A flat, pancake-shaped Arab bread, chewy and split in the middle.

Falafel: Sold like hot dogs by street vendors, falafel consists of small balls of deep-fried ground chickpeas, spiced with peppers, plus salad, coleslaw, tchina, and condiments, and eaten within the split pita.

Hummus: A paste made from ground chickpeas and olive oil.

Tchina: Like hummus, but made from ground sesame seeds, giving it a peanut-butterish sort of taste.

Eshel, leben: Like sour cream, only thinner.

Shamenet: Like sour cream, only thicker.

Kebab: Chopped and spiced lamb or turkey broiled on a skewer.

Shishlik: Pieces of lamb or beef or turkey, charcoal-broiled on a skewer, flavored with onions and tomatoes.

Bamia: Okra prepared with a thick, juicy tomato sauce.

Shwarma: Lamb or turkey, grilled on a spit and served in small pieces.

And don't forget that when you order coffee in a café, you might get one of four varieties. Be specific: there's Turkish coffee, thick and sweet; Nescafé, sometimes called Nes; *ragil* (regular); and *botz* (literally, mud), which is coffee grounds with boiling water poured on top.

One last note: Israel is a hot country and sanitary precautions should be observed. Wash all fruit and vegetables and resist meat from outdoor street stands when in doubt.

Vegetarian diners find life in Israel fairly easy, as there are so many dairy restaurants that serve no meat. Even if you don't eat eggs, finding good, delicious food is not difficult. At breakfast there are always fruits and vegetables, cheeses and yogurt-like eshel, leben and shamenet. The many pizzerias and blintz houses found in every Israeli city are usually "dairy" restaurants, meaning that they will use cheese, but not meat. In addition, Jerusalem has several restaurants which specialize in vegetarian fare.

4. A Hebrew and Arabic Glossary

My final task is to provide a few guideposts to the languages of the country. The Hebrew alphabet is, of course, entirely unlike our Latin ABCs. Fortunately for us, however, Israelis use the same numerals that we use: 1, 2, 3, 4, etc.

Hebrew has a number of sounds that we don't use in English. They are difficult to communicate in writing, and until you hear them spoken correctly, you may not get the flavor of them. The first is the "ch" or "kh" sound—which you'll find repeatedly in many words throughout the vocabulary. This is not the sound of "ch" in either "change" or "champagne." We don't use this sound in English, and the closest to it are the "ch" sounds in the German exclamation "ach," and in the Yiddish-Hebrew toast "le-chaim." It's a raspy, hacking sound that comes from the back of the mouth.

Another difficult sound, and also very common in Hebrew words, is the "o" sound. The best advice for practicing this sound is to say the word "oh" and halfway through saying the word suddenly cut your voice off. That's what many call a short "o." You get an approximation with the "o" sound in the word "on" and the German word "Von," although they're not exactly it either. You just have to cut the "o" short, so when you say the Hebrew word "boker," meaning "morning," you don't "bowker."

Now that you're sufficiently confused, here are some of those words:

HEBREW TERMS AND EXPRESSIONS

USEFUL WORDS

hello	sha-*lom*	see you later	le-hit-rah-*ott*
goodbye	sha-*lom*	friend	cha-*vare*
good night	*lie*-la-tov	excuse me	slee-*cha*
I	ah-*nee*	I speak English	ah-nee m'dah-*berh* ang-*leet*
you	ah-*tah*		
he	hoo	I don't speak Hebrew	ah-nee
she	hee		lo m'dah-*behr*
we	an-*nach*-noo		ee-*vreet*
there is	yesh	yesterday	et-*mohl*
there isn't	ain	right (correct)	na-*chon*
little	m'*aat*	too much	yo-*tair* mee-*die*
much	har-*beh*	patience	*sav*-la-*noot*
very	m'*od*	hands off	*blee* yah-*die*-im
so-so	*ka*-cha-*ka*-cha	what	mah
good	tov	why	*la*-ma
hot	chaam	how	aych
bad	rah	when	mah-tiee

cold	car	movie	cine-*ma* (also *kol*-no-*ah*)
today	hah-*yom*	house	bah-yit
tomorrow	ma-char	white	lah-*vaahn*
yes	ken	black	sha-*chor*
no	lo	synagogue	bait k-*ness*-et
good morning	*bo*-ker tov	school	bait say-*fer*
good evening	*Erev* tov	newspaper	ee-*tahn*
thank you	to-*dah* rah-*bah*	healthy	ba-*ree*
please	be-va-ka-*sha*	sick	cho-*leh*
you are welcome	al low da-*vaar*		

HOTEL TALK

hotel	meh-*lon*	dining room	*che*-der *oh*-chel
room	che-der	bill	*chesh*-bon
water	my-im	Mr. (sir)	ah-don-*ee*
toilet	bait key-*say*, no-chi	Mrs. (madam)	g'*ver*-et
	yoot, she-roo-*teem*	where is	*ay*-fo
money	*kes*-sef	key	maf-*tay*-ach
bank	bank	manager	min-ah-*hel*
do you speak English?	ah-*tah*	accommodations	ma-*kom*
	m'dah-*behr* ang-*leet*?	balcony	meer-*pes*-eth

LOCAL TRAVELING

station	ta-cha-nah	far	rah-*chok*
railroad	rah-*keh*-vet	central	meer-ka-*zith*
airport	sde t'u*fah*	from	may
bus	auto-boos	bus stop	ta-cha-*naht* ha-auto-
taxi	taxi		boos
taxi (sherut)	shay-*root*	which bus goes to . . . ?	
straight ahead	ya-*shar*		*eh*-zeh auto-boos
street	re-*chov*		no-*say*-ah le . . . ?
to the right	yeh-*mean*-ah	stop here	ah-*tsor* kahn
to the left	smol-*ah*	north	tsa-*fon*
south	da-*rom*	near	ka-*rov*
east	miz-*rach*	to	le
west	m'ar-*av*	wait	*reg*-gah

RESTAURANT AND FOOD

restaurant	*miss*-ah-*dah*	ice cream	glee-*dah*
food	*o*-chel	wine	*yah*-yin
cafe	ca-*fe*	milk	cha-*lav*
breakfast	ah-roo-*chat bo*-ker	ice	ker-*ach*

lunch	ah-roo-*chat* tsa-ha-rye-im	tea	tay
dinner	ah-roo-*chat* erev	coffee	cafe
waiter	mel-*tsar*	vegetables	yeh-rah-*koht*
menu	taf-*reet*	salad	salat
butter	chem-*ah*	fruit	pay-*rote*
cheese	g'*vee*-nah	apple	ta-*poo*-ach
egg	bay-*tsa*	orange	tapooz
hard-boiled egg	bay-*tsa* ka-sha	tomatoes	ag-von-ee-*oat*
soft-boiled egg	bay-*tsa* rah-kah	cucumber	mah-la-fe-*fon*
scrambled eggs	bay-*tsim* m-bull-*bell*-et	pepper	pil-*pel*
fried eggs	bay-*tsee*-ah ma-*rock*	salt	me-*lach*
soup	bah-*sahr*	sugar	sue-*car*
meat	e-gel	omelet	cha-vi-*tah*
veal	tar-ne-*gol*-et	sour	cha-*muts*
chicken	dag	sweet	mah-*tok*
fish	le-eh-*chol*	bread	*lech*-hem
to eat		satisfy	save'a
		hungry	ra'ev
		pleasant	nah-*im*
		excellent	met-soo-*yan*
		to drink	lish-toth

POST OFFICE

post office	dough-are	postcard	gloo-yah
letter	mich-tav	telegram	miv-rock
stamp	bool (bool-im pl.)	airmail	dough-are ah-*veer*
envelopes	ma-ata-*foth*		

SHOPPING AND STORES

how much is it?	*ka*-mah zeh oh-leh	manicure	*mah*-nee-*koor*
		appointment	p'gee-*shah*
store	cha-*noot*	doctor	row-*feh*
pharmacy	bait mer-kah-*chat*	dentist	row-*feh* shin-*eye*-yim
barber, hairdresser	mahs-peh-rah	expensive	ya-*kar*
shampoo	ha-fee-*fah*	cheap	zol

THE COUNTRYSIDE

sea	*yaam*	village	k'far
sand	chol	road	*der*-ech
desert	mid-*bar*	mountain	har
forest	yah-*are*	hill	giv-*ah*

| farm | *mesh*-ekh | spring, well | ayn, ma-ay-in, ay-in |
| valley | *eh*-mek | trip | tee-*yule* |

DAYS AND TIME

Sunday	*yom* ree-*shon*	minute	da-*kah*
Monday	*yom* shay-*nee*	hour	sha-ah
Tuesday	*yom* shlee-*shee*	seven o'clock	ha-sha-*ah shay*-va
Wednesday	*yom* reh-vee-*ee*		
Thursday	*yom* cha-mee *shee*	day	yom
Friday	*yom* shee-*shee*	week	sha-voo-ah
Saturday	sha-*bot* (as in "hot")	month	*cho*-desh
what time	*ma* ha-sha-*ah*	year	sha-*nah*

NUMBERS

1	eh-*had*	20	ess-*reem*
2	*shta*-yim	21	ess-*reem* v'eh-*had*
3	sha-*losh*	30	shlo-*sheem*
4	*ar*-bah	50	cha-mee-*sheem*
5	cha-*maysh*	100	*may*-ah
6	shaysh	200	mah-tah-*yeem*
7	*shev*-vah	300	shlosh may-*oat*
8	sh-*mo*-neh	500	cha-*maysh* may-*oat*
9	*tay*-shah	1000	elef
10	*ess*-er	3000	shlosh-*et* elef-*eem*
11	eh-*had* ess-ray	5000	cha-maysh-*et* elef-*eem*
12	*shtaym*-ess-ray		

ARABIC TERMS AND EXPRESSIONS

please	min fadlach	pardon	sa-mech-nee
how much is this?	ah-desh	one	wa-had
	hadah	two	tinen
thank you	shoo-khraan	three	talatay
goodbye	salaam aleichem, ma-ah-salameh	four	arbaha
		five	chamseh
hello	a-halan, mahr-haba	six	sitteh
do you speak English?	tech-kee Ingleesi?	seven	sabah
		eight	tamanyeh
yes	ay-wah	nine	taisah
no	la	ten	ahsharah
right	yemine	coffee	kah-wah
left	she-mal	scram; beat it	rooch min-hon
straight	doo-ree		

NOW, SAVE MONEY ON ALL YOUR TRAVELS!
Join Arthur Frommer's $25-A-Day Travel Club™

Saving money while traveling is never a simple matter, which is why, over 25 years ago, the **$25-A-Day Travel Club** was formed. Actually, the idea came from readers of the Arthur Frommer Publications who felt that such an organization could bring financial benefits, continuing travel information, and a sense of community to economy-minded travelers all over the world.

In keeping with the money-saving concept, the annual membership fee is low—$18 (U.S. residents) or $20 U.S. (Canadian, Mexican, and foreign residents)—and is immediately exceeded by the value of your benefits which include:

(1) The latest edition of any TWO of the books listed on the following pages.

(2) An annual subscription to an 8-page quarterly newspaper *The Wonderful World of Budget Travel* which keeps you up-to-date on fastbreaking developments in low-cost travel in all parts of the world—bringing you the kind of information you'd have to pay over $25 a year to obtain elsewhere. This consumer-conscious publication also includes the following columns:

Hospitality Exchange—members all over the world who are willing to provide hospitality to other members as they pass through their home cities.

Share-a-Trip—requests from members for travel companions who can share costs and help avoid the burdensome single supplement.

Readers Ask . . . Readers Reply—travel questions from members to which other members reply with authentic firsthand information.

(3) A copy of *Arthur Frommer's Guide to New York.*

(4) Your personal membership card which entitles you to purchase through the Club all Arthur Frommer Publications for a third to a half off their regular retail prices during the term of your membership.

So why not join this hardy band of international budgeteers NOW and participate in its exchange of information and hospitality? Simply send $18 (U.S. residents) or $20 U.S. (Canadian, Mexican, and other foreign residents) along with your name and address to: $25-A-Day Travel Club, Inc., Gulf + Western Building, One Gulf + Western Plaza, New York, NY 10023. Remember to specify which *two* of the books in section (1) above you wish to receive in your initial package of member's benefits. Or tear out the next page, check off any two of the books listed on either side, and send it to us with your membership fee.

Date_____

FROMMER BOOKS
PRENTICE HALL PRESS
ONE GULF + WESTERN PLAZA
NEW YORK, NY 10023

Friends:

Please send me the books checked below:

FROMMER'S $-A-DAY GUIDES™

(In-depth guides to sightseeing and low-cost tourist accommodations and facilities.)

☐ Europe on $25 a Day $12.95	☐ New Zealand on $25 a Day $10.95
☐ Australia on $25 a Day $10.95	☐ New York on $45 a Day $9.95
☐ Eastern Europe on $25 a Day $10.95	☐ Scandinavia on $50 a Day $10.95
☐ England on $35 a Day $10.95	☐ Scotland and Wales on $35 a Day $10.95
☐ Greece on $25 a Day $10.95	☐ South America on $30 a Day $10.95
☐ Hawaii on $50 a Day $10.95	☐ Spain and Morocco (plus the Canary
☐ India on $15 & $25 a Day $9.95	Is.) on $40 a Day $10.95
☐ Ireland on $30 a Day $10.95	☐ Turkey on $25 a Day $10.95
☐ Israel on $30 & $35 a Day $10.95	☐ Washington, D.C., on $40 a Day $10.95
☐ Mexico on $20 a Day $10.95	

FROMMER'S DOLLARWISE GUIDES™

(Guides to sightseeing and tourist accommodations and facilities from budget to deluxe, with emphasis on the medium-priced.)

☐ Alaska $12.95	☐ Cruises (incl. Alaska, Carib, Mex,
☐ Austria & Hungary $11.95	Hawaii, Panama, Canada, & US) $12.95
☐ Belgium, Holland, Luxembourg $11.95	☐ California & Las Vegas $11.95
☐ Egypt $11.95	☐ Florida $10.95
☐ England & Scotland $11.95	☐ Mid-Atlantic States $12.95
☐ France $11.95	☐ New England $11.95
☐ Germany $11.95	☐ New York State $11.95
☐ Italy $11.95	☐ Northwest $11.95
☐ Japan & Hong Kong $12.95	☐ Skiing in Europe $12.95
☐ Portugal (incl. Madeira & the Azores) . $11.95	☐ Skiing USA—East $10.95
☐ South Pacific $12.95	☐ Skiing USA—West $10.95
☐ Switzerland & Liechtenstein $11.95	☐ Southeast & New Orleans $11.95
☐ Bermuda & The Bahamas $10.95	☐ Southwest $11.95
☐ Canada $12.95	☐ Texas $11.95
☐ Caribbean $12.95	

TURN PAGE FOR ADDITIONAL BOOKS AND ORDER FORM.

THE ARTHUR FROMMER GUIDES™

(Pocket-size guides to sightseeing and tourist accommodations and facilities in all price ranges.)

☐ Amsterdam/Holland	$5.95	☐ Mexico City/Acapulco	$5.95
☐ Athens	$5.95	☐ Minneapolis/St. Paul	$5.95
☐ Atlantic City/Cape May	$5.95	☐ Montreal/Quebec City	$5.95
☐ Boston	$5.95	☐ New Orleans	$5.95
☐ Cancún/Cozumel/Yucatán	$5.95	☐ New York	$5.95
☒ Dublin/Ireland	$5.95	☐ Orlando/Disney World/EPCOT	$5.95
☐ Hawaii	$5.95	☐ Paris	$5.95
☐ Las Vegas	$5.95	☐ Philadelphia	$5.95
☐ Lisbon/Madrid/Costa del Sol	$5.95	☐ Rome	$5.95
☐ London	$5.95	☐ San Francisco	$5.95
☐ Los Angeles	$5.95	☐ Washington, D.C.	$5.95

FROMMER'S TOURING GUIDES™

(Color illustrated guides that include walking tours, cultural & historic sites, and other vital travel information.)

☐ Egypt	$8.95	☐ Paris	$8.95
☐ Florence	$8.95	☐ Venice	$8.95
☐ London	$8.95		

SPECIAL EDITIONS

☐ A Shopper's Guide to the Best Buys in England, Scotland, & Wales	$10.95	☐ Marilyn Wood's Wonderful Weekends (NY, Conn, Mass, RI, Vt, NH, NJ, Del, Pa)	$11.95
☐ A Shopper's Guide to the Caribbean	$10.95	☐ Motorist's Phrase Book (Fr/Ger/Sp)	$4.95
☐ Bed & Breakfast—N. America	$8.95	☐ Swap and Go (Home Exchanging)	$10.95
☐ Fast 'n' Easy Phrase Book (Fr/Ger/Ital/Sp in *one* vol.)	$6.95	☐ The Candy Apple (NY for Kids)	$11.95
☐ Honeymoons Guide (US, Canada, Mexico, & Carib)	$12.95	☐ Travel Diary and Record Book	$5.95
☐ How to Beat the High Cost of Travel	$4.95	☐ Where to Stay USA (Lodging from $3 to $30 a night)	$9.95

ORDER NOW!

In U.S. include $1.50 shipping UPS for 1st book; 50¢ ea. add'l book Outside U.S. $2 and 50¢, respectively.

Enclosed is my check or money order for $_____

NAME _____

ADDRESS _____

CITY _____ STATE _____ ZIP _____

It's 2 am.
It's far from home.
It's more than
a tummyache.

American Express Cardmembers can get emergency medical and legal referrals, worldwide. Simply by calling Global Assist.℠

What if it really is more than a tummyache? What if your back goes out? What if you get into a legal fix?

Call Global Assist – a new emergency referral service for the exclusive use of American Express Cardmembers. Just call. Toll-free. 24 hours a day. Every day. Virtually anywhere in the world.

Your call helps find a doctor, lawyer, dentist, optician, chiropractor, nurse, pharmacist, or an interpreter.

All this costs nothing, except for the medical and legal bills you would normally expect to pay.

Global Assist. One more reason to have the American Express® Card. Or, to get one.

For an application, call 1-800-THE-CARD.

Don't leave home without it.®

If you lose cash on vacation, don't count on a Boy Scout finding it.

Honestly.

How many people can you trust to give back hundreds of dollars in cash? Not too many.

That's why it's so important to help protect your vacation with American Express® Travelers Cheques.

If they're lost, you can get them back from over 100,000 refund locations th[...] out the world. Or you can hope a Boy [...] finds it.

Protect your vacation.